Data Mining

D0138972

Data Mining
Practical Machine Learning Tools and Techniques
Fourth Edition

Ian H. Witten
University of Waikato, Hamilton, New Zealand

Eibe Frank
University of Waikato, Hamilton, New Zealand

Mark A. Hall
University of Waikato, Hamilton, New Zealand

Christopher J. Pal
Polytechnique Montréal, Montreal, Quebec, Canada

ELSEVIER

AMSTERDAM • BOSTON • HEIDELBERG • LONDON
NEW YORK • OXFORD • PARIS • SAN DIEGO
SAN FRANCISCO • SINGAPORE • SYDNEY • TOKYO

Morgan Kaufmann is an imprint of Elsevier

Morgan Kaufmann is an imprint of Elsevier
50 Hampshire Street, 5th Floor, Cambridge, MA 02139, United States

Copyright © 2017, 2011, 2005, 2000 Elsevier Inc. All rights reserved.

No part of this publication may be reproduced or transmitted in any form or by any means, electronic
or mechanical, including photocopying, recording, or any information storage and retrieval system,
without permission in writing from the publisher. Details on how to seek permission, further
information about the Publisher's permissions policies and our arrangements with organizations
such as the Copyright Clearance Center and the Copyright Licensing Agency, can be found at our
website: www.elsevier.com/permissions.

This book and the individual contributions contained in it are protected under copyright by the
Publisher (other than as may be noted herein).

Notices
Knowledge and best practice in this field are constantly changing. As new research and experience
broaden our understanding, changes in research methods, professional practices, or medical treatment
may become necessary.

Practitioners and researchers must always rely on their own experience and knowledge in evaluating
and using any information, methods, compounds, or experiments described herein. In using such
information or methods they should be mindful of their own safety and the safety of others, including
parties for whom they have a professional responsibility.

To the fullest extent of the law, neither the Publisher nor the authors, contributors, or editors, assume
any liability for any injury and/or damage to persons or property as a matter of products liability,
negligence or otherwise, or from any use or operation of any methods, products, instructions, or ideas
contained in the material herein.

British Library Cataloguing-in-Publication Data
A catalogue record for this book is available from the British Library

Library of Congress Cataloging-in-Publication Data
A catalog record for this book is available from the Library of Congress

ISBN: 978-0-12-804291-5

For Information on all Morgan Kaufmann publications
visit our website at https://www.elsevier.com

Working together
to grow libraries in
developing countries

ELSEVIER   Book Aid International

www.elsevier.com • www.bookaid.org

Publisher: Todd Green
Acquisition Editor: Tim Pitts
Editorial Project Manager: Charlotte Kent
Production Project Manager: Nicky Carter
Designer: Matthew Limbert

Typeset by MPS Limited, Chennai, India

Contents

List of Figures...xv
List of Tables..xxi
Preface xxiii

PART I INTRODUCTION TO DATA MINING

CHAPTER 1   What's it all about? 3
   1.1 Data Mining and Machine Learning...4
     Describing Structural Patterns 6
     Machine Learning 7
     Data Mining 9
   1.2 Simple Examples: The Weather Problem and Others..................9
     The Weather Problem..10
     Contact Lenses: An Idealized Problem.......................12
     Irises: A Classic Numeric Dataset 14
     CPU Performance: Introducing Numeric Prediction 16
     Labor Negotiations: A More Realistic Example......................16
     Soybean Classification: A Classic Machine Learning
       Success 19
   1.3 Fielded Applications 21
     Web Mining 21
     Decisions Involving Judgment 22
     Screening Images...23
     Load Forecasting 24
     Diagnosis..25
     Marketing and Sales 26
     Other Applications..27
   1.4 The Data Mining Process...28
   1.5 Machine Learning and Statistics...30
   1.6 Generalization as Search..31
     Enumerating the Concept Space 32
     Bias 33
   1.7 Data Mining and Ethics 35
     Reidentification..36
     Using Personal Information...37
     Wider Issues...38
   1.8 Further Reading and Bibliographic Notes...................................38

CHAPTER 2   Input: concepts, instances, attributes **43**
    2.1 What's a Concept? 44
    2.2 What's in an Example? 46
        Relations 47
        Other Example Types 51
    2.3 What's in an Attribute? 53
    2.4 Preparing the Input 56
        Gathering the Data Together 56
        ARFF Format 57
        Sparse Data 60
        Attribute Types 61
        Missing Values 62
        Inaccurate Values 63
        Unbalanced Data 64
        Getting to Know Your Data 65
    2.5 Further Reading and Bibliographic Notes 65

CHAPTER 3   Output: knowledge representation **67**
    3.1 Tables 68
    3.2 Linear Models 68
    3.3 Trees 70
    3.4 Rules 75
        Classification Rules 75
        Association Rules 79
        Rules With Exceptions 80
        More Expressive Rules 82
    3.5 Instance-Based Representation 84
    3.6 Clusters 87
    3.7 Further Reading and Bibliographic Notes 88

CHAPTER 4   Algorithms: the basic methods **91**
    4.1 Inferring Rudimentary Rules 93
        Missing Values and Numeric Attributes 94
    4.2 Simple Probabilistic Modeling 96
        Missing Values and Numeric Attributes 100
        Naïve Bayes for Document Classification 103
        Remarks 105
    4.3 Divide-and-Conquer: Constructing Decision Trees 105
        Calculating Information 108
        Highly Branching Attributes 110

4.4 Covering Algorithms: Constructing Rules 113

Rules Versus Trees 114

A Simple Covering Algorithm 115

Rules Versus Decision Lists 119

4.5 Mining Association Rules 120

Item Sets 120

Association Rules 122

Generating Rules Efficiently 124

4.6 Linear Models 128

Numeric Prediction: Linear Regression 128

Linear Classification: Logistic Regression 129

Linear Classification Using the Perceptron 131

Linear Classification Using Winnow 133

4.7 Instance-Based Learning 135

The Distance Function 135

Finding Nearest Neighbors Efficiently 136

Remarks 141

4.8 Clustering 141

Iterative Distance-Based Clustering 142

Faster Distance Calculations 144

Choosing the Number of Clusters 146

Hierarchical Clustering 147

Example of Hierarchical Clustering 148

Incremental Clustering 150

Category Utility 154

Remarks 156

4.9 Multi-instance Learning 156

Aggregating the Input 157

Aggregating the Output 157

4.10 Further Reading and Bibliographic Notes............................. 158

4.11 WEKA Implementations 160

CHAPTER 5 Credibility: evaluating what's been learned 161

5.1 Training and Testing 163

5.2 Predicting Performance 165

5.3 Cross-Validation 167

5.4 Other Estimates 169

Leave-One-Out 169

The Bootstrap 169

5.5 Hyperparameter Selection 171

5.6 Comparing Data Mining Schemes..172
5.7 Predicting Probabilities..176
    Quadratic Loss Function..177
    Informational Loss Function 178
    Remarks 179
5.8 Counting the Cost 179
    Cost-Sensitive Classification 182
    Cost-Sensitive Learning..183
    Lift Charts 183
    ROC Curves 186
    Recall-Precision Curves..190
    Remarks 190
    Cost Curves 192
5.9 Evaluating Numeric Prediction 194
5.10 The MDL Principle..197
5.11 Applying the MDL Principle to Clustering..200
5.12 Using a Validation Set for Model Selection 201
5.13 Further Reading and Bibliographic Notes..202

PART II MORE ADVANCED MACHINE LEARNING SCHEMES

CHAPTER 6 Trees and rules **209**
6.1 Decision Trees..210
    Numeric Attributes 210
    Missing Values 212
    Pruning..213
    Estimating Error Rates 215
    Complexity of Decision Tree Induction..217
    From Trees to Rules 219
    C4.5: Choices and Options..219
    Cost-Complexity Pruning 220
    Discussion 221
6.2 Classification Rules..221
    Criteria for Choosing Tests 222
    Missing Values, Numeric Attributes 223
    Generating Good Rules 224
    Using Global Optimization..226
    Obtaining Rules From Partial Decision Trees 227
    Rules With Exceptions 231
    Discussion 233

  6.3 Association Rules..234
    Building a Frequent Pattern Tree 235
    Finding Large Item Sets 240
    Discussion 241
  6.4 WEKA Implementations...242

CHAPTER 7 Extending instance-based and linear models 243
  7.1 Instance-Based Learning..244
    Reducing the Number of Exemplars.. 245
    Pruning Noisy Exemplars... 245
    Weighting Attributes 246
    Generalizing Exemplars.. 247
    Distance Functions for Generalized Exemplars......................... 248
    Generalized Distance Functions 250
    Discussion 250
  7.2 Extending Linear Models..252
    The Maximum Margin Hyperplane.. 253
    Nonlinear Class Boundaries 254
    Support Vector Regression 256
    Kernel Ridge Regression 258
    The Kernel Perceptron 260
    Multilayer Perceptrons... 261
    Radial Basis Function Networks 270
    Stochastic Gradient Descent.. 270
    Discussion 272
  7.3 Numeric Prediction With Local Linear Models.......................273
    Model Trees 274
    Building the Tree 275
    Pruning the Tree 275
    Nominal Attributes 276
    Missing Values 276
    Pseudocode for Model Tree Induction...................................... 277
    Rules From Model Trees 281
    Locally Weighted Linear Regression 281
    Discussion 283
  7.4 WEKA Implementations...284

CHAPTER 8 Data transformations 285
  8.1 Attribute Selection 288
    Scheme-Independent Selection.. 289
    Searching the Attribute Space 292
    Scheme-Specific Selection 293

8.2 Discretizing Numeric Attributes...296
　　　Unsupervised Discretization... 297
　　　Entropy-Based Discretization....................................... 298
　　　Other Discretization Methods....................................... 301
　　　Entropy-Based Versus Error-Based Discretization.................. 302
　　　Converting Discrete to Numeric Attributes 303
8.3 Projections..304
　　　Principal Component Analysis.. 305
　　　Random Projections... 307
　　　Partial Least Squares Regression 307
　　　Independent Component Analysis..................................... 309
　　　Linear Discriminant Analysis....................................... 310
　　　Quadratic Discriminant Analysis 310
　　　Fisher's Linear Discriminant Analysis.............................. 311
　　　Text to Attribute Vectors.. 313
　　　Time Series 314
8.4 Sampling..315
　　　Reservoir Sampling 315
8.5 Cleansing...316
　　　Improving Decision Trees 316
　　　Robust Regression 317
　　　Detecting Anomalies 318
　　　One-Class Learning 319
　　　Outlier Detection 320
　　　Generating Artificial Data 321
8.6 Transforming Multiple Classes to Binary Ones.....................322
　　　Simple Methods.. 323
　　　Error-Correcting Output Codes 324
　　　Ensembles of Nested Dichotomies.................................... 326
8.7 Calibrating Class Probabilities..................................328
8.8 Further Reading and Bibliographic Notes..........................331
8.9 WEKA Implementations...334

CHAPTER 9 Probabilistic methods **335**
9.1 Foundations 336
　　　Maximum Likelihood Estimation 338
　　　Maximum a Posteriori Parameter Estimation......................... 339
9.2 Bayesian Networks..339
　　　Making Predictions... 340

Learning Bayesian Networks 344

Specific Algorithms 347

Data Structures for Fast Learning 349

9.3 Clustering and Probability Density Estimation 352

The Expectation Maximization Algorithm for a Mixture

of Gaussians 353

Extending the Mixture Model 356

Clustering Using Prior Distributions 358

Clustering With Correlated Attributes 359

Kernel Density Estimation 361

Comparing Parametric, Semiparametric and Nonparametric

Density Models for Classification 362

9.4 Hidden Variable Models 363

Expected Log-Likelihoods and Expected Gradients 364

The Expectation Maximization Algorithm 365

Applying the Expectation Maximization Algorithm

to Bayesian Networks 366

9.5 Bayesian Estimation and Prediction 367

Probabilistic Inference Methods 368

9.6 Graphical Models and Factor Graphs 370

Graphical Models and Plate Notation 371

Probabilistic Principal Component Analysis 372

Latent Semantic Analysis 376

Using Principal Component Analysis for Dimensionality

Reduction 377

Probabilistic LSA 378

Latent Dirichlet Allocation 379

Factor Graphs 382

Markov Random Fields 385

Computing Using the Sum-Product and Max-Product

Algorithms 386

9.7 Conditional Probability Models 392

Linear and Polynomial Regression as Probability

Models 392

Using Priors on Parameters 393

Multiclass Logistic Regression 396

Gradient Descent and Second-Order Methods 400

Generalized Linear Models 400

Making Predictions for Ordered Classes 402

Conditional Probabilistic Models Using Kernels 402

9.8   Sequential and Temporal Models.................................403
    Markov Models and *N*-gram Methods 403
    Hidden Markov Models...404
    Conditional Random Fields...406
9.9   Further Reading and Bibliographic Notes.........................410
    Software Packages and Implementations..............................414
9.10   WEKA Implementations...416

CHAPTER 10   Deep learning 417
10.1   Deep Feedforward Networks..420
    The MNIST Evaluation 421
    Losses and Regularization...422
    Deep Layered Network Architecture 423
    Activation Functions..424
    Backpropagation Revisited..426
    Computation Graphs and Complex Network Structures 429
    Checking Backpropagation Implementations 430
10.2   Training and Evaluating Deep Networks..............................431
    Early Stopping 431
    Validation, Cross-Validation, and Hyperparameter Tuning ... 432
    Mini-Batch-Based Stochastic Gradient Descent...................433
    Pseudocode for Mini-Batch Based Stochastic Gradient
       Descent...434
    Learning Rates and Schedules..434
    Regularization With Priors on Parameters............................435
    Dropout 436
    Batch Normalization...436
    Parameter Initialization..436
    Unsupervised Pretraining..437
    Data Augmentation and Synthetic Transformations..............437
10.3   Convolutional Neural Networks...437
    The ImageNet Evaluation and Very Deep Convolutional
       Networks 438
    From Image Filtering to Learnable Convolutional Layers.....439
    Convolutional Layers and Gradients....................................443
    Pooling and Subsampling Layers and Gradients 444
    Implementation 445
10.4   Autoencoders..445
    Pretraining Deep Autoencoders With RBMs.........................448
    Denoising Autoencoders and Layerwise Training................448
    Combining Reconstructive and Discriminative Learning.......449

10.5 Stochastic Deep Networks 449

Boltzmann Machines 449

Restricted Boltzmann Machines 451

Contrastive Divergence 452

Categorical and Continuous Variables.....................452

Deep Boltzmann Machines.......................................453

Deep Belief Networks 455

10.6 Recurrent Neural Networks 456

Exploding and Vanishing Gradients 457

Other Recurrent Network Architectures 459

10.7 Further Reading and Bibliographic Notes...............461

10.8 Deep Learning Software and Network Implementations........464

Theano...464

Tensor Flow 464

Torch 465

Computational Network Toolkit................................465

Caffe..465

Deeplearning4j..465

Other Packages: Lasagne, Keras, and cuDNN........465

10.9 WEKA Implementations..466

CHAPTER 11 Beyond supervised and unsupervised learning **467**

11.1 Semisupervised Learning...468

Clustering for Classification.....................................468

Cotraining 470

EM and Cotraining 471

Neural Network Approaches 471

11.2 Multi-instance Learning..472

Converting to Single-Instance Learning 472

Upgrading Learning Algorithms 475

Dedicated Multi-instance Methods...........................475

11.3 Further Reading and Bibliographic Notes...............477

11.4 WEKA Implementations..478

CHAPTER 12 Ensemble learning.. **479**

12.1 Combining Multiple Models....................................480

12.2 Bagging 481

Bias—Variance Decomposition 482

Bagging With Costs..483

12.3 Randomization 484

Randomization Versus Bagging 485

Rotation Forests 486

12.4 Boosting 486
    AdaBoost..487
    The Power of Boosting..489
12.5 Additive Regression...490
    Numeric Prediction...491
    Additive Logistic Regression 492
12.6 Interpretable Ensembles..493
    Option Trees 494
    Logistic Model Trees 496
12.7 Stacking...497
12.8 Further Reading and Bibliographic Notes..........................499
12.9 WEKA Implementations..501

CHAPTER 13 **Moving on: applications and beyond...................503**
13.1 Applying Machine Learning...504
13.2 Learning From Massive Datasets...506
13.3 Data Stream Learning..509
13.4 Incorporating Domain Knowledge.......................................512
13.5 Text Mining...515
    Document Classification and Clustering...........................516
    Information Extraction..517
    Natural Language Processing 518
13.6 Web Mining...519
    Wrapper Induction..519
    Page Rank 520
13.7 Images and Speech 522
    Images 523
    Speech 524
13.8 Adversarial Situations...524
13.9 Ubiquitous Data Mining 527
13.10 Further Reading and Bibliographic Notes 529
13.11 WEKA Implementations 532

Appendix A: Theoretical foundations..533
Appendix B: The WEKA workbench...553
References...573
Index 601

List of Figures

Figure 1.1	Rules for the contact lens data.	13
Figure 1.2	Decision tree for the contact lens data.	14
Figure 1.3	Decision trees for the labor negotiations data.	18
Figure 1.4	Life cycle of a data mining project.	29
Figure 2.1	A family tree and two ways of expressing the *sister-of* relation.	48
Figure 2.2	ARFF file for the weather data.	58
Figure 2.3	Multi-instance ARFF file for the weather data.	60
Figure 3.1	A linear regression function for the CPU performance data.	69
Figure 3.2	A linear decision boundary separating *Iris setosas* from *Iris versicolors*.	70
Figure 3.3	Constructing a decision tree interactively: (A) creating a rectangular test involving *petallength* and *petalwidth*; (B) the resulting (unfinished) decision tree.	73
Figure 3.4	Models for the CPU performance data: (A) linear regression; (B) regression tree; (C) model tree.	74
Figure 3.5	Decision tree for a simple disjunction.	76
Figure 3.6	The *exclusive-or* problem.	77
Figure 3.7	Decision tree with a replicated subtree.	77
Figure 3.8	Rules for the iris data.	81
Figure 3.9	The shapes problem.	82
Figure 3.10	Different ways of partitioning the instance space.	86
Figure 3.11	Different ways of representing clusters.	88
Figure 4.1	Pseudocode for 1R.	93
Figure 4.2	Tree stumps for the weather data.	106
Figure 4.3	Expanded tree stumps for the weather data.	108
Figure 4.4	Decision tree for the weather data.	109
Figure 4.5	Tree stump for the *ID code* attribute.	111
Figure 4.6	Covering algorithm: (A) covering the instances; (B) decision tree for the same problem.	113
Figure 4.7	The instance space during operation of a covering algorithm.	115
Figure 4.8	Pseudocode for a basic rule learner.	118

Figure 4.9	(A) Finding all item sets with sufficient coverage; (B) finding all sufficiently accurate association rules for a k-item set.	127
Figure 4.10	Logistic regression: (A) the logit transform; (B) example logistic regression function.	130
Figure 4.11	The perceptron: (A) learning rule; (B) representation as a neural network.	132
Figure 4.12	The Winnow algorithm: (A) unbalanced version; (B) balanced version.	134
Figure 4.13	A kD-tree for four training instances: (A) the tree; (B) instances and splits.	137
Figure 4.14	Using a kD-tree to find the nearest neighbor of the star.	137
Figure 4.15	Ball tree for 16 training instances: (A) instances and balls; (B) the tree.	139
Figure 4.16	Ruling out an entire ball (gray) based on a target point (star) and its current nearest neighbor.	140
Figure 4.17	Iterative distance-based clustering.	143
Figure 4.18	A ball tree: (A) two cluster centers and their dividing line; (B) corresponding tree.	145
Figure 4.19	Hierarchical clustering displays.	149
Figure 4.20	Clustering the weather data.	151
Figure 4.21	Hierarchical clusterings of the iris data.	153
Figure 5.1	A hypothetical lift chart.	185
Figure 5.2	Analyzing the expected benefit of a mailing campaign when the cost of mailing is (A) \$0.50 and (B) \$0.80.	187
Figure 5.3	A sample ROC curve.	188
Figure 5.4	ROC curves for two learning schemes.	189
Figure 5.5	Effect of varying the probability threshold: (A) error curve; (B) cost curve.	193
Figure 6.1	Example of subtree raising, where node C is "raised" to subsume node B.	214
Figure 6.2	Pruning the labor negotiations decision tree.	216
Figure 6.3	Algorithm for forming rules by incremental reduced-error pruning.	226
Figure 6.4	RIPPER: (A) algorithm for rule learning; (B) meaning of symbols.	228
Figure 6.5	Algorithm for expanding examples into a partial tree.	229
Figure 6.6	Example of building a partial tree.	230
Figure 6.7	Rules with exceptions for the iris data.	232

Figure 6.8	Extended prefix trees for the weather data: (A) the full data; (B) the data conditional on *temperature = mild*; (C) the data conditional on *humidity = normal*.	238
Figure 7.1	A boundary between two rectangular classes.	249
Figure 7.2	A maximum margin hyperplane.	253
Figure 7.3	Support vector regression: (A) $\varepsilon = 1$; (B) $\varepsilon = 2$; (C) $\varepsilon = 0.5$.	257
Figure 7.4	Example data sets and corresponding perceptrons.	262
Figure 7.5	Step vs sigmoid: (A) step function; (B) sigmoid function.	264
Figure 7.6	Gradient descent using the error function $w^2 + 1$.	265
Figure 7.7	Multilayer perceptron with a hidden layer (omitting bias inputs).	267
Figure 7.8	Hinge, squared and 0−1 loss functions.	271
Figure 7.9	Pseudocode for model tree induction.	278
Figure 7.10	Model tree for a data set with nominal attributes.	279
Figure 8.1	Attribute space for the weather dataset.	292
Figure 8.2	Discretizing the *temperature* attribute using the entropy method.	299
Figure 8.3	The result of discretizing the *temperature* attribute.	299
Figure 8.4	Class distribution for a two-class, two-attribute problem.	302
Figure 8.5	Principal component transform of a dataset: (A) variance of each component; (B) variance plot.	306
Figure 8.6	Comparing principal component analysis and Fisher's linear discriminant analysis.	312
Figure 8.7	Number of international phone calls from Belgium, 1950−1973.	318
Figure 8.8	Overoptimistic probability estimation for a two-class problem.	329
Figure 9.1	A simple Bayesian network for the weather data.	341
Figure 9.2	Another Bayesian network for the weather data.	342
Figure 9.3	The Markov blanket for variable x_6 in a 10-variable Bayesian network.	348
Figure 9.4	The weather data: (A) reduced version; (B) corresponding AD tree.	350
Figure 9.5	A two-class mixture model.	354
Figure 9.6	DensiTree showing possible hierarchical clusterings of a given data set.	360
Figure 9.7	Probability contours for three types of model, all based on Gaussians.	362

Figure 9.8	(A) Bayesian network for a mixture model; (B) multiple copies of the Bayesian network, one for each observation; (C) plate notation version of (B).	371
Figure 9.9	(A) Bayesian network for probabilistic PCA; (B) equal-probability contour for a Gaussian distribution along with its covariance matrix's principal eigenvector.	372
Figure 9.10	The singular value decomposition of a t by d matrix.	377
Figure 9.11	Graphical models for (A) pLSA, (B) LDA^b, and (C) smoothed LDA^b.	379
Figure 9.12	(A) Bayesian network and (B) corresponding factor graph.	382
Figure 9.13	The Markov blanket for variable x_6 in a 10-variable factor graph.	383
Figure 9.14	(A) and (B) Bayesian network and corresponding factor graph; (C) and (D) Naïve Bayes model and corresponding factor graph.	384
Figure 9.15	(A) Bayesian network representing the joint distribution of y and its parents; (B) factor graph for a logistic regression for the conditional distribution of y given its parents.	384
Figure 9.16	(A) Undirected graph representing a Markov random field structure; (B) corresponding factor graph.	385
Figure 9.17	Message sequence in an example factor graph.	389
Figure 9.18	(A) and (B) First- and second-order Markov models for a sequence of variables; (C) Hidden Markov model; (D) Markov random field.	404
Figure 9.19	Mining emails for meeting details.	406
Figure 9.20	(A) Dynamic Bayesian network representation of a hidden Markov model; (B) similarly structured Markov random field; (C) factor graph for (A); and (D) factor graph for a linear chain conditional random field.	407
Figure 10.1	A feedforward neural network.	424
Figure 10.2	Computation graph showing forward propagation in a deep network.	426
Figure 10.3	Backpropagation in a deep network (the forward computation is shown with gray arrows).	429
Figure 10.4	Parameter updates that follow the forward and backward propagation steps (shown with gray arrows).	430
Figure 10.5	Typical learning curves for the training and validation sets.	431

Figure 10.6	Pseudocode for mini-batch based stochastic gradient descent.	435
Figure 10.7	Typical convolutional neural network architecture.	439
Figure 10.8	Original image; filtered with the two Sobel operators; magnitude of the result.	441
Figure 10.9	Examples of what random neurons detect in different layers of a convolutional neural network using the visualization approach of Zeiler and Fergus (2013). Underlying imagery kindly provided by Matthew Zeiler.	442
Figure 10.10	Example of the convolution, pooling, and decimation operations used in convolutional neural networks.	443
Figure 10.11	A simple autoencoder.	445
Figure 10.12	A deep autoencoder with multiple layers of transformation.	447
Figure 10.13	Low-dimensional principal component space (left) compared with one learned by a deep autoencoder (right).	447
Figure 10.14	Boltzmann machines: (A) fully connected; (B) restricted; (C) more general form of (B).	450
Figure 10.15	(A) Deep Boltzmann machine and (B) deep belief network.	453
Figure 10.16	(A) Feedforward network transformed into a recurrent network; (B) hidden Markov model; and (C) recurrent network obtained by unwrapping (A).	456
Figure 10.17	Structure of a "long short-term memory" unit.	459
Figure 10.18	Recurrent neural networks: (A) bidirectional, (B) encoder-decoder.	460
Figure 10.19	A deep encoder-decoder recurrent network.	460
Figure 12.1	Algorithm for bagging.	483
Figure 12.2	Algorithm for boosting.	488
Figure 12.3	Algorithm for additive logistic regression.	493
Figure 12.4	Simple option tree for the weather data.	494
Figure 12.5	Alternating decision tree for the weather data.	495
Figure 13.1	A tangled web.	521

List of Tables

Table 1.1	The Contact Lens Data	7
Table 1.2	The Weather Data	11
Table 1.3	Weather Data With Some Numeric Attributes	12
Table 1.4	The Iris Data	15
Table 1.5	The CPU Performance Data	16
Table 1.6	The Labor Negotiations Data	17
Table 1.7	The Soybean Data	20
Table 2.1	Iris Data as a Clustering Problem	46
Table 2.2	Weather Data With a Numeric Class	47
Table 2.3	Family Tree	48
Table 2.4	The Sister-of Relation	49
Table 2.5	Another Relation	52
Table 3.1	A New Iris Flower	80
Table 3.2	Training Data for the Shapes Problem	83
Table 4.1	Evaluating the Attributes in the Weather Data	94
Table 4.2	The Weather Data, With Counts and Probabilities	97
Table 4.3	A New Day	98
Table 4.4	The Numeric Weather Data With Summary Statistics	101
Table 4.5	Another New Day	102
Table 4.6	The Weather Data with Identification Codes	111
Table 4.7	Gain Ratio Calculations for the Tree Stumps of Fig. 4.2	112
Table 4.8	Part of the Contact Lens Data for which *Astigmatism = Yes*	116
Table 4.9	Part of the Contact Lens Data for Which *Astigmatism = Yes* and *Tear Production Rate = Normal*	117
Table 4.10	Item Sets for the Weather Data With Coverage 2 or Greater	121
Table 4.11	Association Rules for the Weather Data	123
Table 5.1	Confidence Limits for the Normal Distribution	166
Table 5.2	Confidence Limits for Student's Distribution With 9 Degrees of Freedom	174
Table 5.3	Different Outcomes of a Two-Class Prediction	180
Table 5.4	Different Outcomes of a Three-Class Prediction: (A) Actual; (B) Expected	181
Table 5.5	Default Cost Matrixes: (A) Two-Class Case; (B) Three-Class Case	182

Table 5.6   Data for a Lift Chart   184

Table 5.7   Different Measures Used to Evaluate the False Positive   191
             Versus False Negative Tradeoff

Table 5.8   Performance Measures for Numeric Prediction   195

Table 5.9   Performance Measures for Four Numeric Prediction   197
             Models

Table 6.1   Preparing the Weather Data for Insertion Into an FP-tree: 236
             (A) The Original Data; (B) Frequency Ordering of Items
             With Frequent Item Sets in Bold; (C) The Data With Each
             Instance Sorted Into Frequency Order; (D) The Two
             Multiple-Item Frequent Item Sets

Table 7.1   Linear Models in the Model Tree   280

Table 8.1   The First Five Instances From the CPU Performance Data;   308
             (A) Original Values; (B) The First Partial Least Squares
             Direction; (C) Residuals From the First Direction

Table 8.2   Transforming a Multiclass Problem Into a Two-Class One: 324
             (A) Standard Method; (B) Error-Correcting Code

Table 8.3   A Nested Dichotomy in the Form of a Code Matrix   327

Table 9.1   Highest Probability Words and User Tags From a Sample   381
             of Topics Extracted From a Collection of Scientific
             Articles

Table 9.2   Link Functions, Mean Functions, and Distributions Used in   401
             Generalized Linear Models

Table 10.1   Summary of Performance on the MNIST Evaluation   421

Table 10.2   Loss Functions, Corresponding Distributions, and   423
             Activation Functions

Table 10.3   Activation Functions and Their Derivatives   425

Table 10.4   Convolutional Neural Network Performance on the   439
             ImageNet Challenge

Table 10.5   Components of a "Long Short-Term Memory" Recurrent   459
             Neural Network

Table 13.1   The Top 10 Algorithms in Data Mining, According to a   504
             2006 Poll

Preface

The convergence of computing and communication has produced a society that feeds on information. Yet most of the information is in its raw form: data. If *data* is characterized as recorded facts, then *information* is the set of patterns, or expectations, that underlie the data. There is a huge amount of information locked up in databases—information that is potentially important but has not yet been discovered or articulated. Our mission is to bring it forth.

Data mining is the extraction of implicit, previously unknown, and potentially useful information from data. The idea is to build computer programs that sift through databases automatically, seeking regularities or patterns. Strong patterns, if found, will likely generalize to make accurate predictions on future data. Of course, there will be problems. Many patterns will be banal and uninteresting. Others will be spurious, contingent on accidental coincidences in the particular dataset used. And real data is imperfect: some parts will be garbled, some missing. Anything that is discovered will be inexact: there will be exceptions to every rule and cases not covered by any rule. Algorithms need to be robust enough to cope with imperfect data and to extract regularities that are inexact but useful.

Machine learning provides the technical basis of data mining. It is used to extract information from the raw data in databases—information i.e., ideally, expressed in a comprehensible form and can be used for a variety of purposes. The process is one of abstraction: taking the data, warts and all, and inferring whatever structure underlies it. This book is about the tools and techniques of machine learning that are used in practical data mining for finding, and if possible describing, structural patterns in data.

As with any burgeoning new technology that enjoys intense commercial attention, the use of machine learning is surrounded by a great deal of hype in the technical—and sometimes the popular—press. Exaggerated reports appear of the secrets that can be uncovered by setting learning algorithms loose on oceans of data. But there is no magic in machine learning, no hidden power, no alchemy. Instead there is an identifiable body of simple and practical techniques that can often extract useful information from raw data. This book describes these techniques and shows how they work.

In many applications machine learning enables the acquisition of structural descriptions from examples. The kind of descriptions that are found can be used for prediction, explanation, and understanding. Some data mining applications focus on prediction: forecasting what will happen in new situations from data that describe what happened in the past, often by guessing the classification of new examples. But we are equally—perhaps more—interested in applications where the result of "learning" is an actual description of a structure that can be used to classify examples. This structural description supports explanation and understanding as well as prediction. In our experience, insights gained by the user are of most interest in the majority of practical data mining applications; indeed, this is one of machine learning's major advantages over classical statistical modeling.

The book explains a wide variety of machine learning methods. Some are pedagogically motivated: simple schemes that are designed to explain clearly how the basic ideas work. Others are practical: real systems that are used in applications today. Many are contemporary and have been developed only in the last few years.

A comprehensive software resource has been created to illustrate the ideas in the book. Called the Waikato Environment for Knowledge Analysis, or WEKA[1] for short, it is available as Java source code at www.cs.waikato.ac.nz/ml/weka. It is a full, industrial-strength implementation of most of the techniques that are covered in this book. It includes illustrative code and working implementations of machine learning methods. It offers clean, spare implementations of the simplest techniques, designed to aid understanding of the mechanisms involved. It also provides a workbench that includes full, working, state-of-the-art implementations of many popular learning schemes that can be used for practical data mining or for research. Finally, it contains a framework, in the form of a Java class library, that supports applications that use embedded machine learning and even the implementation of new learning schemes.

The objective of this book is to introduce the tools and techniques for machine learning that are used in data mining. After reading it, you will understand what these techniques are and appreciate their strengths and applicability. If you wish to experiment with your own data, you will be able to do this easily with the WEKA software. But WEKA is by no means the only choice. For example, the freely available statistical computing environment R includes many machine learning algorithms. Devotees of the Python programming language might look at a popular library called *scikit-learn*. Modern "big data" frameworks for distributed computing, such as Apache Spark, include support for machine learning. There is a plethora of options for deploying machine learning in practice. This book discusses fundamental learning algorithms without delving into software-specific implementation details. When appropriate, we point out where the algorithms we discuss can be found in the WEKA software. We also briefly introduce other machine learning software for so-called "deep learning" from high-dimensional data. However, most software-specific information is relegated to appendices.

The book spans the gulf between the intensely practical approach taken by trade books that provide case studies on data mining and the more theoretical, principle-driven exposition found in current textbooks on machine learning. (A brief description of these books appears in the *Further reading* section at the end of chapter: What's it all about?) This gulf is rather wide. To apply machine learning techniques productively, you need to understand something about how

---

[1]Found only on the islands of New Zealand, the *weka* (pronounced to rhyme with "Mecca") is a flightless bird with an inquisitive nature.

they work; this is not a technology that you can apply blindly and expect to get good results. Different problems yield to different techniques, but it is rarely obvious which techniques are suitable for a given situation: you need to know something about the range of possible solutions. And we cover an extremely wide range of techniques. We can do this because, unlike many trade books, this volume does not promote any particular commercial software or approach. We include a large number of examples, but they use illustrative datasets that are small enough to allow you to follow what is going on. Real datasets are far too large to show this (and in any case are usually company confidential). Our datasets are chosen not to illustrate actual large-scale practical problems, but to help you understand what the different techniques do, how they work, and what their range of application is.

The book is aimed at the technically aware general reader who is interested in the principles and ideas underlying the current practice of machine learning. It will also be of interest to information professionals who need to become acquainted with this new technology, and to all those who wish to gain a detailed technical understanding of what machine learning involves. It is written for an eclectic audience of information systems practitioners, programmers, consultants, developers, data scientists, information technology managers, specification writers, patent examiners, curious lay people—as well as students and professors—who need an easy-to-read book with lots of illustrations that describes what the major machine learning techniques are, what they do, how they are used, and how they work. It is practically oriented, with a strong "how to" flavor, and includes algorithms, and often pseudo-code. All those involved in practical data mining will benefit directly from the techniques described. The book is aimed at people who want to cut through to the reality that underlies the hype about machine learning and who seek a practical, nonacademic, unpretentious approach. In most of the book we have avoided requiring any specific theoretical or mathematical knowledge. However, recognizing the growing complexity of the subject as it matures, we have included substantial theoretical material in Chapter 9, Probabilistic methods, and Chapter 10, Deep learning, because this is necessary for a full appreciation of recent practical techniques, in particular deep learning.

The book is organized in layers that make the ideas accessible to readers who are interested in grasping the basics, as well as to those who would like more depth of treatment, along with full details on the techniques covered. We believe that consumers of machine learning need to have some idea of how the algorithms they use work. It is often observed that data models are only as good as the person who interprets them, and that person needs to know something about how the models are produced to appreciate the strengths, and limitations, of the technology. However, it is not necessary for all users to have a deep understanding of the finer details of the algorithms.

We address this situation by describing machine learning methods at successive levels of detail. The book is divided into two parts. Part I is an introduction to machine learning for data mining. The reader will learn the basic ideas, the topmost level, by reading the first three chapters. Chapter 1, What's it all about?, describes, through examples, what machine learning is, where it can be used; it also provides actual practical applications. Chapter 2, Input: concepts, instances, attributes, and Chapter 3, Output: knowledge representation, cover the different kinds of input and output—or *knowledge representation*—that are involved. Different kinds of output dictate different styles of algorithm, and Chapter 4, Algorithms: the basic methods, describes the basic methods of machine learning, simplified to make them easy to comprehend. Here the principles involved are conveyed in a variety of algorithms without getting involved in intricate details or tricky implementation issues. To make progress in the application of machine learning techniques to particular data mining problems, it is essential to be able to measure how well you are doing. Chapter 5, Credibility: evaluating what's been learned, which can be read out of sequence, equips the reader to evaluate the results that are obtained from machine learning, addressing the sometimes complex issues involved in performance evaluation.

Part II introduces advanced techniques of machine learning for data mining. At the lowest and most detailed level, Chapter 6, Trees and rules, and Chapter 7, Extending instance-based and linear models, expose in naked detail the nitty-gritty issues of implementing a spectrum of machine learning algorithms, including the complexities that are necessary for them to work well in practice (but omitting the heavy mathematical machinery that is required for a few of the algorithms). Although many readers may want to ignore such detailed information, it is at this level that full working implementations of machine learning schemes are written. Chapter 8, Data transformations, describes practical topics involved with engineering the input and output to machine learning—e.g., selecting and discretizing attributes. Chapter 9, Probabilistic methods, and Chapter 10, Deep learning, provide a rigorous account of probabilistic methods for machine learning and deep learning respectively. Chapter 11, Beyond supervised and unsupervised learning, looks at semisupervised and multi-instance learning, while Chapter 12, Ensemble learning, covers techniques of "ensemble learning," which combine the output from different learning techniques. Chapter 13, Moving on: applications and beyond, looks to the future.

The book describes most methods used in practical machine learning. However, it does not cover reinforcement learning because it is rarely applied in practical data mining; nor genetic algorithm approaches because these are really just optimization techniques that are not specific to machine learning; nor relational learning and inductive logic programming because they are not very commonly used in mainstream data mining applications.

An Appendix covers some mathematical background needed to follow the material in Chapter 9, Probabilistic methods, and Chapter 10, Deep learning. Another Appendix introduces the WEKA data mining workbench, which provides implementations of most of the ideas described in Parts I and II. We have done this in order to clearly separate conceptual material from the practical aspects of how to use it. At the end of each chapter in Parts I and II are pointers to related WEKA algorithms. You can ignore these, or look at them as you go along, or skip directly to the WEKA material if you are in a hurry to get on with analyzing your data and don't want to be bothered with the technical details of how the algorithms work.

UPDATED AND REVISED CONTENT

We finished writing the first edition of this book in 1999, the second and third in 2005 and 2011 respectively, and now, in May 2016, are just polishing this fourth edition. How things have changed over the past couple of decades! While the basic core of material remains the same, we have made the most of opportunities to update it and add new material, and as a result the book has doubled in size to reflect the changes that have taken place. Of course, there have also been errors to fix, errors that we had accumulated in our publicly available errata file (available through the book's home page at http://www.cs.waikato.ac.nz/ml/weka/book. html).

SECOND EDITION

The major change in the second edition of the book was a separate part at the end of the book that included all the material on the WEKA machine learning workbench. This allowed the main part of the book to stand alone, independent of the workbench. At that time WEKA, a widely used and popular feature of the first edition, had just acquired a radical new look in the form of an interactive graphical user interface—or rather, three separate interactive interfaces—which made it far easier to use. The primary one is the "Explorer," which gives access to all of WEKA's facilities using menu selection and form filling. The others are the Knowledge Flow interface, which allows you to design configurations for streamed data processing, and the Experimenter, with which you set up automated experiments that run selected machine learning algorithms with different parameter settings on a corpus of datasets, collect performance statistics, and perform significance tests on the results. These interfaces lower the bar for becoming a practitioner of machine learning, and the second edition included a full description of how to use them.

It also contained much new material that we briefly mention here. We extended the sections on rule learning and cost-sensitive evaluation. Bowing to popular demand, we added information on neural networks: the perceptron and the closely related Winnow algorithm; the multilayer perceptron and backpropagation algorithm. Logistic regression was also included. We described how to implement nonlinear decision boundaries using both the kernel perceptron and radial basis function networks, and also included support vector machines for regression. We incorporated a new section on Bayesian networks, again in response to readers' requests and WEKA's new capabilities in this regard, with a description of how to learn classifiers based on these networks, and how to implement them efficiently using AD trees.

The previous 5 years (1999–2004) had seen great interest in data mining for text, and this was reflected in the introduction of string attributes in WEKA, multinomial Bayes for document classification, and text transformations. We also described efficient data structures for searching the instance space: kD-trees and ball trees for finding nearest neighbors efficiently, and for accelerating distance-based clustering. We described new attribute selection schemes such as race search and the use of support vector machines; new methods for combining models such as additive regression, additive logistic regression, logistic model trees, and option trees. We also covered recent developments in using unlabeled data to improve classification, including the cotraining and co-EM methods.

THIRD EDITION

For the third edition, we thoroughly edited the second edition and brought it up to date, including a great many new methods and algorithms. WEKA and the book were closely linked together—pretty well everything in WEKA was covered in the book. We also included far more references to the literature, practically tripling the number of references that were in the first edition.

As well as becoming far easier to use, WEKA had grown beyond recognition over the previous decade, and matured enormously in its data mining capabilities. It incorporates an unparalleled range of machine learning algorithms and related techniques. The growth has been partly stimulated by recent developments in the field, and is partly user-led and demand-driven. This puts us in a position where we know a lot about what actual users of data mining want, and we have capitalized on this experience when deciding what to include in this book.

Here are a few of the highlights of the material that was added in the third edition. A section on web mining was included, and, under ethics, a discussion of how individuals can often be "reidentified" from supposedly anonymized data. Other additions included techniques for multi-instance learning, new material on interactive cost-benefit analysis, cost-complexity pruning, advanced association rule algorithms that use extended prefix trees to store a compressed version of the dataset in main memory, kernel ridge regression, stochastic gradient descent, and hierarchical clustering methods. We added new data transformations: partial least squares regression, reservoir sampling, one-class learning, decomposing multi-class classification problems into ensembles of nested dichotomies, and calibrating class probabilities. We added new information on ensemble learning techniques: randomization vs. bagging, and rotation forests. New sections on data stream learning and web mining were added as well.

FOURTH EDITION

One of the main drivers behind this fourth edition was a desire to add comprehensive material on the topic of deep learning, a new development that is essentially enabled by the emergence of truly vast data resources in domains like image and speech processing, and the availability of truly vast computational resources, including server farms and graphics processing units. However, deep learning techniques are heavily based on a potent mix of theory and practice. And we had also received other requests asking us to include more, and more rigorous, theoretical material.

This forced us to rethink the role of theory in the book. We bit the bullet and added two new theoretically oriented chapters. Chapter 10, Deep learning, covers deep learning itself, and its predecessor, Chapter 9, Probabilistic methods, gives a principled theoretical development of probabilistic methods that is necessary to understand a host of other new algorithms. We recognize that many of our readers will not want to stomach all this theory, and we assure them that the remainder of the book has intentionally been left at a far simpler mathematical level. But this additional theoretical base puts some key material in the hands of readers who aspire to understand rapidly advancing techniques from the research world.

Developments in WEKA have proceeded apace. It now provides ways of reaching out and incorporating other languages and systems, such as the popular R statistical computing language, the Spark and Hadoop frameworks for distributed computing, the Python and Groovy languages for scripting, and the MOA system for stream-oriented learning—to name but a few. Recognizing that it is not possible, and perhaps not desirable, to document such a comprehensive and fast-evolving system in a printed book, we have created a series of open online courses, *Data Mining with Weka*, *More Data Mining with Weka*, and *Advanced Data Mining with Weka*, to accompany the book (at https://weka.waikato.ac.nz).

The fourth edition contains numerous other updates and additions, and far more references to the literature. But enough of this: dive in and see for yourself.

ACKNOWLEDGMENTS

Writing the acknowledgments is always the nicest part! A lot of people have helped us, and we relish this opportunity to thank them. This book has arisen out of the machine learning research project in the Computer Science Department at the University of Waikato, New Zealand. We have received generous encouragement and assistance from the academic staff members early on in that project: John Cleary, Sally Jo Cunningham, Matt Humphrey, Lyn Hunt, Bob McQueen, Lloyd Smith, and Tony Smith. We also benefited greatly from interactions with staff members who arrived later: Michael Mayo and Robert Durrant. Special thanks go to Geoff Holmes, who led the project for many years, and Bernhard Pfahringer, who had significant input into many different aspects of the WEKA software. All who have worked on the machine learning project here have contributed to our thinking: we would particularly like to mention early students Steve Garner,

Stuart Inglis and Craig Nevill-Manning for helping us to get the project off the ground in the beginning when success was less certain and things were more difficult.

The WEKA system that illustrates the ideas in this book forms a crucial component of it. It was conceived by the authors and designed and implemented principally by Eibe Frank, Mark Hall, Peter Reutemann, and Len Trigg, but many people in the machine learning laboratory at Waikato made significant contributions. Since the first edition of the book the WEKA team has expanded considerably: so many people have contributed that it is impossible to acknowledge everyone properly. We are grateful to Chris Beckham, for contributing several packages to WEKA, Remco Bouckaert for his Bayes net package and many other contributions, Lin Dong for her implementations of multi-instance learning methods, Dale Fletcher for many database-related aspects, Kurt Driessens for his implementation of Gaussian process regression, James Foulds for his work on multi-instance filtering, Anna Huang for information bottleneck clustering, Martin Gütlein for his work on feature selection, Kathryn Hempstalk for her one-class classifier, Ashraf Kibriya and Richard Kirkby for contributions far too numerous to list, Nikhil Kishore for his implementation of elastic net regression, Niels Landwehr for logistic model trees, Chi-Chung Lau for creating all the icons for the Knowledge Flow interface, Abdelaziz Mahoui for the implementation of K*, Jonathan Miles for his implementation of kernel filtering, Stefan Mutter for association rule mining, Malcolm Ware for numerous miscellaneous contributions, Haijian Shi for his implementations of tree learners, Marc Sumner for his work on speeding up logistic model trees, Tony Voyle for least-median-of-squares regression, Yong Wang for Pace regression and the original implementation of M5′, Benjamin Weber for his great unification of WEKA parsing modules, and Xin Xu for his multi-instance learning package, *JRip*, logistic regression and many other contributions. Our sincere thanks go to all these people for their dedicated work, and also to the many contributors to WEKA from outside our group at Waikato.

Tucked away as we are in a remote (but very pretty) corner of the southern hemisphere, we greatly appreciate the visitors to our department who play a crucial role in acting as sounding boards and helping us to develop our thinking. We would like to mention in particular Rob Holte, Carl Gutwin, and Russell Beale, each of whom visited us for several months; David Aha, who although he only came for a few days did so at an early and fragile stage of the project and performed a great service by his enthusiasm and encouragement; and Kai Ming Ting, who worked with us for 2 years on many of the topics in this book, and helped to bring us into the mainstream of machine learning. More recent visitors included Arie Ben-David, Carla Brodley, Gregory Butler, Stefan Kramer, Johannes Schneider, Jan van Rijn and Michalis Vlachos, and many others who have given talks at our department. We would particularly like to thank Albert Bifet, who gave us detailed feedback on a draft version of the third edition—most of which we have incorporated.

Students at Waikato have played a significant role in the development of the project. Many of them are in the above list of WEKA contributors, but they have also contributed in other ways. In the early days, Jamie Littin worked on ripple-down rules and relational learning. Brent Martin explored instance-based learning and nested instance-based representations. Murray Fife slaved over relational learning, Nadeeka Madapathage investigated the use of functional languages for expressing machine learning algorithms. Kathryn Hempstalk worked on one-class learning and Richard Kirkby on data streams. Gabi Schmidberger worked on density estimation trees, Lan Huang on concept-based text clustering, and Alyona Medelyan on keyphrase extraction. More recently, Felipe Bravo has worked on sentiment classification for Twitter, Mi Li on fast clustering methods, and Tim

Leathart on ensembles of nested dichotomies. Other graduate students have influenced us in numerous ways, particularly Gordon Paynter, YingYing Wen, and Zane Bray, who have worked with us on text mining, and Quan Sun and Xiaofeng Yu. Colleagues Steve Jones and Malika Mahoui have also made far-reaching contributions to these and other machine learning projects. We have also learned much from our many visiting students from Freiburg, including Nils Weidmann.

Ian Witten would like to acknowledge the formative role of his former students at Calgary, particularly Brent Krawchuk, Dave Maulsby, Thong Phan, and Tanja Mitrovic, all of whom helped him develop his early ideas in machine learning, as did faculty members Bruce MacDonald, Brian Gaines, and David Hill at Calgary, and John Andreae at the University of Canterbury.

Eibe Frank is indebted to his former supervisor at the University of Karlsruhe, Klaus-Peter Huber, who infected him with the fascination of machines that learn. On his travels Eibe has benefited from interactions with Peter Turney, Joel Martin, and Berry de Bruijn in Canada; Luc de Raedt, Christoph Helma, Kristian Kersting, Stefan Kramer, Ulrich Rückert, and Ashwin Srinivasan in Germany.

Mark Hall thanks his former supervisor Lloyd Smith, now at Missouri State University, who exhibited the patience of Job when his thesis drifted from its original topic into the realms of machine learning. The many and varied people who have been part of, or have visited, the machine learning group at the University of Waikato over the years deserve a special thanks for their valuable insights and stimulating discussions.

Chris Pal thanks his coauthors for the invitation to help write this fourth edition; and his family for accommodating the extra time spent writing. He thanks Polytechique Montréal for the sabbatical that allowed him to travel to New Zealand, leading to this fruitful collaboration; and the University of Waikato Department of Computer Science for hosting him. He also thanks his many mentors, academic family, coauthors, and colleagues over the years, whose perspectives have been enriching and have influenced the presentation here, including: Brendan Frey, Geoff Hinton, Yoshua Bengio, Sam Roweis, Andrew McCallum, and Charles Sutton among many others. Particular thanks goes to Hugo Larochelle for his pedagogical perspectives on deep learning. Chris also thanks his friends and colleagues at the Montréal Institute for Learning Algorithms, the Theano development team and all his current and former students for helping to create such a great environment for machine learning research. Particular thanks goes to Chris Beckham who provided excellent feedback on earlier drafts of the new chapters in this edition.

Charlie Kent and Tim Pitts of Morgan Kaufmann have worked hard to shape this book, and Nicky Carter, our production editor, has made the process go very smoothly. We would like to thank the librarians of the Repository of Machine Learning Databases at the University of California, Irvine, whose carefully collected datasets have been invaluable in our research.

Our research has been funded by the New Zealand Foundation for Research, Science and Technology and the Royal Society of New Zealand Marsden Fund. The Department of Computer Science at the University of Waikato has generously supported us in all sorts of ways, and we owe a particular debt of gratitude to Mark Apperley for his enlightened leadership and warm encouragement. Part of the first edition was written while both authors were visiting the University of Calgary, Canada, and the support of the Computer Science department there is gratefully acknowledged—as well as the positive and helpful attitude of the long-suffering students in the machine learning course, on whom we experimented. Part of the second edition was written at the University of Lethbridge in Southern Alberta on a visit supported by Canada's Informatics Circle of Research Excellence.

Last, and most of all, we are grateful to our families and partners. Pam, Anna and Nikki were all too well aware of the implications of having an author in the house ("not again!") but let Ian go ahead and write the book anyway. Julie was always supportive, even when Eibe had to burn the midnight oil in the machine learning lab, and Immo and Ollig provided exciting diversions. Bernadette too was very supportive, somehow managing to keep the combined noise output of Charlotte, Luke, Zach, Kyle, and Francesca to a level that allowed Mark to concentrate. Between us we hail from Canada, England, Germany, Ireland, New Zealand, and Samoa: New Zealand has brought us together and provided an ideal, even idyllic, place to do this work.

Introduction to data mining

What's it all about?

CHAPTER OUTLINE

1.1 **Data Mining and Machine Learning** 4
   Describing Structural Patterns 6
   Machine Learning 7
   Data Mining 9
1.2 **Simple Examples: The Weather Problem and Others** 9
   The Weather Problem 10
   Contact Lenses: An Idealized Problem 12
   Irises: A Classic Numeric Dataset 14
   CPU Performance: Introducing Numeric Prediction 16
   Labor Negotiations: A More Realistic Example 16
   Soybean Classification: A Classic Machine Learning Success 19
1.3 **Fielded Applications** 21
   Web Mining 21
   Decisions Involving Judgment 22
   Screening Images 23
   Load Forecasting 24
   Diagnosis 25
   Marketing and Sales 26
   Other Applications 27
1.4 **The Data Mining Process** 28
1.5 **Machine Learning and Statistics** 30
1.6 **Generalization as Search** 31
   Enumerating the Concept Space 32
   Bias 33
1.7 **Data Mining and Ethics** 35
   Reidentification 36
   Using Personal Information 37
   Wider Issues 38
1.8 **Further Reading and Bibliographic Notes** 38

Data Mining.
© 2017 Elsevier Inc. All rights reserved.

Human in vitro fertilization involves collecting several eggs from a woman's ovaries, which, after fertilization with partner or donor sperm, produce several embryos. Some of these are selected and transferred to the woman's uterus. The problem is to select the "best" embryos to use—the ones that are most likely to survive. Selection is based on around 60 recorded features of the embryos—characterizing their morphology, oocyte, follicle, and sperm sample. The number of features is sufficiently large that it is difficult for an embryologist to assess them all simultaneously and correlate historical data with the crucial outcome of whether that embryo did or did not result in a live child. In a research project in England, machine learning has been investigated as a technique for making the selection, using historical records of embryos and their outcome as training data.

Every year, dairy farmers in New Zealand have to make a tough business decision: which cows to retain in their herd and which to sell off to an abattoir. Typically, one-fifth of the cows in a dairy herd are culled each year near the end of the milking season as feed reserves dwindle. Each cow's breeding and milk production history influences this decision. Other factors include age (a cow is nearing the end of its productive life at 8 years), health problems, history of difficult calving, undesirable temperament traits (kicking or jumping fences), and not being in calf for the following season. About 700 attributes for each of several million cows have been recorded over the years. Machine learning has been investigated as a way of ascertaining what factors are taken into account by successful farmers—not to automate the decision but to propagate their skills and experience to others.

Life and death. From Europe to the antipodes. Family and business. Machine learning is a burgeoning new technology for mining knowledge from data, a technology that a lot of people are starting to take seriously.

1.1 DATA MINING AND MACHINE LEARNING

We are overwhelmed with data. The amount of data in the world, in our lives, seems ever-increasing—and there's no end in sight. Omnipresent computers make it too easy to save things that previously we would have trashed. Inexpensive disks and online storage make it too easy to postpone decisions about what to do with all this stuff—we simply get more memory and keep it all. Ubiquitous electronics record our decisions, our choices in the supermarket, our financial habits, our comings and goings. We swipe our way through the world, every swipe a record in a database. The World Wide Web overwhelms us with information; meanwhile, every choice we make is recorded. And all these are just personal choices: they have countless counterparts in the world of commerce and industry. We would all testify to the growing gap between the *generation of data* and the *benefit we get from it*. Large corporations have seized the opportunity, but the tools needed to unlock this potential—the tools we describe in this book—are available to everyone. Lying hidden in all this data is information, potentially useful information, that we rarely make explicit or take advantage of.

This book is about looking for patterns in data. There is nothing new about this. People have been seeking patterns in data ever since human life began. Hunters seek patterns in animal migration behavior, farmers seek patterns in crop growth, politicians seek patterns in voter opinion, and lovers seek patterns in their partners' responses. A scientist's job (like a baby's) is to make sense of data, to discover the patterns that govern how the physical world works, and encapsulate them in theories that can be used for predicting what will happen in new situations. The entrepreneur's job is to identify opportunities, that is, patterns in behavior that can be turned into a profitable business, and exploit them.

In *data mining*, the data is stored electronically and the search is automated—or at least augmented—by computer. Even this is not particularly new. Economists, statisticians, forecasters, and communication engineers have long worked with the idea that patterns in data can be sought automatically, identified, validated, and used for prediction. What is new is the staggering increase in opportunities for finding patterns in data. The unbridled growth of databases in recent years, databases on such everyday activities as customer choices, brings data mining to the forefront of new business technologies. It has been estimated that the amount of data stored in the world's databases doubles every 20 months, and although it would surely be difficult to justify this figure in any quantitative sense, we can all relate to the pace of growth qualitatively. As the flood of data swells and machines that can undertake the searching become commonplace, the opportunities for data mining increase. As the world grows in complexity, overwhelming us with the data it generates, data mining becomes our only hope for elucidating hidden patterns. Intelligently analyzed data is a valuable resource. It can lead to new insights, better decision making, and, in commercial settings, competitive advantages.

Data mining is about solving problems by analyzing data already present in databases. Suppose, to take a well-worn example, the problem is fickle customer loyalty in a highly competitive marketplace. A database of customer choices, along with customer profiles, holds the key to this problem. Patterns of behavior of former customers can be analyzed to identify distinguishing characteristics of those likely to switch products and those likely to remain loyal. Once such characteristics are found, they can be put to work to identify present customers who are likely to jump ship. This group can be targeted for special treatment, treatment too costly to apply to the customer base as a whole. More positively, the same techniques can be used to identify customers who might be attracted to another service the enterprise provides, one they are not presently enjoying, to target them for special offers that promote this service. In today's highly competitive, customer-centered, service-oriented economy, data is the raw material that fuels business growth.

Data mining is defined as the process of discovering patterns in data. The process must be automatic or (more usually) semiautomatic. The patterns discovered must be meaningful in that they lead to some advantage—e.g., an economic advantage. The data is invariably present in substantial quantities.

And how are the patterns expressed? Useful patterns allow us to make nontrivial predictions on new data. There are two extremes for the expression of a pattern: as a black box whose innards are effectively incomprehensible and as a transparent box whose construction reveals the structure of the pattern. Both, we are assuming, make good predictions. The difference is whether or not the patterns that are mined are represented in terms of a structure that can be examined, reasoned about, and used to inform future decisions. Such patterns we call *structural* because they capture the decision structure in an explicit way. In other words, they help to explain something about the data.

Most of this book is about techniques for finding and describing structural patterns in data, but there are applications where black-box methods are more appropriate because they yield greater predictive accuracy, and we also cover those. Many of the techniques that we cover have developed within a field known as *machine learning*.

DESCRIBING STRUCTURAL PATTERNS

What is meant by *structural patterns*? How do you describe them? And what form does the input take? We will answer these questions by way of illustration rather than by attempting formal, and ultimately sterile, definitions. There will be plenty of examples later in this chapter, but let's examine one right now to get a feeling for what we're talking about.

Look at the contact lens data in Table 1.1. This gives the conditions under which an optician might want to prescribe soft contact lenses, hard contact lenses, or no contact lenses at all; we will say more about what the individual features mean later. Each line of the table is one of the examples. Part of a structural description of this information might be as follows:

```
If tear production rate = reduced then recommendation = none
Otherwise, if age = young and astigmatic = no then recommendation = soft
```

Structural descriptions need not necessarily be couched as rules such as these. Decision trees, which specify the sequences of decisions that need to be made along with the resulting recommendation, are another popular means of expression.

This example is a very simplistic one. For a start, all combinations of possible values are represented in the table. There are 24 rows, representing 3 possible values of age and 2 values each for spectacle prescription, astigmatism, and tear production rate ($3 \times 2 \times 2 \times 2 = 24$). The rules do not really generalize from the data; they merely summarize it. In most learning situations, the set of examples given as input is far from complete, and part of the job is to generalize to other, new examples.

Table 1.1 The Contact Lens Data

Age	Spectacle Prescription	Astigmatism	Tear Production Rate	Recommended Lenses
Young	Myope	No	Reduced	None
Young	Myope	No	Normal	Soft
Young	Myope	Yes	Reduced	None
Young	Myope	Yes	Normal	Hard
Young	Hypermetrope	No	Reduced	None
Young	Hypermetrope	No	Normal	Soft
Young	Hypermetrope	Yes	Reduced	None
Young	Hypermetrope	Yes	Normal	Hard
Prepresbyopic	Myope	No	Reduced	None
Prepresbyopic	Myope	No	Normal	Soft
Prepresbyopic	Myope	Yes	Reduced	None
Prepresbyopic	Myope	Yes	Normal	Hard
Prepresbyopic	Hypermetrope	No	Reduced	None
Prepresbyopic	Hypermetrope	No	Normal	Soft
Prepresbyopic	Hypermetrope	Yes	Reduced	None
Prepresbyopic	Hypermetrope	Yes	Normal	None
Presbyopic	Myope	No	Reduced	None
Presbyopic	Myope	No	Normal	None
Presbyopic	Myope	Yes	Reduced	None
Presbyopic	Myope	Yes	Normal	Hard
Presbyopic	Hypermetrope	No	Reduced	None
Presbyopic	Hypermetrope	No	Normal	Soft
Presbyopic	Hypermetrope	Yes	Reduced	None
Presbyopic	Hypermetrope	Yes	Normal	None

You can imagine omitting some of the rows in the table for which tear production rate is *reduced* and still coming up with the rule.

```
If tear production rate = reduced then recommendation = none
```

which would generalize to the missing rows and fill them in correctly. Second, values are specified for all the features in all the examples. Real-life datasets often contain examples in which the values of some features, for some reason or other, are unknown—e.g., measurements were not taken or were lost. Third, the preceding rules classify the examples correctly, whereas often, because of errors or *noise* in the data, misclassifications occur even on the data that is used to create the classifier.

MACHINE LEARNING

Now that we have some idea of the inputs and outputs, let's turn to machine learning. What is learning, anyway? What is *machine* learning? These are philosophical questions, and we will not be much concerned with philosophy in this book; our emphasis is firmly on the practical. However, it is worth spending a few moments at the outset on fundamental issues, just to see how tricky they are, before rolling up our sleeves and looking at machine learning in practice. Our dictionary defines "to learn" as

to get knowledge of by study, experience, or being taught;
to become aware by information or from observation;
to commit to memory;
to be informed of, ascertain;
to receive instruction.

These meanings have some shortcomings when it comes to talking about computers. For the first two, it is virtually impossible to test whether learning has been achieved or not. How do you know whether a machine has "got knowledge of" something? You probably can't just ask it questions; even if you could, you wouldn't be testing its ability to learn but its ability to answer questions. How do you know whether it has "become aware" of something? The whole question of whether computers can be aware, or conscious, is a burning philosophical issue. As for the last three meanings, although we can see what they denote in human terms, merely "committing to memory" and "receiving instruction" seem to fall far short of what we might mean by machine learning. They are too passive, and we know that computers find these tasks trivial. Instead, we are interested in improvements in performance, or at least in the potential for performance, in new situations. You can "commit something to memory" or "be informed of something" by rote learning without being able to apply the new knowledge to new situations. You can receive instruction without benefiting from it at all.

Earlier we defined data mining operationally, as the process of discovering patterns, automatically or semiautomatically, in large quantities of data—and the patterns must be useful. An operational definition can be formulated in the same way for learning. How about things learnt when they change their behavior in a way that makes them perform better in the future.

This ties learning to *performance* rather than *knowledge*. You can test learning by observing the behavior and comparing it with past behavior. This is a much more objective kind of definition and appears to be far more satisfactory.

But still there's a problem. Learning is a rather slippery concept. Lots of things change their behavior in ways that make them perform better in the future, yet we wouldn't want to say that they have actually *learned*. A good example is a comfortable slipper. Has it *learned* the shape of your foot? It has certainly changed its behavior to make it perform better as a slipper! Yet we would hardly want to call this *learning*. In everyday language, we often use the word "*training*" to denote a mindless kind of learning. We train animals and even plants, although it would be stretching the word a bit to talk of training objects such as slippers that are not in any sense alive. But learning is different. Learning implies thinking. Learning implies purpose. Something that learns has to do so intentionally. That is why we wouldn't say that a vine has learned to grow round a trellis in a vineyard—we'd say it has been *trained*. Learning without purpose is merely training. Or, more to the point, in learning the purpose is the learner's, whereas in training it is the teacher's.

Thus on closer examination the second definition of learning, in operational, performance-oriented terms, has its own problems when it comes to talking about computers. To decide whether something has actually learned, you need to see whether it intended to, whether there was any purpose involved. That makes the concept moot when applied to machines because whether artifacts can behave purposefully is unclear. Philosophical discussions of what is *really* meant by "learning," like discussions of what is *really* meant by "intention" or "purpose," are fraught with difficulty. Even courts of law find intention hard to grapple with.

DATA MINING

Fortunately the kind of learning techniques explained in this book do not present these conceptual problems—they are called "machine learning" without really presupposing any particular philosophical stance about what learning actually is. Data mining is a practical topic and involves learning in a practical, not a theoretical, sense. We are interested in techniques for finding patterns in data, patterns that provide insight or enable fast and accurate decision making. The data will take the form of a set of examples—examples of customers who have switched loyalties, for instance, or situations in which certain kinds of contact lenses can be prescribed. The output takes the form of predictions on new examples—a prediction of whether a particular customer will switch or a prediction of what kind of lens will be prescribed under given circumstances.

Many learning techniques look for structural descriptions of what is learned, descriptions that can become fairly complex and are typically expressed as sets of rules such as the ones described previously or the decision trees described later in this chapter. Because they can be understood by people, these descriptions serve to explain what has been learned, in other words, to explain the basis for new predictions. Experience shows that in many applications of machine learning to data mining, the explicit knowledge structures that are acquired, the structural descriptions, are at least as important as the ability to perform well on new examples. People frequently use data mining to gain knowledge, not just predictions. Gaining knowledge from data certainly sounds like a good idea if you can do it. To find out how, read on!

1.2 SIMPLE EXAMPLES: THE WEATHER PROBLEM AND OTHERS

We will be using a lot of examples in this book, which seems particularly appropriate considering that the book is all about learning from examples! There are several standard datasets that we will come back to repeatedly. Different datasets tend to expose new issues and challenges, and it is interesting and instructive to have in mind a variety of problems when considering learning methods. In fact, the need to work with different datasets is so important that a corpus containing more than 100 example problems has been gathered together so that different algorithms can be tested and compared on the same set of problems.

The illustrations in this section are all unrealistically simple. Serious application of machine learning involve thousands, hundreds of thousands, or even millions of individual cases. But when explaining what algorithms do and how they work, we need simple examples that enable us to capture the essence of the problem yet small enough to be comprehensible in every detail. We will be working with the illustrations in this section throughout the book, and they are intended to be "academic" in the sense that they will help us to understand what is going on. Some actual fielded applications of learning techniques are discussed in Section 1.3, and many more are covered in the books mentioned in the *Further Reading* section at the end of the chapter.

Another problem with actual real-life datasets is that they are often proprietary. No one is going to share their customer and product choice database with you so that you can understand the details of their data mining application and how it works. Corporate data is a valuable asset, one whose value has increased enormously with the development of machine learning techniques such as those described in this book. Yet we are concerned here with understanding how these methods work, understanding their details so that we can trace their operation on actual data. That is why our illustrations are simple ones. But they are not *simplistic*: they exhibit the features of real datasets.

THE WEATHER PROBLEM

The weather problem is a tiny dataset that we will use repeatedly to illustrate machine learning methods. Entirely fictitious, it supposedly concerns the conditions that are suitable for playing some unspecified game. In general, examples in a dataset are characterized by the values of features, or *attributes*, that measure different aspects of the example. In this case there are four attributes: *outlook*, *temperature*, *humidity*, and *windy*. The outcome is whether to play or not.

In its simplest form, shown in Table 1.2, all four attributes have values that are symbolic categories rather than numbers. Outlook can be *sunny, overcast*, or *rainy*; temperature can be *hot, mild*, or *cool*; humidity can be *high* or *normal*; and windy can be *true* or *false*. This creates 36 possible combinations $(3 \times 3 \times 2 \times 2 = 36)$, of which 14 are present in the set of input examples.

A set of rules learned from this information—not necessarily a very good one—might look like this:

```
If outlook = sunny and humidity = high    then play = no
If outlook = rainy and windy = true       then play = no
If outlook = overcast                     then play = yes
If humidity = normal                      then play = yes
If none of the above                      then play = yes
```

Table 1.2 The Weather Data

Outlook	Temperature	Humidity	Windy	Play
Sunny	Hot	High	False	No
Sunny	Hot	High	True	No
Overcast	Hot	High	False	Yes
Rainy	Mild	High	False	Yes
Rainy	Cool	Normal	False	Yes
Rainy	Cool	Normal	True	No
Overcast	Cool	Normal	True	Yes
Sunny	Mild	High	False	No
Sunny	Cool	Normal	False	Yes
Rainy	Mild	Normal	False	Yes
Sunny	Mild	Normal	True	Yes
Overcast	Mild	High	True	Yes
Overcast	Hot	Normal	False	Yes
Rainy	Mild	High	True	No

These rules are meant to be interpreted in order: the first one; then, if it doesn't apply, the second; and so on. A set of rules that are intended to be interpreted in sequence is called a *decision list*. Interpreted as a decision list, the rules correctly classify all of the examples in the table, whereas taken individually, out of context, some of the rules are incorrect. For example, the rule *if humidity = normal then play = yes* gets one of the examples wrong (check which one). The meaning of a set of rules depends on how it is interpreted—not surprisingly!

n the slightly more complex form shown in Table 1.3, two of the attributes—temperature and humidity—have numeric values. This means that any learning scheme must create inequalities involving these attributes, rather than simple equality tests as in the former case. This is called a *numeric-attribute problem*—in this case, a *mixed-attribute problem* because not all attributes are numeric.

Now the first rule given earlier might take the form:

```
If outlook = sunny and humidity > 83 then play = no
```

A slightly more complex process is required to come up with rules that involve numeric tests.

The rules we have seen so far are *classification rules*: they predict the classification of the example in terms of whether to play or not. It is equally possible to disregard the classification and just look for any rules that strongly associate different attribute values. These are called *association rules*. Many

Table 1.3 Weather Data With Some Numeric Attributes

Outlook	Temperature	Humidity	Windy	Play
Sunny	85	85	False	No
Sunny	80	90	True	No
Overcast	83	86	False	Yes
Rainy	70	96	False	Yes
Rainy	68	80	False	Yes
Rainy	65	70	True	No
Overcast	64	65	True	Yes
Sunny	72	95	False	No
Sunny	69	70	False	Yes
Rainy	75	80	False	Yes
Sunny	75	70	True	Yes
Overcast	72	90	True	Yes
Overcast	81	75	False	Yes
Rainy	71	91	True	No

association rules can be derived from the weather data in Table 1.2. Some good ones are:

```
If temperature = cool                       then humidity = normal
If humidity = normal and windy = false      then play = yes
If outlook = sunny and play = no            then humidity = high
If windy = false and play = no              then outlook = sunny
                                             and humidity = high.
```

All these rules are 100% correct on the given data: they make no false predictions. The first two apply to four examples in the dataset, the next to three examples, and the fourth to two examples. And there are many other rules: in fact, nearly 60 association rules can be found that apply to two or more examples of the weather data and are completely correct on this data. And if you look for rules that are less than 100% correct, then you will find many more. There are so many because unlike classification rules, association rules can "predict" any of the attributes, not just a specified class, and can even predict more than one thing. For example, the fourth rule predicts both that *outlook* will be *sunny* and that *humidity* will be *high*.

CONTACT LENSES: AN IDEALIZED PROBLEM

The contact lens data introduced earlier tells you the kind of contact lens to prescribe, given certain information about a patient. Note that this example is intended for illustration only: it grossly oversimplifies the problem and should certainly not be used for diagnostic purposes!

```
If tear production rate = reduced then recommendation = none.
If age = young and astigmatic = no and tear production rate = normal
   then recommendation = soft
If age = pre-presbyopic and astigmatic = no and tear production
   rate = normal then recommendation = soft
If age = presbyopic and spectacle prescription = myope and
   astigmatic = no then recommendation = none
If spectacle prescription = hypermetrope and astigmatic = no and
   tear production rate = normal then recommendation = soft
If spectacle prescription = myope and astigmatic = yes and
   tear production rate = normal then recommendation = hard
If age = young and astigmatic = yes and tear production rate = normal
   then recommendation = hard
If age = pre-presbyopic and spectacle prescription = hypermetrope
   and astigmatic = yes then recommendation = none
If age = presbyopic and spectacle prescription = hypermetrope
   and astigmatic = yes then recommendation = none
```

FIGURE 1.1

Rules for the contact lens data.

The first column of Table 1.1 gives the age of the patient. In case you're wondering, *presbyopia* is a form of long-sightedness that accompanies the onset of middle age. The second gives the spectacle prescription: *myope* means short-sighted and *hypermetrope* means longsighted. The third shows whether the patient is astigmatic, while the fourth relates to the rate of tear production, which is important in this context because tears lubricate contact lenses. The final column shows which kind of lenses to prescribe, whether *hard*, *soft*, or *none*. All possible combinations of the attribute values are represented in Table 1.1.

A sample set of rules learned from this information is shown in Fig. 1.1. This is a rather large set of rules, but they do correctly classify all the examples. These rules are complete and deterministic: they give a unique prescription for every conceivable example. Generally this is not the case. Sometimes there are situations in which no rule applies; other times more than one rule may apply, resulting in conflicting recommendations. Sometimes probabilities or weights may be associated with the rules themselves to indicate that some are more important, or more reliable, than others.

You might be wondering whether there is a smaller rule set that performs as well. If so, would you be better off using the smaller rule set, and, if so, why? These are exactly the kinds of questions that will occupy us in this book. Because the examples form a complete set for the problem space, the rules do no more than summarize all the information that is given, expressing it in a different and more concise way. Even though it involves no generalization, this is often a very useful thing to do! People frequently use machine learning techniques to gain insight into the structure of their data rather than to make predictions for new cases. In fact, a prominent and successful line of research in machine learning began as an attempt to compress a huge database of possible chess endgames and their outcomes into a data structure of reasonable size.

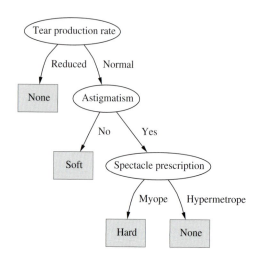

FIGURE 1.2

Decision tree for the contact lens data.

The data structure chosen for this enterprise was not a set of rules but a decision tree.

Fig. 1.2 shows a structural description for the contact lens data in the form of a decision tree, which for many purposes is a more concise and perspicuous representation of the rules and has the advantage that it can be visualized more easily. (However, this decision tree—in contrast to the rule set given in Fig. 1.1—classifies two examples incorrectly.) The tree calls first for a test on *tear production rate*, and the first two branches correspond to the two possible outcomes. If *tear production rate* is *reduced* (the left branch), the outcome is *none*. If it is *normal* (the right branch), a second test is made, this time on *astigmatism*. Eventually, whatever the outcome of the tests, a leaf of the tree is reached that dictates the contact lens recommendation for that case. The question of what is the most natural and easily understood format for the output from a machine learning scheme is one that we will return to in Chapter 3, Output: knowledge representation.

IRISES: A CLASSIC NUMERIC DATASET

The iris dataset, which dates back to seminal work by the eminent statistician R.A. Fisher in the mid-1930s and is arguably the most famous dataset used in machine learning, contains 50 examples each of three types of plant: *Iris setosa*, *Iris versicolor*, and *Iris virginica*. It is excerpted in Table 1.4. There are four attributes: *sepal length*, *sepal width*, *petal length*, and *petal width* (all measured in centimeters). Unlike previous datasets, all attributes have values that are numeric.

Table 1.4 The Iris Data

	Sepal Length	Sepal Width	Petal Length	Petal Width	Type
1	5.1	3.5	1.4	0.2	Iris setosa
2	4.9	3.0	1.4	0.2	I. setosa
3	4.7	3.2	1.3	0.2	I. setosa
4	4.6	3.1	1.5	0.2	I. setosa
5	5.0	3.6	1.4	0.2	I. setosa
...					
51	7.0	3.2	4.7	1.4	Iris versicolor
52	6.4	3.2	4.5	1.5	I. versicolor
53	6.9	3.1	4.9	1.5	I. versicolor
54	5.5	2.3	4.0	1.3	I. versicolor
55	6.5	2.8	4.6	1.5	I. versicolor
...					
101	6.3	3.3	6.0	2.5	Iris virginica
102	5.8	2.7	5.1	1.9	I. virginica
103	7.1	3.0	5.9	2.1	I. virginica
104	6.3	2.9	5.6	1.8	I. virginica
105	6.5	3.0	5.8	2.2	I. virginica
...					

The following set of rules might be learned from this dataset:

```
If petal-length < 2.45 then Iris-setosa
If sepal-width < 2.10 then Iris-versicolor
If sepal-width < 2.45 and petal-length < 4.55 then Iris-versicolor
If sepal-width < 2.95 and petal-width < 1.35 then Iris-versicolor
If petal-length ≥ 2.45 and petal-length < 4.45 then Iris-versicolor
If sepal-length ≥ 5.85 and petal-length < 4.75 then Iris-versicolor
If sepal-width < 2.55 and petal-length < 4.95 and petal-width < 1.55 then
    Iris-versicolor
If petal-length ≥ 2.45 and petal-length < 4.95 and petal-width < 1.55 then
    Iris-versicolor
If sepal-length ≥ 6.55 and petal-length < 5.05 then Iris-versicolor
If sepal-width < 2.75 and petal-width < 1.65 and sepal-length < 6.05
    then Iris-versicolor
If sepal-length ≥ 5.85 and sepal-length < 5.95 and petal-length < 4.85
    then Iris-versicolor
If petal-length ≥ 5.15 then Iris-virginica
If petal-width ≥ 1.85 then Iris-virginica
If petal-width ≥ 1.75 and sepal-width < 3.05 then Iris-virginica
If petal-length ≥ 4.95 and petal-width < 1.55 then Iris-virginica
```

These rules are very cumbersome, and we will see in Chapter 3, Output: knowledge representation, how more compact rules can be expressed that convey the same information.

Table 1.5 The CPU Performance Data

| | Cycle Time (ns) | Main Memory (Kb) | | Cache (KB) | Channels | | Performance |
| | | Min | Max | | Min | Max | |
	MYCT	MMIN	MMAX	CACH	CHMIN	CHMAX	PRP
1	125	256	6000	256	16	128	198
2	29	8000	32,000	32	8	32	269
3	29	8000	32,000	32	8	32	220
4	29	8000	32,000	32	8	32	172
5	29	8000	16,000	32	8	16	132
...							
207	125	2000	8000	0	2	14	52
208	480	512	8000	32	0	0	67
209	480	1000	4000	0	0	0	45

CPU PERFORMANCE: INTRODUCING NUMERIC PREDICTION

Although the iris dataset involves numeric attributes, the outcome—the type of iris—is a category, not a numeric value. Table 1.5 shows some data for which both the outcome and the attributes are numeric. It concerns the relative performance of computer processing power on the basis of a number of relevant attributes: each row represents 1 of 209 different computer configurations.

The classic way of dealing with continuous prediction is to write the outcome as a linear sum of the attribute values with appropriate weights, e.g.,

$$PRP = -55.9 + 0.0489 \text{ MYCT} + 0.0153 \text{ MMIN} + 0.0056 \text{ MMAX}$$
$$+ 0.6410 \text{ CACH} - 0.2700 \text{ CHMIN} + 1.480 \text{ CHMAX}$$

(The abbreviated variable names are given in the second row of the table.) This is called a *linear regression* equation, and the process of determining the weights is called *linear regression*, a well-known procedure in statistics that we will review in Chapter 4, Algorithms: the basic methods. The basic regression method is incapable of discovering nonlinear relationships, but variants exist—we encounter them later in this book. In Chapter 3, Output: knowledge representation, we will examine other representations that can be used for predicting numeric quantities.

In the iris and central processing unit (CPU) performance data, all the attributes have numeric values. Practical situations frequently present a mixture of numeric and nonnumeric attributes.

LABOR NEGOTIATIONS: A MORE REALISTIC EXAMPLE

The labor negotiations dataset in Table 1.6 summarizes the outcome of Canadian labor contract negotiations in 1987 and 1988. It includes all collective

Table 1.6 The Labor Negotiations Data

Attribute	Type	1	2	3	...	40
Duration	(Number of years)	1	2	3		2
Wage increase 1st year	Percentage	2%	4%	4.3%		4.5
Wage increase 2nd year	Percentage	?	5%	4.4%		4.0
Wage increase 3rd year	Percentage	?	?	?		?
Cost of living adjustment	{None, tcf, tc}	None	Tcf	?		None
Working hours per week	(Number of hours)	28	35	38		40
Pension	{None, ret-allw, empl-cntr}	None	?	?		?
Standby pay	Percentage	?	13%	?		?
Shift-work supplement	Percentage	?	5%	4%		4
Education allowance	{Yes, no}	Yes	?	?		?
Statutory holidays	(Number of days)	11	15	12		12
Vacation	{Below-avg, avg, gen}	Avg	Gen	Gen		Avg
Long-term disability assistance	{Yes, no}	No	?	?		Yes
Dental plan contribution	{None, half, full}	None	?	Full		Full
Bereavement assistance	{Yes, no}	No	?	?		Yes
Health-plan contribution	{None, half, full}	None	?	Full		Half
Acceptability of contract	{Good, bad}	Bad	Good	Good		Good

agreements reached in the business and personal services sector for organizations with at least 500 members (teachers, nurses, university staff, police, etc.). Each case concerns one contract, and the outcome is whether the contract is deemed *acceptable* or *unacceptable*. The acceptable contracts are ones in which agreements were accepted by both labor and management. The unacceptable ones are either known offers that fell through because one party would not accept them or acceptable contracts that had been significantly perturbed to the extent that, in the view of experts, they would not have been accepted.

There are 40 examples in the dataset (plus another 17 that are normally reserved for test purposes). Unlike the other tables here, Table 1.6 presents the examples as columns rather than as rows; otherwise, it would have to be stretched over several pages. Many of the values are unknown or missing, as indicated by question marks.

This is a much more realistic dataset than the others we have seen. It contains many missing values, and it seems unlikely that an exact classification can be obtained.

Fig. 1.3 shows two decision trees that represent the dataset. Fig. 1.3A is simple and approximate: it doesn't represent the data exactly. For example, it will

(A)   (B)

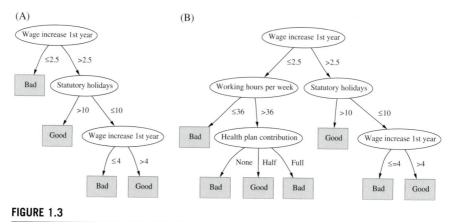

FIGURE 1.3

Decision trees for the labor negotiations data.

predict *bad* for some contracts that are actually marked *good*. But it does make intuitive sense: a contract is bad (for the employee!) if the wage increase in the first year is too small (less than 2.5%). If the first-year wage increase is larger than this, it is good if there are lots of statutory holidays (more than 10 days). Even if there are fewer statutory holidays, it is good if the first-year wage increase is large enough (more than 4%).

Fig. 1.3B is a more complex decision tree that represents the same dataset. Take a detailed look down the left branch. At first sight it doesn't seem to make sense intuitively that, if the working hours exceed 36, a contract is bad if there is no health-plan contribution or a full health-plan contribution but is good if there is a half health-plan contribution. It is certainly reasonable that the health-plan contribution plays a role in the decision, but it seems anomalous that half is good and both full and none are bad. However, on reflection this could make sense after all, because "good" contracts are ones that have been accepted by *both* parties: labor and management. Perhaps this structure reflects compromises that had to be made to get agreement. This kind of detailed reasoning about what parts of decision trees mean is a good way of getting to know your data and think about the underlying problem.

In fact, Fig. 1.3B is a more accurate representation of the training dataset than Fig. 1.3A. But it is not necessarily a more accurate representation of the underlying concept of good versus bad contracts. Although it is more accurate on the data that was used to train the classifier, it may perform less well on an independent set of test data. It may be "overfitted" to the training data—following it too slavishly. The tree in Fig. 1.3A is obtained from the one in Fig. 1.3B by a process of pruning, which we will learn more about in Chapter 6, Trees and rules.

SOYBEAN CLASSIFICATION: A CLASSIC MACHINE LEARNING SUCCESS

An often quoted early success story in the application of machine learning to practical problems is the identification of rules for diagnosing soybean diseases. The data is taken from questionnaires describing plant diseases. There are about 680 examples, each representing a diseased plant. Plants were measured on 35 attributes, each one having a small set of possible values. Examples are labeled with the diagnosis of an expert in plant biology: there are 19 disease categories altogether—horrible-sounding diseases such as diaporthe stem canker, rhizoctonia root rot, and bacterial blight, to mention just a few.

Table 1.7 gives the attributes, the number of different values that each can have, and a sample record for one particular plant. The attributes are placed into different categories just to make them easier to read.

Here are two example rules, learned from this data:

```
If   leaf condition = normal and
     stem condition = abnormal and
     stem cankers = below soil line and
     canker lesion color = brown
then
     diagnosis is rhizoctonia root rot

If   leaf malformation = absent and
     stem condition = abnormal and
     stem cankers = below soil line and
     canker lesion color = brown
then
     diagnosis is rhizoctonia root rot
```

These rules nicely illustrate the potential role of prior knowledge—often called *domain knowledge*—in machine learning, for in fact the only difference between the two descriptions is *leaf condition is normal* versus *leaf malformation is absent*. Now, in this domain, if the leaf condition is normal then leaf malformation is necessarily absent, so one of these conditions happens to be a special case of the other. Thus if the first rule is true, the second is necessarily true as well. The only time the second rule comes into play is when leaf malformation is absent but leaf condition is *not* normal, i.e., when something other than malformation is wrong with the leaf. This is certainly not apparent from a casual reading of the rules.

Research on this problem in the late 1970s found that these diagnostic rules could be generated by a machine learning algorithm, along with rules for every other disease category, from about 300 training examples. These training examples were carefully selected from the corpus of cases as being quite different from one another—"far apart" in the example space. At the same time, the plant pathologist who had produced the diagnoses was interviewed, and his expertise

Table 1.7 The Soybean Data

	Attribute	Number of Values	Sample Value
Environment	Time of occurrence	7	July
	Precipitation	3	Above normal
	Temperature	3	Normal
	Cropping history	4	Same as last year
	Hail damage	2	Yes
	Damaged area	4	Scattered
	Severity	3	Severe
	Plant height	2	Normal
	Plant growth	2	Abnormal
	Seed treatment	3	Fungicide
	Germination	3	Less than 80%
Seed	Condition	2	Normal
	Mold growth	2	Absent
	Discoloration	2	Absent
	Size	2	Normal
	Shriveling	2	Absent
Fruit	Condition of fruit pods	3	Normal
	Fruit spots	5	—
Leaves	Condition	2	Abnormal
	Leaf spot size	3	—
	Yellow leaf spot halo	3	Absent
	Leaf spot margins	3	—
	Shredding	2	Absent
	Leaf malformation	2	Absent
	Leaf mildew growth	3	Absent
Stem	Condition	2	Abnormal
	Stem lodging	2	Yes
	Stem cankers	4	Above soil line
	Canker lesion color	3	—
	Fruiting bodies on stems	2	Present
	External decay of stem	3	Firm and dry
	Mycelium on stem	2	Absent
	Internal discoloration	3	None
	Sclerotia	2	Absent
Roots	Condition	3	Normal
Diagnosis		19	Diaporthe stem canker

was translated into diagnostic rules. Surprisingly, the computer-generated rules outperformed the expert-derived rules on the remaining test examples. They gave the correct disease top ranking 97.5% of the time compared with only 72% for the expert-derived rules. Furthermore, not only did the learning algorithm find rules that outperformed those of the expert collaborator, but the same expert was so impressed that he allegedly adopted the discovered rules in place of his own!

1.3 FIELDED APPLICATIONS

The examples that we opened with are speculative research projects, not production systems. And most of the illustrations above are toy problems: they are deliberately chosen to be small so that we can use them to work through algorithms later in the book. Where's the beef? Here are some applications of machine learning that have actually been put into use.

Being fielded applications, the illustrations that follow tend to stress the use of learning in performance situations, in which the emphasis is on the ability to perform well on new examples. This book also describes the use of learning systems to gain knowledge from decision structures that are inferred from the data. We believe that this is as important a use of the technology as making high-performance predictions. Still, it will tend to be underrepresented in fielded applications because when learning techniques are used to gain insight, the result is not normally a system that is put to work as an application in its own right. Nevertheless, in three of the examples below, the fact that the decision structure is comprehensible is a key feature in the successful adoption of the application.

WEB MINING

Mining information on the World Wide Web is a huge application area. Search engine companies examine the hyperlinks in web pages to come up with a measure of "prestige" for each web page and website. Dictionaries define *prestige* as "high standing achieved through success or influence." A metric called PageRank, introduced by the founders of Google and used in various guises by other search engine developers too, attempts to measure the standing of a web page. The more pages that link to your website, the higher its prestige. And prestige is greater if the pages that link in have high prestige themselves. The definition sounds circular, but it can be made to work. Search engines use PageRank (among other things) to sort web pages into order before displaying the result of your search.

Another way in which search engines tackle the problem of how to rank web pages is to use machine learning based on a training set of example queries—documents that contain the terms in the query and human judgments about how relevant the documents are to that query. Then a learning algorithm analyzes this training data and comes up with a way to predict the relevance judgment for any document and query. For each document a set of feature values is calculated that depend on the query term—e.g., whether it occurs in the title tag, whether it occurs in the document's URL, how often it occurs in the document itself, and how often it appears in the anchor text of hyperlinks that point to this document. For multiterm queries, features include how often two different terms appear close together in the document, and so on. There are many possible features: typical algorithms for learning ranks use hundreds or thousands of them.

Search engines mine the content of the Web. They also mine the content of your queries—the terms you search for—to select advertisements that you might be interested in. They have a strong incentive to do this accurately, because they only get paid by advertisers when users click on their links. Search engine companies mine your very clicks, because knowledge of which results you click on can be used to improve the search next time. Online booksellers mine the purchasing database to come up with recommendations such as "users who bought this book also bought these ones"; again they have a strong incentive to present you with compelling, personalized choices. Movie sites recommend movies based on your previous choices and other people's choices: they win if they make recommendations that keep customers coming back to their website.

And then there are social networks and other personal data. We live in the age of selfrevelation: people share their innermost thoughts in blogs and tweets, their photographs, their music and movie tastes, their opinions of books, software, gadgets, and hotels, their social life. They may believe they are doing this anonymously, or pseudonymously, but often they are incorrect (see Section 1.6). There is huge commercial interest in making money by mining the Web.

DECISIONS INVOLVING JUDGMENT

When you apply for a loan, you have to fill out a questionnaire asking for relevant financial and personal information. This information is used by the loan company as the basis for its decision as to whether to lend you money. Such decisions are often made in two stages: first, statistical methods are used to determine clear "accept" and "reject" cases. The remaining borderline cases are more difficult and call for human judgment. For example, one loan company uses a statistical decision procedure to calculate a numeric parameter based on the information supplied in the questionnaire. Applicants are accepted if this parameter exceeds a preset threshold and rejected if it falls below a second threshold. This accounts for 90% of cases, and the remaining 10% are referred to loan officers for a decision. On examining historical data on whether applicants did indeed repay their loans, however, it turned out that half of the borderline applicants who were granted loans actually defaulted. Although it would be tempting simply to deny credit to borderline customers, credit industry professionals pointed out that if only their repayment future could be reliably determined it is precisely these customers whose business should be wooed; they tend to be active customers of a credit institution because their finances remain in a chronically volatile condition. A suitable compromise must be reached between the viewpoint of a company accountant, who dislikes bad debt, and that of a sales executive, who dislikes turning business away.

Enter machine learning. The input was 1000 training examples of borderline cases for which a loan had been made that specified whether the borrower had finally paid off or defaulted. For each training example, about 20 attributes were extracted from the questionnaire, such as age, years with current employer, years at current address, years with the bank, and other credit cards possessed. A machine learning procedure was used to produce a small set of classification rules that made correct predictions on two-thirds of the borderline cases in an independently chosen test set. Not only did these rules improve the success rate of the loan decisions, but the company also found them attractive because they could be used to explain to applicants the reasons behind the decision. Although the project was an exploratory one that took only a small development effort, the loan company was apparently so pleased with the result that the rules were put into use immediately.

SCREENING IMAGES

Since the early days of satellite technology, environmental scientists have been trying to detect oil slicks from satellite images to give early warning of ecological disasters and deter illegal dumping. Radar satellites provide an opportunity for monitoring coastal waters day and night, regardless of weather conditions. Oil slicks appear as dark regions in the image whose size and shape evolve depending on weather and sea conditions. However, other look-alike dark regions can be caused by local weather conditions such as high wind. Detecting oil slicks is an expensive manual process requiring highly trained personnel who assess each region in the image.

A hazard detection system has been developed to screen images for subsequent manual processing. Intended to be marketed worldwide to a wide variety of users—government agencies and companies—with different objectives, applications, and geographical areas, it needs to be highly customizable to individual circumstances. Machine learning allows the system to be trained on examples of spills and nonspills supplied by the user and lets the user control the tradeoff between undetected spills and false alarms. Unlike other machine learning applications, which generate a classifier that is then deployed in the field, here it is the learning scheme itself that will be deployed.

The input is a set of raw pixel images from a radar satellite, and the output is a much smaller set of images with putative oil slicks marked by a colored border. First, standard image-processing operations are applied to normalize the image.

Then, suspicious dark regions are identified. Several dozen attributes are extracted from each region, characterizing its size, shape, area, intensity, sharpness, and jaggedness of the boundaries, proximity to other regions, and information about the background in the vicinity of the region. Finally, standard learning techniques are applied to the resulting attribute vectors. (An alternative, omitting explicit feature extraction steps, would be to use the deep learning approach discussed in Chapter 10, Deep learning).

Several interesting problems were encountered. One is the scarcity of training data. Oil slicks are (fortunately) very rare, and manual classification is extremely costly. Another is the unbalanced nature of the problem: of the many dark regions in the training data, only a very small fraction are actual oil slicks. A third is that the examples group naturally into batches, with regions drawn from each image forming a single batch, and background characteristics vary from one batch to another. Finally, the performance task is to serve as a filter, and the user must be provided with a convenient means of varying the false-alarm rate.

LOAD FORECASTING

In the electricity supply industry, it is important to determine future demand for power as far in advance as possible. If accurate estimates can be made for the maximum and minimum load for each hour, day, month, season, and year, utility companies can make significant economies in areas such as setting the operating reserve, maintenance scheduling, and fuel inventory management.

An automated load-forecasting assistant has been operating at a major utility supplier for more than a decade to generate hourly forecasts 2 days in advance. The first step was to use data collected over the previous 15 years to create a sophisticated load model manually. This model had three components: base load for the year, load periodicity over the year, and effect of holidays. To normalize for the base load, the data for each previous year was standardized by subtracting the average load for that year from each hourly reading and dividing by the standard deviation over the year. Electric load shows periodicity at three fundamental frequencies: diurnal, where usage has an early morning minimum and midday and afternoon maxima; weekly, where demand is lower at weekends; and seasonal, where increased demand during winter and summer for heating and cooling, respectively, creates a yearly cycle. Major holidays such as Thanksgiving, Christmas, and New Year's Day show significant variation from the normal load and are each modeled separately by averaging hourly loads for that day over the past 15 years. Minor official holidays, such as Columbus Day, are lumped together as school holidays and treated as an offset to the normal diurnal pattern. All of these effects are incorporated by reconstructing a year's load as a sequence of typical days, fitting the holidays in their correct position, and denormalizing the load to account for overall growth.

Thus far, the load model is a static one, constructed manually from historical data, and implicitly assumes "normal" climatic conditions over the year. The final step was to take weather conditions into account by locating the previous day most similar to the current circumstances and using the historical information from that day as a predictor. The prediction is treated as an additive correction to the static load model. To guard against outliers, the eight most similar days are located and their additive corrections averaged. A database was constructed of temperature, humidity, wind speed, and cloud cover at three local weather centers for each hour of the 15-year historical record, along with the difference between the actual load and that predicted by the static model. A linear regression analysis was performed to determine the relative effects of these observations on load, and the coefficients were applied to weight the distance function used to locate the most similar days.

The resulting system yielded the same performance as trained human forecasters but was far quicker—taking seconds rather than hours to generate a daily forecast. Human operators can analyze the forecast's sensitivity to simulated changes in weather and bring up for examination the "most similar" days that the system used for weather adjustment.

DIAGNOSIS

Diagnosis is one of the principal application areas of expert systems. Although the hand-crafted rules used in expert systems often perform well, machine learning can be useful in situations in which producing rules manually is too labor intensive.

Preventative maintenance of electromechanical devices such as motors and generators can forestall failures that disrupt industrial processes. Technicians regularly inspect each device, measuring vibrations at various points to determine whether the device needs servicing. Typical faults include shaft misalignment, mechanical loosening, faulty bearings, and unbalanced pumps. A particular chemical plant uses more than 1000 different devices, ranging from small pumps to very large turbo-alternators, which used to be diagnosed by a human expert with 20 years of experience. Faults are identified by measuring vibrations at different places on the device's mounting and using Fourier analysis to check the energy present in three different directions at each harmonic of the basic rotation speed. This information, which is very noisy because of limitations in the measurement and recording procedure, can be studied by the expert to arrive at a diagnosis. Although handcrafted expert system rules had been elicited for some situations, the elicitation process would have to be repeated several times for different types of machinery; so a learning approach was investigated.

Six hundred faults, each comprising a set of measurements along with the expert's diagnosis, were available, representing 20 years of experience. About half were unsatisfactory for various reasons and had to be discarded; the remainder were used as training examples. The goal was not to determine whether or not a fault existed, but to diagnose the kind of fault, given that one was there. Thus there was no need to include fault-free cases in the training set. The measured attributes were rather low level and had to be augmented by intermediate concepts, i.e., functions of basic attributes, which were defined in consultation with the expert and embodied some causal domain knowledge. The derived attributes were run through an induction algorithm to produce a set of diagnostic rules. Initially, the expert was not satisfied with the rules because he could not relate them to his own knowledge and experience. For him, mere statistical evidence was not, by itself, an adequate explanation. Further background knowledge had to be used before satisfactory rules were generated. Although the resulting rules were quite complex, the expert liked them because he could justify them in light of his mechanical knowledge. He was pleased that a third of the rules coincided with ones he used himself and was delighted to gain new insight from some of the others.

Performance tests indicated that the learned rules were slightly superior to the handcrafted ones that had previously been elicited from the expert, and this result was confirmed by subsequent use in the chemical factory. It is interesting to note, however, that the system was put into use not because of its good performance but because the domain expert approved of the rules that had been learned.

MARKETING AND SALES

Some of the most active applications of data mining have been in the area of marketing and sales. These are domains in which companies possess massive volumes of precisely recorded data, data that is potentially extremely valuable. In these applications, predictions themselves are the chief interest: the structure of how decisions are made is often completely irrelevant.

We have already mentioned the problem of fickle customer loyalty and the challenge of detecting customers who are likely to defect so that they can be wooed back into the fold by giving them special treatment. Banks were early adopters of data mining technology because of their successes in the use of machine learning for credit assessment. Data mining is now being used to reduce customer attrition by detecting changes in individual banking patterns that may herald a change of bank, or even life changes—such as a move to another city—that could result in a different bank being chosen. It may reveal, e.g., a group of customers with above-average attrition rate who do most of their banking by phone after hours when telephone response is slow. Data mining may determine groups for whom new services are appropriate, such as a cluster of profitable, reliable customers who rarely get cash advances from their credit card except in November and December, when they are prepared to pay exorbitant interest rates to see them through the holiday season. In another domain, cellular phone companies fight *churn* by detecting patterns of behavior that could benefit from new services, and then advertise such services to retain their customer base. Incentives provided specifically to retain existing customers can be expensive, and successful data mining allows them to be precisely targeted to those customers who are likely to yield maximum benefit.

Market basket analysis is the use of association techniques to find groups of items that tend to occur together in transactions, e.g., supermarket checkout data. For many retailers this is the only source of sales information that is available for data mining. For example, automated analysis of checkout data may uncover the fact that customers who buy beer also buy chips, a discovery that could be significant from the supermarket operator's point of view (although rather an obvious one that probably does not need a data mining exercise to discover). Or it may come up with the fact that on Thursdays, customers often purchase diapers and beer together, an initially surprising result that, on reflection, makes some sense as young parents stock up for a weekend at home. Such information could be used for many purposes: planning store layouts, limiting special discounts to just one of a set of items that tend to be purchased together, offering coupons for a matching product when one of them is sold alone, and so on.

There is enormous added value in being able to identify individual customer's sales histories. Discount or "loyalty" cards let retailers identify all the purchases that each individual customer makes. This personal data is far more valuable than the cash value of the discount. Identification of individual customers not only allows historical analysis of purchasing patterns but also permits precisely targeted special offers to be mailed out to prospective customers—or perhaps personalized coupons can be printed in real time at the checkout for use during the next grocery run. Supermarkets want you to feel that although we may live in a world of inexorably rising prices, they don't increase so much *for you* because the bargains offered by personalized coupons make it attractive for you to stock up on things that you wouldn't normally have bought.

Direct marketing is another popular domain for data mining. Bulk-mail promotional offers are expensive, and have a low—but highly profitable—response rate. Anything that helps focus promotions, achieving the same or nearly the same response from a smaller sample, is valuable. Commercially available databases containing demographic information that characterize neighborhoods based on ZIP codes can be correlated with information on existing customers to predict what kind of people might buy which items. This model can be trialed on information gained in response to an initial mailout, where people send back a response card or call an 800 number for more information, to predict likely future customers. Unlike shopping-mall retailers, direct mail companies have complete purchasing histories for each individual customer and can use data mining to determine those likely to respond to special offers. Targeted campaigns save money—and reduce annoyance—by directing offers only to those likely to want the product.

OTHER APPLICATIONS

There are countless other applications of machine learning. We briefly mention a few more areas to illustrate the breadth of what has been done.

Sophisticated manufacturing processes often involve tweaking control parameters. Separating crude oil from natural gas is an essential prerequisite to oil refinement, and controlling the separation process is a tricky job. British Petroleum used machine learning to create rules for setting the parameters. Setting parameters using these rules takes just 10 minutes, whereas human experts take more than a day. Westinghouse faced problems in their process for manufacturing nuclear fuel pellets and used machine learning to create rules to control the process. This was reported to save them more than $10 million per year (in 1984). The Tennessee printing company R.R. Donnelly applied the same idea to control rotogravure printing presses to reduce artifacts caused by inappropriate parameter settings, reducing the number of artifacts from more than 500 each year to less than 30.

In the realm of customer support and service, we have already described adjudicating loans, and marketing and sales applications. Another example arises when a customer reports a telephone problem and the company must decide what kind of technician to assign to the job. An expert system developed by Bell Atlantic in 1991 to make this decision was replaced in 1999 by a set of rules learned using machine learning, which saved more than $10 million per year by making fewer incorrect decisions.

There are many scientific applications. In biology, machine learning is used to help identify the thousands of genes within each new genome. In biomedicine, it is used to predict drug activity by analyzing not just the chemical properties of drugs but also their three-dimensional structure. This accelerates drug discovery and reduces its cost. In astronomy, machine learning has been used to develop a fully automatic cataloguing system for celestial objects that are too faint to be seen by visual inspection. In chemistry, it has been used to predict the structure of certain organic compounds from magnetic resonance spectra. In all these applications, machine learning techniques have attained levels of performance—or should we say skill?—that rival or surpass human experts.

Automation is especially welcome in situations involving continuous monitoring, a job that is time consuming and exceptionally tedious for humans. Ecological applications include the oil spill monitoring described earlier. Some other applications are rather less consequential—e.g., machine learning is being used to predict preferences for TV programs based on past choices and advise viewers about the available channels. Still others may save lives. Intensive care patients may be monitored to detect changes in variables that cannot be explained by circadian rhythm, medication, and so on, raising an alarm when appropriate. Finally, in a world that relies on vulnerable networked computer systems and is increasingly concerned about cybersecurity, machine learning is used to detect intrusion by recognizing unusual patterns of operation.

1.4 THE DATA MINING PROCESS

This book is about machine learning techniques for data mining: the technical core of practical data mining applications. Successful implementation of these techniques in a business context requires an understanding of important aspects that we do not—and cannot—cover in this book.

Fig. 1.4 shows the life cycle of a data mining project, as defined by the CRISP-DM reference model. Before data mining can be applied, you need to understand

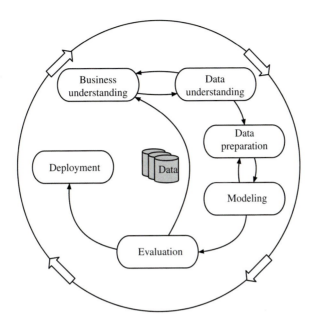

FIGURE 1.4

Life cycle of a data mining project.

what you want to achieve by implementing it. This is the "business understanding" phase: investigating the business objectives and requirements, deciding whether data mining can be applied to meet them, and determining what kind of data can be collected to build a deployable model. In the next phase, "data understanding," an initial dataset is established and studied to see whether it is suitable for further processing. If the data quality is poor, it may be necessary to collect new data based on more stringent criteria. Insights into the data that are gained at this stage may also trigger reconsideration of the business context—perhaps the objective of applying data mining needs to be reviewed?

The next three steps—data preparation, modeling, and evaluation—are what this book deals with. Preparation involves preprocessing the raw data so that machine learning algorithms can produce a model—ideally, a structural description of the information that is implicit in the data. Preprocessing may include model building activities as well, because many preprocessing tools build an internal model of the data to transform it. In fact, data preparation and modeling usually go hand in hand. It is almost always necessary to iterate: results obtained during modeling provide new insights that affect the choice of preprocessing techniques.

The next phase in any successful application of data mining—and its importance cannot be overstated!—is *evaluation*. Do the structural descriptions inferred from the data have any predictive value, or do they simply reflect spurious regularities? This book explains many techniques for estimating the predictive performance of models built by machine learning. If the evaluation step shows that the model is poor, you may need to reconsider the entire project and return to the business understanding step to identify more fruitful business objectives or avenues for data collection. If, on the other hand, the model's accuracy is sufficiently high, the next step is to deploy it in practice. This normally involves integrating it into a larger software system, so the model needs to be handed over to the project's software engineers. This is the stage where the implementation details of the modeling techniques matter. For example, to slot the model into the software system it may be necessary to reimplement it in a different programming language.

1.5 MACHINE LEARNING AND STATISTICS

What's the difference between machine learning and statistics? Cynics, looking wryly at the explosion of commercial interest (and hype) in this area, equate data mining to statistics plus marketing. In truth, you should not look for a dividing line between machine learning and statistics because there is a continuum—and a multidimensional one at that—of data analysis techniques. Some derive from the skills taught in standard statistics courses, and others are more closely associated with the kind of machine learning that has arisen out of computer science. Historically, the two sides have had rather different traditions. If forced to point to a single difference of emphasis, it might be that statistics has been more concerned with testing hypotheses, whereas machine learning has been more concerned with formulating the process of generalization as a search through possible hypotheses. But this is a gross oversimplification: statistics is far more than just hypothesis-testing, and many machine learning techniques do not involve any searching at all.

In the past, very similar schemes have developed in parallel in machine learning and statistics. One is decision tree induction. Four statisticians at Californian universities published a book on *Classification and regression trees* in the mid-1980s, and throughout the 1970s and early 1980s a prominent Australian machine learning researcher, J. Ross Quinlan, was developing a system for inferring classification trees from examples. These two independent projects produced quite similar schemes for generating trees from examples, and the researchers only became aware of one another's work much later. A second area where similar methods have arisen involves the use of nearest-neighbor methods for classification. These are standard statistical techniques that have been extensively adapted by machine learning researchers, both to improve classification performance and to make the procedure more efficient computationally. We will examine both decision tree induction and nearest-neighbor methods in Chapter 4, Algorithms: the basic methods.

But now the two perspectives have converged. The techniques we will examine in this book incorporate a great deal of statistical thinking. Right from the beginning, when constructing and refining the initial example set, standard statistical methods apply: visualization of data, selection of attributes, discarding outliers, and so on. Many learning algorithms use statistical tests when constructing rules or trees and for correcting models that are "overfitted" in that they depend too strongly on the details of the particular examples used to produce them (we have already seen an example of this in the two decision trees of Fig. 1.3 for the labor negotiations problem). Statistical tests are used to validate machine learning models and to evaluate machine learning algorithms. In our study of practical techniques for data mining, we will learn a great deal about statistics.

1.6 GENERALIZATION AS SEARCH

One way of visualizing the problem of learning—and one that distinguishes it from statistical approaches—is to imagine a search through a space of possible concept descriptions for one that fits the data. Although the idea of generalization as search is a powerful conceptual tool for thinking about machine learning, it is not essential for understanding the practical schemes described in this book. That is why this section is marked *optional*, as indicated by the gray bar in the margin.

Suppose, for definiteness, that *concept descriptions*—the result of learning—are expressed as rules such as the ones given for the weather problem in Section 1.2 (although other concept description languages would do just as well). Suppose that we list all possible sets of rules and then look for ones that satisfy a given set of examples. A big job? Yes. An *infinite* job? At first glance it seems so because there is no limit to the number of rules there might be. But actually the number of possible rule sets is finite. Note first that each individual rule is no greater than a fixed maximum size, with at most one term for each attribute: for the weather data of Table 1.2 this involves four terms in all. Because the number of possible rules is finite, the number of possible rule *sets* is finite too, although extremely large. However, we'd hardly be interested in sets that contained a very large number of rules. In fact, we'd hardly be interested in sets that had more rules than there are examples because it is difficult to imagine needing more than one rule for each example. So if we were to restrict consideration to rule sets smaller than that, the problem would be substantially reduced, although still very large.

The threat of an infinite number of possible concept descriptions seems more serious for the second version of the weather problem in Table 1.3 because these rules contain numbers. If they are real numbers, you can't enumerate them, even in principle. However, on reflection the problem again disappears because the numbers really just represent breakpoints in the numeric values that appear in the examples. For instance, consider the *temperature* attribute in Table 1.3. It involves the numbers 64, 65, 68, 69, 70, 71, 72, 75, 80, 81, 83, and 85—12 different numbers. There are 13 possible places in which we might want to put a breakpoint for a rule involving temperature. The problem isn't infinite after all.

So the process of generalization with rule sets can be regarded as a search through an enormous, but finite, search space. In principle, the problem can be solved by enumerating descriptions and striking out those that do not fit the examples presented—assuming there is no noise in the examples, and the description language is sufficiently expressive. A positive example eliminates all descriptions that it does not match, and a negative one eliminates those it does match. With each example the set of remaining descriptions shrinks (or stays the same). If only one is left, it is the target description—the target concept.

If several descriptions are left, they may still be used to classify unknown objects. An unknown object that matches all remaining descriptions should be classified as matching the target; if it fails to match any description it should be classified as being outside the target concept. Only when it matches some descriptions but not others is there ambiguity. In this case if the classification of the unknown object were revealed, it would cause the set of remaining descriptions to shrink because rule sets that classified the object the wrong way would be rejected.

ENUMERATING THE CONCEPT SPACE

Regarding it as search is a good way of looking at the learning process. However, the search space, although finite, is extremely big, and it is generally quite impractical to enumerate all possible descriptions and then see which ones fit. In the weather problem there are $4 \times 4 \times 3 \times 3 \times 2 = 288$ possibilities for each rule. There are four possibilities for the *outlook* attribute: *sunny*, *overcast*, *rainy*, or it may not participate in the rule at all. Similarly, there are four for *temperature*, three for *windy* and *humidity*, and two for the class. If we restrict the rule set to contain no more than 14 rules (because there are 14 examples in the training set), there are around 2.7×10^{34} possible different rule sets. That's a lot to enumerate, especially for such a patently trivial problem.

Although there are ways of making the enumeration procedure more feasible, a serious problem remains: in practice, it is rare for the process to converge on a unique acceptable description. Either many descriptions are still in the running after the examples are processed or the descriptors are all eliminated. The first case arises when the examples are not sufficiently comprehensive to eliminate all possible descriptions except for the "correct" one. In practice, people often want a single "best" description, and it is necessary to apply some other criteria to select the best one from the set of remaining descriptions. The second problem arises either because the description language is not expressive enough to capture the actual concept or because of noise in the examples. If an example comes in with the "wrong" classification due to an error in some of the attribute values or in the class that is assigned to it, this will likely eliminate the correct description from the space. The result is that the set of remaining descriptions becomes empty.

This situation is very likely to happen if the examples contain any noise at all, which inevitably they do except in artificial situations.

Another way of looking at generalization as search is to imagine it not as a process of enumerating descriptions and striking out those that don't apply but as a kind of hill-climbing in description space to find the description that best matches the set of examples according to some prespecified matching criterion. This is the way that most practical machine learning methods work. However, it is often impractical to search the whole space exhaustively; many practical algorithms involve heuristic search and cannot guarantee to find the optimal description.

BIAS

Viewing generalization as a search in a space of possible concepts makes it clear that the most important decisions in a machine learning system are:

- the concept description language;
- the order in which the space is searched;
- the way that overfitting to the particular training data is avoided.

These three properties are generally referred to as the *bias* of the search and are called *language bias*, *search bias*, and *overfitting-avoidance bias*. You bias the learning scheme by choosing a language in which to express concepts, by searching in a particular way for an acceptable description, and by deciding when the concept has become so complex that it needs to be simplified.

Language bias

The most important question for language bias is whether the concept description language is universal or whether it imposes constraints on what concepts can be learned. If you consider the set of all possible examples, a concept is really just a division of it into subsets. In the weather example, if you were to enumerate all possible weather conditions, the *play* concept is a subset of possible weather conditions. A "universal" language is one that is capable of expressing every possible subset of examples. In practice, the set of possible examples is generally huge, and in this respect our perspective is a theoretical, not a practical, one.

If the concept description language permits statements involving logical *or*, i.e., *disjunctions* (as well as logical *and*, i.e., *conjunctions*), then any subset can be represented. If the description language is rule-based, disjunction can be achieved by using separate rules. For example, one possible concept representation is just to enumerate the examples:

```
If outlook = overcast and temperature = hot and humidity = high
    and windy = false then play = yes
If outlook = rainy and temperature = mild and humidity = high
    and windy = false then play = yes
```

```
If outlook = rainy and temperature = cool and humidity = normal
    and windy = false then play = yes
If outlook = overcast and temperature = cool and humidity = normal
    and windy = true then play = yes
...
If none of the above then play = no
```

This is not a particularly enlightening concept description: it simply records the positive examples that have been observed and assumes that all the rest are negative. Each positive example is given its own rule, and the concept is the disjunction of the rules. Alternatively, you could imagine having individual rules for each of the negative examples, too—an equally uninteresting concept. In either case the concept description does not perform any generalization; it simply records the original data.

On the other hand, if disjunction is *not* allowed, some possible concepts—sets of examples—may not be able to be represented at all. In that case, a machine learning scheme may simply be unable to achieve good performance.

Another kind of language bias is that obtained from knowledge of the particular domain being used. For example, it may be that some combinations of attribute values can never happen. This would be the case if one attribute implied another. We saw an example of this when considering the rules for the soybean problem described above. Then, it would be pointless to even consider concepts that involved redundant or impossible combinations of attribute values. Domain knowledge can be used to cut down the search space, but specialized techniques may be needed for this. Knowledge is power: a little goes a long way, and even a small hint can reduce the search space dramatically.

Search bias

In realistic data mining problems, there are many alternative concept descriptions that fit the data, and the problem is to find the "best" one according to some criterion—usually simplicity. We use the term *fit* in a statistical sense; we seek the best description that fits the data reasonably well. Moreover, it is often computationally infeasible to search the whole space and guarantee that the description found really is the best. Consequently, the search procedure is heuristic, and no guarantees can be made about the optimality of the final result. This leaves plenty of room for bias: different search heuristics bias the search in different ways.

For example, a learning algorithm might adopt a "greedy" search for rules by trying to find the best rule at each stage and adding it in to the rule set. However, it may be that the best *pair* of rules is not just the two rules that are individually found best. Or when building a decision tree, a commitment to split early on using a particular attribute might turn out later to be ill considered in light of how the tree develops below that node. To get around these problems, a *beam search* could be used where irrevocable commitments are not made but instead a set of several active alternatives—whose number is the *beam width*—are pursued in parallel. This will complicate the learning algorithm quite considerably but has the potential to avoid the myopia associated with a greedy search. Of course, if the beam width is not large enough, myopia may still occur. There are more complex search strategies that help to overcome this problem.

A more general and higher level kind of search bias concerns whether the search is done by starting with a general description and refining it, or by starting with a specific example and generalizing it. The former is called a *general-to-specific* search bias, the latter a *specific-to-general* one. Many learning algorithms adopt the former policy, starting with an empty decision tree, or a very general rule, and specializing it to fit the examples. However, it is perfectly possible to work in the other direction. Instance-based methods start with a particular example and see how it can be generalized to cover other nearby examples in the same class.

Overfitting-avoidance bias

Overfitting-avoidance bias is often just another kind of search bias. But because it addresses a rather special problem, we treat it separately. Recall the disjunction problem described previously. The problem is that if disjunction is allowed, useless concept descriptions that merely summarize the data become possible, whereas if it is prohibited, some concepts are unlearnable. To get around this problem, it is common to search the concept space starting with the simplest concept descriptions and proceeding to more complex ones: simplest-first ordering. This biases the search in favor of simple concept descriptions.

Using a simplest-first search and stopping when a sufficiently complex concept description is found is a good way of avoiding overfitting. It is sometimes called *forward pruning* or *prepruning* because complex descriptions are pruned away before they are reached. The alternative, *backward pruning* or *postpruning*, is also viable. Here, we first find a description that fits the data well and then prune it back to a simpler description that also fits the data. This is not as redundant as it sounds: often the best way to arrive at a simple theory is to find a complex one and then simplify it. Forward and backward pruning are both a kind of overfitting-avoidance bias.

In summary, although generalization as search is a nice way to think about the learning problem, bias is the only way to make it feasible in practice. Different learning algorithms correspond to different concept description spaces searched with different biases. This is what makes it interesting: different description languages and biases serve some problems well and other problems badly. There is no universal "best" learning method—as every teacher knows!

1.7 DATA MINING AND ETHICS

The use of data—particularly data about people—for data mining has serious ethical implications, and practitioners of data mining techniques must act responsibly by making themselves aware of the ethical issues that surround their particular application.

When applied to people, data mining is frequently used to discriminate—who gets the loan, who gets the special offer, and so on. Certain kinds of discrimination—racial, sexual, religious, and so on—are not only unethical but also illegal. However, the situation is complex: everything depends on the application. Using sexual and racial information for medical diagnosis is certainly ethical, but using the same information when mining loan payment behavior is not. Even when sensitive information is discarded, there is a risk that models will be built that rely on variables that can be shown to substitute for racial or sexual characteristics. For example, people frequently live in areas that are associated with particular ethnic identities, and so using a ZIP code runs the risk of building models that are based on race—even though racial information has been explicitly excluded from the data.

REIDENTIFICATION

Work on what are being called "reidentification" techniques has provided sobering insights into the difficulty of anonymizing data. It turns out, e.g., that over 85% of Americans can be identified from publicly available records using just three pieces of information: five-digit ZIP code, birthdate (including year), and sex. Don't know the ZIP code?—over half of Americans can be identified from just city, birthdate, and sex. When the state of Massachusetts released medical records summarizing every state employee's hospital record in the mid-1990s, the Governor gave a public assurance that it had been anonymized by removing all identifying information such as name, address, and social security number. He was surprised to receive his own health records (which included diagnoses and prescriptions) in the mail.

Stories abound of companies releasing allegedly anonymous data in good faith, only to find that many individuals are easily identifiable. In 2006 an Internet services company released to the research community the records of 20 million user searches. The records were anonymized by removing all personal information—or so the company thought. But pretty soon journalists from *The New York Times* were able to identify the actual person corresponding to user number 4417749 (they sought her permission before exposing her). They did so by analyzing the search terms she used, which included queries for landscapers in her home town, and several people with the same last name as her, which reporters correlated with public databases.

Two months later, Netflix, an online movie rental service, released 100 million records of movie ratings (from 1 to 5), with their dates. To their surprise, it turned out to be quite easy to identify people in the database and thus discover all the movies they had rated. For example, if you know approximately when (give or take 2 weeks) a person in the database rated six movies, and the ratings, you can identify 99% of the people in the database. Knowing only two movies with their ratings and dates give or take 3 days, nearly 70% of people can be identified.

From just a little information about your friends (or enemies) you can determine all the movies they have rated on Netflix.

The moral is that if you really do remove all possible identification information from a database, you will probably be left with nothing useful.

USING PERSONAL INFORMATION

It is widely accepted that before people make a decision to provide personal information they need to know how it will be used and what it will be used for, what steps will be taken to protect its confidentiality and integrity, what the consequences of supplying or withholding the information are, and any rights of redress they may have. Whenever such information is collected, individuals should be told these things—not in legalistic small print but straightforwardly in plain language they can understand.

The potential use of data mining techniques means that the ways in which a repository of data can be used may stretch far beyond what was conceived when the data was originally collected. This creates a serious problem: it is necessary to determine the conditions under which the data was collected and for what purposes it may be used. Does the ownership of data bestow the right to use it in ways other than those purported when it was originally recorded? Clearly in the case of explicitly collected personal data it does not. But in general the situation is complex.

Surprising things emerge from data mining. For example, it has been reported that one of the leading consumer groups in France has found that people with red cars are more likely to default on their car loans. What is the status of such a "discovery"? What information is it based on? Under what conditions was that information collected? In what ways is it ethical to use it? Clearly, insurance companies are in the business of discriminating among people based on stereotypes—young males pay heavily for automobile insurance—but such stereotypes are not based solely on statistical correlations; they also draw on common-sense knowledge about the world as well. Whether the preceding finding says something about the kind of person who chooses a red car, or whether it should be discarded as an irrelevancy, is a matter for human judgment based on knowledge of the world rather than on purely statistical criteria.

When presented with data, it is important to ask who is permitted to have access to it, for what purpose it was collected, and what kind of conclusions is it legitimate to draw from it. The ethical dimension raises tough questions for those involved in practical data mining. It is necessary to consider the norms of the community that is used to dealing with the kind of data involved, standards that may have evolved over decades or centuries but ones that may not be known to the information specialist. For example, did you know that in the library community, it is taken for granted that the privacy of readers is a right that is jealously protected? If you call your university library and ask who has such-and-such a textbook out on loan, they will not tell you. This prevents a student being subjected to pressure from an irate professor to yield access to a book that she desperately needs for her latest grant application. It also prohibits enquiry into the dubious recreational reading tastes of the university ethics committee chairperson. Those who build, say, digital libraries may not be aware of these sensitivities and might incorporate data mining systems that analyze and compare individuals' reading habits to recommend new books—perhaps even selling the results to publishers.

WIDER ISSUES

In addition to community standards for the use of data, logical and scientific standards must be adhered to when drawing conclusions from data. If conclusions are derived (such as red car owners being greater credit risks), caveats need to be attached unless they can be backed up by arguments other than purely statistical ones. The point is that data mining is just a tool in the whole process: it is people who take the results, along with other knowledge, and decide what action to apply.

Data mining prompts another question, which is really a political one concerning the use to which society's resources are being put. We mentioned earlier the application of data mining to basket analysis, where supermarket checkout records are analyzed to detect associations among items that people purchase. What use should be made of the resulting information? Should the supermarket manager place the beer and chips together, to make it easier for shoppers, or farther apart, making it less convenient for them, to maximize their time in the store and therefore their likelihood of being drawn into further purchases? Should the manager move the most expensive, most profitable diapers near the beer, increasing sales to harried fathers of a high-margin item, and add further luxury baby products nearby?

Of course, anyone who uses advanced technologies should consider the wisdom of what they are doing. If *data* is characterized as recorded facts, then *information* is the set of patterns, or expectations, that underlie the data. You could go on to define *knowledge* as the accumulation of your set of expectations and *wisdom* as the value attached to knowledge. Although we will not pursue it further here, this issue is worth pondering.

As we saw at the very beginning of this chapter, the techniques described in this book may be called upon to help make some of the most profound and intimate decisions that life presents. Machine learning is a technology that we need to take seriously.

1.8 FURTHER READING AND BIBLIOGRAPHIC NOTES

To avoid breaking up the flow of the main text, all references are collected in a section at the end of each chapter. This first such section describes papers, books, and other resources relevant to the material covered in this chapter. The human in vitro fertilization research mentioned in the opening was undertaken by the Oxford University Computing Laboratory, and the research on cow culling was performed in the Computer Science Department at Waikato University, New Zealand.

The weather problem is from Quinlan (1986) and has been widely used to explain machine learning schemes. The corpus of example problems mentioned in the introduction to Section 1.2 is available from Lichman (2013). The contact lens example is from Cendrowska (1987), who introduced the PRISM rule-learning algorithm that we will encounter in Chapter 4, Algorithms: the basic methods. The iris dataset was described in a classic early paper on statistical inference (Fisher, 1936). The labor negotiations data is from the *Collective bargaining review*, a publication of Labour Canada issued by the Industrial Relations Information Service (BLI, 1988), and the soybean problem was first described by Michalski and Chilausky (1980).

Some of the applications in Section 1.3 are covered in an excellent paper that gives plenty of other applications of machine learning and rule induction (Langley & Simon, 1995); another source of fielded applications is a special issue of the *Machine Learning Journal* (Kohavi & Provost, 1988). Chakrabarti (2003) has written an excellent and comprehensive book on techniques of Web mining; another is Liu's *Web data mining* (2009). The loan company application is described in more detail by Michie (1989); the oil slick detector is due to Kubat, Holte, and Matwin (1998); the electric load forecasting work is by Jabbour, Riveros, Landsbergen, and Meyer (1988); and the application to preventative maintenance of electromechanical devices is from Saitta and Neri (1998). Fuller descriptions of some of the other projects mentioned in Section 1.3 (including the figures of dollars saved, and related literature references) appeared at the website of the Alberta Ingenuity Centre for Machine Learning. Luan (2002) described applications for data mining in higher education. Dasu, Koutsofios, and Wright (2006) have some recommendations for successful data mining. Another special issue of the *Machine Learning Journal* addresses the lessons that have been learned from data mining applications and collaborative problem solving (Lavrac et al., 2004).

The "diapers and beer" story is legendary. According to an article in London's *Financial Times* (February 7, 1996), "The oft-quoted example of what data mining can achieve is the case of a large US supermarket chain which discovered a strong association for many customers between a brand of babies nappies (diapers) and a brand of beer. Most customers who bought the nappies also bought the beer. The best hypothesizers in the world would find it difficult to propose this combination but data mining showed it existed, and the retail outlet was able to exploit it by moving the products closer together on the shelves." However, it seems that it is just a legend after all; Power (2002) traced its history.

Shearer (2000) discussed the data mining process, including the Cross Industry Standard Process for Data Mining (CRISP-DM) depicted in Fig. 1.4.

The book *Classification and regression trees* mentioned in Section 1.5 is by Breiman, Friedman, Olshen, and Stone (1984), and Quinlan's (1993) independently derived but similar scheme was described in a series of papers that eventually led to a book.

The first book on data mining appeared in 1991 (Piatetsky-Shapiro & Frawley, 1991)—a collection of papers presented at a workshop on knowledge discovery in databases in the late 1980s. Another book from the same stable has appeared since (Fayyad, Piatetsky-Shapiro, Smyth, & Uthurusamy, 1996) from a 1994 workshop. There followed a rash of business-oriented books on data mining, focusing mainly on practical aspects of how it can be put into practice with only rather superficial descriptions of the technology that underlies the methods used. They are valuable sources of applications and inspiration. For example, Adriaans and Zantige (1996) from Syllogic, a European systems and database consultancy, is an early introduction to data mining. Berry and Linoff (1997), from a Pennsylvania-based firm specializing in data warehousing and data mining, gave an excellent and example-studded review of data mining techniques for marketing, sales, and customer support. Cabena, Hadjinian, Stadler, Verhees, and Zanasi (1998), written by people from five international IBM laboratories, overviews the data mining process with many examples of real-world applications. Dhar and Stein (1997) gave a business perspective on data mining and include broad-brush, popularized reviews of many of the technologies involved. Groth (1998), working for a provider of data mining software, gave a brief introduction to data mining and then a fairly extensive review of data mining software products; the book includes a CD-ROM containing a demo version of his company's product. Weiss and Indurkhya (1998) looked at a wide variety of statistical techniques for making predictions from what they call "big data." Han, Kamber, and Pei (2011) covered data mining from a database perspective, focusing on the discovery of knowledge in large corporate databases; they also discussed mining complex types of data. Hand, Manilla, and Smyth (2001) produced an interdisciplinary book on data mining from an international group of authors who are well respected in the field. Finally, Nisbet, Elder, and Miner (2009) have produced a comprehensive handbook of statistical analysis and data mining applications.

Books on machine learning, on the other hand, tend to be academic texts suited for use in university courses rather than practical guides. Mitchell (1997) wrote an excellent book that covers many techniques of machine learning, including some—notably genetic algorithms, and reinforcement learning—that are not covered here. Langley (1996) offered another good text. Although the previously mentioned book by Quinlan (1993) concentrated on a particular learning algorithm, C4.5, which we will cover in detail in Chapters 4 and 6, it is a good introduction to some of the problems and techniques of machine learning. An absolutely excellent book on machine learning from a statistical perspective is Hastie, Tibshirani, and Friedman (2009). This is quite a theoretically oriented work, and is beautifully produced with apt and telling illustrations. Another excellent book, covering machine learning from a probabilistic perspective, is Murphy (2012). Russell and Norvig's (2009) *Artificial intelligence: A modern approach* is the third edition of a classic text that includes a great deal of information on machine learning and data mining.

Pattern recognition is a topic that is closely related to machine learning, and many of the same techniques apply. Duda, Hart, and Stork (2001) was the second edition of a classic and successful book on pattern recognition (Duda & Hart, 1973). Ripley (1996) and Bishop (1995) described the use of neural networks for pattern recognition; Bishop had a more recent book *Pattern recognition and machine learning* (2006). Data mining with neural networks is the subject of a book by Bigus (1996) of IBM, which features the IBM Neural Network Utility Product that he developed. A very recent textbook on deep learning is Goodfellow, Bengio, and Courville (2016).

Support vector machines and kernel-based learning is an important topic in machine learning. Cristianini and Shawe-Taylor (2000) gave a nice introduction, and a follow-up work generalized this to cover additional algorithms, kernels and solutions with applications to pattern discovery problems in fields such as bioinformatics, text analysis, and image analysis (Shawe-Taylor & Cristianini, 2004). Schölkopf and Smola (2002) provided a comprehensive introduction to support vector machines and related kernel methods.

The emerging area of reidentification techniques was explored, along with its implications for anonymization, by Ohm (2009).

Input: concepts, instances, attributes

2

CHAPTER OUTLINE

2.1 What's a Concept? 44
2.2 What's in an Example? 46
    Relations 47
    Other Example Types 51
2.3 What's in an Attribute? 53
2.4 Preparing the Input 56
    Gathering the Data Together 56
    ARFF Format..57
    Sparse Data 60
    Attribute Types..61
    Missing Values 62
    Inaccurate Values 63
    Unbalanced Data...64
    Getting to Know Your Data..65
2.5 Further Reading and Bibliographic Notes 65

Before delving into the question of how machine learning schemes operate, we begin by looking at the different forms the input might take and, in Chapter 3, Output: knowledge representation, the different kinds of output that might be produced. With any software system, understanding what the inputs and outputs are is far more important than knowing what goes on in between, and machine learning is no exception.

The input takes the form of *concepts*, *instances*, and *attributes*. We call the thing that is to be learned a *concept description*. The idea of a concept, like the very idea of learning in the first place, is hard to pin down precisely, and we won't spend time philosophizing about just what it is and isn't. In a sense, what we are trying to find—the result of the learning process—is a description of the concept that is, ideally, *intelligible* in that it can be understood, discussed, and disputed, and *operational* in that it can be applied to actual examples. Section 2.1 explains some distinctions among different kinds of learning problems, distinctions that are very concrete and very important in practical data mining.

Data Mining.
© 2017 Elsevier Inc. All rights reserved.

The information that the learner is given takes the form of a set of *instances*. In the illustrations in Chapter 1, What's it all about?, each instance was an individual, independent example of the concept to be learned. Of course there are many things you might like to learn for which the raw data cannot be expressed as individual, independent instances. Perhaps background knowledge should be taken into account as part of the input. Perhaps the raw data is an agglomerated mass that cannot be fragmented into individual instances. Perhaps it is a single sequence, say a time sequence, that cannot meaningfully be cut into pieces. This book is about simple, practical methods of data mining, and we focus on situations where the information can be supplied in the form of individual examples. However, we do introduce one slightly more complicated scenario where the examples for learning contain multiple instances.

Each instance is characterized by the values of attributes that measure different aspects of the instance. There are many different types of attribute, although typical machine learning schemes deal only with numeric and *nominal*, or categorical, ones.

Finally, we examine the question of preparing input for data mining and introduce a simple format—the one that is used by the Weka system that accompanies this book—for representing the input information as a text file.

2.1 WHAT'S A CONCEPT?

Four basically different styles of learning commonly appear in data mining applications. In *classification learning*, the learning scheme is presented with a set of classified examples from which it is expected to learn a way of classifying unseen examples. In *association learning*, any association among features is sought, not just ones that predict a particular *class* value. In *clustering*, groups of examples that belong together are sought. In *numeric prediction*, the outcome to be predicted is not a discrete class but a numeric quantity. Regardless of the type of learning involved, we call the thing to be learned the *concept* and the output produced by a learning scheme the *concept description*.

Most of the examples in Chapter 1, What's it all about?, are classification problems. The weather data (Tables 1.2 and 1.3) presents a set of days together with a decision for each as to whether to play the game or not. The problem is to learn how to classify new days as play or don't play. Given the contact lens data (Table 1.1), the problem is to learn how to determine a lens recommendation for a new patient—or more precisely, since every possible combination of attributes is present in the data, the problem is to learn a way of summarizing the given data. For the irises (Table 1.4), the problem is to learn how to determine whether a new iris flower is *setosa*, *versicolor*, or *virginica*, given its sepal length and width and petal length and width. For the labor negotiations data (Table 1.6), the problem is to determine whether a new contract is acceptable or not, on the basis of its duration; wage increase in the first, second, and third years; cost of living adjustment; and so forth.

We assume throughout this book that each example belongs to one, and only one, class. However, there exist classification scenarios in which individual examples may belong to multiple classes. In technical jargon, these are called "multilabeled instances." One simple way to deal with such situations is to treat them as several different classification problems, one for each possible class, where the problem is to determine whether instances belong to that class or not.

Classification learning is sometimes called *supervised* because, in a sense, the scheme operates under supervision by being provided with the actual outcome for each of the training examples—the play or don't play judgment, the lens recommendation, the type of iris, the acceptability of the labor contract. This outcome is called the *class* of the example. The success of classification learning can be judged by trying out the concept description that is learned on an independent set of test data for which the true classifications are known but not made available to the machine. The success rate on test data gives an objective measure of how well the concept has been learned. In many practical data mining applications, success is measured more subjectively in terms of how acceptable the learned description—such as the rules or decision tree—are to a human user.

Most of the examples in Chapter 1, What's it all about?, can equally well be used for association learning, in which there is no specified class. Here, the problem is to discover any structure in the data that is "interesting." Some association rules for the weather data were given in Section 1.2. Association rules differ from classification rules in two ways: they can "predict" any attribute, not just the class, and they can predict more than one attribute's value at a time. Because of this there are far more association rules than classification rules, and the challenge is to avoid being swamped by them. For this reason, association rules are often limited to those that apply to a certain minimum number of examples—say 80% of the dataset—and have greater than a certain minimum accuracy level—say 95% accurate. Even then, there are usually lots of them, and they have to be examined manually to determine whether they are meaningful or not. Association rules usually involve only nonnumeric attributes: thus you wouldn't normally look for association rules in the iris dataset.

When there is no specified class, clustering is used to group items that seem to fall naturally together. Imagine a version of the iris data in which the type of iris is omitted, such as in Table 2.1. Then it is likely that the 150 instances fall into natural clusters corresponding to the three iris types. The challenge is to find these clusters and assign the instances to them—and to be able to assign new instances to the clusters as well. It may be that one or more of the iris types split naturally into subtypes, in which case the data will exhibit more than three natural clusters. The success of clustering is often measured subjectively in terms of how useful the result appears to be to a human user. It may be followed by a second step of classification learning in which rules are learned that give an intelligible description of how new instances should be placed into the clusters.

Table 2.1 Iris Data as a Clustering Problem

	Sepal Length	Sepal Width	Petal Length	Petal Width
1	5.1	3.5	1.4	0.2
2	4.9	3.0	1.4	0.2
3	4.7	3.2	1.3	0.2
4	4.6	3.1	1.5	0.2
5	5.0	3.6	1.4	0.2
...				
51	7.0	3.2	4.7	1.4
52	6.4	3.2	4.5	1.5
53	6.9	3.1	4.9	1.5
54	5.5	2.3	4.0	1.3
55	6.5	2.8	4.6	1.5
...				
101	6.3	3.3	6.0	2.5
102	5.8	2.7	5.1	1.9
103	7.1	3.0	5.9	2.1
104	6.3	2.9	5.6	1.8
105	6.5	3.0	5.8	2.2
...				

Numeric prediction is a variant of classification learning in which the outcome is a numeric value rather than a category. The CPU performance problem is one example. Another, shown in Table 2.2, is a version of the weather data in which what is to be predicted is not play or don't play but rather is the time (in minutes) to play. With numeric prediction problems, as with other machine learning situations, the predicted value for new instances is often of less interest than the structure of the description that is learned, expressed in terms of what the important attributes are and how they relate to the numeric outcome.

2.2 WHAT'S IN AN EXAMPLE?

The input to a machine learning scheme is a set of instances. These instances are the things that are to be classified, or associated, or clustered. Although until now we have called them *examples*, henceforth we will generally use the more specific term *instances* to refer to the input. In the standard scenario, each instance is an individual, independent example of the concept to be learned. Instances are characterized by the values of a set of predetermined attributes. This was the case in all the sample datasets described in Chapter 1, What's it all about? (weather, contact lens, the iris, and labor negotiations problems). Each dataset is represented

Table 2.2 Weather Data With a Numeric Class

Outlook	Temperature	Humidity	Windy	Play-time
Sunny	85	85	False	5
Sunny	80	90	True	0
Overcast	83	86	False	55
Rainy	70	96	False	40
Rainy	68	80	False	65
Rainy	65	70	True	45
Overcast	64	65	True	60
Sunny	72	95	False	0
Sunny	69	70	False	70
Rainy	75	80	False	45
Sunny	75	70	True	50
Overcast	72	90	True	55
Overcast	81	75	False	75
Rainy	71	91	True	10

as a matrix of instances versus attributes, which in database terms is a single relation, or a *flat file*.

Expressing the input data as a set of independent instances is by far the most common situation for practical data mining. However, it is a rather restrictive way of formulating problems, and it is worth spending some time reviewing why. Problems often involve relationships between objects, rather than separate, independent instances. Suppose, to take a specific situation, a family tree is given, and we want to learn the concept *sister*. Imagine your own family tree, with your relatives (and their genders) placed at the nodes. This tree is the input to the learning process, along with a list of pairs of people and an indication of whether they are sisters or not.

RELATIONS

Fig. 2.1 shows part of a family tree, below which are two tables that each define sisterhood in a slightly different way. A *yes* in the third column of the tables means that the person in the second column is a sister of the person in the first column (that's just an arbitrary decision we've made in setting up this example).

The first thing to notice is that there are a lot of *nos* in the third column of the table on the left—because there are 12 people and $12 \times 12 = 144$ pairs of people in all, and most pairs of people aren't sisters. The table on the right, which gives the same information, records only the positive examples and assumes that all others are negative. The idea of specifying only positive examples and adopting a standing assumption that the rest are negative is called the *closed world assumption*. It is frequently assumed in theoretical studies; however, it may be less appropriate in real-life problems.

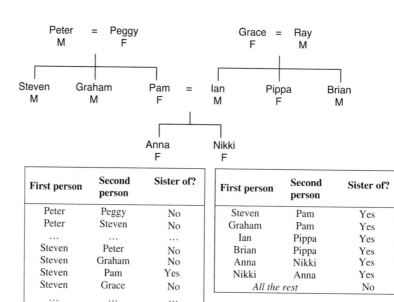

First person	Second person	Sister of?
Peter	Peggy	No
Peter	Steven	No
...	...	...
Steven	Peter	No
Steven	Graham	No
Steven	Pam	Yes
Steven	Grace	No
...	...	...
Ian	Pippa	Yes
...	...	...
Anna	Nikki	Yes
...	...	...
Nikki	Anna	Yes

First person	Second person	Sister of?
Steven	Pam	Yes
Graham	Pam	Yes
Ian	Pippa	Yes
Brian	Pippa	Yes
Anna	Nikki	Yes
Nikki	Anna	Yes
All the rest		No

FIGURE 2.1

A family tree and two ways of expressing the *sister-of* relation.

Table 2.3 Family Tree

Name	Gender	Parent1	Parent2
Peter	Male	?	?
Peggy	Female	?	?
Steven	Male	Peter	Peggy
Graham	Male	Peter	Peggy
Pam	Female	Peter	Peggy
Ian	Male	Grace	Ray

Neither table in Fig. 2.1 is of any use without the family tree itself. This tree can also be expressed in the form of a table, part of which is shown in Table 2.3. Now the problem is expressed in terms of two relationships. But these tables do not contain independent sets of instances because values in the Name, Parent1, and Parent2 columns of the *sister-of* relation refer to rows of the family tree relation. We can make them into a single set of instances by collapsing the two tables into the single one of Table 2.4.

Table 2.4 The Sister-of Relation

First Person				Second Person				Sister-of?
Name	Gender	Parent1	Parent2	Name	Gender	Parent1	Parent2	
Steven	Male	Peter	Peggy	Pam	Female	Peter	Peggy	Yes
Graham	Male	Peter	Peggy	Pam	Female	Peter	Peggy	Yes
Ian	Male	Grace	Ray	Pippa	Female	Grace	Ray	Yes
Brian	Male	Grace	Ray	Pippa	Female	Grace	Ray	Yes
Anna	Female	Pam	Ian	Nikki	Female	Pam	Ian	Yes
Nikki	Female	Pam	Ian	Anna	Female	Pam	Ian	Yes
				All the rest				No

We have at last succeeded in transforming the original relational problem into the form of instances, each of which is an individual, independent example of the concept that is to be learned. Of course, the instances are not really independent—there are plenty of relationships among different rows of the table!—but they are independent as far as the concept of sisterhood is concerned. Most machine learning schemes will still have trouble dealing with this kind of data, as we will see in Section 3.6, but at least the problem has been recast into the right form. A simple rule for the sister-of relation is.

```
If second person's gender = female
   and first person's parent1 = second person's parent1
   then sister-of = yes.
```

This example shows how you can take a relationship between different nodes of a tree and recast it into a set of independent instances. In database terms, you take two relations and join them together to make one, a process of flattening that is technically called *denormalization*. It is always possible to do this with any (finite) set of (finite) relations, but denormalization may yield sets of rows that need to be aggregated to form independent instances.

The structure of Table 2.4 can be used to describe any relationship between two people—grandparenthood, second cousins twice removed, and so on. Relationships among more people would require a larger table. Relationships in which the maximum number of people is not specified in advance pose a more serious problem. If we want to learn the concept of *nuclear family* (parents and their children), the number of people involved depends on the size of the largest nuclear family, and although we could guess at a reasonable maximum (10? 20?), the actual number can only be found by scanning the tree itself. Nevertheless, given a finite set of finite relations we could, at least in principle, form a new "superrelation" that contained one row for *every* combination of people, and this would be enough to express any relationship between people no matter how many were involved. The computational and storage costs would, however, be prohibitive.

Another problem with denormalization is that it produces apparent regularities in the data that are completely spurious and are in fact merely reflections of the original database structure. For example, imagine a supermarket database with a relation for customers and the products they buy, one for products and their suppliers, and one for suppliers and their address. Denormalizing this will produce a flat file that contains, for each instance, customer, product, supplier, and supplier address. A database mining tool that seeks structure in the database may come up with the fact that customers who buy beer also buy chips, a discovery that could be significant from the supermarket manager's point of view. However, it may also come up with the fact that supplier address can be predicted exactly from supplier—a "discovery" that will not impress the supermarket manager at all. This fact masquerades as a significant discovery from the flat file but is present explicitly in the original database structure.

Many abstract computational problems involve relations that are not finite, although clearly any actual set of input examples must be finite. Concepts such as *ancestor-of* involve arbitrarily long paths through a tree, and although the human race, and hence its family tree, may be finite (although prodigiously large), many artificial problems generate data that truly is infinite. Although it may sound abstruse, this situation is the norm in areas such as list processing and logic programming and is addressed in a subdiscipline of machine learning called *inductive logic programming*. Computer scientists usually use recursion to deal with situations in which the number of possible examples is infinite. For example,

```
If person1 is a parent of person2
   then person1 is an ancestor of person2
If person1 is a parent of person2
   and person2 is an ancestor of person3
   then person1 is an ancestor of person3
```

is a simple recursive definition of *ancestor* that works no matter how distantly two people are related. Techniques of inductive logic programming can learn recursive rules such as these from a finite set of instances such as those in Table 2.5.

The real drawbacks of such techniques, however, are that they do not cope well with noisy data, and they tend to be so slow as to be unusable on anything but small artificial datasets. They are not covered in this book.

OTHER EXAMPLE TYPES

As we have seen, general relations present substantial challenges and this book will deal with them no further. Structured examples such as graphs and trees can be viewed as special cases of relations that are often mapped into independent instances by extracting local or global features based on their structure and representing them as attributes. Similarly, sequences of items may be treated by describing them, or their individual items, in terms of a fixed set of properties represented by attributes. Fortunately most practical data mining problems can be expressed quite effectively as a set of instances, each one being an example of the concept to be learned.

In some situations, instead of the individual instances being examples of the concept, each individual example comprises a set of instances that are described by the same attributes. This "multi-instance" setting covers some important real-world applications. One concerns the inference of characteristics of active drug molecules, where *activity* corresponds to how well a drug molecule bonds to a "bonding site" on a target molecule. The problem is that the drug molecule can assume alternative shapes by rotating its bonds. It is classed as positive if just one of these shapes actually binds to the site and has the desired effect—but it is not known which shape it is. On the other hand, a drug molecule is negative if none

Table 2.5 Another Relation

First Person				Second Person				Ancestor of?
Name	Gender	Parent1	Parent2	Name	Gender	Parent1	Parent2	
Peter	Male	?	?	Steven	Male	Peter	Peggy	Yes
Peter	Male	?	?	Pam	Female	Peter	Peggy	Yes
Peter	Male	?	?	Anna	Female	Pam	Ian	Yes
Peter	Male	?	?	Nikki	Female	Pam	Ian	Yes
Pam	Female	Peter	Peggy	Nikki	Female	Pam	Ian	Yes
Grace	Female	?	?	Ian	Male	Grace	Ray	Yes
Grace	Female	?	?	Nikki	Female	Pam	Ian	Yes
Other examples here								Yes
All the rest								No

of the shapes bind successfully. In this case, a multiple instance is a set of shapes, and the entire set is classified as positive or negative.

Multi-instance problems often also arise naturally when relations from a database are joined, i.e., when several rows from a secondary relation are associated with the same row in the target relation. For example, we may want to classify computer users as experts or novices based on descriptions of user sessions that are stored in a secondary table. The target relation just has the classification and the user ID. Joining the two tables creates a flat file. However, the rows pertaining to an individual user are not independent. Classification is performed on a per-user basis, so the set of session instances associated with the same user should be viewed as a single example for learning.

The goal of multi-instance learning is still to produce a concept description, but now the task is more difficult because the learning algorithm has to contend with incomplete information about each training example. Rather than seeing each example in terms of a single definitive attribute vector, the learning algorithm sees each example as a set of attribute vectors. Things would be easy if only it knew which member of the set was responsible for the example's classification—but this is not known.

Several special learning algorithms have been developed to tackle the multi-instance problem: we describe some of them in Chapter 4, Algorithms: the basic methods. It is also possible to apply standard machine learning schemes by recasting the problem as a single table comprising independent instances. Chapter 4, Algorithms: the basic methods, gives some ways of achieving this.

In summary, the input to a data mining scheme is generally expressed as a table of independent instances of the concept to be learned. Because of this it has been suggested, disparagingly, that we should really talk of *file mining* rather than *database mining*. Relational data is more complex than a flat file. A finite set of finite relations can always be recast into a single table, although often at enormous cost in space. Moreover, denormalization can generate spurious regularities in the data, and it is essential to check the data for such artifacts before applying a learning scheme. Potentially infinite concepts can be dealt with by learning rules that are recursive, although that is beyond the scope of this book. Finally, some important real-world problems are most naturally expressed in a multi-instance format, where each example is actually a separate set of instances.

2.3 WHAT'S IN AN ATTRIBUTE?

Each instance that provides the input to machine learning is characterized by its values on a fixed, predefined set of features or *attributes*. The instances are the rows of the tables that we have shown for the weather, contact lens, iris, and CPU performance problems, and the attributes are the columns. (The labor negotiations data was an exception: we presented this with instances in columns and attributes in rows for space reasons.)

The use of a fixed set of features imposes another restriction on the kinds of problems generally considered in practical data mining. What if different instances have different features? If the instances were transportation vehicles, then *number of wheels* is a feature that applies to many vehicles but not to ships, e.g., whereas *number of masts* might be a feature that applies to ships but not to land vehicles. The standard workaround is to make each possible feature an attribute and to use a special "irrelevant value" flag to indicate that a particular attribute is not available for a particular case. A similar situation arises when the existence of one feature (say, spouse's name) depends on the value of another (married or single).

The value of an attribute for a particular instance is a measurement of the quantity to which the attribute refers. There is a broad distinction between attributes that are *numeric* and ones that are *nominal*. Numeric attributes, sometimes called *continuous* attributes, measure numbers—either real or integer valued. Note that the term *continuous* is routinely abused in this context: integer-valued attributes are certainly not continuous in the mathematical sense. Nominal attributes take on values in a prespecified, finite set of possibilities and are sometimes called *categorical*. But there are other possibilities. Statistics texts often introduce "levels of measurement" such as *nominal*, *ordinal*, *interval*, and *ratio*.

Nominal attributes have values that are distinct symbols. The values themselves serve just as labels or names—hence the term *nominal*, which comes from the Latin word for *name*. For example, in the weather data the attribute *outlook* has values *sunny*, *overcast*, and *rainy*. No relation is implied among these three—no ordering or distance measure. It certainly does not make sense to add the values together, multiply them, or even compare their size. A rule using such an attribute can only test for equality or inequality, as in

```
outlook: sunny      →   no
         overcast   →   yes
         rainy      →   yes
```

Ordinal attributes are ones that make it possible to rank order the categories. However, although there is a notion of *ordering*, there is no notion of *distance*. For example, in the weather data the attribute *temperature* has values *hot*, *mild*, and *cool*. These are ordered. Whether you say that

$$hot > mild > cool \text{ or } hot < mild < cool$$

is a matter of convention—it does not matter which is used as long as consistency is maintained. What is important is that *mild* lies between the other two. Although it makes sense to compare two values, it does not make sense to add or subtract them—the difference between *hot* and *mild* cannot be compared with the difference between *mild* and *cool*. A rule using such an attribute might involve a comparison, as in

```
temperature = hot → no
temperature < hot → yes
```

Notice that the distinction between nominal and ordinal attributes is not always straightforward and obvious. Indeed, the very example of a nominal attribute that we used above, *outlook*, is not completely clear: you might argue that the three values *do* have an ordering—*overcast* being somehow intermediate between *sunny* and *rainy* as weather turns from good to bad.

Interval quantities have values that are not only ordered but measured in fixed and equal units. A good example is temperature, expressed in degrees (say, degrees Fahrenheit) rather than on the nonnumeric scale implied by cool, mild, and hot. It makes perfect sense to talk about the difference between two temperatures, say 46°C and 48°C, and compare that with the difference between another two temperatures, say 22°C and 24°C. Another example is dates. You can talk about the difference between the years 1939 and 1945 (6 years), or even the average of the years 1939 and 1945 (1942), but it doesn't make much sense to consider the sum of the years 1939 and 1945 (3884) or three times the year 1939 (5817), because the starting point, year 0, is completely arbitrary—indeed, it has changed many times throughout the course of history. (Children sometimes wonder what the year 300 BC was called in 300 BC).

Ratio quantities are ones for which the measurement scheme inherently defines a zero point. For example, when measuring the distance from one object to another, the distance between the object and itself forms a natural zero. Ratio quantities are treated as real numbers: any mathematical operations are allowed. It certainly does make sense to talk about three times the distance, and even to multiply one distance by another to get an area.

However, the question of whether there is an "inherently" defined zero point depends on our scientific knowledge—it's culture relative. For example, Daniel Fahrenheit knew no lower limit to temperature, and his scale is an interval one. Nowadays, however, we view temperature as a ratio scale based on absolute zero. Measurement of time in years since some culturally defined zero such as ad 0 is not a ratio scale; years since the big bang is. Even the zero point of money—where we are usually quite happy to say that something cost twice as much as something else—may not be quite clearly defined for those of us who constantly max out our credit cards.

Many practical data mining systems accommodate just two of these four levels of measurement: nominal and ordinal. Nominal attributes are sometimes called *categorical, enumerated,* or *discrete. Enumerated* is the standard term used in computer science to denote a categorical data type; however, the strict definition of the term—namely, to put into one-to-one correspondence with the natural numbers—implies an ordering, which is specifically not implied in the machine learning context. *Discrete* also has connotations of ordering because you often discretize a continuous numeric quantity. Ordinal attributes are often coded as *numeric* data, or perhaps *continuous* data, but without the implication of mathematical continuity. A special case of the nominal scale is the *dichotomy*, which has only two members—often designated as *true* and *false*, or *yes* and *no* in the weather data. Such attributes are sometimes called *Boolean*.

Machine learning systems can use a wide variety of other information about attributes. For instance, dimensional considerations could be used to restrict the search to expressions or comparisons that are dimensionally correct. Circular ordering could affect the kinds of tests that are considered. For example, in a temporal context, tests on a *day* attribute could involve next day, previous day, next weekday, same day next week. Partial orderings, i.e., generalization or specialization relations, frequently occur in practical situations. Information of this kind is often referred to as *metadata*, data about data. However, the kinds of practical schemes used for data mining are rarely capable of taking metadata into account, although it is likely that these capabilities will develop rapidly in the future.

2.4 PREPARING THE INPUT

Preparing input for a data mining investigation usually consumes the bulk of the effort invested in the entire data mining process. While this book is not really about the problems of data preparation, we want to give you a feeling for the issues involved so that you can appreciate the complexities. Following that, we look at a particular input file format, the attribute-relation file format (ARFF), that is used in the Weka system described in Appendix B. Then we consider issues that arise when converting datasets to such a format, because there are some simple practical points to be aware of. Bitter experience shows that real data is often disappointingly low in quality, and careful checking—a process that has become known as *data cleaning*—pays off many times over.

GATHERING THE DATA TOGETHER

When beginning work on a data mining problem, it is first necessary to bring all the data together into a set of instances. We explained the need to denormalize relational data when describing the family tree example. Although it illustrates the basic issue, this self-contained and rather artificial example does not really convey a feeling for what the process will be like in practice. In a real business application, it will be necessary to bring data together from different departments. For example, in a marketing study data will be needed from the sales department, the customer billing department, and the customer service department.

Integrating data from different sources usually presents many challenges—not deep issues of principle but nasty realities of practice. Different departments will use different styles of record keeping, different conventions, different time periods, different degrees of data aggregation, different primary keys, and will have different kinds of error. The data must be assembled, integrated, and cleaned up.

The idea of company-wide database integration is known as *data warehousing*. Data warehouses provide a single consistent point of access to corporate or organizational data, transcending departmental divisions. They are the place where old data is published in a way that can be used to inform business decisions. The movement toward data warehousing is a recognition of the fact that the fragmented information that an organization uses to support day-to-day operations at a departmental level can have immense strategic value when brought together. Clearly, the presence of a data warehouse is a very useful precursor to data mining, and if it is not available, many of the steps involved in data warehousing will have to be undertaken to prepare the data for mining.

Even a data warehouse may not contain all the necessary data, and you may have to reach outside the organization to bring in data relevant to the problem at hand. For example, weather data had to be obtained in the load forecasting example in Chapter 1, What's it all about?, and demographic data is needed for marketing and sales applications. Sometimes called *overlay data*, this is not normally collected by an organization but is clearly relevant to the data mining problem. It, too, must be cleaned up and integrated with the other data that has been collected.

Another practical question when assembling the data is the degree of aggregation that is appropriate. When a dairy farmer decides which cows to sell off, the milk production records—which an automatic milking machine records twice a day—must be aggregated. Similarly, raw telephone call data is not much use when telecommunications firms study their clients' behavior: the data must be aggregated to the customer level. But do you want usage by month or by quarter, and for how many months or quarters in arrears? Selecting the right type and level of aggregation is usually critical for success.

Because so many different issues are involved, you can't expect to get it right the first time. This is why data assembly, integration, cleaning, aggregating, and general preparation take so long.

ARFF FORMAT

We now look at a standard way of representing datasets, called an *ARFF file*. We describe the regular version, but there is also a version called XRFF, which, as the name suggests, gives ARFF header and instance information in the XML markup language.

Fig. 2.2 shows an ARFF file for the weather data in Table 1.3, the version with some numeric features. Lines beginning with a % sign are comments. Following the comments at the beginning of the file are the name of the relation (*weather*) and a block defining the attributes (*outlook, temperature, humidity, windy, play?*). Nominal attributes are followed by the set of values they can take on, enclosed in curly braces. Values can include spaces; if so, they must be placed within quotation marks. Numeric values are followed by the keyword *numeric*.

the phenomenon

```
% ARFF file for the weather data with some numeric features
%
@relation weather

@attribute outlook { sunny, overcast, rainy }
@attribute temperature numeric
@attribute humidity numeric
@attribute windy { true, false }
@attribute play? { yes, no }

@data
%
% 14 instances
%
sunny, 85, 85, false, no
sunny, 80, 90, true, no
overcast, 83, 86, false, yes
rainy, 70, 96, false, yes
rainy, 68, 80, false, yes
rainy, 65, 70, true, no
overcast, 64, 65, true, yes
sunny, 72, 95, false, no
sunny, 69, 70, false, yes
rainy, 75, 80, false, yes
sunny, 75, 70, true, yes
overcast, 72, 90, true, yes
overcast, 81, 75, false, yes
rainy, 71, 91, true, no
```

nominal and integer

cases

FIGURE 2.2

ARFF file for the weather data.

Although the weather problem is to predict the class value *play?* from the values of the other attributes, the class attribute is not distinguished in any way in the data file. The ARFF format merely gives a dataset; it does not specify which of the attributes is the one that is supposed to be predicted. This means that the same file can be used for investigating how well each attribute can be predicted from the others, or to find association rules, or for clustering.

Following the attribute definitions is an @*data* line that signals the start of the instances in the dataset. Instances are written one per line, with values for each attribute in turn, separated by commas. If a value is missing it is represented by a single question mark (there are no missing values in this dataset). The attribute specifications in ARFF files allow the dataset to be checked to ensure that it contains legal values for all attributes, and programs that read ARFF files do this checking automatically.

As well as nominal and numeric attributes, exemplified by the weather data, the ARFF format has three further attribute types: string attributes, date attributes, and relation-valued attributes. String attributes have values that are textual. Suppose you have a string attribute that you want to call *description*. In the block defining the attributes it is specified like this:

@attribute description string   *may string*

Then, in the instance data, include any character string in quotation marks (to include quotation marks in your string, use the standard convention of preceding each one by a backslash "\"). Strings are stored internally in a string table, and represented by their address in that table. Thus two strings that contain the same characters will have the same value.

String attributes can have values that are very long—even a whole document. To be able to use string attributes for text mining, it is necessary to be able to manipulate them. For example, a string attribute might be converted into many numeric attributes, one for each word in the string, whose value is the number of times that word appears. These transformations are described in Section 8.3.

Date attributes are strings with a special format and are introduced like this:

```
@attribute today date
```

(for an attribute called *today*). Weka uses the ISO-8601 combined date and time format *yyyy-MM-dd'T'HH:mm:ss* with four digits for the year, two each for the month and day, then the letter *T* followed by the time with two digits for each of hours, minutes, and seconds.[1] In the data section of the file dates are specified as the corresponding string representation of the date and time, e.g., 2004-04-03T12:00:00. Although they are specified as strings, dates are converted to numeric form when the input file is read. Dates can also be converted internally to different formats, so you can have absolute timestamps in the data file and use transformations to forms such as time of day or day of the week to detect periodic behavior.

Relation-valued attributes differ from the other types because they allow multi-instance problems to be represented in ARFF format. The value of a relation attribute is a separate set of instances. The attribute is defined with a name and the type *relational*, followed by a nested attribute block that gives the structure of the referenced instances. For example, a relation-valued attribute called *bag* whose value is a dataset with the same structure as the weather data but without the *play* attribute can be specified like this:

```
@attribute bag relational
        @attribute outlook {sunny, overcast, rainy}
        @attribute temperature numeric
        @attribute humidity numeric
        @attribute windy {true, false}
@end bag
```

The *@end bag* indicates the end of the nested attribute block. Fig. 2.3 shows an ARFF file for a multi-instance problem based on the weather data. In this case, each example is made up of an identifier value, two consecutive instances from the original weather data, and a class label. Each value of the attribute is a string that encapsulates two weather instances separated by the "\n" character (which represents an embedded new-line). This might be appropriate for a game

---

[1] Weka contains a mechanism for defining a date attribute to have a different format by including a special string in the attribute definition.

```
% Multiple instance ARFF file for the weather data
%
@relation weather

@attribute bag_ID { 1, 2, 3, 4, 5, 6, 7 }
@attribute bag relational
    @attribute outlook { sunny, overcast, rainy }
    @attribute temperature numeric
    @attribute humidity numeric
    @attribute windy { true, false }
@end bag
@attribute play? { yes, no }

@data
%
% seven "multiple instance" instances
%
1, "sunny, 85, 85, false\nsunny, 80, 90, true", no
2, "overcast, 83, 86, false\nrainy, 70, 96, false", yes
3, "rainy, 68, 80, false\nrainy, 65, 70, true", yes
4, "overcast, 64, 65, true\nsunny, 72, 95, false", yes
5, "sunny, 69, 70, false\nrainy, 75, 80, false", yes
6, "sunny, 75, 70, true\novercast, 72, 90, true", yes
7, "overcast, 81, 75, false\nrainy, 71, 91, true", yes
```

FIGURE 2.3

Multi-instance ARFF file for the weather data.

that lasts 2 days. A similar dataset might be used for games that last for an indeterminate number of days (e.g., first-class cricket takes 3–5 days). Note, however, that in multi-instance learning the *order* in which the instances is given is generally considered unimportant. An algorithm might learn that cricket can be played if none of the days is rainy and at least one is sunny, but not that it can only be played in a certain sequence of weather events.

SPARSE DATA

Sometimes most attributes have a value of 0 for most of the instances. For example, market basket data records purchases made by supermarket customers. No matter how big the shopping expedition, customers never purchase more than a tiny portion of the items a store offers. The market basket data contains the quantity of each item that the customer purchases, and this is 0 for almost all items in stock. The data file can be viewed as a matrix whose rows and columns represent customers and stock items, and the matrix is "sparse"—nearly all its elements are 0. Another example occurs in text mining, where the instances are documents. Here, the columns and rows represent documents and words, and the numbers indicate how many times a particular word appears in a particular document. Most documents have a rather small vocabulary, so most entries are 0.

It can be impractical to represent each element of a sparse matrix explicitly. Instead of representing each value in order, like this:

```
0, X, 0, 0, 0, 0, Y, 0, 0, 0, "class A"
0, 0, 0, W, 0, 0, 0, 0, 0, 0, "class B"
```

the nonzero attributes can be explicitly identified by attribute number and their value stated:

```
{1 X, 6 Y, 10 "class A"}
{3 W, 10 "class B"}
```

Each instance is enclosed in braces and contains the index number of each non-zero attribute (indexes start from 0) and its value. Sparse data files have the same *@relation* and *@attribute* tags, followed by an *@data* line, but the data section is different and contains specifications in braces such as those shown previously. Note that the omitted values have a value of 0—they are not "missing" values! If a value is unknown, it must be explicitly represented with a question mark.

ATTRIBUTE TYPES

The ARFF format accommodates the two basic data types: nominal and numeric. String attributes and date attributes are effectively nominal and numeric, respectively, although before they are used strings are often converted into a numeric form such as a word vector. Relation-valued attributes contain separate sets of instances that have basic attributes, such as numeric and nominal ones. How the two basic types are interpreted depends on the learning scheme being used. For example, many schemes treat numeric attributes as ordinal scales and only use less-than and greater-than comparisons between the values. However, some treat them as ratio scales and use distance calculations. You need to understand how machine learning schemes work before using them for data mining.

If a learning scheme treats numeric attributes as though they are measured on ratio scales, the question of normalization arises. Attributes are often normalized to lie in a fixed range—usually from zero to one—by dividing all values by the maximum value encountered or by subtracting the minimum value and dividing by the range between the maximum and minimum values. Another normalization technique is to calculate the statistical mean and standard deviation of the attribute values, subtract the mean from each value, and divide the result by the standard deviation. This process is called *standardizing* a statistical variable and results in a set of values whose mean is zero and standard deviation is one.

Some learning schemes—e.g., instance-based and regression methods—deal only with ratio scales because they calculate the "distance" between two instances based on the values of their attributes. If the actual scale is ordinal, a numeric distance function must be defined. One way of doing this is to use a two-level distance: one if the two values are different and zero if they are the same. Any nominal quantity can be treated as numeric by using this distance function. However, it is rather a crude technique and conceals the true degree of variation between instances. Another possibility is to generate several synthetic binary attributes for each nominal attribute: we return to this in Section 7.3 when we look at the use of trees for numeric prediction.

Sometimes there is a genuine mapping between nominal attributes and numeric scales. For example, postal ZIP codes indicate areas that could be represented by geographical coordinates; the leading digits of telephone numbers may do so too, depending on where you live. The first two digits of a student's identification number may be the year in which she first enrolled.

It is very common for practical datasets to contain nominal values that are coded as integers. For example, an integer identifier may be used as a code for an attribute such as *part number*, yet such integers are not intended for use in less-than or greater-than comparisons. If this is the case, it is important to specify that the attribute is nominal rather than numeric.

It is quite possible to treat an ordinal attribute as though it were nominal. Indeed, some machine learning schemes only deal with nominal elements. For example, in the contact lens problem the age attribute is treated as nominal, and the rules generated included these:

```
If age = young and astigmatic = no
    and tear production rate = normal
    then recommendation = soft
If age = pre-presbyopic and astigmatic = no
    and tear production rate = normal
    then recommendation = soft
```

But in fact age, specified in this way, is really an ordinal attribute for which the following is true:

```
young < pre-presbyopic < presbyopic.
```

If it were treated as ordinal, the two rules could be collapsed into one:

```
If age ≤ pre-presbyopic and astigmatic = no
    and tear production rate = normal
    then recommendation = soft
```

which is a more compact, and hence more satisfactory, way of saying the same thing.

MISSING VALUES

Most datasets encountered in practice, such as the labor negotiations data in Table 1.6, contain missing values. Missing values are frequently indicated by out-of-range entries; perhaps a negative number (e.g., -1) in a numeric field that is normally only positive, or a 0 in a numeric field that can never normally be 0. For nominal attributes, missing values may be indicated by blanks or dashes. Sometimes different kinds of missing values are distinguished (e.g., unknown vs unrecorded vs irrelevant values) and perhaps represented by different negative integers (-1, -2, etc.).

You have to think carefully about the significance of missing values. They may occur for a number of reasons, such as malfunctioning measurement equipment, changes in experimental design during data collection, and collation of several similar but not identical datasets. Respondents in a survey may refuse to answer certain questions such as age or income. In an archeological study, a specimen such as a skull may be damaged so that some variables cannot be measured. In a biological one, plants or animals may die before all variables have been measured. What do these things *mean* about the example under consideration? Might the skull damage have some significance in itself, or is it just because of some random event? Does a plant's early death have some bearing on the case or not?

Most machine learning schemes make the implicit assumption that there is no particular significance in the fact that a certain instance has an attribute value missing: the value is simply not known. However, there may be a good reason why the attribute's value is unknown—perhaps a decision was taken, on the evidence available, not to perform some particular test—and that might convey some information about the instance other than the fact that the value is simply missing. If this is the case, then it would be more appropriate to record *not tested* as another possible value for this attribute or perhaps as another attribute in the dataset. As the preceding examples illustrate, only someone familiar with the data can make an informed judgment about whether a particular value being missing has some extra significance or whether it should simply be coded as an ordinary missing value. Of course, if there seem to be several types of missing value, that is prima facie evidence that something is going on that needs to be investigated.

If missing values mean that an operator has decided not to make a particular measurement, that may convey a great deal more than the mere fact that the value is unknown. For example, people analyzing medical databases have noticed that cases may, in some circumstances, be diagnosable simply from the tests that a doctor decides to make regardless of the outcome of the tests. Then a record of which values are "missing" is all that is needed for a complete diagnosis—the actual values can be ignored completely!

INACCURATE VALUES

It is important to check data mining files carefully for rogue attributes and attribute values. The data used for mining has almost certainly not been gathered expressly for that purpose. When originally collected, many of the fields probably didn't matter and were left blank or unchecked. Provided it does not affect the original purpose of the data, there is no incentive to correct it. However, when the same database is used for mining, the errors and omissions suddenly start to assume great significance. For example, banks do not really need to know the age of their customers, so their databases may contain many missing or incorrect values. But age may be a very significant feature in mined rules.

Typographic errors in a dataset will obviously lead to incorrect values. Often the value of a nominal attribute is misspelled, creating an extra possible value for that attribute. Or perhaps it is not a misspelling but different names for the same thing, such as Pepsi and Pepsi Cola. Obviously the point of a defined format such as ARFF is to allow data files to be checked for internal consistency. However, errors that occur in the original data file are often preserved through the conversion process into the file that is used for data mining; thus the list of possible values that each attribute takes on should be examined carefully.

Typographical or measurement errors in numeric values generally cause outliers that can be detected by graphing one variable at a time. Erroneous values often deviate significantly from the pattern that is apparent in the remaining values. Sometimes, however, inaccurate values are hard to find, particularly without specialist domain knowledge.

Duplicate data presents another source of error. Most machine learning tools will produce different results if some of the instances in the data files are duplicated, because repetition gives them more influence on the result.

People often make deliberate errors when entering personal data into databases. They might make minor changes in the spelling of their street to try to identify whether the information they have provided ends up being sold to advertising agencies that burden them with junk mail. They might adjust the spelling of their name when applying for insurance if they have had insurance refused in the past. Rigid computerized data entry systems often impose restrictions that require imaginative workarounds. One story tells of a foreigner renting a vehicle in the United States. Being from abroad, he had no ZIP code; yet the computer insisted on one; in desperation the operator suggested that he use the ZIP code of the rental agency. If this is common practice, future data mining projects may notice a cluster of customers who apparently live in the same district as the agency! Similarly, a supermarket checkout operator sometimes uses his own frequent buyer card when the customer does not supply one, either so that the customer can get a discount that would otherwise be unavailable or simply to accumulate credit points in the cashier's account. Only a deep semantic knowledge of what is going on will be able to explain systematic data errors like these.

Finally, data goes stale. Many items change as circumstances change. For example, items in mailing lists—names, addresses, telephone numbers, and so on—change frequently. You need to consider whether the data you are mining is still current.

UNBALANCED DATA

In practical applications of classification schemes, it is very often the case that one class is far more prevalent than the others. For example, when predicting the weather in Ireland, it is pretty safe to predict that tomorrow will be *rainy* rather than *sunny*. Given a dataset in which these two values form the class attribute, with information relevant to the forecast in the other attributes, excellent accuracy is obtained by predicting *rainy* regardless of the values of the attributes. In fact, it might be very difficult to come up with a prediction that is numerically more accurate. (A more serious example is the image screening problem of Section 1.3: of the many dark regions in the training data, only a very small fraction are actual oil slicks—fortunately).

Suppose the accuracy if the same class value is predicted for every instance, regardless of the other attributes' values, is (say) 99%. It's hard to imagine that a more sophisticated rule could do better. It's true that there may be better ways of predicting the minority outcome, but these will inevitably make some errors on some cases with the majority outcome. The advantage of better predictions in the 1% of minority-outcome cases will almost certainly be overwhelmed by sacrificing even a tiny bit of accuracy on the 99% cases with the majority outcome.

Always predicting the majority outcome rarely says anything interesting about the data. The problem is that raw accuracy, measured by the proportion of correct predictions, is not necessarily the best criterion of success. In practice, different costs may be associated with the two types of error. If preventative measures are available, the cost of predicting a nuclear disaster (or a death) which turns out not to happen may be serious, but is overwhelmed by the cost of not predicting a nuclear disaster (or a death) if one actually happens. We will consider cost-sensitive evaluation, classification, and learning later in this book.

GETTING TO KNOW YOUR DATA

There is no substitute for getting to know your data. Simple tools that show histograms of the distribution of values of nominal attributes, and graphs of the values of numeric attributes (perhaps sorted or simply graphed against instance number), are very helpful. These graphical visualizations of the data make it easy to identify outliers, which may well represent errors in the data file—or arcane conventions for coding unusual situations, such as a missing year as 9999 or a missing weight as -1 kg, that no one has thought to tell you about. Domain experts need to be consulted to explain anomalies, missing values, the significance of integers that represent categories rather than numeric quantities, and so on. Pairwise plots of one attribute against another, or each attribute against the class value, can be extremely revealing.

Data cleaning is a time-consuming and labor-intensive procedure, but one that is absolutely necessary for successful data mining. With a large dataset, people often give up—How can they possibly check it all? Instead, you should sample a few instances and examine them carefully. You'll be surprised at what you find. Time looking at your data is always well spent.

2.5 FURTHER READING AND BIBLIOGRAPHIC NOTES

Pyle (1999) provided an extensive guide to data preparation for data mining. There is also a great deal of interest in data warehousing and the problems it entails. Kimball and Ross (2002) is the best introduction to these that we know of. Cabena et al. (1998) estimated that data preparation accounts for 60% of the effort involved in a data mining application, and they write at some length about the problems involved.

The area of inductive logic programming, which deals with finite and infinite relations, was covered by Bergadano and Gunetti (1996). The different "levels of measurement" for attributes were introduced by Stevens (1946) and are well described in the manuals for statistical packages such as SPSS (Nie, Hull, Jenkins, Steinbrenner, & Bent, 1970).

The multi-instance learning setting in its original, quite specific sense, and the drug activity prediction problem that motivated it, was introduced by Dietterich, Lathrop, and Lozano-Perez (1997). The multilabeled instance problem, mentioned near the beginning of Section 2.1, is quite a different setting; Read, Pfahringer, Holmes, and Frank (2009) discussed some approaches for tackling it using standard classification algorithms.

Output: knowledge representation

3

CHAPTER OUTLINE

3.1 Tables...68
3.2 Linear Models...68
3.3 Trees 70
3.4 Rules 75
    Classification Rules 75
    Association Rules 79
    Rules With Exceptions 80
    More Expressive Rules 82
3.5 Instance-Based Representation 84
3.6 Clusters...87
3.7 Further Reading and Bibliographic Notes 88

Many of the techniques in this book produce easily comprehensible descriptions of the structural patterns in the data. Before looking at how these techniques work, we have to see how structural patterns can be expressed. There are many different ways for representing the patterns that can be discovered by machine learning, and each one dictates the kind of technique that can be used to infer that output structure from data. Once you understand how the output is represented, you have come a long way toward understanding how it can be generated.

We saw many examples of machine learning in Chapter 1, What's it all about?. In these cases the output took the form of decision trees and classification rules, which are basic knowledge representation styles that many machine learning methods use. *Knowledge* is really too imposing a word for a decision tree or a collection of rules, and by using it we don't really mean to imply that these structures vie with the *real* kind of knowledge that we carry in our heads: it's just that we need some word to refer to the structures that learning methods produce. There are more complex varieties of rules that allow exceptions to be specified, and ones that can express relations among the values of the attributes of different instances. Some problems have a numeric class, and—as mentioned in chapter: What's it all about?—the classic way of dealing with these is to use linear models. Linear models can also be adapted to deal with binary classification. Moreover, special forms of trees can be developed for numeric prediction.

Instance-based representations focus on the instances themselves rather than rules that govern their attribute values. Finally, some learning schemes generate clusters of instances. These different knowledge representation methods parallel the different kinds of learning problems introduced in Chapter 2, Input: concepts, instances, attributes.

3.1 TABLES

The simplest, most rudimentary way of representing the output from machine learning is to make it just the same as the input—a table. For example, Table 1.2 is a decision table for the weather data: you just look up the appropriate conditions to decide whether or not to play. Exactly the same process can be used for numeric prediction too—in this case, the structure is sometimes referred to as a *regression table*. Less trivially, creating a decision or regression table might involve selecting some of the attributes. If temperature is irrelevant to the decision, e.g., a smaller, condensed table with that attribute missing would be a better guide. The problem is, of course, to decide which attributes to leave out without affecting the final decision. Attribute selection is discussed in Chapter 8, Data transformations.

3.2 LINEAR MODELS

Another simple style of representation is a "linear model," whose output is just the sum of the attribute values, except that weights are applied to each attribute before adding them together. The trick is to come up with good values for the weights—ones that make the model's output match the desired output. Here, the output and the inputs—attribute values—are all numeric. Statisticians use the word *regression* for the process of predicting a numeric quantity, and "linear regression model" is another term for this kind of model. Unfortunately this does not really relate to the ordinary use of the word "regression," which means to return to a previous state.

Linear models are easiest to visualize in two dimensions, where they are tantamount to drawing a straight line through a set of data points. Fig. 3.1 shows a line fitted to the CPU performance data described in Chapter 1, What's it all about? (Table 1.5), where only the *cache* attribute is used as input. The class attribute *performance* is shown on the vertical axis, with *cache* on the horizontal axis: both are numeric. The straight line represents the "best fit" prediction equation:

$$PRP = 37.06 + 2.47 \; CACH.$$

Given a test instance, a prediction can be produced by plugging the observed value of *cache* into this expression to obtain a value for *performance*. Here the

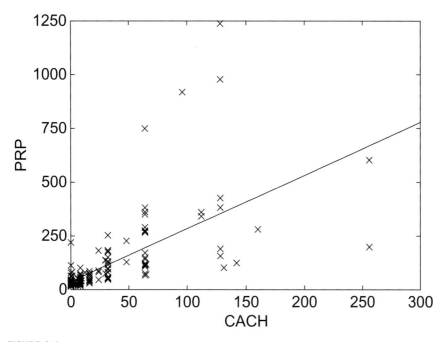

FIGURE 3.1

A linear regression function for the CPU performance data.

expression comprises a constant "bias" term (37.06) and a weight for the *cache* attribute (2.47). Of course, linear models can be extended beyond a single attribute—the trick is to come up with suitable values for each attribute's weight, and a bias term, that together give a good fit to the training data.

Linear models can also be applied to binary classification problems. In this case, the line produced by the model separates the two classes: it defines where the decision changes from one class value to the other. Such a line is often referred to as the *decision boundary*. Fig. 3.2 shows a decision boundary for the iris data that separates the *Iris setosas* from the *Iris versicolors*. In this case, the data is plotted using two of the input attributes—petal length and petal width—and the straight line defining the decision boundary is a function of these two attributes. Points lying on the line are given by the equation:

$$2.0 - 0.5 \text{ PETAL-LENGTH} - 0.8 \text{ PETAL-WIDTH} = 0.$$

As before, given a test instance, a prediction is produced by plugging the observed values of the attributes in question into the expression. But here we check the result and predict one class if it is greater than or equal to 0 (in this case, *Iris setosa*) and the other if it is less than 0 (*I. versicolor*). Again, the model can be extended to multiple attributes, in which case the boundary becomes

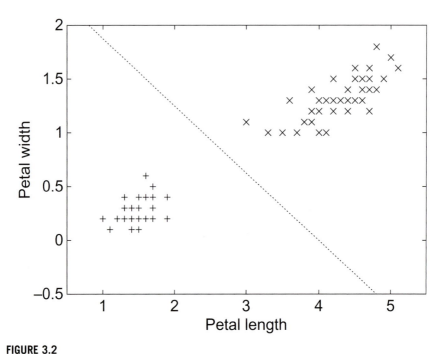

FIGURE 3.2

A linear decision boundary separating *Iris setosas* from *Iris versicolors*.

a high-dimensional plane or "hyperplane" in the instance space. The task is to find values for the weights so that the training data is correctly classified by the hyperplane.

In Figs. 3.1 and 3.2, a different fit to the data could be obtained by changing the position and orientation of the line, i.e., by changing the weights. The weights for Fig. 3.1 were found by a method called *least squares linear regression*; those for Fig. 3.2 were found by the perceptron training rule. Both methods are described in Chapter 4, Algorithms: the basic methods.

3.3 TREES

A "divide-and-conquer" approach to the problem of learning from a set of independent instances leads naturally to a style of representation called a *decision tree*. We have seen some examples of decision trees, for the contact lens (Fig. 1.2) and labor negotiations (Fig. 1.3) datasets. Nodes in a decision tree involve testing a particular attribute. Usually, the test compares an attribute value with a constant. Leaf nodes give a classification that applies to all instances that reach the leaf, or a set of classifications, or a probability distribution over all possible classifications. To classify an unknown instance, it is routed down the tree according to the values of the attributes tested in successive nodes, and when a leaf is reached the instance is classified according to the class assigned to the leaf.

If the attribute that is tested at a node is a nominal one, the number of children is usually the number of possible values of the attribute. In this case, because there is one branch for each possible value, the same attribute will not be retested further down the tree. Sometimes the attribute values are divided into two subsets, and the tree branches just two ways depending on which subset the value lies in the tree; in that case, the attribute might be tested more than once in a path.

If the attribute is numeric, the test at a node usually determines whether its value is greater or less than a predetermined constant, giving a two-way split. Alternatively, a three-way split may be used, in which case there are several different possibilities. If *missing value* is treated as an attribute value in its own right, that will create a third branch. An alternative for an integer-valued attribute would be a three-way split into *less than*, *equal to*, and *greater than*. An alternative for a real-valued attribute, for which *equal to* is not such a meaningful option, would be to test against an interval rather than a single constant, again giving a three-way split: *below*, *within*, and *above*. A numeric attribute is often tested several times in any given path down the tree from root to leaf, each test involving a different constant. We return to this when describing the handling of numeric attributes in Section 6.1.

Missing values pose an obvious problem. It is not clear which branch should be taken when a node tests an attribute whose value is missing. Sometimes, as described in Section 2.4, *missing value* is treated as an attribute value in its own right. If this is not the case, missing values should be treated in a special way rather than being considered just another possible value that the attribute might take. A simple solution is to record the number of elements in the training set that go down each branch and to use the most popular branch if the value for a test instance is missing.

A more sophisticated solution is to notionally split the instance into pieces and send part of it down each branch and from there right on down to the leaves of the subtrees involved. The split is accomplished using a numeric weight between 0 and 1, and the weight for a branch is chosen to be proportional to the number of training instances going down that branch, all weights summing to 1. A weighted instance may be further split at a lower node. Eventually, the various parts of the instance will each reach a leaf node, and the decisions at these leaf nodes must be recombined using the weights that have percolated down to the leaves. We return to this in Section 6.1.

So far we've described decision trees that divide the data at a node by comparing the value of some attribute with a constant. This is the most common approach. If you visualize this with two input attributes in two dimensions, comparing the value of one attribute with a constant splits the data parallel to that axis. However, there are other possibilities. Some trees compare two attributes with one another, while others compute some function of several attributes. For example, using a hyperplane as described in Section 3.2 results in an *oblique* split that is not parallel to an axis. A *functional tree* can have oblique splits as well as linear models at the leaf nodes, which are used for prediction. It is also possible for some nodes in the tree to specify alternative splits on different attributes, as though the tree designer couldn't make up their mind which one to choose. This might be useful if the attributes seem to be equally useful for classifying the data. Such nodes are called *option* nodes, and when classifying an unknown instance all branches leading from an option node are followed. This means that the instance will end up in more than one leaf, giving various alternative predictions, which are then combined in some fashion—e.g., using majority voting.

It is instructive and can even be entertaining to build a decision tree for a dataset manually. To do so effectively, you need a good way of visualizing the data so that you can decide which are likely to be the best attributes to test and what an appropriate test might be. The Weka Explorer, described in Appendix B, has a User Classifier facility that allows users to construct a decision tree interactively. It presents you with a scatter plot of the data against two selected attributes, which you choose. When you find a pair of attributes that discriminates the classes well, you can create a two-way split by drawing a polygon around the appropriate data points on the scatter plot.

For example, in Fig. 3.3A the user is operating on a dataset with three classes, the iris dataset, and has found two attributes, *petallength* and *petalwidth*, that do a good job of splitting up the classes. A rectangle has been drawn, manually, to separate out one of the classes (*I. versicolor*). Then the user switches to the decision tree view in Fig. 3.3B to see the tree so far. The left-hand leaf node contains predominantly irises of one type (*I. versicolor*, contaminated by only one *virginica*); the right-hand one contains predominantly two types (*I. setosa* and *virginica*, contaminated by only three *versicolors*). The user will probably select the right-hand leaf and work on it next, splitting it further with another rectangle—perhaps based on a different pair of attributes (although, from Fig. 3.3A, these two look pretty good).

The kinds of decision trees we've been looking at are designed for predicting categories rather than numeric quantities. When it comes to predicting numeric quantities, as with the CPU performance data in Table 1.5, the same kind of tree can be used, but each leaf would contain a numeric value that is the average of all the training set values to which the leaf applies. Because a numeric quantity is what is predicted, decision trees with averaged numeric values at the leaves are called *regression trees*.

Fig. 3.4A shows a regression equation for the CPU performance data, and Fig. 3.4B shows a regression tree. The leaves of the tree are numbers that represent the average outcome for instances that reach the leaf. The tree is much larger and more complex than the regression equation, and if we calculate the

(A)
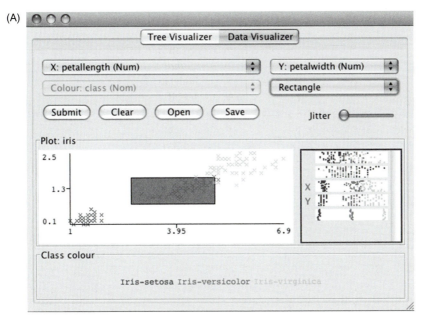

(B)
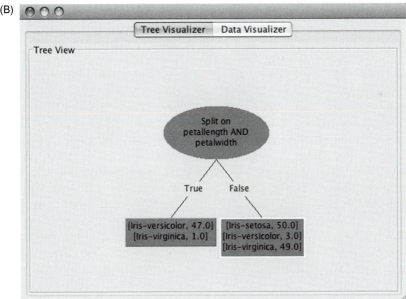

FIGURE 3.3

Constructing a decision tree interactively: (A) creating a rectangular test involving *petallength* and *petalwidth*; (B) the resulting (unfinished) decision tree.

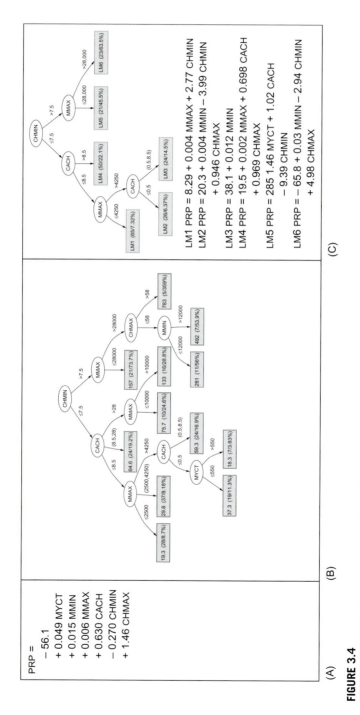

PRP =
    − 56.1
    + 0.049 MYCT
    + 0.015 MMIN
    + 0.006 MMAX
    + 0.630 CACH
    − 0.270 CHMIN
    + 1.46 CHMAX

(A)

(B)

LM1 PRP = 8.29 + 0.004 MMAX + 2.77 CHMIN
LM2 PRP = 20.3 + 0.004 MMIN − 3.99 CHMIN
    + 0.946 CHMAX
LM3 PRP = 38.1 + 0.012 MMIN
LM4 PRP = 19.5 + 0.002 MMAX + 0.698 CACH
    + 0.969 CHMAX
LM5 PRP = 285 1.46 MYCT + 1.02 CACH
    − 9.39 CHMIN
LM6 PRP = − 65.8 + 0.03 MMIN − 2.94 CHMIN
    + 4.98 CHMAX

(C)

FIGURE 3.4

Models for the CPU performance data: (A) linear regression; (B) regression tree; (C) model tree.

average of the absolute values of the errors between the predicted and actual CPU performance measures, it turns out to be significantly less for the tree than for the regression equation. The regression tree is more accurate because a simple linear model poorly represents the data in this problem. However, the tree is cumbersome and difficult to interpret because of its large size.

It is possible to combine regression equations with regression trees. Fig. 3.4C is a tree whose leaves contain linear expressions—i.e., regression equations—rather than single predicted values. This is called a *model tree*. Fig. 3.4C contains the six linear models that belong at the six leaves, labeled LM1 through LM6. The model tree approximates continuous functions by linear "patches," a more sophisticated representation than either linear regression or regression trees. Although the model tree is smaller and more comprehensible than the regression tree, the average error values on the training data are lower. (However, we will see in Chapter 5, Credibility: evaluating what's been learned, that calculating the average error on the training set is not in general a good way of assessing the performance of models.)

3.4 RULES

Rules are a popular alternative to decision trees, and we have already seen examples for the weather, contact lens, iris, and soybean datasets. The *antecedent*, or precondition, of a rule is a series of tests just like the tests at nodes in decision trees, while the *consequent*, or conclusion, gives the class or classes that apply to instances covered by that rule, or perhaps gives a probability distribution over the classes. Generally, the preconditions are logically ANDed together, and all the tests must succeed if the rule is to fire. However, in some rule formulations the preconditions are general logical expressions rather than simple conjunctions. We often think of the individual rules as being effectively logically ORed together: if any one applies, the class (or probability distribution) given in its conclusion is applied to the instance. However, conflicts arise when several rules with different conclusions apply; we will return to this shortly.

CLASSIFICATION RULES

It is easy to read a set of classification rules directly off a decision tree. One rule is generated for each leaf. The antecedent of the rule includes a condition for every node on the path from the root to that leaf, and the consequent of the rule is the class assigned by the leaf. This procedure produces rules that are unambiguous in that the order in which they are executed is irrelevant. However, in general, rules that are read directly off a decision tree are far more complex than necessary, and rules derived from trees are usually pruned to remove redundant tests.

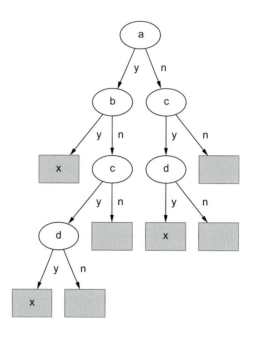

FIGURE 3.5

Decision tree for a simple disjunction.

Because decision trees cannot easily express the disjunction implied among the different rules in a set, transforming a general set of rules into a tree is not quite so straightforward. A good illustration of this occurs when the rules have the same structure but different attributes, like:

```
If a and b then x
If c and d then x
```

Then it is necessary to break the symmetry and choose a single test for the root node. If, e.g., *a* is chosen, the second rule must, in effect, be repeated twice in the tree, as shown in Fig. 3.5. This is known as the *replicated subtree problem*.

The replicated subtree problem is sufficiently important that it is worth looking at a couple more examples. The diagram on the left of Fig. 3.6 shows an *exclusive-or* function for which the output is *a* if $x = 1$ or $y = 1$ but not both. To make this into a tree, you have to split on one attribute first, leading to a structure like the one shown in the center. In contrast, rules can faithfully reflect the true symmetry of the problem with respect to the attributes, as shown on the right.

In this example the rules are not notably more compact than the tree. In fact, they are just what you would get by reading rules off the tree in the obvious way. But in other situations, rules are much more compact than trees, particularly if it is possible to have a "default" rule that covers cases not specified by the other rules. For example, to capture the effect of the rules in Fig. 3.7, in which there

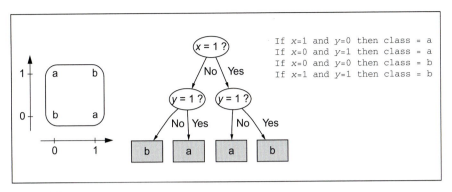

FIGURE 3.6

The *exclusive-or* problem.

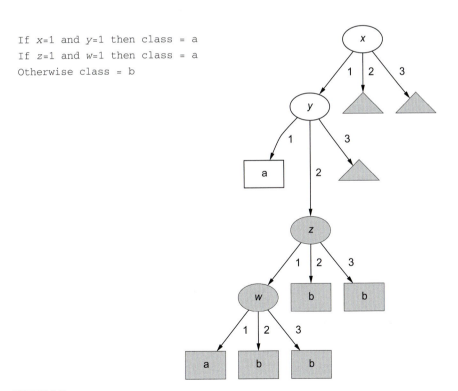

FIGURE 3.7

Decision tree with a replicated subtree.

are four attributes—*x*, *y*, *z*, and *w*, which can each be 1, 2, or 3—requires the tree shown on the right. Each of the three small gray triangles to the upper right should actually contain the whole three-level subtree that is displayed in gray, a rather extreme example of the replicated subtree problem. This is a distressingly complex description of a rather simple concept.

One reason why rules are popular is that each rule seems to represent an independent "nugget" of knowledge. New rules can be added to an existing rule set without disturbing ones already there, whereas to add to a tree structure may require reshaping the whole tree. However, this independence is something of an illusion, because it ignores the question of how the rule set is executed. We explained earlier the fact that if rules are meant to be interpreted *in order* as a "decision list," some of them, taken individually and out of context, may be incorrect. On the other hand, if the order of interpretation is supposed to be immaterial, then it is not clear what to do when different rules lead to different conclusions for the same instance. This situation cannot arise for rules that are read directly off a decision tree because the redundancy included in the structure of the rules prevents any ambiguity in interpretation. But it does arise when rules are generated in other ways.

If a rule set gives multiple classifications for a particular example, one solution is to give no conclusion at all. Another is to count how often each rule fires on the training data and go with the most popular one. These strategies can lead to radically different results. A different problem occurs when an instance is encountered that the rules fail to classify at all. Again, this cannot occur with decision trees, or with rules read directly off them, but it can easily happen with general rule sets. One way of dealing with this situation is to fail to classify such an example; another is to choose the most frequently occurring class as a default. Again, radically different results may be obtained for these strategies. Individual rules are simple, and sets of rules seem deceptively simple—but given just a set of rules with no additional information, it is not clear how it should be interpreted.

A particularly straightforward situation occurs when rules lead to a class that is Boolean (say, *yes* and *no*), and when only rules leading to one outcome (say, *yes*) are expressed. The assumption is that if a particular instance is not in class *yes*, then it must be in class *no*—a form of closed world assumption. If this is the case, rules cannot conflict and there is no ambiguity in rule interpretation: any interpretation strategy will give the same result. Such a set of rules can be written as a logic expression in what is called *disjunctive normal form*: i.e., as a disjunction (OR) of conjunctive (ANDed) conditions.

It is this simple special case that seduces people into assuming that rules are very easy to deal with, for here each rule really does operate as a new, independent piece of information that contributes in a straightforward way to the disjunction. Unfortunately, it only applies to Boolean outcomes and requires the closed world assumption, and these constraints are unrealistic in many practical situations. Machine learning algorithms that generate rules invariably produce ordered rule sets in multiclass situations, and this sacrifices any possibility of modularity because the order of execution is critical.

ASSOCIATION RULES

Association rules are no different from classification rules except that they can predict any attribute, not just the class, and this gives them the freedom to predict combinations of attributes too. Also, association rules are not intended to be used together as a set, as classification rules are. Different association rules express different regularities that underlie the dataset, and they generally predict different things.

Because so many different association rules can be derived from even a tiny dataset, interest is restricted to those that apply to a reasonably large number of instances and have a reasonably high accuracy on the instances to which they apply. The *coverage* of an association rule is the number of instances for which it predicts correctly—this is often called its *support*. Its *accuracy*—often called *confidence*—is the number of instances that it predicts correctly, expressed as a proportion of all instances to which it applies. For example, with the rule:

```
If temperature = cool then humidity = normal
```

the coverage is the number of days that are both cool and have normal humidity (4 in the data of Table 1.2), and the accuracy is the proportion of cool days that have normal humidity (100% in this case). It is usual to specify minimum coverage and accuracy values, and to seek only those rules whose coverage and accuracy are both at least these specified minima. In the weather data, e.g., there are 58 rules whose coverage and accuracy are at least 2 and 95%, respectively. (It may also be convenient to specify coverage as a percentage of the total number of instances instead.)

Association rules that predict multiple consequences must be interpreted rather carefully. For example, with the weather data in Table 1.2 we saw this rule:

```
If windy = false and play = no then outlook = sunny
                                and humidity = high.
```

This is *not* just a shorthand expression for the two separate rules:

```
If windy = false and play = no then outlook = sunny
If windy = false and play = no then humidity = high
```

It does indeed imply that these exceed the minimum coverage and accuracy figures—but it also implies more. The original rule means that the number of examples that are nonwindy, nonplaying, with sunny outlook and high humidity, is at least as great as the specified minimum coverage figure. It also means that the number of such days, expressed as a proportion of nonwindy, nonplaying days, is at least the specified minimum accuracy figure. This implies that the rule

```
If humidity = high and windy = false and play = no then outlook = sunny
```

also holds, because it has the same coverage as the original rule, and its accuracy must be at least as high as the original rule's because the number of high-humidity, nonwindy, nonplaying days is necessarily less than that of nonwindy, nonplaying days—which makes the accuracy greater.

As we have seen, there are relationships between particular association rules: some rules imply others. To reduce the number of rules that are produced, in cases where several rules are related it makes sense to present only the strongest one to the user. In the above example, only the first rule should be printed.

RULES WITH EXCEPTIONS

Returning to classification rules, a natural extension is to allow them to have *exceptions*. Then incremental modifications can be made to a rule set by expressing exceptions to existing rules rather than reengineering the entire set. For example, consider the iris problem described earlier. Suppose a new flower was found with the dimensions given in Table 3.1, and an expert declared it to be an instance of *I. setosa*. If this flower was classified by the rules given in Chapter 1, What's it all about?, for this problem, it would be misclassified by two of them:

```
If petal-length ≥ 2.45 and petal-length < 4.45 then Iris-versicolor
If petal-length ≥ 2.45 and petal-length < 4.95 and petal-width < 1.55
    then Iris-versicolor
```

These rules require modification so that the new instance can be treated correctly. However, simply changing the bounds for the attribute–value tests in these rules may not suffice because the instances used to create the rule set may then be misclassified. Fixing up a rule set is not as simple as it sounds.

Instead of changing the tests in the existing rules, an expert might be consulted to explain why the new flower violates them, giving explanations that could be used to extend the relevant rules only. For example, the first of these two rules misclassifies the new *I. setosa* as an instance of the genus *I. versicolor*. Instead of altering the bounds on any of the inequalities in the rule, an exception can be made based on some other attribute:

```
If petal-length ≥ 2.45 and petal-length < 4.45 then Iris-versicolor
    EXCEPT if petal-width < 1.0 then Iris-setosa
```

This rule says that a flower is *I. versicolor* if its petal length is between 2.45 and 4.45 cm *except* when its petal width is less than 1.0 cm, in which case it is *I. setosa*.

Of course, we might have exceptions to the exceptions, exceptions to these, and so on, giving the rule set something of the character of a tree. As well as being

Table 3.1 A New Iris Flower

Sepal Length	Sepal Width	Petal Length	Petal Width	Type
5.1	3.5	2.6	0.2	?

```
Default: Iris-setosa                                                    1
except if petal-length ≥ 2.45 and petal-length < 5.355                  2
            and petal-width < 1.75                                      3
        then Iris-versicolor                                            4
            except if petal-length ≥ 4.95 and petal-width < 1.55        5
                    then Iris-virginica                                 6
                    else if sepal-length < 4.95 and sepal-width ≥ 2.45  7
                        then Iris-virginica                             8
        else if petal-length ≥ 3.35                                     9
            then Iris-virginica                                        10
                except if petal-length < 4.85 and sepal-length < 5.95  11
                    then Iris-versicolor                               12
```

FIGURE 3.8

Rules for the iris data.

used to make incremental changes to existing rule sets, rules with exceptions can be used to represent the entire concept description in the first place.

Fig. 3.8 shows a set of rules that correctly classify all examples in the iris dataset given earlier. These rules are quite difficult to comprehend at first. Let's follow them through. A default outcome has been chosen, *I. setosa*, and is shown in the first line. For this dataset, the choice of default is rather arbitrary because there are 50 examples of each type. Normally, the most frequent outcome is chosen as the default.

Subsequent rules give exceptions to this default. The first *if . . . then*, on lines 2 through 4, gives a condition that leads to the classification *I. versicolor*. However, there are two exceptions to this rule (lines 5 through 8), which we will deal with in a moment. If the conditions on lines 2 and 3 fail, the *else* clause on line 9 is reached, which essentially specifies a second exception to the original default. If the condition on line 9 holds, the classification is *Iris virginica* (line 10). Again, there is an exception to this rule (on lines 11 and 12).

Now return to the exception on lines 5 through 8. This overrides the *I. versicolor* conclusion on line 4 if either of the tests on lines 5 and 7 holds. As it happens, these two exceptions both lead to the same conclusion, *I. virginica* (lines 6 and 8). The final exception is the one on lines 11 and 12, which overrides the *I. virginica* conclusion on line 10 when the condition on line 11 is met, and leads to the classification *I. versicolor*.

You will probably need to ponder these rules for some minutes before it becomes clear how they are intended to be read. Although it takes some time to get used to reading them, sorting out the *excepts* and *if . . . then . . . elses* becomes easier with familiarity. People often think of real problems in terms of rules, exceptions, and exceptions to the exceptions, so it is often a good way to express a complex rule set. But the main point in favor of this way of representing rules is that it scales up well. Although the whole rule set is a little hard to comprehend, each individual conclusion, each individual *then* statement, can be considered just in the context of the rules and exceptions that lead to it; whereas with decision lists, all prior rules need to be reviewed to determine the precise effect of an individual rule. This locality property is crucial when trying to understand large rule sets. Psychologically, people familiar with the data think of a particular set of cases, or kind of case, when looking at any one conclusion in the exception structure, and when one of these cases turns out to be an exception to the conclusion, it is easy to add an *except* clause to cater for it.

It is worth pointing out that the *default ... except if ... then ...* structure is logically equivalent to an *if ... then ... else ...*, where the *else* is unconditional and specifies exactly what the default did. An unconditional *else* is, of course, a default. (Note that there are no unconditional *elses* in the preceding rules.) Logically, the exception-based rules can very simply be rewritten in terms of regular *if ... then ... else* clauses. What is gained by the formulation in terms of exceptions is not *logical* but *psychological*. We assume that the defaults and the tests that occur early on apply more widely than the exceptions further down. If this is indeed true for the domain, and the user can see that it is plausible, the expression in terms of (common) rules and (rare) exceptions will be easier to grasp than a different, but logically equivalent, structure.

MORE EXPRESSIVE RULES

We have assumed implicitly that the conditions in rules involve testing an attribute value against a constant. But this may not be ideal. Suppose, to take a concrete example, we have the set of eight building blocks of the various shapes and sizes illustrated in Fig. 3.9, and we wish to learn the concept of *standing up*. This is a classic two-class problem with classes *standing* and *lying*. The four shaded blocks are positive (*standing*) examples of the concept, and the unshaded blocks are negative (*lying*) examples. The only information the learning algorithm will be given is the *width*, *height*, and *number of sides* of each block. The training data is shown in Table 3.2.

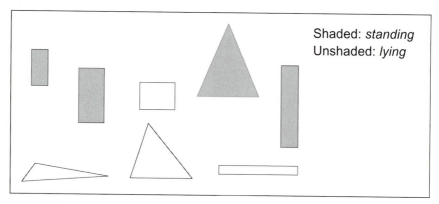

FIGURE 3.9

The shapes problem.

Table 3.2 Training Data for the Shapes Problem

Width	Height	Sides	Class
2	4	4	Standing
3	6	4	Standing
4	3	4	Lying
7	8	3	Standing
7	6	3	Lying
2	9	4	Standing
9	1	4	Lying
10	2	3	Lying

A conventional rule set that might be produced for this data is:

```
if width ≥ 3.5 and height < 7.0 then lying
if height ≥ 3.5 then standing
```

In case you're wondering, 3.5 is chosen as the breakpoint for *width* because it is halfway between the width of the thinnest lying block, namely 4, and the width of the fattest standing block whose height is less than 7, namely 3. Also, 7.0 is chosen as the breakpoint for *height* because it is halfway between the height of the tallest lying block, namely 6, and the shortest standing block whose width is greater than 3.5, namely 8. It is common to place numeric thresholds halfway between the values that delimit the boundaries of a concept.

Although these two rules work well on the examples given, they are not very good. Many new blocks would not be classified by either rule (e.g., one with width 1 and height 2), and it is easy to devise many legitimate blocks that the rules would not fit.

A person classifying the eight blocks would probably notice that "standing blocks are those that are taller than they are wide." This rule does not compare attribute values with constants, it compares attributes with one another:

```
if width > height then lying
if height > width then standing
```

The actual values of the *height* and *width* attributes are not important: just the result of comparing the two.

Many machine learning schemes do not consider relations between attributes because there is a considerable cost in doing so. One way of rectifying this is to add extra, secondary attributes that say whether two primary attributes are equal or not, or give the difference between them if they are numeric. For example, we might add a binary attribute *is width < height?* to Table 3.2. Such attributes are often added as part of the data engineering process.

With a seemingly rather small further enhancement, the expressive power of the knowledge representation can be extended very greatly. The trick is to express rules in a way that makes the role of the instance explicit:

```
if width(block) > height(block) then lying(block)
if height(block) > width(block) then standing(block)
```

Although this may not seem like much of an extension, it is if instances can be decomposed into parts. For example, if a *tower* is a pile of blocks, one on top of the other, the fact that the topmost block of the tower is standing can be expressed by:

```
if height(tower.top) > width(tower.top) then standing(tower.top)
```

Here, *tower.top* is used to refer to the topmost block. So far, nothing has been gained. But if *tower.rest* refers to the rest of the tower, then the fact that the tower is composed *entirely* of standing blocks can be expressed by the rules:

```
if height(tower.top) > width(tower.top) and standing(tower.rest)
   then standing(tower)
```

The apparently minor addition of the condition *standing(tower.rest)* is a recursive expression that will turn out to be true only if the rest of the tower is composed of standing blocks. That will be tested by a recursive application of the same rule. Of course, it is necessary to ensure that the recursion "bottoms out" properly by adding a further rule, such as:

```
if tower = empty then standing(tower.top)
```

Sets of rules like this are called *logic programs*, and this area of machine learning is called *inductive logic programming*. We will not be treating it further in this book.

3.5 INSTANCE-BASED REPRESENTATION

The simplest form of learning is plain memorization, or *rote learning*. Once a set of training instances has been memorized, on encountering a new instance the memory is searched for the training instance that most strongly resembles the new one. The only problem is how to interpret "resembles": we will explain that shortly. First, however, note that this is a completely different way of representing the "knowledge" extracted from a set of instances: just store the instances themselves and operate by relating new instances whose class is unknown to existing ones whose class is known. Instead of trying to create rules, work directly from the examples themselves. This is known as *instance-based* learning. In a sense all the other learning methods are "instance-based" too, because we always start with a set of instances as the initial training information. But the instance-based knowledge representation uses the instances themselves to represent what is learned, rather than inferring a rule set or decision tree and storing it instead.

In instance-based learning, all the real work is done when the time comes to classify a new instance rather than when the training set is processed. In a sense, then, the difference between this method and the others that we have seen is the time at which the "learning" takes place. Instance-based learning is lazy, deferring the real work as long as possible, whereas other methods are eager, producing a generalization as soon as the data has been seen. In instance-based classification, each new instance is compared with existing ones using a distance metric, and the closest existing instance is used to assign the class to the new one. This is called the *nearest-neighbor* classification method. Sometimes more than one nearest neighbor is used, and the majority class of the closest k neighbors (or the distance-weighted average, if the class is numeric) is assigned to the new instance. This is termed the *k-nearest-neighbor* method.

Computing the distance between two examples is trivial when examples have just one numeric attribute: it is just the difference between the two attribute values. It is almost as straightforward when there are several numeric attributes: generally, the standard Euclidean distance is used. However, this assumes that the attributes are normalized and are of equal importance, and one of the main problems in learning is to determine which are the important features.

When nominal attributes are present, it is necessary to come up with a "distance" between different values of that attribute. What are the distances between, say, the values *red*, *green*, and *blue*? Usually a distance of zero is assigned if the values are identical; otherwise, the distance is one. Thus the distance between *red* and *red* is zero but that between *red* and *green* is one. However, it may be desirable to use a more sophisticated representation of the attributes. For example, with more colors one could use a numeric measure of hue in color space, making *yellow* closer to *orange* than it is to *green* and *ocher* closer still.

Some attributes will be more important than others, and this is usually reflected in the distance metric by some kind of attribute weighting. Deriving suitable attribute weights from the training set is a key problem in instance-based learning.

It may not be necessary, or desirable, to store *all* the training instances. For one thing, this may make the nearest-neighbor calculation unbearably slow. For another, it may consume unrealistic amounts of storage. Generally some regions of attribute space are more stable than others with regard to class, and just a few exemplars are needed inside stable regions. For example, you might expect the required density of exemplars that lie well inside class boundaries to be much less than the density that is needed near class boundaries. Deciding which instances to save and which to discard is another key problem in instance-based learning.

An apparent drawback to instance-based representations is that they do not make explicit the structures that are learned. In a sense this violates the notion of

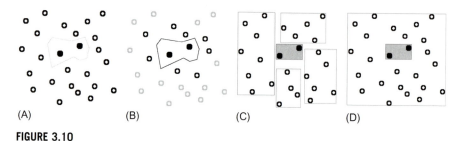

FIGURE 3.10

Different ways of partitioning the instance space.

"learning" that we presented at the beginning of this book; instances do not really "describe" the patterns in data. However, the instances combine with the distance metric to carve out boundaries in instance space that distinguish one class from another, and this is a kind of explicit representation of knowledge. For example, given a single instance of each of two classes, the nearest-neighbor rule effectively splits the instance space along the perpendicular bisector of the line joining the instances. Given several instances of each class, the space is divided by a set of lines that represent the perpendicular bisectors of selected lines joining an instance of one class to one of another class. Fig. 3.10A illustrates a nine-sided polygon that separates the filled-circle class from the open-circle class. This polygon is implicit in the operation of the nearest-neighbor rule.

When training instances are discarded, the result is to save just a few critical examples of each class. Fig. 3.10B shows only the examples that actually get used in nearest-neighbor decisions: the others (the light gray ones) can be discarded without affecting the result. These examples serve as a kind of explicit knowledge representation.

Some instance-based representations go further and explicitly generalize the instances. Typically this is accomplished by creating rectangular regions that enclose examples of the same class. Fig. 3.10C shows the rectangular regions that might be produced. Unknown examples that fall within one of the rectangles will be assigned the corresponding class: ones that fall outside all rectangles will be subject to the usual nearest-neighbor rule. Of course this produces different decision boundaries from the straightforward nearest-neighbor rule, as can be seen by superimposing the polygon in Fig. 3.10A onto the rectangles. Any part of the polygon that lies within a rectangle will be chopped off and replaced by the rectangle's boundary.

Rectangular generalizations in instance space are just like rules with a special form of condition, one that tests a numeric variable against an upper and lower bound and selects the region in between. Different dimensions of the rectangle correspond to tests on different attributes being ANDed together. Choosing snugly fitting rectangular regions as tests leads to much more conservative rules than those generally produced by rule-based machine learning schemes, because for each boundary of the region, there is an actual instance that lies on (or just inside) that boundary. Tests such as $x < a$ (where x is an attribute value and a is a constant) encompass an entire half-space—they apply no matter how small x is as long as it is less than a. When doing rectangular generalization in instance space you can afford to be conservative because if a new example is encountered that lies outside all regions, you can fall back on the nearest-neighbor metric. With rule-based methods the example cannot be classified, or receives just a default classification, if no rules apply to it. The advantage of more conservative rules is that, although incomplete, they may be more perspicuous than a complete set of rules that covers all cases. Finally, ensuring that the regions do not overlap is tantamount to ensuring that at most one rule can apply to an example, eliminating another of the difficulties of rule-based systems—what to do when several rules apply.

A more complex kind of generalization is to permit rectangular regions to nest one within another. Then a region that is basically all one class can contain an inner region with a different class, as illustrated in Fig. 3.10D. It is possible to allow nesting within nesting so that the inner region can itself contain its own inner region of a different class—perhaps the original class of the outer region. This is analogous to allowing rules to have exceptions and exceptions to the exceptions, as in Section 3.5.

It is worth pointing out a slight danger to the technique of visualizing instance-based learning in terms of boundaries in example space: it makes the implicit assumption that attributes are numeric rather than nominal. If the various values that a nominal attribute can take on were laid out along a line, generalizations involving a segment of that line would make no sense: each test involves either one value for the attribute or all values for it (or perhaps an arbitrary subset of values). Although you can more or less easily imagine extending the examples in Fig. 3.10 to several dimensions, it is much harder to imagine how rules involving nominal attributes will look in multidimensional instance space. Many machine learning situations involve numerous attributes, and our intuitions tend to lead us astray when extended to high-dimensional spaces.

3.6 CLUSTERS

When clusters rather than a classifier is learned, the output takes the form of a diagram that shows how the instances fall into clusters. In the simplest case this involves associating a cluster number with each instance, which might be depicted by laying the instances out in two dimensions and partitioning the space to show each cluster, as illustrated in Fig. 3.11A.

Some clustering algorithms allow one instance to belong to more than one cluster, so the diagram might lay the instances out in two dimensions and draw overlapping subsets representing each cluster—a Venn diagram, as in Fig. 3.11B.

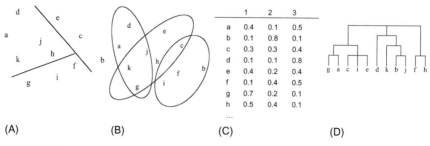

(A)   (B)   (C)   (D)

FIGURE 3.11

Different ways of representing clusters.

Some algorithms associate instances with clusters probabilistically rather than categorically. In this case, for every instance there is a probability or degree of membership with which it belongs to each of the clusters. This is shown in Fig. 3.11C. This particular association is meant to be a probabilistic one, so the numbers for each example sum to one—although that is not always the case. Other algorithms produce a hierarchical structure of clusters so that at the top level the instance space divides into just a few clusters, each of which divides into its own subclusters at the next level down, and so on. In this case a diagram such as the one in Fig. 3.11D is used, in which elements joined together at lower levels are more tightly clustered than ones joined together at higher levels. Such diagrams are called *dendrograms*. This term means just the same thing as *tree diagrams* (the Greek word *dendron* means a "tree"), but in clustering the more exotic version seems to be preferred—perhaps because biological species are a prime application area for clustering techniques, and ancient languages are often used for naming in biology.

Clustering is often followed by a stage in which a decision tree or rule set is inferred that allocates each instance to the cluster in which it belongs. Then, the clustering operation is just one step on the way to a structural description.

3.7 FURTHER READING AND BIBLIOGRAPHIC NOTES

Knowledge representation is a key topic in classical artificial intelligence and early work is well represented by a comprehensive series of papers edited by Brachman and Levesque (1985). The area of inductive logic programming and associated topics are well covered by de Raedt's (2008) book *Logical and relational learning*.

We mentioned the problem of dealing with conflict among different rules. Various ways of doing this, called *conflict resolution strategies*, have been developed for use with rule-based programming systems. These are described in books on rule-based programming, such as Brownstown, Farrell, Kant, and Martin (1985).

Again, however, they are designed for use with handcrafted rule sets rather than ones that have been learned. The use of handcrafted rules with exceptions for a large dataset has been studied by Gaines and Compton (1995), and Richards and Compton (1998) describe their role as an alternative to classic knowledge engineering.

Further information on the various styles of concept representation can be found in the papers that describe machine learning methods for inferring concepts from examples, and these are covered in the *Further reading* section of Chapter 4, Algorithms: the basic methods, and the *Discussion* sections of Chapter 6, Trees and rules, and Chapter 7, Extending instance-based and linear models. Finally, graphical models for representing concepts in the form of probability distributions are discussed in Chapter 9, Probabilistic methods.

Algorithms: the basic methods

4

CHAPTER OUTLINE

4.1 Inferring Rudimentary Rules 93
    Missing Values and Numeric Attributes 94
4.2 Simple Probabilistic Modeling 96
    Missing Values and Numeric Attributes 100
    Naïve Bayes for Document Classification 103
    Remarks 105
4.3 Divide-and-Conquer: Constructing Decision Trees 105
    Calculating Information...108
    Highly Branching Attributes 110
4.4 Covering Algorithms: Constructing Rules 113
    Rules Versus Trees...114
    A Simple Covering Algorithm 115
    Rules Versus Decision Lists 119
4.5 Mining Association Rules 120
    Item Sets..120
    Association Rules...122
    Generating Rules Efficiently 124
4.6 Linear Models...128
    Numeric Prediction: Linear Regression 128
    Linear Classification: Logistic Regression 129
    Linear Classification Using the Perceptron..131
    Linear Classification Using Winnow...133
4.7 Instance-Based Learning 135
    The Distance Function 135
    Finding Nearest Neighbors Efficiently 136
    Remarks 141
4.8 Clustering..141
    Iterative Distance-Based Clustering...142
    Faster Distance Calculations 144
    Choosing the Number of Clusters 146
    Hierarchical Clustering 147
    Example of Hierarchical Clustering 148
    Incremental Clustering...150

© 2017 Elsevier Inc. All rights reserved.

Category Utility 154
Remarks 156
4.9 **Multi-instance Learning** 156
Aggregating the Input 157
Aggregating the Output 157
4.10 **Further Reading and Bibliographic Notes** 158
4.11 **WEKA Implementations** 160

Now that we've seen how the inputs and outputs can be represented, it's time to look at the learning algorithms themselves. This chapter explains the basic ideas behind the techniques that are used in practical data mining. We will not delve too deeply into the trickier issues—advanced versions of the algorithms, optimizations that are possible, complications that arise in practice. These topics are deferred to Part II, where we come to grips with more advanced machine learning schemes and data transformations. It is important to understand these more advanced issues so that you know what is really going on when you analyze a particular dataset.

In this chapter we look at the basic ideas. One of the most instructive lessons is that simple ideas often work very well, and we strongly recommend the adoption of a "simplicity-first" methodology when analyzing practical datasets. There are many different kinds of simple structure that datasets can exhibit. In one dataset, there might be a single attribute that does all the work and the others are irrelevant or redundant. In another dataset, the attributes might contribute independently and equally to the final outcome. A third might have a simple logical structure, involving just a few attributes, which can be captured by a decision tree. In a fourth, there may be a few independent rules that govern the assignment of instances to different classes. A fifth might exhibit dependencies among different subsets of attributes. A sixth might involve linear dependence among numeric attributes, where what matters is a weighted sum of attribute values with appropriately chosen weights. In a seventh, classifications appropriate to particular regions of instance space might be governed by the distances between the instances themselves. And in an eighth, it might be that no class values are provided: the learning is unsupervised.

In the infinite variety of possible datasets there are many different kinds of structure that can occur, and a data mining tool—no matter how capable—i.e., looking for one class of structure may completely miss regularities of a different kind, regardless of how rudimentary those may be. The result is a baroque and opaque classification structure of one kind instead of a simple, elegant, immediately comprehensible structure of another.

Each of the eight examples of different kinds of datasets sketched above leads to a different machine learning scheme that is well suited to discovering the underlying concept. The sections of this chapter look at each of these structures in turn. A final section introduces simple ways of dealing with multi-instance problems, where each example comprises several different instances.

4.1 INFERRING RUDIMENTARY RULES

Here's an easy way to find very simple classification rules from a set of instances. Called *1R* for *1-rule*, it generates a one-level decision tree expressed in the form of a set of rules that all test one particular attribute. 1R is a simple, cheap method that often comes up with quite good rules for characterizing the structure in data. It turns out that simple rules frequently achieve surprisingly high accuracy. Perhaps this is because the structure underlying many real-world datasets is quite rudimentary, and just one attribute is sufficient to determine the class of an instance quite accurately. In any event, it is always a good plan to try the simplest things first.

The idea is this: we make rules that test a single attribute and branch accordingly. Each branch corresponds to a different value of the attribute. It is obvious what is the best classification to give each branch: use the class that occurs most often in the training data. Then the error rate of the rules can easily be determined. Just count the errors that occur on the training data, i.e., the number of instances that do not have the majority class.

Each attribute generates a different set of rules, one rule for every value of the attribute. Evaluate the error rate for each attribute's rule set and choose the best. It's that simple! Fig. 4.1 shows the algorithm in the form of pseudocode.

To see the 1R method at work, consider the weather data of Table 1.2 (we will encounter it many times again when looking at how learning algorithms work). To classify on the final column, *play*, 1R considers four sets of rules, one for each attribute. These rules are shown in Table 4.1. An asterisk indicates that a random choice has been made between two equally likely outcomes. The number of errors is given for each rule, along with the total number of errors for the rule set as a whole. 1R chooses the attribute that produces rules with the smallest number of errors—i.e., the first and third rule sets. Arbitrarily breaking the tie between these two rule sets gives:

```
outlook: sunny   →no
         overcast →yes
         rainy    →yes
```

We noted at the outset that the game for the weather data is unspecified. Oddly enough, it is apparently played when it is overcast or rainy but not when it is sunny. Perhaps it's an indoor pursuit.

```
For each attribute,
  For each value of that attribute, make a rule as follows:
    count how often each class appears
    find the most frequent class
    make the rule assign that class to this attribute-value.
  Calculate the error rate of the rules.
Choose the rules with the smallest error rate.
```

FIGURE 4.1

Pseudocode for 1R.

Table 4.1 Evaluating the Attributes in the Weather Data

	Attribute	Rules	Errors	Total Errors
1	Outlook	Sunny → no	2/5	4/14
		Overcast → yes	0/4	
		Rainy → yes	2/5	
2	Temperature	Hot → no*	2/4	5/14
		Mild → yes	2/6	
		Cool → yes	1/4	
3	Humidity	High → no	3/7	4/14
		Normal → yes	1/7	
4	Windy	False → yes	2/8	5/14
		True → no*	3/6	

Surprisingly, despite its simplicity 1R can do well in comparison with more sophisticated learning schemes. Rules that test a single attribute are often a viable alternative to more complex structures, and this strongly encourages a simplicity-first methodology in which the baseline performance is established using simple, rudimentary techniques before progressing to more sophisticated learning schemes, which inevitably generate output that is harder for people to interpret.

MISSING VALUES AND NUMERIC ATTRIBUTES

Although a very rudimentary learning scheme, 1R does accommodate both missing values and numeric attributes. It deals with these in simple but effective ways. *Missing* is treated as just another attribute value so that, e.g., if the weather data had contained missing values for the *outlook* attribute, a rule set formed on *outlook* would specify four possible class values, one for each of *sunny*, *overcast*, and *rainy* and a fourth for *missing*.

We can convert numeric attributes into nominal ones using a simple discretization method. First, sort the training examples according to the values of the numeric attribute. This produces a sequence of class values. For example, sorting the numeric version of the weather data (Table 1.3) according to the values of *temperature* produces the sequence

64	65	68	69	70	71	72	72	75	75	80	81	83	85
Yes	No	Yes	Yes	Yes	No	No	Yes	Yes	Yes	No	Yes	Yes	No

Discretization involves partitioning this sequence by placing breakpoints in it. One possibility is to place breakpoints wherever the class changes, producing eight categories:

Yes| No| Yes Yes Yes | No No | Yes Yes Yes | No | Yes Yes | No

Choosing breakpoints halfway between the examples on either side places them at 64.5, 66.5, 70.5, 72, 77.5, 80.5, and 84. However, the two instances with value 72 cause a problem because they have the same value of *temperature* but fall into different classes. The simplest fix is to move the breakpoint at 72 up one example, to 73.5, producing a mixed partition in which *no* is the majority class.

A more serious problem is that this procedure tends to form a large number of categories. The 1R method will naturally gravitate toward choosing an attribute that splits into many categories, because this will partition the dataset into many classes, making it more likely that instances will have the same class as the majority in their partition. In fact, the limiting case is an attribute that has a different value for each instance—i.e., an *identification code* attribute that pinpoints instances uniquely—and this will yield a zero error rate on the training set because each partition contains just one instance. Of course, highly branching attributes do not usually perform well on new examples; indeed the identification code attribute will never get any examples outside the training set correct. This phenomenon is known as *overfitting*; we have already described overfitting-avoidance bias in Chapter 1, What's it all about?, and we will encounter this problem repeatedly in the subsequent chapters.

For 1R, overfitting is likely to occur whenever an attribute has a large number of possible values. Consequently, when discretizing a numeric attribute a minimum limit is imposed on the number of examples of the majority class in each partition. Suppose that minimum is set at three. This eliminates all but two of the preceding partitions. Instead, the partitioning process begins

```
Yes    No    Yes    Yes |    Yes    ...
```

ensuring that there are three occurrences of *yes*, the majority class, in the first partition. However, because the next example is also *yes*, we lose nothing by including that in the first partition, too. This leads to a new division.

```
Yes No Yes Yes Yes | No No Yes Yes Yes | No Yes Yes No
```

where each partition contains at least three instances of the majority class, except the last one, which will usually have less. Partition boundaries always fall between examples of different classes.

Whenever adjacent partitions have the same majority class, as do the first two partitions above, they can be merged together without affecting the meaning of the rule sets. Thus the final discretization is

```
Yes No Yes Yes Yes No No Yes Yes Yes | No Yes Yes No
```

which leads to the rule set.

```
temperature: ≤77.5 → yes
             >77.5 → no
```

The second rule involved an arbitrary choice: as it happens, *no* was chosen. If *yes* had been chosen instead, there would be no need for any breakpoint at all— and as this example illustrates, it might be better to use the adjacent categories to help to break ties. In fact this rule generates five errors on the training set and so is less effective than the preceding rule for *outlook*. However, the same procedure leads to this rule for *humidity*:

```
humidity: ≤82.5 →yes
          >82.5 and ≤95.5 →no
          >95.5 →yes
```

This generates only three errors on the training set and is the best "1-rule" for the data in Table 1.3.

Finally, if a numeric attribute has missing values, an additional category is created for them, and the discretization procedure is applied just to the instances for which the attribute's value is defined.

4.2 SIMPLE PROBABILISTIC MODELING

The 1R method uses a single attribute as the basis for its decisions and chooses the one that works best. Another simple technique is to use all attributes and allow them to make contributions to the decisions that are *equally important* and *independent* of one another, given the class. This is unrealistic, of course: what makes real-life datasets interesting is that the attributes are certainly not equally important or independent. But it leads to a simple scheme that again works surprisingly well in practice.

Table 4.2 shows a summary of the weather data obtained by counting how many times each attribute–value pair occurs with each value (*yes* and *no*) for *play*. For example, you can see from Table 1.2 that *outlook* is *sunny* for five examples, two of which have *play = yes* and three of which have *play = no*. The cells in the first row of the new table simply count these occurrences for all possible values of each attribute, and the *play* figure in the final column counts the total number of occurrences of *yes* and *no*. The lower part of the table contains the same information expressed as fractions, or observed probabilities. For example, of the 9 days that *play* is yes, *outlook* is *sunny* for two, yielding a fraction of 2/9. For *play* the fractions are different: they are the proportion of days that *play* is *yes* and *no*, respectively.

Now suppose we encounter a new example with the values that are shown in Table 4.3. We treat the five features in Table 4.2—*outlook, temperature, humidity, windy*, and the overall likelihood that *play* is *yes* or *no*—as equally important, independent pieces of evidence and multiply the corresponding fractions. Looking at the outcome *yes* gives:

Likelihood of *yes* = $2/9 \times 3/9 \times 3/9 \times 3/9 \times 9/14 = 0.0053$.

Table 4.2 The Weather Data, With Counts and Probabilities

	Outlook		Temperature			Humidity			Windy			Play	
	Yes	No		Yes	No		Yes	No		Yes	No	Yes	No
Sunny	2	3	Hot	2	2	High	3	4	False	6	2	9	5
Overcast	4	0	Mild	4	2	Normal	6	1	True	3	3		
Rainy	3	2	Cool	3	1								
Sunny	2/9	3/5	Hot	2/9	2/5	High	3/9	4/5	False	6/9	2/5	9/14	5/14
Overcast	4/9	0/5	Mild	4/9	2/5	Normal	6/9	1/5	True	3/9	3/5		
Rainy	3/9	2/5	Cool	3/9	1/5								

Table 4.3 A New Day

Outlook	Temperature	Humidity	Windy	Play
Sunny	Cool	High	True	?

The fractions are taken from the *yes* entries in the table according to the values of the attributes for the new day, and the final 9/14 is the overall fraction representing the proportion of days on which *play* is *yes*. A similar calculation for the outcome *no* leads to

$$\text{Likelihood of } no = 3/5 \times 1/5 \times 4/5 \times 3/5 \times 5/14 = 0.0206.$$

This indicates that for the new day, *no* is more likely than *yes*—four times more likely. The numbers can be turned into probabilities by normalizing them so that they sum to 1:

$$\text{Probability of } yes = \frac{0.0053}{0.0053 + 0.0206} = 20.5\%,$$

$$\text{Probability of } no = \frac{0.0206}{0.0053 + 0.0206} = 79.5\%.$$

This simple and intuitive method is based on Bayes' rule of conditional probability. Bayes' rule says that if you have a hypothesis H and evidence E that bears on that hypothesis, then

$$P(E|H) = N! \times \prod_{i=1}^{k} \frac{P_i^{n_j}}{n_j!} \tag{4.1}$$

We use the notation that $P(A)$ denotes the probability of an event A and $P(A|B)$ denotes the probability of A conditional on another event B. The hypothesis H is that *play* will be, say, *yes*, and $P(H|E)$ is going to turn out to be 20.5%, just as determined previously. The evidence E is the particular combination of attribute values for the new day, *outlook* = *sunny*, *temperature* = *cool*, *humidity* = *high*, and *windy* = *true*. Let's call these four pieces of evidence E_1, E_2, E_3, and E_4, respectively. Assuming that these pieces of evidence are independent (given the class), their combined probability is obtained by multiplying the probabilities:

$$P(yes|E) = \frac{P(E_1|yes) \times P(E_2|yes) \times P(E_3|yes) \times P(E_4|yes) \times P(yes)}{P(E)}. \tag{4.2}$$

Don't worry about the denominator: we will ignore it and eliminate it in the final normalizing step when we make the probabilities of yes and no sum to 1, just as we did previously. The $P(yes)$ at the end is the probability of a yes outcome without knowing any of the evidence E, i.e., without knowing anything about the particular day in question—it's called the prior probability of the hypothesis H. In this case, it's just 9/14, because 9 of the 14 training examples had a yes value for play.

Substituting the fractions in Table 4.2 for the appropriate evidence probabilities
leads to

$$P(yes|E) = \frac{2/9 \times 3/9 \times 3/9 \times 3/9 \times 9/14}{P(E)},$$

just as we calculated previously. Again, the $P(E)$ in the denominator will disap-
pear when we normalize.

This method goes by the name of *Naïve Bayes*, because it's based on Bayes' rule
and "naïvely" assumes independence—it is only valid to multiply probabilities when
the events are independent. The assumption that attributes are independent (given
the class) in real life certainly is a simplistic one. But despite the disparaging name,
Naïve Bayes works very well when tested on actual datasets, particularly when combined with some of the attribute selection procedures introduced in Chapter 8, Data
transformations, that eliminate redundant, and hence nonindependent, attributes.

Things go badly awry in Naïve Bayes if a particular attribute value does not
occur in the training set in conjunction with *every* class value. Suppose that in the
training data the attribute value *outlook = sunny* was always associated with the
outcome *no*. Then the probability of *outlook = sunny* given a *yes*, i.e.,
$P(outlook = sunny|yes)$, would be zero, and because the other probabilities are
multiplied by this the final probability of *yes* in the above example would be zero
no matter how large they were. Probabilities that are zero hold a veto over the
other ones. This is not a good idea. But the bug is easily fixed by minor adjustments to the method of calculating probabilities from frequencies.

For example, the upper part of Table 4.2 shows that for *play = yes*, *outlook* is
sunny for two examples, *overcast* for four, and *rainy* for three, and the lower part
gives these events probabilities of 2/9, 4/9, and 3/9, respectively. Instead, we could
add 1 to each numerator, and compensate by adding 3 to the denominator, giving
probabilities of 3/12, 5/12, and 4/12, respectively. This will ensure that an attribute
value that occurs zero times receives a probability which is nonzero, albeit small.
The strategy of adding 1 to each count is a standard technique called the *Laplace
estimator* after the great 18th century French mathematician Pierre Laplace.
Although it works well in practice, there is no particular reason for adding 1 to the
counts: we could instead choose a small constant μ and use

$$\frac{2 + \mu/3}{9 + \mu}, \frac{4 + \mu/3}{9 + \mu}, \quad \text{and} \quad \frac{3 + \mu/3}{9 + \mu}.$$

The value of μ, which was set to 3 above, effectively provides a weight that
determines how influential the a priori values of 1/3, 1/3, and 1/3 are for each of
the three possible attribute values. A large μ says that these priors are very important compared with the new evidence coming in from the training set, whereas a
small one gives them less influence. Finally, there is no particular reason for dividing μ into three *equal* parts in the numerators: we could use

$$\frac{2 + \mu p_1}{9 + \mu}, \frac{4 + \mu p_2}{9 + \mu} \quad \text{and} \quad \frac{3 + \mu p_3}{9 + \mu}.$$

instead, where p_1, p_2, and p_3 sum to 1. Effectively, these three numbers are a priori probabilities of the values of the *outlook* attribute being *sunny*, *overcast*, and *rainy*, respectively.

This technique of smoothing parameters using pseudocounts for imaginary data can be rigorously justified using a probabilistic framework. Think of each parameter—in this case, the three numbers—as having an associated probability distribution. This is called a Bayesian formulation, to which we will return in greater detail in Chapter 9, Probabilistic methods. The initial "prior" distributions dictate how important the prior information is, and when new evidence comes in from the training set they can be updated to "posterior" distributions, which take that information into account. If the prior distributions have a particular form, namely, "Dirichlet" distributions, then the posterior distributions have the same form. Dirichlet distributions are defined in Appendix A.2, which contains a more detailed theoretical explanation.

The upshot is that the mean values for the posterior distribution are computed from the prior distribution in a way that generalizes the above example. Thus this heuristic smoothing technique can be justified theoretically as corresponding to the use of a Dirichlet prior with a nonzero mean for the parameter, then taking the value of the posterior mean as the updated estimate for the parameter.

This Bayesian formulation has the advantage of deriving from a rigorous theoretical framework. However, from a practical point of view it does not really help in determining just how to assign the prior probabilities. In practice, so long as zero values are avoided in the parameter estimates, the prior probabilities make little difference given a sufficient number of training instances, and people typically just estimate frequencies using the Laplace estimator by initializing all counts to one instead of zero.

MISSING VALUES AND NUMERIC ATTRIBUTES

One of the really nice things about Naïve Bayes is that missing values are no problem at all. For example, if the value of *outlook* were missing in the example of Table 4.3, the calculation would simply omit this attribute, yielding

$$\text{Likelihood of } yes = 3/9 \times 3/9 \times 3/9 \times 9/14 = 0.0238$$
$$\text{Likelihood of } no = 1/5 \times 4/5 \times 3/5 \times 5/14 = 0.0343.$$

These two numbers are individually a lot higher than they were before, because one of the fractions is missing. But that's not a problem because a fraction is missing in both cases, and these likelihoods are subject to a further normalization process. This yields probabilities for *yes* and *no* of 41% and 59%, respectively.

If a value is missing in a training instance, it is simply not included in the frequency counts, and the probability ratios are based on the number of values that actually occur rather than on the total number of instances.

Numeric values are usually handled by assuming that they have a "normal" or "Gaussian" probability distribution. Table 4.4 gives a summary of the weather

Table 4.4 The Numeric Weather Data With Summary Statistics

Outlook	Yes	No	Temperature	Yes	No	Humidity	Yes	No	Windy	Yes	No	Play	Yes	No
Sunny	2	3		83	85		86	85	False	6	2		9	5
Overcast	4	0		70	80		96	90	True	3	3			
Rainy	3	2		68	65		80	70						
				64	72		65	95						
				69	71		70	91						
				75			80							
				75			70							
				72			90							
				81			75							
Sunny	2/9	3/5	Mean	73	74.6	Mean	79.1	86.2	False	6/9	2/5		9/14	5/14
Overcast	4/9	0/5	Std dev	6.2	7.9	Std dev	10.2	9.7	True	3/9	3/5			
Rainy	3/9	2/5												

data with numeric features from Table 1.3. For nominal attributes, we calculate counts as before, while for numeric ones we simply list the values that occur. Then, instead of normalizing counts into probabilities as we do for nominal attributes, we calculate the mean and standard deviation for each class and each numeric attribute. The mean value of *temperature* over the *yes* instances is 73, and its standard deviation is 6.2. The mean is simply the average of the values, i.e., the sum divided by the number of values. The standard deviation is the square root of the sample variance, which we calculate as follows: subtract the mean from each value, square the result, sum them together, and then divide by one less than the number of values. After we have found this "sample variance," take its square root to yield the standard deviation. This is the standard way of calculating mean and standard deviation of a set of numbers (the "one less than" is to do with the number of degrees of freedom in the sample, a statistical notion that we don't want to get into here).

The probability density function for a normal distribution with mean μ and standard deviation σ is given by the rather formidable expression

$$f(x) = \frac{1}{\sqrt{2\pi}\sigma}e^{-\frac{(x-\mu)^2}{2\sigma^2}}.$$

But fear not! All this means is that if we are considering a *yes* outcome when *temperature* has a value, say, of 66, we just need to plug $x = 66$, $\mu = 73$, and $\sigma = 6.2$ into the formula. So the value of the probability density function is

$$f(temperature = 66 | yes) = \frac{1}{\sqrt{2\pi}\cdot 6.2}e^{-\frac{(66-73)^2}{2\cdot 6.2^2}} = 0.0340.$$

And by the same token, the probability density of a *yes* outcome when *humidity* has a value, say, of 90 is calculated in the same way:

$$f(humidity = 90 | yes) = 0.0221.$$

The probability density function for an event is very closely related to its probability. However, it is not quite the same thing. If temperature is a continuous scale, the probability of the temperature being *exactly* 66—or *exactly* any other value, such as 63.14159262—is zero. The real meaning of the density function $f(x)$ is that the probability that the quantity lies within a small region around x, say, between $x - \varepsilon/2$ and $x + \varepsilon/2$, is $\varepsilon \cdot f(x)$. You might think we ought to factor in the accuracy figure ε when using these density values, but that's not necessary. The same ε would appear in both the *yes* and *no* likelihoods that follow and cancel out when the probabilities were calculated.

Using these probabilities for the new day in Table 4.5 yields

Table 4.5 Another New Day

Outlook	Temperature	Humidity	Windy	Play
Sunny	66	90	True	?

Likelihood of $yes = 2/9 \times 0.0340 \times 0.0221 \times 3/9 \times 9/14 = 0.000036,$
Likelihood of $no = 3/5 \times 0.0279 \times 0.0381 \times 3/5 \times 5/14 = 0.000137;$

which leads to probabilities

$$\text{Probability of } yes = \frac{0.000036}{0.000036 + 0.000137} = 20.8\%,$$

$$\text{Probability of } no = \frac{0.000137}{0.000036 + 0.000137} = 79.2\%.$$

These figures are very close to the probabilities calculated earlier for the new day in Table 4.3, because the *temperature* and *humidity* values of 66 and 90 yield similar probabilities to the *cool* and *high* values used before.

The normal-distribution assumption makes it easy to extend the Naïve Bayes classifier to deal with numeric attributes. If the values of any numeric attributes are missing, the mean and standard deviation calculations are based only on the ones that are present.

NAÏVE BAYES FOR DOCUMENT CLASSIFICATION

An important domain for machine learning is document classification, in which each instance represents a document and the instance's class is the document's topic. Documents might be news items and the classes might be domestic news, overseas news, financial news, and sport. Documents are characterized by the words that appear in them, and one way to apply machine learning to document classification is to treat the presence or absence of each word as a Boolean attribute. Naïve Bayes is a popular technique for this application because it is very fast and quite accurate.

However, this does not take into account the number of occurrences of each word, which is potentially useful information when determining the category of a document. Instead, a document can viewed as a *bag of words*—a set that contains all the words in the document, with multiple occurrences of a word appearing multiple times (technically, a *set* includes each of its members just once, whereas a *bag* can have repeated elements). Word frequencies can be accommodated by applying a modified form of Naïve Bayes called *multinominal* Naïve Bayes.

Suppose $n_1, n_2, \ldots, n_k$ is the number of times word i occurs in the document, and $P_1, P_2, \ldots, P_k$ is the probability of obtaining word i when sampling from all the documents in category H. Assume that the probability is independent of the word's context and position in the document. These assumptions lead to a *multinomial distribution* for document probabilities. For this distribution, the probability of a document E given its class H—in other words, the formula for computing the probability $P(E|H)$ in Bayes' rule—is

$$P(E|H) = N! \times \prod_{i=1}^{k} \frac{P_i^{n_i}}{n_i!}$$

where $N = n_1 + n_2 + \cdots + n_k$ is the number of words in the document. The reason for the factorials is to account for the fact that the ordering of the occurrences of each word is immaterial according to the bag-of-words model. P_i is estimated by computing the relative frequency of word i in the text of all training documents pertaining to category H. In reality there could be a further term that gives the probability that the model for category H generates a document whose length is the same as the length of E, but it is common to assume that this is the same for all classes and hence can be dropped.

For example, suppose there are only two words, *yellow* and *blue*, in the vocabulary, and a particular document class H has $P(\textit{yellow} \mid H) = 75\%$ and $P(\textit{blue} \mid H) = 25\%$ (you might call H the class of *yellowish green* documents). Suppose E is the document *blue yellow blue* with a length of $N = 3$ words. There are four possible bags of three words. One is {*yellow yellow yellow*}, and its probability according to the preceding formula is

$$P(\{\textit{yellow yellow yellow}\} \mid H) = 3! \times \frac{0.75^3}{3!} \times \frac{0.25^0}{0!} = \frac{27}{64}$$

The other three, with their probabilities, are

$$P(\{\textit{blue blue blue}\} \mid H) = \frac{1}{64}$$

$$P(\{\textit{yellow yellow blue}\} \mid H) = \frac{27}{64}$$

$$P(\{\textit{yellow blue blue}\} \mid H) = \frac{9}{64}$$

E corresponds to the last case (recall that in a bag of words the order is immaterial); thus its probability of being generated by the *yellowish green* document model is 9/64, or 14%. Suppose another class, *very bluish green* documents (call it H'), has $P(\textit{yellow} \mid H') = 10\%$ and $P(\textit{blue} \mid H') = 90\%$. The probability that E is generated by this model is 24%.

If these are the only two classes, does that mean that E is in the *very bluish green* document class? Not necessarily. Bayes' rule, given earlier, says that you have to take into account the prior probability of each hypothesis. If you know that in fact *very bluish green* documents are twice as rare as *yellowish green* ones, this would be just sufficient to outweigh the 14−24% disparity and tip the balance in favor of the *yellowish green* class.

The factorials in the probability formula don't actually need to be computed because—being the same for every class—they drop out in the normalization process anyway. However, the formula still involves multiplying together many small probabilities, which soon yields extremely small numbers that cause underflow on large documents. The problem can be avoided by using logarithms of the probabilities instead of the probabilities themselves.

In the multinomial Naïve Bayes formulation a document's class is determined not just by the words that occur in it but also by the number of times they occur. In general it performs better than the ordinary Naïve Bayes model for document classification, particularly for large dictionary sizes.

REMARKS

Naïve Bayes gives a simple approach, with clear semantics, to representing, using, and learning probabilistic knowledge. It can achieve impressive results. People often find that Naïve Bayes rivals, and indeed outperforms, more sophisticated classifiers on many datasets. The moral is, always try the simple things first. Over and over again people have eventually, after an extended struggle, managed to obtain good results using sophisticated learning schemes, only to discover later that simple methods such as 1R and Naïve Bayes do just as well—or even better. The primary reason for its effectiveness in classification problems is that maximizing classification accuracy does not require particularly accurate probability estimates; it is sufficient for the correct class to receive the greatest probability.

There are many datasets for which Naïve Bayes does not do well, however, and it is easy to see why. Because attributes are treated as though they were independent given the class, the addition of redundant ones skews the learning process. As an extreme example, if you were to include a new attribute with the same values as *temperature* to the weather data, the effect of the *temperature* attribute would be multiplied: all of its probabilities would be squared, giving it a great deal more influence in the decision. If you were to add 10 such attributes, the decisions would effectively be made on *temperature* alone. Dependencies between attributes inevitably reduce the power of Naïve Bayes to discern what is going on. They can, however, be ameliorated by using a subset of the attributes in the decision procedure, making a careful selection of which ones to use. Chapter 8, Data transformations, shows how.

The normal-distribution assumption for numeric attributes is another restriction on Naïve Bayes as we have formulated it here. Many features simply aren't normally distributed. However, there is nothing to prevent us from using other distributions: there is nothing magic about the normal distribution. If you know that a particular attribute is likely to follow some other distribution, standard estimation procedures for that distribution can be used instead. If you suspect it isn't normal but don't know the actual distribution, there are procedures for "kernel density estimation" that do not assume any particular distribution for the attribute values. Another possibility is simply to discretize the data first.

Naïve Bayes is a very simple probabilistic model, and we examine far more sophisticated ones in Chapter 9, Probabilistic methods.

4.3 DIVIDE-AND-CONQUER: CONSTRUCTING DECISION TREES

The problem of constructing a decision tree can be expressed recursively. First, select an attribute to place at the root node, and make one branch for each possible value. This splits up the example set into subsets, one for every value of the attribute. Now the process can be repeated recursively for each branch, using only those instances that actually reach the branch. If at any time all instances at a node have the same classification, stop developing that part of the tree.

The only thing left is how to determine which attribute to split on, given a set of examples with different classes. Consider (again!) the weather data. There are four possibilities for each split, and at the top level they produce the trees in Fig. 4.2 Which is the best choice? The number of *yes* and *no* classes are shown at the leaves. Any leaf with only one class—*yes* or *no*—will not have to be split further, and the recursive process down that branch will terminate. Because we seek small trees, we would like this to happen as soon as possible. If we had a measure of the purity of each node, we could choose the attribute that produces the purest daughter nodes. Take a moment to look at Fig. 4.2 and ponder which attribute you think is the best choice.

The measure of purity that we will use is called the *information* and is measured in units called *bits*. Associated with a node of the tree, it represents the expected amount of information that would be needed to specify whether a new instance should be classified *yes* or *no*, given that the example reached that node. Unlike the bits in computer memory, the expected amount of information usually involves fractions of a bit—and is often less than one! It is calculated based on the number of *yes* and *no* classes at the node; we will look at the details of the

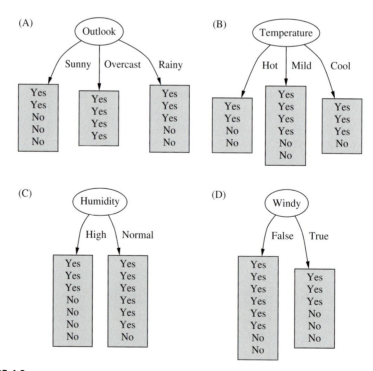

FIGURE 4.2

Tree stumps for the weather data.

calculation shortly. But first let's see how it's used. When evaluating the first tree in Fig. 4.2, the number of *yes* and *no* classes at the leaf nodes are [2, 3], [4, 0], and [3, 2], respectively, and the information values of these nodes are:

$$\text{Info}([2, 3]) = 0.971 \text{ bits}$$
$$\text{Info}([4, 0]) = 0.0 \text{ bits}$$
$$\text{Info}([3, 2]) = 0.971 \text{ bits}$$

We calculate the average information value of these, taking into account the number of instances that go down each branch—five down the first and third and four down the second:

$$\text{Info}([2, 3], [4, 0], [3, 2]) = (5/14) \times 0.971 + (4/14) \times 0 + (5/14) \times 0.971$$
$$= 0.693 \text{ bits}.$$

This average represents the amount of information that we expect would be necessary to specify the class of a new instance, given the tree structure in Fig. 4.2A.

Before any of the nascent tree structures in Fig. 4.2 were created, the training examples at the root comprised nine *yes* and five *no* nodes, corresponding to an information value of

$$\text{Info}([9, 5]) = 0.940 \text{ bits}.$$

Thus the tree in Fig. 4.2A is responsible for an information gain of

$$\text{Gain}(outlook) = \text{info}([9, 5]) - \text{info}([2, 3], [4, 0], [3, 2]) = 0.940 - 0.693$$
$$= 0.247 \text{ bits},$$

which can be interpreted as the informational value of creating a branch on the *outlook* attribute.

The way forward is clear. We calculate the information gain for each attribute and split on the one that gains the most information. In the situation of Fig. 4.2,

$$\text{Gain}(outlook) = 0.247 \text{ bits}$$
$$\text{Gain}(temperature) = 0.029 \text{ bits}$$
$$\text{Gain}(humidity) = 0.152 \text{ bits}$$
$$\text{Gain}(windy) = 0.048 \text{ bits},$$

so we select *outlook* as the splitting attribute at the root of the tree. Hopefully this accords with your intuition as the best one to select. It is the only choice for which one daughter node is completely pure, and this gives it a considerable advantage over the other attributes. *Humidity* is the next best choice because it produces a larger daughter node that is almost completely pure.

Then we continue, recursively. Fig. 4.3 shows the possibilities for a further branch at the node reached when *outlook* is *sunny*. Clearly, a further split on *outlook* will produce nothing new, so we only consider the other three attributes. The information gain for each turns out to be

$$\text{Gain}(temperature) = 0.571 \text{ bits}$$
$$\text{Gain}(humidity) = 0.971 \text{ bits}$$
$$\text{Gain}(windy) = 0.020 \text{ bits},$$

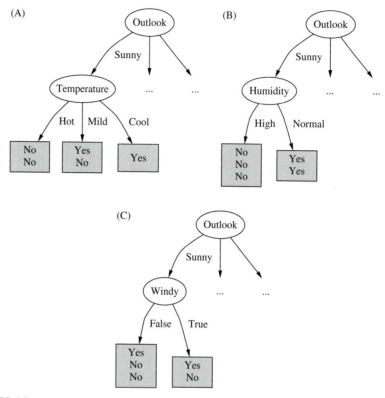

FIGURE 4.3

Expanded tree stumps for the weather data.

so we select *humidity* as the splitting attribute at this point. There is no need to split these nodes any further, so this branch is finished.

Continued application of the same idea leads to the decision tree of Fig. 4.4 for the weather data. Ideally the process terminates when all leaf nodes are pure, i.e., when they contain instances that all have the same classification. However, it might not be possible to reach this happy situation because there is nothing to stop the training set containing two examples with identical sets of attributes but different classes. Consequently we stop when the data cannot be split any further. Alternatively, one could stop if the information gain is zero. This is slightly more conservative, because it is possible to encounter cases where the data can be split into subsets exhibiting identical class distributions, which would make the information gain zero.

CALCULATING INFORMATION

Now it is time to explain how to calculate the information measure that is used as a basis for evaluating different splits. We describe the basic idea in this

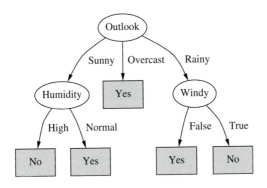

FIGURE 4.4

Decision tree for the weather data.

section, then in the next we examine a correction that is usually made to counter a bias toward selecting splits on attributes with large numbers of possible values.

Before examining the detailed formula for calculating the amount of information required to specify the class of an example given that it reaches a tree node with a certain number of *yes*'s and *no*'s, consider first the kind of properties we would expect this quantity to have:

1. When the number of either *yes*'s or *no*'s is zero, the information is zero;
2. When the number of *yes*'s and *no*'s is equal, the information reaches a maximum.

Moreover, the measure should be applicable to multiclass situations, not just to two-class ones.

The information measure relates to the amount of information obtained by making a decision, and a more subtle property of information can be derived by considering the nature of decisions. Decisions can be made in a single stage, or they can be made in several stages, and the amount of information involved is the same in both cases. For example, the decision involved in

$$\mathrm{Info}([2, 3, 4])$$

can be made in two stages. First decide whether it's the first case or one of the other two cases:

$$\mathrm{Info}([2, 7])$$

and then decide which of the other two cases it is:

$$\mathrm{Info}([3, 4])$$

In some cases the second decision will not need to be made, namely, when the decision turns out to be the first one. Taking this into account leads to the equation

$$\text{Info}([2, 3, 4]) = \text{info}([2, 7]) + (7/9) \times \text{info}([3, 4]).$$

Of course, there is nothing special about these particular numbers, and a similar relationship should hold regardless of the actual values. Thus we could add a further criterion to the list above:

3. The information should obey the multistage property that we have illustrated.

Remarkably, it turns out that there is only one function that satisfies all these properties, and it is known as the *information value* or *entropy*:

$$\text{Entropy}(p_1, p_2, \ldots, p_n) = - p_1 \log p_1 - p_2 \log p_2 \ldots - p_n \log p_n$$

The reason for the minus signs is that logarithms of the fractions $p_1, p_2, \ldots, p_n$ are negative, so the entropy is actually positive. Usually the logarithms are expressed in base 2, and then the entropy is in units called *bits*—just the usual kind of bits used with computers.

The arguments $p_1, p_2, \ldots$ of the entropy formula are expressed as fractions that add up to one, so that, e.g.,

$$\text{Info}([2, 3, 4]) = \text{entropy}(2/9, 3/9, 4/9).$$

Thus the multistage decision property can be written in general as

$$\text{Entropy}(p, q, r) = \text{entropy}(p, q + r) + (q + r) \cdot \text{entropy}\left(\frac{q}{q+r}, \frac{r}{q+r}\right)$$

where $p + q + r = 1$.

Because of the way the log function works, you can calculate the information measure without having to work out the individual fractions:

$$\text{Info}([2, 3, 4]) = - 2/9 \times \log 2/9 - 3/9 \times \log 3/9 - 4/9 \times \log 4/9$$
$$= [- 2 \log 2 - 3 \log 3 - 4 \log 4 + 9 \log 9]/9.$$

This is the way that the information measure is usually calculated in practice. So the information value for the first node of the first tree in Fig. 4.2 is

$$\text{Info}([2, 3]) = - 2/5 \times \log 2/5 - 3/5 \times \log 3/5 = 0.971 \text{ bits,}$$

as stated earlier.

HIGHLY BRANCHING ATTRIBUTES

When some attributes have a large number of possible values, giving rise to a multiway branch with many child nodes, a problem arises with the information gain calculation. The problem can best be appreciated in the extreme case when an attribute has a different value for each instance in the dataset—as, e.g., an identification code attribute might.

Table 4.6 The Weather Data with Identification Codes

ID Code	Outlook	Temperature	Humidity	Windy	Play
a	Sunny	Hot	High	False	No
b	Sunny	Hot	High	True	No
c	Overcast	Hot	High	False	Yes
d	Rainy	Mild	High	False	Yes
e	Rainy	Cool	Normal	False	Yes
f	Rainy	Cool	Normal	True	No
g	Overcast	Cool	Normal	True	Yes
h	Sunny	Mild	High	False	No
i	Sunny	Cool	Normal	False	Yes
j	Rainy	Mild	Normal	False	Yes
k	Sunny	Mild	Normal	True	Yes
l	Overcast	Mild	High	True	Yes
m	Overcast	Hot	Normal	False	Yes
n	Rainy	Mild	High	True	No

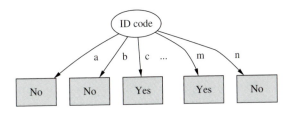

FIGURE 4.5

Tree stump for the *ID code* attribute.

Table 4.6 gives the weather data with this extra attribute. Branching on *ID code* produces the tree stump in Fig. 4.5. The expected information required to specify the class given the value of this attribute is

$$\frac{1}{14}(\text{info}([0, 1]) + \text{info}([0, 1]) + \text{info}([1, 0]) + \cdots + \text{info}([1, 0]) + \text{info}([0, 1])),$$

which is zero because each of the 14 terms is zero. This is not surprising: the *ID code* attribute identifies the instance, which determines the class without any ambiguity—just as Table 4.6 shows. Consequently, the information gain of this attribute is just the information at the root, info([9,5]) = 0.940 bits. This is greater than the information gain of any other attribute, and so *ID code* will inevitably be chosen as the splitting attribute. But branching on the identification code is no good for predicting the class of unknown instances.

The overall effect is that the information gain measure tends to prefer attributes with large numbers of possible values. To compensate for this, a modification of the measure called the *gain ratio* is widely used. The gain ratio is derived by taking into account the number and size of daughter nodes into which an attribute splits the dataset, disregarding any information about the class. In the situation shown in Fig. 4.5, all counts have a value of 1, so the information value of the split is

$$\text{Info}([1, 1, \ldots, 1]) = -1/14 \times \log 1/14 \times 14,$$

because the same fraction, 1/14, appears 14 times. This amounts to log 14, or 3.807 bits, which is a very high value. This is because the information value of a split is the number of bits needed to determine to which branch each instance is assigned, and the more branches there are, the greater this value is. The gain ratio is calculated by dividing the original information gain, 0.940 in this case, by the information value of the attribute, 3.807—yielding a gain ratio value of 0.247 for the *ID code* attribute.

Returning to the tree stumps for the weather data in Fig. 4.2, *outlook* splits the dataset into three subsets of size 5, 4, and 5 and thus has an intrinsic information value of

$$\text{Info}([5, 4, 5]) = 1.577$$

without paying any attention to the classes involved in the subsets. As we have seen, this intrinsic information value is greater for a more highly branching attribute such as the hypothesized *ID code*. Again we can correct the information gain by dividing by the intrinsic information value to get the gain ratio.

The results of these calculations for the tree stumps of Fig. 4.2 are summarized in Table 4.7 *Outlook* still comes out on top, but *humidity* is now a much closer contender because it splits the data into two subsets instead of three. In this particular example, the hypothetical *ID code* attribute, with a gain ratio of 0.247, would still be preferred to any of these four. However, its advantage is greatly reduced. In practical implementations, we can use an ad hoc test to guard against splitting on such a useless attribute.

Unfortunately, in some situations the gain ratio modification overcompensates and can lead to preferring an attribute just because its intrinsic information is much lower than for the other attributes. A standard fix is to choose the attribute that maximizes the gain ratio, provided that the information gain for that attribute is at least as great as the average information gain for all the attributes examined.

Table 4.7 Gain Ratio Calculations for the Tree Stumps of Fig. 4.2

Outlook		Temperature		Humidity		Windy	
Info:	0.693	Info:	0.911	Info:	0.788	Info:	0.892
Gain: 0.940−0.693	0.247	Gain: 0.940−0.911	0.029	Gain: 0.940−0.788	0.152	Gain: 0.940−0.892	0.048
Split info: info([5,4,5])	1.577	Split info: info([4,6,4])	1.557	Split info: info([7,7])	1.000	Split info: info([8,6])	0.985
Gain ratio: 0.247/1.577	0.156	Gain ratio: 0.029/1.557	0.019	Gain ratio: 0.152/1	0.152	Gain ratio: 0.048/0.985	0.049

The basic information-gain algorithm we have described is called ID3. A series of improvements to ID3, including the gain ratio criterion, culminated in a practical and influential system for decision tree induction called C4.5. Further improvements include methods for dealing with numeric attributes, missing values, noisy data, and generating rules from trees, and they are described in Section 6.1.

4.4 COVERING ALGORITHMS: CONSTRUCTING RULES

As we have seen, decision tree algorithms are based on a divide-and-conquer approach to the classification problem. They work top-down, seeking at each stage an attribute to split on that best separates the classes, and then recursively processing the subproblems that result from the split. This strategy generates a decision tree, which can if necessary be converted into a set of classification rules—although if it is to produce effective rules, the conversion is not trivial.

An alternative approach is to take each class in turn and seek a way of covering all instances in it, at the same time excluding instances not in the class. This is called a *covering* approach because at each stage you identify a rule that "covers" some of the instances. By its very nature, this covering approach leads to a set of rules rather than to a decision tree.

The covering method can readily be visualized in a two-dimensional space of instances as shown in Fig. 4.6A. We first make a rule covering the *a*'s. For the

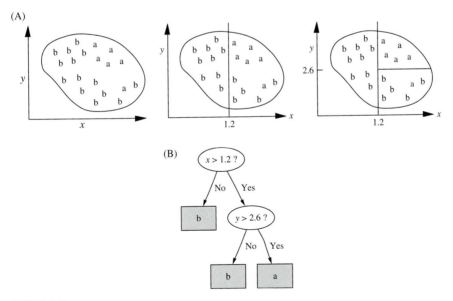

FIGURE 4.6

Covering algorithm: (A) covering the instances; (B) decision tree for the same problem.

first test in the rule, split the space vertically as shown in the center picture. This gives the beginnings of a rule:

```
If x > 1.2 then class = a
```

However, the rule covers many b's as well as a's, so a new test is added to the rule by further splitting the space horizontally as shown in the third diagram:

```
If x > 1.2 and y > 2.6 then class = a
```

This gives a rule covering all but one of the a's. It's probably appropriate to leave it at that, but if it were felt necessary to cover the final a, another rule would be necessary—perhaps.

```
If x > 1.4 and y < 2.4 then class = a
```

The same procedure leads to two rules covering the b's:

```
If x ≤ 1.2 then class = b
If x > 1.2 and y ≤ 2.6 then class = b
```

Again, one a is erroneously covered by these rules. If it were necessary to exclude it, more tests would have to be added to the second rule, and additional rules would be needed to cover the b's that these new tests exclude.

RULES VERSUS TREES

A top-down divide-and-conquer algorithm operates on the same data in a manner, i.e., at least superficially, quite similar to a covering algorithm. It might first split the dataset using the x attribute, and would probably end up splitting it at the same place, $x = 1.2$. However, whereas the covering algorithm is concerned only with covering a single class, the division would take both classes into account, because divide-and-conquer algorithms create a single concept description that applies to all classes. The second split might also be at the same place, $y = 2.6$, leading to the decision tree in Fig. 4.6B. This tree corresponds exactly to the set of rules, and in this case there is no difference in effect between the covering and the divide-and-conquer algorithms.

But in many situations there *is* a difference between rules and trees in terms of the perspicuity of the representation. For example, when we described the replicated subtree problem in Section 3.4, we noted that rules can be symmetric whereas trees must select one attribute to split on first, and this can lead to trees that are much larger than an equivalent set of rules. Another difference is that, in the multiclass case, a decision tree split takes all classes into account, trying to maximize the purity of the split, whereas the rule-generating method concentrates on one class at a time, disregarding what happens to the other classes.

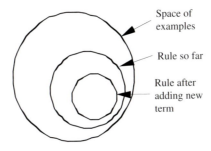

FIGURE 4.7

The instance space during operation of a covering algorithm.

A SIMPLE COVERING ALGORITHM

Covering algorithms operate by adding tests to the rule that is under construction, always striving to create a rule with maximum accuracy. In contrast, divide-and-conquer algorithms operate by adding tests to the tree that is under construction, always striving to maximize the separation between the classes. Each of these involves finding an attribute to split on. But the criterion for the best attribute is different in each case. Whereas divide-and-conquer algorithms such as ID3 choose an attribute to maximize the information gain, the covering algorithm we will describe chooses an attribute–value pair to maximize the probability of the desired classification.

Fig. 4.7 gives a picture of the situation, showing the space containing all the instances, a partially constructed rule, and the same rule after a new term has been added. The new term restricts the coverage of the rule: the idea is to include as many instances of the desired class as possible and exclude as many instances of other classes as possible. Suppose the new rule will cover a total of t instances, of which p are positive examples of the class and $t-p$ are in other classes—i.e., they are errors made by the rule. Then choose the new term to maximize the ratio p/t.

An example will help. For a change, we use the contact lens problem of Table 1.1. We will form rules that cover each of the three classes, *hard*, *soft*, and *none*, in turn. To begin, we seek a rule:

```
If ? then recommendation = hard.
```

For the unknown term "?," we have nine choices:

age = young	2/8
age = pre-presbyopic	1/8
age = presbyopic	1/8
spectacle prescription = myope	3/12
spectacle prescription = hypermetrope	1/12
astigmatism = no	0/12
astigmatism = yes	4/12
tear production rate = reduced	0/12
tear production rate = normal	4/12

The numbers on the right show the fraction of "correct" instances in the set singled out by that choice. In this case, *correct* means that the recommendation is *hard*. For instance, *age = young* selects eight instances, two of which recommend hard contact lenses, so the first fraction is 2/8. (To follow this, you will need to look back at the contact lens data in Table 1.1 and count up the entries in the table.) We select the largest fraction, 4/12, arbitrarily choosing between the seventh and the last choice in the list, and create the rule:

    If astigmatism = yes then recommendation = hard

This rule is quite inaccurate, getting only 4 instances correct out of the 12 that it covers, shown in Table 4.8. So we refine it further:

    If astigmatism = yes and ? then recommendation = hard

Considering the possibilities for the unknown term ? yields the seven choices:

age = young	2/4
age = pre-presbyopic	1/4
age = presbyopic	1/4
spectacle prescription = myope	3/6
spectacle prescription = hypermetrope	1/6
tear production rate = reduced	0/6
tear production rate = normal	4/6

Table 4.8 Part of the Contact Lens Data for which *Astigmatism = Yes*

Age	Spectacle Prescription	Astigmatism	Tear Production Rate	Recommended Lenses
Young	Myope	Yes	Reduced	None
Young	Myope	Yes	Normal	Hard
Young	Hypermetrope	Yes	Reduced	None
Young	Hypermetrope	Yes	Normal	Hard
Prepresbyopic	Myope	Yes	Reduced	None
Prepresbyopic	Myope	Yes	Normal	Hard
Prepresbyopic	Hypermetrope	Yes	Reduced	None
Prepresbyopic	Hypermetrope	Yes	Normal	None
Presbyopic	Myope	Yes	Reduced	None
Presbyopic	Myope	Yes	Normal	Hard
Presbyopic	Hypermetrope	Yes	Reduced	None
Presbyopic	Hypermetrope	Yes	Normal	None

(Again, count the entries in Table 4.8.) The last is a clear winner, getting four instances correct out of the six that it covers, and corresponds to the rule.

```
If astigmatism = yes and tear production rate = normal
   then recommendation = hard
```

Should we stop here? Perhaps. But let's say we are going for exact rules, no matter how complex they become. Table 4.9 shows the cases that are covered by the rule so far. The possibilities for the next term are now.

age = young	2/2
age = pre-presbyopic	1/2
age = presbyopic	1/2
spectacle prescription = myope	3/3
spectacle prescription = hypermetrope	1/3

We need to choose between the first and fourth. So far we have treated the fractions numerically, but although these two are equal (both evaluate to 1), they have different coverage: one selects just two correct instances and the other selects three. In the event of a tie, we choose the rule with the greater coverage, giving the final rule:

```
If astigmatism = yes and tear production rate = normal
   and spectacle prescription = myope then recommendation = hard
```

This is indeed one of the rules given for the contact lens problem. But it only covers three out of the four *hard* recommendations. So we delete these three from the set of instances and start again, looking for another rule of the form:

```
If ? then recommendation = hard
```

Table 4.9 Part of the Contact Lens Data for Which *Astigmatism = Yes* and *Tear Production Rate = Normal*

Age	Spectacle Prescription	Astigmatism	Tear Production Rate	Recommended Lenses
Young	Myope	Yes	Normal	Hard
Young	Hypermetrope	Yes	Normal	Hard
Prepresbyopic	Myope	Yes	Normal	Hard
Prepresbyopic	Hypermetrope	Yes	Normal	None
Presbyopic	Myope	Yes	Normal	Hard
Presbyopic	Hypermetrope	Yes	Normal	None

Following the same process, we will eventually find that *age* = *young* is the best choice for the first term. Its coverage is one out of seven; the reason for the seven is that 3 instances have been removed from the original set, leaving 21 instances altogether. The best choice for the second term is *astigmatism* = *yes*, selecting 1/3 (actually, this is a tie); *tear production rate* = *normal* is the best for the third, selecting 1/1.

```
If age = young and astigmatism = yes
    and tear production rate = normal
    then recommendation = hard
```

This rule actually covers two of the original set of instances, one of which is covered by the previous rule—but that's all right because the recommendation is the same for each rule.

Now that all the hard-lens cases are covered, the next step is to proceed with the soft-lens ones in just the same way. Finally, rules are generated for the *none* case—unless we are seeking a rule set with a default rule, in which case explicit rules for the final outcome are unnecessary.

What we have just described is the PRISM method for constructing rules. It generates only correct or "perfect" rules. It measures the success of a rule by the accuracy formula *p/t*. Any rule with accuracy less than 100% is "incorrect" in that it assigns cases to the class in question that actually do not have that class. PRISM continues adding clauses to each rule until it is perfect: its accuracy is 100%. Fig. 4.8 gives a summary of the algorithm. The outer loop iterates over the classes, generating rules for each class in turn. Note that we reinitialize to the full set of examples each time round. Then we create rules for that class and remove the examples from the set until there are none of that class left. Whenever we create a rule, start with an empty rule (which covers all the examples), and then restrict it by adding tests until it covers only examples of the desired class. At each stage choose the most promising test, i.e., the one that

```
For each class C
  Initialize E to the instance set
  While E contains instances in class C
    Create a rule R with an empty left-hand side that predicts class C
    Until R is perfect (or there are no more attributes to use) do
      For each attribute A not mentioned in R, and each value v,
        Consider adding the condition A=v to the LHS of R
        Select A and v to maximize the accuracy p/t
          (break ties by choosing the condition with the largest p)
      Add A=v to R
    Remove the instances covered by R from E
```

FIGURE 4.8

Pseudocode for a basic rule learner.

maximizes the accuracy of the rule. Finally, break ties by selecting the test with greatest coverage.

RULES VERSUS DECISION LISTS

Consider the rules produced for a particular class, i.e., the algorithm in Fig. 4.8 with the outer loop removed. It seems clear from the way that these rules are produced that they are intended to be interpreted in order, i.e., as a decision list, testing the rules in turn until one applies and then using that. This is because the instances covered by a new rule are removed from the instance set as soon as the rule is completed (in the last line of the code in Fig. 4.8): thus subsequent rules are designed for instances that are *not* covered by the rule. However, although it appears that we are supposed to check the rules in turn, we do not have to do so. Consider that any subsequent rules generated for this class will have the same effect—they all predict the same class. This means that it does not matter what order they are executed in: either a rule will be found that covers this instance, in which case the class in question is predicted, or no such rule is found, in which case the class is not predicted.

Now return to the overall algorithm. Each class is considered in turn, and rules are generated that distinguish instances in that class from the others. No ordering is implied between the rules for one class and those for another. Consequently the rules that are produced can be executed in any order.

As described in Section 3.4, order-independent rules seem to provide more modularity by acting as independent nuggets of "knowledge," but they suffer from the disadvantage that it is not clear what to do when conflicting rules apply. With rules generated in this way, a test example may receive multiple classifications, i. e., it may satisfy rules that apply to different classes. Other test examples may receive no classification at all. A simple strategy to force a decision in ambiguous cases is to choose, from the classifications that are predicted, the one with the most training examples or, if no classification is predicted, to choose the category with the most training examples overall. These difficulties do not occur with decision lists because they are meant to be interpreted in order and execution stops as soon as one rule applies: the addition of a default rule at the end ensures that any test instance receives a classification. It is possible to generate good decision lists for the multiclass case using a slightly different method, as we shall see in Section 6.2.

Methods such as Prism can be described as *separate-and-conquer* algorithms: you identify a rule that covers many instances in the class (and excludes ones not in the class), separate out the covered instances because they are already taken care of by the rule, and continue the process on those that are left. This contrasts with the divide-and-conquer approach of decision trees. The "separate" step results in an efficient method because the instance set continually shrinks as the operation proceeds.

4.5 MINING ASSOCIATION RULES

Association rules are like classification rules. You could find them in the same way, by executing a separate-and-conquer rule-induction procedure for each possible expression that could occur on the right-hand side of the rule. But not only might any attribute occur on the right-hand side with any possible value; a single association rule often predicts the value of more than one attribute. To find such rules, you would have to execute the rule induction procedure once for every possible *combination* of attributes, with every possible combination of values, on the right-hand side. That would result in an enormous number of association rules, which would then have to be pruned down on the basis of their *coverage* (the number of instances that they predict correctly) and their *accuracy* (the same number expressed as a proportion of the number of instances to which the rule applies). This approach is quite infeasible. (Note that, as we mentioned in Section 3.4, what we are calling *coverage* is often called *support* and what we are calling *accuracy* is often called *confidence*.)

Instead, we capitalize on the fact that we are only interested in association rules with high coverage. We ignore, for the moment, the distinction between the left- and right-hand sides of a rule and seek combinations of attribute—value pairs that have a prespecified minimum coverage. These are called *frequent item sets*: an attribute—value pair is an *item*. The terminology derives from market basket analysis, in which the items are articles in your shopping cart and the supermarket manager is looking for associations among these purchases.

ITEM SETS

The first column of Table 4.10 shows the individual items for the weather data of Table 1.2, with the number of times each item appears in the dataset given at the right. These are the one-item sets. The next step is to generate the two-item sets by making pairs of one-item ones. Of course, there is no point in generating a set containing two different values of the same attribute (such as *outlook = sunny* and *outlook = overcast*), because that cannot occur in any actual instance.

Assume that we seek association rules with minimum coverage 2: thus we discard any item sets that cover fewer than two instances. This leaves 47 two-item sets, some of which are shown in the second column along with the number of times they appear. The next step is to generate the three-item sets, of which 39 have a coverage of 2 or greater. There are 6 four-item sets, and no five-item sets—for this data, a five-item set with coverage 2 or greater could only correspond to a repeated instance. The first rows of the table, e.g., show that there are 5 days when *outlook = sunny*, two of which have *temperature = hot*, and, in fact, on both of those days *humidity = high* and *play = no* as well.

Table 4.10 Item Sets for the Weather Data With Coverage 2 or Greater

#	One-Item Sets		Two-Item Sets		Three-Item Sets		Four-Item Sets	
1	Outlook = sunny	5	Outlook = sunny temperature = mild	2	Outlook = sunny temperature = hot humidity = high	2	Outlook = sunny temperature = hot humidity = high play = no	2
2	Outlook = overcast	4	Outlook = sunny temperature = hot	2	Outlook = sunny temperature = hot play = no	2	Outlook = sunny humidity = high windy = false play = no	2
3	Outlook = rainy	5	Outlook = sunny humidity = normal	2	Outlook = sunny humidity = normal play = yes	2	Outlook = overcast temperature = hot windy = false play = yes	2
4	Temperature = cool	4	Outlook = sunny humidity = high	3	Outlook = sunny humidity = high windy = false	3	Outlook = rainy temperature = mild windy = false play = yes	2
5	Temperature = mild	6	Outlook = sunny windy = true	2	Outlook = sunny humidity = high play = no	2	Outlook = rainy humidity = normal windy = false play = yes	2
6	Temperature = hot	4	Outlook = sunny windy = false	3	Outlook = sunny windy = false play = no	3	Temperature = cool humidity = normal windy = false play = yes	2
7	Humidity = normal	7	Outlook = sunny play = yes	2	Outlook = overcast temperature = hot windy = false	2		
8	Humidity = high	7	Outlook = sunny play = no	3	Outlook = overcast temperature = hot play = yes	3		
9	Windy = true	6	Outlook = overcast temperature = hot	2	Outlook = overcast humidity = normal play = yes	2		
10	Windy = false	8	Outlook = overcast humidity = normal	2	Outlook = overcast humidity = high play = yes	2		
11	Play = yes	9	Outlook = overcast humidity = high	2	Outlook = overcast windy = true play = yes	2		
12	Play = no	5	Outlook = overcast windy = true	2	Outlook = overcast windy = false play = yes	2		
13			Outlook = overcast windy = false	2	Outlook = rainy temperature = cool humidity = normal	2		
...								
38			Humidity = normal windy = false	4	Humidity = normal windy = false play = yes	4		
39			Humidity = normal play = yes	4	Humidity = high windy = false play = no	2		
40			Humidity = high windy = true	3				
...								
47			Windy = false play = no	2				

ASSOCIATION RULES

Shortly we will explain how to generate these item sets efficiently. But first let us finish the story. Once all item sets with the required coverage have been generated, the next step is to turn each into a rule, or set of rules, with at least the specified minimum accuracy. Some item sets will produce more than one rule; others will produce none. For example, there is one three-item set with a coverage of 4 (row 38 of Table 4.10):

```
humidity = normal, windy = false, play = yes
```

This set leads to seven potential rules:

If humidity = normal and windy = false then play = yes	4/4
If humidity = normal and play = yes then windy = false	4/6
If windy = false and play = yes then humidity = normal	4/6
If humidity = normal then windy = false and play = yes	4/7
If windy = false then humidity = normal and play = yes	4/8
If play = yes then humidity = normal and windy = false	4/9
If−then humidity = normal and windy = false and play = yes	4/14

The figures at the right show the number of instances for which all three conditions are true—i.e., the coverage—divided by the number of instances for which the conditions in the antecedent are true. Interpreted as a fraction, they represent the proportion of instances on which the rule is correct—i.e., its accuracy. Assuming that the minimum specified accuracy is 100%, only the first of these rules will make it into the final rule set. The denominators of the fractions are readily obtained by looking up the antecedent expression in Table 4.10 (although some are not shown in the table). The final rule above has no conditions in the antecedent, and its denominator is the total number of instances in the dataset.

Table 4.11 shows the final rule set for the weather data, with minimum coverage 2 and minimum accuracy 100%, sorted by coverage. There are 58 rules, 3 with coverage 4, 5 with coverage 3, and 50 with coverage 2. Only 7 have two conditions in the consequent, and none has more than two. The first rule comes from the item set described previously. Sometimes several rules arise from the same item set. For example, rules 9, 10, and 11 all arise from the four-item set in row 6 of Table 4.10:

```
temperature = cool, humidity = normal, windy = false, play = yes
```

which has coverage 2. Three subsets of this item set also have coverage 2:

```
temperature = cool, windy = false
temperature = cool, humidity = normal, windy = false
temperature = cool, windy = false, play = yes
```

Table 4.11 Association Rules for the Weather Data

	Association Rule			Coverage	Accuracy (%)
1	Humidity = normal windy = false	⇒	Play = yes	4	100
2	Temperature = cool	⇒	Humidity = normal	4	100
3	Outlook = overcast	⇒	Play = yes	4	100
4	Temperature = cool play = yes	⇒	Humidity = normal	3	100
5	Outlook = rainy windy = false	⇒	Play = yes	3	100
6	Outlook = rainy play = yes	⇒	Windy = false	3	100
7	Outlook = sunny humidity = high	⇒	Play = no	3	100
8	Outlook = sunny play = no	⇒	Humidity = high	3	100
9	Temperature = cool windy = false	⇒	Humidity = normal play = yes	2	100
10	Temperature = cool humidity = normal windy = false ⇒	⇒	Play = yes	2	100
11	Temperature = cool windy = false play = yes	⇒	Humidity = normal	2	100
12	Outlook = rainy humidity = normal windy = false	⇒	Play = yes	2	100
13	Outlook = rainy humidity = normal play = yes	⇒	Windy = false	2	100
14	Outlook = rainy temperature = mild windy = false	⇒	Play = yes	2	100
15	Outlook = rainy temperature = mild play = yes	⇒	Windy = false	2	100
16	Temperature = mild windy = false play = yes	⇒	Outlook = rainy	2	100
17	Outlook = overcast temperature = hot	⇒	Windy = false play = yes	2	100
18	Outlook = overcast windy = false	⇒	Temperature = hot play = yes	2	100
19	Temperature = hot play = yes	⇒	Outlook = overcast windy = false	2	100
20	Outlook = overcast temperature = hot windy = false ⇒	⇒	Play = yes	2	100

(Continued)

Table 4.11 Association Rules for the Weather Data *Continued*

	Association Rule			Coverage	Accuracy (%)
21	Outlook = overcast temperature = hot play = yes	⇒	Windy = false	2	100
22	Outlook = overcast windy = false play = yes	⇒	Temperature = hot	2	100
23	Temperature = hot windy = false play = yes	⇒	Outlook = overcast	2	100
24	Windy = false play = no	⇒	Outlook = sunny humidity = high	2	100
25	Outlook = sunny humidity = high windy = false	⇒	Play = no	2	100
26	Outlook = sunny windy = false play = no	⇒	Humidity = high	2	100
27	Humidity = high windy = false play = no	⇒	Outlook = sunny	2	100
28	Outlook = sunny temperature = hot	⇒	Humidity = high play = no	2	100
29	Temperature = hot play = no	⇒	Outlook = sunny humidity = high	2	100
30	Outlook = sunny temperature = hot humidity = high	⇒	Play = no	2	100
31	Outlook = sunny temperature = hot play = no	⇒	Humidity = high	2	100
...	...	...	...		
58	Outlook = sunny temperature = hot	⇒	Humidity = high	2	100

and these lead to rules 9, 10, and 11, all of which are 100% accurate (on the training data).

GENERATING RULES EFFICIENTLY

We now consider in more detail an algorithm for producing association rules with specified minimum coverage and accuracy. There are two stages: generating item sets with the specified minimum coverage, and from each item set determining the rules that have the specified minimum accuracy.

The first stage proceeds by generating all one-item sets with the given minimum coverage (the first column of Table 4.10) and then using this to generate the two-item sets (second column), three-item sets (third column), and so on.

Each operation involves a pass through the dataset to count the items in each set, and after the pass the surviving item sets are stored in a hash table—a standard data structure that allows elements stored in it to be found very quickly. From the one-item sets, candidate two-item sets are generated, and then a pass is made through the dataset, counting the coverage of each two-item set; at the end the candidate sets with less than minimum coverage are removed from the table. The candidate two-item sets are simply all of the one-item sets taken in pairs, because a two-item set cannot have the minimum coverage unless both its constituent one-item sets have the minimum coverage, too. This applies in general: a three-item set can only have the minimum coverage if all three of its two-item subsets have minimum coverage as well, and similarly for four-item sets.

An example will help to explain how candidate item sets are generated. Suppose there are five three-item sets: (A B C), (A B D), (A C D), (A C E), and (B C D)—where, e.g., A is a feature such as *outlook = sunny*. The union of the first two, (A B C D), is a candidate four-item set because its other three-item subsets (A C D) and (B C D) have greater than minimum coverage. If the three-item sets are sorted into lexical order, as they are in this list, then we need only consider pairs whose first two members are the same. For example, we do not consider (A C D) and (B C D) because (A B C D) can also be generated from (A B C) and (A B D), and if these two are not three-item sets with minimum coverage then (A B C D) cannot be a candidate four-item set. This leaves the pairs (A B C) and (A B D), which we have already explained, and (A C D) and (A C E). This second pair leads to the set (A C D E) whose three-item subsets do not all have the minimum coverage, so it is discarded. The hash table assists with this check: we simply remove each item from the set in turn and check that the remaining three-item set is indeed present in the hash table. Thus in this example there is only one candidate four-item set, (A B C D). Whether or not it actually has minimum coverage can only be determined by checking the instances in the dataset.

The second stage of the procedure takes each item set and generates rules from it, checking that they have the specified minimum accuracy. If only rules with a single test on the right-hand side were sought, it would be simply a matter of considering each condition in turn as the consequent of the rule, deleting it from the item set, and dividing the coverage of the entire item set by the coverage of the resulting subset—obtained from the hash table—to yield the accuracy of the corresponding rule. Given that we are also interested in association rules with multiple tests in the consequent, it looks like we have to evaluate the effect of placing each *subset* of the item set on the right-hand side, leaving the remainder of the set as the antecedent.

This brute-force method will be excessively computation intensive unless item sets are small, because the number of possible subsets grows exponentially with the size of the item set. However, there is a better way. We observed when describing association rules in Section 3.4 that if the double-consequent rule

```
If windy = false and play = no
   then outlook = sunny and humidity = high
```

holds with a given minimum coverage and accuracy, then both single-consequent rules formed from the same item set must also hold:

```
If humidity = high and windy = false and play = no
   then outlook = sunny
If outlook = sunny and windy = false and play = no
   then humidity = high
```

Conversely, if one or other of the single-consequent rules does not hold, there is no point in considering the double-consequent one. This gives a way of building up from single-consequent rules to candidate double-consequent ones, from double-consequent rules to candidate triple-consequent ones, and so on. Of course, each candidate rule must be checked against the hash table to see if it really does have more than the specified minimum accuracy. But this generally involves checking far fewer rules than the brute force method. It is interesting that this way of building up candidate $(n + 1)$-consequent rules from actual n-consequent ones is really just the same as building up candidate $(n + 1)$-item sets from actual n-item sets, described earlier.

Fig. 4.9 shows pseudocode for the two parts of the association rule mining process. Fig. 4.9A shows how to find all item sets of sufficient coverage. In an actual implementation, the minimum coverage (or support) would be specified by a parameter whose value the user can specify. Fig. 4.9B shows how to find all rules that are sufficiently accurate, for a particular item set found by the previous algorithm. Again, in practice, minimum accuracy (or confidence) would be determined by a user-specified parameter.

To find all rules for a particular dataset, the process shown in the second part would be applied to all the item sets found using the algorithm in the first part. Note that the code in the second part requires access to the hash tables established by the first part, which contain all the sufficiently frequent item sets that have been found, along with their coverage. In this manner, the algorithm in Fig. 4.9B does not need to revisit the original data at all: accuracy can be estimated based on the information in these tables.

Association rules are often sought for very large datasets, and efficient algorithms are highly valued. The method we have described makes one pass through the dataset for each different size of item set. Sometimes the dataset is too large to read in to main memory and must be kept on disk; then it may be worth reducing the number of passes by checking item sets of two consecutive sizes in one go. For example, once sets with two items have been generated, all sets of three items could be generated from them before going through the instance set to count the actual number of items in the sets. More three-item sets than necessary would be considered, but the number of passes through the entire dataset would be reduced.

(A)

```
Set k to 1
Find all k-item sets with sufficient coverage and store them in hash table #1
While some k-item sets with sufficient coverage have been found
    Increment k
    Find all pairs of (k-1)-item sets in hash table #(k-1) that differ only in
    their last item
    Create a k-item set for each pair by combining the two (k-1)-item sets
    that are paired
    Remove all k-item sets containing any (k-1)-item sets that are not in the
    #(k-1)hash table
    Scan the data and remove all remaining k-item sets that do not have
    sufficient coverage
    Store the remaining k-item sets and their coverage in hash table #k,
    sorting items in lexical order
```

(B)

```
Set n to 1
Find all sufficiently accurate n-consequent rules for the k-item set and
    store them in hash table #1, computing accuracy using the hash tables
    found for item sets
While some sufficiently accurate n-consequent rules have been found
    Increment n
    Find all pairs of (n-1)-consequent rules in hash table #(n-1) whose
    consequents differ only in their last item
    Create an n-consequent rule for each pair by combining the two (n-1)-
    consequent rules that are paired
    Remove all n-consequent rules that are insufficiently accurate, computing
    accuracy using the hash tables found for item sets
    Store the remaining n-consequent rules and their accuracy in hash table
    #k, sorting items for each consequent in lexical order
```

FIGURE 4.9

(A) Finding all item sets with sufficient coverage; (B) finding all sufficiently accurate
association rules for a k-item set.

In practice, the amount of computation needed to generate association rules
depends critically on the minimum coverage specified. The accuracy has less
influence because it does not affect the number of passes that must be made
through the dataset. In many situations we would like to obtain a certain number
of rules—say 50—with the greatest possible coverage at a prespecified minimum
accuracy level. One way to do this is to begin by specifying the coverage to be
rather high and to then successively reduce it, reexecuting the entire rule-finding
algorithm for each coverage value and repeating until the desired number of rules
has been generated.

The tabular input format that we use throughout this book, and in particular
the standard ARFF format based on it, is very inefficient for many association-
rule problems. Association rules are often used in situations where attributes are
binary—either present or absent—and most of the attribute values associated with
a given instance are absent. This is a case for the sparse data representation
described in Section 2.4; the same algorithm for finding association rules applies.

4.6 LINEAR MODELS

The methods we have been looking at for decision trees and rules work most naturally with nominal attributes. They can be extended to numeric attributes either by incorporating numeric-value tests directly into the decision tree or rule induction scheme, or by prediscretizing numeric attributes into nominal ones. We will see how in Chapter 6, Trees and rules, and Chapter 8, Data transformations. However, there are methods that work most naturally with numeric attributes, namely, the linear models introduced in Section 3.2; we examine them in more detail here. They can form components or starting points for more complex learning methods, which we will investigate later.

NUMERIC PREDICTION: LINEAR REGRESSION

When the outcome, or class, is numeric, and all the attributes are numeric, linear regression is a natural technique to consider. This is a staple method in statistics. The idea is to express the class as a linear combination of the attributes, with predetermined weights:

$$x = w_0 + w_1 a_1 + w_2 a_2 + \cdots + w_k a_k$$

where x is the class; $a_1, a_2, \ldots, a_k$ are the attribute values; and $w_0, w_1, \ldots, w_k$ are weights.

The weights are calculated from the training data. Here the notation gets a little heavy, because we need a way of expressing the attribute values for each training instance. The first instance will have a class, say $x^{(1)}$, and attribute values, $a_1^{(1)}, a_2^{(1)}, \ldots, a_k^{(1)}$, where the superscript denotes that it is the first example. Moreover, it is notationally convenient to assume an extra attribute a_0, whose value is always 1.

The predicted value for the first instance's class can be written as

$$w_0 a_0^{(1)} + w_1 a_1^{(1)} + w_2 a_2^{(1)} + \cdots + w_k a_k^{(1)} = \sum_{j=0}^{k} w_j a_j^{(1)}.$$

This is the predicted, not the actual, value for the class. Of interest is the difference between the predicted and actual values. The method of least-squares linear regression is to choose the coefficients w_j—there are $k + 1$ of them—to minimize the sum of the squares of these differences over all the training instances. Suppose there are n training instances: denote the ith one with a superscript (i). Then the sum of the squares of the differences is

$$\sum_{i=1}^{n} \left(x^{(i)} - \sum_{j=0}^{k} w_j a_j^{(i)} \right)^2$$

where the expression inside the parentheses is the difference between the *i*th instance's actual class and its predicted class. This sum of squares is what we have to minimize by choosing the coefficients appropriately.

This is all starting to look rather formidable. However, the minimization technique is straightforward if you have the appropriate math background. Suffice it to say that given enough examples—roughly speaking, more examples than attributes—choosing weights to minimize the sum of the squared differences is really not difficult. It does involve a matrix inversion operation, but this is readily available as prepackaged software.

Once the math has been accomplished, the result is a set of numeric weights, based on the training data, which can be used to predict the class of new instances. We saw an example of this when looking at the CPU performance data, and the actual numeric weights are given in Fig. 3.4A. This formula can be used to predict the CPU performance of new test instances.

Linear regression is an excellent, simple method for numeric prediction, and it has been widely used in statistical applications for decades. Of course, basic linear models suffer from the disadvantage of, well, linearity. If the data exhibits a nonlinear dependency, the best-fitting straight line will be found, where "best" is interpreted as the least mean-squared difference. This line may not fit very well. However, linear models serve well as building blocks or starting points for more complex learning methods.

LINEAR CLASSIFICATION: LOGISTIC REGRESSION

Linear regression can easily be used for classification in domains with numeric attributes. Indeed, we can use *any* regression technique for classification. The trick is to perform a regression for each class, setting the output equal to one for training instances that belong to the class and zero for those that do not. The result is a linear expression for the class. Then, given a test example of unknown class, calculate the value of each linear expression and choose the one that is largest. When used with linear regression, this scheme is sometimes called *multiresponse linear regression*.

One way of looking at multiresponse linear regression is to imagine that it approximates a numeric *membership function* for each class. The membership function is 1 for instances that belong to that class and 0 for other instances. Given a new instance we calculate its membership for each class and select the biggest.

Multiresponse linear regression often yields good results in practice. However, it has two drawbacks. First, the membership values it produces are not proper probabilities because they can fall outside the range 0−1. Second, least-squares regression assumes that the errors are not only statistically independent, but are also normally distributed with the same standard deviation, an assumption that is blatantly violated when the method is applied to classification problems because the observations only ever take on the values 0 and 1.

A related statistical technique called *logistic regression* does not suffer from these problems. Instead of approximating the 0 and 1 values directly, thereby risking illegitimate probability values when the target is overshot, logistic regression builds a linear model based on a transformed target variable.

Suppose first that there are only two classes. Logistic regression replaces the original target variable

$$\Pr[1|a_1, a_2, \ldots, a_k],$$

which cannot be approximated accurately using a linear function, by

$$\log[\Pr[1|a_1, a_2, \ldots, a_k]/(1 - \Pr[1|a_1, a_2, \ldots, a_k]).$$

The resulting values are no longer constrained to the interval from 0 to 1 but can lie anywhere between negative infinity and positive infinity. Fig. 4.10A plots the transformation function, which is often called the *logit transformation.*

The transformed variable is approximated using a linear function just like the ones generated by linear regression. The resulting model is

$$\Pr[1|a_1, a_2, \ldots, a_k] = 1/(1 + \exp(-w_0 - w_1 a_1 - \cdots - w_k a_k)),$$

with weights w. Fig. 4.10B shows an example of this function in one dimension, with two weights $w_0 = -1.25$ and $w_1 = 0.5$.

Just as in linear regression, weights must be found that fit the training data well. Linear regression measures goodness of fit using the squared error. In logistic regression the *log-likelihood* of the model is used instead. This is given by

$$\sum_{i=1}^{n}(1 - x^{(i)})\log(1 - \Pr[1|a_1^{(i)}, a_2^{(i)}, \ldots, a_k^{(i)}]) + x^{(i)}\log(\Pr[1|a_1^{(i)}, a_2^{(i)}, \ldots, a_k^{(i)}])$$

where the $x^{(i)}$ are either zero or one.

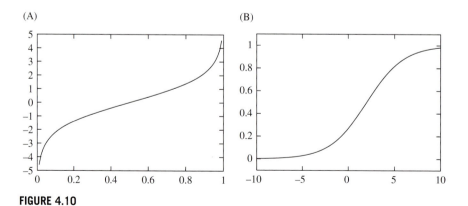

FIGURE 4.10

Logistic regression: (A) the logit transform; (B) example logistic regression function.

The weights w_i need to be chosen to maximize the log-likelihood. There are several methods for solving this maximization problem. A simple one is to iteratively solve a sequence of weighted least-squares regression problems until the log-likelihood converges to a maximum, which usually happens in a few iterations.

To generalize logistic regression to several classes, one possibility is to proceed in the way described above for multiresponse linear regression by performing logistic regression independently for each class. Unfortunately, the resulting probability estimates will not generally sum to one. To obtain proper probabilities it is necessary to couple the individual models for each class. This yields a joint optimization problem, and there are efficient solution methods for this.

The use of linear functions for classification can easily be visualized in instance space. The decision boundary for two-class logistic regression lies where the prediction probability is 0.5, i.e.:

$$\Pr[1|a_1, a_2, \ldots, a_k] = 1/(1 + \exp(-w_0 - w_1 a_1 - \cdots - w_k a_k)) = 0.5.$$

This occurs when

$$-w_0 - w_1 a_1 - \cdots - w_k a_k = 0.$$

Because this is a linear equality in the attribute values, the boundary is a plane, or *hyperplane*, in instance space. It is easy to visualize sets of points that cannot be separated by a single hyperplane, and these cannot be discriminated correctly by logistic regression.

Multiresponse linear regression suffers from the same problem. Each class receives a weight vector calculated from the training data. Focus for the moment on a particular pair of classes. Suppose the weight vector for class 1 is

$$w_0^{(1)} + w_1^{(1)} a_1 + w_2^{(1)} a_2 + \cdots + w_k^{(1)} a_k$$

and the same for class 2 with appropriate superscripts. Then, an instance will be assigned to class 1 rather than class 2 if

$$w_0^{(1)} + w_1^{(1)} a_1 + \cdots + w_k^{(1)} a_k > w_0^{(2)} + w_1^{(2)} a_1 + \cdots + w_k^{(2)} a_k$$

In other words, it will be assigned to class 1 if

$$(w_0^{(1)} - w_0^{(2)}) + (w_1^{(1)} - w_1^{(2)}) a_1 + \cdots + (w_k^{(1)} - w_k^{(2)}) a_k > 0.$$

This is a linear inequality in the attribute values, so the boundary between each pair of classes is a hyperplane.

LINEAR CLASSIFICATION USING THE PERCEPTRON

Logistic regression attempts to produce accurate probability estimates by maximizing the probability of the training data. Of course, accurate probability estimates lead to accurate classifications. However, it is not necessary to perform probability estimation if the sole purpose of the model is to predict class labels. A different approach is to learn a hyperplane that separates the instances pertaining to the different classes—let's assume that there are only two of them. If the data can be separated perfectly into two groups using a hyperplane, it is said to be *linearly separable*. It turns out that if the data is linearly separable, there is a very simple algorithm for finding a separating hyperplane.

The algorithm is called the *perceptron learning rule*. Before looking at it in detail, let's examine the equation for a hyperplane again:

$$w_0 a_0 + w_1 a_1 + w_2 a_2 + \cdots + w_k a_k = 0.$$

Here, $a_1, a_2, \ldots, a_k$ are the attribute values, and $w_0, w_1, \ldots, w_k$ are the weights that define the hyperplane. We will assume that each training instance $a_1, a_2, \ldots$ is extended by an additional attribute a_0 that always has the value 1 (as we did in the case of linear regression). This extension, which is called the *bias*, just means that we don't have to include an additional constant element in the sum. If the sum is greater than zero, we will predict the first class; otherwise, we will predict the second class. We want to find values for the weights so that the training data is correctly classified by the hyperplane.

Fig. 4.11A gives the perceptron learning rule for finding a separating hyperplane. The algorithm iterates until a perfect solution has been found, but it will only work properly if a separating hyperplane exists, i.e., if the data is linearly

(A)

```
Set all weights to zero
Until all instances in the training data are classified correctly
   For each instance I in the training data
      If I is classified incorrectly by the perceptron
         If I belongs to the first class add it to the weight vector
         else subtract it from the weight vector
```

(B)

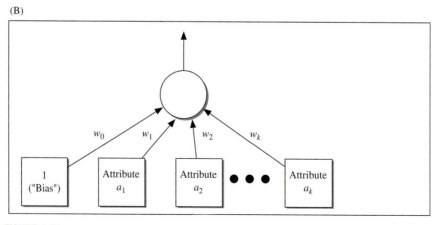

FIGURE 4.11

The perceptron: (A) learning rule; (B) representation as a neural network.

separable. Each iteration goes through all the training instances. If a misclassified instance is encountered, the parameters of the hyperplane are changed so that the misclassified instance moves closer to the hyperplane or maybe even across the hyperplane onto the correct side. If the instance belongs to the first class, this is done by adding its attribute values to the weight vector; otherwise, they are subtracted from it.

To see why this works, consider the situation after an instance a pertaining to the first class has been added:

$$(w_0 + a_0)a_0 + (w_1 + a_1)a_1 + (w_2 + a_2)a_2 + \cdots + (w_k + a_k)a_k.$$

This means the output for a has increased by

$$a_0 \times a_0 + a_1 \times a_1 + a_2 \times a_2 + \cdots + a_k \times a_k.$$

This number is always positive. Thus the hyperplane has moved in the correct direction for classifying instance a as positive. Conversely, if an instance belonging to the second class is misclassified, the output for that instance decreases after the modification, again moving the hyperplane in the correct direction.

These corrections are incremental, and can interfere with earlier updates. However, it can be shown that the algorithm converges into a finite number of iterations if the data is linearly separable. Of course, if the data is not linearly separable, the algorithm will not terminate, so an upper bound needs to be imposed on the number of iterations when this method is applied in practice.

The resulting hyperplane is called a *perceptron*, and it's the grandfather of neural networks (we return to neural networks in Section 7.2 and chapter: Deep learning). Fig. 4.11B represents the perceptron as a graph with nodes and weighted edges, imaginatively termed a "network" of "neurons." There are two layers of nodes: input and output. The input layer has one node for every attribute, plus an extra node that is always set to one. The output layer consists of just one node. Every node in the input layer is connected to the output layer. The connections are weighted, and the weights are those numbers found by the perceptron learning rule.

When an instance is presented to the perceptron, its attribute values serve to "activate" the input layer. They are multiplied by the weights and summed up at the output node. If the weighted sum is greater than 0 the output signal is 1, representing the first class; otherwise, it is −1, representing the second.

LINEAR CLASSIFICATION USING WINNOW

The perceptron algorithm is not the only method that is guaranteed to find a separating hyperplane for a linearly separable problem. For datasets with binary attributes there is an alternative known as *Winnow*, shown in Fig. 4.12A. The structure of the two algorithms is very similar. Like the perceptron, Winnow only updates the weight vector when a misclassified instance is encountered—it is *mistake driven*.

(A)

```
While some instances are misclassified
  for every instance a
    classify a using the current weights
    if the predicted class is incorrect
      if a belongs to the first class
        for each aᵢ that is 1, multiply wᵢ by α
        (if aᵢ is 0, leave wᵢ unchanged)
      otherwise
        for each aᵢ that is 1, divide wᵢ by α
        (if aᵢ is 0, leave wᵢ unchanged)
```

(B)

```
While some instances are misclassified
  for every instance a
    classify a using the current weights
    if the predicted class is incorrect
      if a belongs to the first class
        for each aᵢ that is 1,
          multiply wᵢ⁺ by α
          divide wᵢ⁻ by α
          (if aᵢ is 0, leave wᵢ⁺ and wᵢ⁻ unchanged)
      otherwise
          multiply wᵢ⁻ by α
          divide wᵢ⁺ by α
          (if aᵢ is 0, leave wᵢ⁺ and wᵢ⁻ unchanged)
```

FIGURE 4.12

The Winnow algorithm: (A) unbalanced version; (B) balanced version.

The two methods differ in how the weights are updated. The perceptron rule employs an additive mechanism that alters the weight vector by adding (or subtracting) the instance's attribute vector. Winnow employs multiplicative updates and alters weights individually by multiplying them by a user-specified parameter α (or its inverse). The attribute values a_i are either 0 or 1 because we are working with binary data. Weights are unchanged if the attribute value is 0, because then they do not participate in the decision. Otherwise, the multiplier is α if that attribute helps to make a correct decision and $1/\alpha$ if it does not.

Another difference is that the threshold in the linear function is also a user-specified parameter. We call this threshold θ and classify an instance as belonging to class 1 if and only if

$$w_0 a_0 + w_1 a_1 + w_2 a_2 + \cdots + w_k a_k > \theta.$$

The multiplier α needs to be greater than one. The w_i are set to a constant at the start.

The algorithm we have described doesn't allow for negative weights, which—depending on the domain—can be a drawback. However, there is a version, called *Balanced Winnow*, which does allow them. This version maintains two weight vectors, one for each class. An instance is classified as belonging to class 1 if:

$$(w_0^+ - w_0^-)a_0 + (w_1^+ - w_1^-)a_1 + \cdots + (w_k^+ - w_k^-)a_k > \theta.$$

Fig. 4.12B shows the balanced algorithm.

Winnow is very effective in homing in on the relevant features in a dataset—therefore it is called an *attribute-efficient* learner. That means that it may be a good candidate algorithm if a dataset has many (binary) features and most of them are irrelevant. Both Winnow and the perceptron algorithm can be used in an online setting in which new instances arrive continuously, because they can incrementally update their concept descriptions as new instances arrive.

4.7 INSTANCE-BASED LEARNING

In instance-based learning the training examples are stored verbatim, and a distance function is used to determine which member of the training set is closest to an unknown test instance. Once the nearest training instance has been located, its class is predicted for the test instance. The only remaining problem is defining the distance function, and that is not very difficult to do, particularly if the attributes are numeric.

THE DISTANCE FUNCTION

Although there are other possible choices, most instance-based learners use Euclidean distance. The distance between an instance with attribute values $a_1^{(1)}$, $a_2^{(1)}, \ldots, a_k^{(1)}$ (where k is the number of attributes) and one with values $a_1^{(2)}, a_2^{(2)}, \ldots, a_k^{(2)}$ is defined as

$$\sqrt{(a_1^{(1)}-a_1^{(2)})^2 + (a_2^{(1)}-a_2^{(2)})^2 + \cdots + (a_k^{(1)}-a_k^{(2)})^2}.$$

When comparing distances it is not necessary to perform the square root operation: the sums of squares can be compared directly. One alternative to the Euclidean distance is the Manhattan or city-block metric, where the difference between attribute values is not squared but just added up (after taking the absolute value). Others are obtained by taking powers higher than the square. Higher powers increase the influence of large differences at the expense of small differences. Generally, the Euclidean distance represents a good compromise. Other distance metrics may be more appropriate in special circumstances. The key is to think of actual instances and what it means for them to be separated by a certain distance—What would twice that distance mean, for example?

Different attributes are measured on different scales, so if the Euclidean distance formula were used directly, the effect of some attributes might be completely dwarfed by others that had larger scales of measurement. Consequently, it is usual to normalize all attribute values to lie between 0 and 1, by calculating

$$a_i = \frac{v_i - \min v_i}{\max v_i - \min v_i}$$

where v_i is the actual value of attribute i, and the maximum and minimum are taken over all instances in the training set.

These formulae implicitly assume numeric attributes. Here the difference between two values is just the numerical difference between them, and it is this difference that is squared and added to yield the distance function. For nominal attributes that take on values that are symbolic rather than numeric, the difference between two values that are not the same is often taken to be one, whereas if the values are the same the difference is zero. No scaling is required in this case because only the values 0 and 1 are used.

A common policy for handling missing values is as follows: for nominal attributes, assume that a missing feature is maximally different from any other feature value. Thus if either or both values are missing, or if the values are different, the difference between them is taken as one; the difference is zero only if they are not missing and both are the same. For numeric attributes, the difference between two missing values is also taken as one. However, if just one value is missing, the difference is often taken as either the (normalized) size of the other value or one minus that size, whichever is larger. This means that if values are missing, the difference is as large as it can possibly be.

FINDING NEAREST NEIGHBORS EFFICIENTLY

Although instance-based learning is simple and effective, it is often slow. The obvious way to find which member of the training set is closest to an unknown test instance is to calculate the distance from every member of the training set and select the smallest. This procedure is linear in the number of training instances: in other words, the time it takes to make a single prediction is proportional to the number of training instances. Processing an entire test set takes time proportional to the product of the number of instances in the training and test sets.

Nearest neighbors can be found more efficiently by representing the training set as a tree, although it is not quite obvious how. One suitable structure is a *kD-tree*. This is a binary tree that divides the input space with a hyperplane and then splits each partition again, recursively. All splits are made parallel to one of the axes, either vertically or horizontally, in the two-dimensional case. The data structure is called a *kD-tree* because it stores a set of points in k-dimensional space, k being the number of attributes.

Fig. 4.13A gives a small example with $k = 2$, and Fig. 4.13B shows the four training instances it represents, along with the hyperplanes that constitute the tree. Note that these hyperplanes are *not* decision boundaries: decisions are made on a nearest-neighbor basis as explained later. The first split is horizontal (*h*), through the point (7,4)—this is the tree's root. The left branch is not split further: it contains the single point (2,2), which is a leaf of the tree. The right branch is split vertically (*v*) at the point (6,7). Its right child is empty, and its left child contains the point (3,8). As this example illustrates, each region contains just one point—or, perhaps, no points. Sibling branches of the tree—e.g., the two

(A)   (B)

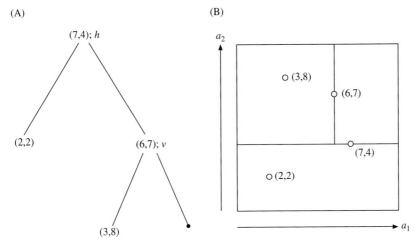

FIGURE 4.13

A *k*D-tree for four training instances: (A) the tree; (B) instances and splits.

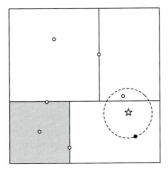

FIGURE 4.14

Using a *k*D-tree to find the nearest neighbor of the star.

daughters of the root in Fig. 4.13A—are not necessarily developed to the same depth. Every point in the training set corresponds to a single node, and up to half are leaf nodes.

How do you build a *k*D-tree from a dataset? Can it be updated efficiently as new training examples are added? And how does it speed up nearest-neighbor calculations? We tackle the last question first.

To locate the nearest neighbor of a given target point, follow the tree down from its root to locate the region containing the target. Fig. 4.14 shows a space like that of Fig. 4.13B but with a few more instances and an extra boundary. The target, which is not one of the instances in the tree, is marked by a star. The leaf node of the region containing the target is colored black. This is not necessarily the target's closest neighbor, as this example illustrates, but it is a good first approximation. In particular, any nearer neighbor must lie closer—within the dashed circle in Fig. 4.14. To determine whether one exists, first check whether it is possible for a closer neighbor to lie within the node's sibling. The black node's sibling is shaded in Fig. 4.14, and the circle does not intersect it, so the sibling cannot contain a closer neighbor. Then back up to the parent node and check *its* sibling—which here covers everything above the horizontal line. In this case it *must* to be explored, because the area it covers intersects with the best circle so far. To explore it, find its daughters (the original point's two aunts), check whether they intersect the circle (the left one does not, but the right one does), and descend to see if it contains a closer point (it does).

In a typical case, this algorithm is far faster than examining all points to find the nearest neighbor. The work involved in finding the initial approximate nearest neighbor—the black point in Fig. 4.14—depends on the depth of the tree, given by the logarithm $\log_2 n$ of the number of nodes n, if the tree is well balanced. The amount of work involved in backtracking to check whether this really is the nearest neighbor depends a bit on the tree, and on how good the initial approximation is. But for a well-constructed tree whose nodes are approximately square, rather than long skinny rectangles, it can also be shown to be logarithmic in the number of nodes (if the number of attributes in the dataset is not too large).

How do you build a good tree for a set of training examples? The problem boils down to selecting the first training instance to split at and the direction of the split. Once you can do that, apply the same method recursively to each child of the initial split to construct the entire tree.

To find a good direction for the split, calculate the variance of the data points along each axis individually, select the axis with the greatest variance, and create a splitting hyperplane perpendicular to it. To find a good place for the hyperplane, locate the median value along that axis and select the corresponding point. This makes the split perpendicular to the direction of greatest spread, with half the points lying on either side. This produces a well-balanced tree. To avoid long skinny regions it is best for successive splits to be along different axes, which is likely because the dimension of greatest variance is chosen at each stage. However, if the distribution of points is badly skewed, choosing the median value may generate several successive splits in the same direction, yielding long, skinny hyperrectangles. A better strategy is to calculate the mean rather than the median and use the point closest to that. The tree will not be perfectly balanced, but its regions will tend to be squarish because there is a greater chance that different directions will be chosen for successive splits.

An advantage of instance-based learning over most other machine learning methods is that new examples can be added to the training set at any time. To retain this advantage when using a kD-tree, we need to be able to update it incrementally with new data points. To do this, determine which leaf node contains the new point and find its hyperrectangle. If it is empty, simply place the new point there. Otherwise split the hyperrectangle, splitting it along its longest dimension to preserve squareness. This simple heuristic does not guarantee that adding a series of points will preserve the tree's balance, nor that the hyperrectangles will be well shaped for nearest-neighbor search. It is a good idea to rebuild the tree from scratch occasionally—e.g., when its depth grows to twice the best possible depth.

As we have seen, kD-trees are good data structures for finding nearest neighbors efficiently. However, they are not perfect. Skewed datasets present a basic conflict between the desire for the tree to be perfectly balanced and the desire for regions to be squarish. More importantly, rectangles—even squares—are not the best shape to use anyway, because of their corners. If the dashed circle in Fig. 4.14 were any bigger, which it would be if the black instance were a little further from the target, it would intersect the lower right-hand corner of the rectangle at the top left and then that rectangle would have to be investigated, too—despite the fact that the training instances that define it are a long way from the corner in question. The corners of rectangular regions are awkward.

The solution? Use hyperspheres, not hyperrectangles. Neighboring spheres may overlap whereas rectangles can abut, but this is not a problem because the nearest-neighbor algorithm for kD-trees does not depend on the regions being disjoint. A data structure called a *ball tree* defines k-dimensional hyperspheres (balls) that cover the data points, and arranges them into a tree.

Fig. 4.15A shows 16 training instances in two-dimensional space, overlaid by a pattern of overlapping circles, and Fig. 4.15B shows a tree formed from these circles. Circles at different levels of the tree are indicated by different styles of dash, and the smaller circles are drawn in shades of gray. Each node of the tree represents a ball, and the node is dashed or shaded according to the same convention so that you can identify which level the balls are at. To help you understand the tree, numbers are placed on the nodes to show how many data points are

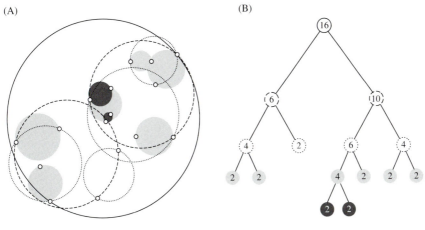

(A)   (B)

FIGURE 4.15

Ball tree for 16 training instances: (A) instances and balls; (B) the tree.

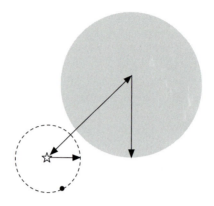

FIGURE 4.16

Ruling out an entire ball (gray) based on a target point (star) and its current nearest neighbor.

deemed to be inside that ball. But be careful: this is not necessarily the same as the number of points falling within the spatial region that the ball represents. The regions at each level sometimes overlap, but points that fall into the overlap area are assigned to only one of the overlapping balls (the diagram does not show which one). Instead of the occupancy counts in Fig. 4.15B the nodes of actual ball trees store the center and radius of their ball; leaf nodes record the points they contain as well.

To use a ball tree to find the nearest neighbor to a given target, start by traversing the tree from the top down to locate the leaf that contains the target and find the closest point to the target in that ball. (If no ball contains the instance, pick the closest ball.) This gives an upper bound for the target's distance from its nearest neighbor. Then, just as for the kD-tree, examine the sibling node. If the distance from the target to the sibling's center exceeds its radius plus the current upper bound, it cannot possibly contain a closer point; otherwise the sibling must be examined by descending the tree further. In Fig. 4.16 the target is marked with a star and the black dot is its closest currently known neighbor. The entire contents of the gray ball can be ruled out: it cannot contain a closer point because its center is too far away. Proceed recursively back up the tree to its root, examining any ball that may possibly contain a point nearer than the current upper bound.

Ball trees are built from the top down, and as with kD-trees the basic problem is to find a good way of splitting a ball containing a set of data points into two. In practice you do not have to continue until the leaf balls contain just two points: you can stop earlier, once a predetermined minimum number is reached—and the same goes for kD-trees. Here is one possible splitting method. Choose the point in the ball that is farthest from its center, and then a second point that is farthest from the first one. Assign all data points in the ball to the closest one of these two provisional cluster centers, then compute the centroid of each cluster and the minimum radius required for it to enclose all the data points it represents. This method has the merit that the cost of splitting a ball containing n points is only linear in n. There are more elaborate algorithms that produce tighter balls, but they require more computation. We will not describe sophisticated algorithms for constructing ball trees or updating them incrementally as new training instances are encountered.

REMARKS

Nearest-neighbor instance-based learning is simple and often works very well. In the scheme we have described each attribute has exactly the same influence on the decision, just as it does in the Naïve Bayes method. Another problem is that the database can easily become corrupted by noisy exemplars. One solution is to adopt the k-nearest neighbor strategy, where some fixed, small, number k of nearest neighbors—say five—are located and used together to determine the class of the test instance through a simple majority vote. (Note that earlier we used k to denote the number of attributes; this is a different, independent usage.) Another way of proofing the database against noise is to choose the exemplars that are added to it selectively and judiciously. Improved procedures, described in Section 7.1, address these shortcomings.

The nearest-neighbor method originated many decades ago, and statisticians analyzed k-nearest-neighbor schemes in the early 1950s. If the number of training instances is large, it makes intuitive sense to use more than one nearest neighbor, but clearly this is dangerous if there are few instances. It can be shown that when k and the number n of instances both become infinite in such a way that $k/n \rightarrow 0$, the probability of error approaches the theoretical minimum for the dataset. The nearest-neighbor method was adopted as a classification scheme in the early 1960s and has been widely used in the field of pattern recognition for almost half a century.

Nearest-neighbor classification was notoriously slow until kD-trees began to be applied in the early 1990s, although the data structure itself was developed much earlier. In practice, these trees become inefficient when the dimension of the space increases and are only worthwhile when the number of attributes is relatively small. Ball trees were developed much more recently and are an instance of a more general structure called a *metric tree*.

4.8 CLUSTERING

Clustering techniques apply when there is no class to be predicted but rather when the instances are to be divided into natural groups. These clusters presumably reflect some mechanism at work in the domain from which instances are drawn, a mechanism that causes some instances to bear a stronger resemblance to each other than they do to the remaining instances. Clustering naturally requires different techniques to the classification and association learning methods that we have considered so far.

As we saw in Section 3.6, there are different ways in which the result of clustering can be expressed. The groups that are identified may be exclusive: any instance belongs in only one group. Or they may be overlapping: an instance may fall into several groups. Or they may be probabilistic: an instance belongs to each group with a certain probability. Or they may be hierarchical: a rough division of instances into groups at the top level and each group refined further—perhaps all the way down to individual instances. Really, the choice among these possibilities should be dictated by the nature of the mechanisms that are thought to underlie the particular clustering phenomenon. However, because these mechanisms are rarely known—the very existence of clusters is, after all, something that we're trying to discover—and for pragmatic reasons too, the choice is usually dictated by the clustering tools that are available.

We will begin by examining an algorithm that works in numeric domains, partitioning instances into disjoint clusters. Like the basic nearest-neighbor method of instance-based learning, it is a simple and straightforward technique that has been used for several decades. The algorithm is known as k-means and many variations of the procedure have been developed.

In the basic formulation k initial points are chosen to represent initial cluster centers, all data points are assigned to the nearest one, the mean value of the points in each cluster is computed to form its new cluster center, and iteration continues until there are no changes in the clusters. This procedure only works when the number of clusters is known in advance. This leads to the natural question: How do you choose k? Often nothing is known about the likely number of clusters, and the whole point of clustering is to find out. We therefore go on to discuss what to do when the number of clusters is not known in advance.

Some techniques produce a hierarchical clustering by applying the algorithm with $k = 2$ to the overall dataset and then repeating, recursively, within each cluster. We go on to look at techniques for creating a hierarchical clustering structure by "agglomeration," i.e., starting with the individual instances and successively joining them up into clusters. Then we look at a method that works incrementally, processing each new instance as it appears. This method was developed in the late 1980s and embodied in a pair of systems called Cobweb (for nominal attributes) and Classit (for numeric attributes). Both come up with a hierarchical grouping of instances, and use a measure of cluster "quality" called *category utility*.

ITERATIVE DISTANCE-BASED CLUSTERING

The classic clustering technique is called k-*means*. First, you specify in advance how many clusters are being sought: this is the parameter k. Then k points are chosen at random as cluster centers. All instances are assigned to their closest cluster center according to the ordinary Euclidean distance metric. Next the centroid, or mean, of the instances in each cluster is calculated—this is the "means" part. These centroids are taken to be new center values for their respective clusters. Finally, the whole process is repeated with the new cluster centers. Iteration continues until the same points are assigned to each cluster in consecutive rounds, at which stage the cluster centers have stabilized and will remain the same forever.

Fig. 4.17 shows an example of how this process works, based on scatter plots of a simple dataset with 15 instances and 2 numeric attributes. Each of the four columns corresponds to one iteration of the k-means algorithm. This example assumes we are seeing three clusters; thus we set $k = 3$. Initially, at the top left, three cluster centers, represented by different geometric shapes, are placed randomly. Then, in the plot, instances are tentatively assigned to clusters by finding the closest cluster center for each instance. This completes the first iteration of the algorithm. So far, the clustering looks messy—which is not surprising because the initial cluster centers were random. The key is to update the centers based on the assignment that has just been created. In the next iteration, the cluster centers are recalculated based on the instances that have been assigned to each cluster, to obtain the upper plot in the second column. Then instances are reassigned to these new centers to obtain the plot below. This produces a much nicer set of clusters. However, the centers are still not in the middle of their clusters; moreover, one triangle is still incorrectly clustered as a circle. Thus, the two steps—center recalculation and instance reassignment—need to be repeated. This yields Step 2, in which the clusters look very plausible. But the two top-most cluster centers still need to be updated, because they are based on the old

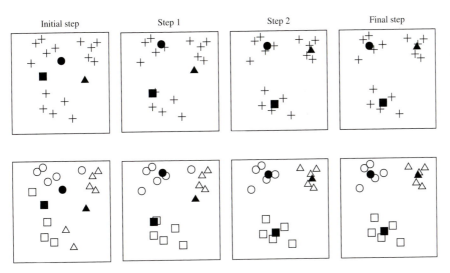

FIGURE 4.17

Iterative distance-based clustering.

assignment of instances to clusters. Recomputing the assignments in the next and final iteration shows that all instances remain assigned to the same cluster centers. The algorithm has converged.

This clustering method is simple and effective. It is easy to prove that choosing the cluster center to be the centroid minimizes the total squared distance from each of the cluster's points to its center. Once the iteration has stabilized, each point is assigned to its nearest cluster center, so the overall effect is to minimize the total squared distance from all points to their cluster centers. But the minimum is a local one: there is no guarantee that it is the global minimum. The final clusters are quite sensitive to the initial cluster centers. Completely different arrangements can arise from small changes in the initial random choice. In fact, this is true of all practical clustering techniques: it is almost always infeasible to find globally optimal clusters. To increase the chance of finding a global minimum people often run the algorithm several times with different initial choices and choose the best final result—the one with the smallest total squared distance.

It is easy to imagine situations in which k-means fails to find a good clustering. Consider four instances arranged at the vertices of a rectangle in two-dimensional space. There are two natural clusters, formed by grouping together the two vertices at either end of a short side. But suppose the two initial cluster centers happen to fall at the midpoints of the *long* sides. This forms a stable configuration. The two clusters each contain the two instances at either end of a long side—no matter how great the difference between the long and the short sides.

k-means clustering can be dramatically improved by careful choice of the initial cluster centers, often called "seeds." Instead of beginning with an arbitrary set of seeds, here is a better procedure. Choose the initial seed at random from the entire space, with a uniform probability distribution. Then choose the second seed with a probability that is proportional to the square of the distance from the first. Proceed, at each stage choosing the next seed with a probability proportional to the square of the distance from the closest seed that has already been chosen. This procedure, called k-means++, improves both speed and accuracy over the original algorithm with random seeds.

FASTER DISTANCE CALCULATIONS

The k-means clustering algorithm usually requires several iterations, each involving finding the distance of k cluster centers from every instance to determine its cluster. There are simple approximations that speed this up considerably. For example, you can project the dataset and make cuts along selected axes, instead of using the arbitrary hyperplane divisions that are implied by choosing the nearest cluster center. But this inevitably compromises the quality of the resulting clusters.

Here's a better way of speeding things up. Finding the closest cluster center is not so different from finding nearest neighbors in instance-based learning. Can the same efficient solutions—kD-trees and ball trees—be used? Yes! Indeed they can be applied in an even more efficient way, because in each iteration of *k*-means all the data points are processed together, whereas in instance-based learning test instances are processed individually.

First, construct a *k*D-tree or ball tree for all the data points, which will remain static throughout the clustering procedure. Each iteration of *k*-means produces a set of cluster centers, and all data points must be examined and assigned to the nearest center. One way of processing the points is to descend the tree from the root until reaching a leaf, and then check each individual point in the leaf to find its closest cluster center. But it may be that the region represented by a higher interior node falls entirely within the domain of a single cluster center. In that case all the data points under that node can be processed in one blow!

The aim of the exercise, after all, is to find new positions for the cluster centers by calculating the centroid of the points they contain. The centroid can be calculated by keeping a running vector sum of the points in the cluster, and a count of how many there are so far. At the end, just divide one by the other to find the centroid. Suppose that with each node of the tree we store the vector sum of the points within that node and a count of the number of points. If the whole node falls within the ambit of a single cluster, the running totals for that cluster can be updated immediately. If not, look inside the node by proceeding recursively down the tree.

Fig. 4.18 shows the same instances and ball tree as Fig. 4.15, but with two cluster centers marked as black stars. Because all instances are assigned to the closest center, the space is divided into two by the thick line shown in Fig. 4.18A. Begin at the root of the tree in Fig. 4.18B, with initial values for the vector sum and counts for each cluster; all initial values are zero. Proceed recursively down the tree. When node A is reached, all points within it lie in cluster 1,

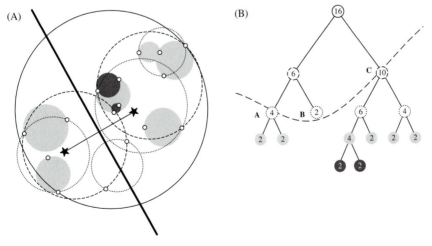

FIGURE 4.18

A ball tree: (A) two cluster centers and their dividing line; (B) corresponding tree.

so cluster 1's sum and count can be updated with the sum and count for node A, and we need descend no further. Recursing back to node B, its ball straddles the boundary between the clusters, so its points must be examined individually. When node C is reached, it falls entirely within cluster 2; again, we can update cluster 2 immediately and need descend no further. The tree is only examined down to the frontier marked by the dashed line in Fig. 4.18B, and the advantage is that the nodes below need not be opened—at least, not on this particular iteration of k-means. Next time, the cluster centers will have changed and things may be different.

CHOOSING THE NUMBER OF CLUSTERS

Suppose you are using k-means but do not know the number of clusters in advance. One solution is to try out different possibilities and see which is best. A simple strategy is to start from a given minimum, perhaps $k = 1$, and work up to a small fixed maximum. Note that on the training data the "best" clustering according to the total squared distance criterion will always be to choose as many clusters as there are data points! To penalize solutions with many clusters you will have to apply something like the minimum description length (MDL) criterion of Section 5.10.

Another possibility is to begin by finding a few clusters and determining whether it is worth splitting them. You could choose $k = 2$, perform k-means clustering until it terminates, and then consider splitting each cluster. Computation time will be reduced considerably if the initial two-way clustering is considered irrevocable and splitting is investigated for each component independently. One way to split a cluster is to make a new seed, one standard deviation away from the cluster's center in the direction of its greatest variation, and make a second seed the same distance in the opposite direction. (Alternatively, if this is too slow, choose a distance proportional to the cluster's bounding box and a random direction.) Then apply k-means to the points in the cluster with these two new seeds.

Having tentatively split a cluster, is it worthwhile retaining the split or is the original cluster equally plausible by itself? It's no good looking at the total squared distance of all points to their cluster center—this is bound to be smaller for two subclusters. A penalty should be incurred for inventing an extra cluster, and this is a job for the MDL criterion. That principle can be applied to see whether the information required to specify the two new cluster centers, along with the information required to specify each point with respect to them, exceeds the information required to specify the original center and all the points with respect to *it*. If so, the new clustering is unproductive and should be abandoned.

If the split is retained, try splitting each new cluster further. Continue the process until no worthwhile splits remain.

Additional implementation efficiency can be achieved by combining this iterative clustering process with kD-tree or ball tree data structures. Then, the data points are reached by working down the tree from the root. When considering splitting a cluster, there is no need to consider the whole tree, just look at those parts of it that are needed to cover the cluster. For example, when deciding whether to split the lower left cluster in Fig. 4.18A (below the thick line), it is only necessary to consider nodes A and B of the tree in Fig. 4.18B, because node C is irrelevant to that cluster.

HIERARCHICAL CLUSTERING

Forming an initial pair of clusters and then recursively considering whether it is worth splitting each one further produces a hierarchy that can be represented as a binary tree called a *dendrogram*. In fact, we illustrated a dendrogram in Fig. 3.11D (there, some of the branches were three-way). The same information could be represented as a Venn diagram of sets and subsets: the constraint that the structure is hierarchical corresponds to the fact that although subsets can include one another, they cannot intersect. In some cases there exists a measure of the degree of dissimilarity between the clusters in each set; then, the height of each node in the dendrogram can be made proportional to the dissimilarity between its children. This provides an easily interpretable diagram of a hierarchical clustering.

An alternative to the top-down method for forming a hierarchical structure of clusters is to use a bottom-up approach, which is called *agglomerative* clustering. This idea was proposed many years ago and has recently enjoyed a resurgence in popularity. The basic algorithm is simple. All you need is a measure of distance (or alternatively, a similarity measure) between any two clusters. You begin by regarding each instance as a cluster in its own right, find the two closest clusters, merge them, and keep on doing this until only one cluster is left. The record of mergings forms a hierarchical clustering structure—a binary dendrogram.

There are numerous possibilities for the distance measure. One is the minimum distance between the clusters—the distance between their two closest members. This yields what is called the *single-linkage* clustering algorithm. Since this measure takes into account only the two closest members of a pair of clusters, the procedure is sensitive to outliers: the addition of just a single new instance can radically alter the entire clustering structure. Also, if we define the diameter of a cluster to be the greatest distance between its members, single-linkage clustering can produce clusters with very large diameters. Another measure is the maximum distance between the clusters, instead of the minimum. Two clusters are considered close only if all instances in their union are relatively similar—sometimes called the *complete-linkage* method. This measure, which is also sensitive to outliers, seeks compact clusters with small diameters. However, some instances may end up much closer to other clusters than they are to the rest of their own cluster.

There are other measures that represent a compromise between the extremes of minimum and maximum distance between cluster members. One is to represent clusters by the centroid of their members, as the *k*-means algorithm does, and use the distance between centroids—the *centroid-linkage* method. This works well when the instances are positioned in multidimensional Euclidean space and the notion of centroid is clear, but not if all we have is a pairwise similarity measure between instances, because centroids are not instances and the similarity between them may be impossible to define. Another measure, which avoids this problem, is to calculate the average distance between each pair of members of the two clusters—the *average-linkage* method. Although this seems like a lot of work, you would have to calculate all pairwise distances in order to find the maximum or minimum anyway, and averaging them isn't much additional burden. Both these measures have a technical deficiency: their results depend on the numerical scale on which distances are measured. The minimum and maximum distance measures produce a result that depends only on the *ordering* between the distances involved. In contrast, the result of both centroid-based and average-distance clustering can be altered by a monotonic transformation of all distances, even though it preserves their relative ordering.

Another method, called *group-average* clustering, uses the average distance between all members of the merged cluster. This differs from the "average" method just described because it includes in the average pairs from the same original cluster. Finally, *Ward's* clustering method calculates the increase in the sum of squares of the distances of the instances from the centroid before and after fusing two clusters. The idea is to minimize the increase in this squared distance at each clustering step.

All these measures will produce the same hierarchical clustering result if the clusters are compact and well separated. However, in other cases they can yield quite different structures.

EXAMPLE OF HIERARCHICAL CLUSTERING

Fig. 4.19 shows displays of the result of agglomerative hierarchical clustering. (These visualizations have been generated using the FigTree program. (http://tree. bio.ed.ac.uk/software/figtree/)) In this case the dataset contained 50 examples of different kinds of creatures, from dolphin to mongoose, from giraffe to lobster. There was one numeric attribute (number of legs, ranging from 0 to 6, but scaled to the range [0, 1]) and fifteen Boolean attributes such as *has feathers*, *lays eggs*, and *venomous*, which are treated as binary attributes with values 0 and 1 in the distance calculation.

Two kinds of display are shown: a standard dendrogram and a polar plot. Fig. 4.19A and B shows the output from an agglomerative clusterer plotted in two different ways, and Fig. 4.19C and D shows the result of a different agglomerative clusterer plotted in the same two ways. The difference is that the pair at the top was produced using the complete-linkage measure and the pair beneath was produced using the single-linkage measure. You can see that the complete-linkage method tends to produce compact clusters while the single-linkage method produces clusters with large diameters at fairly low levels of the tree.

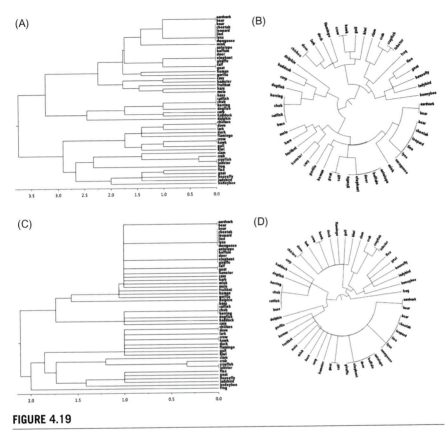

FIGURE 4.19

Hierarchical clustering displays.

In all four methods the height of each node in the dendrogram is proportional to the dissimilarity between its children, measured as the Euclidean distance between instances. A numeric scale is provided beneath Fig. 4.19A and C. The total dissimilarity from root to leaf is far greater for the complete-linkage method at the top than for the single-linkage method at the bottom since the former involves the maximum distance and the latter the minimum distance between instances in each cluster. In the first case the total dissimilarity is a little less than 3.75, which is almost the maximum possible distance between instances—the distance between two instances that differ in 14 of the 15 attributes is $\sqrt{14} \approx 3.74$. In the second it is a little greater than 2 (i.e., $\sqrt{4}$), which is what a difference in four Boolean attributes would produce.

For the complete-linkage method (Fig. 4.19A), many elements join together at a dissimilarity of 1, which corresponds to a difference in a single Boolean attribute. Only one pair has a smaller dissimilarity: this is *crab* and *crayfish*, which differ only in the number of legs (4/6 and 6/6, respectively, after scaling). Other popular dissimilarities are $\sqrt{2}$, $\sqrt{3}$, $\sqrt{4}$, and so on, corresponding to differences in two, three, and four Boolean attributes. For the single-linkage method (Fig. 4.19C) that uses the minimum distance between clusters, even more elements join together at a dissimilarity of 1.

Which of the two display methods—the standard dendrogram and the polar plot—is more useful is a matter of taste. Although more unfamiliar at first, the polar plot spreads the visualization more evenly over the space available.

INCREMENTAL CLUSTERING

Whereas the k-means algorithm iterates over the whole dataset until convergence is reached and the hierarchical method examines all the clusters present so far at each stage of merging, the clustering methods we examine next work incrementally, instance by instance. At any stage the clustering forms a tree with instances at the leaves and a root node that represents the entire dataset. In the beginning the tree consists of the root alone. Instances are added one by one, and the tree is updated appropriately at each stage. Updating may merely be a case of finding the right place to put a leaf representing the new instance, or it may involve a radical restructuring of the part of the tree that is affected by the new instance. The key to deciding how and where to update is a quantity called *category utility*, which measures the overall quality of a partition of instances into clusters. We defer detailed consideration of how this is defined until Category Utility section and look first at how the clustering algorithm works.

The procedure is best illustrated by an example. We will use the familiar weather data again, but without the *play* attribute. To track progress, the 14 instances are labeled a, b, c,..., n (as in Table 4.6), and for interest we include the class *yes* or *no* in the label—although it should be emphasized that for this artificial dataset there is little reason to suppose that the two classes of instance should fall into separate categories. Fig. 4.20 shows the situation at salient points throughout the clustering procedure.

At the beginning, when new instances are absorbed into the structure, they each form their own subcluster under the overall top-level cluster. Each new instance is processed by tentatively placing it into each of the existing leaves and evaluating the category utility of the resulting set of the top-level node's children to see if the leaf is a good "host" for the new instance. For each of the first five instances, there is no such host: it is better, in terms of category utility, to form a new leaf for each instance. With the sixth it finally becomes beneficial to form a cluster, joining the new instance f with the old one—the host—e. If you look at Table 4.6 you will see that the fifth and sixth instances are indeed very similar, differing only in the *windy* attribute (and *play*, which is being ignored here). The next example, g, is placed in the same cluster (it differs from f only in *outlook*). This involves another call to the clustering procedure. First, g is evaluated to see which of the five children of the root makes the best host: it turns out to be the rightmost, the one that is already a cluster. Then the clustering algorithm is

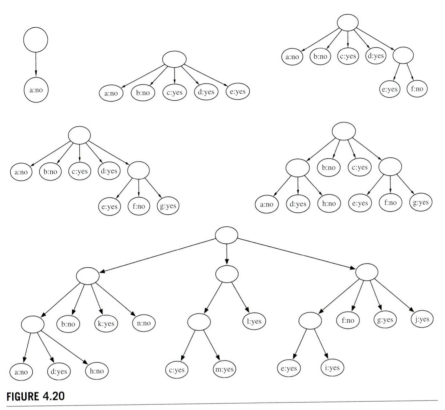

FIGURE 4.20

Clustering the weather data.

invoked with this as the root, and its two children are evaluated to see which would make the better host. In this case it proves best, according to the category utility measure, to add the new instance as a subcluster in its own right.

If we were to continue in this vein, there would be no possibility of any radical restructuring of the tree, and the final clustering would be excessively dependent on the ordering of examples. To avoid this, there is provision for restructuring, and you can see it come into play when instance h is added in the next step shown in Fig. 4.20. In this case two existing nodes are *merged* into a single cluster: nodes a and d are merged before the new instance h is added. One way of accomplishing this would be to consider all pairs of nodes for merging and evaluate the category utility of each pair. However, that would be computationally expensive, and would involve a lot of repeated work if it were undertaken whenever a new instance was added.

Instead, whenever the nodes at a particular level are scanned for a suitable host, both the best-matching node—the one that produces the greatest category utility for the split at that level—and the runner-up are noted. The best one will form the host for the new instance (unless that new instance is better off in a cluster of its own). However, before setting to work on putting the new instance in with the host, consideration is given to merging the host and the runner-up. In this case, *a* is the preferred host and *d* is the runner-up. When a merge of *a* and *d* is evaluated, it turns out that it would improve the category utility measure. Consequently, these two nodes are merged, yielding a version of the fifth hierarchy before *h* is added. Then, consideration is given to the placement of *h* in the new, merged node; and it turns out to be best to make it a subcluster in its own right, as shown.

An operation converse to merging is also implemented, called *splitting*. Whenever the best host is identified, and merging has not proved beneficial, consideration is given to splitting the host node. Splitting has exactly the opposite effect of merging, taking a node and replacing it with its children. For example, splitting the rightmost node in the fourth hierarchy of Fig. 4.20 would raise the *e*, *f*, and *g* leaves up a level, making them siblings of *a*, *b*, *c*, and *d*. Merging and splitting provide an incremental way of restructuring the tree to compensate for incorrect choices caused by infelicitous ordering of examples.

The final hierarchy for all 14 examples is shown at the end of Fig. 4.20. There are three major clusters, each of which subdivides further into its own subclusters. If the *play/don't play* distinction really represented an inherent feature of the data, a single cluster would be expected for each outcome. No such clean structure is observed, although a (very) generous eye might discern a slight tendency at lower levels for *yes* instances to group together, and likewise with *no* instances.

Exactly the same scheme works for numeric attributes. Category utility is defined for these as well, based on an estimate of the mean and standard deviation of the value of that attribute. Details are deferred to the Category Utility section. However, there is just one problem that we must attend to here: when estimating the standard deviation of an attribute for a particular node, the result will be zero if the node contains only one instance, as it does more often than not. Unfortunately, zero variances produce infinite values in the category utility formula. A simple heuristic solution is to impose a minimum variance on each attribute. It can be argued that because no measurement is completely precise, it is reasonable to impose such a minimum: it represents the measurement error in a single sample. This parameter is called *acuity*.

Fig. 4.21 shows, at the top, a hierarchical clustering produced by the incremental algorithm for part of the iris dataset (30 instances, 10 from each class). At the top level there are two clusters (i.e., subclusters of the single node representing the whole dataset). The first contains both *Iris virginicas* and *Iris versicolors*, and the second contains only *Iris setosas*. The *I. setosas* themselves split into two subclusters, one with four cultivars and the other with six. The other top-level cluster splits into three subclusters, each with a fairly complex structure. Both the first and second contain only *I. versicolors*, with one exception, a stray *I. virginica*, in each case; the third contains only *I. virginicas*. This represents a fairly satisfactory clustering of the iris data: it shows that the three genera are not artificial at all but reflect genuine differences in the data. This is, however a

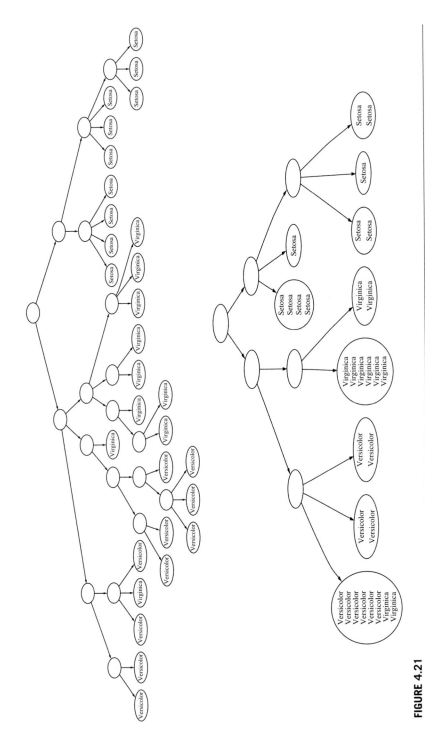

FIGURE 4.21

Hierarchical clusterings of the iris data.

slightly overoptimistic conclusion, because quite a bit of experimentation with the acuity parameter was necessary to obtain such a nice division.

The clusterings produced by this scheme contain one leaf for every instance. This produces an overwhelmingly large hierarchy for datasets of any reasonable size, corresponding, in a sense, to overfitting the particular dataset. Consequently a second numerical parameter called *cutoff* is used to suppress growth. Some instances are deemed to be sufficiently similar to others to not warrant formation of their own child node, and this parameter governs the similarity threshold. Cutoff is specified in terms of category utility: when the increase in category utility from adding a new node is sufficiently small, that node is cut off.

Fig. 4.21B shows the same iris data, clustered with cutoff in effect. Many leaf nodes contain several instances: these are children of the parent node that have been cut off. The division into the three types of iris is a little easier to see from this hierarchy because some of the detail is suppressed. Again, however, some experimentation with the cutoff parameter was necessary to get this result, and in fact a sharper cutoff leads to much less satisfactory clusters.

Similar clusterings are obtained if the full iris dataset of 150 instances is used. However, the results depend on the ordering of examples: Fig. 4.21 was obtained by alternating the three varieties of iris in the input file. If all *I. setosas* are presented first, followed by all *I. versicolors* and then all *I. virginicas*, the resulting clusters are quite unsatisfactory.

CATEGORY UTILITY

Now we look at how the category utility, which measures the overall quality of a partition of instances into clusters, is calculated. In Section 5.9 we will see how the MDL measure could, in principle, be used to evaluate the quality of clustering. Category utility is not MDL-based but rather resembles a kind of quadratic loss function defined on conditional probabilities.

The definition of category utility is rather formidable:

$$CU(C_1, C_2, \ldots, C_k) = \frac{\sum_{\ell} P(C_\ell) \sum_i \sum_j (P(a_i = v_{ij} | C_\ell)^2 - P(a_i = v_{ij})^2)}{k},$$

where $C_1, C_2, \ldots, C_k$ are the k clusters; the outer summation is over these clusters; the next inner one sums over the attributes; a_i is the ith attribute; and it takes on values $v_{i1}, v_{i2}, \ldots$, which are dealt with by the sum over j. Note that the probabilities themselves are obtained by summing over all instances: thus there is a further implied level of summation.

This expression makes a great deal of sense if you take the time to examine it. The point of having a cluster is that it will give some advantage in predicting the values of attributes of instances in that cluster—i.e., $P(a_i = v_{ij} | C_\ell)$ is a better estimate of the probability that attribute a_i has value v_{ij}, for an instance in cluster C_ℓ, than $P(a_i = v_{ij})$ because it takes account of the cluster the instance is in. If that information doesn't help, the clusters aren't doing much good! So what the measure calculates, inside the multiple summation, is the amount by which that information *does* help in terms of the differences between squares of probabilities. This is not quite the standard squared-difference metric, because that sums the squares of the differences (which produces a symmetric result), and the present measure sums the difference of the squares (which, appropriately, does not produce a symmetric result). The differences between squares of probabilities are summed over all attributes, and all their possible values, in the inner double summation. Then it is summed over all clusters, weighted by their probabilities, in the outer summation.

The overall division by k is a little hard to justify because the squared differences have already been summed over the categories. It essentially provides a "per cluster" figure for the category utility that discourages overfitting. Otherwise, because the probabilities are derived by summing over the appropriate instances, the very best category utility would be obtained by placing each instance in its own cluster. Then, $P(a_i = v_{ij}|C_\ell)$ would be 1 for the value that attribute a_i actually has for the single instance in category C_ℓ and 0 for all other values; and the numerator of the category utility formula will end up as

$$n - \sum_i \sum_j P(a_i = v_{ij})^2,$$

where n is the total number of attributes. This is the greatest value that the numerator can have; and so if it were not for the additional division by k in the category utility formula, there would never be any incentive to form clusters containing more than one member. This extra factor is best viewed as a rudimentary overfitting-avoidance heuristic.

This category utility formula applies only to nominal attributes. However, it can easily be extended to numeric attributes by assuming that their distribution is normal with a given (observed) mean μ and standard deviation σ. The probability density function for an attribute a is

$$f(a) = \frac{1}{\sqrt{2\pi}\sigma} \exp\left(-\frac{(a-\mu)^2}{2\sigma^2}\right).$$

The analog of summing the squares of attribute-value probabilities is

$$\sum_j P(a_i = v_{ij})^2 \Leftrightarrow \int f(a_i)^2 da_i = \frac{1}{2\sqrt{\pi}\sigma_i},$$

where σ_i is the standard deviation of the attribute a_i. Thus for a numeric attribute, we estimate the standard deviation from the data, both within the cluster (σ_i') and for the data over all clusters (σ_i), and use these in the category utility formula:

$$CU(C_1, C_2, \ldots, C_k) = \frac{1}{k} \sum_\ell P(C_\ell) \frac{1}{2\sqrt{\pi}} \sum_i \left(\frac{1}{\sigma_i'} - \frac{1}{\sigma_i}\right).$$

Now the problem mentioned above that occurs when the standard deviation estimate is zero becomes apparent: a zero standard deviation produces an infinite value of the category utility formula. Imposing a prespecified minimum variance on each attribute, the acuity, is a rough-and-ready solution to the problem.

REMARKS

Many of the concepts and techniques presented above are easily adapted to the probabilistic setting, where the task of clustering can be viewed as that of probability density estimation. In Chapter 9, Probabilistic methods, we revisit clustering and examine a statistical clustering based on a mixture model of different probability distributions, one for each cluster. It does not partition instances into disjoint clusters as k-means does, but instead assigns them to classes probabilistically, not deterministically. We explain the basic technique and sketch the working of a comprehensive clustering scheme called AutoClass.

The clustering methods that have been described produce different kinds of output. All are capable of taking new data in the form of a test set and classifying it according to clusters that were discovered by analyzing a training set. However, the hierarchical and incremental clustering methods are the only ones that generate an explicit knowledge structure that describes the clustering in a way that can be visualized and reasoned about. The other algorithms produce clusters that can be visualized in instance space if the dimensionality is not too high.

If a clustering method were used to label the instances of the training set with cluster numbers, that labeled set could then be used to train a rule or decision tree learner. The resulting rules or tree would form an explicit description of the classes. A probabilistic clustering scheme could be used for the same purpose, except that each instance would have multiple weighted labels and the rule or decision tree learner would have to be able to cope with weighted instances—as many can.

Another application of clustering is to fill in any values of the attributes that may be missing. For example, it is possible to make a statistical estimate of the value of unknown attributes of a particular instance, based on the class distribution for the instance itself and the values of the unknown attributes for other examples. We will return to these types of ideas in Chapter 9, Probabilistic methods.

4.9 MULTI-INSTANCE LEARNING

In Chapter 2, Input: concepts, instances, attributes, we introduced *multi-instance* learning, where each example in the data comprises several different instances. We call these examples "bags" (in mathematics, a bag is the same as a set except that particular elements can appear more than once, whereas sets cannot contain duplicates). In supervised multi-instance learning, a class label is associated with each bag, and the goal of learning is to determine how the class can be inferred from the instances that make up the bag. While advanced algorithms have been devised to tackle such problems, it turns out that the "simplicity first" methodology can be applied here with surprisingly good results. A simple but effective approach is to manipulate the input data in such a fashion as to transform it to a single-instance learning problem, and then apply standard learning methods—such as the ones described in this chapter. Two such approaches are described below.

AGGREGATING THE INPUT

You can convert a multiple-instance problem to a single-instance one by calculating values such as mean, mode, minimum, and maximum that summarize the instances in the bag and adding these as new attributes. Each "summary" instance retains the class label of the bag it was derived from. To classify a new bag the same process is used: a single aggregated instance is created with attributes that summarize the instances in the bag. Surprisingly, for the original drug activity dataset that spurred the development of multi-instance learning, results comparable with special-purpose multi-instance learners can be obtained using just the minimum and maximum values of each attribute for each bag, combined with a support vector machine classifier (see Section 7.2). One potential drawback of this approach is that the best summary statistics to compute depend on the problem at hand. However, the additional computational cost associated with exploring combinations of different summary statistics is offset by the fact that the summarizing process means that fewer instances are processed by the learning algorithm.

AGGREGATING THE OUTPUT

Instead of aggregating the instances in each bag, another approach is to learn a classifier directly from the original instances that comprise the bag. To achieve this, the instances in a given bag are all assigned the bag's class label. At classification time, a prediction is produced for each instance in the bag to be predicted, and the predictions are aggregated in some fashion to form a prediction for the bag as a whole. One approach is to treat the predictions as votes for the various class labels. If the classifier is capable of assigning probabilities to the class labels, these could be averaged to yield an overall probability distribution for the bag's class label. This method treats the instances independently, and gives them equal influence on the predicted class label.

One problem is that the bags in the training data can contain different numbers of instances. Ideally, each bag should have the same influence on the final model that is learned. If the learning algorithm can accept instance-level weights this can be achieved by assigning each instance in a given bag a weight inversely proportional to the bag's size. If a bag contains n instances, giving each one a weight of $1/n$ ensures that the instances contribute equally to the bag's class label and each bag receives a total weight of 1.

Both these ways of tackling multi-instance problems disregard the original assumption of supervised multi-instance learning that a bag is positive if and only if at least one of its instances is positive. Instead, making each instance in a bag contribute equally to its label is the key element that allows standard learning algorithms to be applied. Otherwise, it is necessary to try to identify the "special" instances that are the key to determining the bag's label.

4.10 FURTHER READING AND BIBLIOGRAPHIC NOTES

The 1R scheme was proposed and thoroughly investigated by Holte (1993). It was never really intended as a machine learning "method": the point was more to demonstrate that very simple structures underlie most of the practical datasets being used to evaluate machine learning schemes at the time and that putting high-powered inductive inference schemes to work on simple datasets was like using a sledgehammer to crack a nut. Why grapple with a complex decision tree when a simple rule will do?

Bayes (1763) was an 18th century English philosopher who set out his theory of probability in an "Essay towards solving a problem in the doctrine of chances," published in the *Philosophical Transactions of the Royal Society of London* ; the rule that bears his name has been a cornerstone of probability theory ever since. The difficulty with the application of Bayes' rule in practice is the assignment of prior probabilities. With a particular dataset, prior probabilities for Naïve Bayes are usually reasonably easy to estimate, which encourages a Bayesian approach to learning.

The fact that Naïve Bayes performs well in classification tasks even when the independence assumption that it rests upon is violated was explored by Domingos and Pazzani (1997). Nevertheless, the assumption is a great stumbling block, and there are ways to apply Bayes' rule without assuming independence. The resulting models are called *Bayesian networks* (Heckerman, Geiger, & Chickering, 1995), and we describe them in Section 9.2.

Bayesian techniques had been used in the field of pattern recognition (Duda & Hart, 1973) for 20 years before they were adopted by machine learning researchers (e.g., see Langley, Iba, & Thompson, 1992) and made to work on datasets with redundant attributes (Langley & Sage, 1994) and numeric attributes (John & Langley, 1995). The label *Naïve Bayes* is unfortunate because it is hard to use this method without feeling simpleminded. However, there is nothing naïve about its use in appropriate circumstances. The multinomial Naïve Bayes model, which is particularly useful for text classification, was investigated by McCallum and Nigam (1998).

The classic paper on decision tree induction was written by Quinlan (1986), who described the basic ID3 procedure developed in this chapter. A comprehensive description of the method, including the improvements that are embodied in C4.5, appears in a classic book by Quinlan (1993), which gives a listing of the complete C4.5 system, written in the C programming language. Prism was developed by Cendrowska (1987), who also introduced the contact lens dataset.

Association rules are introduced and described in the database literature rather than in the machine learning literature. Here the emphasis is very much on dealing with huge amounts of data rather than on sensitive ways of testing and evaluating algorithms on limited datasets. The algorithm introduced in this chapter is the Apriori method developed by Agrawal and his associates (Agrawal, Imielinski, & Swami, 1993a, 1993b; Agrawal & Srikant, 1994). A survey of association-rule mining appears in an article by Chen, Jan, and Yu (1996).

Linear regression is described in most standard statistical texts, and a particularly comprehensive treatment can be found in Lawson and Hanson (1995). The use of linear models for classification enjoyed a great deal of popularity in the 1960s; Nilsson (1965) is an excellent reference. He defined a *linear threshold unit* as a binary test of whether a linear function is greater or less than zero and a *linear machine* as a set of linear functions, one for each class, whose value for an unknown example was compared and the largest chosen as its predicted class. In the distant past, perceptrons fell out of favor on publication of an influential book that showed that they had fundamental limitations (Minsky & Papert, 1969); however, more complex systems of linear functions have enjoyed a resurgence in recent years in the form of neural networks, described in Section 7.2 and Chapter 10, Deep learning. The Winnow algorithms were introduced by Nick Littlestone in his PhD thesis (Littlestone, 1988, 1989). Multiresponse linear classifiers have found application in an operation called *stacking* that combines the output of other learning algorithms, described in Chapter 12, Ensemble learning (see Wolpert, 1992).

Fix and Hodges (1951) performed the first analysis of the nearest-neighbor method, and Johns (1961) pioneered its use in classification problems. Cover and Hart (1967) obtained the classic theoretical result that, for large enough datasets, its probability of error never exceeds twice the theoretical minimum; Devroye, Györfi, and Lugosi (1996) showed that k-nearest neighbor is asymptotically optimal for large k and n with $k/n \rightarrow 0$. Nearest-neighbor methods gained popularity in machine learning through the work of Aha (1992), who showed that instance-based learning can be combined with noisy exemplar pruning and attribute weighting and that the resulting methods perform well in comparison with other learning methods. We take this up again in Chapter 7, Extending instance-based and linear models.

The kD-tree data structure was developed by Friedman, Bentley, and Finkel (1977). Our description closely follows an explanation given by Andrew Moore in his PhD thesis (Moore, 1991), who, along with Omohundro (1987), pioneered its use in machine learning. Moore (2000) described sophisticated ways of constructing ball trees that perform well even with thousands of attributes. We took our ball tree example from lecture notes by Alexander Gray of Carnegie-Mellon University.

The k-means algorithm is a classic technique, and many descriptions and variations are available (e.g., Hartigan, 1975). The k-means++ variant, which yields a significant improvement by choosing the initial seeds more carefully, was introduced as recently as 2007 by Arthur and Vassilvitskii (2007). Our description of how to modify k-means to find a good value of k by repeatedly splitting clusters and seeing whether the split is worthwhile follows the *X*-means algorithm of Moore and Pelleg (2000). However, instead of the MDL principle they use a probabilistic scheme called the Bayes Information Criterion (Kass & Wasserman, 1995). Efficient agglomerative methods for hierarchical clustering were developed by Day and Edelsbrünner (1984), and the ideas are described in recent books (Duda et al., 2001; Hastie et al., 2009). The incremental clustering procedure, based on the merging and splitting operations, was introduced in systems called Cobweb for nominal attributes (Fisher, 1987) and Classit for numeric attributes (Gennari, Langley, & Fisher, 1990). Both are based on a measure of category utility that had been defined previously (Gluck & Corter, 1985).

A hierarchical clustering method called BIRCH (for "balanced iterative reducing and clustering using hierarchies") has been developed specifically for large multidimensional datasets, where it is necessary for efficient operation to minimize input—output costs (Zhang, Ramakrishnan, & Livny, 1996). It incrementally and dynamically clusters multidimensional metric data points, seeking the best clustering within given memory and time constraints. It typically finds a good clustering with a single scan of the data, which can then be improved by further scans.

The method of dealing with multi-instance learning problems by applying standard single instance learners to summarize bag-level data was applied in conjunction with support vector machines by Gärtner, Flach, Kowalczyk, and Smola (2002). The alternative approach of aggregating the output was explained by Frank and Xu (2003).

4.11 WEKA IMPLEMENTATIONS

- Inferring rudimentary rules: *OneR*
- Statistical modeling
  NaiveBayes and many variants, including *NaiveBayesMultinomial*
- Decision trees: *Id3* (in the *simpleEducationalLearningSchemes* package)
- Decision rules: *Prism* (in the *simpleEducationalLearningSchemes* package)
- Association rules: *Apriori*
- Linear models
  SimpleLinearRegression, LinearRegression, Logistic (regression),
  Winnow (in the *Winnow* package)
- Instance-based learning:
  IB1 (in the *simpleEducationalLearningSchemes* package)
- Clustering:
  SimpleKMeans
  Cobweb (which includes *Classit*)
  HierarchicalClusterer (hierarchical clustering using various link functions)
- Multi-instance learning:
  SimpleMI, MIWrapper (available in the *multi-InstanceLearning* package)

Credibility: evaluating what's been learned

5

CHAPTER OUTLINE

5.1 Training and Testing 163
5.2 Predicting Performance 165
5.3 Cross-Validation 167
5.4 Other Estimates..169
    Leave-One-Out 169
    The Bootstrap 169
5.5 Hyperparameter Selection 171
5.6 Comparing Data Mining Schemes 172
5.7 Predicting Probabilities..176
    Quadratic Loss Function 177
    Informational Loss Function 178
    Remarks 179
5.8 Counting the Cost..179
    Cost-Sensitive Classification..182
    Cost-Sensitive Learning...183
    Lift Charts 183
    ROC Curves 186
    Recall-Precision Curves...190
    Remarks 190
    Cost Curves..192
5.9 Evaluating Numeric Prediction 194
5.10 The MDL Principle...197
5.11 Applying the MDL Principle to Clustering 200
5.12 Using a Validation Set for Model Selection...201
5.13 Further Reading and Bibliographic Notes..202

Evaluation is the key to making real progress in data mining. There are lots of ways of inferring structure from data: we have encountered many already and will see further refinements, and new methods, throughout the rest of this book. But to determine which ones to use on a particular problem we need systematic ways to evaluate how well different methods work and to compare one with another. But evaluation is not as simple as it might appear at first sight.

What's the problem? We have the training set; surely we can just look at how well different methods do on that. Well, no: as we will see very shortly, performance on the training set is definitely not a good indicator of performance on an independent test set. We need ways of predicting performance bounds in practice, based on experiments with whatever data can be obtained.

When a vast supply of data is available, this is no problem: just make a model based on a large training set, and try it out on another large test set. But although data mining sometimes involves "big data"—particularly in marketing, sales, and customer support applications—it is often the case that labeled data, quality data, is scarce. The oil slicks mentioned in Chapter 1, What's it all about?, had to be detected and marked manually—a skilled and labor-intensive process—before being used as training data. Even in the credit card application, there turned out to be only 1000 training examples of the appropriate type. The electricity supply data went back 15 years, 5000 days—but only 15 Christmas days and Thanksgivings, and just 4 February 29s and presidential elections. The electromechanical diagnosis application was able to capitalize on 20 years of recorded experience, but this yielded only 300 usable examples of faults. Marketing and sales applications certainly involve big data, but many others do not: training data frequently relies on specialist human expertise—and that is always in short supply.

The question of predicting performance based on limited data is an interesting one. We will encounter many different techniques, of which one—repeated cross-validation—is probably the method of choice in most practical limited-data situations. Comparing the performance of different machine learning schemes on a given problem is another matter that is not so easy as it sounds: to be sure that apparent differences are not caused by chance effects, statistical tests are needed.

So far we have tacitly assumed that what is being predicted is the ability to classify test instances accurately; however, some situations involve predicting class probabilities rather than the classes themselves, and others involve predicting numeric rather than nominal values. Different methods are needed in each case. Then we look at the question of cost. In most practical machine learning situations the cost of a misclassification error depends on the type of error it is—whether, e.g., a positive example was erroneously classified as negative or vice versa. When doing machine learning, and evaluating its performance, it is often essential to take these costs into account. Fortunately, there are simple techniques to make most learning schemes cost sensitive without grappling with the internals of the algorithm. Finally, the whole notion of evaluation has fascinating philosophical connections. For 2000 years philosophers have debated the question of how to evaluate scientific theories, and the issues are brought into sharp focus by machine learning because what is extracted is essentially a "theory" of the data.

5.1 **TRAINING AND TESTING**

For classification problems, it is natural to measure a classifier's performance in terms of the *error rate*. The classifier predicts the class of each instance: if it is correct, that is counted as a *success*; if not, it is an *error*. The error rate is just the proportion of errors made over a whole set of instances, and it measures the overall performance of the classifier.

Of course, what we are interested in is the likely future performance on new data, not the past performance on old data. We already know the classifications of each instance in the training set, which after all is why we can use it for training. We are not generally interested in learning about those classifications—although we might be if our purpose is data cleansing rather than prediction. So the question is, is the error rate on old data likely to be a good indicator of the error rate on new data? The answer is a resounding *no*—not if the old data was used during the learning process to train the classifier.

This is a surprising fact, and a very important one. Error rate on the training set is *not* likely to be a good indicator of future performance. Why? Because the classifier has been learned from the very same training data, any estimate of performance based on that data will be optimistic, and may be hopelessly optimistic.

We have already seen an example of this in the labor relations dataset. Fig. 1.3B was generated directly from the training data, and Fig. 1.3A was obtained from it by a process of pruning. The former is potentially more accurate on the data that was used to train the classifier, but may perform less well on independent test data because it may be overfitted to the training data. The first tree will look good according to the error rate on the training data, better than the second tree. But this does not necessarily reflect how they will perform on independent test data.

The error rate on the training data is called the *resubstitution error*, because it is calculated by resubstituting the training instances into a classifier that was constructed from them. Although it is not a reliable predictor of the true error rate on new data, it is nevertheless often useful to know.

To predict the performance of a classifier on new data, we need to assess its error rate on a dataset that played no part in the formation of the classifier. This independent dataset is called the *test set*. We assume that both the training data and the test data are representative samples of the underlying problem.

In some cases the test data might be distinct in nature from the training data. Consider, e.g., the credit risk problem from Section 1.3. Suppose the bank had training data from branches in New York City and Florida and wanted to know how well a classifier trained on one of these datasets would perform in a new branch in Nebraska. It should probably use the Florida data as test data for evaluating the New York–trained classifier and the New York data to evaluate the Florida-trained classifier. If the datasets were amalgamated before training, performance on the test data would probably not be good indicator of performance on future data in a completely different state.

It is important that the test data is not used *in any way* to create the classifier. For example, some learning schemes involve two stages, one to come up with a basic structure and the second to optimize parameters involved in that structure, and separate sets of data may be needed in the two stages. Or you might try out several learning schemes on the training data and then evaluate them—on a fresh dataset, of course—to see which one works best. But none of this data may be used to determine an estimate of the future error rate. In such situations people often talk about three datasets: the *training* data, the *validation* data, and the *test* data. The training data is used by one or more learning schemes to come up with classifiers. The validation data is used to optimize parameters of those classifiers, or to select a particular one. Then the test data is used to calculate the error rate of the final, optimized, method. Each of the three sets must be chosen independently: the validation set must be different from the training set to obtain good performance in the optimization or selection stage, and the test set must be different from both to obtain a reliable estimate of the true error rate.

It may be that once the error rate has been determined, the test data is bundled back into the training data to produce a new classifier for actual use. There is nothing wrong with this: it is just a way of maximizing the amount of data used to generate the classifier that will actually be employed in practice. With well-behaved learning schemes, this should not decrease predictive performance. Also, once the validation data has been used—maybe to determine the best type of learning scheme to use—then it can be bundled back into the training data to retrain that learning scheme, maximizing the use of data.

If lots of data is available, there is no problem: we take a large sample and use it for training; then another, independent large sample of different data and use it for testing. Provided both samples are representative, the error rate on the test set will give a good indication of future performance. Generally, the larger the training sample the better the classifier, although the returns begin to diminish once a certain volume of training data is exceeded. And the larger the test sample, the more accurate the error estimate. The accuracy of the error estimate can be quantified statistically, as we will see in Section 5.2.

The real problem occurs when there is not a vast supply of data available. In many situations the training data must be classified manually—and so must the test data, of course, to obtain error estimates. This limits the amount of data that can be used for training, validation, and testing, and the problem becomes how to make the most of a limited dataset. From this dataset, a certain amount is held over for testing—this is called the *holdout* procedure—and the remainder used for training (and, if necessary, part of that is set aside for validation). There's a dilemma here: to find a good classifier, we want to use as much of the data as possible for training; to obtain a good error estimate, we want to use as much of it as possible for testing. Sections 5.3 and 5.4 review widely used methods for dealing with this dilemma.

5.2 PREDICTING PERFORMANCE

Suppose we measure the error of a classifier on a test set and obtain a certain numerical error rate—say 25%. Actually, in this section we talk about success rate rather than error rate, so this corresponds to a success rate of 75%. Now, this is only an estimate. What can you say about the *true* success rate on the target population? Sure, it's expected to be close to 75%. But how close?—within 5%? 10%? It must depend on the size of the test set. Naturally we would be more confident of the 75% figure if it was based on a test set of 10,000 instances than a test set of 100 instances. But how much more confident would we be?

To answer these questions, we need some statistical reasoning. In statistics, a succession of independent events that either succeed or fail is called a *Bernoulli process*. The classic example is coin tossing. Each toss is an independent event. Let's say we always predict heads; but rather than "heads" or "tails," each toss is considered a "success" or a "failure." Let's say the coin is biased, but we don't know what the probability of heads is. Then, if we actually toss the coin 100 times and 75 of them are heads, we have a situation very like the one described above for a classifier with an observed 75% success rate on a test set. What can we say about the true success probability? In other words, imagine that there is a Bernoulli process—a biased coin—whose true (but unknown) success rate is p. Suppose that out of N trials, S are successes: thus the observed success rate is $f = S/N$. The question is, what does this tell you about the true success rate p?

The answer to this question is usually expressed as a confidence interval; i.e., p lies within a certain specified interval with a certain specified confidence. For example, if $S = 750$ successes are observed out of $N = 1000$ trials, this indicates that the true success rate must be around 75%. But how close to 75%? It turns out that with 80% confidence, the true success rate p lies between 73.2% and 76.7%. If $S = 75$ successes are observed out of $N = 100$ trials, this also indicates that the true success rate must be around 75%. But the experiment is smaller, and so the 80% confidence interval for p is wider, stretching from 69.1% to 80.1%.

These figures are easy to relate to qualitatively, but how are they derived quantitatively? We reason as follows: the mean and variance of a single Bernoulli trial with success rate p are p and $p(1 - p)$, respectively. If N trials are taken from a Bernoulli process, the expected success rate $f = S/N$ is a random variable with the same mean p; the variance is reduced by a factor of N to $p(1 - p)/N$. For large N, the distribution of this random variable approaches the normal distribution. These are all facts of statistics: we will not go into how they are derived.

The probability that a random variable X, with zero mean, lies within a certain confidence range of width $2z$ is

$$P(-z \leq X \leq z) = c.$$

For a normal distribution, values of c and corresponding values of z are given in tables printed at the back of most statistical texts. However, the tabulations conventionally take a slightly different form: they give the confidence that X will lie outside the range, and they give it for the upper part of the range only:

$$P(X \geq z).$$

This is called a *one-tailed* probability because it refers only to the upper "tail" of the distribution. Normal distributions are symmetric, so the probabilities for the lower tail.

$$P(X \leq -z)$$

are just the same.

Table 5.1 gives an example. Like other tables for the normal distribution, this assumes that the random variable X has a mean of 0 and a variance of 1. Alternatively, you might say that the z figures are measured in *standard deviations from the mean*. Thus the figure for $P(X \geq z) = 5\%$ implies that there is a 5% chance that X lies more than 1.65 standard deviations above the mean. Because the distribution is symmetric, the chance that X lies more than 1.65 standard deviations from the mean (above or below) is 10%, or

$$P(-1.65 \leq X \leq 1.65) = 90\%.$$

All we need do now is reduce the random variable f to have zero mean and unit variance. We do this by subtracting the mean p and dividing by the standard deviation $\sqrt{p(1-p)/N}$. This leads to

$$P\left(-z < \frac{f-p}{\sqrt{p(1-p)/N}} < z\right) = c.$$

Now here is the procedure for finding confidence limits. Given a particular confidence figure c, consult Table 5.1 for the corresponding z value. To use the table you will first have to subtract c from 1 and then halve the result, so that for $c = 90\%$ you use the table entry for 5%. Linear interpolation can be used for intermediate confidence levels. Then write the inequality in the preceding expression as an equality and invert it to find an expression for p.

Table 5.1 Confidence Limits for the Normal Distribution

$P(X \geq z)$ (%)	z
0.1	3.09
0.5	2.58
1	2.33
5	1.65
10	1.28
20	0.84
40	0.25

The final step involves solving a quadratic equation. Although not hard to do, it leads to an unpleasantly formidable expression for the confidence limits:

$$p = \left(f + \frac{z^2}{2N} \pm z\sqrt{\frac{f}{N} - \frac{f^2}{N} + \frac{z^2}{4N^2}} \right) \Bigg/ \left(1 + \frac{z^2}{N} \right).$$

The $\pm$ in this expression gives two values for p that represent the upper and lower confidence boundaries. Although the formula looks complicated, it is not hard to work out in particular cases.

This result can be used to obtain the values in the numeric example given earlier. Setting $f = 75\%$, $N = 1000$, and $c = 80\%$ (so that $z = 1.28$) leads to the interval [0.732, 0.767] for p, and $N = 100$ leads to [0.691, 0.801] for the same level of confidence. Note that the normal distribution assumption is only valid for large N (say, $N > 100$). Thus $f = 75\%$ and $N = 10$ leads to confidence limits [0.549, 0.881]—but these should be taken with a grain of salt.

5.3 CROSS-VALIDATION

Now consider what to do when the amount of data for training and testing is limited. The holdout method reserves a certain amount for testing, and uses the remainder for training (and sets part of that aside for validation, if required). In practical terms, it is common to hold one-third of the data out for testing and use the remaining two-thirds for training.

Of course, you may be unlucky: the sample used for training (or testing) might not be representative. In general, you cannot tell whether a sample is representative or not. But there is one simple check that might be worthwhile: each class in the full dataset should be represented in about the right proportion in the training and testing sets. If, by bad luck, all examples with a certain class were omitted from the training set, you could hardly expect a classifier learned from that data to perform well on examples of that class—and the situation would be exacerbated by the fact that the class would necessarily be overrepresented in the test set, because none of its instances made it into the training set! Instead, you should ensure that the random sampling is done in a way that guarantees that each class is properly represented in both training and test sets. This procedure is called *stratification*, and we might speak of *stratified holdout*. While it is generally well worth doing, stratification provides only a primitive safeguard against uneven representation in training and test sets.

A more general way to mitigate any bias caused by the particular sample chosen for holdout is to repeat the whole process, training and testing, several times with different random samples. In each iteration a certain proportion—say two-thirds—of the data is randomly selected for training, possibly with stratification, and the remainder used for testing. The error rates on the different iterations are averaged to yield an overall error rate. This is the *repeated holdout* method of error rate estimation.

In a single holdout procedure, you might consider swapping the roles of the testing and training data—i.e., train the system on the test data and test it on the training data—and average the two results, thus reducing the effect of uneven representation in training and test sets. Unfortunately, this is only really plausible with a 50:50 split between training and test data, which is generally not ideal—it is better to use more than half the data for training even at the expense of test data. However, a simple variant forms the basis of an important statistical technique called *cross-validation*. In cross-validation, you decide on a fixed number of *folds*, or partitions of the data. Suppose we use three. Then the data is split into three approximately equal partitions: each in turn is used for testing and the remainder is used for training. That is, use two-thirds for training and one-third for testing, and repeat the procedure three times so that in the end, every instance has been used exactly once for testing. This is called *threefold cross-validation*, and if stratification is adopted as well—which it often is—it is *stratified threefold cross-validation*.

The standard way of predicting the error rate of a learning technique given a single, fixed sample of data is to use stratified 10-fold cross-validation. The data is divided randomly into 10 parts in which the class is represented in approximately the same proportions as in the full dataset. Each part is held out in turn and the learning scheme trained on the remaining nine-tenths; then its error rate is calculated on the holdout set. Thus the learning procedure is executed a total of 10 times on different training sets (each of which have a lot in common). Finally, the 10 error estimates are averaged to yield an overall error estimate.

Why 10? Extensive tests on numerous different datasets, with different learning techniques, have shown that 10 is about the right number of folds to get the best estimate of error, and there is also some theoretical evidence that backs this up. Although these arguments are by no means conclusive, 10-fold cross-validation has become the standard method in practical terms. Tests have also shown that the use of stratification improves results slightly. Thus the standard evaluation technique in situations where only limited data is available is stratified 10-fold cross-validation. Note that neither the stratification nor the division into 10 folds has to be exact: it is enough to divide the data into 10 approximately equal sets in which the various class values are represented in approximately the right proportion. Moreover, there is nothing magic about the exact number 10: 5-fold or 20-fold cross-validation is likely to be almost as good.

A single 10-fold cross-validation might not be enough to get a reliable error estimate if the data is limited. Different 10-fold cross-validation experiments with the same learning scheme and dataset often produce different results, because of the effect of random variation in choosing the folds themselves. Stratification reduces the variation, but it certainly does not eliminate it entirely. When seeking an accurate error estimate with limited data, it is standard procedure to repeat the cross-validation process 10 times—i.e., 10 times 10-fold cross-validation—and average the results. This involves invoking the learning algorithm 100 times on datasets that are all nine-tenths the size of the original. Getting a good measure of performance is a computation-intensive undertaking.

5.4 OTHER ESTIMATES

Tenfold cross-validation is the standard way of measuring the error rate of a learning scheme on limited data; for reliable results, 10 times 10-fold cross-validation. But many other methods are used instead. Two that are particularly prevalent are *leave-one-out* cross-validation and the *bootstrap*.

LEAVE-ONE-OUT

Leave-one-out cross-validation is simply n-fold cross-validation, where n is the number of instances in the dataset. Each instance in turn is left out, and the learning scheme is trained on all the remaining instances. It is judged by its correctness on the remaining instance—1or 0 for success or failure. The results of all n judgments, one for each member of the dataset, are averaged, and that average represents the final error estimate.

This procedure is an attractive one for two reasons. First, the greatest possible amount of data is used for training in each case, which presumably increases the chance that the classifier is an accurate one. Second, the procedure is deterministic: no random sampling is involved. There is no point in repeating it 10 times, or repeating it at all: the same result will be obtained each time. Set against this is the high computational cost, because the entire learning procedure must be executed n times and this is usually quite infeasible for large datasets. Nevertheless, leave-one-out seems to offer a chance of squeezing the maximum out of a small dataset and getting as accurate an estimate as possible.

But there is a disadvantage to leave-one-out cross-validation, apart from the computational expense. By its very nature, it cannot be stratified—worse than that, it *guarantees* a nonstratified sample. Stratification involves getting the correct proportion of examples in each class into the test set, and this is impossible when the test set contains only a single example. A dramatic, although highly artificial, illustration of the problems this might cause is to imagine a completely random dataset that contains exactly the same number of instances of each of two classes. The best that an inducer can do with random data is to predict the majority class, giving a true error rate of 50%. But in each fold of leave-one-out, the opposite class to the test instance is in the majority—and therefore the predictions will always be incorrect, leading to an estimated error rate of 100%!

THE BOOTSTRAP

The second estimation method we describe, the bootstrap, is based on the statistical procedure of sampling *with replacement*. Previously, whenever a sample was taken from the dataset to form a training or test set, it was drawn without replacement. That is, the same instance, once selected, could not be selected again. It is like picking teams for football: you cannot choose the same person twice. But dataset instances are not like people. Most learning schemes can use the same instance twice, and it makes a difference in the result of learning if it is present in the training set twice. (Mathematical sticklers will notice that we should not really be talking about "sets" at all if the same object can appear more than once.)

The idea of the bootstrap is to sample the dataset with replacement to form a training set. We will describe a particular variant, mysteriously (but for a reason that will soon become apparent) called the *0.632 bootstrap*. For this, a dataset of n instances is sampled n times, with replacement, to give another dataset of n instances. Because some elements in this second dataset will (almost certainly) be repeated, there must be some instances in the original dataset that have not been picked: we will use these as test instances.

What is the chance that a particular instance will not be picked for the training set? It has a $1/n$ probability of being picked each time, and so a $1 - 1/n$ probability of *not* being picked. Multiply these probabilities together for a sufficient number of picking opportunities, n, and the result is a figure of

$$\left(1 - \frac{1}{n}\right)^n \approx e^{-1} = 0.368$$

(where e is the base of natural logarithms, 2.7183, not the error rate!). This gives the chance of a particular instance not being picked at all. Thus for a reasonably large dataset, the test set will contain about 36.8% of the instances and the training set will contain about 63.2% of them (now you can see why it's called the *0.632 bootstrap*). Some instances will be repeated in the training set, bringing it up to a total size of n, the same as in the original dataset.

The figure obtained by training a learning system on the training set and calculating its error over the test set will be a pessimistic estimate of the true error rate, because the training set, although its size is n, nevertheless contains only 63% of the instances, which is not a great deal compared, e.g., with the 90% used in 10-fold cross-validation. To compensate for this, we combine the test-set error rate with the resubstitution error on the instances in the training set. The resubstitution figure, as we warned earlier, gives a very optimistic estimate of the true error and should certainly not be used as an error figure on its own. But the bootstrap procedure combines it with the test error rate to give a final estimate e as follows:

$$e = 0.632 \cdot e_{\text{test instances}} + 0.368 \cdot e_{\text{training instances}}.$$

Then, the whole bootstrap procedure is repeated several times, with different replacement samples for the training set, and the results averaged.

The bootstrap procedure may be the best way of estimating error for very small datasets. However, like leave-one-out cross-validation, it has disadvantages that can be illustrated by considering a special, artificial situation. In fact, the very dataset we considered above will do: a completely random dataset with two classes of equal size. The true error rate is 50% for any prediction rule. But a scheme that memorized the training set would give a perfect resubstitution score of 100%, so that $e_{\text{training instances}} = 0$, and the 0.632 bootstrap will mix this in with a weight of 0.368 to give an overall error rate of only 31.6% ($0.632 \times 50\%$ + $0.368 \times 0\%$), which is misleadingly optimistic.

5.5 HYPERPARAMETER SELECTION

Many learning algorithms have parameters that can be tuned to optimize their behavior. These are called "hyperparameters" to distinguish them from basic parameters such as the coefficients in linear regression models. An example is the parameter k that determines the number of neighbors used in a k-nearest-neighbor classifier. Normally, best performance on a test set is achieved by adjusting the value of this hyperparameter to suit the characteristics of the data. However, frustratingly, it is very important not to use performance on the test data to choose the best value for k! This is because peeking at the test data to make choices automatically introduces optimistic bias in the performance score obtained from this same data. Performance on future new data will very likely be worse than the estimate.

What to do? The trick, as mentioned earlier in this chapter, is to split the original training set into a smaller, new training set and a validation set. (The split is normally done randomly.) Then the algorithm is run several times with different hyperparameter values on this reduced training set, and each of the resulting models is evaluated on the validation set. Once the hyperparameter value that gives best performance on the validation set has been determined, a final model is built by running the algorithm with that hyperparameter value on the original, full training set. Note that the test data is not involved in any of this! Only after the final model is fixed are we allowed to use the test data to obtain an estimate of the performance of this model on new, unseen data. Basically, the test data can only be used once, to establish the final performance score.

This also applies when using methods, such as cross-validation, with multiple training and testing splits. Hyperparameter choice must be based on the training set only. When applying the above parameter selection process multiple times within a cross-validation, once for each fold, it is entirely possible that the hyperparameter values will be slightly different from fold to fold. This does not matter: hyperparameter selection is part of the overall process of learning a model, and these models will normally differ from fold to fold anyway. In other words, what is being evaluated with cross-validation is the learning process, not one particular model.

There is a drawback to this process for hyperparameter selection: if the original training data is small—and the training folds in a cross-validation often are—then splitting off a validation set will further reduce the size of the set available for training; and the validation set will be small too. This means that the choice of hyperparameter may not be reliable. This is analogous to the problem with the simple holdout estimate we encountered earlier in this chapter, and the same remedy applies: use cross-validation instead. This means that a so-called "inner" cross-validation is applied to determine the best value of the hyperparameter for each fold of the "outer" cross-validation used to obtain the final performance estimate for the learning algorithm.

This kind of nested cross-validation process is expensive, particularly considering that the inner cross-validation must be run for each value of the hyperparameter that we want to evaluate. Things become worse with multiple hyperparameters. If a grid search is used to find the best parameter value, then with two hyperparameters and a 10×10 grid 100 inner cross-validations are needed, and this must be done for each fold of the outer cross-validation. Assuming that 10 folds are used for both the inner and outer cross-validation, the learning algorithm must be run 10 times 10 times 100 times—10,000 times! And then we might want to repeat the outer cross-validation 10 times to get a more reliable final performance estimate.

Fortunately, this process can easily be distributed across multiple computers. Nevertheless, it may be infeasible, at least with the above configuration, and it is common practice to use a smaller number of folds for the internal cross-validation, perhaps just twofolds.

5.6 COMPARING DATA MINING SCHEMES

We often need to compare two different learning schemes on the same problem to see which is the better one to use. It seems simple: estimate the error using cross-validation (or any other suitable estimation procedure), perhaps repeated several times, and choose the scheme whose estimate is smaller. And this is quite sufficient in many practical applications: if one scheme has a lower estimated error than another on a particular dataset, the best we can do is to use the former scheme's model. However, it may be that the difference is simply caused by estimation error, and in some circumstances it is important to determine whether one scheme is *really* better than another on a particular problem. This is a standard challenge for machine learning researchers. If a new learning algorithm is proposed, its proponents must show that it improves on the state of the art for the problem at hand and demonstrate that the observed improvement is not just a chance effect in the estimation process.

This is a job for a statistical test that is based on confidence bounds, the kind we met previously when trying to predict true performance from a given test-set error rate. If there were unlimited data, we could use a large amount for training and evaluate performance on a large independent test set, obtaining confidence bounds just as before. However, if the difference turns out to be significant we must ensure that this is not just because of the particular dataset we happened to base the experiment on. What we want to determine is whether one scheme is better or worse than another on average, across all possible training and test datasets that can be drawn from the domain. Because the amount of training data naturally affects performance, all datasets should be the same size: indeed, the experiment might be repeated with different sizes to obtain a learning curve.

For the moment, assume that the supply of data is unlimited. For definiteness, suppose that cross-validation is being used to obtain the error estimates (other estimators, such as repeated cross-validation, are equally viable). For each learning scheme we can draw several datasets of the same size, obtain an accuracy estimate for each dataset using cross-validation, and compute the mean of the estimates. Each cross-validation experiment yields a different, independent error estimate. What we are interested in is the mean accuracy across all possible datasets of the same size, and whether this mean is greater for one scheme or the other.

From this point of view, we are trying to determine whether the mean of a set of samples—cross-validation estimates for the various datasets that we sampled from the domain—is significantly greater than, or significantly less than, the mean of another. This is a job for a statistical device known as the *t-test*, or *Student's t-test*. Because the same cross-validation experiment can be used for both learning schemes to obtain a matched pair of results for each dataset, a more sensitive version of the *t*-test known as a *paired t-test* can be used.

We need some notation. There is a set of samples $x_1, x_2, \ldots, x_k$ obtained by successive 10-fold cross-validations using one learning scheme, and a second set of samples $y_1, y_2, \ldots, y_k$ obtained by successive 10-fold cross-validations using the other. Each cross-validation estimate is generated using a different dataset (but all datasets are of the same size and from the same domain). We will get best results if exactly the same cross-validation partitions are used for both schemes, so that x_1 and y_1 are obtained using the same cross-validation split, as are x_2 and y_2, and so on. Denote the mean of the first set of samples by $\bar{x}$ and the mean of the second set by $\bar{y}$. We are trying to determine whether $\bar{x}$ is significantly different from $\bar{y}$.

If there are enough samples, the mean ($\bar{x}$) of a set of independent samples ($x_1, x_2, \ldots, x_k$) has a normal (i.e., Gaussian) distribution, regardless of the distribution underlying the samples themselves. Call the true value of the mean μ. If we knew the variance of that normal distribution, so that it could be reduced to have zero mean and unit variance, we could obtain confidence limits on μ given the mean of the samples ($\bar{x}$). However, the variance is unknown, and the only way we can obtain it is to estimate it from the set of samples.

That is not hard to do. The variance of $\bar{x}$ can be estimated by dividing the variance calculated from the samples $x_1, x_2, \ldots, x_k$—call it σ_x^2—by k. We can reduce the distribution of $\bar{x}$ to have zero mean and unit variance by using

$$\frac{\bar{x} - \mu}{\sqrt{\sigma_x^2/k}}.$$

The fact that we have to *estimate* the variance changes things somewhat. Because the variance is only an estimate, this does *not* have a normal distribution (although it does become normal for large values of k). Instead, it has what is called a *Student's distribution with $k - 1$ degrees of freedom*. What this means in practice is that we have to use a table of confidence intervals for Student's

Table 5.2 Confidence Limits for Student's Distribution With 9 Degrees of Freedom

Pr[X ≥ z] (%)	z
0.1	4.30
0.5	3.25
1	2.82
5	1.83
10	1.38
20	0.88

distribution rather than the confidence table for the normal distribution given earlier. For 9 degrees of freedom (which is the correct number if we are using the average of 10 cross-validations) the appropriate confidence limits are shown in Table 5.2. If you compare them with Table 5.1 you will see that the Student's figures are slightly more conservative—for a given degree of confidence, the interval is slightly wider—and this reflects the additional uncertainty caused by having to estimate the variance. Different tables are needed for different numbers of degrees of freedom, and if there are more than 100 degrees of freedom the confidence limits are very close to those for the normal distribution. Like Table 5.1, the figures in Table 5.2 are for a "one-sided" confidence interval.

To decide whether the means $\bar{x}$ and $\bar{y}$, each an average of the same number k of samples, are the same or not, we consider the differences d_i between corresponding observations, $d_i = x_i - y_i$. This is legitimate because the observations are paired. The mean of this difference is just the difference between the two means, $\bar{d} = \bar{x} - \bar{y}$, and, like the means themselves, it has a Student's distribution with $k - 1$ degrees of freedom. If the means are the same, the difference is zero (this is called the *null hypothesis*); if they're significantly different, the difference will be significantly different from zero. So for a given confidence level, we will check whether the actual difference exceeds the confidence limit.

First, reduce the difference to a zero-mean, unit-variance variable called the *t*-statistic:

$$t = \frac{\bar{d}}{\sqrt{\sigma_d^2/k}}$$

where σ_d^2 is the variance of the difference samples. Then, decide on a confidence level—generally, 5% or 1% is used in practice. From this the confidence limit z is determined using Table 5.2 if k is 10; if it is not, a confidence table of the Student distribution for the k value in question is used. A two-tailed test is appropriate because we do not know in advance whether the mean of the x's is likely to be greater than that of the y's or vice versa: thus for a 1% test we use the value corresponding to 0.5% in Table 5.2. If the value of t according to the formula above is greater than z, or less than $-z$, we reject the null hypothesis that the means are the same and conclude that there really is a significant difference between the two learning methods on that domain for that dataset size.

Two observations are worth making on this procedure. The first is technical: what if the observations were not paired? That is, what if we were unable, for some reason, to assess the error of each learning scheme on the same datasets? What if the number of datasets for each scheme was not even the same? These conditions could arise if someone else had evaluated one of the schemes and published several different estimates for a particular domain and dataset size—or perhaps just their mean and variance—and we wished to compare this with a different learning scheme. Then it is necessary to use a regular, nonpaired t-test. Instead of taking the mean of the difference, $\bar{d}$, we use the difference of the means, $\bar{x} - \bar{y}$. Of course, that's the same thing: the mean of the difference *is* the difference of the means. But the variance of the difference $\bar{d}$ is *not* the same. If the variance of the samples $x_1, x_2, \ldots, x_k$ is σ_x^2 and the variance of the samples $y_1, y_2, \ldots, y_\ell$ is σ_y^2,

$$\frac{\sigma_x^2}{k} + \frac{\sigma_y^2}{\ell}.$$

is a good estimate of the variance of the difference of the means. It is this variance (or rather, its square root) that should be used as the denominator of the t-statistic given previously. The degrees of freedom, necessary for consulting Student's confidence tables, should be taken conservatively to be the minimum of the degrees of freedom of the two samples. Essentially, knowing that the observations are paired allows the use of a better estimate for the variance, which will produce tighter confidence bounds.

The second observation concerns the assumption that there is essentially unlimited data so that several independent datasets of the right size can be used. In practice there is usually only a single dataset of limited size. What can be done? We could split the data into subsets (perhaps 10) and perform a cross-validation on each one. However, the overall result will only tell us whether a learning scheme is preferable for that particular size—one-tenth of the original dataset. Alternatively, the original dataset could be reused—e.g., with different randomizations of the dataset for each cross-validation. However, the resulting cross-validation estimates will not be independent because they are not based on independent datasets. In practice, this means that a difference may be judged to be significant when in fact it is not. Indeed, just increasing the number of samples k, i.e., the number of cross-validation runs, will eventually yield an apparently significant difference because the value of the t-statistic increases without bound.

Various modifications of the standard t-test have been proposed to circumvent this problem, all of them heuristic and somewhat lacking in theoretical justification. One that appears to work well in practice is the *corrected resampled t-test*. Assume for the moment that the repeated holdout method is used instead of cross-validation, repeated k times on different random splits of the same dataset to obtain accuracy estimates for two learning schemes. Each time, n_1 instances are used for training and n_2 for testing, and differences d_i are computed from performance on the test data. The corrected resampled t-test uses the modified statistic.

$$t = \frac{\bar{d}}{\sqrt{\left(\frac{1}{k} + \frac{n_2}{n_1}\right)\sigma_d^2}}$$

in exactly the same way as the standard t-statistic. A closer look at the formula shows that its value cannot be increased simply by increasing k. The same modified statistic can be used with repeated cross-validation, which is just a special case of repeated holdout in which the individual test sets for *one* cross-validation do not overlap. For 10-fold cross-validation repeated 10 times, $k = 100$, $n_2/n_1 = 0.1/0.9$, and σ_d^2 is based on 100 differences.

5.7 PREDICTING PROBABILITIES

Throughout this section we have tacitly assumed that the goal is to maximize the success rate of the predictions. The outcome for each test instance is either *correct*, if the prediction agrees with the actual value for that instance, or *incorrect*, if it does not. There are no grays: everything is black or white, correct or incorrect. In many situations, this is the most appropriate perspective. If the learning scheme, when it is actually applied, results in either a correct or an incorrect prediction, success is the right measure to use. This is sometimes called a $0 - 1$ *loss function*: the "loss" is either zero if the prediction is correct or one if it is not. The use of *loss* is conventional, although a more optimistic terminology might couch the outcome in terms of profit instead.

Other situations are softer edged. Most learning schemes can associate a probability with each prediction (as the Naïve Bayes scheme does). It might be more natural to take this probability into account when judging correctness. For example, a correct outcome predicted with a probability of 99% should perhaps weigh more heavily than one predicted with a probability of 51%, and, in a two-class situation, perhaps the latter is not all that much better than an *incorrect* outcome predicted with probability 51%. Whether it is appropriate to take prediction probabilities into account depends on the application. If the ultimate application really is just a prediction of the outcome, and no prizes are awarded for a realistic assessment of the likelihood of the prediction, it does not seem appropriate to use probabilities. If the prediction is subject to further processing, however—perhaps involving assessment by a person, or a cost analysis, or maybe even serving as input to a second-level learning process—then it may well be appropriate to take prediction probabilities into account.

QUADRATIC LOSS FUNCTION

Suppose for a single instance there are k possible outcomes, or classes, and for a given instance the learning scheme comes up with a probability vector $p_1, p_2, \ldots, p_k$ for the classes (where these probabilities sum to 1). The actual outcome for that instance will be one of the possible classes. However, it is convenient to express it as a vector $a_1, a_2, \ldots, a_k$ whose ith component, where i is the actual class, is 1 and all other components are 0. We can express the penalty associated with this situation as a loss function that depends on both the p vector and the a vector.

One criterion that is frequently used to evaluate probabilistic prediction is the *quadratic loss function*:

$$\sum_j (p_j - a_j)^2.$$

Note that this is for a single instance: the summation is over possible outputs not over different instances. Just one of the a's will be 1 and the rest 0, so the sum contains contributions of p_j^2 for the incorrect predictions and $(1 - p_i)^2$ for the correct one: consequently it can be written.

$$1 - 2p_i + \sum_j p_j^2,$$

where i is the correct class. When the test set contains several instances, the loss function is summed over them all.

It is an interesting theoretical fact that if you seek to minimize the value of the quadratic loss function in a situation where the actual class is generated probabilistically, the best strategy is to choose for the p vector the actual probabilities of the different outcomes, i.e., $p_i = P(\text{class} = i)$. If the true probabilities are known, they will be the best values for p. If they are not, a system that strives to minimize the quadratic loss function will be encouraged to use its best estimate of $P(\text{class} = i)$ as the value for p_i.

This is quite easy to see. Denote the true probabilities by $p_1^*, p_2^*, \ldots, p_k^*$ so that $p_i^* = P(\text{class} = i)$. The expected value of the quadratic loss function over test instances can be rewritten as follows:

$$E\left[\sum_j (p_j - a_j)^2\right] = \sum_j (E[p_j^2] - 2E[p_j a_j] + E[a_j^2])$$
$$= \sum_j (p_j^2 - 2p_j p_j^* + p_j^*) = \sum_j ((p_j - p_j^*)^2 + p_j^*(1 - p_j^*)).$$

The first stage just involves bringing the expectation inside the sum and expanding the square. For the second, p_j is just a constant and the expected value of a_j is simply p_j^*; moreover, because a_j is either 0 or 1, $a_j^2 = a_j$ and its expected value is p_j^* too. The third stage is straightforward algebra. To minimize the resulting sum, it is clear that it is best to choose $p_j = p_j^*$ so that the squared term disappears and all that is left is a term that is just the variance of the true distribution governing the actual class.

Minimizing the squared error has a long history in prediction problems. In the present context, the quadratic loss function forces the predictor to be honest about choosing its best estimate of the probabilities—or, rather, it gives preference to predictors that are able to make the best guess at the true probabilities. Moreover, the quadratic loss function has some useful theoretical properties that we will not go into here. For all these reasons it is frequently used as the criterion of success in probabilistic prediction situations.

INFORMATIONAL LOSS FUNCTION

Another popular criterion for the evaluation of probabilistic prediction is the *informational loss function*:

$$-\log_2 p_i$$

where the ith prediction is the correct one. This is in fact identical to the negative of the log-likelihood function that is optimized by logistic regression, described in Section 4.6 (modulo a constant factor, which is determined by the base of the logarithm). It represents the information (in bits) required to express the actual class i with respect to the probability distribution $p_1, p_2, \ldots, p_k$. In other words, if you were given the probability distribution and someone had to communicate to you which class was the one that actually occurred, this is the number of bits they would need to encode the information if they did it as effectively as possible. (Of course, it is always possible to use *more* bits.) Because probabilities are always less than one, their logarithms are negative, and the minus sign makes the outcome positive. For example, in a two-class situation—heads or tails—with an equal probability of each class, the occurrence of a head would take 1 bit to transmit, because $-\log_2 1/2$ is 1.

The expected value of the informational loss function, if the true probabilities are $p_1^*, p_2^*, \ldots, p_k^*$, is

$$-p_1^* \log_2 p_1 - p_2^* \log_2 p_2 - \ldots - p_k^* \log_2 p_k.$$

Like the quadratic loss function, this expression is minimized by choosing $p_j = p_j^*$, in which case the expression becomes the entropy of the true distribution:

$$-p_1^* \log_2 p_1^* - p_2^* \log_2 p_2^* - \ldots - p_k^* \log_2 p_k^*.$$

Thus the informational loss function also rewards honesty in predictors that know the true probabilities, and encourages predictors that do not to put forward their best guess.

One problem with the informational loss function is that if you assign a probability of zero to an event that actually occurs, the function's value is infinity. This corresponds to losing your shirt when gambling. Prudent predictors operating under the informational loss function do not assign zero probability to any outcome. This does lead to a problem when no information is available about that outcome on which to base a prediction: i.e., called the *zero-frequency problem*, and various plausible solutions have been proposed, such as the Laplace estimator discussed earlier for Naïve Bayes.

REMARKS

If you are in the business of evaluating predictions of probabilities, which of the two loss functions should you use? That's a good question, and there is no universally agreed-upon answer—it's really a matter of taste. They both do the fundamental job expected of a loss function: they give maximum reward to predictors that are capable of predicting the true probabilities accurately. However, there are some objective differences between the two that may help you form an opinion.

The quadratic loss function takes account not only of the probability assigned to the event that actually occurred, but also the other probabilities. For example, in a four-class situation, suppose you assigned 40% to the class that actually came up, and distributed the remainder among the other three classes. The quadratic loss will depend on how you distributed it because of the sum of the p_j^2 that occurs in the expression given earlier for the quadratic loss function. The loss will be smallest if the 60% was distributed evenly among the three classes: an uneven distribution will increase the sum of the squares. The informational loss function, on the other hand, depends solely on the probability assigned to the class that actually occurred. If you're gambling on a particular event coming up, and it does, who cares about potential winnings from other events?

If you assign a very small probability to the class that actually occurs, the information loss function will penalize you massively. The maximum penalty, for a zero probability, is infinite. The quadratic loss function, on the other hand, is milder, being bounded by

$$1 + \sum_j p_j^2,$$

which can never exceed 2.

Finally, proponents of the informational loss function point to a general theory of performance assessment in learning called the *minimum description length (MDL) principle*. They argue that the size of the structures that a scheme learns can be measured in bits of information, and if the same units are used to measure the loss, the two can be combined in useful and powerful ways. We return to this in Section 5.10.

5.8 COUNTING THE COST

The evaluations that have been discussed so far do not take into account the cost of making wrong decisions, wrong classifications. Optimizing classification rate without considering the cost of the errors often leads to strange results. In one case, machine learning was being used to determine the exact day that each cow in a dairy herd was in estrus, or "in heat." Cows were identified by electronic ear tags, and various attributes were used such as milk volume and chemical composition (recorded automatically by a high-tech milking machine), and milking order—for cows are regular beasts and generally arrive in the milking shed in the same order, except in unusual circumstances such as estrus. In a modern dairy operation it's important to know when a cow is ready: animals are fertilized by artificial insemination and missing a cycle will delay calving unnecessarily, causing complications down the line. In early experiments, machine learning schemes stubbornly predicted that each cow was *never* in estrus. Like humans, cows have a menstrual cycle of approximately 30 days, so this "null" rule is correct about 97% of the time—an impressive degree of accuracy in any agricultural domain! What was wanted, of course, were rules that predicted the "in estrus" situation more accurately than the "not in estrus" one: the costs of the two kinds of error were different. Evaluation by classification accuracy tacitly assumes equal error costs.

Other examples where errors cost different amounts include loan decisions: the cost of lending to a defaulter is far greater than the lost-business cost of refusing a loan to a nondefaulter. And oil-slick detection: the cost of failing to detect an environment-threatening real slick is far greater than the cost of a false alarm. And load forecasting: the cost of gearing up electricity generators for a storm that doesn't hit is far less than the cost of being caught completely unprepared. And diagnosis: the cost of misidentifying problems with a machine that turns out to be free of faults is less than the cost of overlooking problems with one that is about to fail. And promotional mailing: the cost of sending junk mail to a household that doesn't respond is far less than the lost-business cost of not sending it to a household that would have responded. Why—these are all the examples of Chapter 1, What's it all about?! In truth, you'd be hard pressed to find an application in which the costs of different kinds of error were the same.

In the two-class case with classes *yes* and *no*, lend or not lend, mark a suspicious patch as an oil-slick or not, and so on, a single prediction has the four different possible outcomes shown in Table 5.3. The *true positives* (TP) and *true negatives* (TN) are correct classifications. A *false positive* (FP) is when the outcome is incorrectly predicted as *yes* (or positive) when it is actually *no* (negative). A *false negative* (FN) is when the outcome is incorrectly predicted as negative when it is actually positive. The *TP rate* is TP divided by the total number of positives, which is TP + FN; the *FP rate* is FP divided by the total number of

Table 5.3 Different Outcomes of a Two-Class Prediction

		Predicted Class	
		Yes	No
Actual class	Yes	True positive	False negative
	No	False positive	True negative

negatives, FP + TN. The overall success rate is the number of correct classifications divided by the total number of classifications:

$$\frac{TP + TN}{TP + TN + FP + FN}.$$

Finally, the error rate is one minus this.

In a multiclass prediction, the result on a test set is often displayed as a two-dimensional *confusion matrix* with a row and column for each class. Each matrix element shows the number of test examples for which the actual class is the row and the predicted class is the column. Good results correspond to large numbers down the main diagonal and small, ideally zero, off-diagonal elements. Table 5.4A shows a numeric example with three classes. In this case the test set has 200 instances (the sum of the nine numbers in the matrix), and 88 + 40 + 12 = 140 of them are predicted correctly, so the success rate is 70%.

But is this a fair measure of overall success? How many agreements would you expect *by chance*? This predictor predicts a total of 120 *a*'s, 60 *b*'s, and 20 *c*'s; What if you had a random predictor that predicted the same total numbers of the three classes? The answer is shown in Table 5.4B. Its first row divides the 100 *a*'s in the test set into these overall proportions, and the second and third rows do the same thing for the other two classes. Of course, the row and column totals for this matrix are the same as before—the number of instances hasn't changed, and we have ensured that the random predictor predicts the same number of *a*'s, *b*'s and *c*'s as the actual predictor.

This random predictor gets 60 + 18 + 4 = 82 instances correct. A measure called the *Kappa statistic* takes this expected figure into account by deducting it from the predictor's successes and expressing the result as a proportion of the total for a perfect predictor, to yield 140 − 82 = 58 extra successes out of a possible total of 200 − 82 = 118, or 49.2%. The maximum value of Kappa is 100%, and the expected value for a random predictor with the same column totals is zero. In summary, the Kappa statistic is used to measure the agreement between predicted and observed categorizations of a dataset, while correcting for agreement that occurs by chance. However, like the plain success rate, it does not take costs into account.

Table 5.4 Different Outcomes of a Three-Class Prediction: (A) Actual; (B) Expected

(A) Actual class		Predicted Class				(B) Actual Class		Predicted Class			
		a	*b*	*c*	*total*			*a*	*b*	*c*	*total*
	a	88	10	2	*100*		*a*	60	30	10	*100*
	b	14	40	6	*60*		*b*	36	18	6	*60*
	c	18	10	12	*40*		*c*	24	12	4	*40*
	total	*120*	*60*	*20*			*total*	*120*	*60*	*20*	

Table 5.5 Default Cost Matrixes: (A) Two-Class Case; (B) Three-Class Case

(A)		Predicted Class			(B)		Predicted Class		
		Yes	No				a	b	c
Actual class	Yes	0	1		Actual class	a	0	1	1
	No	1	0			b	1	0	1
						c	1	1	0

COST-SENSITIVE CLASSIFICATION

If the costs are known, they can be incorporated into a financial analysis of the decision-making process. In the two-class case, in which the confusion matrix is like that of Table 5.3, the two kinds of error—FPs and FNs—will have different costs; likewise, the two types of correct classification may have different benefits. In the two-class case, costs can be summarized in the form of a 2×2 matrix in which the diagonal elements represent the two types of correct classification and the off-diagonal elements represent the two types of error. In the multiclass case this generalizes to a square matrix whose size is the number of classes, and again the diagonal elements represent the cost of correct classification. Table 5.5A and 5.5B shows default cost matrixes for the two- and three-class cases whose values simply give the number of errors: misclassification costs are all 1.

Taking the cost matrix into account replaces the success rate by the average cost (or, thinking more positively, profit) per decision. Although we will not do so here, a complete financial analysis of the decision-making process might also take into account the cost of using the machine-learning tool—including the cost of gathering the training data—and the cost of using the model, or decision structure, that it produces—including the cost of determining the attributes for the test instances. If all costs are known, and the projected number of the four different outcomes in the cost matrix can be estimated—say, using cross-validation—it is straightforward to perform this kind of financial analysis.

Given a cost matrix, you can calculate the cost of a particular learned model on a given test set just by summing the relevant elements of the cost matrix for the model's prediction for each test instance. Here, the costs are ignored when making predictions, but taken into account when evaluating them.

If the model outputs the probability associated with each prediction, it can be adjusted to minimize the expected cost of the predictions. Given a set of predicted probabilities for each outcome on a certain test instance, one normally selects the most likely outcome. Instead, the model could predict the class with the smallest expected misclassification cost. For example, suppose in a three-class situation the model assigns the classes a, b, and c to a test instance with probabilities p_a, p_b, and p_c, and the cost matrix is that in Table 5.5B. If it predicts a, the expected cost of the prediction is obtained by multiplying the first column of the matrix,

[0,1,1], by the probability vector, $[p_a, p_b, p_c]$, yielding $p_b + p_c$, or $1 - p_a$ because the three probabilities sum to 1. Similarly, the costs for predicting the other two classes are $1 - p_b$ and $1 - p_c$. For this cost matrix, choosing the prediction with the lowest expected cost is the same as choosing the one with the greatest probability. For a different cost matrix it might be different.

We have assumed that the learning scheme outputs probabilities, as Naïve Bayes does. Even if they do not normally output probabilities, most classifiers can easily be adapted to compute them. In a decision tree, e.g., the probability distribution for a test instance is just the distribution of classes at the corresponding leaf.

COST-SENSITIVE LEARNING

We have seen how a classifier, built without taking costs into consideration, can be used to make predictions that are sensitive to the cost matrix. In this case, costs are ignored at training time but used at prediction time. An alternative is to do just the opposite: take the cost matrix into account during the training process and ignore costs at prediction time. In principle, better performance might be obtained if the classifier were tailored by the learning algorithm to the cost matrix.

In the two-class situation, there is a simple and general way to make any learning scheme cost sensitive. The idea is to generate training data with a different proportion of *yes* and *no* instances. Suppose you artificially increase the number of *no* instances by a factor of 10 and use the resulting dataset for training. If the learning scheme is striving to minimize the number of errors, it will come up with a decision structure that is biased toward avoiding errors on the *no* instances, because such errors are effectively penalized 10-fold. If data with the original proportion of *no* instances is used for testing, fewer errors will be made on these than on *yes* instances—i.e., there will be fewer FPs than FNs—because FPs have been weighted 10 times more heavily than FNs. Varying the proportion of instances in the training set is a general technique for building cost-sensitive classifiers.

One way to vary the proportion of training instances is to duplicate instances in the dataset. However, many learning schemes allow instances to be weighted. (As we mentioned in Section 3.3, this is a common technique for handling missing values.) Instance weights are normally initialized to one. To build cost-sensitive classifiers the weights can be initialized to the relative cost of the two kinds of error, FPs, and FNs.

LIFT CHARTS

In practice, costs are rarely known with any degree of accuracy, and people will want to ponder various different scenarios. Imagine you're in the direct mailing business and are contemplating a mass mail-out of a promotional offer to 1,000,000 households—most of whom won't respond, of course. Let us say that, based on previous experience, the proportion who normally respond is known to be 0.1% (1000 respondents). Suppose a data mining tool is available that, based on known information about the households, identifies a subset of 100,000 for which the response rate is 0.4% (400 respondents). It may well pay off to restrict the mail-out to these 100,000 households—that depends on the mailing cost compared with the return gained for each response to the offer. In marketing terminology, the increase in response rate, a factor of four in this case, is known as the *lift* factor yielded by the learning tool. If you knew the costs, you could determine the payoff implied by a particular lift factor.

But you probably want to evaluate other possibilities too. The same data mining scheme, with different parameter settings, may be able to identify 400,000 households for which the response rate will be 0.2% (800 respondents), corresponding to a lift factor of two. Again, whether this would be a more profitable target for the mail-out can be calculated from the costs involved. It may be necessary to factor in the cost of creating and using the model—including collecting the information that is required to come up with the attribute values. After all, if developing the model is very expensive, a mass mailing may be more cost effective than a targeted one.

Given a learning scheme that outputs probabilities for the predicted class of each member of the set of test instances (as Naïve Bayes does), your job is to find subsets of test instances that have a high proportion of positive instances, higher than in the test set as a whole. To do this, the instances should be sorted in descending order of predicted probability of *yes*. Then, to find a sample of a given size with the greatest possible proportion of positive instances, just read the requisite number of instances off the list, starting at the top. If each test instance's class is known, you can calculate the lift factor by simply counting the number of positive instances that the sample includes, dividing by the sample size to obtain a success proportion and dividing by the success proportion for the complete test set to determine the lift factor.

Table 5.6 shows an example, for a small dataset with 120 instances, of which 60 are *yes* responses—an overall success proportion of 50%. The instances have

Table 5.6 Data for a Lift Chart

Rank	Predicted	Actual	Rank	Predicted	Actual Class
1	0.95	Yes	11	0.77	No
2	0.93	Yes	12	0.76	Yes
3	0.93	No	13	0.73	Yes
4	0.88	Yes	14	0.65	No
5	0.86	Yes	15	0.63	Yes
6	0.85	Yes	16	0.58	No
7	0.82	Yes	17	0.56	Yes
8	0.80	Yes	18	0.49	No
9	0.80	No	19	0.48	Yes
10	0.79	Yes	...	...	...

been sorted in descending probability order according to the predicted probability of a *yes* response. The first instance is the one that the learning scheme thinks is most likely to be positive, the second is the next most likely, and so on. The numeric values of the probabilities are unimportant: rank is the only thing that matters. With each rank is given the actual class of the instance. Thus the learning scheme was right about items 1 and 2—they are indeed positives—but wrong about item 3, which turned out to be a negative. Now, if you were seeking the most promising sample of size 10 but only knew the predicted probabilities and not the actual classes, your best bet would be the top ten ranking instances. Eight of these are positive, so the success proportion for this sample is 80%, corresponding to a lift factor of about 2.4.

If you knew the different costs involved, you could work them out for each sample size and choose the most profitable. But a graphical depiction of the various possibilities will often be far more revealing than presenting a single "optimal" decision. Repeating the operation for different-sized samples allows you to plot a lift chart like that of Fig. 5.1. The horizontal axis shows the sample size as a proportion of the total possible mail-out. The vertical axis shows the number of responses obtained. The lower left and upper right points correspond to no mail-out at all, with a response of 0, and a full mail-out, with a response of 1000. The diagonal line gives the expected result for different-sized random samples. But we do not choose random samples, we choose those instances that, according to the data mining tool, are most likely to generate a positive response. These correspond to the upper line, which is derived by summing the actual responses over the corresponding percentage of the instance list sorted in probability order. The two particular scenarios described previously are marked: a 10% mail-out that yields 400 respondents and a 40% one that yields 800.

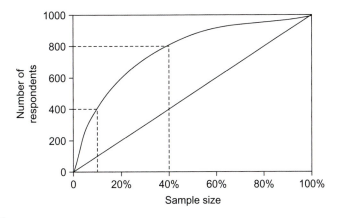

FIGURE 5.1

A hypothetical lift chart.

Where you'd like to be in a lift chart is near the upper left-hand corner: at the very best, 1000 responses from a mail-out of just 1000, where you send only to those households that will respond and are rewarded with a 100% success rate. Any selection procedure worthy of the name will keep you above the diagonal—otherwise, you'd be seeing a response that was worse than for random sampling. So the operating part of the diagram is the upper triangle, and the farther to the northwest the better.

Fig. 5.2A shows a visualization that allows various cost scenarios to be explored in an interactive fashion (called the "cost/benefit analyzer," it forms part of the Weka workbench described in Appendix B). Here it is displaying results for predictions generated by the Naïve Bayes classifier on a real-world direct-mail dataset. In this example, 47,706 instances were used for training and a further 47,706 for testing. The test instances were ranked according to the predicted probability of a response to the mail-out. The graphs show a lift chart on the left and the total cost (or benefit), plotted against sample size, on the right. At the lower left is a confusion matrix; at the lower right a cost matrix. Cost or benefit values associated with incorrect or correct classifications can be entered into the matrix and affect the shape of the curve above. The horizontal slider in the middle allows users to vary the percentage of the population that is selected from the ranked list. Alternatively, one can determine the sample size by adjusting the recall level (the proportion of positives to be included in the sample) or by adjusting a threshold on the probability of the positive class, which here corresponds to a response to the mail-out. When the slider is moved, a large cross shows the corresponding point on both graphs. The total cost or benefit associated with the selected sample size is shown at the lower right, along with the expected response to a random mail-out of the same size.

In the cost matrix in Fig. 5.2A, a cost of $0.50—the cost of mailing—has been associated with nonrespondents and a benefit of $15.00 with respondents (after deducting the mailing cost). Under these conditions, and using the Naïve Bayes classifier, there it is no subset from the ranked list of prospects that yields a greater profit than mailing to the entire population. However, a slightly higher mailing cost changes the situation dramatically, and Fig. 5.2B shows what happens when it is increased to $0.80. Assuming the same profit of $15.00 per respondent, a maximum profit of $4,560.60 is achieved by mailing to the top 46.7% of the population. In this situation, a random sample of the same size achieves a loss of $99.59.

ROC CURVES

Lift charts are a valuable tool, widely used in marketing. They are closely related to a graphical technique for evaluating data mining schemes known as *ROC curves*, which are used in just the same situation, where the learner is trying to select samples of test instances that have a high proportion of positives. The acronym stands for *receiver operating characteristic* (ROC), a term used in signal

(A)

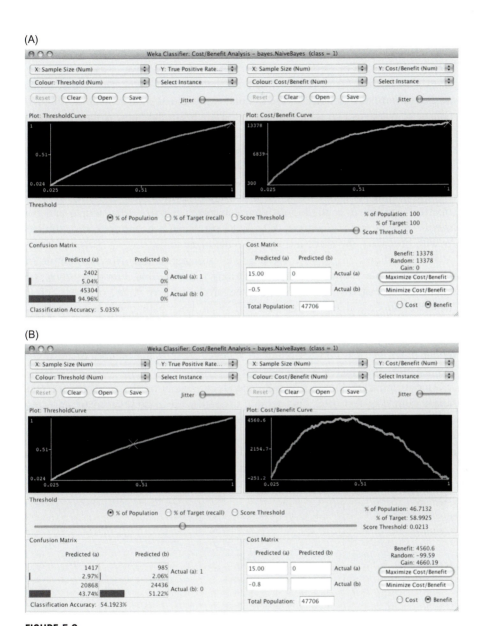

(B)

FIGURE 5.2

Analyzing the expected benefit of a mailing campaign when the cost of mailing is
(A) $0.50 and (B) $0.80.

detection to characterize the tradeoff between hit rate and false alarm rate over a noisy channel. ROC curves depict the performance of a classifier without regard to class distribution or error costs. They plot the "true positive" rate on the vertical axis against the "false positive" rate on the horizontal axis. The former is the number of positives included in the sample, expressed as a percentage of the total number of positives (TP Rate = $100 \times TP/(TP + FN)$); the latter is the number of negatives included in the sample, expressed as a percentage of the total number of negatives (FP Rate = $100 \times FP/(FP + TN)$). The vertical axis is the same as the lift chart's except that it is expressed as a percentage. The horizontal axis is slightly different—number of negatives rather than sample size. However, in direct marketing situations where the proportion of positives is very small anyway (like 0.1%), there is negligible difference between the size of a sample and the number of negatives it contains, so the ROC curve and lift chart look very similar. As with lift charts, the northwest corner is the place to be.

Fig. 5.3 shows an example ROC curve—the jagged line—for the sample of test data in Table 5.6. You can follow it along with the table. From the origin: go up two (two positives), along one (one negative), up five (five positives), along (negative), up one, along one, up two, and so on. Each point corresponds to drawing a line at a certain position on the ranked list, counting the *yes*'s and *no*'s above it, and plotting them vertically and horizontally, respectively. As you go farther down the list, corresponding to a larger sample, the number of positives and negatives both increase.

The jagged ROC line in Fig. 5.3 depends intimately on the details of the particular sample of test data. This sample dependence can be reduced by applying cross-validation. For each different number of *no*'s—i.e., each position along the horizontal axis—take just enough of the highest-ranked instances to include that number of *no*'s, and count the number of *yes*'s they contain. Finally, average that

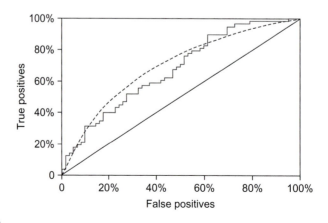

FIGURE 5.3

A sample ROC curve.

number over different folds of the cross-validation. The result is a smooth curve like that in Fig. 5.3—although in reality such curves do not generally look quite so smooth.

This is just one way of using cross-validation to generate ROC curves. A simpler approach is to collect the predicted probabilities for all the various test sets (of which there are 10 in a 10-fold cross-validation), along with the true class labels of the corresponding instances, and generate a single ranked list based on this data. This assumes that the probability estimates from the classifiers built from the different training sets are all based on equally sized random samples of the data. It is not clear which method is preferable. However, the latter method is easier to implement.

If the learning scheme does not allow the instances to be ordered, you can first make it cost-sensitive as described earlier. For each fold of a 10-fold cross-validation, weigh the instances for a selection of different cost ratios, train the scheme on each weighted set, count the TPs and FPs in the test set, and plot the resulting point on the ROC axes. (It doesn't matter whether the test set is weighted or not because the axes in the ROC diagram are expressed as the percentage of true and FPs.)

It is instructive to look at ROC curves obtained using different learning schemes. For example, in Fig. 5.4, method A excels if a small, focused sample is sought; i.e., if you are working toward the left-hand side of the graph. Clearly, if you aim to cover just 40% of the TPs you should choose method A, which gives a FP rate of around 5%, rather than method B, which gives more than 20% FPs. But method B excels if you are planning a large sample: if you are covering 80% of the TPs, B will give a FP rate of 60% as compared with method A's 80%. The shaded area is called the *convex hull* of the two curves, and you should always operate at a point that lies on the upper boundary of the convex hull.

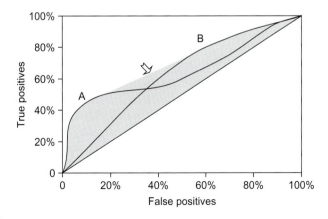

FIGURE 5.4

ROC curves for two learning schemes.

What about the region in the middle where neither method A nor method B lies on the convex hull? It is a remarkable fact that you can get anywhere in the shaded region by combining methods A and B and using them at random with appropriate probabilities. To see this, choose a particular probability cutoff for method A that gives true and FP rates of t_A and f_A, respectively, and another cutoff for method B that gives t_B and f_B. If you use these two schemes at random with probability p and q, where $p + q = 1$, then you will get true and FP rates of $p \cdot t_A + q \cdot t_B$ and $p \cdot f_A + q \cdot f_B$. This represents a point lying on the straight line joining the points (t_A, f_A) and (t_B, f_B), and by varying p and q you can trace out the whole line between these two points. By this device, the entire shaded region can be reached. Only if a particular scheme generates a point that lies on the convex hull should it be used alone: otherwise, it would always be better to use a combination of classifiers corresponding to a point that lies on the convex hull.

RECALL-PRECISION CURVES

People have grappled with the fundamental tradeoff illustrated by lift charts and ROC curves in a wide variety of domains. Information retrieval is a good example. Given a query, a Web search engine produces a list of hits that represent documents supposedly relevant to the query. Compare one system that locates 100 documents, 40 of which are relevant, with another that locates 400 documents, 80 of which are relevant. Which is better? The answer should now be obvious: it depends on the relative cost of FPs, documents returned that aren't relevant, and FNs, documents that are relevant but aren't returned. Information retrieval researchers define parameters called *recall* and *precision*:

$$\text{Recall} = \frac{\text{Number of documents retrieved that are relevant}}{\text{Total number of documents that are relevant}}$$

$$\text{Precision} = \frac{\text{Number of documents retrieved that are relevant}}{\text{Total number of documents that are retrieved}}.$$

For example, if the list of *yes*'s and *no*'s in Table 5.6 represented a ranked list of retrieved documents and whether they were relevant or not, and the entire collection contained a total of 40 relevant documents, then "recall at 10" would refer to recall for the top ten documents, i.e., $8/40 = 20\%$; while "precision at 10" would be $8/10 = 80\%$. Information retrieval experts use *recall–precision curves* that plot one against the other, for different numbers of retrieved documents, in just the same way as ROC curves and lift charts—except that because the axes are different, the curves are hyperbolic in shape and the desired operating point is toward the upper right.

REMARKS

Table 5.7 summarizes the three different ways we have met of evaluating the same basic tradeoff: TP, FP, TN, and FN are the number of TPs, FPs, TNs, and

Table 5.7 Different Measures Used to Evaluate the False Positive Versus False Negative Tradeoff

	Domain	Plot	Axes
Lift chart	Marketing	TP vs subset size	TP number of true positives subset size $\dfrac{TP + FP}{TP + FP + TN + FN} \times 100\%$
ROC curve	Communications	TP rate vs FP rate	TP rate $tp = \dfrac{TP}{TP + FN} \times 100\%$ FP rate $fp = \dfrac{FP}{FP + TN} \times 100\%$
Recall-precision curve	Information retrieval	Recall vs precision	Recall same as TP rate tp above precision $\dfrac{TP}{TP + FP} \times 100\%$

FNs, respectively. You want to choose a set of instances with a high proportion of *yes* instances and a high coverage of the *yes* instances: you can increase the proportion by (conservatively) using a smaller coverage, or (liberally) increase the coverage at the expense of the proportion. Different techniques give different tradeoffs, and can be plotted as different lines on any of these graphical charts.

People also seek single measures that characterize performance. Two that are used in information retrieval are *3-point average recall*, which gives the average precision obtained at recall values of 20%, 50%, and 80%, and *11-point average recall*, which gives the average precision obtained at recall values of 0%, 10%, 20%, 30%, 40%, 50%, 60%, 70%, 80%, 90%, and 100%. Also used in information retrieval is the *F-measure*, which is

$$\frac{2 \times \text{recall} \times \text{precision}}{\text{recall} + \text{precision}} = \frac{2 \cdot TP}{2 \cdot TP + FP + FN}.$$

Different terms are used in different domains. Medics, e.g., talk about the *sensitivity* and *specificity* of diagnostic tests. Sensitivity refers to the proportion of people with disease who have a positive test result, i.e., tp. Specificity refers to the proportion of people without disease who have a negative test result, which is $1 - fp$. Sometimes the product of these is used as an overall measure:

$$\text{sensitivity} \times \text{specificity} = tp(1 - fp) = \frac{TP \cdot TN}{(TP + FN) \cdot (FP + TN)}$$

Finally, of course, there is our old friend the success rate:

$$\frac{TP + TN}{TP + FP + TN + FN}.$$

To summarize ROC curves in a single quantity, people use the area under the curve because, roughly speaking, the larger the area the better the model. The area also has a nice interpretation as the probability that the classifier ranks a randomly chosen positive instance above a randomly chosen negative one. Although such measures may be useful if costs and class distributions are unknown and one scheme must be chosen to handle all situations, no single number is able to capture the tradeoff. That can only be done by two-dimensional depictions such as lift charts, ROC curves, and recall-precision diagrams.

Several methods are commonly employed for computing the area under the ROC curve. One, corresponding to a geometric interpretation, is to approximate it by fitting several trapezoids under the curve and summing up their area. Another is to compute the probability that the classifier ranks a randomly chosen positive instance above a randomly chosen negative one. This can be accomplished by calculating the Mann−Whitney U statistic, or, more specifically, the ρ statistic from the U statistic. This value is easily obtained from a list of test instances sorted in descending order of predicted probability of the positive class. For each positive instance, count how many negative ones are ranked below it (increase the count by $\frac{1}{2}$ if positive and negative instances tie in rank). The U statistic is simply the total of these counts. The ρ statistic is obtained by dividing U by the product of the number of positive and negative instances in the test set—in other words, the U value that would result if all positive instances were ranked above the negative ones.

The area under the precision-recall curve is an alternative summary statistic that is preferred by some practitioners, particularly in the information retrieval area.

COST CURVES

ROC curves and their relatives are very useful for exploring the tradeoffs among different classifiers over a range of scenarios. However, they are not ideal for evaluating machine learning models in situations with known error costs. For example, it is not easy to read off the expected cost of a classifier for a fixed cost matrix and class distribution. Neither can you easily determine the ranges of applicability of different classifiers. For example, from the crossover point between the two ROC curves in Fig. 5.4 it is hard to tell for what cost and class distributions classifier A outperforms classifier B.

Cost curves are a different kind of display on which a single classifier corresponds to a straight line that shows how the performance varies as the class distribution changes. Again, they work best in the two-class case, although you can always make a multiclass problem into a two-class one by singling out one class and evaluating it against the remaining ones.

Fig. 5.5A plots the expected error against the probability of one of the classes. You could imagine adjusting this probability by resampling the test set in a non-uniform way. We denote the two classes by + and −. The diagonals show the performance of two extreme classifiers: one always predicts +, giving an expected error of one if the dataset contains no + instances and zero if all its instances are +; the other always predicts −, giving the opposite performance. The dashed horizontal line shows the performance of the classifier that is always wrong, and the x-axis itself represents the classifier that is always correct. In practice, of course, neither of these is realizable. Good classifiers have low error rates, so where you want to be is as close to the bottom of the diagram as possible.

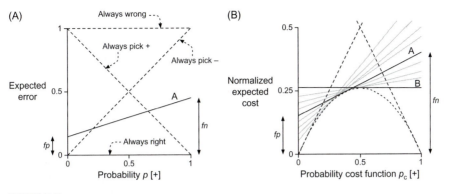

FIGURE 5.5

Effect of varying the probability threshold: (A) error curve; (B) cost curve.

The line marked A represents the error rate of a particular classifier. If you calculate its performance on a certain test set, its FP rate *fp* is its expected error on a subsample of the test set that contains only negative examples $(P(+) = 0)$, and its FN rate *fn* is the error on a subsample that contains only positive examples $(P(+) = 1)$. These are the values of the intercepts at the left and right, respectively. You can see immediately from the plot that if $P(+)$ is smaller than about 0.2, predictor A is outperformed by the extreme classifier that always predicts $-$, while if it is larger than about 0.65, the other extreme classifier is better.

So far we have not taken costs into account, or rather we have used the default cost matrix in which all errors cost the same. Cost curves, which do take cost into account, look very similar—very similar indeed—but the axes are different. Fig. 5.5B shows a cost curve for the same classifier A (note that the vertical scale has been enlarged, for convenience, and ignore the gray lines for now). It plots the expected cost of using A against the *probability cost function*, which is a distorted version of $P(+)$ that retains the same extremes: zero when $P(+) = 0$ and one when $P(+) = 1$. Denote by $C[+|-]$ the cost of predicting $+$ when the instance is actually $-$, and the reverse by $C[-|+]$. Then the axes of Fig. 5.5B are

$$\text{Normalized expected cost} = fn \times P_C(+) + fp \times (1 - P_C(+))$$

$$\text{Probability cost function } P_C(+) = \frac{P(+)C[-|+]}{P(+)C[-|+] + P(-)C[+|-]}.$$

We are assuming here that correct predictions have no cost: $C[+|+] = C[-|-] = 0$. If that is not the case the formulas are a little more complex.

The maximum value that the normalized expected cost can have is 1—i.e., why it is "normalized." One nice thing about cost curves is that the extreme cost values at the left and right sides of the graph are *fp* and *fn*, just as they are for the error curve, so you can draw the cost curve for any classifier very easily.

Fig. 5.5B also shows classifier B, whose expected cost remains the same across the range—i.e., its FP and FN rates are equal. As you can see, it outperforms classifier A if the probability cost function exceeds about 0.45, and knowing the costs we could easily work out what this corresponds to in terms of class distribution. In situations that involve different class distributions, cost curves make it easy to tell when one classifier will outperform another.

In what circumstances might this be useful? To return to our example of predicting when cows will be in estrus, their 30-day cycle, or 1/30 prior probability, is unlikely to vary greatly (barring a genetic cataclysm!). But a particular herd may have different proportions of cows that are likely to reach estrus in any given week, perhaps synchronized with—Who knows?—the phase of the moon. Then, different classifiers would be appropriate at different times. In the oil spill example, different batches of data may have different spill probabilities. In these situations cost curves can help to show which classifier to use when.

Each point on a lift chart, ROC curve, or recall-precision curve represents a classifier, typically obtained by using different threshold values for a method such as Naïve Bayes. Cost curves represent each classifier by a straight line, and a suite of classifiers will sweep out a curved envelope whose lower limit shows how well that type of classifier can do if the parameter is well chosen. Fig. 5.5B indicates this with a few gray lines. If the process were continued, it would sweep out the dotted parabolic curve.

The operating region of classifier B ranges from a probability cost value of about 0.25 to a value of about 0.75. Outside this region, classifier B is outperformed by the trivial classifiers represented by dashed lines. Suppose we decide to use classifier B within this range and the appropriate trivial classifier below and above it. All points on the parabola are certainly better than this scheme. But how much better? It is hard to answer such questions from an ROC curve, but the cost curve makes them easy. The performance difference is negligible if the probability cost value is around 0.5, and below a value of about 0.2 and above 0.8 it is barely perceptible. The greatest difference occurs at probability cost values of 0.25 and 0.75 and is about 0.04, or 4% of the maximum possible cost figure.

5.9 EVALUATING NUMERIC PREDICTION

All the evaluation measures we have described pertain to classification rather than numeric prediction. The basic principles—using an independent test set rather than the training set for performance evaluation, the holdout method, cross-validation—apply equally well to numeric prediction. But the basic quality measure offered by the error rate is no longer appropriate: errors are not simply present or absent, they come in different sizes.

Several alternative measures, some of which are summarized in Table 5.8, can be used to evaluate the success of numeric prediction. The predicted values on the test instances are $p_1, p_2, \ldots, p_n$; the actual values are $a_1, a_2, \ldots, a_n$. Notice that p_i means something very different here to what it did in the last section: there

Table 5.8 Performance Measures for Numeric Prediction

Mean-squared error	$\dfrac{(p_1-a_1)^2 + \cdots + (p_n-a_n)^2}{n}$
Root mean-squared error	$\sqrt{\dfrac{(p_1-a_1)^2 + \cdots + (p_n-a_n)^2}{n}}$
Mean absolute error	$\dfrac{|p_1-a_1| + \cdots + |p_n - a_n|}{n}$
Relative squared error	$\dfrac{(p_1-a_1)^2 + \cdots + (p_n-a_n)^2}{(a_1-\bar{a})^2 + \cdots + (a_n-\bar{a})^2}$ (in this formula and the following two, $\bar{a}$ is the mean value over the training data)
Root relative squared error	$\sqrt{\dfrac{(p_1-a_1)^2 + \cdots + (p_n-a_n)^2}{(a_1-\bar{a})^2 + \cdots + (a_n-\bar{a})^2}}$
Relative absolute error	$\dfrac{|p_1-a_1| + \cdots + |p_n - a_n|}{|a_1 - \bar{a}| + \cdots + |a_n - \bar{a}|}$
Correlation coefficient	$\dfrac{S_{PA}}{\sqrt{S_P S_A}}$, where $S_{PA} = \dfrac{\sum_i(p_i - \bar{p})(a_i - \bar{a})}{n-1}$, $S_P = \dfrac{\sum_i(p_i - \bar{p})^2}{n-1}$, $S_A = \dfrac{\sum_i(a_i - \bar{a})^2}{n-1}$ (here, $\bar{a}$ is the mean value over the test data)

it was the probability that a particular prediction was in the ith class; here it refers to the numerical value of the prediction for the ith test instance.

Mean-squared error is the principal and most commonly used measure; sometimes the square root is taken to give it the same dimensions as the predicted value itself. Many mathematical techniques (such as linear regression, explained in chapter: Algorithms: the basic methods) use the mean-squared error because it tends to be the easiest measure to manipulate mathematically: it is, as mathematicians say, "well behaved." However, here we are considering it as a performance measure: all the performance measures are easy to calculate, so mean-squared error has no particular advantage. The question is, is it an appropriate measure for the task at hand?

Mean absolute error is an alternative: just average the magnitude of the individual errors without taking account of their sign. Mean-squared error tends to exaggerate the effect of outliers—instances whose prediction error is larger than the others—but absolute error does not have this effect: all sizes of error are treated evenly according to their magnitude.

Sometimes it is the *relative* rather than *absolute* error values that are of importance. For example, if a 10% error is equally important whether it is an error of 50 in a prediction of 500 or an error of 0.2 in a prediction of 2, then averages of absolute error will be meaningless: relative errors are appropriate. This effect would be taken into account by using the relative errors in the mean-squared error calculation or the mean absolute error calculation.

Relative squared error in Table 5.8 refers to something quite different. The error is made relative to what it would have been if a simple predictor had been used. The simple predictor in question is just the average of the actual values from the training data, denoted by $\bar{a}$. Thus relative squared error takes the total squared error and normalizes it by dividing by the total squared error of the default predictor. The root relative squared error is obtained in the obvious way.

The next error measure goes by the glorious name of *relative absolute error* and is just the total absolute error, with the same kind of normalization. In these three relative error measures, the errors are normalized by the error of the simple predictor that predicts average values.

The final measure in Table 5.8 is the *correlation coefficient*, which measures the statistical correlation between the a's and the p's. The correlation coefficient ranges from 1 for perfectly correlated results, through 0 when there is no correlation, to -1 when the results are perfectly correlated negatively. Of course, negative values should not occur for reasonable prediction methods. Correlation is slightly different from the other measures because it is scale independent in that, if you take a particular set of predictions, the error is unchanged if all the predictions are multiplied by a constant factor and the actual values are left unchanged. This factor appears in every term of S_{PA} in the numerator and in every term of S_P in the denominator, thus canceling out. (This is not true for the relative error figures, despite normalization: if you multiply all the predictions by a large constant, then the difference between the predicted and actual values will change dramatically, as will the percentage errors.) It is also different in that good performance leads to a large value of the correlation coefficient, whereas because the other methods measure error, good performance is indicated by small values.

Which of these measures is appropriate in any given situation is a matter that can only be determined by studying the application itself. What are we trying to minimize? What is the cost of different kinds of error? Often it is not easy to decide. The squared error measures and root squared error measures weigh large discrepancies much more heavily than small ones, whereas the absolute error measures do not. Taking the square root (root mean-squared error) just reduces the figure to have the same dimensionality as the quantity being predicted. The relative error figures try to compensate for the basic predictability or unpredictability of the output variable: if it tends to lie fairly close to its average value, then you expect prediction to be good and the relative figure compensates for this. Otherwise, if the error figure in one situation is far greater than in another situation, it may be because the quantity in the first situation is inherently more variable and therefore harder to predict, not because the predictor is any worse.

Fortunately, it turns out that in most practical situations the best numerical prediction method is still the best no matter which error measure is used. For example, Table 5.9 shows the result of four different numeric prediction techniques on a given dataset, measured using cross-validation. Method D is the best according to all five metrics: it has the smallest value for each error measure and the largest correlation coefficient. Method C is the second best by all five metrics. The performance of A and B is open to dispute: they have the same correlation coefficient, A is better than B according to mean-squared and relative squared

Table 5.9 Performance Measures for Four Numeric Prediction Models

	A	B	C	D
Root mean-squared error	67.8	91.7	63.3	57.4
Mean absolute error	41.3	38.5	33.4	29.2
Root relative squared error	42.2%	57.2%	39.4%	35.8%
Relative absolute error	43.1%	40.1%	34.8%	30.4%
Correlation coefficient	0.88	0.88	0.89	0.91

errors, and the reverse is true for absolute and relative absolute error. It is likely that the extra emphasis that the squaring operation gives to outliers accounts for the differences in this case.

When comparing two different learning schemes that involve numeric prediction, the methodology developed in Section 5.5 still applies. The only difference is that success rate is replaced by the appropriate performance measure (e.g., root mean-squared error) when performing the significance test.

5.10 THE MDL PRINCIPLE

What is learned by a machine learning scheme is a kind of "theory" of the domain from which the examples are drawn, a theory that is predictive in that it is capable of generating new facts about the domain—in other words, the class of unseen instances. Theory is rather a grandiose term: we are using it here only in the sense of a predictive model. Thus theories might comprise decision trees, or sets of rules—they don't have to be any more "theoretical" than that.

There is a long-standing tradition in science that, other things being equal, simple theories are preferable to complex ones. This is known as *Occam's Razor* after the medieval philosopher William of Occam (or Ockham). Occam's Razor shaves philosophical hairs off a theory. The idea is that the best scientific theory is the smallest one that explains all the facts. As Einstein is reputed to have said, "Everything should be made as simple as possible, but no simpler." Of course, quite a lot is hidden in the phrase "other things being equal," and it can be hard to assess objectively whether a particular theory really does "explain" all the facts on which it is based—that's what controversy in science is all about.

In our case, in machine learning, most theories make errors. And if what is learned is a theory, then the errors it makes are like *exceptions* to the theory. One way to ensure that other things *are* equal is to insist that the information embodied in the exceptions is included as part of the theory when its "simplicity" is judged.

Imagine an imperfect theory for which there are a few exceptions. Not all the data is explained by the theory, but most is. What we do is simply adjoin the exceptions to the theory, specifying them explicitly as exceptions. This new theory is larger: i.e., a price that, quite justifiably, has to be paid for its inability to explain all the data. However, it may be that the simplicity—Is it too much to call it *elegance*?—of the original theory is sufficient to outweigh the fact that it does not quite explain everything compared with a large, baroque theory that is more comprehensive and accurate.

For example, if Kepler's three laws of planetary motion did not at the time account for the known data quite so well as Copernicus's latest refinement of the Ptolemaic theory of epicycles, they had the advantage of being far less complex, and that would have justified any slight apparent inaccuracy. Kepler was well aware of the benefits of having a theory that was compact, despite the fact that his theory violated his own esthetic sense because it depended on "ovals" rather than pure circular motion. He expressed this in a forceful metaphor: "I have cleared the Augean stables of astronomy of cycles and spirals, and left behind me only a single cartload of dung."

The MDL principle takes the stance that the best theory for a body of data is one that minimizes the size of the theory plus the amount of information necessary to specify the exceptions relative to the theory—the smallest cartload of dung. In statistical estimation theory, this has been applied successfully to various parameter-fitting problems. It applies to machine learning as follows: given a set of instances, a learning scheme infers a theory—be it ever so simple; unworthy, perhaps, to be called a "theory"—from them. Using a metaphor of communication, imagine that the instances are to be transmitted through a noiseless channel. Any similarity that is detected among them can be exploited to give a more compact coding. According to the MDL principle, the best theory is the one that minimizes the number of bits required to communicate the theory, along with the labels of the examples from which it was made.

Now the connection with the informational loss function introduced in Section 5.7 should be starting to emerge. That function measures the error in terms of the number of bits required to transmit the instances' class labels, given the probabilistic predictions made by the theory. According to the MDL principle we need to add to this the "size" of the theory in bits, suitably encoded, to obtain an overall figure for complexity. However, the MDL principle refers to the information required to transmit the examples from which the theory was formed, i.e., the *training* instances—not a test set. The overfitting problem is avoided because a complex theory that overfits will be penalized relative to a simple one by virtue of the fact that it takes more bits to encode. At one extreme is a very complex, highly overfitted theory that makes no errors on the training set. At the other is a very simple theory—the null theory—which does not help at all when transmitting the training set. And in between are theories of intermediate complexity, which make probabilistic predictions that are imperfect and need to be corrected by transmitting some information about the training set. The MDL principle provides a means of comparing all these possibilities on an equal footing to see which is the best. We have found the Holy Grail: an evaluation scheme that works on the training set alone and does not need a separate test set. But the devil is in the details, as we will see.

Suppose a learning scheme comes up with a theory T, based on a training set E of examples, that requires a certain number of bits $L(T)$ to encode (L for *length*). We are only interested in predicting class labels correctly, so we assume that E stands for the collection of class labels in the training set. Given the theory, the training set itself can be encoded in a certain number of bits, $L(E|T)$. $L(E|T)$ is in fact given by the informational loss function summed over all members of the training set. Then the total description length of theory plus training set is

$$L(T) + L(E|T)$$

and the MDL principle recommends choosing the theory T that minimizes this sum.

There is a remarkable connection between the MDL principle and basic probability theory. Given a training set E, we seek the "most likely" theory T, i.e., the theory for which the a posteriori probability $P(T|E)$—the probability after the examples have been seen—is maximized. Bayes' rule of conditional probability, the very same rule that we encountered in Section 4.2, dictates that

$$P(T|E) = \frac{P(E|T)P(T)}{P(E)}.$$

Taking negative logarithms,

$$-\log P(T|E) = -\log P(E|T) - \log P(T) + \log P(E).$$

Maximizing the probability is the same as minimizing its negative logarithm. Now (as we saw in Section 5.7) the number of bits required to code something is just the negative logarithm of its probability. Furthermore, the final term, $\log P(E)$, depends solely on the training set and not on the learning method. Thus choosing the theory that maximizes the probability $P(T|E)$ is tantamount to choosing the theory that minimizes.

$$L(E|T) + L(T)$$

—in other words, the MDL principle!

This astonishing correspondence with the notion of maximizing the a posteriori probability of a theory after the training set has been taken into account gives credence to the MDL principle. But it also points out where the problems will sprout when the principle is applied in practice. The difficulty with applying Bayes' rule directly is in finding a suitable prior probability distribution $P(T)$ for the theory. In the MDL formulation, that translates into finding how to code the theory T into bits in the most efficient way. There are many ways of coding things, and they all depend on presuppositions that must be shared by encoder and decoder. If you know in advance that the theory is going to take a certain form, you can use that information to encode it more efficiently. How are you going to actually encode T? The devil is in the details.

Encoding E with respect to T to obtain $L(E|T)$ seems a little more straightforward: we have already met the informational loss function. But actually, when you encode one member of the training set after another, you are encoding a *sequence* rather than a *set*. It is not necessary to transmit the training set in any particular order, and it ought to be possible to use that fact to reduce the number of bits required. Often, this is simply approximated by subtracting log n! (where n is the number of elements in E), which is the number of bits needed to specify a particular permutation of the training set (and because this is the same for all theories, it doesn't actually affect the comparison between them). But one can imagine using the frequency of the individual errors to reduce the number of bits needed to code them. Of course, the more sophisticated the method that is used to code the errors, the less the need for a theory in the first place—so whether a theory is justified or not depends to some extent on how the errors are coded. The details, the details.

We end this section as we began, on a philosophical note. It is important to appreciate that Occam's Razor, the preference of simple theories over complex ones, has the status of a philosophical position or "axiom" rather than something that can be proven from first principles. While it may seem self-evident to us, this is a function of our education and the times we live in. A preference for simplicity is—or may be—culture specific rather than absolute.

The Greek philosopher Epicurus (who enjoyed good food and wine and supposedly advocated sensual pleasure—in moderation—as the highest good) expressed almost the opposite sentiment. His *principle of multiple explanations* advises "if more than one theory is consistent with the data, keep them all" on the basis that if several explanations are equally in agreement, it may be possible to achieve a higher degree of precision by using them together—and anyway, it would be unscientific to discard some arbitrarily. This brings to mind instance-based learning, in which all the evidence is retained to provide robust predictions, and resonates strongly with decision combination methods such as bagging and boosting (described in Chapter 12: Ensemble learning) that actually do gain predictive power by using multiple explanations together.

5.11 APPLYING THE MDL PRINCIPLE TO CLUSTERING

One of the nice things about the MDL principle is that unlike other evaluation criteria, it can be applied under widely different circumstances. Although in some sense equivalent to Bayes' rule in that, as we have seen, devising a coding scheme for theories is tantamount to assigning them a prior probability distribution, schemes for coding are somehow far more tangible and easier to think about in concrete terms than intuitive prior probabilities. To illustrate this we will briefly describe—without entering into coding details—how you might go about applying the MDL principle to clustering.

Clustering seems intrinsically difficult to evaluate. Whereas classification or association learning has an objective criterion of success—predictions made on test cases are either right or wrong—this is not so with clustering. It seems that the only realistic evaluation is whether the result of learning—the clustering—proves useful in the application context. (It is worth pointing out that really this is the case for all types of learning, not just clustering.)

Despite this, clustering can be evaluated from a description length perspective. Suppose a cluster-learning technique divides the training set E into k clusters. If these clusters are natural ones, it should be possible to use them to encode E more efficiently. The best clustering will support the most efficient encoding.

One way of encoding the instances in E with respect to a given clustering is to start by encoding the cluster centers—the average value of each attribute over all instances in the cluster. Then, for each instance in E, transmit which cluster it belongs to (in $\log_2 k$ bits) followed by its attribute values with respect to the cluster center—perhaps as the numeric difference of each attribute value from the center. Couched as it is in terms of averages and differences, this description presupposes numeric attributes and raises thorny questions of how to code numbers efficiently. Nominal attributes can be handled in a similar manner: for each cluster there is a probability distribution for the attribute values, and the distributions are different for different clusters. The coding issue becomes more straightforward: attribute values are coded with respect to the relevant probability distribution, a standard operation in data compression.

If the data exhibits extremely strong clustering, this technique will result in a smaller description length than simply transmitting the elements of E without any clusters. However, if the clustering effect is not so strong, it will likely increase rather than decrease the description length. The overhead of transmitting cluster-specific distributions for attribute values will more than offset the advantage gained by encoding each training instance relative to the cluster it lies in. This is where more sophisticated coding techniques come in. Once the cluster centers have been communicated, it is possible to transmit cluster-specific probability distributions adaptively, in tandem with the relevant instances: the instances themselves help to define the probability distributions, and the probability distributions help to define the instances. We will not venture further into coding techniques here. The point is that the MDL formulation, properly applied, may be flexible enough to support the evaluation of clustering. But actually doing it satisfactorily in practice is not easy.

5.12 USING A VALIDATION SET FOR MODEL SELECTION

The MDL principle is an example of a so-called model selection criterion, which can be used to determine the appropriate complexity of a model for a given dataset. Adding unnecessary structure to a model can result in overfitting and a consequent drop in predictive performance. Conversely, insufficient model complexity implies that the information in the training data cannot be completely exploited: the model will underfit. Model selection criteria such as the MDL principle can be used as tools for guessing the right complexity.

A classic model selection problem in statistics is to determine, for a given dataset, what subset of attributes to use in a linear regression model for the data. (Even a simple technique such as linear regression can overfit!) However, the problem is ubiquitous in machine learning because learning algorithms inevitably need to choose how much structure to add to a model. Examples include pruning subtrees in a decision tree, determining the number of instances to retain in a nearest-neighbor classifier, and picking the number and size of the layers in an artificial neural network.

Many model selection strategies similar to the MDL principle exist, based on various theoretical approaches and corresponding underlying assumptions. They all follow the same strategy: the predictive performance on the training data is balanced with the complexity of the model. The aim is to find a sweet spot. Whether they succeed depends on whether the underlying assumptions are appropriate for the problem at hand. This is difficult to know in practice. The good news is that there is a simple alternative approach to guessing what model complexity will maximize predictive performance on new data: we can simply use a validation set for model selection, just as we did in Section 5.5 for tuning hyperparameters. Alternatively, if the dataset is small, we can use cross-validation, or maybe the bootstrap.

5.13 FURTHER READING AND BIBLIOGRAPHIC NOTES

The statistical basis of confidence tests is well covered in most statistics texts, which also gives tables of the normal distribution and Student's distribution. (We use an excellent course text by Wild and Seber (1995), which we recommend very strongly if you can get hold of it). "Student" is the nom de plume of a statistician called William Gosset, who obtained a post as a chemist in the Guinness brewery in Dublin, Ireland, in 1899 and invented the t-test to handle small samples for quality control in brewing. The corrected resampled t-test was proposed by Nadeau and Bengio (2003). Cross-validation is a standard statistical technique, and its application in machine learning has been extensively investigated and compared with the bootstrap by Kohavi (1995a). The bootstrap technique itself is thoroughly covered by Efron and Tibshirani (1993).

The Kappa statistic was introduced by Cohen (1960). Ting (2002) has investigated a heuristic way of generalizing to the multiclass case the algorithm given in Section 5.8 to make two-class learning schemes cost sensitive. Lift charts are described by Berry and Linoff (1997). The use of ROC analysis in signal detection theory is covered by Egan (1975); this work has been extended for visualizing and analyzing the behavior of diagnostic systems (Swets, 1988) and is also used in medicine (Beck & Schultz, 1986). Provost and Fawcett (1997) brought the idea of ROC analysis to the attention of the machine learning and data mining community. Witten, Moffat, and Bell (1999b) explain the use of recall and precision in information retrieval systems; the *F*-measure is described by van Rijsbergen (1979). Drummond and Holte (2000) introduced cost curves and investigated their properties.

The MDL principle was formulated by Rissanen (1985). Kepler's discovery of his economical three laws of planetary motion, and his doubts about them, are recounted by Koestler (1964).

Epicurus's principle of multiple explanations is mentioned by Li and Vitanyi (1992), quoting from Asmis (1984).

More advanced machine learning schemes

We have seen the basic ideas of several machine learning methods and studied in detail how to assess their performance on practical data mining problems. Now we are well prepared to look at more powerful and advanced machine learning algorithms. Our aim is to explain these both at a conceptual level and with a fair amount of technical detail, so that you can understand them fully and appreciate the key implementation issues that arise.

There are substantial differences between the simple methods described in Chapter 4, Algorithms: the basic methods, and the more sophisticated algorithms required to achieve state-of-the-art performance on many real-world problems, but the principles are the same. So are the inputs and, in many cases, the outputs—the methods of knowledge representation. But the algorithms are more complex—e.g., they may have to be extended to deal with numeric attributes, missing values, and—most challenging of all—noisy data.

Chapter 4, Algorithms: the basic methods, opened with an explanation of how to infer rudimentary rules, and went on to examine probabilistic modeling and decision trees. Then we returned to rule induction, and continued with association rules, linear models, the nearest-neighbor method of instance-based learning, clustering, and multi-instance learning. In Part II, we develop all these topics further, and also encounter some new ones.

We begin, in Chapter 6, Trees and rules, with decision tree induction, working up to a full description of the C4.5 system, a landmark decision tree program that is one of the most widely used workhorses of machine learning. Next we describe decision rule induction. Despite the simplicity of the idea, inducing rules that perform comparably with state-of-the-art decision trees turns out to be quite difficult in practice. Most high-performance rule inducers find an initial rule set and then refine it using a rather complex optimization stage that discards or adjusts individual rules to make them work better together. We describe the ideas that underlie rule learning in the presence of noise, and then go on to cover a scheme that operates by forming partial decision trees, an approach that has been demonstrated to perform well, while avoiding complex heuristics. Following this, we take a brief look at how to generate rules with exceptions, which were described in Section 3.4, and examine fast data structures for learning association rules.

Chapter 7, Extending instance-based and linear models, extends instance-based learning methods and linear models. There has been a resurgence of interest in linear models with the introduction of *support vector machines*, a blend of linear modeling and instance-based learning. These select a small number of critical boundary instances called "support vectors" from each class and build a linear discriminant function that separates them as widely as possible. This instance-based approach transcends the limitations of linear boundaries by making it practical to include further terms in the function that allow quadratic, cubic, and higher order decision boundaries. The same techniques can be applied to the perceptron described in Section 4.6 to implement complex decision boundaries, and also to least squares regression. An older but also very powerful technique for extending the perceptron is to connect units together into multilayer "neural networks." We cover all these ideas in Chapter 7, Extending instance-based and linear models.

Chapter 7, Extending instance-based and linear models, also describes classic instance-based learners, developing the simple nearest-neighbor method introduced in Section 4.7 and showing some more powerful alternatives that perform explicit generalization. The final part of the chapter extends linear regression for numeric prediction to a more sophisticated procedure that comes up with the tree representation introduced in Section 3.3, and goes on to describe locally weighted regression, an instance-based strategy for numeric prediction.

Chapter 8, Data transformations, discusses methods for transforming data to improve machine learning. We look primarily at techniques that process the input to machine learning to make it more amenable to learning. We cover selection of informative attributes, discretization of numeric attributes, data projections for dimensionality reduction and learning from text data, efficient sampling from large datasets, data cleansing using such techniques as anomaly detection; and also consider transforming multiclass classification problems to two-class problems, and calibrating class probability estimates to make them more accurate.

Chapter 9, Probabilistic methods, covers probabilistic modeling approaches that go far beyond the simple Naïve Bayes classifier introduced in Chapter 4, Algorithms: the basic methods. We begin with a review of some fundamental concepts, such as maximum likelihood estimation, that form the basis of probabilistic approaches. Then we examine Bayesian networks, a powerful way of extending the Naïve Bayes method to make it less "naïve" by accommodating datasets that have internal dependencies. Next we consider how clustering can be viewed from a probabilistic perspective as fitting a mixture of probability distributions to a dataset. This is essentially a form of density estimation, and we also discuss the alternative approach of kernel density estimation to model the distribution of a dataset.

Except for the brief review of foundations at the beginning, this initial part of Chapter 9, Probabilistic methods, is fairly light on mathematics. However, the remainder of the material in the chapter requires a more mathematical approach. We look at general approaches for fitting models with unknown variables—hidden attributes that are not explicitly included in a dataset—before considering truly Bayesian methods for estimation and prediction. The next big topic is how to represent probability distributions using graphical models such as factor graphs. We will encounter probabilistic principal component analysis and Markov random fields, as well as (probabilistic) latent semantic analysis and latent Dirichlet allocation, two well-known models for working with text data. We will also see how to efficiently compute probabilities for tree-structured graphical models using the sum-product and max-product algorithms.

Up to now, most of the techniques described in this book have twin goals: maximizing predictive accuracy and producing comprehensible models. Chapter 10, Data transformations, however, breaks away and focuses exclusively on maximizing modeling accuracy; it makes no attempt to provide insight by generating interpretable models. Here we enter the domain of "deep learning," the idea of learning very complex artificial neural networks that implicitly extract increasingly more abstract representations of the underlying patterns in a dataset. We first cover the nuts and bolts of deep feedforward networks, including commonly used loss functions and activation functions, before delving into the details of training and evaluating deep networks, including hyperparameter tuning, data augmentation, and pretraining. Next, we introduce a particular type of feedforward network, called a convolutional neural network, that reduces the number of parameters to be learned by weight sharing. We also describe autoencoders and Boltzmann machines, which are network models for unsupervised learning; and recurrent networks, which are designed for sequential data. Chapter 10, Deep learning, closes with some pointers to software implementations of deep learning methods.

The main focus of this book is on supervised techniques for machine learning, although we also consider unsupervised learning in the form of clustering and association rule mining. However, there are other, less conventional learning settings. In fact, we have already encountered one in Chapter 4, Algorithms: the basic methods—multi-instance learning (although it can also be interpreted as a form of supervised learning with bag-based examples). Chapter 8, Data transformations, covers more advanced techniques for multi-instance learning than those in Chapter 4, Algorithms: the basic methods. We also look at semisupervised learning, which, by combining supervised and unsupervised learning, promises a tantalizing opportunity to exploit unlabeled data for learning more accurate classification and numeric prediction models.

To maximize accuracy in practical applications, advantage can often be gained by combining multiple models. A wealth of practical experience has shown that ensembles of models are often necessary to squeeze out the last drops of predictive accuracy. Chapter 12, Ensemble learning, introduces various popular methods of ensemble learning—bagging, boosting, and randomization, including the renowned random forest variant—before going on to show how boosting can be interpreted as a form of additive regression, a statistical model building approach. A major drawback of most ensemble techniques is lack of interpretability, but alternating decision trees and related tree-based approaches offer the prospect of high accuracy while also providing insight. Finally we examine stacking, an intuitive method for combining a diverse set of models to maximize accuracy.

Chapter 13, Moving on: Applications and beyond, provides an outlook and overview of applications. We discuss learning from massive datasets and data streams, consider the use of domain knowledge, and provide an overview of application areas such as text mining, web mining, computer vision, speech recognition, and natural language processing, before briefly discussing the scenario of adversarial learning—learning with a malevolent teacher. At the very end, we imagine a future in which machine learning pervades our everyday activities.

Because of the nature of the material, this second part of the book differs from Part I in how you can approach it. Chapters can be read independently. Each is selfcontained, including references to further reading and to the research literature.

Trees and rules

CHAPTER OUTLINE

6.1 **Decision Trees**...210
   Numeric Attributes 210
   Missing Values 212
   Pruning 213
   Estimating Error Rates..215
   Complexity of Decision Tree Induction..217
   From Trees to Rules..219
   C4.5: Choices and Options...219
   Cost-Complexity Pruning 220
   Discussion 221
6.2 **Classification Rules** 221
   Criteria for Choosing Tests...222
   Missing Values, Numeric Attributes..223
   Generating Good Rules 224
   Using Global Optimization..226
   Obtaining Rules From Partial Decision Trees.......................................227
   Rules With Exceptions 231
   Discussion 233
6.3 **Association Rules** 234
   Building a Frequent Pattern Tree 235
   Finding Large Item Sets...240
   Discussion 241
6.4 **WEKA Implementations**..242

Decision tree learners are the workhorses of many practical applications of machine learning because they are fast and produce intelligible output that is often surprisingly accurate. This chapter explains how to make decision tree learning robust and versatile enough to cope with the demands of real-world datasets. It shows how to deal with numeric attributes and missing values, and how to prune away those parts of a tree that do not actually enjoy sufficient support from the data. Our discussion is based on how these issues are addressed in the classic C4.5 algorithm for decision tree learning, but we will also see how cross-validation is used by the famous CART decision tree learner to implement a more robust pruning strategy.

The second topic in this chapter is rule learning. When implemented appropriately, this shares the advantages of decision tree learning, at a somewhat higher cost in runtime, and often yields even more concise classification models. Surprisingly, rules are less popular than decision trees in practice—perhaps because rule learning algorithms are quite heuristic and are not often considered outside the artificial intelligence community. We will see how to make the basic rule learning strategy from Chapter 4, Algorithms: the basic methods, less prone to overfitting, how to deal with missing values and numeric attributes, and how to select and prune good rules. Generating concise and accurate rule sets is trickier than learning concise and accurate decision trees. We will discuss two strategies for achieving this: one based on global optimization of a rule set and another based on extracting rules from partially grown and pruned decision trees. We will also briefly look at the advantages of representing learned knowledge using rules sets with exceptions.

6.1 DECISION TREES

The first machine learning scheme that we will develop in detail, the C4.5 algorithm, derives from the simple divide-and-conquer algorithm for producing decision trees that was described in Section 4.3. It needs to be extended in several ways before it is ready for use on real-world problems. First we consider how to deal with numeric attributes, and, after that, missing values. Then we look at the all-important problem of pruning decision trees, because trees constructed by the basic divide-and-conquer algorithm as described perform well on the training set, but are usually overfitted to it and do not generalize well to independent test sets. We then briefly consider how to convert decision trees to classification rules, and examine the options provided by the C4.5 algorithm itself. Finally, we look at an alternative pruning strategy that is implemented in the famous CART system for learning classification and regression trees.

NUMERIC ATTRIBUTES

The method we described in Section 4.3 only works when all the attributes are nominal, whereas, as we have seen, most real datasets contain some numeric attributes. It is not too difficult to extend the algorithm to deal with these. For a numeric attribute we will restrict the possibilities to a two-way, or binary, split.

Suppose we use the version of the weather data that has some numeric features (Table 1.3). Then, when temperature is being considered for the first split, the temperature values involved are

64	65	68	69	70	71	72	75	80	81	83	85
Yes	No	Yes	Yes	Yes	No	No	Yes	No	Yes	Yes	No
						Yes	Yes				

(Repeated values have been collapsed together), and there are only 11 possible positions for the breakpoint—8 if the breakpoint is not allowed to separate items of the same class. The information gain for each can be calculated in the usual way. For example, the test *temperature* < 71.5 produces four *yes*'s and two *no*'s, whereas *temperature* > 71.5 produces five *yes*'s and three *no*'s, and so the information value of this test is

$$\text{Info}([4, 2], [5, 3]) = (6/14) \times \text{info}([4, 2]) + (8/14) \times \text{info}([5, 3]) = 0.939 \text{ bits}.$$

It is common to place numeric thresholds halfway between the values that delimit the boundaries of a concept, although something might be gained by adopting a more sophisticated policy. For example, we will see below that although the simplest form of instance-based learning puts the dividing line between concepts in the middle of the space between them, other methods that involve more than just the two nearest examples have been suggested.

When creating decision trees using the divide-and-conquer method, once the first attribute to split on has been selected, a top-level tree node is created that splits on that attribute, and the algorithm proceeds recursively on each of the child nodes. For each numeric attribute, it appears that the subset of instances at each child node must be re-sorted according to that attribute's values—and, indeed, this is how programs for inducing decision trees are usually written. However, it is not actually necessary to re-sort because the sort order at a parent node can be used to derive the sort order for each child, leading to a speedier implementation, at the expense of storage. Consider the temperature attribute in the weather data, whose sort order (this time including duplicates) is

64	65	68	69	70	71	72	72	75	75	80	81	83	85
7	*6*	*5*	*9*	*4*	*14*	*8*	*12*	*10*	*11*	*2*	*13*	*3*	*1*

The italicized number below each temperature value gives the number of the instance that has that value: thus instance number 7 has temperature value 64, instance 6 has temperature 65, and so on. Suppose we decide to split at the top level on the attribute *outlook*. Consider the child node for which *outlook* = *sunny*—in fact the examples with this value of *outlook* are numbers 1, 2, 8, 9, and 11. If the italicized sequence is stored with the example set (and a different sequence must be stored for each numeric attribute)—i.e., instance 7 contains a pointer to instance 6, instance 6 points to instance 5, instance 5 points to instance 9, and so on—then it is a simple manner to read off the examples for which *outlook* = *sunny* in order. All that is necessary is to scan through the instances in the indicated order, checking the *outlook* attribute for each and writing down the ones with the appropriate value:

9	8	11	2	1

Thus repeated sorting can be avoided by storing with each subset of instances the sort order for that subset according to each numeric attribute. The sort order must be determined for each numeric attribute at the beginning; no further sorting is necessary thereafter.

When a decision tree tests a nominal attribute as described in Section 4.3, a branch is made for each possible value of the attribute. However, we have restricted splits on numeric attributes to be binary. This creates an important difference between numeric attributes and nominal ones: once you have branched on a nominal attribute, you have used all the information that it offers, whereas successive splits on a numeric attribute may continue to yield new information. Whereas a nominal attribute can only be tested once on any path from the root of a tree to the leaf, a numeric one can be tested many times. This can yield trees that are messy and difficult to understand because the tests on any single numeric attribute are not located together but can be scattered along the path. An alternative, which is harder to accomplish but produces a more readable tree, is to allow a multiway test on a numeric attribute, testing against several different constants at a single node of the tree. A simpler but less powerful solution is to prediscretize the attribute as described in Section 8.2.

MISSING VALUES

The next enhancement to the decision tree-building algorithm deals with the problems of missing values. Missing values are endemic in real-world datasets. As explained in Chapter 2, Input: concepts, instances, attributes, one way of handling them is to treat them as just another possible value of the attribute; this is appropriate if the fact that the attribute is missing is significant in some way. In that case no further action need be taken. But if there is no particular significance in the fact that a certain instance has a missing attribute value, a more subtle solution is needed. It is tempting to simply ignore all instances in which some of the values are missing, but this solution is often too draconian to be viable. Instances with missing values often provide a good deal of information. Sometimes the attributes whose values are missing play no part in the decision, in which case these instances are as good as any other.

One question is how to apply a decision tree, once it has been constructed, to an instance in which some of the attributes to be tested have missing values. We outlined a solution in Section 3.3. It involves notionally splitting the instance into pieces, using a numeric weighting scheme, and sending part of it down each branch in proportion to the number of training instances going down that branch. Eventually, the various parts of the instance will each reach a leaf node, and the decisions at these leaf nodes must be recombined using the weights that have percolated to the leaves.

A second question, which precedes the first one because it applies to training, is how to partition the training set once a splitting attribute has been chosen, to allow recursive application of the decision tree formation procedure on each of the daughter nodes. The same weighting procedure is used. Instances for which the relevant attribute value is missing are notionally split into pieces, one piece for each branch, in the same proportion as the known instances go down the various branches. Pieces of the instance contribute to decisions at lower nodes in the usual way through the information gain or gain ratio calculation, except that they are weighted accordingly. The calculations described in Section 4.3 can also be applied to partial instances. Instead of having integer counts, the weights are used when computing both gain figures. Instances may be further split at lower nodes, of course, if the values of other attributes are unknown as well.

PRUNING

Fully expanded decision trees often contain unnecessary structure, and it is generally advisable to simplify them before they are deployed. Now it is time to learn how to prune decision trees.

By building the complete tree and pruning it afterward we are adopting a strategy of *postpruning* (sometimes called *backward pruning*) rather than *prepruning* (or *forward pruning*). Prepruning would involve trying to decide during the tree-building process when to stop developing subtrees—quite an attractive prospect because that would avoid all the work of developing subtrees only to throw them away afterward. However, postpruning does seem to offer some advantages. For example, situations occur in which two attributes individually seem to have nothing to contribute but are powerful predictors when combined—a sort of combination-lock effect in which the correct combination of the two attribute values is very informative whereas the attributes taken individually are not. Most decision tree builders postprune.

Two rather different operations have been considered for postpruning: *subtree replacement* and *subtree raising*. At each node, a learning scheme might decide whether it should perform subtree replacement, subtree raising, or leave the subtree as it is, unpruned. Subtree replacement is the primary pruning operation, and we look at it first. The idea is to select some subtrees and replace them with single leaves. For example, the whole subtree in Fig. 1.3B, involving two internal nodes and four leaf nodes, has been replaced by the single leaf *bad*. This will certainly cause the accuracy on the training set to decrease if the original tree is produced by the decision tree algorithm described previously, because that continues to build the tree until all leaf nodes are pure (or until all attributes have been tested). However, it may increase the accuracy on an independently chosen test set.

When subtree replacement is implemented, it proceeds from the leaves and works back up toward the root. In the Fig. 1.3 example, the whole subtree in (b) would not be replaced at once. First, consideration would be given to replacing the three daughter nodes in the *health plan contribution* subtree with a single leaf node. Assume that a decision is made to perform this replacement—we will explain how shortly. Then, continuing to work back from the leaves, consideration would be given to replacing the *working hours per week* subtree, which now has just two daughter nodes, by a single leaf node. In the Fig. 1.3 example this replacement was indeed made, which accounts for the entire subtree in (b) being replaced by a single leaf marked *bad*. Finally, consideration would be given to replacing the two daughter nodes in the *wage increase 1st year* subtree with a single leaf node. In this case that decision was not made, so the tree remains as shown in Fig. 1.3A. Again, we will examine how these decisions are actually made shortly.

The second pruning operation, subtree raising, is more complex, and it is not clear that it is necessarily always worthwhile. However, because it is used in the influential decision tree building system C4.5, we describe it here. Subtree raising does not occur in the Fig. 1.3 example, so use the artificial example of Fig. 6.1 for illustration. Here, consideration is given to pruning the tree in Fig. 6.1A, and the result is shown in Fig. 6.1B. The entire subtree from C downward has been "raised" to replace the B subtree. Note that although the daughters of B and C are shown as leaves, they can be entire subtrees. Of course, if we perform this raising operation, it is necessary to reclassify the examples at the nodes marked 4 and 5 into the new subtree headed by C. This is why the daughters of that node are marked with primes: 1′, 2′, and 3′—to indicate that they are not the same as the original daughters 1, 2, and 3 but differ by the inclusion of the examples originally covered by 4 and 5.

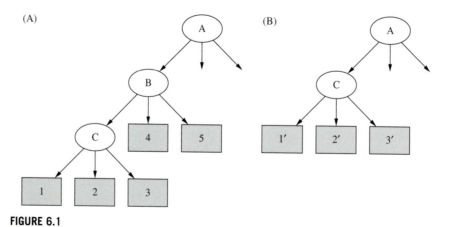

FIGURE 6.1

Example of subtree raising, where node C is "raised" to subsume node B.

Subtree raising is a potentially time-consuming operation. In actual implementations it is generally restricted to raising the subtree of the most popular branch. That is, we consider doing the raising illustrated in Fig. 6.1 provided that the branch from B to C has more training examples than the branches from B to node 4 or from B to node 5. Otherwise, if (e.g.) node 4 were the majority daughter of B, we would consider raising node 4 to replace B and reclassifying all examples under C, as well as the examples from node 5, into the new node.

ESTIMATING ERROR RATES

So much for the two pruning operations. Now we must address the question of how to decide whether to replace an internal node by a leaf (for subtree replacement), or whether to replace an internal node by one of the nodes below it (for subtree raising). To make this decision rationally, it is necessary to estimate the error rate that would be expected at a particular node given an independently chosen test set. We need to estimate the error at internal nodes as well as at leaf nodes. If we had such an estimate, it would be clear whether to replace, or raise, a particular subtree simply by comparing the estimated error of the subtree with that of its proposed replacement. Before estimating the error for a subtree proposed for raising, examples that lie under siblings of the current node—the examples at 4 and 5 of Fig. 6.1—would have to be temporarily reclassified into the raised tree.

It is no use taking the training set error as the error estimate: that would not lead to any pruning because the tree has been constructed expressly for that particular training set. One way of coming up with an error estimate is the standard verification technique: hold back some of the data originally given and use it as an independent test set to estimate the error at each node. This is called *reduced-error* pruning. It suffers from the disadvantage that the actual tree is based on less data.

The alternative is to try to make some estimate of error based on the training data itself. That is what C4.5 does, and we will describe its method here. It is a heuristic based on some statistical reasoning, but the statistical underpinning is rather weak. However, it seems to work well in practice. The idea is to consider the set of instances that reach each node and imagine that the majority class is chosen to represent that node. That gives us a certain number of "errors," E, out of the total number of instances, N. Now imagine that the true probability of error at the node is q, and that the N instances are generated by a Bernoulli process with parameter q, of which E turn out to be errors.

This is almost the same situation as we considered when looking at the hold-out method in Section 5.2, where we calculated confidence intervals on the true success probability p given a certain observed success rate. There are two differences. One is trivial: here we are looking at the error rate q rather than the success rate p; these are simply related by $p + q = 1$. The second is more serious: here the figures E and N are measured from the training data, whereas in

Section 5.2 we were considering independent test data instead. Because of this difference we make a pessimistic estimate of the error rate by using the upper confidence limit rather than stating the estimate as a confidence range.

The mathematics involved is just the same as before. Given a particular confidence c (the default figure used by C4.5 is $c = 25\%$), we find confidence limits z such that

$$\Pr\left[\frac{f - q}{\sqrt{q(1-q)/N}} > z\right] = c,$$

where N is the number of samples, $f = E/N$ is the observed error rate, and q is the true error rate. As before, this leads to an upper confidence limit for q. Now we use that upper confidence limit as a (pessimistic) estimate for the error rate e at the node:

$$e = \frac{f + \frac{z^2}{2N} + z\sqrt{\frac{f}{N} - \frac{f^2}{N} + \frac{z^2}{4N^2}}}{1 + \frac{z^2}{N}}.$$

Note the use of the $+$ sign before the square root in the numerator to obtain the upper confidence limit. Here, z is the number of standard deviations corresponding to the confidence c, which for $c = 25\%$ is $z = 0.69$.

To see how all this works in practice, let's look again at the labor negotiations decision tree of Fig. 1.3, salient parts of which are reproduced in Fig. 6.2 with the number of training examples that reach the leaves added. We use the above formula with a 25% confidence figure, i.e., with $z = 0.69$. Consider the lower left

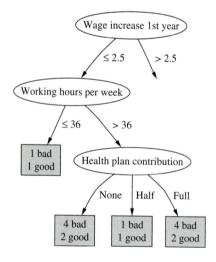

FIGURE 6.2

Pruning the labor negotiations decision tree.

leaf, for which $E = 2$, $N = 6$, and so $f = 0.33$. Plugging these figures into the formula, the upper confidence limit is calculated as $e = 0.47$. That means that instead of using the training set error rate for this leaf, which is 33%, we will use the pessimistic estimate of 47%. This is pessimistic indeed, considering that it would be a bad mistake to let the error rate exceed 50% for a two-class problem. But things are worse for the neighboring leaf, where $E = 1$ and $N = 2$, because the upper confidence limit becomes $e = 0.72$. The third leaf has the same value of e as the first. The next step is to combine the error estimates for these three leaves in the ratio of the number of examples they cover, 6: 2:6, which leads to a combined error estimate of 0.51. Now we consider the error estimate for the parent node, *health plan contribution*. This covers nine bad examples and five good ones, so the training set error rate is $f = 5/14$. For these values, the above formula yields a pessimistic error estimate of $e = 0.46$. Because this is less than the combined error estimate of the three children, they are pruned away.

The next step is to consider the *working hours per week* node, which now has two children that are both leaves. The error estimate for the first, with $E = 1$ and $N = 2$, is $e = 0.72$, while for the second it is $e = 0.46$ as we have just seen. Combining these in the appropriate ratio of 2:14 leads to a value that is higher than the error estimate for the *working hours* node, so the subtree is pruned away and replaced by a leaf node.

The estimated error figures obtained in these examples should be taken with a grain of salt because the estimate is only a heuristic one and is based on a number of shaky assumptions: the use of the upper confidence limit; the assumption of a normal distribution; and the fact that statistics from the training set are used. However, the qualitative behavior of the error formula is correct and the method seems to work reasonably well in practice. If necessary, the underlying confidence level, which we have taken to be 25%, can be tweaked to produce more satisfactory results.

COMPLEXITY OF DECISION TREE INDUCTION

Now that we have learned how to accomplish the pruning operations, we have finally covered all the central aspects of decision tree induction. Let's take stock and examine the computational complexity of inducing decision trees. We will use the standard order notation: $O(n)$ stands for a quantity that grows at most linearly with n, $O(n^2)$ grows at most quadratically with n, and so on.

Suppose the training data contains n instances and m attributes. We need to make some assumption about the size of the tree, and we will assume that its depth is on the order of $\log n$, i.e., $O(\log n)$. This is the standard rate of growth of a tree with n leaves, provided that it remains "bushy" and does not degenerate into a few very long, stringy branches. Note that we are tacitly assuming that most of the instances are different from each other, and—this is almost the same thing—that the m attributes provide enough tests to allow the instances to be differentiated. For example, if there were only a few binary attributes, they would allow only so many instances to be differentiated and the tree could not grow past a certain point, rendering an "in the limit" analysis meaningless.

The computational cost of building the tree in the first place is

$$O(mn \log n)$$

Consider the amount of work done for one attribute over all nodes of the tree. Not all the examples need to be considered at each node, of course. But at each possible tree depth, the entire set of n instances must be considered. And because there are $\log n$ different depths in the tree, the amount of work for this one attribute is $O(n \log n)$. At each node all attributes are considered, so the total amount of work is $O(mn \log n)$.

This reasoning makes some assumptions. If some attributes are numeric, they must be sorted, but once the initial sort has been done there is no need to re-sort at each tree depth if the appropriate algorithm is used (described earlier). The initial sort takes $O(n \log n)$ operations for each of up to m attributes: thus the above complexity figure is unchanged. If the attributes are nominal, all attributes do *not* have to be considered at each tree node—because attributes that are used further up the tree cannot be reused. However, if attributes are numeric, they can be reused and so they have to be considered at every tree level.

Next, consider pruning by subtree replacement. First an error estimate must be made for every tree node. Provided that counts are maintained appropriately, this is linear in the number of nodes in the tree. Then each node needs to be considered for replacement. The tree has at most n leaves, one for each instance. If it were a binary tree, each attribute being numeric or two-valued, that would give it $2n - 1$ nodes; multiway branches would only serve to decrease the number of internal nodes. Thus the complexity of subtree replacement is

$$O(n)$$

Finally, subtree lifting has a basic complexity equal to subtree replacement. But there is an added cost because instances need to be reclassified during the lifting operation. During the whole process, each instance may have to be reclassified at every node between its leaf and the root, i.e., as many as $O(\log n)$ times. That makes the total number of reclassifications $O(n \log n)$. And reclassification is not a single operation: one that occurs near the root will take $O(\log n)$ operations, and one of average depth will take half of this. Thus the total complexity of subtree lifting is as follows:

$$O(n(\log n)^2).$$

Taking into account all these operations, the full complexity of decision tree induction is

$$O(mn \log n) + O(n(\log n)^2).$$

FROM TREES TO RULES

It is possible to read a set of rules directly off a decision tree, as noted in Section 3.4, by generating a rule for each leaf and making a conjunction of all the tests encountered on the path from the root to that leaf. This produces rules that are unambiguous in that it does not matter in what order they are executed. However, the rules are more complex than necessary.

The estimated error rate described previously provides exactly the mechanism necessary to prune the rules. Given a particular rule, each condition in it is considered for deletion by tentatively removing it, working out which of the training examples are now covered by the rule, calculating from this a pessimistic estimate of the error rate of the new rule, and comparing this with the pessimistic estimate for the original rule. If the new rule is better, delete that condition and carry on, looking for other conditions to delete. Leave the rule when there are no conditions left that will improve it if they are removed. Once all rules have been pruned in this way, it is necessary to see if there are any duplicates and remove them from the rule set.

This is a greedy approach to detecting redundant conditions in a rule, and there is no guarantee that the best set of conditions will be removed. An improvement would be to consider all subsets of conditions, but this is usually prohibitively expensive. Another solution might be to use an optimization technique such as simulated annealing or a genetic algorithm to select the best version of this rule. However, the simple greedy solution seems to produce quite good rule sets.

The problem, even with the greedy method, is computational cost. For every condition that is a candidate for deletion, the effect of the rule must be reevaluated on all the training instances. This means that rule generation from trees tends to be very slow, and Section 6.2: Classification Rules describes much faster methods that generate classification rules directly without forming a decision tree first.

C4.5: CHOICES AND OPTIONS

C4.5 works essentially as described in the "From Trees to Rules" sections. The default confidence value is set at 25% and works reasonably well in most cases; possibly it should be altered to a lower value, which causes more drastic pruning, if the actual error rate of pruned trees on test sets is found to be much higher than the estimated error rate. There is one other important parameter whose effect is to eliminate tests for which almost all of the training examples have the same outcome. Such tests are often of little use. Consequently tests are not incorporated into the decision tree unless they have at least two outcomes that have at least a minimum number of instances. The default value for this minimum is 2, but it is controllable and should perhaps be increased for tasks that have a lot of noisy data.

Another heuristic in C4.5 is that candidate splits on numeric attributes are only considered if they cut off a certain minimum number of instances: at least 10% of the average number of instances per class at the current node, or 25 instances, whichever value is smaller (but the above minimum, 2 by default, is also enforced).

C4.5 Release 8, the version of C4.5 implemented in the Weka software, includes an MDL-based adjustment to the information gain for splits on numeric attributes. More specifically, if there are S candidate splits on a certain numeric attribute at the node currently considered for splitting, $\log2(S)/N$ is subtracted from the information gain, where N is the number of instances at the node. This heuristic is designed to prevent overfitting. The information gain may be negative after subtraction, and tree growing will stop if there are no attributes with positive information gain—a form of prepruning. We mention this here because it can be surprising to obtain a pruned tree even if postpruning has been turned off!

Finally, C4.5 does not actually place the split point for a numeric attribute halfway between two values. Once a split has been chosen, the entire training set is searched to find the greatest value for that attribute that does not exceed the provisional split point, and this becomes the actual split point. This adds a quadratic term $O(n^2)$ to the time complexity because it can happen at any node, which we have ignored above.

COST-COMPLEXITY PRUNING

As mentioned above, the postpruning method in C4.5 is based on shaky statistical assumptions and it turns out that it often does not prune enough. On the other hand, it is very fast and thus popular in practice. However, in many applications it is worthwhile expending more computational effort to obtain a more compact decision tree. Experiments have shown that C4.5's pruning method can yield unnecessary additional structure in the final tree: tree size continues to grow when more instances are added to the training data even when this does not further increase performance on independent test data. In that case the more conservative *cost-complexity pruning* method from the CART tree learning system may be more appropriate.

Cost-complexity pruning is based on the idea of first pruning those subtrees that, relative to their size, lead to the smallest increase in error on the training data. The increase in error is measured by a quantity α that is defined to be the average error increase per leaf of the subtree concerned. By monitoring this quantity as pruning progresses, the algorithm generates a sequence of successively smaller pruned trees. In each iteration it prunes all subtrees that exhibit the smallest value of α amongst the remaining subtrees in the current version of the tree.

Each candidate tree in the resulting sequence of pruned trees corresponds to one particular threshold value α_i. The question becomes: which tree should be chosen as the final classification model? To determine the most predictive tree, cost-complexity pruning either uses a holdout set to estimate the error rate of each tree, or, if data is limited, employs cross-validation.

Using a holdout set is straightforward. However, cross-validation poses the problem of relating the α values observed in the sequence of pruned trees for training fold k of the cross-validation to the α values from the sequence of trees for the full dataset: these values are usually different. This problem is solved by first computing the geometric average of α_i and α_{i+1} for tree i from the full dataset. Then, for each fold k of the cross-validation, the tree that exhibits the largest α value smaller than this average is picked. The average of the error estimates for these trees from the k folds, estimated from the corresponding test datasets, is the cross-validation error for tree i from the full dataset.

DISCUSSION

Top-down induction of decision trees is probably the most extensively researched method of machine learning used in data mining. Researchers have investigated a panoply of variations for almost every conceivable aspect of the learning process—e.g., different criteria for attribute selection or modified pruning methods. However, they are rarely rewarded by substantial improvements in accuracy over a spectrum of diverse datasets. As discussed above, the pruning method used by the CART system for learning decision trees (Breiman et al., 1984) can often produce smaller trees than C4.5's pruning method. This has been investigated empirically by Oates and Jensen (1997).

The decision tree program C4.5 and its successor C5.0 were devised by Ross Quinlan over a 20-year period beginning in the late 1970s. A complete description of C4.5, the early 1990s version, appears as a excellent and readable book (Quinlan, 1993), along with the full source code. The MDL heuristic for C4.5 Release 8 is described by Quinlan (1996). The more recent version, C5.0, is also available as open-source code.

In our description of decision trees, we have assumed that only one attribute is used to split the data into subsets at each node of the tree. However, it is possible to allow tests that involve several attributes at a time. For example, with numeric attributes each test can be on a linear combination of attribute values. Then the final tree consists of a hierarchy of linear models of the kind described in Section 4.6, and the splits are no longer restricted to being axis-parallel. The CART system has the option of generating such tests. They are often more accurate and smaller than standard trees, but take much longer to generate and are also more difficult to interpret. We briefly mention one way of generating them under principal component analysis in Section 8.3.

6.2 CLASSIFICATION RULES

We call the basic covering algorithm for generating rules that was described in Section 4.4 a separate-and-conquer technique because it identifies a rule that covers instances in the class (and excludes ones not in the class), separates them out, and continues on those that are left. Such algorithms have been used as the basis of many systems that generate rules. There we described a simple correctness-based measure for choosing what test to add to the rule at each stage. However, there are many other possibilities, and the particular criterion that is used has a significant effect on the rules produced. We examine different criteria for choosing tests in this section. We also look at how the basic rule-generation algorithm can be extended to more practical situations by accommodating missing values and numeric attributes.

But the real problem with all these rule-generation schemes is that they tend to overfit the training data and do not generalize well to independent test sets, particularly on noisy data. To be able to generate good rule sets for noisy data, it is necessary to have some way of measuring the real worth of individual rules. The standard approach to assessing the worth of rules is to evaluate their error rate on an independent set of instances, held back from the training set, and we explain this next. After that, we describe two industrial-strength rule learners: one that combines the simple separate-and-conquer technique with a global optimization step, and another one that works by repeatedly building partial decision trees and extracting rules from them. Finally, we consider how to generate rules with exceptions, and exceptions to the exceptions.

CRITERIA FOR CHOOSING TESTS

When we introduced the basic rule learner in Section 4.4, we had to figure out a way of deciding which of many possible tests to add to a rule to prevent it from covering any negative examples. For this we used the test that maximizes the ratio

$$p/t$$

where t is the total number of instances that the new rule will cover, and p is the number of these that are positive—i.e., belong to the class in question. This attempts to maximize the "correctness" of the rule on the basis that the higher the proportion of positive examples it covers, the more correct a rule is. One alternative is to calculate an information gain:

$$p\left[\log\frac{p}{t} - \log\frac{P}{T}\right],$$

where p and t are the number of positive instances and the total number of instances covered by the new rule, as before, and P and T are the corresponding number of instances that satisfied the rule *before* the new test was added. The rationale for this is that it represents the total information gained regarding the current positive examples, which is given by the number of them that satisfy the new test, multiplied by the information gained regarding each one.

The basic criterion for choosing a test to add to a rule is to find one that covers as many positive examples as possible, while covering as few negative examples as possible. The original correctness-based heuristic, which is just the percentage of positive examples among all examples covered by the rule, attains a maximum when no negative examples are covered regardless of the number of positive examples covered by the rule. Thus a test that makes the rule exact will be preferred to one that makes it inexact, no matter how few positive examples the former rule covers, nor how many positive examples the latter covers. For example, if we can choose between a test that covers one example, which is positive, this criterion will prefer it over a test that covers 1000 positive examples along with one negative one.

The information-based heuristic, on the other hand, places far more emphasis on covering a large number of positive examples regardless of whether the rule so created is exact. Of course, both algorithms continue adding tests until the final rule produced is exact, which means that the rule will be finished earlier using the correctness measure, whereas more terms will have to be added if the information-based measure is used. Thus the correctness-based measure might find special cases and eliminate them completely, saving the larger picture for later (when the more general rule might be simpler because awkward special cases have already been dealt with), whereas the information-based one will try to generate high-coverage rules first and leave the special cases until later. It is by no means obvious that either strategy is superior to the other at producing an exact rule set. Moreover, the whole situation is complicated by the fact that, as described below, rules may be pruned and inexact ones tolerated.

MISSING VALUES, NUMERIC ATTRIBUTES

As with divide-and-conquer decision tree algorithms, the nasty practical considerations of missing values and numeric attributes need to be addressed. In fact, there is not much more to say. Now that we know how these problems can be solved for decision tree induction, appropriate solutions for rule induction are easily given.

When producing rules using covering algorithms, missing values can best be treated as though they don't match any of the tests. This is particularly suitable when a decision list is being produced because it encourages the learning algorithm to separate out positive instances using tests that are known to succeed. It has the effect that either instances with missing values are dealt with by rules involving other attributes that are not missing, or any decisions about them are deferred until most of the other instances have been taken care of, at which time tests will probably emerge that involve other attributes. Covering algorithms for decision lists have a decided advantage over decision tree algorithms in this respect: tricky examples can be left until late in the process, at which time they will appear less tricky because most of the other examples have already been classified and removed from the instance set.

Numeric attributes can be dealt with in exactly the same way as they are for trees. For each numeric attribute, instances are sorted according to the attribute's value and, for each possible threshold, a binary less-than/greater-than test is considered and evaluated in exactly the same way that a binary attribute would be.

GENERATING GOOD RULES

Suppose you don't want to generate perfect rules that guarantee to give the correct classification on all instances in the training set, but would rather generate "sensible" ones that avoid overfitting the training set and thereby stand a better chance of performing well on new test instances. How do you decide which rules are worthwhile? How do you tell when it becomes counterproductive to continue adding terms to a rule to exclude a few pesky instances of the wrong type, all the while excluding more and more instances of the right type, too?

Let's look at a few examples of possible rules—some good and some bad—for the contact lens problem in Table 1.1. Consider first the rule

```
If astigmatism = yes and tear production rate = normal
        then recommendation = hard.
```

This gives a correct result for four out of the six cases that it covers; thus its success fraction is 4/6. Suppose we add a further term to make the rule a "perfect" one:

```
If astigmatism = yes and tear production rate = normal
        and age = young then recommendation = hard.
```

This improves accuracy to 2/2. Which rule is better? The second one is more accurate on the training data but covers only two cases, whereas the first one covers six. It may be that the second version is just overfitting the training data. For a practical rule learner we need a principled way of choosing the appropriate version of a rule, preferably one that maximizes accuracy on future test data.

Suppose we split the training data into two parts that we will call a *growing set* and a *pruning set*. The growing set is used to form a rule using the basic covering algorithm. Then a test is deleted from the rule, and the effect is evaluated by trying out the truncated rule on the pruning set and seeing whether it performs better than the original rule. This pruning process repeats until the rule cannot be improved by deleting any further tests. The whole procedure is repeated for each class, obtaining one best rule for each class, and the overall best rule is established by evaluating the rules on the pruning set. This rule is then added to the rule set, the instances it covers removed from the training data—from both growing and pruning sets—and the process is repeated.

Why not do the pruning as we build the rule up, rather than building up the whole thing and then throwing parts away? That is, why not preprune rather than postprune? Just as when pruning decision trees it is often best to grow the tree to its maximum size and then prune back, so with rules it is often best to make a perfect rule and then prune it. Who knows?—adding that last term may make a really good rule, a situation that we might never have noticed had we adopted an aggressive prepruning strategy.

It is essential that the growing and pruning sets are separate, because it is misleading to evaluate a rule on the very data that was used to form it: that would lead to serious errors by preferring rules that were overfitted. Usually the training set is split so that two-thirds of instances are used for growing and one-third for pruning. A disadvantage, of course, is that learning occurs from instances in the growing set only, so the algorithm might miss important rules because some key instances had been assigned to the pruning set. Moreover, the wrong rule might be preferred because the pruning set contains only one-third of the data and may not be completely representative. These effects can be ameliorated by resplitting the training data into growing and pruning sets at each cycle of the algorithm, i.e., after each rule is finally chosen.

The idea of using a separate pruning set for pruning—which is applicable to decision trees as well as rule sets—is called *reduced-error pruning*. The variant described above prunes a rule immediately after it has been grown, and is called *incremental reduced-error pruning*. Another possibility is to build a full, unpruned, rule set first, pruning it afterwards by discarding individual tests. However, this method is much slower.

Of course, there are many different ways to assess the worth of a rule based on the pruning set. A simple measure is to consider how well the rule would do at discriminating the predicted class from other classes if it were the only rule in the rule set, operating under the closed world assumption. Suppose it gets p instances right out of the t instances that it covers, and there are P instances of this class out of a total T of instances altogether. The instances that it does not cover include $N - n$ negative ones, where $n = t - p$ is the number of negative instances that the rule covers and $N = T - P$ is the total number of negative instances. Thus in total the rule makes correct decisions on $p + (N - n)$ instances, and so has an overall success ratio of

$$[p + (N - n)]/T.$$

This quantity, evaluated on the test set, has been used to evaluate the success of a rule when using reduced-error pruning.

This measure is open to criticism because it treats noncoverage of negative examples as equally important as coverage of positive ones, which is unrealistic in a situation where what is being evaluated is one rule that will eventually serve alongside many others. For example, a rule that gets $p = 2000$ instances right out of a total coverage of 3000 (i.e., it gets $n = 1000$ wrong) is judged as more successful than one that gets $p = 1000$ out of a total coverage of 1001 (i.e., $n = 1$ wrong), because $[p + (N - n)]/T$ is $[1000 + N]/T$ in the first case but only $[999 + N]/T$ in the second. This is counterintuitive: the first rule is clearly less predictive than the second, because it has 33.3% as opposed to only 0.1% chance of being incorrect.

```
Initialize E to the instance set
Split E into Grow and Prune in the ratio 2:1
  For each class C for which Grow and Prune both contain an instance
    Use the basic covering algorithm to create the best perfect rule for class C
    Calculate the worth w(R) for the rule on Prune, and of the rule with the
    final condition omitted w(R-)
    While w(R-) > w(R), remove the final condition from the rule and repeat the
    previous step
  From the rules generated, select the one with the largest w(R)
  Print the rule
  Remove the instances covered by the rule from E
Continue
```

FIGURE 6.3

Algorithm for forming rules by incremental reduced-error pruning.

Using the success rate p/t as a measure, as was done in the original formulation of the covering algorithm (Fig. 4.8), is not the perfect solution either, because it will prefer a rule that gets a single instance right ($p = 1$) out of a total coverage of 1 (so $n = 0$) to the far more useful rule that gets 1000 right out of 1001. Another heuristic that has been used is $(p - n)/t$, but that suffers from exactly the same problem because $(p - n)/t = 2p/t - 1$ and so the result, when comparing one rule with another, is just the same as with the success rate. It seems hard to find a simple measure of the worth of a rule that corresponds with intuition in all cases.

Whatever heuristic is used to measure the worth of a rule, the incremental reduced-error pruning algorithm is the same. A possible rule learning algorithm based on this idea is given in Fig. 6.3. It generates a decision list, creating rules for each class in turn and choosing at each stage the best version of the rule according to its worth on the pruning data. The basic covering algorithm for rule generation (Fig. 4.8) is used to come up with good rules for each class, choosing conditions to add to the rule using the accuracy measure p/t that we described earlier.

This method has been used to produce rule induction schemes that can process vast amounts of data and operate very quickly. It can be accelerated by generating rules for the classes in order rather than generating a rule for each class at every stage and choosing the best. A suitable ordering is the increasing order in which they occur in the training set so that the rarest class is processed first and the most common ones are processed later. Another significant speedup is obtained by stopping the whole process when a rule of sufficiently low accuracy is generated, so as not to spend time generating a lot of rules at the end with very small coverage. However, very simple terminating conditions (such as stopping when the accuracy for a rule is lower than the default accuracy for the class it predicts) do not give the best performance. One criterion that seems to work well is a rather complicated one based on the MDL principle, described below.

USING GLOBAL OPTIMIZATION

In general, rules generated using incremental reduced-error pruning in this manner perform quite well, particularly on large datasets. However, it has been found that a worthwhile performance advantage can be obtained by performing a global optimization step on the set of rules induced. The motivation is to increase the accuracy of the rule set by revising or replacing individual rules. Experiments show that both the size and the performance of rule sets are significantly improved by postinduction optimization. On the other hand, the process itself is rather complex.

To give an idea of how elaborate industrial-strength rule learners become, Fig. 6.4 shows an algorithm called RIPPER, an acronym for *repeated incremental pruning to produce error reduction*. Classes are examined in increasing size and an initial set of rules for the class is generated using incremental reduced-error pruning. An extra stopping condition is introduced that depends on the description length (DL) of the examples and rule set. The description length *DL* is a complex formula that takes into account the number of bits needed to send a set of examples with respect to a set of rules, the number of bits required to send a rule with k conditions, and the number of bits needed to send the integer k—times an arbitrary factor of 50% to compensate for possible redundancy in the attributes. Having produced a rule set for the class, each rule is reconsidered and two variants produced, again using reduced-error pruning—but at this stage, instances covered by other rules for the class are removed from the pruning set, and success rate on the remaining instances is used as the pruning criterion. If one of the two variants yields a better DL, it replaces the rule. Next we reactivate the original building phase to mop up any newly uncovered instances of the class. A final check is made to ensure that each rule contributes to the reduction of DL, before proceeding to generate rules for the next class.

OBTAINING RULES FROM PARTIAL DECISION TREES

There is an alternative approach to rule induction that avoids global optimization but nevertheless produces accurate and fairly compact rule sets. The method combines the divide-and-conquer strategy for decision tree learning with the separate-and-conquer one for rule learning. It adopts the separate-and-conquer strategy in that it builds a rule, removes the instances it covers, and continues creating rules recursively for the remaining instances until none are left. However, it differs from the standard approach in the way that each rule is created. In essence, to make a single rule, a pruned decision tree is built for the current set of instances, the leaf with the largest coverage is made into a rule, and the tree is discarded.

The prospect of repeatedly building decision trees only to discard most of them is not as bizarre as it first seems. Using a pruned tree to obtain a rule instead of pruning a rule incrementally by removing conjunctions one at a time avoids a tendency to overprune that is a characteristic problem of the basic separate-and-conquer rule learner. Using the separate-and-conquer methodology in conjunction with decision trees adds flexibility and speed. It is indeed wasteful to build a full decision tree just to obtain a single rule, but the process can be accelerated significantly without sacrificing the advantages.

(A)

```
Initialize E to the instance set
For each class C, from smallest to largest
     BUILD:
          Split E into Growing and Pruning sets in the ratio 2:1
          Repeat until (a) there are no more uncovered examples of C; or(b) the
                description length (DL) of ruleset and examples is 64 bits greater
                than the smallest DL found so far, or(c) the error rate exceeds
                50%:
          GROW phase: Grow a rule by greedily adding conditions until the rule is
                100% accurate by testing every possible value of each attribute and
                selecting the condition with greatest information gain G
          PRUNE phase: Prune conditions in last-to-first order. Continue as long
                as the worth W of the rule increases
     OPTIMIZE:
          GENERATE VARIANTS:
          For each rule R for class C,
               Split E afresh into Growing and Pruning sets
               Remove all instances from the Pruning set that are covered by other
               rules for C
               Use GROW and PRUNE to generate and prune two competing rules from the
               newly split data:
                    R1 is a new rule, rebuilt from scratch;
                    R2 is generated by greedily adding antecedents to R.
               Prune using the metric A (instead of W) on this reduced data
          SELECT REPRESENTATIVE:
          Replace R by whichever of R, R1 and R2 has the smallest DL.
     MOP UP:
          If there are residual uncovered instances of class C, return to the
                BUILD stage to generate more rules based on these instances.
     CLEAN UP:
          Calculate DL for the whole ruleset and for the ruleset with each rule in
                turn omitted; delete any rule that increases the DL
          Remove instances covered by the rules just generated
Continue
```

(B)   *DL*: see text

$$G = p[\log(p/t) - \log(P/T)]$$

$$W = \frac{p+1}{t+2}$$

$$A = \frac{p+n'}{T}; \text{accuracy for this rule}$$

p = number of positive examples covered by this rule (true positives)
n = number of negative examples covered by this rule (false negatives)
$t = p + n$; total number of examples covered by this rule
$n' = N - n$; number of negative examples not covered by this rule (true negatives)
P = number of positive examples of this class
N = number of negative examples of this class
$T = P + N$; total number of examples of this class

FIGURE 6.4

RIPPER: (A) algorithm for rule learning; (B) meaning of symbols.

The key idea is to build a partial decision tree instead of a fully explored one. A partial decision tree is an ordinary decision tree that contains branches to undefined subtrees. To generate such a tree, the construction and pruning operations are integrated in order to find a "stable" subtree that can be simplified no further. Once this subtree has been found, tree building ceases and a single rule is read off.

```
Expand-subset (S):
  Choose a test T and use it to split the set of examples into subsets
  Sort subsets into increasing order of average entropy
  while (there is a subset X that has not yet been expanded
        AND all subsets expanded so far are leaves)
    expand-subset(X)
  if (all the subsets expanded are leaves
      AND estimated error for subtree ≥ estimated error for node)
    undo expansion into subsets and make node a leaf
```

FIGURE 6.5

Algorithm for expanding examples into a partial tree.

The tree-building algorithm is summarized in Fig. 6.5: it splits a set of instances recursively into a partial tree. The first step chooses a test and divides the instances into subsets accordingly. The choice is made using the same information-gain heuristic that is normally used for building decision trees (Section 4.3). Then the subsets are expanded in increasing order of their average entropy. The reason for this is that the later subsets will most likely not end up being expanded, and a subset with low average entropy is more likely to result in a small subtree and therefore produce a more general rule. This proceeds recursively until a subset is expanded into a leaf, and then continues further by backtracking. But as soon as an internal node appears that has all its children expanded into leaves, the algorithm checks whether that node is better replaced by a single leaf. This is just the standard subtree replacement operation of decision tree pruning (Section 6.1). If replacement is performed the algorithm backtracks in the standard way, exploring siblings of the newly replaced node. However, if during backtracking a node is encountered not all of whose children expanded so far are leaves—and this will happen as soon as a potential subtree replacement is *not* performed—then the remaining subsets are left unexplored and the corresponding subtrees are left undefined. Due to the recursive structure of the algorithm, this event automatically terminates tree generation.

Fig. 6.6 shows a step-by-step example. During the stages in Fig. 6.6A–C, tree building continues recursively in the normal way—except that at each point the lowest-entropy sibling is chosen for expansion: node 3 between stages (A) and (B). Gray elliptical nodes are as yet unexpanded; rectangular ones are leaves. Between stages (B) and (C), the rectangular node will have lower entropy than its sibling, node 5, but cannot be expanded further because it is a leaf. Backtracking occurs and node 5 is chosen for expansion. Once stage (C) is reached, there is a node—node 5—that has all its children expanded into leaves, and this triggers pruning. Subtree replacement for node 5 is considered and accepted, leading to stage (D). Now node 3 is considered for subtree replacement, and this operation is again accepted. Backtracking continues, and node 4, having lower entropy than node 2, is expanded into two leaves. Now subtree replacement is considered for node 4: suppose that node 4 is not replaced. At this point, the process terminates with the three-leaf partial tree of stage (E).

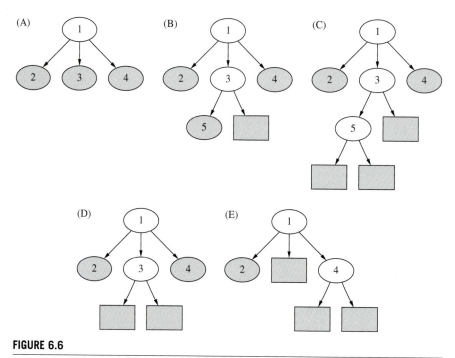

FIGURE 6.6

Example of building a partial tree.

If the data is noise-free and contains enough instances to prevent the algorithm from doing any pruning, just one path of the full decision tree has to be explored. This achieves the greatest possible performance gain over the naïve method that builds a full decision tree each time. The gain decreases as more pruning takes place. For datasets with numeric attributes, the asymptotic time complexity of the algorithm is the same as building the full decision tree, because in this case the complexity is dominated by the time required to sort the attribute values in the first place.

Once a partial tree has been built, a single rule is extracted from it. Each leaf corresponds to a possible rule, and we seek the "best" leaf of those subtrees (typically a small minority) that have been expanded into leaves. Experiments show that it is best to aim at the most general rule by choosing the leaf that covers the greatest number of instances.

When a dataset contains missing values, they can be dealt with exactly as they are when building decision trees. If an instance cannot be assigned to any given branch because of a missing attribute value, it is assigned to each of the branches with a weight proportional to the number of training instances going down that branch, normalized by the total number of training instances with known values at the node. During testing, the same procedure is applied separately to each rule, thus associating a weight with the application of each rule to the test instance. That weight is deducted from the instance's total weight before it is passed to the next rule in the list. Once the weight has reduced to zero, the predicted class probabilities are combined into a final classification according to the weights.

This yields a simple but surprisingly effective method for learning decision lists for noisy data. Its main advantage over other comprehensive rule-generation schemes is simplicity, because it does not require a complex global optimization stage.

RULES WITH EXCEPTIONS

In Section 3.4 we learned that a natural extension of rules is to allow them to have exceptions, and exceptions to the exceptions, and so on—indeed the whole rule set can be considered as exceptions to a default classification rule that is used when no other rules apply. The method of generating a "good" rule, using one of the measures described previously provides exactly the mechanism needed to generate rules with exceptions.

First, a default class is selected for the top-level rule: it is natural to use the class that occurs most frequently in the training data. Then, a rule is found pertaining to any class other than the default one. Of all such rules it is natural to seek the one with the most discriminatory power, e.g., the one with the best evaluation on a test set. Suppose this rule has the form

```
if <condition> then class = <new class>
```

It is used to split the training data into two subsets: one containing instances for which the rule's condition is *true* and the other containing those for which it is *false*. If either subset contains instances of more than one class, the algorithm is invoked recursively on that subset. For the subset for which the condition is *true*, the "default class" is the new class as specified by the rule; for the subset where the condition is *false*, the default class remains as it was before.

Let's examine how this algorithm would work for the rules with exceptions that were given in Section 3.4 for the iris data of Table 1.4. We will represent the rules in the graphical form shown in Fig. 6.7, which is in fact equivalent to the textual rules we showed before in Fig. 3.8. The default of *Iris setosa* is the entry node at the top left. Horizontal, dotted paths show exceptions, so the next box, which contains a rule that concludes *Iris versicolor*, is an exception to the default. Below this is an alternative, a second exception—alternatives are shown by vertical, solid lines—leading to the conclusion *Iris virginica*. Following the upper path along horizontally leads to an exception to the *Iris versicolor* rule that overrides it whenever the condition in the top right box holds, with the conclusion *I. virginica*. Below this is an alternative, leading (as it happens) to the same conclusion. Returning to the box at bottom center, this has its own exception, the lower right box, which gives the conclusion *Iris versicolor*. The numbers at the lower right of each box give the "coverage" of the rule, expressed as the number of

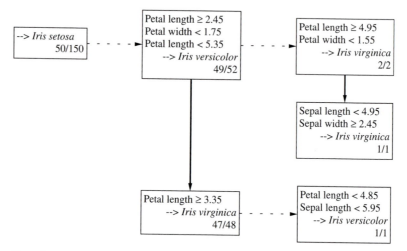

Exceptions are represented as dotted paths, alternatives as solid ones.

FIGURE 6.7

Rules with exceptions for the iris data.

examples that satisfy it divided by the number that satisfy its condition but not its conclusion. For example, the condition in the top center box applies to 52 of the examples, and 49 of them are *Iris versicolor*. The strength of this representation is that you can get a very good feeling for the effect of the rules from the boxes toward the left-hand side; the boxes at the right cover just a few exceptional cases.

To create these rules, the default is first set to *I. setosa* by taking the most frequently occurring class in the dataset. This is an arbitrary choice because for this dataset all classes occur exactly 50 times; as shown in Fig. 6.7 this default "rule" is correct in 50 out of 150 cases. Then the best rule that predicts another class is sought. In this case it is

```
if petal-length ≥ 2.45 and petal-length < 5.355 and petal-width < 1.75
    then Iris-versicolor
```

This rule cover 52 instances, of which 49 are *Iris versicolor*. It divides the dataset into two subsets: the 52 instances that satisfy the condition of the rule and the remaining 98 that do not.

We work on the former subset first. The default class for these instances is *Iris versicolor*: there are only three exceptions, all of which happen to be *I. virginica*. The best rule for this subset that does not predict *Iris versicolor* is identified next:

```
if petal-length ≥ 4.95 and petal-width < 1.55 then Iris-virginica
```

It covers two of the three *I. virginicas* and nothing else. Again it divides the subset into two: those instances that satisfy its condition and those that do not.

Fortunately, in this case, all those instances that satisfy the condition do indeed have class *I. virginica*, so there is no need for a further exception. However, the remaining instances still include the third *I. virginica*, along with 49 *Iris versicolors*, which are the default at this point. Again the best rule is sought:

```
if sepal-length < 4.95 and sepal-width ≥ 2.45 then Iris-virginica
```

This rule covers the remaining *I. virginica* and nothing else, so it also has no exceptions. Furthermore, all remaining instances in the subset that do not satisfy its condition have the class *Iris versicolor*, which is the default, so no more needs to be done.

Return now to the second subset created by the initial rule, the instances that do not satisfy the condition

```
petal-length ≥ 2.45 and petal-length < 5.355 and petal-width < 1.75
```

Of the rules for these instances that do not predict the default class *I. setosa*, the best is

```
if petal-length ≥ 3.35 then Iris-virginica
```

It covers all 47 *Iris virginicas* that are in the example set (3 were removed by the first rule, as explained previously). It also covers 1 *Iris versicolor*. This needs to be taken care of as an exception, by the final rule:

```
if petal-length < 4.85 and sepal-length < 5.95 then Iris-versicolor
```

Fortunately, the set of instances that do *not* satisfy its condition are all the default, *I. setosa*. Thus the procedure is finished.

The rules that are produced have the property that most of the examples are covered by the high-level rules and the lower-level ones really do represent exceptions. For example, the last exception clause and the deeply nested *else* clause both cover a solitary example, and removing them would have little effect. Even the remaining nested exception rule covers only two examples. Thus one can get an excellent feeling for what the rules do by ignoring all the deeper structure and looking only at the first level or two. That is the attraction of rules with exceptions.

DISCUSSION

All algorithms for producing classification rules that we have describe use the basic covering or separate-and-conquer approach. For the simple, noise-free case this produces PRISM (Cendrowska, 1987), an algorithm that is simple and easy to understand. When applied to two-class problems with the closed world assumption, it is only necessary to produce rules for one class: then the rules are in disjunctive normal form and can be executed on test instances without any ambiguity arising. When applied to multiclass problems, a separate rule set is produced for each class: thus a test instance may be assigned to more than one class, or to no class, and further heuristics are necessary if a unique prediction is sought.

To reduce overfitting in noisy situations, it is necessary to produce rules that are not "perfect" even on the training set. To do this it is necessary to have a measure for the "goodness," or worth, of a rule. With such a measure it is then possible to abandon the class-by-class approach of the basic covering algorithm and start by generating the very best rule, regardless of which class it predicts, and then remove all examples covered by this rule and continue the process. This yields a method for producing a decision list rather than a set of independent classification rules, and decision lists have the important advantage that they do not generate ambiguities when interpreted.

The idea of incremental reduced-error pruning is due to Fürnkranz and Widmer (1994) and forms the basis for fast and effective rule induction. The RIPPER rule learner is due to Cohen (1995), although the published description appears to differ from the implementation in precisely how the DL affects the stopping condition. What we have presented here is the basic idea of the algorithm; there are many more details in the implementation.

The whole question of measuring the value of a rule is a difficult one. Many different measures have been proposed, some blatantly heuristic and others based on information-theoretical or probabilistic grounds. However, there seems to be no consensus on what the best measure to use is. An extensive theoretical study of various criteria has been performed by Fürnkranz and Flach (2005).

The rule learning scheme based on partial decision trees was developed by Frank and Witten (1998). On standard benchmark datasets it produces rule sets that are as accurate as rules generated by the C4.5 rule learner, and often more accurate than those of RIPPER; however, it produces larger rule sets than RIPPER. Its main advantage over other schemes is not performance but simplicity: by combining top-down decision tree induction with separate-and-conquer rule learning, it produces good rule sets without any need for global optimization.

The procedure for generating rules with exceptions was developed as an option in the Induct system by Gaines and Compton (1995), who called them *ripple-down* rules. In an experiment with a large medical dataset (22,000 instances, 32 attributes, and 60 classes), they found that people can understand large systems of rules with exceptions more readily than equivalent systems of regular rules because that is the way that they think about the complex medical diagnoses that are involved. Richards and Compton (1998) describe their role as an alternative to classic knowledge engineering.

6.3 ASSOCIATION RULES

In Section 4.5 we studied the Apriori algorithm for generating association rules that meet minimum support and confidence thresholds. Apriori follows a generate-and-test methodology for finding frequent item sets, generating successively longer candidate item sets from shorter ones that are known to be frequent. Each different size of candidate item set requires a scan through the dataset in order to determine whether its frequency exceeds the minimum support threshold. Although some improvements to the algorithm have been suggested to reduce the number of scans of the dataset, the combinatorial nature of this generation process can prove costly—particularly if there are many item sets or item sets are large. Both these conditions readily occur even for modest datasets when low support thresholds are used. Moreover, no matter how high the threshold, if the data is too large to fit in main memory it is undesirable to have to scan it repeatedly—and many association rule applications involve truly massive datasets.

These effects can be ameliorated by using appropriate data structures. We describe a method called FP-growth that uses an extended prefix tree—a frequent pattern tree or "FP-tree"—to store a compressed version of the dataset in main memory. Only two passes are needed to map a dataset into an FP-tree. The algorithm then processes the tree in a recursive fashion to grow large item sets directly, instead of generating candidate item sets and then having to test them against the entire database.

BUILDING A FREQUENT PATTERN TREE

Like Apriori, the FP-growth algorithm begins by counting the number of times individual items (i.e., attribute—value pairs) occur in the dataset. After this initial pass, a tree structure is created in a second pass. Initially the tree is empty and the structure emerges as each instance in the dataset is inserted into it.

The key to obtaining a compact tree structure that can be quickly processed to find large item sets is to sort the items in each instance in descending order of their frequency of occurrence in the dataset, which has already been recorded in the first pass, before inserting them into the tree. Individual items in each instance that do not meet the minimum support threshold are not inserted into the tree, effectively removing them from the dataset. The hope is that many instances will share those items that occur most frequently individually, resulting in a high degree of compression close to the tree's root.

We illustrate the process with the weather data, reproduced in Table 6.1A, using a minimum support threshold of 6. The algorithm is complex, and its complexity far exceeds what would be reasonable for such a trivial example, but a small illustration is the best way of explaining it. Table 6.1B shows the individual items, with their frequencies, that are collected in the first pass. They are sorted into descending order and ones whose frequency exceeds the minimum threshold are in bold. Table 6.1C shows the original instances, numbered as in Table 6.1A, with the items in each instance sorted into descending frequency order. Finally, to give an advance peek at the final outcome, Table 6.1D shows the only two multiple-item sets whose frequency satisfies the minimum support threshold. Along with the six single-item sets shown in bold in Table 6.1B, these form the

Table 6.1 Preparing the Weather Data for Insertion Into an FP-tree: (A) The Original Data; (B) Frequency Ordering of Items With Frequent Item Sets in Bold; (C) The Data With Each Instance Sorted Into Frequency Order; (D) The Two Multiple-Item Frequent Item Sets

		Outlook	Temperature	Humidity	Windy	Play
(A)	1	Sunny	Hot	High	False	No
	2	Sunny	Hot	High	True	No
	3	Overcast	Hot	High	False	Yes
	4	Rainy	Mild	High	False	Yes
	5	Rainy	Cool	Normal	False	Yes
	6	Rainy	Cool	Normal	True	No
	7	Overcast	Cool	Normal	True	Yes
	8	Sunny	Mild	High	False	No
	9	Sunny	Cool	Normal	False	Yes
	10	Rainy	Mild	Normal	False	Yes
	11	Sunny	Mild	Normal	True	Yes
	12	Overcast	Mild	High	True	Yes
	13	Overcast	Hot	Normal	False	Yes
	14	Rainy	Mild	High	True	No

(B)		
Play = yes	9	
Windy = false	8	
Humidity = normal	7	
Humidity = high	7	
Windy = true	6	
Temperature = mild	6	
Play = no	5	
Outlook = sunny	5	
Outlook = rainy	5	
Temperature = hot	4	
Temperature = cool	4	
Outlook = overcast	4	

(C)		
	1	**Windy = false, humidity = high**, play = no, outlook = sunny, temperature = hot
	2	**Humidity = high, windy = true**, play = no, outlook = sunny, temperature = hot
	3	**Play = yes, windy = false, humidity = high**, temperature = hot, outlook = overcast
	4	**Play = yes, windy = false, humidity = high, temperature = mild**, outlook = rainy
	5	**Play = yes, windy = false, humidity = normal**, outlook = rainy, temperature = cool
	6	**Humidity = normal, windy = true**, play = no, outlook = rainy, temperature = cool
	7	**Play = yes, humidity = normal, windy = true**, temperature = cool, outlook = overcast

	8	Windy = false, humidity = high, temperature = mild, play = no, outlook = sunny	
	9	Play = yes, windy = false, humidity = normal, outlook = sunny, temperature = cool	
	10	Play = yes, windy = false, humidity = normal, temperature = mild, outlook = rainy	
	11	Play = yes, humidity = normal, windy = true, temperature = mild, outlook = sunny	
	12	Play = yes, humidity = high, windy = true, temperature = mild, outlook = overcast	
	13	Play = yes, windy = false, humidity = normal, temperature = hot, outlook = overcast	
	14	Humidity = high, windy = true, temperature = mild, play = no, outlook = rainy	
(D)	Play = yes & windy = false	6	
	Play = yes & humidity = normal	6	

final answer: a total of eight item sets. We are going to have to do a lot of work to find the two multiple-item sets in Table 6.1D using the FP-tree method.

Fig. 6.8A shows the FP-tree structure that results from this data with a minimum support threshold of 6. The tree itself is shown with solid arrows. The numbers at each node show how many times the sorted prefix of items, up to and including the item at that node, occur in the dataset. For example, following the third branch from the left in the tree we can see that, after sorting, two instances begin with the prefix *humidity = high*—the second and last instances of Table 6.1C. Continuing down that branch, the next node records that the same two instances also have *windy = true* as their next most frequent item. The lowest node in the branch shows that one of these two instances (the last in Table 6.1C) contain *temperature = mild* as well. The other instance (the second in the Table) drops out at this stage because its next most frequent item does not meet the minimum support constraint and is therefore omitted from the tree.

On the left-hand side of the diagram a "header table" shows the frequencies of the individual items in the dataset (Table 6.1B). These items appear in descending frequency order, and only those with at least minimum support are included. Each item in the header table points to its first occurrence in the tree, and subsequent items in the tree with the same name are linked together to form a list. These lists, emanating from the header table, are shown in Fig. 6.8A by dashed arrows.

It is apparent from the tree that only two nodes have counts that satisfy the minimum support threshold, corresponding to the item sets *play = yes* (count of 9) and *play = yes* & *windy = false* (count of 6) in the leftmost branch. Each entry in the header table is itself a single-item set that also satisfies the threshold. This identifies as part of the final answer all the bold items in Table 6.1B and the first item set in Table 6.1D. Since we know the outcome in advance we can see that there is only one more item set to go—the second in Table 6.1D. But there is no hint of it in the data structure of Fig. 6.8A, and we will have to do a lot of work to discover it!

(A)

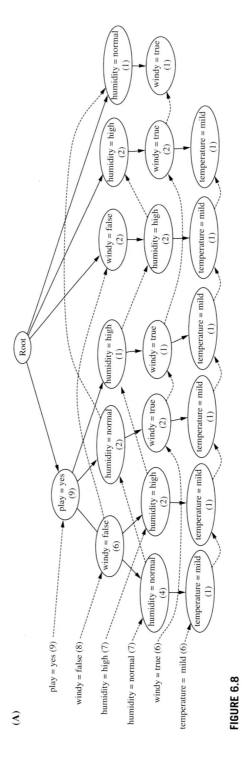

FIGURE 6.8

Extended prefix trees for the weather data: (A) the full data; (B) the data conditional on *temperature = mild*; (C) the data conditional on *humidity = normal*.

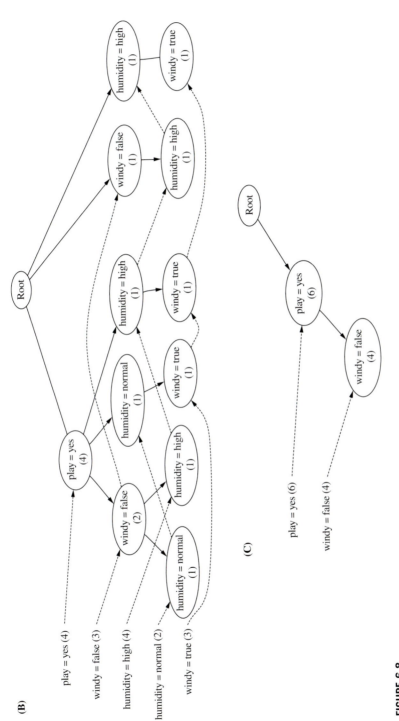

(B)

play = yes (4)

windy = false (3)

humidity = high (4)

humidity = normal (2)

windy = true (3)

(C)

play = yes (6)

windy = false (4)

FIGURE 6.8

(Continued)

FINDING LARGE ITEM SETS

The purpose of the links from the header table into the tree structure is to facilitate traversal of the tree to find other large item sets, apart from the two that are already in the tree. This is accomplished by a divide-and-conquer approach that recursively processes the tree to grow large item sets. Each header table list is followed in turn, starting from the bottom of the table and working upwards. Actually, the header table can be processed in any order, but it is easier to think about processing the longest paths in the tree first, and these correspond to the lower-frequency items.

Starting from the bottom of the header table, we can immediately add *temperature = mild* to the list of large item sets. Fig. 6.8B shows the result of the next stage, which is an FP-tree for just those instances in the dataset that include *temperature = mild*. This tree was not created by rescanning the dataset but by further processing of the tree in Fig. 6.8A, as follows.

To see if a larger item set containing *temperature = mild* can be grown, we follow its link from the header table. This allows us to find all instances that contain *temperature = mild*. From here the new tree in Fig. 6.8B is created, with counts projected from the original tree corresponding to the set of instances that are conditional on the presence of *temperature = mild*. This is done by propagating the counts from the *temperature = mild* nodes up the tree, each node receiving the sum of its children's counts.

A quick glance at the header table for this new FP-tree shows that the *temperature = mild* pattern cannot be grown any larger because there are no individual items, conditional on *temperature = mild*, that meet the minimum support threshold. Note, however, that it is necessary to create the whole Fig. 6.8B tree in order to discover this, because it is effectively being created bottom up and the counts in the header table to the left are computed from the numbers in the tree. The recursion exits at this point, and processing continues on the remaining header table items in the original FP-tree.

Fig. 6.8C shows a second example, the FP-tree that results from following the header table link for *humidity = normal*. Here the *windy = false* node has a count of 4, corresponding to the four instances that had *humidity = normal* in its left branch in the original tree. Similarly, *play = yes* has a count of 6, corresponding to the four instances from *windy = false* and the two instances that contain *humidity = normal* from the middle branch of the subtree rooted at *play = yes* in Fig. 6.8A.

Processing the header list for this FP-tree shows that the *humidity = normal* item set can be grown to include *play = yes* since these two occur together six times, which meets the minimum support constraint. This corresponds to the second item set in Table 6.1D, which in fact completes the output. However, in order to be sure that there are no other eligible item sets it is necessary to continue processing the entire header link table in Fig. 6.8A.

Once the recursive tree mining process is complete all large item sets that meet the minimum support threshold have been found. Then association rules are created using the approach explained in Section 4.5. Studies have claimed that the FP-growth algorithm is up to an order of magnitude faster than Apriori at finding large item sets, although this depends on the details of the implementation and the nature of the dataset.

DISCUSSION

The process of recursively creating projected FP-trees can be efficiently implemented within a single prefix tree structure by having a list of frequencies, indexed by recursion depth, at each node in the tree and each element of the header table. The tree structure itself is usually far smaller than the original dataset, and if the dataset is dense it achieves a high level of compression. This outweighs the overhead imposed by the pointers and counters that must be maintained at each node. Only when the support threshold is set very low does the FP-tree's ability to compress the dataset degrade. Under these conditions, the tree becomes bushy, with little node sharing. On massive datasets for which the FP-tree exceeds main memory, disk-resident trees can be constructed using indexing techniques that have been developed for relational database systems.

The FP-tree data structure and FP-growth algorithm for finding large item sets without candidate generation were introduced by Han, Pei, and Yin (2000) following pioneering work by Zaki, Parthasarathy, Ogihara, and Li (1997); Han, Pei, Yin, and Mao (2004) give a more comprehensive description. It has been extended in various ways. Wang, Han, and Pei (2003) develop an algorithm called CLOSET+ to mine closed item sets, i.e., sets for which there is no proper superset that has the same support. Finding large closed item sets provides essentially the same information as finding the complete set of large item sets, but produces few redundant rules and thus eases the task that users face when examining the output of the mining process. GSP, for Generalized Sequential Patterns, is a method based on the Apriori algorithm for mining patterns in databases of event sequences (Srikant & Agrawal, 1996). A similar approach to FP-growth is used for event sequences by algorithms called PrefixSpan (Pei et al., 2004) and CloSpan (Yan, Han, & Afshar, 2003), and for graph patterns by algorithms called gSpan (Yan & Han, 2002) and CloseGraph (Yan & Han, 2003).

Ceglar and Roddick (2006) provide a comprehensive survey of association rule mining. Some authors have worked on integrating association rule mining with classification. For example, Liu, Hsu, and Ma (1998) mine a kind of association rule that they call a "class association rule," and build a classifier on the rules that are found using a technique they call CBA. Mutter, Hall, and Frank (2004) use classification to evaluate the output of confidence-based association rule mining, and find that standard learners for classification rules are generally preferable to CBA when run time and size of the rule sets is of concern.

6.4 WEKA IMPLEMENTATIONS

- Decision trees
    J48 (implementation of C4.5)
    SimpleCart (minimum cost-complexity pruning à la CART, in the
        simpleCART package)
    REPTree (reduced-error pruning)
- Classification rules
    JRip (RIPPER rule learner)
    Part (rules from partial decision trees)
    Ridor (ripple-down rule learner, in the *ridor* package)
- Association rules
    FPGrowth (frequent pattern trees).
    GeneralizedSequentialPatterns (find large item trees in sequential data, in
        the *generalizedSequentialPatterns* package)
    CBA (mining class association rules, in the *classAssociationRules* package)

CHAPTER

Extending instance-based and linear models

7

CHAPTER OUTLINE

7.1 Instance-Based Learning 244
  Reducing the Number of Exemplars 245
  Pruning Noisy Exemplars 245
  Weighting Attributes 246
  Generalizing Exemplars...247
  Distance Functions for Generalized Exemplars 248
  Generalized Distance Functions 250
  Discussion 250
7.2 Extending Linear Models 252
  The Maximum Margin Hyperplane...253
  Nonlinear Class Boundaries...254
  Support Vector Regression...256
  Kernel Ridge Regression 258
  The Kernel Perceptron 260
  Multilayer Perceptrons 261
  Radial Basis Function Networks...270
  Stochastic Gradient Descent..270
  Discussion 272
7.3 Numeric Prediction With Local Linear Models 273
  Model Trees 274
  Building the Tree..275
  Pruning the Tree..275
  Nominal Attributes 276
  Missing Values 276
  Pseudocode for Model Tree Induction.......................................277
  Rules From Model Trees..281
  Locally Weighted Linear Regression 281
  Discussion 283
7.4 WEKA Implementations...284

Instance-based learning and fitting linear models are both classic techniques that have been used for many decades to solve prediction tasks in statistics. In this chapter, we show how these basic methods can be extended to tackle more challenging tasks.

Basic instance-based learning using the nearest-neighbor classifier is quite fickle in the presence of noise and irrelevant attributes, and its predictive performance hinges on employing a distance function that matches the task at hand. It requires the entire training data to be stored, which may not be desirable or even feasible in practice. Finally, it provides no insight into what has been "learned." To address these deficiencies, we will show how to reduce the number of training examples, how to guard against noisy examples, how to weight attributes to take account of their importance, how to generalize examples to rules to provide insight, and how to generalize distance functions to different types of data.

For linear models, we discuss several ways of extending their applicability to situations where the output is not a linear function of the original attributes. One is to increase the mathematical complexity of the model by forming new attributes based on the original ones, or by combining the output of many linear models to form a far more complex function. The first approach, applied naïvely, greatly increases the computational demands of the learning problem. However, it turns out that there is a neat mathematical device—known as the "kernel trick"—that resolves this issue. We discuss several kernel-based learning methods: support vector machines, kernel regression, and kernel perceptrons. The second approach, based on nonlinear transformations of the outputs of linear models, yields what is known as an artificial neural network. We will discuss multilayer perceptrons, a widely used type of neural network for classification and regression. We will also explain stochastic gradient descent, a simple and fast technique for learning many of the models we discuss—both basic linear models and their extended versions.

We also discuss two other ways to extend linear models. One is to build local linear models by dividing the instance space into regions using a tree learner and fitting models to the leaves of the tree, yielding so-called model trees. Another is to combine instance-based learning with linear models, yielding locally weighted regression. The former approach produces an intelligible model, in contrast to most of the other approaches discussed in this chapter; the latter naturally accommodates incremental learning.

7.1 INSTANCE-BASED LEARNING

In Section 4.7 we saw how the nearest-neighbor rule can be used to implement a basic form of instance-based learning. There are several practical problems with this simple scheme. First, it tends to be slow for large training sets, because the entire set must be searched for each test instance—unless sophisticated data structures such as kD-trees or ball trees are used. Second, it performs badly with noisy data, because the class of a test instance is determined by its single nearest neighbor without any "averaging" to help eliminate noise. Third, it performs badly when different attributes affect the outcome to different extents—in the extreme case, when some attributes are completely irrelevant—because all attributes contribute equally to the distance formula. Fourth, it does not perform explicit generalization, although we intimated in Section 3.5 (and illustrated in Fig. 3.10) that some instance-based learning systems do indeed perform explicit generalization.

REDUCING THE NUMBER OF EXEMPLARS

The plain nearest-neighbor rule stores a lot of redundant exemplars. Yet it is almost always completely unnecessary to save all the examples seen so far. A simple variant is to classify each example with respect to the examples already seen and to save only ones that are misclassified. We use the term *exemplars* to refer to the already-seen instances that are used for classification. Discarding correctly classified instances reduces the number of exemplars and proves to be an effective way to prune the exemplar database. Ideally, only a single exemplar is stored for each important region of the instance space. However, early in the learning process examples may be discarded that later turn out to be important, possibly leading to some decrease in predictive accuracy. As the number of stored instances increases, the accuracy of the model improves, and so the system makes fewer mistakes.

Unfortunately, the strategy of only storing misclassified instances does not work well in the face of noise. Noisy examples are very likely to be misclassified, and so the set of stored exemplars tends to accumulate those that are least useful. This effect is easily observed experimentally. Thus this strategy is only a stepping stone on the way toward more effective instance-based learners.

PRUNING NOISY EXEMPLARS

Noisy exemplars inevitably lower the performance of any nearest-neighbor scheme that does not suppress them, because they have the effect of repeatedly misclassifying new instances. There are two ways of dealing with this. One is to locate, instead of the single nearest neighbor, the k nearest neighbors for some predetermined constant k, and assign the majority class to the unknown instance. The only problem here is determining a suitable value of k. Plain nearest-neighbor learning corresponds to $k = 1$. The more noise, the greater the optimal value of k. One way to proceed is to perform cross-validation tests with several different values and choose the best. Although this is expensive in computation time, it often yields excellent predictive performance.

A second solution is to monitor the performance of each exemplar that is stored and discard ones that do not perform well. This can be done by keeping a record of the number of correct and incorrect classification decisions that each exemplar makes. Two predetermined thresholds are set on the success ratio. When an exemplar's performance drops below the lower one, it is deleted from the exemplar set. If its performance exceeds the upper threshold, it is used for predicting the class of new instances. If its performance lies between the two, it is not used for prediction but, whenever it is the closest exemplar to the new instance (and thus would have been used for prediction if its performance record had been good enough), its success statistics are updated as though it had been used to classify that new instance.

To accomplish this, we use the confidence limits on the success probability of a Bernoulli process that we derived in Section 5.2. Recall that we took a certain number of successes S out of a total number of trials N as evidence on which to base confidence limits on the true underlying success rate p. Given a certain confidence level of, say, 5%, we can calculate upper and lower bounds and be 95% sure that p lies between them.

To apply this to the problem of deciding when to accept a particular exemplar, suppose that it has been used n times to classify other instances and that s of these have been successes. That allows us to estimate bounds, at a particular confidence level, on the true success rate of this exemplar. Now suppose that the exemplar's class has occurred c times out of a total number N of training instances. This allows us to estimate bounds on the default success rate, i.e., the probability of successfully classifying an instance of this class without any information about the attribute values. We insist that the *lower* confidence bound on an exemplar's success rate exceeds the *upper* confidence bound on the default success rate. We use the same method to devise a criterion for rejecting a poorly performing exemplar, requiring that the *upper* confidence bound on its success rate lies below the *lower* confidence bound on the default success rate.

With suitable choice of thresholds, this scheme works well. In a particular implementation, called *IB3* for *Instance-Based learner version 3*, a confidence level of 5% is used to determine acceptance, whereas a level of 12.5% is used for rejection. The lower percentage figure produces a wider confidence interval, which makes for a more stringent criterion because it is harder for the lower bound of one interval to lie above the upper bound of the other. The criterion for acceptance is more stringent than for rejection, making it more difficult for an instance to be accepted. The reason for a less stringent rejection criterion is that there is little to be lost by dropping instances with only moderately poor classification accuracies: they will probably be replaced by similar instances later. Using these thresholds has been found to improve the performance of instance-based learning and, at the same time, dramatically reduce the number of exemplars—particularly noisy exemplars—that are stored.

WEIGHTING ATTRIBUTES

The Euclidean distance function, modified to scale all attribute values to between 0 and 1, works well in domains in which the attributes are equally relevant to the outcome. Such domains, however, are the exception rather than the rule. In most domains some attributes are irrelevant, and some relevant ones are less important than others. The next improvement in instance-based learning is to learn the relevance of each attribute incrementally by dynamically updating feature weights.

In some schemes, the weights are class specific in that an attribute may be more important to one class than to another. To cater for this, a description is produced for each class that distinguishes its members from members of all other classes. This leads to the problem that an unknown test instance may be assigned to several different classes, or no classes at all—a problem that is all too familiar from our description of rule induction. Heuristic solutions are applied to resolve these situations.

The weighted Euclidean distance metric incorporates the feature weights w_1, $w_2, \ldots, w_n$ on each dimension:

$$\sqrt{w_1^2(x_1 - y_1)^2 + w_2^2(x_2 - y_2)^2 + \cdots + w_n^2(x_n - y_n)^2}.$$

In the case of class-specific feature weights, there will be a separate set of weights for each class.

All attribute weights are updated after each training instance is classified, and the most similar exemplar (or the most similar exemplar of each class) is used as the basis for updating. Call the training instance x and the most similar exemplar y. For each attribute i, the difference $|x_i - y_i|$ is a measure of the contribution of that attribute to the decision. If this difference is small then the attribute contributes positively, whereas if it is large it may contribute negatively. The basic idea is to update the ith weight on the basis of the size of this difference and whether the classification was indeed correct. If the classification is correct the associated weight is increased and if it is incorrect it is decreased, the amount of increase or decrease being governed by the size of the difference: large if the difference is small and vice versa. The weight change is generally followed by a renormalization step. A simpler strategy, which may be equally effective, is to leave the weights alone if the decision is correct and if it is incorrect to increase the weights for those attributes that differ most greatly, accentuating the difference.

A good test of whether an attribute weighting scheme works is to add irrelevant attributes to all examples in a data set. Ideally, the introduction of irrelevant attributes should not affect either the quality of predictions or the number of exemplars stored.

GENERALIZING EXEMPLARS

Removing training exemplars that are noisy or redundant aids understanding of the structure of the data—to some extent. To improve interpretability further, exemplars need to be generalized.

Generalized exemplars are rectangular regions of instance space, called *hyperrectangles* because they are high-dimensional. When classifying new instances it is necessary to modify the distance function as described below to allow the distance to a hyperrectangle to be computed. When a new exemplar is classified correctly, it is generalized by simply merging it with the nearest exemplar of the same class. The nearest exemplar may be either a single instance or a hyperrectangle. In the former case, a new hyperrectangle is created that covers the old and the new instance. In the latter, the hyperrectangle is enlarged to encompass the new instance. Finally, if the prediction is incorrect and it was a hyperrectangle that was responsible for the incorrect prediction, the hyperrectangle's boundaries are altered so that it shrinks away from the new instance.

It is necessary to decide at the outset whether overgeneralization caused by nesting or overlapping hyperrectangles is to be permitted or not. If it is to be avoided, a check is made before generalizing a new example to see whether any regions of feature space conflict with the proposed new hyperrectangle. If they do, the generalization is aborted and the example is stored verbatim. Note that overlapping hyperrectangles are precisely analogous to situations in which the same example is covered by two or more rules in a rule set.

In some schemes generalized exemplars can be nested in that they may be completely contained within one another in the same way that, in some representations, rules may have exceptions. To do this, whenever an example is incorrectly classified, a fallback heuristic is tried using the second nearest neighbor if it would have produced a correct prediction in a further attempt to perform generalization. This second-chance mechanism promotes nesting of hyperrectangles. If an example falls within a rectangle of the wrong class that already contains an exemplar of the same class, the two are generalized into a new "exception" hyperrectangle nested within the original one. For nested generalized exemplars, the learning process frequently begins with a small number of seed instances to prevent all examples of the same class from being generalized into a single rectangle that covers most of the problem space.

DISTANCE FUNCTIONS FOR GENERALIZED EXEMPLARS

With generalized exemplars it is necessary to generalize the distance function to compute the distance from an instance to a generalized exemplar, as well as to another instance. The distance from an instance to a hyperrectangle is defined to be zero if the point lies within the hyperrectangle. The simplest way to generalize the distance function to compute the distance from an exterior point to a hyperrectangle is to choose the closest instance within it and measure the distance to that. However, this reduces the benefit of generalization because it reintroduces dependence on a particular single example. More precisely, whereas new instances that happen to lie within a hyperrectangle continue to benefit from generalizations, ones that lie outside do not. It might be better to use the distance from the nearest part of the hyperrectangle instead.

Fig. 7.1 shows the implicit boundaries that are formed between two rectangular classes if the distance metric is adjusted to measure distance to the nearest

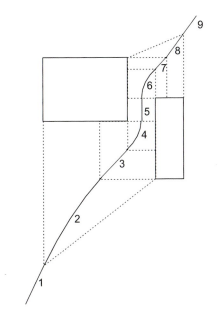

FIGURE 7.1

A boundary between two rectangular classes.

point of a rectangle. Even in two dimensions the boundary contains a total of nine regions (they are numbered for easy identification); the situation will be more complex for higher-dimensional hyperrectangles.

Proceeding from the lower left, the first region, in which the boundary is linear, lies outside the extent of both rectangles—to the left of both borders of the larger one and below both borders of the smaller one. The second is within the extent of one rectangle—to the right of the leftmost border of the larger rectangle—but outside that of the other—below both borders of the smaller one. In this region the boundary is parabolic, because the locus of a point that is the same distance from a given line as from a given point is a *parabola*. The third region is where the boundary meets the lower border of the larger rectangle when projected upward and the left border of the smaller one when projected to the right. The boundary is linear in this region, because it is equidistant from these two borders. The fourth is where the boundary lies to the right of the larger rectangle but below the bottom of that rectangle. In this case the boundary is parabolic because it is the locus of points equidistant from the lower right corner of the larger rectangle and the left side of the smaller one. The fifth region lies between the two rectangles: here the boundary is vertical. The pattern is repeated in the upper right part of the diagram: first parabolic, then linear, then parabolic (although this particular parabola is almost indistinguishable from a straight line), and finally linear as the boundary finally escapes from the scope of both rectangles.

This simple situation certainly defines a complex boundary! Of course it is not necessary to represent the boundary explicitly; it is generated implicitly by the nearest-neighbor calculation. Nevertheless, the solution is still not a very good one. Whereas taking the distance from the nearest instance within a hyperrectangle is overly dependent on the position of that particular instance, taking the distance to the nearest point of the hyperrectangle is overly dependent on that corner of the rectangle—the nearest example might be a long way from the corner.

A final problem concerns measuring the distance to hyperrectangles that overlap or are nested. This complicates the situation because an instance may fall within more than one hyperrectangle. A suitable heuristic for use in this case is to choose the class of the most specific hyperrectangle containing the instance, i.e., the one covering the smallest area of instance space.

Whether or not overlap or nesting is permitted, the distance function should be modified to take account of both the observed prediction accuracy of exemplars and the relative importance of different features, as described in the sections above on pruning noisy exemplars and attribute weighting.

GENERALIZED DISTANCE FUNCTIONS

There are many different ways of defining a distance function, and it is hard to find rational grounds for any particular choice. An elegant solution is to consider one instance being transformed into another through a sequence of predefined elementary operations and to calculate the probability of such a sequence occurring if operations are chosen randomly. Robustness is improved if all possible transformation paths are considered, weighted by their probabilities, and the scheme generalizes naturally to the problem of calculating the distance between an instance and a set of other instances by considering transformations to all instances in the set. Through such a technique it is possible to consider each instance as exerting a "sphere of influence," but a sphere with soft boundaries rather than the hard-edged cutoff implied by the k-nearest-neighbor rule, in which any particular example is either "in" or "out" of the decision.

With such a measure, given a test instance whose class is unknown, its distance to the set of all training instances in each class in turn is calculated, and the closest class is chosen. It turns out that nominal and numeric attributes can be treated in a uniform manner within this transformation-based approach by defining different transformation sets, and it is even possible to take account of unusual attribute types—such as degrees of arc or days of the week, which are measured on a circular scale.

DISCUSSION

Nearest-neighbor methods gained popularity in machine learning through the work of Aha (1992), who showed that, when combined with noisy exemplar pruning and attribute weighting, instance-based learning performs well in comparison with other methods. It is worth noting that although we have described it solely in the context of classification rather than numeric prediction problems, it applies to these equally well: predictions can be obtained by combining the predicted values of the k nearest neighbors and weighting them by distance.

Viewed in instance space, the standard rule- and tree-based representations are only capable of representing class boundaries that are parallel to the axes defined by the attributes. This is not a handicap for nominal attributes, but it is for numeric ones. Nonaxis-parallel class boundaries can only be approximated by covering the region above or below the boundary with several axis-parallel rectangles, the number of rectangles determining the degree of approximation. In contrast, the instance-based method can easily represent arbitrary linear boundaries. Even with just one example of each of two classes, the boundary implied by the nearest-neighbor rule is a straight line of arbitrary orientation, namely, the perpendicular bisector of the line joining the examples.

Plain instance-based learning does not produce explicit knowledge representations except by selecting representative exemplars. However, when combined with exemplar generalization, a set of rules can be obtained that may be compared with those produced by other machine learning schemes. The rules tend to be more conservative because the distance metric, modified to incorporate generalized exemplars, can be used to process examples that do not fall within the rules. This reduces the pressure to produce rules that cover the whole example space or even all of the training examples. On the other hand, the incremental nature of the instance-based learning scheme we have described means that rules are formed eagerly, after only part of the training set has been seen; and this inevitably reduces their quality.

We have not given precise algorithms for variants of instance-based learning that involve generalization because it is not clear what the best way to do generalization is. Salzberg (1991) suggested that generalization with nested exemplars can achieve a high degree of classification of accuracy on a variety of different problems, a conclusion disputed by Wettschereck and Dietterich (1994), who argued that these results were fortuitous and did not hold in other domains. Martin (1995) explored the idea that it is not generalization but the overgeneralization that occurs when hyperrectangles nest or overlap that is responsible for poor performance and demonstrated that if nesting and overlapping are avoided excellent results are achieved in a large number of domains. The generalized distance function based on transformations is described by Cleary and Trigg (1995).

Exemplar generalization is a rare example of a learning strategy in which the search proceeds from specific to general rather than from general to specific as in the case of the tree and rule induction schemes we have described. There is no particular reason why specific-to-general searching should necessarily be handicapped by forcing the examples to be considered in a strictly incremental fashion, and batch-oriented approaches exist that generate rules using a basic instance-based approach. Moreover, it seems that the idea of producing conservative generalizations and coping with instances that are not covered by choosing the "closest" generalization may be generally useful for tree and rule inducers.

7.2 EXTENDING LINEAR MODELS

Section 4.6 described how simple linear models can be used for classification in situations where all attributes are numeric. Their biggest disadvantage is that they can only represent linear boundaries between classes, which makes them too simple for many practical applications. Support vector machines use linear models to implement nonlinear class boundaries. (Although it is a widely used term, *support vector machines* is something of a misnomer: these are algorithms, not machines.) How can this be possible? The trick is easy: transform the input using a nonlinear mapping. In other words, transform the instance space into a new space. With a nonlinear mapping, a straight line in the new space does not look straight in the original instance space. A linear model constructed in the new space can represent a nonlinear decision boundary in the original space.

Imagine applying this idea directly to the ordinary linear models in Section 4.6. For example, the original set of attributes could be replaced by one giving all products of n factors that can be constructed from these attributes. An example for two attributes, including all products with three factors, is

$$x = w_1 a_1^3 + w_2 a_1^2 a_2 + w_3 a_1 a_2^2 + w_4 a_2^3.$$

Here, x is the outcome, a_1 and a_2 are the two attribute values, and there are four weights w_i to be learned. As described in Section 4.6, the result can be used for classification by training one linear system for each class and assigning an unknown instance to the class that gives the greatest output x—the standard technique of multiresponse linear regression. Then, a_1 and a_2 will be the attribute values for the test instance. To generate a linear model in the space spanned by these products, each training instance is mapped into the new space by computing all possible three-factor products of its two attribute values. The learning algorithm is then applied to the transformed instances. To classify an instance, it is processed by the same transformation prior to classification. There is nothing to stop us from adding in more synthetic attributes. For example, if a constant term were included, the original attributes and all two-factor products of them would yield a total of ten weights to be learned. (Alternatively, adding an additional attribute with a constant value would have the same effect.) Indeed, polynomials of sufficiently high degree can approximate arbitrary decision boundaries to any required accuracy.

It seems too good to be true—and it is. As you will probably have guessed, problems arise with this procedure due to the large number of coefficients introduced by the transformation in any realistic setting. The first snag is computational complexity. With 10 attributes in the original data set, suppose we want to include all products with 5 factors: then the learning algorithm will have to determine more than 2000 coefficients. If its run time is cubic in the number of attributes, as it is for linear regression, training will be infeasible. That is a problem of practicality. The second problem is one of principle: overfitting. If the number of coefficients is large relative to the number of training instances, the resulting model will be "too nonlinear"—it will overfit the training data. There are just too many parameters in the model.

THE MAXIMUM MARGIN HYPERPLANE

Support vector machines address both problems. They are based on an algorithm that finds a special kind of linear model: the *maximum margin hyperplane*. We already know what a hyperplane is—it is just another term for a linear model. To visualize a maximum margin hyperplane, imagine a two-class data set whose classes are linearly separable; i.e., there is a hyperplane in instance space that classifies all training instances correctly. The maximum margin hyperplane is the one that gives the greatest separation between the classes—it comes no closer to either than it has to. An example is shown in Fig. 7.2, where the classes are represented by open and filled circles, respectively. Technically, the *convex hull* of a set of points is the tightest enclosing convex polygon: its outline emerges when you connect every point of the set to every other point. Because we have supposed that the two classes are linearly separable, their convex hulls cannot overlap. Among all hyperplanes that separate the classes, the maximum margin hyperplane is the one that is as far as possible from both convex hulls—it is the perpendicular bisector of the shortest line connecting the hulls, which is shown dashed in the figure.

The instances that are closest to the maximum margin hyperplane—the ones with minimum distance to it—are called *support vectors*. There is always at least one support vector for each class, and often there are more. The important thing

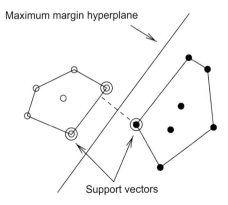

FIGURE 7.2

A maximum margin hyperplane.

is that the set of support vectors uniquely defines the maximum margin hyper-plane for the learning problem. Given the support vectors for the two classes, we can easily construct the maximum margin hyperplane. All other training instances are irrelevant—they can be deleted without changing the position and orientation of the hyperplane.

A hyperplane separating the two classes might be written

$$x = w_0 + w_1 a_1 + w_2 a_2$$

in the two-attribute case, where a_1 and a_2 are the attribute values, and there are three weights w_i to be learned. However, the equation defining the maximum margin hyperplane can be written in another form, in terms of the support vectors. Write the class value y of a training instance as either 1 (for *yes*, it is in this class) or -1 (for *no*, it is not). Then the maximum margin hyperplane can be written

$$x = b + \sum_{i \text{ is support vector}} \alpha_i y_i \mathbf{a(i)} \cdot \mathbf{a}.$$

Here, y_i is the class value of training instance $\mathbf{a(i)}$, while b and α_i are numeric parameters that have to be determined by the learning algorithm. Note that $\mathbf{a(i)}$ and $\mathbf{a}$ are vectors. The vector $\mathbf{a}$ represents a test instance—just as the vector $[a_1, a_2]$ represented a test instance in the earlier formulation. The vectors $\mathbf{a(i)}$ are the support vectors, those circled in Fig. 7.2; they are selected members of the training set. The term $\mathbf{a(i)} \cdot \mathbf{a}$ represents the dot product of the test instance with one of the support vectors: $\mathbf{a(i)} \cdot \mathbf{a} = \sum_j a(i)_j a_j$. If you are not familiar with dot product notation, you should still be able to understand the gist of what follows: just think of $\mathbf{a(i)}$ as the whole set of attribute values for the i-th support vector. Finally, b and α_i are parameters that determine the hyperplane, just as the weights w_0, w_1, and w_2 are parameters that determine the hyperplane in the earlier formulation.

It turns out that finding the support vectors for the training instances and determining the parameters b and α_i belong to a standard class of optimization problems known as *constrained quadratic optimization* problems. There are off-the-shelf software packages for solving these problems. However, the computa-tional complexity can be reduced, and learning accelerated, if special purpose algorithms for training support vector machines are applied—but the details of these algorithms lie beyond the scope of this book.

NONLINEAR CLASS BOUNDARIES

We motivated the introduction of support vector machines by claiming that they can be used to model nonlinear class boundaries. However, so far we have only described the linear case. Consider what happens when an attribute transformation, as described above, is applied to the training data before determining the maximum margin hyperplane. Recall that there are two problems with the straightforward application of such transformations to linear models: computational complexity, on the one hand, and overfitting, on the other.

With support vectors, overfitting is reduced. The reason is that it is inevitably associated with instability: with an algorithm that overfits, changing one or two instance vectors will make sweeping changes to large sections of the decision boundary. But the maximum margin hyperplane is relatively stable: it only moves if training instances are added or deleted that are support vectors—and this is true even in the high-dimensional space spanned by the nonlinear transformation. Overfitting is caused by too much flexibility in the decision boundary. The support vectors are global representatives of the whole set of training points, and there are often relatively few of them, which gives little flexibility. Thus overfitting is less likely to occur.

What about computational complexity? This is still a problem. Suppose that the transformed space is a high-dimensional one so that the transformed support vectors and test instance have many components. According to the preceding equation, every time an instance is classified its dot product with all support vectors must be calculated. In the high-dimensional space produced by the nonlinear mapping this is rather expensive. Obtaining the dot product involves one multiplication and one addition for each attribute, and the number of attributes in the new space can be huge. This problem occurs not only during classification but also during training, because the optimization algorithms have to calculate the same dot products very frequently.

Fortunately, it turns out that it is possible to calculate the dot product *before* the nonlinear mapping is performed, on the original attribute set. A high-dimensional version of the preceding equation is simply

$$x = b + \sum \alpha_i y_i (\mathbf{a(i)} \cdot \mathbf{a})^n,$$

where n is chosen as the number of factors in the transformation (three in the example we used earlier). If you expand the term $(\mathbf{a(i)} \cdot \mathbf{a})^n$, you will find that it contains all the high-dimensional terms that would have been involved if the test and training vectors were first transformed by including all products of n factors and the dot product was taken of the result. (If you actually do the calculation, you will notice that some constant factors—binomial coefficients—are introduced. However, it is primarily the dimensionality of the space that concerns us; the constants merely scale the axes.) Because of this mathematical equivalence, the dot products can be computed in the original low-dimensional space, and the problem becomes feasible. In implementation terms, you take a software package for constrained quadratic optimization and every time $\mathbf{a(i)} \cdot \mathbf{a}$ is evaluated you evaluate $(\mathbf{a(i)} \cdot \mathbf{a})^n$ instead. It is as simple as that, because in both the optimization and the classification algorithms these vectors are only ever used in this dot product form. The training vectors, including the support vectors, and the test instance all remain in the original low-dimensional space throughout the calculations.

The function $(\mathbf{x} \cdot \mathbf{y})^n$, which computes the dot product of two vectors $\mathbf{x}$ and $\mathbf{y}$ and raises the result to the power n, is called a *polynomial kernel*. A good way of choosing the value of n is to start with 1 (a linear model) and increment it until the estimated error ceases to improve. Usually, quite small values suffice. To include lower-order terms, we can use the kernel $(\mathbf{x} \cdot \mathbf{y} + 1)^n$.

Other kernel functions can be used instead to implement different nonlinear mappings. Two that are often suggested are the *radial basis function (RBF) kernel* and the *sigmoid kernel*. Which one produces the best results depends on the application, although the differences are rarely large in practice. It is interesting to note that a support vector machine with the RBF kernel corresponds to a type of neural network called an *RBF network* (which we describe later), and one with the sigmoid kernel implements another type of neural network, a multilayer perceptron with one hidden layer (also described later).

Mathematically, any function $K(\mathbf{x}, \mathbf{y})$ is a kernel function if it can be written $K(\mathbf{x}, \mathbf{y}) = \Phi(\mathbf{x}) \cdot \Phi(\mathbf{y})$, where Φ is a function that maps an instance into a (potentially high-dimensional) feature space. In other words, the kernel function represents a dot product in the feature space created by Φ. Practitioners sometimes apply functions that are not proper kernel functions (the sigmoid kernel with certain parameter settings is an example). Despite the lack of theoretical guarantees, this can nevertheless produce accurate classifiers.

Throughout this section, we have assumed that the training data is linearly separable—either in the instance space or in the new space spanned by the nonlinear mapping. It turns out that support vector machines can be generalized to the case where the training data is not separable. This is accomplished by placing an upper bound C on the coefficients α_i. Unfortunately this parameter must be chosen by the user, and the best setting can only be determined by experimentation. Also, except in trivial cases, it is not possible to determine a priori whether the data is linearly separable or not.

Finally, we should mention that compared with other methods such as decision tree learners, even the fastest training algorithms for support vector machines are slow when applied in the nonlinear setting. On the other hand, they often produce very accurate classifiers because subtle and complex decision boundaries can be obtained.

SUPPORT VECTOR REGRESSION

The concept of a maximum margin hyperplane only applies to classification. However, support vector machine algorithms have been developed for numeric prediction that share many of the properties encountered in the classification case: they produce a model that can usually be expressed in terms of a few support vectors and can be applied to nonlinear problems using kernel functions. As with regular support vector machines, we will describe the concepts involved but do not attempt to describe the algorithms that actually perform the work.

As with linear regression, covered in Section 4.6, the basic idea is to find a function that approximates the training points well by minimizing the prediction error. The crucial difference is that all deviations up to a user-specified parameter

ε are simply discarded. Also, when minimizing the error, the risk of overfitting is reduced by simultaneously trying to maximize the flatness of the function. Another difference is that what is minimized is normally the predictions' absolute error instead of the squared error used in linear regression. (There are, however, versions of the algorithm that use the squared error instead.)

A user-specified parameter ε defines a tube around the regression function in which errors are ignored: for linear support vector regression, the tube is a cylinder. If all training points can fit within a tube of width 2ε, the algorithm outputs the function in the middle of the flattest tube that encloses them. In this case the total perceived error is zero. Fig. 7.3A shows a regression problem with one attribute, a numeric class, and eight instances. In this case ε was set to 1, so the width of the tube around the regression function (indicated by dotted lines) is 2. Fig. 7.3B shows the outcome of the learning process when ε is set to 2. As you can see, the wider tube makes it possible to learn a flatter function.

The value of ε controls how closely the function will fit the training data. Too large a value will produce a meaningless predictor—in the extreme case, when 2ε exceeds the range of class values in the training data, the regression line is horizontal and the algorithm just predicts the mean class value. On the other hand, for small values of ε there may be no tube that encloses all the data. In that case some training points will have nonzero error, and there will be a tradeoff between the prediction error and the tube's flatness. In Fig. 7.3C, ε was set to 0.5 and there is no tube of width 1 that encloses all the data.

For the linear case, the support vector regression function can be written

$$x = b + \sum_{i \text{ is support vector}} \alpha_i \mathbf{a(i)} \cdot \mathbf{a}.$$

As with classification, the dot product can be replaced by a kernel function for nonlinear problems. The support vectors are all those points that do not fall strictly within the tube—i.e., the points outside the tube and on its border. As with classification, all other points have coefficient 0 and can be deleted from the training data without changing the outcome of the learning process—just as in the classification case, we obtain a so-called sparse model. In contrast to the classification case, the α_i may be negative.

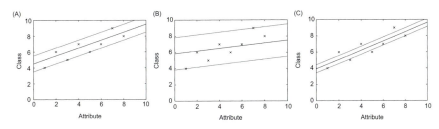

FIGURE 7.3

Support vector regression: (A) $\varepsilon = 1$; (B) $\varepsilon = 2$; (C) $\varepsilon = 0.5$.

We have mentioned that as well as minimizing the error, the algorithm simultaneously tries to maximize the flatness of the regression function. In Fig. 7.3A and B, where there is a tube that encloses all the training data, the algorithm simply outputs the flattest tube that does so. However, in Fig. 7.3C there is no tube with error 0, and a tradeoff is struck between the prediction error and the tube's flatness. This tradeoff is controlled by enforcing an upper limit C on the absolute value of the coefficients α_i. The upper limit restricts the influence of the support vectors on the shape of the regression function and is a parameter that the user must specify in addition to ε. The larger C is, the more closely the function can fit the data. In the degenerate case $\varepsilon = 0$ the algorithm simply performs least-absolute-error regression under the coefficient size constraint, and all training instances become support vectors. Conversely, if ε is large enough that the tube can enclose all the data, the error becomes zero, there is no tradeoff to make, and the algorithm outputs the flattest tube that encloses the data irrespective of the value of C.

KERNEL RIDGE REGRESSION

Chapter 4, Algorithms: the basic methods, introduced classic least-squares linear regression as a technique for predicting numeric quantities. In "Nonlinear class boundaries" section we saw how the powerful idea of support vector machines can be applied to regression, and, furthermore, how nonlinear problems can be tackled by replacing the dot product in the support vector formulation by a kernel function—this is often known as the "kernel trick." For classic linear regression using squared loss, only simple matrix operations are needed to find the model, but this is not the case for support vector regression with the user-specified loss parameter ε. It would be nice to combine the power of the kernel trick with the simplicity of standard least-squares regression. Kernel ridge regression does just that. In contrast to support vector regression, it does not ignore errors smaller than ε, and the squared error is used instead of the absolute error.

Instead of expressing the linear regression model's predicted class value for a given test instance $\mathbf{a}$ as a weighted sum of the attribute values, as in Chapter 4, Algorithms: the basic methods, it can be expressed as a weighted sum over the dot products of each training instance $\mathbf{a}_j$ and the test instance in question:

$$\sum_{j=1}^{n} \alpha_j \mathbf{a}_j \cdot \mathbf{a}$$

where we assume that the function goes through the origin and an intercept is not required. This involves a coefficient α_j for each training instance, which resembles the situation with support vector machines—except that here j ranges over *all* instances in the training data, not just the support vectors. Again, the dot product can be replaced by a kernel function to yield a nonlinear model.

The sum of the squared errors of the model's predictions on the training data is given by

$$\sum_{i=1}^{n}\left(y_i - \sum_{j=1}^{n}\alpha_j\mathbf{a}_j\cdot\mathbf{a}_i\right)^2.$$

This is the squared loss, just as in Chapter 4, Algorithms: the basic methods, and again we seek to minimize it by choosing appropriate α_j's. But now there is a coefficient for each training instance, not just for each attribute, and most data sets have far more instances than attributes. This means that there is a serious risk of overfitting the training data when a kernel function is used instead of the dot product to obtain a nonlinear model.

That is where the *ridge* part of kernel ridge regression comes in. Instead of minimizing the squared loss, we trade closeness of fit against model complexity by introducing a penalty term:

$$\sum_{i=1}^{n}\left(y_i - \sum_{j=1}^{n}\alpha_j\mathbf{a}_j\cdot\mathbf{a}_i\right)^2 + \lambda\sum_{i,j=1}^{n}\alpha_i\alpha_j\mathbf{a}_j\cdot\mathbf{a}_i.$$

The second sum penalizes large coefficients. This prevents the model from placing too much emphasis on individual training instances by giving them large coefficients, unless this yields a correspondingly large drop in error. The parameter λ controls the tradeoff between closeness of fit and model complexity. When matrix operations are used to solve for the coefficients of the model, the ridge penalty also has the added benefit of stabilizing degenerate cases. For this reason, it is often applied in standard least-squares linear regression as well.

Although kernel ridge regression has the advantage over support vector machines of computational simplicity, one disadvantage is that there is no sparseness in the vector of coefficients—in other words, no concept of "support vectors." This makes a difference at prediction time, because support vector machines have to sum only over the set of support vectors, not the entire training set.

In a typical situation with more instances than attributes, kernel ridge regression is more computationally expensive than standard linear regression—even when using the dot product rather than a kernel. This is because of the complexity of the matrix inversion operation used to find the model's coefficient vector. Standard linear regression requires inverting an $m \times m$ matrix, which has complexity $O(m^3)$ where m is the number of attributes in the data. Kernel ridge regression, on the other hand, involves an $n \times n$ matrix, with complexity $O(n^3)$ where n is the number of *instances* in the training data. Nevertheless, it is advantageous to use kernel ridge regression in cases where a nonlinear fit is desired, or where there are more attributes than training instances.

THE KERNEL PERCEPTRON

In Section 4.6 we introduced the perceptron algorithm for learning a linear classifier. It turns out that the kernel trick can also be used to upgrade this algorithm to learn nonlinear decision boundaries. To see this, we first revisit the linear case. The perceptron algorithm repeatedly iterates through the training data instance by instance and updates the weight vector every time one of these instances is misclassified based on the weights learned so far. The weight vector is updated simply by adding or subtracting the instance's attribute values to or from it. This means that the final weight vector is just the sum of the instances that have been misclassified. The perceptron makes its predictions based on whether

$$\sum_i w_i a_i$$

is greater or less than zero—where w_i is the weight for the ith attribute and a_i the corresponding attribute value of the instance that we wish to classify. Instead, we could use

$$\sum_i \sum_j y(j) a'(j)_i a_i.$$

Here, $a'(j)$ is the jth misclassified training instance, $a'(j)_i$ its ith attribute value, and $y(j)$ its class value (either $+1$ or -1). To implement this we no longer keep track of an explicit weight vector: we simply store the instances that have been misclassified so far and use the above expression to make a prediction.

It looks like we have gained nothing—in fact, the algorithm is much slower because it iterates through all misclassified training instances every time a prediction is made. However, closer inspection of this formula reveals that it can be expressed in terms of dot products between instances. First, swap the summation signs to yield

$$\sum_j y(j) \sum_i a'(j)_i a_i.$$

The second sum is just a dot product between two instances and can be written

$$\sum_j y(j) \mathbf{a}'(\mathbf{j}) \cdot \mathbf{a}.$$

This rings a bell! A similar expression for support vector machines enabled the use of kernels. Indeed, we can apply exactly the same trick here and use a kernel function instead of the dot product. Writing this function as $K(\ldots)$ gives

$$\sum_j y(j) K(\mathbf{a}'(\mathbf{j}), \mathbf{a}).$$

In this way the perceptron algorithm can learn a nonlinear classifier simply by keeping track of the instances that have been misclassified during the training process and using this expression to form each prediction.

If a separating hyperplane exists in the high-dimensional space implicitly created by the kernel function, this algorithm will learn one. However, it won't learn the maximum-margin hyperplane found by a support vector machine classifier. This means that classification performance is usually worse. On the plus side, the algorithm is easy to implement and supports incremental learning.

This classifier is called the *kernel perceptron*. It turns out that all sorts of algorithms for learning linear models can be upgraded by applying the kernel trick in a similar fashion. For example, logistic regression can be turned into *kernel logistic regression*. As we saw above, the same applies to regression problems: linear regression can also be upgraded using kernels. Again, a drawback of these advanced methods for linear and logistic regression (if they are done in a straightforward manner) is that the solution is not "sparse": every training instance contributes to the solution vector. In support vector machines and the kernel perceptron, only some of the training instances affect the solution, and this can make a big difference to computational efficiency.

The solution vector found by the perceptron algorithm depends greatly on the order in which the instances are encountered. One way to make the algorithm more stable is to use all the weight vectors encountered during learning, not just the final one, letting them vote on a prediction. Each weight vector contributes a certain number of votes. Intuitively, the "correctness" of a weight vector can be measured roughly as the number of successive trials after its inception in which it correctly classified subsequent instances and thus didn't have to be changed. This measure can be used as the number of votes given to the weight vector, giving an algorithm known as the *voted perceptron* that performs almost as well as a support vector machine. (Note that, as mentioned earlier, the various weight vectors in the voted perceptron don't need to be stored explicitly, and the kernel trick can be applied here too.)

MULTILAYER PERCEPTRONS

Using a kernel is not the only way to create a nonlinear classifier based on the perceptron. In fact, kernel functions are a fairly recent development in machine learning. Previously, neural network proponents used a different approach for nonlinear classification: they connected many simple perceptron-like models in a hierarchical structure. This approach has seen a dramatic resurgence in the form of deep learning, which we cover in Chapter 10, Deep learning.

Section 4.6 explained that a perceptron represents a hyperplane in instance space. We mentioned there that it is sometimes described as an artificial "neuron." Of course, human and animal brains successfully undertake very complex classification tasks—e.g., image recognition. The functionality of each individual neuron in a brain is certainly not sufficient to perform these feats. How can they be solved by brain-like structures? The answer must lie in the fact that the neurons in the brain are massively interconnected, allowing a problem to be decomposed into subproblems that can be solved at the neuron level. This observation inspired the development of artificial networks of neurons—neural nets.

Consider the simple data sets in Fig. 7.4. Fig. 7.4A shows a two-dimensional instance space with four instances having classes 0 and 1, represented by white and black dots, respectively. No matter how you draw a straight line through this space, you will not be able to find one that separates all the black points from all the white ones. In other words, the problem is not linearly separable, and the simple perceptron algorithm will fail to generate a separating hyperplane (in this two-dimensional instance space a hyperplane is just a straight line). The situation is different in Fig. 7.4B and C: both these problems are linearly separable. The same holds for Fig. 7.4D, which shows two points in a one-dimensional instance space (in the case of one dimension the separating hyperplane degenerates to a separating point).

If you are familiar with propositional logic, you may have noticed that the four situations in Fig. 7.4 correspond to four types of logical connectives. Fig. 7.4A represents a logical XOR, where the class is 1 if and only if exactly one of the attributes has value 1. Fig. 7.4B represents logical AND, where the class is 1 if and only if both attributes have value 1. Fig. 7.4C represents OR, where the class is 0 only if both attributes have value 0. Fig. 7.4D represents NOT, where the class is 0 if and only if the attribute has value 1. Because the last three are linearly separable, a perceptron can represent AND, OR, and NOT. Indeed, perceptrons for the corresponding data sets are shown in Fig. 7.4F, G, and H, respectively. However, a simple perceptron cannot represent XOR, because that is not linearly separable. To build a classifier for this type of problem a single perceptron is not sufficient: we need several of them.

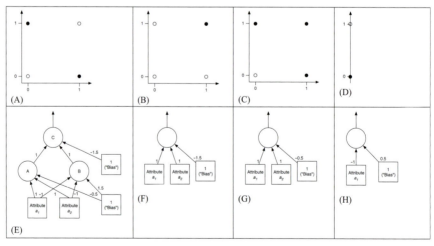

FIGURE 7.4

Example data sets and corresponding perceptrons.

Fig. 7.4E shows a network with three perceptrons, or *units*, labeled A, B, and C. The first two are connected to what is sometimes called the *input layer* of the network, representing the attributes in the data. As in a simple perceptron, the input layer has an additional constant input called the *bias*. However, the third unit does not have any connections to the input layer. Its input consists of the output of units A and B (either 0 or 1) and another constant bias unit. These three units make up the *hidden layer* of the multilayer perceptron. They are called "hidden" because the units have no direct connection to the environment. This layer is what enables the system to represent XOR. You can verify this by trying all four possible combinations of input signals. For example, if attribute a_1 has value 1 and a_2 has value 1, then unit A will output 1 (because $1 \times 1 + 1 \times 1 - 0.5 \times 1 > 0$), unit B will output 0 (because $-1 \times 1 + -1 \times 1 + 1.5 \times 1 < 0$), and unit C will output 0 (because $1 \times 1 + 1 \times 0 + -1.5 \times 1 < 0$). This is the correct answer. Closer inspection of the behavior of the three units reveals that the first one represents OR, the second represents NAND (NOT combined with AND), and the third represents AND. Together they represent the expression (a_1 OR a_2) AND (a_1 NAND a_2), which is precisely the definition of XOR.

As this example illustrates, any expression from propositional logic can be converted into a multilayer perceptron, because the three connectives AND, OR, and NOT are sufficient for this and we have seen how each can be represented using a perceptron. Individual units can be connected together to form arbitrarily complex expressions. Hence, a multilayer perceptron has the same expressive power as, say, a decision tree. In fact, it turns out that a two-layer perceptron (not counting the input layer) is sufficient. In this case, each unit in the hidden layer corresponds to a variant of AND—a variant because we assume that it may negate some of the inputs before forming the conjunction—joined by an OR that is represented by a single unit in the output layer. In other words, in this particular neural network setup each node in the hidden layer has the same role as a leaf in a decision tree or a single rule in a set of decision rules.

The big question is how to learn a multilayer perceptron. There are two aspects to the problem: learning the structure of the network and learning the connection weights. It turns out that there is a relatively simple algorithm for determining the weights given a fixed network structure. This algorithm is called *backpropagation* and is described in "Backpropagation" section. However, although there are many algorithms that attempt to identify network structure, this aspect of the problem is commonly solved by experimentation—perhaps combined with a healthy dose of expert knowledge. Sometimes the network can be separated into distinct modules that represent identifiable subtasks (e.g., recognizing different components of an object in an image recognition problem), which opens up a way of incorporating domain knowledge into the learning process. Often a single hidden layer is all that is necessary, and an appropriate number of units for that layer is determined by maximizing the estimated accuracy.

Backpropagation

Suppose we have some data and seek a multilayer perceptron that is an accurate predictor for the underlying classification problem. Given a fixed network structure, we must determine appropriate weights for the connections in the network. In the absence of hidden layers, the perceptron learning rule from Section 4.6 can be used to find suitable values. But suppose there are hidden units. We know what the output unit should predict, and could adjust the weights of the connections leading to that unit based on the perceptron rule. But the correct outputs for the hidden units are unknown, so the rule cannot be applied there.

It turns out that, roughly speaking, the solution is to modify the weights of the connections leading to the hidden units based on the strength of each unit's contribution to the final prediction. There is a standard mathematical optimization algorithm, called *gradient descent*, which achieves exactly that. The standard gradient descent algorithm requires taking derivatives, and the step function that the simple perceptron uses to convert the weighted sum of the inputs into a 0/1 prediction is not differentiable. We need to see whether the step function can be replaced by something else.

Fig. 7.5A shows the step function: if the input is smaller than zero, it outputs zero; otherwise, it outputs one. We want a function that is similar in shape but differentiable. A commonly used replacement is shown in Fig. 7.5B. In neural networks terminology it is called the *sigmoid* function, and it is defined by

$$f(x) = \frac{1}{1 + e^{-x}}.$$

We encountered it in Section 4.6 when we described the logit transform used in logistic regression. In fact, learning a multilayer perceptron is closely related to logistic regression.

To apply the standard gradient descent procedure, the error function—the thing that is to be minimized by adjusting the weights—must also be

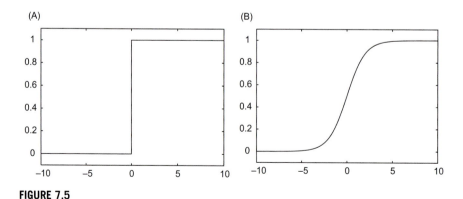

FIGURE 7.5

Step vs sigmoid: (A) step function; (B) sigmoid function.

differentiable. The number of misclassifications—measured by the discrete 0–1 loss mentioned in Section 5.7—does not fulfill this criterion. Instead, multilayer perceptrons are usually trained by minimizing the squared error of the network's output, essentially treating it as an estimate of the class probability. (Other loss functions are also applicable. For example, if the negative log-likelihood is used instead of the squared error, learning a sigmoid-based perceptron is identical to logistic regression.)

We work with the squared-error loss function because it is most widely used. For a single training instance, it is

$$E = \frac{1}{2}(y - f(x))^2,$$

where $f(x)$ is the network's prediction obtained from the output unit and y is the instance's class label (in this case, it is assumed to be either 0 or 1). The factor 1/2 is included just for convenience, and will drop out when we start taking derivatives.

Gradient descent exploits information given by the derivative of the function that is to be minimized—in this case, the error function. As an example, consider a hypothetical error function that happens to be identical to $w^2 + 1$, shown in Fig. 7.6. The x-axis represents a hypothetical parameter w that is to be optimized. The derivative of $w^2 + 1$ is simply $2w$. The crucial observation is that, based on the derivative, we can figure out the slope of the function at any particular point. If the derivative is negative, the function slopes downward to the right; if it is positive, it slopes downward to the left; and the size of the derivative determines how steep the decline is. Gradient descent is an iterative optimization procedure that uses this information to adjust a function's parameters. It takes the value of the derivative, multiplies it by a small constant called the *learning rate*, and

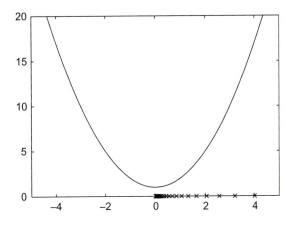

FIGURE 7.6

Gradient descent using the error function $w^2 + 1$.

subtracts the result from the current parameter value. This is repeated for the new parameter value, and so on, until a minimum is reached.

Returning to the example, assume that the learning rate is set to 0.1 and the current parameter value w is 4. The derivative is double this—8 at this point. Multiplying by the learning rate yields 0.8, and subtracting this from 4 gives 3.2, which becomes the new parameter value. Repeating the process for 3.2, we get 2.56, then 2.048, and so on. The little crosses in Fig. 7.6 show the values encountered in this process. The process stops once the change in parameter value becomes too small. In the example this happens when the value approaches 0, the value corresponding to the location on the x-axis where the minimum of the hypothetical error function is located.

The learning rate determines the step size and hence how quickly the search converges. If it is too large and the error function has several minima, the search may overshoot and miss a minimum entirely, or it may oscillate wildly. If it is too small, progress toward the minimum may be slow. Note that gradient descent can only find a *local* minimum. If the function has several minima—and error functions for multilayer perceptrons usually have many—it may not find the best one. This is a significant drawback of standard multilayer perceptrons compared with, e.g., support vector machines.

To use gradient descent to find the weights of a multilayer perceptron, the derivative of the squared error must be determined with respect to each parameter—i.e., each weight in the network. Let us start with a simple perceptron without a hidden layer. Differentiating the error function with respect to a particular weight w_i yields

$$\frac{dE}{dw_i} = (f(x) - y)\frac{f(x)}{dw_i}.$$

Here, $f(x)$ is the perceptron's output and x is the weighted sum of the inputs.

To compute the second factor on the right-hand side, the derivative of the sigmoid function $f(x)$ is needed. It turns out that this has a particularly simple form that can be written in terms of $f(x)$ itself:

$$\frac{df(x)}{dx} = f(x)(1 - f(x)).$$

We use $f'(x)$ to denote this derivative. But we seek the derivative with respect to w_i, not x. Because

$$x = \sum_i w_i a_i,$$

the derivative of $f(x)$ with respect to w_i is

$$\frac{df(x)}{dw_i} = f'(x)a_i.$$

Plugging this back into the derivative of the error function yields

$$\frac{dE}{dw_i} = (f(x) - y)f'(x)a_i.$$

This expression gives all that is needed to calculate the change of weight w_i caused by a particular example vector **a** (extended by 1 to represent the bias, as explained previously). Having repeated this computation for each training instance, we add up the changes associated with a particular weight w_i, multiply by the learning rate, and subtract the result from w_i's current value.

So far so good. But all this assumes that there is no hidden layer. With a hidden layer, things get a little trickier. Suppose $f(x_i)$ is the output of the ith hidden unit, w_{ij} is the weight of the connection from input j to the ith hidden unit, and w_i is the weight of the ith hidden unit to the output unit. The situation is depicted in Fig. 7.7, where, for simplicity, we have omitted bias inputs for all units. As before, $f(x)$ is the output of the single unit in the output layer. The update rule for the weights w_i is essentially the same as above, except that a_i is replaced by the output of the ith hidden unit:

$$\frac{dE}{dw_i} = (f(x) - y)f'(x)f(x_i).$$

However, to update the weights w_{ij} the corresponding derivatives must be calculated. Applying the chain rule gives

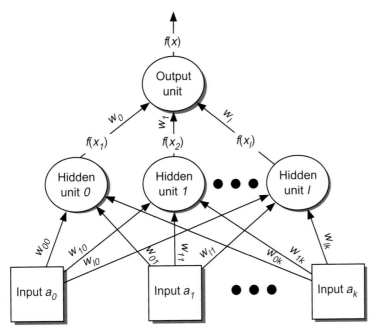

FIGURE 7.7

Multilayer perceptron with a hidden layer (omitting bias inputs).

$$\frac{dE}{dw_{ij}} = \frac{dE}{dx}\frac{dx}{dw_{ij}} = (f(x) - y)f'(x)\frac{dx}{dw_{ij}}.$$

The first two factors are the same as in the previous equation. To compute the third factor, differentiate further. Because

$$x = \sum_i w_i f(x_i),$$

$$\frac{dx}{dw_{ij}} = w_i \frac{df(x_i)}{dw_{ij}}.$$

Furthermore,

$$x_i = \sum_j w_{ij} a_j,$$

so

$$\frac{df(x_i)}{dw_{ij}} = f'(x_i)\frac{dx_i}{dw_{ij}} = f'(x_i)a_j.$$

This means that we are finished. Putting everything together yields an equation for the derivative of the error function with respect to the weights w_{ij}:

$$\frac{dE}{dw_{ij}} = (f(x) - y)f'(x)w_i f'(x_i)a_j.$$

As before, we calculate this value for every training instance, add up the changes associated with a particular weight w_{ij}, multiply by the learning rate, and subtract the outcome from the current value of w_{ij}.

This derivation applies to a perceptron with one hidden layer. If there are two hidden layers, the same strategy can be applied a second time to update the weights pertaining to the input connections of the first hidden layer, propagating the error from the output unit through the second hidden layer to the first one. Because of this error propagation mechanism, this version of the generic gradient descent strategy is called backpropagation.

We have tacitly assumed that the network's output layer has just one unit, which is appropriate for two-class problems. For more than two classes, a separate network could be learned for each class that distinguishes it from the remaining classes. A more compact classifier can be obtained from a single network by creating an output unit for each class, connecting every unit in the hidden layer to every output unit. The squared error for a particular training instance is the sum of squared errors taken over all output units. The same technique can be applied to predict several targets, or attribute values, simultaneously by creating a separate output unit for each one. Intuitively, this may give better predictive accuracy than building a separate classifier for each class attribute if the underlying learning tasks are in some way related.

We have assumed that weights are only updated after all training instances have been fed through the network and all the corresponding weight changes have been accumulated. This is *batch* learning, because all the training data is processed together. But exactly the same formulas can be used to update the weights incrementally after each training instance has been processed. This is called *stochastic backpropagation* because the overall error does not necessarily decrease after every update. It can be used for online learning, in which new data arrives in a continuous stream and every training instance is processed just once. In both variants of backpropagation, it is often helpful to standardize the attributes, e.g., to have zero mean and unit standard deviation. Before learning starts, each weight is initialized to a small, randomly chosen value based on a normal distribution with zero mean.

Like any other learning scheme, multilayer perceptrons trained with backpropagation may suffer from overfitting—especially if the network is much larger than what is actually necessary to represent the structure of the underlying learning problem. Many modifications have been proposed to alleviate this. A very simple one, called *early stopping*, works like reduced-error pruning in rule learners: a holdout set is used to decide when to stop performing further iterations of the backpropagation algorithm. The error on the holdout set is measured and the algorithm is terminated once the error begins to increase, because that indicates overfitting to the training data. Another method, called *weight decay*, adds to the error function a penalty term that consists of the squared sum of all nonbias weights in the network, as in ridge regression. This attempts to limit the influence of irrelevant connections on the network's predictions by penalizing large weights that do not contribute a correspondingly large reduction in the error.

Although standard gradient descent is the simplest technique for learning the weights in a multilayer perceptron, it is by no means the most efficient one. In practice, it tends to be rather slow when executed on a standard personal computer. A trick that often improves performance is to include a *momentum* term when updating weights: add to the new weight change a small proportion of the update value from the previous iteration. This smooths the search process by making changes in direction less abrupt. More sophisticated methods make use of information obtained from the second derivative of the error function as well; they can converge much more quickly. However, even those algorithms can be very slow compared with other methods of classification learning.

A serious disadvantage of multilayer perceptrons that contain hidden units is that they are essentially opaque. There are several techniques that attempt to extract rules from trained neural networks. However, it is unclear whether they offer any advantages over standard rule learners that induce rule sets directly from data—especially considering that this can generally be done much more quickly than learning a multilayer perceptron in the first place.

Although multilayer perceptrons are the most prominent type of neural network, many others have been proposed. Multilayer perceptrons belong to a class of networks called *feedforward networks* because they do not contain any cycles and the network's output depends only on the current input instance. *Recurrent neural networks* do have cycles. Computations derived from earlier input are fed back into the network, which gives them a kind of memory.

RADIAL BASIS FUNCTION NETWORKS

Another popular type of feedforward network is the radial basis function (RBF) network. It has two layers, not counting the input layer, and differs from a multi-layer perceptron in the way that the hidden units perform computations. Each hidden unit essentially represents a particular point in input space, and its output, or *activation*, for a given instance depends on the distance between its point and the instance—which is just another point. Intuitively, the closer these two points, the stronger the activation. This is achieved by using a nonlinear transformation function to convert the distance into a similarity measure. A bell-shaped Gaussian *activation function*, whose width may be different for each hidden unit, is commonly used for this purpose. The hidden units are called RBFs because the points in instance space for which a given hidden unit produces the same activation form a hypersphere or hyperellipsoid. (In a multilayer perceptron, this is a hyperplane.)

The output layer of an RBF network is the same as that of a multilayer perceptron: it takes a linear combination of the outputs of the hidden units and—in classification problems—pipes it through the sigmoid function (or something with a similar shape).

The parameters that such a network learns are (1) the centers and widths of the RBFs and (2) the weights used to form the linear combination of the outputs obtained from the hidden layer. A significant advantage over multilayer perceptrons is that the first set of parameters can be determined independently of the second set and still produce fairly accurate classifiers.

One way to determine the first set of parameters is to use clustering. The simple *k*-means clustering algorithm described in Section 4.8 can be applied, clustering each class independently to obtain *k* basis functions for each class. Intuitively, the resulting RBFs represent prototype instances. The second set of parameters is then learned by keeping the first parameters fixed. This involves learning a simple linear classifier using one of the techniques we have discussed (e.g., linear or logistic regression). If there are far fewer hidden units than training instances, this can be done very quickly. Note that although this two-stage process is very quick, it is generally not as accurate as training all network parameters using a strategy such as gradient descent.

A disadvantage of RBF networks is that they give every attribute the same weight because all are treated equally in the distance computation, unless attribute weight parameters are included in the overall optimization process. Support vector machines share the same problem. In fact, support vector machines with Gaussian kernels (i.e., "RBF kernels") are a particular type of RBF network, in which one basis function is centered on every training instance, all basis functions have the same width, and the outputs are combined linearly by computing the maximum margin hyperplane. This has the effect that only some of the RBFs have a non-zero weight—the ones that represent the support vectors.

STOCHASTIC GRADIENT DESCENT

We have introduced gradient descent and stochastic backpropagation as optimization methods for learning the weights in a neural network. Gradient descent is, in fact, a general-purpose optimization technique that can be applied whenever the objective function is differentiable. Actually, it turns out that it can even be applied in cases where the objective function is not completely differentiable through use of a device called *subgradients*.

One application is the use of gradient descent to learn linear models such as linear support vector machines or logistic regression. Learning such models using gradient descent is easier than optimizing nonlinear neural networks because the error function has a global minimum rather than many local minima, which is usually the case for nonlinear networks. For linear problems, a stochastic gradient descent procedure can be designed that is computationally simple and converges very rapidly, allowing models such as linear support vector machines and logistic regression to be learned from large data sets. Moreover, stochastic gradient descent allows models to be learned incrementally, in an online setting.

For support vector machines, the error function—the thing that is to be minimized—is called the "hinge loss." Illustrated in Fig. 7.8, this is so named because it comprises a downwards sloping linear segment joined to a horizontal part at $z = 1$—more formally, $E(z) = \max\{0, 1 - z\}$. For comparison, the Figure also shows the 0−1 loss, which is discontinuous, and the squared loss, which is both continuous and differentiable. These functions are plotted as a function of the margin $z = yf(x)$, where the class y is either −1 or +1 and $f(x)$ is the output of the linear model. Misclassification occurs when $z < 0$, so all loss functions incur their most serious penalties in the negative region. In the linearly separable case, the hinge loss is zero for a function that successfully separates the data. The maximum margin hyperplane is given by the smallest weight vector that achieves a zero hinge loss.

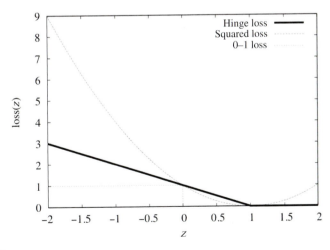

FIGURE 7.8

Hinge, squared and 0−1 loss functions.

The hinge loss is continuous, unlike the $0-1$ loss, but is not differentiable at $z = 1$, unlike the squared loss which is differentiable everywhere. This lack of differentiability presents a problem if gradient descent is used to update the model's weights after a training example has been processed, because the loss function's derivative is needed for this. That is where subgradients come in. The basic idea is that even though the gradient cannot be computed, the minimum will still be found if something resembling a gradient can be substituted. In the case of the hinge loss, the gradient is taken to be zero at the point of nondifferentiability. In fact, since the hinge loss is zero for $z \geq 1$, we can focus on that part of the function that is differentiable ($z < 1$) and proceed as usual.

The weight update for a linear support vector machine using the hinge loss is $\Delta w_i = \eta x_i y$, where η is the learning rate. For stochastic gradient descent, all that is needed to compute z for each training instance is to take the dot product between the current weight vector and the instance, multiply the result by the instance's class value, and check to see if the resulting value is less than 1. If so, the weights are updated accordingly. As with perceptrons, a bias term can be included by extending the weight vector by one element and including an additional attribute with each training instance that always has the value 1.

DISCUSSION

Support vector machines originated from research in statistical learning theory (Vapnik, 1999), and a good starting point for exploration is a tutorial by Burges (1998). A general description, including generalization to the case in which the data is not linearly separable, has been published by Cortes and Vapnik (1995). We have introduced the standard version of support vector regression: Schölkopf, Bartlett, Smola, and Williamson (1999) present a different version that has one parameter instead of two. Smola and Schölkopf (2004) provide an extensive tutorial on support vector regression. Fletcher (1987) covers solution methods for constrained quadratic optimization problems, while Platt (1998) describes the sequential minimal optimization algorithm, which is specifically designed to train support vector machines.

Ridge regression was introduced in statistics by Hoerl and Kennard (1970) and can now be found in standard statistics texts. Hastie et al. (2009) give a good description of kernel ridge regression. Kernel ridge regression is equivalent to a technique called Gaussian process regression, a Bayesian approach that additionally provides estimates of predictive uncertainty. The complexity of the most efficient general matrix inversion algorithm is in fact $O(n^{2.807})$ rather than $O(n^3)$.

The (voted) kernel perceptron is due to Freund and Schapire (1999). Cristianini and Shawe-Taylor (2000) provide a nice introduction to support vector machines and other kernel-based methods, including the optimization theory underlying the support vector learning algorithms. We have barely skimmed the surface of these learning schemes, mainly because advanced mathematics lies just beneath. The idea of using kernels to solve nonlinear problems has been applied to many algorithms, e.g., principal component analysis (described in Section 8.3). A kernel is essentially a similarity function with certain mathematical properties, and it is possible to define kernel functions over all sorts of structures—e.g., sets, strings, trees, and probability distributions. Shawe-Taylor and Cristianini (2004) and Schölkopf and Smola (2002) cover kernel-based learning in detail.

There is extensive literature on neural networks, and Bishop (1995) provides an excellent introduction to both multilayer perceptrons and RBF networks. Interest in neural networks initially declined after the arrival of support vector machines, perhaps because the latter often require fewer parameters to be tuned to achieve the same (or greater) accuracy. However, recent studies have shown that multilayer perceptrons achieve performance competitive with more modern learning techniques on many practical data sets, and they excel in particular when performing deep learning (see chapter: Deep learning).

Gradient methods for learning classifiers are very popular. In particular, sto-chastic gradient methods have been explored because they are applicable to large data sets and online learning scenarios. Kivinen, Smola, and Williamson (2002); Zhang (2004); and Shalev-Shwartz, Singer, and Srebro (2007) explore such meth-ods when applied to learning support vector machines. Kivinen et al. (2002) and Shalev-Shwartz et al. (2007) provide heuristics for setting the learning rate for gradient descent based on the current iteration, and only require the user to pro-vide a value for a single parameter that determines the closeness of fit to the training data (a so-called regularization parameter). In the vanilla approach, regu-larization is performed by limiting the number of updates that can be performed.

7.3 NUMERIC PREDICTION WITH LOCAL LINEAR MODELS

Trees that are used for numeric prediction are just like ordinary decision trees except that at each leaf they store either a class value that represents the average value of instances that reach the leaf, in which case the tree is called a *regression tree*, or a linear regression model that predicts the class value of instances that reach the leaf, in which case it is called a *model tree*. In what follows we will talk about model trees because regression trees are really a special case.

Regression and model trees are constructed by first using a decision tree induction algorithm to build an initial tree. However, whereas most decision tree algorithms choose the splitting attribute to maximize the information gain, it is appropriate for numeric prediction to instead minimize the intrasubset variation in the class values down each branch. Once the basic tree has been formed, consid-eration is given to pruning the tree back from each leaf, just as with ordinary decision trees. The only difference between regression tree and model tree induc-tion is that for the latter, each node is replaced by a regression plane instead of a constant value. The attributes that serve to define that plane are generally those that participate in decisions in the subtree that will be pruned, i.e., in nodes beneath the current one, and perhaps those that occur on the path to the root node.

Following an extensive description of model trees, we briefly explain how to generate rules from model trees, and then describe another approach to numeric prediction based on generating local linear models—locally weighted linear regression. Whereas model trees derive from the basic divide-and-conquer decision tree methodology, locally weighted regression is inspired by the instance-based methods for classification that we described is discussed in Section 4.3. Like instance-based learning, it performs all "learning" at prediction time. Although locally weighted regression resembles model trees in that it uses linear regression to fit models locally to particular areas of instance space, it does so in quite a different way.

MODEL TREES

When a model tree is used to predict the value for a test instance, the tree is followed down to a leaf in the normal way, using the instance's attribute values to make routing decisions at each node. The leaf will contain a linear model based on some of the attribute values, and this is evaluated for the test instance to yield a raw predicted value.

Instead of using this raw value directly, however, it turns out to be beneficial to use a smoothing process to reduce the sharp discontinuities that will inevitably occur between adjacent linear models at the leaves of the pruned tree. This is a particular problem for models constructed from a small number of training instances. Smoothing can be accomplished by producing linear models for each internal node, as well as for the leaves, at the time the tree is built. Then, once the leaf model has been used to obtain the raw predicted value for a test instance, that value is filtered along the path back to the root, smoothing it at each node by combining it with the value predicted by the linear model for that node.

An appropriate smoothing calculation is

$$p' = \frac{np + kq}{n + k},$$

where p' is the prediction passed up to the next higher node, p is the prediction passed to this node from below, q is the value predicted by the model at this node, n is the number of training instances that reach the node below, and k is a smoothing constant. Experiments show that smoothing substantially increases the accuracy of predictions.

However, discontinuities remain and the resulting function is not smooth. In fact, exactly the same smoothing process can be accomplished by incorporating the interior models into each leaf model after the tree has been built. Then, during the classification process, only the leaf models are used. The disadvantage is that the leaf models tend to be larger and more difficult to comprehend, because many coefficients that were previously zero become nonzero when the interior nodes' models are incorporated.

BUILDING THE TREE

The splitting criterion is used to determine which attribute is the best to split that portion T of the training data that reaches a particular node. It is based on treating the standard deviation of the class values in T as a measure of the error at that node, and calculating the expected reduction in error as a result of testing each attribute at that node. The attribute that maximizes the expected error reduction is chosen for splitting at the node.

The expected error reduction, which we call SDR for *standard deviation reduction*, is calculated by

$$SDR = sd(T) - \sum_i \frac{|T_i|}{|T|} \times sd(T_i),$$

where T_1, T_2,... are the sets that result from splitting the node according to the chosen attribute.

The splitting process terminates when the class values of the instances that reach a node vary very slightly, i.e., when their standard deviation is only a small fraction (say, less than 5%) of the standard deviation of the original instance set. Splitting also terminates when just a few instances remain, say four or fewer. Experiments show that the results obtained are not very sensitive to the exact choice of these parameters.

PRUNING THE TREE

As noted earlier, a linear model is needed for each interior node of the tree, not just at the leaves, for use in the smoothing process. Before pruning, a model is calculated for each node of the unpruned tree. The model takes the form

$$w_0 + w_1 a_1 + w_2 a_2 + \cdots + w_k a_k,$$

where $a_1, a_2,..., a_k$ are attribute values. The weights $w_1, w_2,..., w_k$ are calculated using standard regression. However, only a subset of the attributes are generally used here—e.g., those that are tested in the subtree below this node, and perhaps those occurring along the path to the root node. Note that we have tacitly assumed that attributes are numeric: we describe the handling of nominal attributes in "Nominal attributes" section.

The pruning procedure makes use of an estimate, at each node, of the expected error for test data. First, the absolute difference between the predicted value and the actual class value is averaged over each of the training instances that reach that node. Because the tree has been built expressly for this data set, this average will underestimate the expected error for unseen cases. To compensate, it is multiplied by the factor $(n + \nu)/(n - \nu)$, where n is the number of training instances that reach the node and ν is the number of parameters in the linear model that gives the class value at that node.

The expected error for test data at a node is calculated as described previously, using the linear model for prediction. Because of the compensation factor $(n + \nu)/(n - \nu)$, it may be that the linear model can be further simplified by dropping terms to minimize the estimated error. Dropping a term decreases the multiplication factor, which may be enough to offset the inevitable increase in average error over the training instances. Terms are dropped one by one, greedily, as long as the error estimate decreases.

Finally, once a linear model is in place for each interior node, the tree is pruned back from the leaves as long as the expected estimated error decreases. The expected error for the linear model at that node is compared with the expected error from the subtree below. To calculate the latter, the error from each branch is combined into a single, overall value for the node by weighting the branch by the proportion of the training instances that go down it and combining the error estimates linearly using those weights. Alternatively, one can calculate the training error of the subtree and multiply it by the above modification factor based on an ad hoc estimate of the number of parameters in the tree—perhaps adding one for each split point.

NOMINAL ATTRIBUTES

Before constructing a model tree, all nominal attributes are transformed into binary variables that are then treated as numeric. For each nominal attribute, the average class value corresponding to each possible value in the set is calculated from the training instances, and the values are sorted according to these averages. Then, if the nominal attribute has k possible values, it is replaced by $k - 1$ synthetic binary attributes, the ith being 0 if the value is one of the first i in the ordering and 1 otherwise. Thus all splits are binary: they involve either a numeric attribute or a synthetic binary one, treated as a numeric attribute.

It is possible to prove analytically that the best split at a node for a nominal variable with k values is one of the $k - 1$ positions obtained by ordering the average class values for each value of the attribute. This sorting operation should really be repeated at each node; however, there is an inevitable increase in noise due to small numbers of instances at lower nodes in the tree (and in some cases nodes may not represent all values for some attributes), and not much is lost by performing the sorting just once, before starting to build a model tree.

MISSING VALUES

To take account of missing values, a modification is made to the SDR formula. The final formula, including the missing value compensation, is

$$\text{SDR} = \frac{m}{|T|} \times \left[sd(T) - \sum_{j \in \{L,R\}} \frac{|T_j|}{|T|} \times sd(T_j) \right],$$

where m is the number of instances without missing values for that attribute, and T is the set of instances that reach this node. T_L, T_R are sets that result from splitting on this attribute—because all tests on attributes are now binary.

When processing both training and test instances, once an attribute is selected for splitting it is necessary to divide the instances into subsets according to their value for this attribute. An obvious problem arises when the value is missing. An interesting technique called *surrogate splitting* has been developed to handle this situation. It involves finding another attribute to split on in place of the original one and using it instead. The attribute is chosen as the one most highly correlated with the original attribute. However, this technique is both complex to implement and time consuming to execute.

A simpler heuristic is to use the class value as the surrogate attribute, in the belief that, a priori, this is the attribute most likely to be correlated with the one being used for splitting. Of course, this is only possible when processing the training set, because for test examples the class is not known. A simple solution for test examples is simply to replace the unknown attribute value by the average value of that attribute for the training examples that reach the node—which has the effect, for a binary attribute, of choosing the most populous subnode. This simple approach seems to work well in practice.

Let us consider in more detail how to use the class value as a surrogate attribute during the training process. We first deal with all instances for which the value of the splitting attribute is known. We determine a threshold for splitting in the usual way, by sorting the instances according to the splitting attribute's value and, for each possible split point, calculating the SDR according to the preceding formula, choosing the split point that yields the greatest reduction in error. Only the instances for which the value of the splitting attribute is known are used to determine the split point.

Then we divide these instances into the two sets L and R according to the test. We determine whether the instances in L or R have the greater average class value, and we calculate the average of these two averages. Then, an instance for which this attribute value is unknown is placed into L or R according to whether its class value exceeds this overall average or not. If it does, it goes into whichever of L and R has the greater average class value; otherwise, it goes into the one with the smaller average class value. When the splitting stops, all the missing values will be replaced by the average values of the corresponding attributes of the training instances reaching the leaves.

PSEUDOCODE FOR MODEL TREE INDUCTION

Fig. 7.9 gives pseudocode for the model tree algorithm we have described. The two main parts are creating a tree by successively splitting nodes, performed by

```
MakeModelTree (instances)
{
  SD = sd(instances)
  for each k-valued nominal attribute
    convert into k-1 synthetic binary attributes
  root = newNode
  root.instances = instances
  split(root)
  prune(root)
  printTree(root)
}
split(node)
{
  if sizeof(node.instances) < 4 or sd(node.instances) < 0.05*SD
    node.type = LEAF
  else
    node.type = INTERIOR
    for each attribute
      for all possible split positions of the attribute
        calculate the attribute's SDR
    node.attribute = attribute with maximum SDR
    split(node.left)
    split(node.right)
}
prune(node)
{
  if node = INTERIOR then
    prune(node.leftChild)
    prune(node.rightChild)
    node.model = linearRegression(node)
    if subtreeError(node) > error(node) then
      node.type = LEAF
}
subtreeError(node)
{
  l = node.left; r = node.right
  if node = INTERIOR then
    return (sizeof(l.instances)*subtreeError(l)
          + sizeof(r.instances)*subtreeError(r))/sizeof(node.instances)
  else return error(node)
}
```

FIGURE 7.9

Pseudocode for model tree induction.

split, and pruning it from the leaves upward, performed by *prune*. The *node* data structure contains a type flag indicating whether it is an internal node or a leaf, pointers to the left and right child, the set of instances that reach that node, the attribute that is used for splitting at that node, and a structure representing the linear model for the node.

The *sd* function called at the beginning of the main program and again at the beginning of *split* calculates the standard deviation of the class values of a set of instances. Then follows the procedure for obtaining synthetic binary attributes that was described previously. Standard procedures for creating new nodes and printing the final tree are not shown. In *split*, *sizeof* returns the number of elements in a set. Missing attribute values are dealt with as described earlier. The SDR is calculated according to the equation at the beginning of "Missing values" section. Although not shown in the code, it is set to infinity if splitting on the attribute would create a leaf with less than two instances. In *prune*, the *linearRegression* routine recursively descends the subtree collecting attributes, performs a linear regression on the instances at that node as a function of those attributes, and then greedily drops terms if doing so improves the error estimate, as described earlier. Finally, the *error* function returns

$$\frac{n+v}{n-v} \times \frac{\sum_{instances} |\text{deviation from predicted class value}|}{n},$$

where n is the number of instances at the node and v the number of parameters in the node's linear model.

Fig. 7.10 gives an example of a model tree formed by this algorithm for a problem with two numeric and two nominal attributes. What is to be predicted is the rise time of a simulated servo system involving a servo amplifier, motor, lead screw, and sliding carriage. The nominal attributes play important roles. Four synthetic binary attributes have been created for each of the five-valued nominal attributes *motor* and *screw*, and are shown in Table 7.1 in terms of the two sets of values to which they correspond. The ordering of these values—D, E, C, B, A for

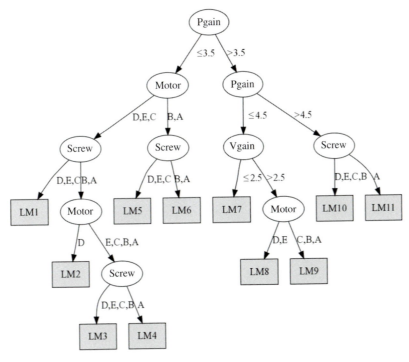

FIGURE 7.10

Model tree for a data set with nominal attributes.

Table 7.1 Linear Models in the Model Tree

Model		LM1	LM2	LM3	LM4	LM5	LM6	LM7	LM8	LM9	LM10	LM11
Constant term		0.96	1.14	1.43	1.52	2.69	2.91	0.88	0.98	1.11	1.06	0.97
Pgain		−0.38	−0.38	−0.38	−0.38	−0.38	−0.38	−0.24	−0.24	−0.24	−0.25	−0.25
Vgain		0.71	0.49	0.49	0.49	0.56	0.45	0.13	0.15	0.15	0.10	0.14
Motor = D	vs E, C, B, A	0.66	1.14	1.06	1.06	0.50	0.50	0.30	0.40	0.30	0.14	0.14
Motor = D, E	vs C, B, A	0.97	0.61	0.65	0.59	0.42	0.42	−0.02	0.06	0.06	0.17	0.22
Motor = D, E, C	vs B, A	0.32	0.32	0.32	0.32	0.41	0.41	0.05				
Motor = D, E, C, B	vs A					0.08	0.05					
Screw = D	vs E, C, B, A	0.13										
Screw = D, E	vs C, B, A	0.49										
Screw = D, E, C	vs B, A		0.54	0.54	0.54	0.39	0.40	0.30	0.20	0.16	0.08	0.08
Screw = D, E, C, B	vs A		1.73	1.79	1.79	0.96	1.13	0.22	0.15	0.15	0.16	0.19

motor and coincidentally D, E, C, B, A for *screw* also—is determined from the training data: the rise time averaged over all examples for which *motor* = D is less than that averaged over examples for which *motor* = E, which is less than when *motor* = C, and so on. It is apparent from the magnitude of the coefficients in Table 7.1 that *motor* = D versus E, C, B, A and *screw* = D, E, C, B versus A play leading roles in the LM2, LM3, and LM4 models (among others). Both *motor* and *screw* also play a minor role in several of the models.

RULES FROM MODEL TREES

Model trees are essentially decision trees with linear models at the leaves. Like decision trees, they may suffer from the replicated subtree problem explained in Section 3.4, and sometimes the structure can be expressed much more concisely using a set of rules instead of a tree. Can we generate *rules* for numeric prediction? Recall the rule learner described in Section 6.2 that uses separate-and-conquer in conjunction with partial decision trees to extract decision rules from trees. The same strategy can be applied to model trees to generate decision lists for numeric prediction.

First build a partial model tree from all the data. Pick one of the leaves and make it into a rule. Remove the data covered by that leaf; then repeat the process with the remaining data. The question is, how to build the partial model tree, i.e., a tree with unexpanded nodes? This boils down to the question of how to pick which node to expand next. The algorithm of Fig. 6.5 (Section 6.2) picks the node whose entropy for the class attribute is smallest. For model trees, whose predictions are numeric, simply use the variance instead. This is based on the same rationale: the lower the variance, the shallower the subtree and the shorter the rule. The rest of the algorithm stays the same, with the model tree learner's split selection method and pruning strategy replacing the decision tree learner's. Because the model tree's leaves are linear models, the corresponding rules will have linear models on the right-hand side.

There is one caveat when using model trees in this fashion to generate rule sets. It turns out that using smoothed model trees does not reduce the error in the final rule set's predictions. This may be because smoothing works best for contiguous data, but the separate-and-conquer scheme removes data covered by previous rules, leaving holes in the distribution. Smoothing, if it is done at all, must be performed after the rule set has been generated.

LOCALLY WEIGHTED LINEAR REGRESSION

An alternative approach to numeric prediction is the method of locally weighted linear regression. With model trees, the tree structure divides the instance space into regions, and a linear model is found for each of them. In effect, the training data determines how the instance space is partitioned. Locally weighted regression, on the other hand, generates local models at prediction time by giving higher weight to instances in the neighborhood of the particular test instance. More specifically, it weights the training instances according to their distance to the test instance and performs a linear regression on the weighted data. Training instances close to the test instance receive a high weight; those far away a low one. In other words, a linear model is tailor made for the particular test instance at hand and used to predict the instance's class value.

To use locally weighted regression, you need to decide on a distance-based weighting scheme for the training instances. A common choice is to weight the instances according to the inverse of their Euclidean distance from the test instance. Another possibility is to use the Euclidean distance in conjunction with a Gaussian kernel function. However, there is no clear evidence that the choice of weighting function is critical. More important is the selection of a "smoothing parameter" that is used to scale the distance function—the distance is multiplied by the inverse of this parameter. If it is set to a small value, only instances very close to the test instance will receive significant weight; if it is large, more distant instances will also have a significant impact on the model. One way of choosing the smoothing parameter is to set it to the distance of the kth nearest training instance so that its value becomes smaller as the volume of training data increases. If the weighting function is linear, say $max(0, 1-smoothed\text{-}distance)$, the weight is zero for all instances further than the kth nearest one. Then the weighting function has bounded support and only the $k-1$ nearest neighbors need to be considered for building the linear model. The best choice of k depends on the amount of noise in the data. The more noise there is, the more neighbors should be included in the linear model. Generally, an appropriate smoothing parameter is found using cross-validation.

Like model trees, locally weighted linear regression is able to approximate nonlinear functions. One of its main advantages is that it is ideally suited for incremental learning: all training is done at prediction time, so new instances can be added to the training data at any time. However, like other instance-based methods, it is slow at deriving a prediction for a test instance. First, the training instances must be scanned to compute their weights; then, a weighted linear regression is performed on these instances. Also, like other instance-based methods, locally weighted regression provides little information about the global structure of the training data set. Note that if the smoothing parameter is based on the kth nearest neighbor and the weighting function gives zero weight to more distant instances, the kD-trees and ball trees described in Section 4.7 can be used to accelerate the process of finding the relevant neighbors.

Locally weighted learning is not restricted to linear regression: it can be applied with any learning technique that can handle weighted instances. In particular, you can use it for classification. Most algorithms can be easily adapted to deal with weights. The trick is to realize that (integer) weights can be simulated by creating several copies of the same instance. Whenever the learning algorithm uses an instance when computing a model, just pretend that it is accompanied by the appropriate number of identical shadow instances. This also works if the weight is not an integer. For example, in the Naïve Bayes algorithm described in Section 4.2, multiply the counts derived from an instance by the instance's weight, and—voilà—you have a version of Naïve Bayes that can be used for locally weighted learning.

It turns out that locally weighted Naïve Bayes works quite well in practice, outperforming both Naïve Bayes itself and the *k*-nearest-neighbor technique. It also compares favorably with more sophisticated ways of enhancing Naïve Bayes by relaxing its intrinsic independence assumption. Locally weighted learning only assumes independence within a neighborhood, not globally in the whole instance space as standard Naïve Bayes does.

In principle, locally weighted learning can also be applied to decision trees and other models that are more complex than linear regression and Naïve Bayes. However, it is less beneficial here because locally weighted learning is primarily a way of allowing simple models to become more flexible by allowing them to approximate arbitrary targets. If the underlying learning algorithm can already do that, there is little point in applying locally weighted learning. Nevertheless it may improve other simple models—e.g., linear support vector machines and logistic regression.

DISCUSSION

Regression trees were introduced in the CART system of Breiman et al. (1984). CART, for *"classification and regression trees,"* incorporated a decision tree inducer for discrete classes like that of C4.5, as well as a scheme for inducing regression trees. Many of the techniques described in this section, such as the method of handling nominal attributes and the surrogate device for dealing with missing values, were included in CART. However, model trees did not appear until much more recently, being first described by Quinlan (1992). Using model trees for generating rule sets (although not partial trees) has been explored by Hall, Holmes, and Frank (1999).

A comprehensive description (and implementation) of model tree induction is given by Wang and Witten (1997). Neural networks are also commonly used for predicting numeric quantities, although they suffer from the disadvantage that the structures they produce are opaque and cannot be used to help understand the nature of the solution. There are techniques for producing understandable insights from the structure of neural networks, but the arbitrary nature of the internal representation means that there may be dramatic variations between networks of identical architecture trained on the same data. By dividing the function being induced into linear patches, model trees provide a representation that is reproducible and at least somewhat comprehensible.

There are many variations of locally weighted learning. For example, statisticians have considered using locally quadratic models instead of linear ones and have applied locally weighted logistic regression to classification problems. Also, many different potential weighting and distance functions can be found in the literature. Atkeson, Schaal, and Moore (1997) have written an excellent survey on locally weighted learning, primarily in the context of regression problems. Frank, Hall, and Pfahringer (2003) evaluated the use of locally weighted learning in conjunction with Naïve Bayes.

7.4 WEKA IMPLEMENTATIONS

- Instance-based learning
    IBk
    KStar
    NNge (rectangular generalizations, in the *NNge* package)
- Linear models and extensions
    SMO and variants
    LibSVM (uses third-party *libsvm* library, in the *LibSVM* package)
    LibLINEAR (uses third-party *liblinear* library, in the *LibLINEAR* package)
    GaussianProcesses (kernel ridge regression, plus estimates of predictive uncertainty)
    VotedPerceptron (voted kernel perceptrons)
    MultiLayerPerceptron, as well as *MLPClassifier* and *MLPRegressor* in the *multiLayerPerceptrons* package
    RBFNetwork, RBFClassifier, and *RBFRegressor* (all in the *RBFNetwork* package)
    SGD (stochastic gradient descent for several loss functions)
- Numeric prediction
    M5P (model trees)
    M5Rules (rules from model trees)
    LWL (locally weighted learning)

Data transformations

CHAPTER OUTLINE

8.1 Attribute Selection 288
    Scheme-Independent Selection 289
    Searching the Attribute Space 292
    Scheme-Specific Selection..293
8.2 Discretizing Numeric Attributes...296
    Unsupervised Discretization 297
    Entropy-Based Discretization..298
    Other Discretization Methods..301
    Entropy-Based Versus Error-Based Discretization.......................302
    Converting Discrete to Numeric Attributes 303
8.3 Projections 304
    Principal Component Analysis 305
    Random Projections..307
    Partial Least Squares Regression 307
    Independent Component Analysis 309
    Linear Discriminant Analysis 310
    Quadratic Discriminant Analysis 310
    Fisher's Linear Discriminant Analysis 311
    Text to Attribute Vectors...313
    Time Series 314
8.4 Sampling 315
    Reservoir Sampling..315
8.5 Cleansing 316
    Improving Decision Trees 316
    Robust Regression..317
    Detecting Anomalies..318
    One-Class Learning...319
    Outlier Detection 320
    Generating Artificial Data..321
8.6 Transforming Multiple Classes to Binary Ones 322
    Simple Methods 323
    Error-Correcting Output Codes 324
    Ensembles of Nested Dichotomies 326

8.7 Calibrating Class Probabilities..328
8.8 Further Reading and Bibliographic Notes..331
8.9 WEKA Implementations...334

In the previous chapters we examined a large array of machine learning methods: decision trees, classification and association rules, linear models, instance-based schemes, numeric prediction techniques, and clustering algorithms. All are sound, robust techniques that are eminently applicable to practical data mining problems.

But successful data mining involves far more than selecting a learning algorithm and running it over your data. For one thing, many learning schemes have various parameters, and suitable values must be chosen for these. In most cases, results can be improved markedly by suitable choice of parameter values, and the appropriate choice depends on the data at hand. For example, decision trees can be pruned or unpruned, and in the former case a pruning parameter may have to be chosen. In the k-nearest-neighbor method of instance-based learning, a value for k will have to be chosen. More generally, the learning scheme itself will have to be chosen from the range of schemes that are available. In all cases, the right choices depend on the data itself.

It is tempting to try out several learning schemes, and several parameter values, on your data, and see which works best. But be careful! The best choice is not necessarily the one that performs best on the training data. We have repeatedly cautioned about the problem of overfitting, where a learned model is too closely tied to the particular training data from which it was built. It is incorrect to assume that performance on the training data faithfully represents the level of performance that can be expected on the fresh data to which the learned model will be applied in practice.

Fortunately, we have already encountered the solution to this problem in Chapter 5, Credibility: evaluating what's been learned. There are two good methods for estimating the expected true performance of a learning scheme: the use of a large dataset that is quite separate from the training data, in the case of plentiful data, and cross-validation (Section 5.3), if data is scarce. In the latter case, a single 10-fold cross-validation is typically used in practice, although to obtain a more reliable estimate the entire procedure should be repeated 10 times. Once suitable parameters have been chosen for the learning scheme, use the whole training set—all the available training instances—to produce the final learned model that is to be applied to fresh data.

Note that the performance obtained with the chosen parameter value during the tuning process is *not* a reliable estimate of the final model's performance, because the final model potentially overfits the data that was used for tuning. We discussed this in Section 5.5. To ascertain how well it will perform, you need yet another large dataset that is quite separate from any data used during learning and tuning. The same is true for cross-validation: you need an "inner" cross-validation for parameter tuning and an "outer" cross-validation for error esti-mation. With 10-fold cross-validation, this involves running the learning scheme 100 times for each parameter setting being considered. To summarize: When assessing the performance of a learning scheme, any parameter tuning that goes on should be treated as though it were an integral part of the training process.

There are other important processes that can materially improve success when applying machine learning techniques to practical data mining problems, and these are the subject of this chapter. They constitute a kind of data engineering: engineering the input data into a form suitable for the learning scheme chosen and engineering the output to make it more effective. You can look on them as a bag of tricks that you can apply to practical machine learning problems to enhance the chance of success. Sometimes they work; other times they do not—and at the present state of the art, it is hard to say in advance whether they will or not. In an area such as this where trial and error is the most reliable guide, it is particularly important to be resourceful and have an understanding of what the tricks are.

In this chapter we examine six different ways in which the input can be mas-saged to make it more amenable for learning methods: attribute selection, attribute discretization, data projections, sampling, data cleansing, and converting multiclass problems to two-class ones. Consider the first, attribute selection. In many practical situations there are far too many attributes for learning schemes to handle, and some of them—perhaps the overwhelming majority—are clearly irrel-evant or redundant. Consequently, the data must be preprocessed to select a subset of the attributes to use in learning. Of course, many learning schemes themselves try to select attributes appropriately and ignore irrelevant or redundant ones, but in practice their performance can frequently be improved by preselection. For exam-ple, experiments show that adding useless attributes causes the performance of learning schemes such as decision trees and rules, linear regression, and instance-based learners to deteriorate.

Discretization of numeric attributes is absolutely essential if the task involves numeric attributes but the chosen learning scheme can only handle categorical ones. Even schemes that can handle numeric attributes often produce better results, or work faster, if the attributes are prediscretized. The converse situation, in which categorical attributes must be represented numerically, also occurs (although less often); and we describe techniques for this case, too.

Data projection covers a variety of techniques. One transformation, which we have encountered before when looking at relational data in Chapter 2, Input: concepts, instances, attributes, and support vector machines in Chapter 7, Extending instance-based and linear models, is to add new, synthetic attributes whose purpose is to present existing information in a form that is suitable for the machine learning scheme to pick up on. More general techniques that do not depend so intimately on the semantics of the particular machine learning problem at hand include principal component analysis and random projections. We also cover dis-criminant analysis for classification and partial least squares regression as a data projection technique for regression problems.

Sampling the input is an important step in many practical data mining applications, and is often the only way in which really large-scale problems can be handled. Although it is fairly simple, we include a brief section on techniques of sampling, including a way of incrementally producing a random sample of given size when the total size of the dataset is not known in advance.

Unclean data plagues data mining. We emphasized in Chapter 2, Input: concepts, instances, attributes, the necessity of getting to know your data: understanding the meaning of all the different attributes, the conventions used in coding them, the significance of missing values and duplicate data, measurement noise, typographical errors, and the presence of systematic errors—even deliberate ones. Various simple visualizations often help with this task. There are also automatic methods of cleansing data, of detecting outliers, and of spotting anomalies, which we describe—including a class of techniques referred to as "one-class learning" in which only a single class of instances is available at training time.

Finally, we examine techniques for refining the output of learning schemes that estimate class probabilities by recalibrating the estimates that they make. This is primarily of importance when accurate probabilities are required, as in cost-sensitive classification, although it can also improve classification performance.

8.1 ATTRIBUTE SELECTION

Most machine learning algorithms are designed to learn which are the most appropriate attributes to use for making their decisions. For example, decision tree methods choose the most promising attribute to split on at each point and should—in theory—never select irrelevant or unhelpful attributes. Having more features should surely—in theory—result in more discriminating power, never less. "What's the difference between theory and practice?" an old question asks. "There is no difference between theory and practice," the answer goes, "—in theory. But in practice, there is." Here there is too: in practice, adding irrelevant or distracting attributes to a dataset often confuses machine learning systems.

Experiments with a decision tree learner (C4.5) have shown that adding to standard datasets a random binary attribute generated by tossing an unbiased coin impacts classification performance, causing it to deteriorate (typically by 5–10% in the situations tested). This happens because at some point in the trees that are learned, the irrelevant attribute is invariably chosen to branch on, causing random errors when test data is processed. How can this be, when decision tree learners are cleverly designed to choose the best attribute for splitting at each node? The reason is subtle. As you proceed further down the tree, less and less data is available to help make the selection decision. At some point, with little data, the random attribute will look good just by chance. Because the number of nodes at each level increases exponentially with depth, the chance of the rogue attribute looking good somewhere along the frontier multiplies up as the tree deepens.

The real problem is that you inevitably reach depths at which only a small amount of data is available for attribute selection. This is known as the fragmentation problem. If the dataset were bigger it wouldn't necessarily help—you'd probably just go deeper.

Divide-and-conquer tree learners and separate-and-conquer rule learners both suffer from this effect because they inexorably reduce the amount of data on which they base judgments. Instance-based learners are very susceptible to irrelevant attributes because they always work in local neighborhoods, taking just a few training instances into account for each decision. Indeed, it has been shown that the number of training instances needed to produce a predetermined level of performance for instance-based learning increases exponentially with the number of irrelevant attributes present. Naïve Bayes, by contrast, does not fragment the instance space and robustly ignores irrelevant attributes. It assumes by design that all attributes are independent of one another, an assumption that is just right for random "distracter" attributes. But through this very same assumption, Naïve Bayes pays a heavy price in other ways because its operation is damaged by adding redundant attributes.

The fact that irrelevant distracters degrade the performance of decision tree and rule learners is, at first, surprising. Even more surprising is that *relevant* attributes can also be harmful. For example, suppose that in a two-class dataset a new attribute were added, which had the same value as the class to be predicted most of the time (65%) and the opposite value the rest of the time, randomly distributed among the instances. Experiments with standard datasets have shown that this can cause classification accuracy to deteriorate (by 1−5% in the situations tested). The problem is that the new attribute is (naturally) chosen for splitting high up in the tree. This has the effect of fragmenting the set of instances available at the nodes below so that other choices are based on sparser data.

Because of the negative effect of irrelevant attributes on most machine learning schemes, it is common to precede learning with an attribute selection stage that strives to eliminate all but the most relevant attributes. The best way to select relevant attributes is manually, based on a deep understanding of the learning problem and what the attributes actually mean. However, automatic methods can also be useful. Reducing the dimensionality of the data by deleting unsuitable attributes improves the performance of learning algorithms. It also speeds them up, although this may be outweighed by the computation involved in attribute selection. More importantly, dimensionality reduction yields a more compact, more easily interpretable representation of the target concept, focusing the user's attention on the most relevant variables.

SCHEME-INDEPENDENT SELECTION

When selecting a good attribute subset, there are two fundamentally different approaches. One is to make an independent assessment based on general characteristics of the data; the other is to evaluate the subset using the machine learning algorithm that will ultimately be employed for learning. The first is called the *filter* method, because the attribute set is filtered to produce the most promising subset before learning commences. The second is the *wrapper* method, because the learning algorithm is wrapped into the selection procedure. Making an independent assessment of an attribute subset would be easy if there were a good way of determining when an attribute was relevant to choosing the class. However, there is no universally accepted measure of "relevance," although several different ones have been proposed.

One simple scheme-independent method of attribute selection is to use just enough attributes to divide up the instance space in a way that separates all the training instances. For example, if just one or two attributes are used, there will generally be several instances that have the same combination of attribute values. At the other extreme, the full set of attributes will likely distinguish the instances uniquely so that no two instances have the same values for all attributes. (This will not necessarily be the case, however; datasets sometimes contain instances with the same attribute values but different classes.) It makes intuitive sense to select the smallest attribute subset that serves to distinguish all instances uniquely. This can easily be found using exhaustive search, although at considerable computational expense. Unfortunately, this strong bias toward consistency of the attribute set on the training data is statistically unwarranted and can lead to overfitting—the algorithm may go to unnecessary lengths to repair an inconsistency that was in fact merely caused by noise.

Machine learning algorithms can be used for attribute selection. For instance, you might first apply a decision tree algorithm to the full dataset, and then select only those attributes that are actually used in the tree. While this selection would have no effect at all if the second stage merely built another tree, it will have an effect on a different learning algorithm. For example, the nearest-neighbor algorithm is notoriously susceptible to irrelevant attributes, and its performance can be improved by using a decision tree builder as a filter for attribute selection first. The resulting nearest-neighbor scheme can also perform better than the decision tree algorithm used for filtering. As another example, the simple 1R scheme described in Chapter 4, Algorithms: the basic methods, has been used to select the attributes for a decision tree learner by evaluating the effect of branching on different attributes (although an error-based method such as 1R may not be the optimal choice for ranking attributes, as we will see later when covering the related problem of supervised discretization). Often the decision tree performs just as well when only the two or three top attributes are used for its construction—and it is much easier to understand.

Another possibility is to use an algorithm that builds a linear model—e.g., a linear support vector machine—and ranks the attributes based on the size of the coefficients. A more sophisticated variant applies the learning algorithm repeatedly. It builds a model, ranks the attributes based on the coefficients, removes the lowest-ranked one, and repeats the process until all attributes have been removed. This method of *recursive feature elimination* has been found to yield better results on certain datasets (e.g., when identifying important genes for cancer classification) than simply ranking attributes based on a single model. With both methods it is important to ensure that the attributes are measured on the same scale; otherwise, the coefficients are not comparable. Note that these techniques just produce a ranking; another method must be used to determine the appropriate number of attributes to use.

Attributes can be selected using instance-based learning methods too. You could sample instances randomly from the training set and check neighboring records of the same and different classes—"near hits" and "near misses." If a near hit has a different value for a certain attribute, that attribute appears to be irrelevant and its weight should be decreased. On the other hand, if a near miss has a different value, the attribute appears to be relevant and its weight should be increased. Of course, this is the standard kind of procedure used for attribute weighting for instance-based learning, described in Section 7.1. After repeating this operation many times, selection takes place: only attributes with positive weights are chosen. As in the standard incremental formulation of instance-based learning, different results will be obtained each time the process is repeated, because of the different ordering of examples. This can be avoided by using all training instances and taking into account all near hits and near misses of each.

A more serious disadvantage is that the method will not detect an attribute that is redundant because it is correlated with another attribute. In the extreme case, two identical attributes would be treated in the same way, either both selected or both rejected. A modification has been suggested that appears to go some way towards addressing this issue by taking the current attribute weights into account when computing the nearest hits and misses.

Another way of eliminating redundant attributes as well as irrelevant ones is to select a subset of attributes that individually correlate well with the class but have little intercorrelation. The correlation between two nominal attributes A and B can be measured using the *symmetric uncertainty*:

$$U(A, B) = 2 \frac{H(A) + H(B) - H(A, B)}{H(A) + H(B)},$$

where H is the entropy function described in Section 4.3. The entropies are based on the probability associated with each attribute value; $H(A,B)$, the joint entropy of A and B, is calculated from the joint probabilities of all combinations of values of A and B. The symmetric uncertainty always lies between 0 and 1. Correlation-based feature selection determines the goodness of a set of attributes using

$$\sum_j U(A_j, C) \Big/ \sqrt{\sum_i \sum_j U(A_i, A_j)},$$

where C is the class attribute and the indices i and j range over all attributes in the set. If all m attributes in the subset correlate perfectly with the class and with one another, the numerator becomes m and the denominator $\sqrt{m^2}$, which is also m.

Hence the measure is 1, which turns out to be the maximum value it can attain (the minimum is 0). Clearly this is not ideal, because we want to avoid redundant attributes. However, any subset of this set will also have value 1. When using this criterion to search for a good subset of attributes it makes sense to break ties in favor of the smallest subset.

SEARCHING THE ATTRIBUTE SPACE

Most methods for attribute selection involve searching the space of attributes for the subset that is most likely to predict the class best. Fig. 8.1 illustrates the attribute space for the—by now all-too-familiar—weather dataset. The number of possible attribute subsets increases exponentially with the number of attributes, making exhaustive search impractical on all but the simplest problems.

Typically the space is searched greedily in one of two directions, top to bottom or bottom to top in the figure. At each stage, a local change is made to the current attribute subset by either adding or deleting a single attribute. The downward direction, where you start with no attributes and add them one at

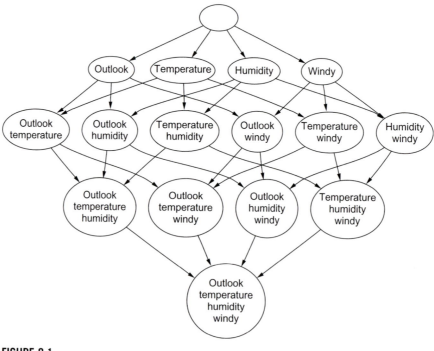

FIGURE 8.1

Attribute space for the weather dataset.

a time, is called *forward selection*. The upward one, where you start with the full set and delete attributes one at a time, is *backward elimination*.

In forward selection, each attribute that is not already in the current subset is tentatively added to it, and the resulting set of attributes is evaluated—using, e.g., cross-validation as described in the following section. This evaluation produces a numeric measure of the expected performance of the subset. The effect of adding each attribute in turn is quantified by this measure, the best one is chosen, and the procedure continues. However, if no attribute produces an improvement when added to the current subset, the search ends. This is a standard greedy search procedure and guarantees to find a locally—but not necessarily globally—optimal set of attributes. Backward elimination operates in an entirely analogous fashion. In both cases a slight bias is often introduced toward smaller attribute sets. This can be done for forward selection by insisting that if the search is to continue, the evaluation measure must not only increase, but must increase by at least a small predetermined quantity. A similar modification works for backward elimination.

More sophisticated search schemes exist. Forward selection and backward elimination can be combined into a bidirectional search; again one can either begin with all the attributes or with none of them. Best-first search is a method that does not just terminate when the performance starts to drop but keeps a list of all attribute subsets evaluated so far, sorted in order of the performance measure, so that it can revisit an earlier configuration instead. Given enough time it will explore the entire space, unless this is prevented by some kind of stopping criterion. Beam search is similar but truncates its list of attribute subsets at each stage so that it only contains a fixed number—the beam width—of most promising candidates. Genetic algorithm search procedures are loosely based on the principle of natural selection: they "evolve" good feature subsets by using random perturbations of a current list of candidate subsets and combining them based on performance.

SCHEME-SPECIFIC SELECTION

The performance of an attribute subset with scheme-specific selection is measured in terms of the learning scheme's classification performance using just those attributes. Given a subset of attributes, accuracy is estimated using the normal procedure of cross-validation described in Section 5.3. Of course, other evaluation methods such as performance on a holdout set (Section 5.2) or the bootstrap estimator (Section 5.4) could equally well be used.

The entire attribute selection process is rather computation intensive. If each evaluation involves a 10-fold cross-validation, the learning procedure must be executed 10 times. With k attributes, the heuristic forward selection or backward elimination multiplies evaluation time by a factor proportional to k^2 in the worst case—and for more sophisticated searches, the penalty will be far greater, up to 2^k for an exhaustive algorithm that examines each of the 2^k possible subsets.

Good results have been demonstrated on many datasets. In general terms, backward elimination produces larger attribute sets than forward selection, but better classification accuracy in some cases. The reason is that the performance measure is only an estimate, and a single optimistic estimate will cause both of these search procedures to halt prematurely—backward elimination with too many attributes and forward selection with not enough. But forward selection is useful if the focus is on understanding the decision structures involved, because it often reduces the number of attributes with only a small effect on classification accuracy. Experience seems to show that more sophisticated search techniques are not generally justified—although they can produce much better results in certain cases.

One way to accelerate the search process is to stop evaluating a subset of attributes as soon as it becomes apparent that it is unlikely to lead to higher accuracy than another candidate subset. This is a job for a paired statistical significance test, performed between the classifier based on this subset and all the other candidate classifiers based on other subsets. The performance difference between two classifiers on a particular test instance can be taken to be -1, 0, or 1 depending on whether the first classifier is worse, the same as, or better than the second on that instance. A paired t-test (described in Section 5.6) can be applied to these figures over the entire test set, effectively treating the results for each instance as an independent estimate of the difference in performance. Then the cross-validation for a classifier can be prematurely terminated as soon as it turns out to be significantly worse than another—which, of course, may never happen. We might want to discard classifiers more aggressively by modifying the t-test to compute the probability that one classifier is better than another classifier by at least a small user-specified threshold. If this probability becomes very small, we can discard the former classifier on the basis that it is very unlikely to perform substantially better than the latter.

This methodology is called *race search* and can be implemented with different underlying search strategies. When used with forward selection, we race all possible single-attribute additions simultaneously and drop those that do not perform well enough. In backward elimination, we race all single-attribute deletions. *Schemata search* is a more complicated method specifically designed for racing; it runs an iterative series of races that each determine whether or not a particular attribute should be included. The other attributes for this race are included or excluded randomly at each point in the evaluation. As soon as one race has a clear winner, the next iteration of races begins, using the winner as the starting point. Another search strategy is to rank the attributes first using, e.g., their information gain (assuming they are discrete), and then race the ranking. In this case the race includes no attributes, the top-ranked attribute, the top two attributes, the top three, and so on.

A simple method for accelerating scheme-specific search is to preselect a given number of attributes by ranking them first using a criterion like the information gain and discarding the rest before applying scheme-specific selection. This has been found to work surprisingly well on high-dimensional datasets such as gene expression and text categorization data, where only a couple of hundred of attributes are used instead of several thousands. In the case of forward selection, a slightly more sophisticated variant is to restrict the number of attributes available for expanding the current attribute subset to a fixed-sized subset chosen from the ranked list of attributes—creating a sliding window of attribute choices—rather than making all (unused) attributes available for consideration in each step of the search process.

Whatever way you do it, scheme-specific attribute selection by no means yields a uniform improvement in performance. Because of the complexity of the process, which is greatly increased by the feedback effect of including a target machine learning algorithm in the attribution selection loop, it is quite hard to predict the conditions under which it will turn out to be worthwhile. As in many machine learning situations, trial and error using your own particular source of data is the final arbiter.

There is one type of classifier for which scheme-specific attribute selection is an essential part of the learning process: the decision table. As mentioned in Section 3.1, the entire problem of learning decision tables consists of selecting the right attributes to be included. Usually this is done by measuring the table's cross-validation performance for different subsets of attributes and choosing the best-performing subset. Fortunately, leave-one-out cross-validation is very cheap for this kind of classifier. Obtaining the cross-validation error from a decision table derived from the training data is just a matter of manipulating the class counts associated with each of the table's entries, because the table's structure doesn't change when instances are added or deleted. The attribute space is generally searched by best-first search because this strategy is less likely to get stuck in a local maximum than others, such as forward selection.

Let's end our discussion with a success story. One learning method for which a simple scheme-specific attribute selection approach has shown good results is Naïve Bayes. Although this method deals well with random attributes, it has the potential to be misled when there are dependencies among attributes, and particularly when redundant ones are added. However, good results have been reported using the forward selection algorithm—which is better able to detect when a redundant attribute is about to be added than the backward elimination approach—in conjunction with a very simple, almost "naïve," metric that determines the quality of an attribute subset to be simply the performance of the learned algorithm on the *training* set. As was emphasized in Chapter 5, Credibility: evaluating what's been learned, training set performance is certainly not a reliable indicator of test set performance; however, Naïve Bayes is less likely to overfit than other learning algorithms. Experiments show that this simple modification to Naïve Bayes markedly improves its performance on those standard datasets for which it does not do so well as tree- or rule-based classifiers, and does not have any negative effect on results on datasets on which Naïve Bayes already does well. *Selective* Naïve Bayes, as this learning method is called, is a viable machine learning technique that performs reliably and well in practice.

8.2 DISCRETIZING NUMERIC ATTRIBUTES

Some classification and clustering algorithms deal with nominal attributes only and cannot handle ones measured on a numeric scale. To use them on general datasets, numeric attributes must first be "discretized" into a small number of distinct ranges. Even learning algorithms that do handle numeric attributes sometimes process them in ways that are not altogether satisfactory. Statistical clustering methods often assume that numeric attributes have a normal distribution—often not a very plausible assumption in practice—and the standard extension of the Naïve Bayes classifier numeric attributes adopts the same assumption. Although most decision tree and decision rule learners can handle numeric attributes, some implementations work more slowly when numeric attributes are present because they repeatedly sort the attribute values. For all these reasons the question arises: what is a good way to discretize numeric attributes into ranges before any learning takes place?

We have already encountered some methods for discretizing numeric attributes. The 1R learning scheme described in Chapter 4, Algorithms: the basic methods, uses a simple but effective technique: sort the instances by the attribute's value and assign the value into ranges at the points that the class value changes—except that a certain minimum number of instances in the majority class (six) must lie in each of the ranges, which means that any given range may include a mixture of class values. This is a "global" method of discretization that is applied to all continuous attributes before learning starts.

Decision tree learners, on the other hand, deal with numeric attributes on a local basis, examining attributes at each node of the tree, when it is being constructed, to see whether they are worth branching on—and only at that point deciding on the best place to split continuous attributes. Although the tree-building method we examined in Chapter 6, Trees and rules, only considers binary splits of continuous attributes, one can imagine a full discretization taking place at that point, yielding a multiway split on a numeric attribute. The pros and cons of the local versus global approach are clear. Local discretization is tailored to the actual context provided by each tree node, and will produce different discretizations of the same attribute at different places in the tree if that seems appropriate. However, its decisions are based on less data as tree depth increases, which compromises their reliability. If trees are developed all the way out to single-instance leaves before being pruned back, as with the normal technique of backward pruning, it is clear that many discretization decisions will be based on data that is grossly inadequate.

When using global discretization before applying a learning scheme, there are two possible ways of presenting the discretized data to the learner. The most obvious is to treat discretized attributes like nominal ones: each discretization interval is represented by one value of the nominal attribute. However, because a discretized attribute is derived from a numeric one, its values are ordered, and treating it as nominal discards this potentially valuable ordering information. Of course, if a learning scheme can handle ordered attributes directly, the solution is obvious: each discretized attribute is declared to be of type "ordered."

If the learning scheme cannot handle ordered attributes, there is still a simple way of enabling it to exploit the ordering information: transform each discretized attribute into a set of binary attributes before the learning scheme is applied. If the discretized attribute has k values, it is transformed into $k-1$ binary attributes. If the original attribute's value is i for a particular instance, the first $i-1$ of these new attributes are set to *false* and the remainder are set to *true*. In other words, the $(i-1)$th binary attribute represents whether the discretized attribute is less than i. If a decision tree learner splits on this attribute, it implicitly utilizes the ordering information it encodes. Note that this transformation is independent of the particular discretization method being applied: it is simply a way of coding an ordered attribute using a set of binary attributes.

UNSUPERVISED DISCRETIZATION

There are two basic approaches to the problem of discretization. One is to quantize each attribute in the absence of any knowledge of the classes of the instances in the training set—so-called *unsupervised* discretization. The other is to take the classes into account when discretizing—*supervised* discretization. The former is the only possibility when dealing with clustering problems where the classes are unknown or nonexistent.

The obvious way of discretizing a numeric attribute is to divide its range into a predetermined number of equal intervals: a fixed, data-independent yardstick. This is frequently done at the time when data is collected. But, like any unsupervised discretization method, it runs the risk of destroying distinctions that would have turned out to be useful in the learning process by using gradations that are too coarse or by unfortunate choices of boundary that needlessly lump together many instances of different classes.

Equal-interval binning often distributes instances very unevenly: some bins contain many instances while others contain none. This can seriously impair the ability of the attribute to help build good decision structures. It is often better to allow the intervals to be of different sizes, choosing them so that the same number of training examples fall into each one. This method, *equal-frequency binning*, divides the attribute's range into a predetermined number of bins based on the distribution of examples along that axis—sometimes called *histogram equalization*, because if you take a histogram of the contents of the resulting bins it will be completely flat. If you view the number of bins as a resource, this method makes best use of it.

However, equal-frequency binning is still oblivious to the instances' classes, and this can cause bad boundaries. For example, if all instances in a bin have one class, and all instances in the next higher bin have another except for the first, which has the original class, surely it makes sense to respect the class divisions and include that first instance in the previous bin, sacrificing the equal-frequency property for the sake of homogeneity. Supervised discretization—taking classes into account during the process—certainly has advantages. Nevertheless it has been found that equal-frequency binning can yield excellent results, at least in conjunction with the Naïve Bayes learning scheme, when the number of bins is chosen in a data-dependent fashion by setting it to the square root of the number of instances. This method is called *proportional k-interval discretization*.

ENTROPY-BASED DISCRETIZATION

Because the criterion used for splitting a numeric attribute during the formation of a decision tree works well in practice, it seems a good idea to extend it to more general discretization by recursively splitting intervals until it is time to stop. In Chapter 6, Trees and rules, we saw how to sort the instances by the attribute's value and consider, for each possible splitting point, the information gain of the resulting split. To discretize the attribute, once the first split is determined the splitting process can be repeated in the upper and lower parts of the range, and so on, recursively.

To see this working in practice, we revisit the example given earlier for discretizing the temperature attribute of the weather data, whose values are

64	65	68	69	70	71	72	75	80	81	83	85
Yes	No	Yes	Yes	Yes	No	No	Yes	No	Yes	Yes	No
						Yes	Yes				

(Repeated values have been collapsed together). The information gain for each of the 11 possible positions for the breakpoint is calculated in the usual way. For example, the information value of the test *temperature* <71.5, which splits the range into four *yes*'s and two *no*'s versus five *yes*'s and three *no*'s, is

$$\text{Info}([4,2],[5,3]) = (6/14) \times \text{info}([4,2]) + (8/14) \times \text{info}([5,3]) = 0.939 \text{ bits}.$$

This represents the amount of information required to specify the individual values of *yes* and *no* given the split. We seek a discretization that makes the sub-intervals as pure as possible; hence, we choose to split at the point where the information value is smallest. (This is the same as splitting where the information *gain*, defined as the difference between the information value without the split and that with the split, is largest.) As before, we place numeric thresholds halfway between the values that delimit the boundaries of a concept.

The graph labeled A in Fig. 8.2 shows the information values at each possible cut point at this first stage. The cleanest division—smallest information value—is at a temperature of 84 (0.827 bits), which separates off just the very final value, a *no* instance, from the preceding list. The instance classes are written below the horizontal axis to make interpretation easier. Invoking the algorithm again on the lower range of temperatures, from 64 to 83, yields the graph labeled B.

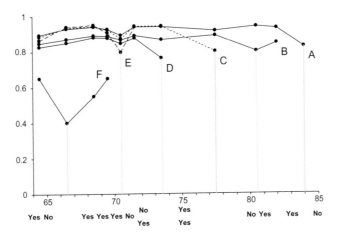

FIGURE 8.2

Discretizing the *temperature* attribute using the entropy method.

64	65	68	69	70	71	72	75	80	81	83	85
Yes	No	Yes	Yes	Yes	No	No Yes	Yes Yes	No	Yes	Yes	No

| | | F | | | E | | D | C | B | | A |
| | | 66.5 | | | 70.5 | | | 73.5 | 77.5 | 80.5 | | 84 |

FIGURE 8.3

The result of discretizing the *temperature* attribute.

This has a minimum at 80.5 (0.800 bits), which splits off the next two values, both *yes* instances. Again invoking the algorithm on the lower range, now from 64 to 80, produces the graph labeled C (shown dotted to help distinguish it from the others). The minimum is at 77.5 (0.801 bits), splitting off another *no* instance. Graph D has a minimum at 73.5 (0.764 bits), splitting off two *yes* instances. Graph E (again dashed, purely to make it more easily visible), for the temperature range 64−72, has a minimum at 70.5 (0.796 bits), which splits off two *nos* and a *yes*. Finally, graph F, for the range 64−70, has a minimum at 66.5 (0.4 bits).

The final discretization of the *temperature* attribute is shown in Fig. 8.3. The fact that recursion only ever occurs in the first interval of each split is an artifact of this example: in general, both the upper and lower intervals will have to be split further. Underneath each division is the label of the graph in Fig. 8.2 that is responsible for it, and below that the actual value of the split point.

It can be shown theoretically that a cut point that minimizes the information value will never occur between two instances of the same class. This leads to a useful optimization: it is only necessary to consider potential divisions that separate instances of different classes. Notice that if class labels were assigned to the intervals based on the majority class in the interval, there would be no guarantee that adjacent intervals would receive different labels. You might be tempted to consider merging intervals with the same majority class (e.g., the first two intervals of Fig. 8.3), but as we will see later this is not a good thing to do in general.

The only problem left to consider is the stopping criterion. In the temperature example most of the intervals that were identified were "pure" in that all their instances had the same class, and there is clearly no point in trying to split such an interval. (Exceptions were the final interval, which we tacitly decided not to split, and the interval from 70.5 to 73.5.) In general, however, things are not so straightforward.

A good way to stop the entropy-based splitting discretization procedure turns out to be the MDL principle that we encountered in Chapter 5, Credibility: evaluating what's been learned. In accordance with that principle, we want to minimize the size of the "theory" plus the size of the information necessary to specify all the data given that theory. In this case, if we do split, the "theory" is the splitting point, and we are comparing the situation in which we split with that in which we do not. In both cases we assume that the instances are known but their class labels are not. If we do not split, the classes can be transmitted by encoding each instance's label. If we do, we first encode the split point (in $\log_2[N-1]$ bits, where N is the number of instances), then the classes of the instances below that point, and then the classes of those above it. You can imagine that if the split is a good one—say, all the classes below it are *yes* and all those above are *no*—then there is much to be gained by splitting. If there is an equal number of *yes* and *no* instances, each instance costs 1 bit without splitting but hardly more than 0 bits with splitting—it is not quite 0 because the class values associated with the split itself must be encoded, but this penalty is amortized across all the instances. In this case, if there are many examples, the penalty of having to encode the split point will be far outweighed by the information saved by splitting.

We emphasized in Section 5.10 that when applying the MDL principle, the devil is in the details. In the relatively straightforward case of discretization, the situation is tractable although not simple. The amounts of information can be obtained exactly under certain reasonable assumptions. We will not go into the details, but the upshot is that the split dictated by a particular cut point is worthwhile if the information gain for that split exceeds a certain value that depends on the number of instances N, the number of classes k, the entropy of the instances E, the entropy of the instances in each subinterval E_1 and E_2, and the number of classes represented in each subinterval k_1 and k_2:

$$Gain > \frac{\log_2(N-1)}{N} + \frac{\log_2(3^k - 2) - kE + k_1E_1 + k_2E_2}{N}.$$

The first component is the information needed to specify the splitting point; the second is a correction due to the need to transmit which classes correspond to the upper and lower subintervals.

When applied to the temperature example, this criterion prevents any splitting at all. The first split removes just the final example, and as you can imagine very little actual information is gained by this when transmitting the classes—in fact, the MDL criterion will never create an interval containing just one example. Failure to discretize *temperature* effectively disbars it from playing any role in the final decision structure because the same discretized value will be given to all instances. In this situation, this is perfectly appropriate: *temperature* does not occur in good decision trees or rules for the weather data. In effect, failure to discretize is tantamount to attribute selection.

OTHER DISCRETIZATION METHODS

The entropy-based method with the MDL stopping criterion is one of the best general techniques for supervised discretization. However, many other methods have been investigated. For example, instead of proceeding top-down by recursively splitting intervals until some stopping criterion is satisfied, you could work bottom-up, first placing each instance into its own interval and then considering whether to merge adjacent intervals. You could apply a statistical criterion to see which would be the best two intervals to merge, and merge them if the statistic exceeds a certain preset confidence level, repeating the operation until no potential merge passes the test. The χ^2 test is a suitable one and has been used for this purpose. Instead of specifying a preset significance threshold, more complex techniques are available to determine an appropriate level automatically.

A rather different approach is to count the number of errors that a discretization makes when predicting each training instance's class, assuming that each interval receives the majority class. For example, the 1R method described earlier is error-based—it focuses on errors rather than the entropy. However, the best possible discretization in terms of error count is obtained by using the largest possible number of intervals, and this degenerate case should be avoided by restricting the number of intervals in advance.

Let's consider the best way to discretize an attribute into k intervals in a way that minimizes the number of errors. The brute-force method of finding this is exponential in k and hence infeasible. However, there are much more efficient schemes that are based on the idea of dynamic programming. Dynamic programming applies not just to the error count measure but to any given additive impurity function, and it can find the partitioning of N instances into k intervals in a way that minimizes the impurity in time proportional to kN^2. This gives a way of finding the best entropy-based discretization, yielding a potential improvement in the quality of the discretization (but in practice a negligible one) over the greedy recursive entropy-based method described previously. The news for error-based discretization is even better, because there is an algorithm that can be used to minimize the error count in time linear in N.

ENTROPY-BASED VERSUS ERROR-BASED DISCRETIZATION

Why not use error-based discretization, since the optimal discretization can be found very quickly? The answer is that there is a serious drawback to error-based discretization: it cannot produce adjacent intervals with the same label (such as the first two of Fig. 8.3). The reason is that merging two such intervals will not affect the error count, but it will free up an interval that can be used elsewhere to reduce the error count.

Why would anyone want to generate adjacent intervals with the same label? The reason is best illustrated with an example. Fig. 8.4 shows the instance space for a simple two-class problem with two numeric attributes ranging from 0 to 1. Instances belong to one class (the dots) if their first attribute ($a1$) is less than 0.3 or if it is less than 0.7 *and* their second attribute ($a2$) is less than 0.5. Otherwise, they belong to the other class (triangles). The data in Fig. 8.4 has been artificially generated according to this rule.

Now suppose we are trying to discretize both attributes with a view to learning the classes from the discretized attributes. The very best discretization splits $a1$ into three intervals (0 through 0.3, 0.3 through 0.7, and 0.7 through 1) and $a2$ into two intervals (0 through 0.5 and 0.5 through 1). Given these nominal attributes, it will be easy to learn how to tell the classes apart with a simple decision tree or rule algorithm. Discretizing $a2$ is no problem. For $a1$, however, the first and last intervals will have opposite labels (*dot* and *triangle*, respectively). The second will have whichever label happens to occur most in the region from 0.3 through 0.7 (it is in fact *dot* for the data in Fig. 8.4). Either way, this label must inevitably be the same as one of the adjacent labels—of course this is true whatever the

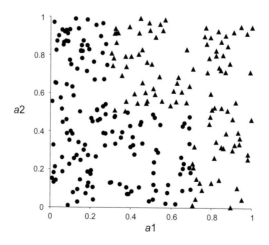

FIGURE 8.4

Class distribution for a two-class, two-attribute problem.

class probability happens to be in the middle region. Thus this discretization will not be achieved by any method that minimizes the error counts, because such a method cannot produce adjacent intervals with the same label.

The point is that what changes as the value of $a1$ crosses the boundary at 0.3 is not the majority class but the class *distribution*. The majority class remains *dot*. The distribution, however, changes markedly, from 100% before the boundary to just over 50% after it. And the distribution changes again as the boundary at 0.7 is crossed, from 50% to 0%. Entropy-based discretization methods are sensitive to changes in the distribution even though the majority class does not change. Error-based methods are not.

CONVERTING DISCRETE TO NUMERIC ATTRIBUTES

There is a converse problem to discretization. Some learning algorithms—notably the nearest-neighbor instance-based method and numeric prediction techniques involving regression—naturally handle only attributes that are numeric. How can they be extended to nominal attributes?

In instance-based learning, as described in Section 4.7, discrete attributes can be treated as numeric by defining the "distance" between two nominal values that are the same as 0 and between two values that are different as 1—regardless of the actual values involved. Rather than modifying the distance function, this can be achieved by an attribute transformation: replace a k-valued nominal attribute by k synthetic binary attributes, one for each value indicating whether the attribute has that value or not. If the attributes are scaled appropriately, this achieves the same effect on the distance function. The distance is insensitive to the attribute values because only "same" or "different" information is encoded, not the shades of difference that may be associated with the various possible values of the attribute. More subtle distinctions can be made if the attributes have weights reflecting their relative importance.

If the values of the attribute can be ordered, more possibilities arise. For a numeric prediction problem, the average class value corresponding to each value of a nominal attribute can be calculated from the training instances and used to determine an ordering—this technique was introduced for model trees in Section 7.3. (It is hard to come up with an analogous way of ordering attribute values for a classification problem.) An ordered nominal attribute can be replaced by an integer in the obvious way—but this implies not just an ordering but also a metric on the attribute's values. The implication of a metric can be avoided by creating $k-1$ synthetic binary attributes for a k-valued nominal attribute, in the manner described earlier. This encoding still implies an ordering among different values of the attribute—adjacent values differ in just one of the synthetic attributes, whereas distant ones differ in several—but does not necessarily imply an equal distance between the attribute values.

8.3 PROJECTIONS

Resourceful data miners have a toolbox full of techniques, such as discretization, for transforming data. As we emphasized in Chapter 2, Input: concepts, instances, attributes, data mining is hardly ever a matter of simply taking a dataset and applying a learning algorithm to it. Every problem is different. You need to think about the data and what it means, and examine it from diverse points of view—creatively!—to arrive at a suitable perspective. Transforming it in different ways can help you get started. In mathematics, a *projection* is a kind of function or mapping that transforms data in some way.

You don't have to make your own toolbox by implementing the projections yourself. Comprehensive environments for machine learning, such as the one described in Appendix B, contain a wide range of suitable tools for you to use. You do not necessarily need a detailed understanding of how they are implemented. What you do need to understand is what the tools do and how they can be applied.

Data often calls for general mathematical transformations of a set of attributes. It might be useful to define new attributes by applying specified mathematical functions to existing ones. Two *date* attributes might be subtracted to give a third attribute representing *age*—an example of a semantic transformation driven by the meaning of the original attributes. Other transformations might be suggested by known properties of the learning algorithm. If a linear relationship involving two attributes, A and B, is suspected, and the algorithm is only capable of axis-parallel splits (as most decision tree and rule learners are), the ratio A/B might be defined as a new attribute. The transformations are not necessarily mathematical ones, but may involve world knowledge such as days of the week, civic holidays, or chemical atomic numbers. They could be expressed as operations in a spreadsheet or as functions that are implemented by arbitrary computer programs. Or you can reduce several nominal attributes to one by concatenating their values, producing a single $k_1 \times k_2$-valued attribute from attributes with k_1 and k_2 values, respectively. Discretization converts a numeric attribute to nominal, and we saw earlier how to convert in the other direction too.

As another kind of transformation, you might apply a clustering procedure to the dataset and then define a new attribute whose value for any given instance is the cluster that contains it using an arbitrary labeling for clusters. Alternatively, with probabilistic clustering, you could augment each instance with its membership probabilities for each cluster, including as many new attributes as there are clusters.

Sometimes it is useful to add noise to data, perhaps to test the robustness of a learning algorithm. To take a nominal attribute and change a given percentage of its values. To obfuscate data by renaming the relation, attribute names, and nominal and string attribute values—because it is often necessary to anonymize sensitive datasets. To randomize the order of instances or produce a random sample of the dataset by resampling it. To reduce a dataset by removing a given percentage of instances, or all instances that have certain values for nominal attributes, or numeric values above or below a certain threshold. Or to remove outliers by applying a classification method to the dataset and deleting misclassified instances.

Different types of input call for their own transformations. If you can input sparse data files (see Section 2.4), you may need to be able to convert datasets to nonsparse form, and vice versa. Textual input and time series input call for their own specialized conversions, described in the subsections that follow. But first we look at general techniques for transforming data with numeric attributes into a lower-dimensional form that may be more useful for mining.

PRINCIPAL COMPONENT ANALYSIS

In a dataset with k numeric attributes, you can visualize the data as a cloud of points in k-dimensional space—the stars in the sky, a swarm of flies frozen in time, a two-dimensional scatter plot on paper. The attributes represent the coordinates of the space. But the axes you use, the coordinate system itself, is arbitrary. You can place horizontal and vertical axes on the paper and represent the points of the scatter plot using those coordinates, or you could draw an arbitrary straight line to represent the x-axis and one perpendicular to it to represent y. To record the positions of the flies you could use a conventional coordinate system with a north–south axis, an east–west axis, and an up–down axis. But other coordinate systems would do equally well. Creatures like flies don't know about north, south, east and west, although, being subject to gravity, they may perceive up–down as something special. And as for the stars in the sky, who's to say what the "right" coordinate system is?

Back to the dataset. Just as in these examples, there is nothing to stop you transforming all the data points into a different coordinate system. But unlike these examples, in data mining there often *is* a preferred coordinate system, defined not by some external convention but by the very data itself. Whatever coordinates you use, the cloud of points has a certain variance in each direction, indicating the degree of spread around the mean value in that direction. It is a curious fact that if you add up the variances along each axis and then transform the points into a different coordinate system and do the same there, you get the same total variance in both cases. This is always true provided the coordinate systems are *orthogonal*, i.e., each axis is at right angles to the others.

The idea of principal component analysis is to use a special coordinate system that depends on the cloud of points as follows: place the first axis in the direction of greatest variance of the points to maximize the variance along that axis. The second axis is perpendicular to it. In two dimensions there is no choice—its direction is determined by the first axis—but in three dimensions it can lie anywhere in the plane perpendicular to the first axis, and in higher dimensions there is even more choice, though it is always constrained to be perpendicular to the first axis. Subject to this constraint, choose the second axis in the way that maximizes the variance along it. And so on, choosing each axis to maximize its share of the remaining variance.

How do you do this? It's not hard, given an appropriate computer program, and it's not hard to understand, given the appropriate mathematical tools. Technically—for those who understand the italicized terms—you calculate the *covariance matrix* of the original coordinates of the points and *diagonalize* it to find the *eigenvectors*. These are the axes of the transformed space, sorted in order of *eigenvalue*—because each eigenvalue gives the variance along its axis.

Fig. 8.5 shows the result of transforming a particular dataset with 10 numeric attributes, corresponding to points in 10-dimensional space. Imagine the original dataset as a cloud of points in 10 dimensions—we can't draw it! Choose the first axis along the direction of greatest variance, the second perpendicular to it along the direction of next greatest variance, and so on. The table gives the variance along each new coordinate axis in the order in which the axes were chosen. Because the sum of the variances is constant regardless of the coordinate system, they are expressed as percentages of that total. We call axes *components* and say that each one "accounts for" its share of the variance. Fig. 8.5B plots the variance that each component accounts for against the component's number. You can use all the components as new attributes for machine learning, or you might want to choose just the first few, the *principal components*, and discard the rest. In this case, three principal components account for 84% of the variance in the dataset; seven account for more than 95%.

On numeric datasets it is common to use principal component analysis prior to data mining as a form of data cleanup and dimensionality reduction. For example, you might want to replace the numeric attributes with the principal component axes or with a subset of them that accounts for a given proportion—say, 95%—of the variance. Note that the scale of the attributes affects the outcome of principal

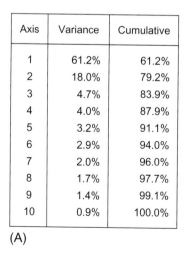

Axis	Variance	Cumulative
1	61.2%	61.2%
2	18.0%	79.2%
3	4.7%	83.9%
4	4.0%	87.9%
5	3.2%	91.1%
6	2.9%	94.0%
7	2.0%	96.0%
8	1.7%	97.7%
9	1.4%	99.1%
10	0.9%	100.0%

(A)

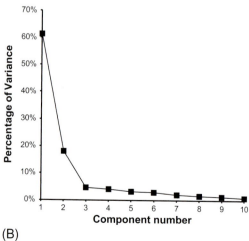

(B)

FIGURE 8.5

Principal component transform of a dataset: (A) variance of each component; (B) variance plot.

component analysis, and it is common practice to standardize all attributes to zero mean and unit variance first.

Another possibility is to apply principal component analysis recursively in a decision tree learner. At each stage an ordinary decision tree learner chooses to split in a direction that is parallel to one of the axes. However, suppose a principal component transform is performed first, and the learner chooses an axis in the transformed space. This equates to a split along an oblique line in the original space. If the transform is performed afresh before each split, the result will be an oblique decision tree whose splits are in directions that are not parallel with the axes or with one another.

RANDOM PROJECTIONS

Principal component analysis transforms the data linearly into a lower-dimensional space. But it's expensive. The time taken to find the transformation (which is a matrix comprising the eigenvectors of the covariance matrix) is cubic in the number of dimensions. This makes it infeasible for datasets with a large number of attributes. A far simpler alternative is to use a random projection of the data into a subspace with a predetermined number of dimensions. It's very easy to find a random projection matrix. But will it be any good?

In fact, theory shows that random projections preserve distance relationships quite well on average. This means that they could be used in conjunction with kD-trees or ball trees to do approximate nearest-neighbor search in spaces with a huge number of dimensions. First transform the data to reduce the number of attributes; then build a tree for the transformed space. In the case of nearest-neighbor classification you could make the result more stable, and less dependent on the choice of random projection, by building an ensemble classifier that uses multiple random matrices.

Not surprisingly, random projections perform worse than ones carefully chosen by principal component analysis when used to preprocess data for a range of standard classifiers. However, experimental results have shown that the difference is not too great—and it tends to decrease as the number of dimensions increases. And of course, random projections are far cheaper computationally.

PARTIAL LEAST SQUARES REGRESSION

As mentioned earlier, principal component analysis is often performed as a preprocessing step before applying a learning algorithm. When the learning algorithm is linear regression, the resulting model is known as *principal component regression*. Since principal components are themselves linear combinations of the original attributes, the output of principal component regression can be re-expressed in terms of the original attributes. In fact, if all the components are used—not just the "principal" ones—the result is the same as that obtained by applying least squares regression to the original input data. Using fewer than the full set of components results in a reduced regression.

Partial least squares differs from principal component analysis in that it takes the class attribute into account, as well as the predictor attributes, when constructing a coordinate system. The idea is to calculate derived directions that, as well as having high variance, are strongly correlated with the class. This can be advantageous when seeking as small a set of transformed attributes as possible to use for supervised learning.

There is a simple iterative method for computing the partial least squares directions that involves only dot product operations. Starting with input attributes that have been standardized to have zero mean and unit variance, the attribute coefficients for the first partial least squares direction are found by taking the dot product between each attribute vector and the class vector in turn. To find the second direction the same approach is used, but the original attribute values are replaced by the difference between the attribute's value and the prediction from a simple univariate regression that uses the first direction as the single predictor of that attribute. These differences are called *residuals*. The process continues in the same fashion for each remaining direction, with residuals for the attributes from the previous iteration forming the input for finding the current partial least squares direction.

Here is a simple worked example that should help make the procedure clear. For the first five instances from the CPU performance data in Table 1.5, Table 8.1A shows the values of CHMIN and CHMAX (after standardization to zero mean and unit variance) and PRP (not standardized). The task is to find an expression for the target attribute PRP in terms of the other two. The attribute coefficients for the first partial least squares direction are found by taking the dot product between the class and each attribute in turn. The dot product between the PRP and CHMIN columns is -0.4472, and that between PRP and CHMAX is 22.981. Thus the first partial least squares direction is

$$PLS1 = -0.4472\ CHMIN + 22.981\ CHMAX.$$

Table 8.1B shows the values for PLS1 obtained from this formula.

Table 8.1 The First Five Instances From the CPU Performance Data; (A) Original Values; (B) The First Partial Least Squares Direction; (C) Residuals From the First Direction

	(A)			(B)	(C)		
	CHMIN	CHMAX	PRP	PLS1	CHMIN	CHMAX	PRP
1	1.7889	1.7678	198	39.825	0.0436	0.0008	198
2	−0.4472	−0.3536	269	−7.925	−0.0999	−0.0019	269
3	−0.4472	−0.3536	220	−7.925	−0.0999	−0.0019	220
4	−0.4472	−0.3536	172	−7.925	−0.0999	−0.0019	172
5	−0.4472	−0.7071	132	−16.05	0.2562	0.005	132

The next step is to prepare the input data for finding the second partial least squares direction. To this end PLS1 is regressed onto CHMIN and CHMAX in turn, resulting in linear equations that predict each of these attributes individually from PLS1. The coefficients are found by taking the dot product between PLS1 and the attribute in question, and dividing the result by the dot product between PLS1 and itself. The resulting univariate regression equations are:

$$\text{CHMIN} = 0.0438 \ \text{PLS1}$$

$$\text{CHMAX} = 0.0444 \ \text{PLS1}.$$

Table 8.1C shows the CPU data in preparation for finding the second partial least squares direction. The original values of CHMIN and CHMAX have been replaced by residuals, i.e., the difference between the original value and the output of the corresponding univariate regression equation given above (the target value PRP remains the same). The entire procedure is repeated using this data as input to yield the second partial least squares direction, which is

$$\text{PLS2} = -23.6002 \ \text{CHMIN} + -0.4593 \ \text{CHMAX}.$$

After this last partial least squares direction has been found, the attribute residuals are all-zero. This reflects the fact that, as with principal component analysis, the full set of directions account for all of the variance in the original data.

When the partial least squares directions are used as input to linear regression, the resulting model is known as a *partial least squares regression model*. As with principal component regression, if all the directions are used, the solution is the same as that obtained by applying linear regression to the original data.

INDEPENDENT COMPONENT ANALYSIS

Principal component analysis finds a coordinate system for a feature space that captures the covariance of the data. In contrast, independent component analysis seeks a projection that decomposes the data into sources that are *statistically independent*.

Consider the "cocktail party problem," where people hear music and the voices of other people: the goal is to un-mix these signals. Of course, there are many other scenarios where a linear mixing of information must be unscrambled. Independent component analysis finds a linear projection of the mixed signal that gives the most statistically independent set of transformed variables.

Principal component analysis is sometimes thought of as seeking to transform correlated variables into linearly uncorrelated variables. However, correlation and statistical independence are two different criteria. *Uncorrelated* variables have correlation coefficients of zero, corresponding to zero entries in a covariance matrix. Two variables are considered *independent* when their joint probability is the product of their marginal probabilities. (We will discuss marginal probabilities in Section 9.1.)

A quantity called *mutual information* measures the amount of information one can obtain from one random variable given another. It can be used as an alternative criterion for finding a projection of data, based on minimizing the mutual information between the dimensions of the data in a linearly transformed space. Given a model $s=Ax$, where A is an orthogonal matrix, x is the input data and s is the decomposition into the source signals, it can be shown that minimizing the mutual information between the dimensions of s corresponds to transforming the data so that the estimated probability distribution of the sources $p(s)$ is as far from Gaussian as possible and the estimates s are constrained to be uncorrelated.

A popular technique for performing independent component analysis known as *fast ICA* uses a quantity known as the *negentropy* $J(s)=H(z)-H(s)$, where z is a Gaussian random variable with the same covariance variance matrix as s and $H(.)$ is the "differential entropy," defined as

$$H(x) = -\int p(x)\log p(x)dx$$

Negentropy measures the departure of s's distribution from the Gaussian distribution. Fast ICA uses simple approximations to the negentropy allowing learning to be performed more quickly.

LINEAR DISCRIMINANT ANALYSIS

Linear discriminant analysis is another way of finding a linear transformation of data that reduces the number of dimensions required to represent it. It is often used for dimensionality reduction prior to classification, but can also be used as a classification technique itself. Unlike principal and independent component analysis, it uses labeled data. The data is modeled by a multivariate Gaussian distribution for each class c, with mean μ_c and a common covariance matrix $\sum$. Because the covariance matrix for each class is assumed to be the same, the posterior distribution over the classes has a linear form, and for each class a *linear discriminant function* $y_c = x^T\sum^{-1}\mu_c - 1/2\mu_c^T\sum^{-1}\mu_c + \log(n_c/n)$ is computed, where n_c is the number of examples of class c and n the total number of examples. The data is classified by choosing the largest y_c. Appendix A.2 gives more information about multivariate Gaussian distributions.

QUADRATIC DISCRIMINANT ANALYSIS

Quadratic discriminant analysis is obtained simply by giving each class its own covariance matrix $\sum_c$ and mean μ_c. The decision boundaries defined by the posterior probability over classes will be described by quadratic equations. The *quadratic discriminant functions* for each class c are

$$f_c(x) = -\frac{1}{2}\log\left|\sum_c\right| - \frac{1}{2}(x-\mu_c)\sum_c^{-1}(x-\mu_c)^T + \log \pi_c,$$

where these functions are produced by taking the log of the corresponding Gaussian model for each class and ignoring the constant terms, since such functions will be compared with one another.

FISHER'S LINEAR DISCRIMINANT ANALYSIS

Linear discriminant analysis of the form discussed above has its roots in an approach developed by the famous statistician R.A. Fisher, who arrived at linear discriminants from a different perspective. He was interested in finding a linear projection for data that maximizes the variance between classes relative to the variance for data from the same class. This approach is known as Fisher's linear discriminant analysis, and can be formulate for two classes or multiple classes.

In the two-class case, we seek a projection vector $\mathbf{a}$ that can be used to compute scalar projections $y = \mathbf{a}\mathbf{x}$ for input vectors $\mathbf{x}$. It is obtained by computing the means of each class, μ_1 and μ_2 in the usual way. Then the *between-class scatter matrix* $\mathbf{S}_B = (\mu_2 - \mu_1)(\mu_2 - \mu_1)^\mathrm{T}$ is calculated (note the use of the outer product of two vectors here, which gives a matrix, rather than the dot product used earlier in the book, which gives a scalar); along with the *within-class scatter matrix*

$$\mathbf{S}_W = \sum_{i:c_i=1}(\mathbf{x}_i - \mu_1)(\mathbf{x}_i - \mu_1)^\mathrm{T} + \sum_{i:c_i=2}(\mathbf{x}_i - \mu_2)(\mathbf{x}_i - \mu_2)^\mathrm{T}$$

$\mathbf{a}$ is found by maximizing the "Rayleigh quotient"

$$J(\mathbf{a}) = \frac{\mathbf{a}^\mathrm{T}\mathbf{S}_B\mathbf{a}}{\mathbf{a}^\mathrm{T}\mathbf{S}_W\mathbf{a}}.$$

This leads to the solution $\mathbf{a} = \mathbf{S}_W^{-1}(\mu_2 - \mu_1)$. The difference between principal component analysis and Fisher's linear discriminant analysis is nicely visualized in Fig. 8.6, which shows the 1-dimensional linear projection obtained by both methods for a two-class problem in two dimensions.

With more than two classes, the problem is to find a projection matrix $\mathbf{A}$ for which the low-dimensional projection given by $\mathbf{y} = \mathbf{A}^\mathrm{T}\mathbf{x}$ yields a cloud of points that are close when they are in the same class relative to the overall spread. To do this, compute the mean μ_c for each class and the global mean μ, and then find the within- and between-class scatter matrices

$$\mathbf{S}_W = \sum_{j=1}^{C}\sum_{i:c_i=j}(\mathbf{x}_i - \mu_j)(\mathbf{x}_i - \mu_j)^\mathrm{T}$$

$$\mathbf{S}_B = \sum_{c=1}^{C}n_c(\mu_c - \mu)(\mu_c - \mu)^\mathrm{T}.$$

$\mathbf{A}$ is the matrix that maximizes

$$J(\mathbf{A}) = \frac{|\mathbf{A}^\mathrm{T}\mathbf{S}_B\mathbf{A}|}{|\mathbf{A}^\mathrm{T}\mathbf{S}_W\mathbf{A}|}.$$

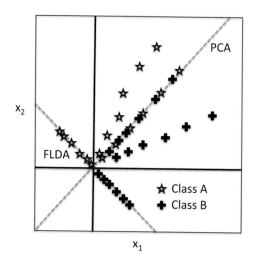

FIGURE 8.6

Comparing principal component analysis and Fisher's linear discriminant analysis.

Adapted from Belhumeur, Hespanha & Kriegman, 1997.

This ratio of determinants is a generalization of the ratio $J(\mathbf{a})$ used above. Determinants serve as analogs of variances computed in multiple dimensions and multiplied together, but computed along the principal directions of the scatter matrices.

Solving this requires sophisticated linear algebra. The idea is to construct something known as a "generalized eigenvalue problem" for each column of the matrix $\mathbf{A}$. The columns of the optimal $\mathbf{A}$ are the generalized eigenvectors $\mathbf{a}_i$ corresponding to the largest eigenvalues λ_i for the equation $\mathbf{S}_B \mathbf{a}_i = \lambda_i \mathbf{S}_W \mathbf{a}_i$. (Appendix A.1 gives more information about eigenvalues and eigenvectors.) It has been shown that solutions have the form $\mathbf{a} = \mathbf{S}_W^{-1/2}\mathbf{U}$, where $\mathbf{U}$ is obtained from the eigenvectors of $\mathbf{S}_W^{-1/2}\mathbf{S}_B\mathbf{S}_W^{-1/2}$.

Fisher's linear discriminant analysis is quite popular for achieving dimensionality reduction, but for C classes it is limited to finding at most a $C-1$ dimensional projection. The *Further reading* section at the end of this chapter discusses a variant that can go beyond $C-1$ dimensions and provide non-linear projections as well.

The above analysis is based on the use of means and scatter matrices, but does not assume an underlying Gaussian distribution as ordinary linear discriminant analysis does. Of course, logistic regression, described in Section 4.6, is an even more direct way to create a linear binary classifier. Logistic regression is one of the most popular methods of applied statistics; we discuss the multiclass version in Section 9.7.

TEXT TO ATTRIBUTE VECTORS

In Section 2.4 we introduced string attributes that contain pieces of text and remarked that the value of a string attribute is often an entire document. String attributes are basically nominal, with an unspecified number of values. If they are treated simply as nominal attributes, models can be built that depend on whether the values of two string attributes are equal or not. But that does not capture any internal structure of the string or bring out any interesting aspects of the text it represents.

You could imagine decomposing the text in a string attribute into paragraphs, sentences, or phrases. Generally, however, the word is the most useful unit. The text in a string attribute is usually a sequence of words, and is often best represented in terms of the words it contains. For example, you might transform the string attribute into a set of numeric attributes, one for each word, that represent how often the word appears. The set of words—i.e., the set of new attributes—is determined from the dataset and is typically quite large. If there are several string attributes whose properties should be treated separately, the new attribute names must be distinguished, perhaps by a user-determined prefix.

Conversion into words—*tokenization*—is not such a simple operation as it sounds. Tokens may be formed from contiguous alphabetic sequences with nonalphabetic characters discarded. If numbers are present, numeric sequences may be retained too. Numbers may involve + or − signs, may contain decimal points, and may have exponential notation—in other words, they must be parsed according to a defined number syntax. An alphanumeric sequence may be regarded as a single token. Perhaps the space character is the token delimiter; perhaps whitespace (including the tab and new-line characters), and perhaps punctuation is too. Periods can be difficult: sometimes they should be considered part of the word (e.g., with initials, titles, abbreviations, and numbers), but sometimes they should not (e.g., if they are sentence delimiters). Hyphens and apostrophes are similarly problematic.

All words may be converted to lower case before being added to the dictionary. Words on a fixed, predetermined list of function words or *stopwords*—such as *the*, *and*, and *but*—could be ignored. Note that stopword lists are language dependent. In fact, so are capitalization conventions (German capitalizes all nouns), number syntax (Europeans use the comma for a decimal point), punctuation conventions (Spanish has an initial question mark), and, of course, character sets. Text is complicated!

Low frequency words such as *hapax legomena*[1] are often discarded too. Sometimes it is found beneficial to keep the most frequent k words after stopwords have been removed—or perhaps the top k words for each class.

Along with all these tokenization options, there is also the question of what the value of each word attribute should be. The value may be the word count—the

---

[1]A *hapax legomena* is a word that only occurs once in a given corpus of text.

number of times the word appears in the string—or it may simply indicate the word's presence or absence. Word frequencies could be normalized to give each document's attribute vector the same Euclidean length. Alternatively, the frequencies f_{ij} for word i in document j can be transformed in various standard ways. One standard logarithmic term frequency measure is $\log(1 + f_{ij})$. A measure that is widely used in information retrieval is TF × IDF, or "term frequency times inverse document frequency." Here, the term frequency is modulated by a factor that depends on how commonly the word is used in other documents. The TF × IDF metric is typically defined as

$$f_{ij} \log \frac{\text{Number of documents}}{\text{Number of documents that include word } i}.$$

The idea is that a document is basically characterized by the words that appear often in it, which accounts for the first factor, except that words used in every document or almost every document are useless as discriminators, which accounts for the second. TF × IDF is used to refer not just to this particular formula but to a general class of measures of the same type. For example, the frequency factor f_{ij} may be replaced by a logarithmic term such as $\log(1 + f_{ij})$.

TIME SERIES

In time series data, each instance represents a different time step and the attributes give values associated with that time—such as in weather forecasting or stock market prediction. You sometimes need to be able to replace an attribute's value in the current instance by the corresponding value in some other instance in the past or the future. Even more common is to replace an attribute's value by the *difference* between the current value and the value in some previous instance. For example, the difference—often called the *Delta*—between the current value and the preceding one is often more informative than the value itself. The first instance, for which the time-shifted value is unknown, may be removed, or replaced with a missing value. The Delta value is essentially the first derivative scaled by some constant that depends on the size of the time step. Successive Delta transformations take higher derivatives.

In some time series, instances do not represent regular samples, but the time of each instance is given by a *timestamp* attribute. The difference between timestamps is the step size for that instance, and if successive differences are taken for other attributes they should be divided by the step size to normalize the derivative. In other cases each attribute may represent a different time, rather than each instance, so that the time series is from one attribute to the next rather than one instance to the next. Then, if differences are needed, they must be taken between one attribute's value and the next attribute's value for each instance.

8.4 SAMPLING

In many applications involving a large volume of data it is necessary to come up with a random sample of much smaller size for processing. A random sample is one in which each instance in the original dataset has an equal chance of being included. Given a batch of N instances, a sample of any desired size is easily created: just generate uniform random integers between 1 and N and retrieve the corresponding instances until the appropriate number has been collected. This is sampling *with replacement*, because the same instance might be selected more than once. (In fact, we used sampling with replacement for the bootstrap algorithm in Section 5.4.) For sampling without replacement, simply note when selecting each instance whether it has already been chosen and, if so, discard the second copy. If the sample size is much smaller than the full dataset there is little difference between sampling with and without replacement.

RESERVOIR SAMPLING

Sampling is such a simple procedure that it merits little discussion or explanation. But there is a situation in which producing a random sample of a given size becomes a little more challenging. What if the training instances arrive one by one, but the total number of them—the value of N—is not known in advance? Or suppose we need to be able to run a learning algorithm on a sample of a given size from a continuous stream of instances at any time, without repeatedly performing an entire sampling operation? Or perhaps the number of training instances is so vast that it is impractical to store them all before taking a sample?

All these situations call for a way of generating a random sample of an input stream without storing all the instances up and waiting for the last one to arrive before beginning the sampling procedure. Is it possible to generate a random sample of a given size and still guarantee that each instance has an equal chance of being selected? The answer is yes. Furthermore, there is a simple algorithm to do so.

The idea is to use a "reservoir" of size r, the size of the sample that is to be generated. To begin, place successive instances from the input stream in the reservoir until it is full. If the stream were to stop there, we would have the trivial case of a random sample of size r from an input stream of the same size. But most likely more instances will come in. The next one should be included in the sample with probability $r/(r+1)$—in fact, if the input stream were to stop there ($N = r + 1$) *any* instance should be in the sample with this probability. Consequently, with probability $r/(r+1)$ we replace a random instance in the reservoir with this new instance. And we carry on in the same vein, replacing a random reservoir element with the next instance with probability $r/(r+2)$ and so on. In general, the ith instance in the input stream is placed into the reservoir at a random location with probability r/i. It is easy to show by induction that once this instance has been processed the probability of any particular instance being in the reservoir is just the same, namely r/i. Thus at any point in the procedure, the reservoir contains a random sample of size r from the input stream. You can stop at any time, secure in the knowledge that the reservoir contains the desired random sample.

This method samples without replacement. Sampling with replacement is a little harder—although for large datasets and small reservoirs there is little difference between the two. But if you really want a sample of size r with replacement, you could set up r independent reservoirs, each with size 1. Run the algorithm concurrently for all of these, and at any time their union is a random sample with replacement.

8.5 CLEANSING

A problem that plagues practical machine learning is poor quality of the data. Errors in large databases are extremely common. Attribute values, and class values too, are frequently unreliable and corrupted. Although one way of addressing this problem is to painstakingly check through the data, machine learning techniques themselves can sometimes help to solve the problem.

IMPROVING DECISION TREES

It is a surprising fact that decision trees induced from training data can often be simplified, without loss of accuracy, by discarding misclassified instances from the training set, relearning, and then repeating until there are no misclassified instances. Experiments on standard datasets have shown that this hardly affects the classification accuracy of C4.5, a standard decision tree induction scheme. In some cases it improves slightly; in others it deteriorates slightly. The difference is rarely statistically significant—and even when it is, the advantage can go either way. What the technique does affect is decision tree size. The resulting trees are invariably smaller than the original ones, even though they perform about the same.

What is the reason for this? When a decision tree induction method prunes away a subtree, it applies a statistical test that decides whether that subtree is "justified" by the data. The decision to prune accepts a small sacrifice in classification accuracy on the training set in the belief that this will improve test-set performance. Some training instances that were classified correctly by the unpruned tree will now be misclassified by the pruned one. In effect, the decision has been taken to ignore these training instances.

But that decision has only been applied locally, in the pruned subtree. Its effect has not been allowed to percolate further up the tree, perhaps resulting in different choices being made of attributes to branch on. Removing the misclassified instances from the training set and relearning the decision tree is just taking the pruning decisions to their logical conclusion. If the pruning strategy is a good one, this should not harm performance. And it may improve it by allowing better attribute choices to be made.

It would no doubt be even better to consult a human expert. Misclassified training instances could be presented for verification, and those that were found to be wrong could be deleted—or better still, corrected.

Notice that we are assuming that the instances are not misclassified in any systematic way. If instances are systematically corrupted in both training and test sets—e.g., one class value might be substituted for another—it is only to be expected that training on the erroneous training set will yield better performance on the (also erroneous) test set.

Interestingly enough, it has been shown that when artificial noise is added to attributes (rather than to classes), test-set performance is improved if the same noise is added in the same way to the training set. In other words, when attribute noise is the problem it is not a good idea to train on a "clean" set if performance is to be assessed on a "dirty" one. A learning scheme can learn to compensate for attribute noise, in some measure, if given a chance. In essence, it can learn which attributes are unreliable, and, if they are all unreliable, how best to use them together to yield a more reliable result. To remove noise from attributes for the training set denies the opportunity to learn how best to combat that noise. But with class noise (rather than attribute noise), it is best to train on noise-free instances if possible.

ROBUST REGRESSION

The problems caused by noisy data have been known in linear regression for years. Statisticians often check data for outliers and remove them manually. In the case of linear regression, outliers can be identified visually—although it is never completely clear whether an outlier is an error or just a surprising, but correct, value. Outliers dramatically affect the usual least-squares regression because the squared distance measure accentuates the influence of points far away from the regression line.

Statistical methods that address the problem of outliers are called *robust*. One way of making regression more robust is to use an absolute-value distance measure instead of the usual squared one. This weakens the effect of outliers. Another possibility is to try to identify outliers automatically and remove them from consideration. For example, one could form a regression line and then remove from consideration those 10% of points that lie furthest from the line. A third possibility is to minimize the *median* (rather than the mean) of the squares of the divergences from the regression line. It turns out that this estimator is very robust and actually copes with outliers in the X-direction as well as outliers in the Y-direction—which is the normal direction one thinks of outliers.

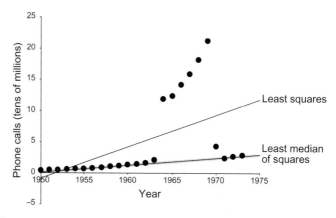

FIGURE 8.7

Number of international phone calls from Belgium, 1950–1973.

A dataset that is often used to illustrate robust regression is a graph of international telephone calls made from Belgium during the years 1950 to 1973, shown in Fig. 8.7. This data is taken from the Belgian Statistical Survey published by the Ministry of Economy. The plot seems to show an upward trend over the years, but there is an anomalous group of points from 1964 to 1969. It turns out that during this period, results were mistakenly recorded as the total number of *minutes* of the calls. The years 1963 and 1970 are also partially affected. This error causes a large fraction of outliers in the Y-direction.

Not surprisingly, the usual least-squares regression line is seriously affected by this anomalous data. However, the least *median* of squares line remains remarkably unperturbed. This line has a simple and natural interpretation. Geometrically, it corresponds to finding the narrowest strip covering half of the observations, where the thickness of the strip is measured in the vertical direction—this strip is marked gray in Fig. 8.7. The least median of squares line lies at the exact center of this band. Note that this notion is often easier to explain and visualize than the normal least-squares definition of regression. Unfortunately, there is a serious disadvantage to median-based regression techniques: they incur high computational cost, which often makes them infeasible for practical problems.

DETECTING ANOMALIES

A serious problem with any form of automatic detection of apparently incorrect data is that the baby may be thrown out with the bathwater. Short of consulting a human expert, there is no way of telling whether a particular instance really is an error or whether it just does not fit the type of model that is being applied. In statistical regression, visualizations help. It will usually be visually apparent, even to the nonexpert, if the wrong kind of curve is being fitted—a straight line is being fitted to data that lies on a parabola, e.g., The outliers in Fig. 8.7 certainly stand out to the eye. But most classification problems cannot be so easily visualized: the notion of "model type" is more subtle than a regression line. And although it is known that good results are obtained on most standard datasets by discarding instances that do not fit a decision tree model, this is not necessarily of great comfort when dealing with a particular new dataset. The suspicion will remain that perhaps the new dataset is simply unsuited to decision tree modeling.

One solution that has been tried is to use several different learning schemes—such as a decision tree, and a nearest-neighbor learner, and a linear discriminant function—to filter the data. A conservative approach is to ask that all three schemes fail to classify an instance correctly before it is deemed erroneous and removed from the data. In some cases, filtering the data in this way and using the filtered data as input to a final learning scheme gives better performance than simply using the three learning schemes and letting them vote on the outcome. Training all three schemes on the *filtered* data and letting them vote can yield even better results. However, there is a danger to voting techniques: some learning algorithms are better suited to certain types of data than others, and the most appropriate scheme may simply get out-voted! We will examine a more subtle method of combining the output from different classifiers, called *stacking*, in Chapter 12, Ensemble learning. The lesson, as usual, is to get to know your data and look at it in many different ways.

One possible danger with filtering approaches is that they might conceivably just be sacrificing instances of a particular class (or group of classes) to improve accuracy on the remaining classes. Although there are no general ways to guard against this, it has not been found to be a common problem in practice.

Finally, it is worth noting once again that automatic filtering is a poor substitute for getting the data right in the first place. And if this is too time-consuming and expensive to be practical, human inspection could be limited to those instances that are identified by the filter as suspect.

ONE-CLASS LEARNING

In most classification problems, training data is available for all classes that can occur at prediction time, and the learning algorithm uses the data for the different classes to determine decision boundaries that discriminate between them. However, some problems exhibit only a single class of instances at training time, while at prediction time new instances with unknown class labels can belong either to this target class or to a new class that was not available during training. Then, two different predictions are possible: *target*, meaning that an instance belongs to the class experienced during training, and *unknown*, where the instance does not appear to belong to that class. This type of learning problem is known as one-class classification.

In many cases, one-class problems can be reformulated into two-class ones because there is data from other classes that can be used for training. However, there are genuine one-class applications where it is impossible or inappropriate to make use of negative data during training. For example, consider password hardening, a biometric system that strengthens a computer login process by not only requiring the correct password to be typed, but also that it be typed with the correct rhythm. This is a one-class problem; a single user must be verified and during training time only data from that user is available—we cannot ask anyone else to provide data without supplying them with the password!

Even in applications where instances from several classes are available at training time, it may be best to focus solely on the target class under consideration—if, e.g., new classes may occur at prediction time that differ from all those available during training. Continuing with the typing-rhythm scenario, suppose we are to recognize typists in a situation where the text is not fixed—the current typist is to be verified as who he or she claims to be from their rhythmic patterns on a block of free text. This task is fundamentally different from distinguishing one user from a group of other users, because we must be prepared to refuse attackers that the system has never seen before.

OUTLIER DETECTION

One-class classification is often called outlier (or novelty) detection because the learning algorithm is being used to differentiate between data that appears normal and abnormal with respect to the distribution of the training data. Earlier in this section we talked about making regression more robust by replacing the usual squared distance measure with the absolute-value one, and about trying to detect anomalies by using several different learning schemes.

A generic statistical approach to one-class classification is to identify outliers as instances that lie beyond a distance d from a given percentage p of the training data. Alternatively, a probability density can be estimated for the target class by fitting a statistical distribution, such as a Gaussian, to the training data; any test instances with a low probability value can be marked as outliers. The challenge is to identify an appropriate distribution for the data at hand. If this cannot be done one can adopt a non-parametric approach such as kernel density estimation (discussed in Section 9.3). An advantage of the density estimation approach is that the threshold can be adjusted at prediction time to obtain a suitable rate of outliers.

Multiclass classifiers can be tailored to the one-class situation by fitting a boundary around the target data and deeming instances that fall outside it to be outliers. The boundary can be generated by adapting the inner workings of existing multiclass classifiers such as support vector machines. These methods rely heavily on a parameter that determines how much of the target data is likely to be classified as outliers. If it is chosen too conservatively, data in the target class will erroneously be rejected. If it is chosen too liberally, the model will overfit and reject too much legitimate data.

GENERATING ARTIFICIAL DATA

Rather than modify the internal workings of a multiclass classifier to form a one-class decision boundary directly, another possibility is to generate artificial data for the outlier class and apply any off-the-shelf classifier. Not only does this allow any classifier to be used, but if the classifier produces class probability estimates the rejection rate can be tuned by altering the threshold.

The most straightforward approach is to generate uniformly distributed data and learn a classifier that can discriminate this from the target. However, different decision boundaries will be obtained for different amounts of artificial data: if too much is generated it will overwhelm the target class and the learning algorithm will always predict the artificial class. This problem can be avoided if the objective of learning is viewed as accurate class probability estimation rather than minimizing the classification error. For example, bagged decision trees (described in Section 12.2), which have been shown to yield good class probability estimators, can be used.

Once a class probability estimation model has been obtained in this fashion, different thresholds on the probability estimates for the target class correspond to different decision boundaries surrounding the target class. This means that, as in the density estimation approach to one-class classification, the rate of outliers can be adjusted at prediction time to yield an outcome appropriate for the application at hand.

There is one significant problem. As the number of attributes increases, it quickly becomes infeasible to generate enough artificial data to obtain adequate coverage of the instance space, and the probability that a particular artificial instance occurs inside or close to the target class diminishes to a point that makes any kind of discrimination impossible.

The solution is to generate artificial data that is as close as possible to the target class. In this case, because it is no longer uniformly distributed, the distribution of this artificial data—call this the "reference" distribution—must be taken into account when computing the membership scores for the resulting one-class model. In other words, the class probability estimates of the two-class classifier must be combined with the reference distribution to obtain membership scores for the target class.

To elaborate a little further, let T denote the target class for which we have training data and seek a one-class model, and A the artificial class, for which we generate data using a known reference distribution. What we would like to obtain is $P(X|T)$, the density function of the target class, for any instance X—of course, we know $P(X|A)$, the density function of the reference distribution. Assume for the moment that we know the true class probability function $P(T|X)$. In practice, we need to estimate this function using a class probability estimator learned from the training data. A simple application of Bayes's rule can be used to express $P(X|T)$ in terms of $P(T)$, $P(T|X)$ and $P(X|A)$:

$$P(X|T) = \frac{(1-P(T))P(T|X)}{P(T)(1-P(T|X))}P(X|A)$$

To use this equation in practice, choose $P(X|A)$, generate a user-specified amount of artificial data from it, label it A, and combine it with instances in the training set for the target class, labeled T. The proportion of target instances is an estimate of $P(T)$, and a standard learning algorithm can be applied to this two-class dataset to obtain a class probability estimator $P(T|X)$. Given that the value for $P(X|A)$ can be computed for any particular instance X, everything is at hand to compute an estimate of the target density function $P(X|T)$ for any instance X. To perform classification we choose an appropriate threshold, adjusted to tune the rejection rate to any desired value.

One question remains, namely, how to choose the reference density $P(X|A)$. We need to be able to generate artificial data from it, and to compute its value for any instance X. Another requirement is that the data it generates should be close to the target class. In fact, ideally the reference density is identical to the target density, in which case $P(T|X)$ becomes a constant function that any learning algorithm should be able to induce—the resulting two-class learning problem becomes trivial. This is unrealistic because it would require us to know the density of the target class. However, this observation gives a clue as to how to proceed: apply any density estimation technique to the target data and use the resulting function to model the artificial class. The better the match between $P(X|A)$ and $P(X|T)$, the easier the resulting two-class class probability estimation task becomes.

In practice, given the availability of powerful methods for class probability estimation and the relative lack of such techniques for density estimation, it may make sense to apply a simple density estimation technique to the target data first to obtain $P(X|A)$ and then employ a state-of-the-art class probability estimation method to the two-class problem that is obtained by combining the artificial data with the data from the target class.

8.6 TRANSFORMING MULTIPLE CLASSES TO BINARY ONES

Recall from Chapter 4, Algorithms: the basic methods, and Chapter 7, Extending instance-based and linear models, that some learning algorithms—e.g., standard support vector machines—only work with two-class problems. In most cases, sophisticated multiclass variants have been developed, but they may be very slow or difficult to implement. As an alternative, it is common practice to transform multiclass problems into multiple two-class ones: the dataset is decomposed into several two-class problems; the algorithm is run on each one; and the outputs of the resulting classifiers are combined. There are several popular techniques that implement this idea. We begin with a very simple one that we already touched on when discussing how to use linear regression for classification, and then move on to pairwise classification and more advanced techniques—error-correcting output codes and ensembles of nested dichotomies—that can often be profitably applied even when the underlying learning algorithm is able to deal with multiclass problems directly.

SIMPLE METHODS

At the beginning of the subsection on *Linear classification* in Section 4.6 we learned how to transform a multiclass dataset for multiresponse linear regression to perform a two-class regression for each class. The idea essentially produces several two-class datasets by discriminating each class against the union of all the other classes. This technique is commonly called the *one-vs-rest* method (or also, somewhat misleadingly, one-vs-all). For each class, a dataset is generated containing a copy of each instance in the original data, but with a modified class value. If the instance has the class associated with the corresponding dataset it is tagged *yes*; otherwise *no*. Then classifiers are built for each of these binary datasets, classifiers that output a confidence figure with their predictions—e.g., the estimated probability that the class is *yes*. During classification, a test instance is fed into each binary classifier, and the final class is the one associated with the classifier that predicts *yes* most confidently.

Of course, this method is sensitive to the accuracy of the confidence figures produced by the classifiers: if some classifiers have an exaggerated opinion of their own predictions, the overall result will suffer. That is why it can be important to carefully tune parameter settings in the underlying learning algorithm. For example, in standard support vector machines for classification, it is generally necessary to tune the parameter C, which provides an upper bound to the influence of each support vector and controls the closeness of fit to the training data, and the value of the kernel parameter—e.g., the size of the exponent in a polynomial kernel. This can be done based on internal cross-validation. It has been found empirically that the one-vs-rest method can be very competitive, at least in the case of kernel-based classifiers, when appropriate parameter tuning is done. Note that it may also be useful to apply techniques for calibrating confidence scores, discussed in Section 8.7: Calibrating class probabilities, to the individual two-class models.

Another simple and general method for multiclass problems is *pairwise classification*. Here a classifier is built for every pair of classes, using only the instances from these two classes. The output on an unknown test example is based on which class receives the most votes. This scheme generally yields accurate results in terms of classification error. It can also be used to produce probability estimates by applying a method called *pairwise coupling*, which calibrates the individual probability estimates from the different classifiers.

If there are k classes, pairwise classification builds a total of $k(k-1)/2$ classifiers. Although this sounds unnecessarily computation intensive, it is not. In fact, if the classes are evenly populated, a pairwise classifier is at least as quick to train as any other multiclass method. The reason is that each of the pairwise learning problems only involves instances pertaining to the two classes under consideration. If n instances are divided evenly among k classes, this amounts to $2n/k$ instances per problem. Suppose the learning algorithm for a two-class problem with n instances takes time proportional to n seconds to execute. Then the run time for pairwise classification is proportional to $k(k-1)/2 \times 2n/k$ seconds, which is $(k-1)n$. In other words, the method scales linearly with the number of classes. If the learning algorithm takes more time—say proportional to n^2—the advantage of the pairwise approach becomes even more pronounced.

ERROR-CORRECTING OUTPUT CODES

The simple methods discussed above are often very effective. Pairwise classification in particular can be a very useful technique. In some cases it can improve accuracy even when the underlying learning algorithm, such as a decision tree learner, can deal with multiclass problems directly. This may be due to the fact that pairwise classification actually generates an ensemble of many classifiers. Ensemble learning is a well-known strategy for obtaining accurate classifiers, and we will discuss several ensemble learning methods in Chapter 12, Ensemble learning. It turns out that there are methods other than pairwise classification that can be used to generate an ensemble classifier by decomposing a multiclass problem into several two-class subtasks. The one we discuss next is based on error-correcting output codes.

Two-class decompositions of multiclass problems can be viewed in terms of the so-called "output codes" they correspond to. Let us revisit the simple one-vs-rest method to see what such codes look like. Consider a multiclass problem with four classes a, b, c, and d. The transformation can be visualized as shown in Table 8.2A, where *yes* and *no* are mapped to 1 and 0, respectively. Each of the original class values is converted into a 4-bit code word, 1 bit per class, and the four classifiers predict the bits independently. Interpreting the classification process in terms of these code words, errors occur when the wrong binary bit receives the highest confidence.

Table 8.2 Transforming a Multiclass Problem Into a Two-Class One: (A) Standard Method; (B) Error-Correcting Code

(A)	Class	Class Vector	(B)	Class	Class Vector
	a	1 0 0 0		*a*	1 1 1 1 1 1 1
	b	0 1 0 0		*b*	0 0 0 0 1 1 1
	c	0 0 1 0		*c*	0 0 1 1 0 0 1
	d	0 0 0 1		*d*	0 1 0 1 0 1 0

However, we do not have to use the particular code words shown. Indeed there is no reason why each class must be represented by 4 bits. Look instead at the code of Table 8.2B, where classes are represented by 7 bits. When applied to a dataset, seven classifiers must be built instead of four. To see what that might buy, consider the classification of a particular instance. Suppose it belongs to class *a*, and that the predictions of the individual classifiers are 1 0 1 1 1 1 1 (respectively). Obviously, comparing this code word with those in Table 8.2B, the second classifier has made a mistake: it predicted 0 instead of 1, *no* instead of *yes*. However, comparing the predicted bits with the code word associated with each class, the instance is clearly closer to *a* than to any other class. This can be quantified by the number of bits that must be changed to convert the predicted code word into those of Table 8.2B: the *Hamming distance*, or the discrepancy between the bit strings, is 1, 3, 3, and 5 for the classes *a*, *b*, *c*, and *d*, respectively. We can safely conclude that the second classifier made a mistake and correctly identify *a* as the instance's true class.

The same kind of error correction is not possible with the code words of Table 8.2A, because any predicted string of 4 bits other than these four 4-bit words has the same distance to at least two of them. The output codes are not "error correcting."

What determines whether a code is error correcting or not? Consider the Hamming distance between the code words representing different classes. The number of errors that can possibly be corrected depends on the minimum distance between any pair of code words, say d. The code can guarantee to correct up to $\lfloor (d-1)/2 \rfloor$ 1-bit errors, because if this number of bits of the correct code word are flipped, it will still be the closest and will therefore be identified correctly. In Table 8.2A the Hamming distance for each pair of code words is 2. Hence, the minimum distance d is also 2, and we can correct no more than 0 errors! However, in the code of Table 8.2B the minimum distance is 4 (in fact, the distance is 4 for all pairs). That means it is guaranteed to correct 1-bit errors.

We have identified one property of a good error-correcting code: the code words must be well separated in terms of their Hamming distance. Because they comprise the rows of the code table, this property is called *row separation*. There is a second requirement that a good error-correcting code should fulfill: *column separation*. The Hamming distance between every pair of columns must be large, as must the distance between each column and the complement of every other column. In Table 8.2B, the seven columns are separated from one another by at least 1 bit.

Column separation is necessary because if two columns are identical (or if one is the complement of another), the corresponding classifiers will make the same errors. Error correction is weakened if the errors are correlated—in other words, if many bit positions are simultaneously incorrect. The greater the distance between columns, the more errors are likely to be corrected.

With fewer than four classes it is hard to construct a really effective error-correcting code because good row separation and good column separation cannot be achieved simultaneously. For example, with three classes there are only eight possible columns (2^3), four of which are complements of the other four. Moreover, columns with all zeroes or all ones provide no discrimination. This leaves just three possible columns, and the resulting code is not error correcting at all. (In fact, it is the standard "one-vs-rest" encoding.)

If there are few classes, an exhaustive error-correcting code such as the one in Table 8.2B can be built. In an exhaustive code for k classes, the columns comprise every possible k-bit string, except for complements and the trivial all-zero or all-one strings. Each code word contains $2^{k-1}-1$ bits. The code is constructed as follows: the code word for the first class consists of all ones; that for the second class has 2^{k-2} zeroes followed by $2^{k-2}-1$ ones; the third has 2^{k-3} zeroes followed by 2^{k-3} ones followed by 2^{k-3} zeroes followed by $2^{k-3}-1$ ones; and so on. The ith code word consists of alternating runs of 2^{k-i} zeroes and ones, the last run being one short.

With more classes, exhaustive codes are infeasible because the number of columns increases exponentially and too many classifiers have to be built. In that case more sophisticated methods are employed, which can build a code with good error-correcting properties from a smaller number of columns, or random codes are used.

Error-correcting output codes do not work for local learning algorithms such as instance-based learners, which predict the class of an instance by looking at nearby training instances. In the case of a nearest-neighbor classifier, all output bits would be predicted using the same training instance. The problem can be circumvented by using different attribute subsets to predict each output bit, decorrelating the predictions.

ENSEMBLES OF NESTED DICHOTOMIES

Error-correcting output codes often produce accurate classifiers for multiclass problems. However, the basic algorithm produces classifications whereas often we would like class probability estimates as well—e.g., to perform cost-sensitive classification using the minimum expected cost approach discussed in Section 5.8. Fortunately, there is a method for decomposing multiclass problems into two-class ones that provides a natural way of computing class probability estimates, so long as the underlying two-class models are able to produce probabilities for the corresponding two-class subtasks.

The idea is to recursively split the full set of classes from the original multiclass problem into smaller and smaller subsets, while splitting the full dataset of instances into subsets corresponding to these subsets of classes. This yields a binary tree of classes. Consider the hypothetical 4-class problem discussed earlier. At the root node are the full set of classes {a, b, c, d}, which are split into disjoint subsets, say {a, c} and {b, d}, along with the instances pertaining to these two subsets of classes. The two subsets form the two successor nodes in the binary tree. These subsets are then split further into one-element sets, yielding successors

Table 8.3 A Nested Dichotomy in the Form of a Code Matrix

Class	Class Vector
a	0 0 X
b	1 X 0
c	0 1 X
d	1 X 1

{a} and {c} for the node {a, c}, and successors {b} and {d} for the node {b, d}. Once we reach one-element subsets, the splitting process stops.

The resulting binary tree of classes is called a *nested dichotomy* because each internal node and its two successors define a dichotomy—e.g., discriminating between classes {a, c} and {b, d} at the root node—and the dichotomies are nested in a hierarchy. We can view a nested dichotomy as a particular type of sparse output code. Table 8.3 shows the output code matrix for the example just discussed. There is one dichotomy for each internal node of the tree structure. Hence, given that the example involves three internal nodes, there are three columns in the code matrix. In contrast to the class vectors considered above, the matrix contains elements marked X that indicate that instances of the corresponding classes are simply omitted from the associated two-class learning problems.

What is the advantage of this kind of output code? It turns out that, because the decomposition is hierarchical and yields disjoint subsets, there is a simple method for computing class probability estimates for each element in the original set of multiple classes, assuming two-class estimates for each dichotomy in the hierarchy. The reason is the chain rule from probability theory, which we will encounter again when discussing Bayesian networks in Section 9.2.

Suppose we want to compute the probability for class a given a particular instance x, i.e., the conditional probability $P(a|x)$. This class corresponds to one of the four leaf nodes in the hierarchy of classes in the above example. First, we learn two-class models that yield class probability estimates for the three two-class datasets at the internal nodes of the hierarchy. Then, from the two-class model at the root node, an estimate of the conditional probability $P(\{a, c\}|x)$—namely, that x belongs to either a or c—can be obtained. Moreover, we can obtain an estimate of $P(\{a\}|x, \{a, c\})$—the probability that x belongs to a given that we already know that it belongs to either a or c—from the model that discriminates between the one-element sets {a} and {c}. Now, based on the chain rule, $P(\{a\}|x) = P(\{a\}|\{a, c\}, x) \times P(\{a, c\}|x)$. Hence to compute the probability for any individual class of the original multiclass problem—any leaf node in the tree of classes—we simply multiply together the probability estimates collected from the internal nodes encountered when proceeding from the root node to this leaf node: the probability estimates for all subsets of classes that contain the target class.

Assuming that the individual two-class models at the internal nodes produce accurate probability estimates, there is reason to believe that the multiclass probability estimates obtained using the chain rule will generally be accurate. However, it is clear that estimation errors will accumulate, causing problems for very deep hierarchies. A more basic issue is that in the above example we arbitrarily decided on a particular hierarchical decomposition of the classes. Perhaps there is some background knowledge regarding the domain concerned, in which case one particular hierarchy may be preferable because certain classes are known to be related, but this is generally not the case.

What can be done? If there is no reason a priori to prefer any particular decomposition, perhaps all of them should be considered, yielding an *ensemble* of nested dichotomies. Unfortunately, for any nontrivial number of classes there are too many potential dichotomies, making an exhaustive approach infeasible. But we could consider a subset, taking a random sample of possible tree structures, building two-class models for each internal node of each tree structure (with caching of models, given that the same two-class problem may occur in multiple trees), and then averaging the probability estimates for each individual class to obtain the final estimates.

Empirical experiments show that this approach yields accurate multiclass classifiers and is able to improve predictive performance even in the case of classifiers, such as decision trees, that can deal with multiclass problems directly. In contrast to standard error-correcting output codes, the technique often works well even when the base learner is unable to model complex decision boundaries. The reason is that, generally speaking, learning is easier with fewer classes, so results become more successful the closer we get to the leaf nodes in the tree. This also explains why the pairwise classification technique described earlier works particularly well for simple models such as ones corresponding to hyperplanes: it creates the simplest possible dichotomies! Nested dichotomies appear to strike a useful balance between the simplicity of the learning problems that occur in pairwise classification—after all, the lowest-level dichotomies involve pairs of individual classes—and the power of the redundancy embodied in standard error-correcting output codes.

8.7 CALIBRATING CLASS PROBABILITIES

Class probability estimation is obviously more difficult than classification. Given a way of generating class probabilities, classification error is minimized as long as the correct class is predicted with maximum probability. However, a method for classification does not imply a method of generating accurate probability estimates: the estimates that yield the correct classification may be quite poor when assessed according to the quadratic or informational loss discussed in Section 5.7. Yet—as we have stressed several times—it is often more important to obtain accurate conditional class probabilities for a given instance than to simply place it into one of the classes. Cost-sensitive prediction based on the minimum expected cost approach is one example where accurate class probability estimates are very useful.

Consider the case of probability estimation for a dataset with two classes. If the predicted probabilities are on the correct side of the 0.5 threshold commonly used for classification, no classification errors will be made. However, this does not mean that the probability estimates themselves are accurate. They may be systematically too optimistic—too close to either 0 or 1—or too pessimistic—not close enough to the extremes. This type of bias will increase the measured quadratic or informational loss, and will cause problems when attempting to minimize the expected cost of classifications based on a given cost matrix.

Fig. 8.8 demonstrates the effect of overoptimistic probability estimation for a two-class problem. The x-axis shows the predicted probability of the multinomial Naïve Bayes model from Section 4.2 for one of two classes in a text classification problem with about 1000 attributes representing word frequencies. The y-axis shows the observed relative frequency of the target class. The predicted probabilities and relative frequencies were collected by running a 10-fold cross-validation. To estimate relative frequencies, the predicted probabilities were first discretized into twenty ranges using equal-frequency discretization. Observations corresponding to one interval were then pooled—predicted probabilities on the one hand and corresponding 0/1 values on the other—and the pooled values are shown as the twenty points in the plot.

This kind of plot, known as a *reliability diagram*, shows how reliable the estimated probabilities are. For a well-calibrated class probability estimator, the observed curve will coincide with the diagonal. This is clearly not the case here. The Naïve Bayes model is too optimistic, generating probabilities that are

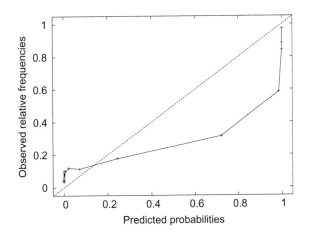

FIGURE 8.8

Overoptimistic probability estimation for a two-class problem.

too close to 0 and 1. This is not the only problem: the curve is quite far from the line that corresponds to the 0.5 threshold that is used for classification. This means that classification performance will be affected by the poor probability estimates that the model generates.

The fact that we seek a curve that lies close to the diagonal makes the remedy clear: systematic mis-estimation should be corrected by using post hoc calibration of the probability estimates to map the empirically observed curve into a diagonal. A coarse way of doing this is to use the data from the reliability diagram directly for calibration, and map the predicted probabilities to the observed relative frequencies in the corresponding discretization intervals. Data for this can be obtained using internal cross-validation or a holdout set, so that the actual test data remains untouched.

Discretization-based calibration is very fast. However, determining appropriate discretization intervals is not easy. With too few, the mapping is too coarse; with too many, each interval contains insufficient data for a reliable estimate of relative frequencies. However, other ways of calibrating can be devised. The key is to realize that calibrating probability estimates for two-class problems is a function estimation problem with one input—the estimated class probability—and one output—the calibrated probability. In principle, complex functions could be used to estimate the mapping—perhaps arbitrary polynomials. However, it makes sense to assume that the observed relationship is at least monotonically increasing, in which case increasing functions should be used.

Assuming that the calibration function is piecewise constant and monotonically increasing, there is an efficient algorithm that minimizes the squared error between the observed class "probabilities" (which are either 0 or 1 when no binning is applied) and the resulting calibrated class probabilities. Estimating a piecewise constant monotonically increasing function is an instance of *isotonic regression*, for which there is a fast algorithm based on the pair-adjacent violators (PAV) approach. The data consists of estimated probabilities and 0/1 values; assume it has been sorted according to the estimated probabilities. The basic PAV algorithm iteratively merges pairs of neighboring data points that violate the monotonicity constraint by computing their weighted mean—initially this will be the mean of 0/1 values—and using it to replace the original data points. This is repeated until all conflicts have been resolved. It can be shown that the order in which data points are merged does not affect the outcome of the process. The result is a function that increases monotonically in a stepwise fashion. This naïve algorithm is quadratic in the number of data points, but there is a clever variant that operates in linear time.

Another popular calibration method, which also presupposes a monotonic relationship, is to assume a linear relation between the log-odds of the estimated class probabilities and the target class probabilities. Here the logistic function is appropriate, and logistic regression can be used to estimate the calibration function, with the caveat that it is important to use log-odds of the estimated class probabilities rather than the raw values as the input for logistic regression.

Given that logistic regression, with only two parameters, uses a simpler model than the PAV approach, it can be more appropriate when little data is available for calibration, but with a large volume of data PAV-based calibration is generally preferable. Logistic regression has the advantage that it can easily be applied to calibrate probabilities for multiclass problems because multiclass versions of logistic regression exist. In the case of isotonic regression it is common to use the one-vs-rest method for problems with more than two classes, but pairwise coupling or ensembles of nested dichotomies—discussed in Section 8.6 above—offer an alternative.

Note that situations exist in which the relationship between the estimated and true probabilities is not monotonic. However, rather than switching to a more complex calibration method—or using discretization-based calibration, which does not assume monotonicity—this should perhaps be taken as an indication that the underlying class probability estimation method is not powerful enough for the problem at hand.

8.8 FURTHER READING AND BIBLIOGRAPHIC NOTES

Attribute selection, under the term *feature selection*, has been investigated in the field of pattern recognition for decades. Backward elimination, e.g., was introduced in the early 1960s (Marill & Green, 1963). Kittler (1978) surveys the feature selection algorithms that have been developed for pattern recognition. Best-first search and genetic algorithms are standard artificial intelligence techniques (Goldberg, 1989; Winston, 1992).

The experiments that show the performance of decision tree learners deteriorating when new attributes are added are reported by John (1997), who gives a nice explanation of attribute selection. Langley and Sage (1997) showed that for an instance-based learner to reach a given performance level, the number of training instances must grow exponentially with the number of attributes. The idea of finding the smallest attribute set that carves up the instances uniquely is from Almuallin and Dietterich (1991, 1992) and was further developed by Liu and Setiono (1996). Kibler and Aha (1987) and Cardie (1993) both investigated the use of decision tree algorithms to identify features for nearest-neighbor learning; Holmes and Nevill-Manning (1995) used 1R to order features for selection. Kira and Rendell (1992) used instance-based methods to select features, leading to a scheme called *RELIEF* for *Recursive Elimination of Features*. Gilad-Bachrach, Navot, and Tishby (2004) show how this scheme can be modified to work better with redundant attributes. The correlation-based feature selection method was developed by Hall (2000).

The use of wrapper methods for feature selection is due to John, Kohavi, and Pfleger (1994) and Kohavi and John (1997), and genetic algorithms have been applied within a wrapper framework by Vafaie and DeJong (1992) and

Cherkauer and Shavlik (1996). The selective Naïve Bayes learning scheme is due to Langley and Sage (1994). Guyon, Weston, Barnhill, and Vapnik (2002) present and evaluate the recursive feature elimination scheme in conjunction with support vector machines. The method of raced search was developed by Moore and Lee (1994). Gütlein, Frank, Hall, and Karwath (2009) investigate how to speed up scheme-specific selection for datasets with many attributes using simple ranking-based methods.

Dougherty, Kohavi, and Sahami (1995) give a brief account of supervised and unsupervised discretization, along with experimental results comparing the entropy-based method with equal-width binning and the 1R method. Frank and Witten (1999) describe the effect of using the ordering information in discretized attributes. Proportional k-interval discretization for Naïve Bayes was proposed by Yang and Webb (2001). The entropy-based method for discretization, including the use of the MDL stopping criterion, was developed by Fayyad and Irani (1993). The bottom-up statistical method using the χ^2 test is due to Kerber (1992), and its extension to an automatically determined significance level is described by Liu and Setiono (1997). Fulton, Kasif, and Salzberg (1995) investigate the use of dynamic programming for discretization and derive the quadratic time bound for a general impurity function (e.g., entropy) and the linear one for error-based discretization. The example used for showing the weakness of error-based discretization is adapted from Kohavi and Sahami (1996), who were the first to clearly identify this phenomenon.

Principal component analysis is a standard technique that can be found in most statistics textbooks. Fradkin and Madigan (2003) analyze the performance of random projections. The algorithm for partial least squares regression is from Hastie et al. (2009). The TF $\times$ IDF metric is described by Witten et al. (1999b).

Hyvärinen and Oja (2000) created the fast ICA method. Duda et al. (2001) and Murphy (2012) explain the algebra underlying solutions to Fisher's linear discriminant analysis. Sugiyama (2007) has extended it in two ways in a variant called "local Fisher discriminant analysis." First, instead of means in the scatter matrix computations, he uses computations between datapoints themselves, which allows the dimensionality of the reduced representation to be increased. Second, he applies Scholköpf and Smola (2002)'s kernel trick to obtain non-linear projections.

There are many alternatives to the type of linear data projections discussed above. For example, multilayer perceptrons provide a way to learn data projections, because their hidden layers can be treated as projections of the data. Chapter 10, Deep learning, examines deep neural networks, including an approach for unsupervised dimensionality reduction based on a type of neural network known as an "autoencoder."

The experiments on using C4.5 to filter its own training data were reported by John (1995). The more conservative approach of a consensus filter involving several different learning algorithms has been investigated by Brodley and Fried (1996). Rousseeuw and Leroy (1987) describe the detection of outliers in statistical regression, including the least median of squares method; they also present the telephone data of Fig. 8.7. It was Quinlan (1986) who noticed that removing noise from the training instance's attributes can decrease a classifier's performance on similarly noisy test instances, particularly at higher noise levels.

Barnett and Lewis (1994) address the general topic of outliers in statistical data, while Pearson (2005) describes the statistical approach of fitting a distribution to the target data. Schölkopf, Williamson, Smola, Shawe-Taylor, and Platt (2000) describe the use of support vector machines for novelty detection, while Abe, Zadrozny, and Langford (2006), amongst others, use artificial data as a second class. Combining density estimation and class probability estimation using artificial data is suggested as a generic approach to unsupervised learning by Hastie et al. (2009) and Hempstalk, Frank, and Witten (2008) describe it in the context of one-class classification. Hempstalk and Frank (2008) discuss the fair comparison of one-class and multiclass classification when several classes are available at training time and we want to discriminate against an entirely new class at prediction time.

Vitter (1985) explored the idea of reservoir sampling; he called the method we described algorithm R. Its computational complexity is $O(N)$ where N is the number of instances in the stream, because a random number must be generated for every instance in order to determine whether to place it in the reservoir, and where. Vitter describes several other algorithms that improve upon R by reducing the number of random numbers that must be generated in order to produce the sample.

Rifkin and Klautau (2004) show that the one-vs-rest method for multiclass classification can work well if appropriate parameter tuning is applied. Friedman (1996) describes the technique of pairwise classification, Fürnkranz (2002) further analyzes it, and Hastie and Tibshirani (1998) extend it to estimate probabilities using pairwise coupling. Fürnkranz (2003) evaluates pairwise classification as a technique for ensemble learning. The idea of using error-correcting output codes for classification gained wide acceptance after a paper by Dietterich and Bakiri (1995); Ricci and Aha (1998) showed how to apply such codes to nearest-neighbor classifiers. Frank and Kramer (2004) introduce ensembles of nested dichotomies for multiclass problems. Dong, Frank, and Kramer (2005) considered using balanced nested dichotomies rather than unrestricted random hierarchies to reduce training time.

The importance of methods for calibrating class probability estimates is now well-established. Zadrozny and Elkan (2002) applied the PAV approach and logistic regression to calibration, and also investigated how to deal with multiclass problems. Niculescu-Mizil and Caruana (2005) compared a variant of logistic regression and the PAV-based method in conjunction with a large set of underlying class probability estimators, and found that the latter is preferable for sufficiently large calibration sets. They also found that multilayer perceptrons and bagged decision trees produce well-calibrated probabilities and do not require an extra calibration step. Stout (2008) describes a linear-time algorithm for isotonic regression based on minimizing the squared error.

8.9 WEKA IMPLEMENTATIONS

Attribute selection
- *CfsSubsetEval* (correlation-based attribute subset evaluator)
- *ConsistencySubsetEval* (measures class consistency for a given set of attributes, in the *consistencySubsetEval* package)
- *ClassifierSubsetEval* (uses a classifier for evaluating subsets of attributes, in the *classifierBasedAttributeSelection* package)
- *SVMAttributeEval* (ranks attributes according to the magnitude of the coefficients learned by a support vector machine, in the *SVMAttributeEval* package)
- *ReliefF* (instance-based approach for ranking attributes)
- *WrapperSubsetEval* (uses a classifier plus cross-validation)
- *GreedyStepwise* (forward selection and backward elimination search)
- *LinearForwardSelection* (forward selection with a sliding window of attribute choices at each step of the search, in the *linearForwardSelection* package)
- *BestFirst* (search method that uses greedy hill-climbing with backtracking)
- *RaceSearch* (uses the race search methodology, in the *raceSearch* package)
- *Ranker* (ranks individual attributes according to their evaluation)

Learning decision tables: *DecisionTable*

Discretization
- *Discretize* (unsupervised and supervised versions)
- *PKIDiscretize* (proportional *k*-interval discretization)

Discriminant analysis for classification
- *LDA, FLDA*, and *QDA* (in the *discriminantAnalysis* package)

Discriminant analysis for dimensionality reduction
- *MultiClassFLDA* (in the *discriminantAnalysis* package)

Other pre- and postprocessing operations
- *PrincipalComponents* and *RandomProjection*
- Arithmetic operations; time-series operations; obfuscation; generating cluster membership values; adding noise; various conversions between numeric, binary, and nominal attributes; and various data cleansing operations
- *PLSFilter* (partial least squares transformation)
- Resampling and reservoir sampling
- *MultiClassClassifier* (includes many ways of handling multiclass problems with two-class classifiers, including error-correcting output codes)
- *FastICA* (independent component analysis, in the *StudentFilters* package)
- *StringToWordVector* (text to attribute vectors)
- *END* (ensembles of nested dichotomies, in the *ensemblesOfNestedDichotomies* package)

Probabilistic methods

CHAPTER OUTLINE

9.1 **Foundations** 336
    Maximum Likelihood Estimation 338
    Maximum a Posteriori Parameter Estimation 339
9.2 **Bayesian Networks**...339
    Making Predictions..340
    Learning Bayesian Networks 344
    Specific Algorithms 347
    Data Structures for Fast Learning...349
9.3 **Clustering and Probability Density Estimation** 352
    The Expectation Maximization Algorithm for a Mixture of Gaussians 353
    Extending the Mixture Model 356
    Clustering Using Prior Distributions 358
    Clustering With Correlated Attributes 359
    Kernel Density Estimation 361
    Comparing Parametric, Semiparametric and Nonparametric Density
    Models for Classification 362
9.4 **Hidden Variable Models** 363
    Expected Log-Likelihoods and Expected Gradients 364
    The Expectation Maximization Algorithm 365
    Applying the Expectation Maximization Algorithm to Bayesian Networks 366
9.5 **Bayesian Estimation and Prediction**..367
    Probabilistic Inference Methods..368
9.6 **Graphical Models and Factor Graphs** 370
    Graphical Models and Plate Notation 371
    Probabilistic Principal Component Analysis 372
    Latent Semantic Analysis..376
    Using Principal Component Analysis for Dimensionality Reduction 377
    Probabilistic LSA..378
    Latent Dirichlet Allocation...379
    Factor Graphs 382
    Markov Random Fields..385
    Computing Using the Sum-Product and Max-Product Algorithms 386

9.7 **Conditional Probability Models** 392
    Linear and Polynomial Regression as Probability Models...........................392
    Using Priors on Parameters 393
    Multiclass Logistic Regression...396
    Gradient Descent and Second-Order Methods 400
    Generalized Linear Models 400
    Making Predictions for Ordered Classes...402
    Conditional Probabilistic Models Using Kernels....................................402
9.8 **Sequential and Temporal Models** 403
    Markov Models and *N*-gram Methods...403
    Hidden Markov Models 404
    Conditional Random Fields..406
9.9 **Further Reading and Bibliographic Notes** 410
    Software Packages and Implementations..414
9.10 **WEKA Implementations** 416

Probabilistic methods form the basis of a plethora of techniques for data mining and machine learning. In Section 4.2, "Simple probabilistic modeling," we encountered the idea of choosing a model that maximizes the likelihood of an event, and have referred to the general idea of maximizing likelihoods several times since. In this chapter we will formalize the notion of likelihoods, and see how maximizing them underpins many estimation problems. We will look at Bayesian networks, and other types of probabilistic models used in machine learning. Let us begin by establishing the foundations: some fundamental rules of probability.

9.1 FOUNDATIONS

In probability modeling, example data or instances are often thought of as being events, observations, or realizations of underlying *random variables*. Given a discrete random variable A, $P(A)$ is a function that encodes the probabilities for each of the categories, classes, or states that A may be in. Similarly, for continuous random variables x, $p(x)$ is a function that assigns a probability density to all possible values of x. In contrast, $P(A = a)$ is the single probability of observing the specific event $A = a$. This notation is often simplified to $P(a)$, but one needs to be careful to remember whether a was defined as a random variable or as an observation. Similarly for the observation that continuous random variable x has the value x_1: it is common to write this probability density as $p(x_1)$, but this is a simplification of the longer but clearer notation $p(x = x_1)$, which emphasizes that it is the scalar value obtained by evaluating the function at $x = x_1$.

There are a few rules of probability theory that are particularly relevant to this book. They go by various names, but we will refer to them as the product rule, the sum (or marginalization) rule, and Bayes' rule. As we will see, these seemingly simple rules can take us far.

Discrete or binary events are used below to keep the notation simple. However, the rules can be applied to *binary*, *discrete*, or *continuous* events and variables. For continuous variables, sums over possible states are replaced by integrals.

The *product rule*, sometimes referred to as the "fundamental rule of probability," states that the joint probability of random variables A and B can be written

$$P(A, B) = P(A|B)P(B).$$

The product rule also applies when A and B are groups or subsets of events or random variables.

The *sum rule* states that given the joint probability of variables $X_1, X_2, \ldots, X_N$, the *marginal probability* for a given variable can be obtained by summing (or integrating) over all the other variables. For example, to obtain the marginal probability of X_1, sum over all the states of all the other variables:

$$P(X_1) = \sum_{x_2} \cdots \sum_{x_N} P(X_1, X_2 = x_2, \ldots, X_N = x_N),$$

The sums are taken over all possible values for the corresponding variable. This notation can be simplified by writing

$$p(x_1) = \sum_{x_2} \cdots \sum_{x_N} P(x_1, x_2, \ldots, x_N).$$

For continuous events and variables $x_1, x_2, \ldots, x_N$, the equivalent formulation is obtained by integrating rather than summing:

$$p(x_1) = \int_{x_2} \cdots \int_{x_N} p(x_1, x_2, \ldots, x_N) dx_1 \ldots dx_N.$$

This can give the marginal distribution of any random variable, or of any subset of random variables.

The famous *Bayes' rule* that was introduced in Chapter 4, Algorithms: the basic methods, can be obtained from the product rule by swapping A and B, observing that $P(B|A)P(A) = P(A|B)P(B)$, and rearranging:

$$P(B|A) = \frac{P(A|B)P(B)}{P(A)}.$$

Suppose we have models for $P(A|B)$ and $P(B)$, observe that event $A = a$, and want to compute $P(B|A = a)$. $P(A = a|B)$ is referred to as the *likelihood*, $P(B)$ as the *prior* distribution of B, and $P(B|A = a)$ as the *posterior* distribution. $P(A = a)$ is obtained from the sum rule:

$$P(A = a) = \sum_b P(A = a, B = b) = \sum_b P(A = a|B = b)P(B = b).$$

These concepts can be applied to random variables, and also to parameters when they are treated as random quantities.

MAXIMUM LIKELIHOOD ESTIMATION

Consider the problem of estimating a set of parameters θ of a probabilistic model, given a set of *observations* $x_1, x_2, \ldots, x_n$. Assume they are continuous-valued observations—but the same idea applies to discrete data too. Maximum likelihood techniques assume that (1) the examples have no dependence on one another, in that the occurrence of one has no effect on the others, and (2) they can each be modeled in exactly the same way. These assumptions are often summarized by saying that events are *independent and identically distributed* (i.i.d.). Although this is rarely completely true, it is sufficiently true in many situations to support useful inferences. Furthermore, as we will see later in this chapter, dependency structure can be captured by more sophisticated models—e.g., by treating interdependent groups of observations as part of a larger instance.

The i.i.d. assumption implies that a model for the joint probability density function for all observations consists of the product of the same probability model $p(x_i; \theta)$ applied to each observation independently. For n observations, this could be written

$$p(x_1, x_2, \ldots, x_n; \theta) = p(x_1; \theta)p(x_2; \theta) \ldots p(x_n; \theta).$$

Each function $p(x_i; \theta)$ has the same parameter values θ, and the aim of parameter estimation is to maximize a joint probability model of this form. Since the observations do not change, this value can only be changed by altering the choice of the parameters θ. We can think about this value as the *likelihood* of the data, and write it as

$$L(\theta; x_1, x_2, \ldots, x_n) = \prod_{i=1}^{n} p(x_i; \theta).$$

Since the data is fixed, it is arguably more useful to think of this as a likelihood function for the parameters, which we are free to choose.

Multiplying many probabilities can lead to very small numbers, and so people often work with the logarithm of the likelihood, or *log-likelihood*:

$$\log L(\theta; x_1, x_2, \ldots, x_n) = \sum_{i=1}^{n} \log p(x_i; \theta),$$

which converts the product into a sum. Since logarithms are strictly monotonically increasing functions, maximizing the log-likelihood is the same as maximizing the likelihood. "Maximum likelihood" learning refers to techniques that search for parameters that do this:

$$\theta_{ML} = \arg \max_{\theta} \sum_{i=1}^{n} \log p(x_i; \theta).$$

The same formulation also works for conditional probabilities and conditional likelihoods. Given some labels y_i that accompany each x_i, e.g., class labels of instances in a classification task, maximum conditional likelihood learning corresponds to determining

$$\theta_{\text{MCL}} = \arg \max_{\theta} \sum_{i=1}^{n} \log p(y_i|x_i; \theta).$$

MAXIMUM A POSTERIORI PARAMETER ESTIMATION

Maximum likelihood assumes that all parameter values are equally likely a priori: we do not judge some parameter values to be more likely than others before we have considered the observations. But suppose we have reason to believe that the model's parameters follow a certain prior distribution. Thinking of them as random variables that specify each instance of the model, Bayes' rule can be applied to compute a posterior distribution of the parameters using the joint probability of data and parameters:

$$p(\theta|x_1, x_2, \ldots, x_n) = \frac{p(x_1, x_2, \ldots, x_n|\theta)p(\theta)}{p(x_1, x_2, \ldots, x_n)}.$$

Since we are computing the posterior distribution over the parameters, we have used | or the "given" notation in place of the semicolon. The denominator is a constant, and assuming i.i.d. observations, the posterior probability of the parameters is proportional to the product of the likelihood and prior:

$$p(\theta|x_1, x_2, \ldots, x_n) \propto \prod_{i=1}^{n} p(x_i; \theta)p(\theta).$$

Switching to logarithms again, the maximum a posteriori parameter estimation procedure seeks a value

$$\theta_{\text{MAP}} = \arg \max_{\theta} \left[\sum_{i=1}^{n} \log p(x_i; \theta) + \log p(\theta) \right].$$

Again, the same idea can be applied to learn conditional probability models.

We have reverted to the semicolon notation to emphasize that maximum a posteriori parameter estimation involves point estimates of the parameters, evaluating them under the likelihood and prior distributions. This contrasts with fully Bayesian methods (discussed below) that explicitly manipulate the distribution of the parameters, typically by integrating over the parameter's uncertainty instead of optimizing a point estimate. The use of the "given" notation in place of the semicolon is more commonly used with fully Bayesian methods, and we will follow this convention.

9.2 BAYESIAN NETWORKS

The Naïve Bayes classifier of Section 4.2 and the logistic regression models of Section 4.6 both produce probability estimates rather than hard classifications.

For each class value, they estimate the probability that a given instance belongs to that class. Most other types of classifiers can be coerced into yielding this kind of information if necessary. For example, probabilities can be obtained from a decision tree by computing the relative frequency of each class in a leaf and from a decision list by examining the instances that a particular rule covers.

Probability estimates are often more useful than plain predictions. They allow predictions to be ranked, and their expected cost to be minimized (see Section 5.8). In fact, there is a strong argument for treating classification learning as the task of learning class probability estimates from data. What is being estimated is the conditional probability distribution of the values of the class attribute given the values of the other attributes. Ideally, the classification model represents this conditional distribution in a concise and easily comprehensible form.

Viewed in this way, Naïve Bayes classifiers, logistic regression models, decision trees, and so on are just alternative ways of representing a conditional probability distribution. Of course, they differ in representational power. Naïve Bayes classifiers and logistic regression models can only represent simple distributions, whereas decision trees can represent—or at least approximate—arbitrary distributions. However, decision trees have their drawbacks: they fragment the training set into smaller and smaller pieces, which inevitably yield less reliable probability estimates, and they suffer from the replicated subtree problem described in Section 3.4. Rule sets go some way toward addressing these shortcomings, but the design of a good rule learner is guided by heuristics with scant theoretical justification.

Does this mean that we have to accept our fate and live with these shortcomings? No! There is a statistically based alternative: a theoretically well-founded way of representing probability distributions concisely and comprehensibly in a graphical manner. The structures are called *Bayesian networks*. They are drawn as a network of nodes, one for each attribute, connected by directed edges in such a way that there are no cycles—a *directed acyclic graph*.

In this section, to explain how to interpret Bayesian networks and how to learn them from data we will make some simplifying assumptions. We assume that all attributes are nominal—they correspond to discrete random variables—and that there are no missing values, so the data is complete. Some advanced learning algorithms can create new attributes in addition to the ones present in the data—so-called hidden attributes corresponding to latent variables whose values cannot be observed. These can support better models if they represent salient features of the underlying problem, and Bayesian networks provide a good way of using them at prediction time. However, they make both learning and prediction far more complex and time consuming, so we will defer considering them to Section 9.4.

MAKING PREDICTIONS

Fig. 9.1 shows a simple Bayesian network for the weather data. It has a node for each of the four attributes *outlook*, *temperature*, *humidity*, and *windy* and one for the class attribute *play*. An edge leads from the *play* node to each of the

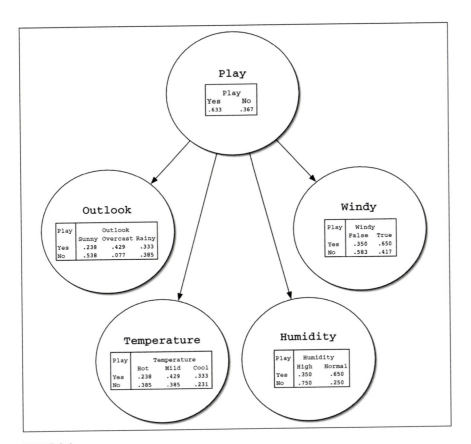

FIGURE 9.1

A simple Bayesian network for the weather data.

other nodes. But in Bayesian networks the structure of the graph is only half the story. Fig. 9.1 shows a table inside each node. The information in the tables defines a probability distribution that is used to predict the class probabilities for any given instance.

Before looking at how to compute this probability distribution, consider the information in the tables. The lower four tables (for *outlook*, *temperature*, *humidity*, and *windy*) have two parts separated by a vertical line. On the left are the values of *play*, and on the right are the corresponding probabilities for each value of the attribute represented by the node. In general, the left side contains a column for every edge pointing to the node, in this case just an edge emanating from the node for the *play* attribute. That is why the table associated with *play* itself does not have a left side: it has no parents. In general, each row of probabilities corresponds to one combination of values of the parent attributes, and the entries in the row show the probability of each value of the node's attribute given this combination. In effect, each row defines a probability distribution over the values of the node's attribute. The entries in a row always sum to 1.

Fig. 9.2 shows a more complex network for the same problem, where three nodes (*windy*, *temperature*, and *humidity*) have two parents. Again, there is one column on the left for each parent and as many columns on the right as the attribute has values. Consider the first row of the table associated with the

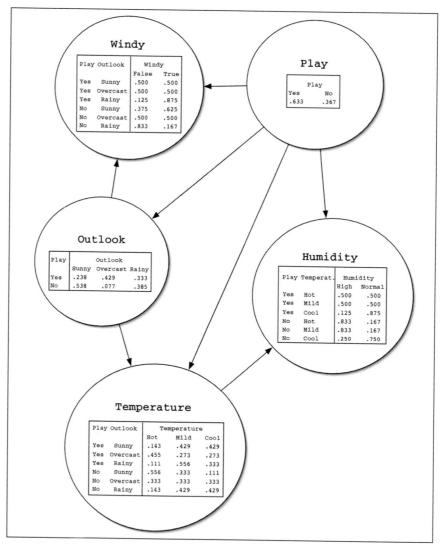

FIGURE 9.2

Another Bayesian network for the weather data.

temperature node. The left side gives a value for each parent attribute, *play* and *outlook*; the right gives a probability for each value of *temperature*. For example, the first number (0.143) is the probability of *temperature* taking on the value *hot*, given that *play* and *outlook* have values *yes* and *sunny*, respectively.

How are the tables used to predict the probability of each class value for a given instance? This turns out to be very easy, because we are assuming that there are no missing values. The instance specifies a value for each attribute. For each node in the network, look up the probability of the node's attribute value based on the row determined by its parents' attribute values. Then just multiply all these probabilities together.

For example, consider an instance with values *outlook* = *rainy*, *temperature* = *cool*, *humidity* = *high*, and *windy* = *true*. To calculate the probability for *play* = *no*, observe that the network in Fig. 9.2 gives probability 0.367 from node *play*, 0.385 from *outlook*, 0.429 from *temperature*, 0.250 from *humidity*, and 0.167 from *windy*. The product is 0.0025. The same calculation for *play* = *yes* yields 0.0077. However, these are clearly not the final answer: the final probabilities must sum to 1, whereas 0.0025 and 0.0077 do not. They are actually the joint probabilities $P(play = no, E)$ and $P(play = yes, E)$, where E denotes all the evidence given by the instance's attribute values. Joint probabilities measure the likelihood of observing an instance that exhibits the attribute values in E as well as the respective class value. They only sum to 1 if they exhaust the space of all possible attribute–value combinations, including the class attribute. This is certainly not the case in our example.

The solution is quite simple (we already encountered it in Section 4.2). To obtain the conditional probabilities $P(play = no|E)$ and $P(play = yes|E)$, normalize the joint probabilities by dividing them by their sum. This gives probability 0.245 for *play* = *no* and 0.755 for *play* = *yes*.

Just one mystery remains: Why multiply all those probabilities together? It turns out that the validity of the multiplication step hinges on a single assumption—namely that, given values for each of a node's parents, knowing the values for any other set of nondescendants does not change the probability associated with each of its possible values. In other words, other sets of nondescendants do not provide any information about the likelihood of the node's values over and above the information provided by the parents. This can be written

$$P(node|parents \text{ plus any other nondescendants}) = P(node|parents),$$

which must hold for all values of the nodes and attributes involved. In statistics this property is called *conditional independence*. Multiplication is valid provided that each node is conditionally independent of its grandparents, great grandparents, and indeed any other set of nondescendants, given its parents. We have discussed above how the *product rule* of probability can be applied to sets of variables. Applying the product rule recursively between a single variable and the rest of the variables gives rise to another rule known as the *chain rule* which states that the joint probability of n attributes A_i can be decomposed into the following product:

$$P(A_1, A_2, \ldots, A_n) = P(A_1) \prod_{i=1}^{n-1} P(A_{i+1} | A_i, A_{i-1}, \ldots, A_1).$$

The multiplications of probabilities in Bayesian networks follow as a direct result of the *chain rule*.

The decomposition holds for any order of the attributes. Because our Bayesian network is an acyclic graph, its nodes can be ordered to give all ancestors of a node a_i indices smaller than i. Then, because of the conditional independence assumption all Bayesian networks can be written in the form

$$P(A_1, A_2, \ldots, A_n) = \prod_{i=1}^{n} P(A_i | \text{Parents}(A_i)),$$

where when a variable has no parents, we use the unconditional probability of that variable. This is exactly the multiplication rule that we applied earlier.

The two Bayesian networks in Figs. 9.1 and 9.2 are fundamentally different. The first (Fig. 9.1) makes stronger independence assumptions because for each of its nodes the set of parents is a subset of the corresponding set of parents in the second (Fig. 9.2). In fact, Fig. 9.1 is almost identical to the simple Naïve Bayes classifier of Section 4.2 (The probabilities are slightly different but only because each count has been initialized to 0.5 to avoid the zero-frequency problem.) The network in Fig. 9.2 has more rows in the conditional probability tables and hence more parameters; it may be a more accurate representation of the underlying true probability distribution that generated the data.

It is tempting to assume that the directed edges in a Bayesian network represent causal effects. But be careful! In our case, a particular value of *play* may enhance the prospects of a particular value of *outlook*, but it certainly does not cause it—it is more likely to be the other way round. Different Bayesian networks can be constructed for the same problem, representing exactly the same probability distribution. This is done by altering the way in which the joint probability distribution is factorized to exploit conditional independencies. The network whose directed edges model causal effects is often the simplest one with the fewest parameters. Hence, human experts who construct Bayesian networks for a particular domain often benefit by representing causal effects by directed edges. However, when machine learning techniques are applied to induce models from data whose causal structure is unknown, all they can do is construct a network based on the correlations that are observed in the data. Inferring causality from correlation is always a dangerous business.

LEARNING BAYESIAN NETWORKS

The way to construct a learning algorithm for Bayesian networks is to define two components: a function for evaluating a given network based on the data and a method for searching through the space of possible networks. The quality of a given network is measured by the probability of the data given the network. We calculate the probability that the network accords to each instance and multiply these probabilities together over all instances. In practice, this quickly yields numbers too small to be represented properly (called *arithmetic underflow*), so we use the sum of the logarithms of the probabilities rather than their product. The resulting quantity is the log-likelihood of the network given the data.

Assume that the structure of the network—the set of edges—is given. It is easy to estimate the numbers in the conditional probability tables: just compute the relative frequencies of the associated combinations of attribute values in the training data. To avoid the zero-frequency problem each count is initialized with a constant as described in Section 4.2. For example, to find the probability that *humidity* = *normal* given that *play* = *yes* and *temperature* = *cool* (the last number of the third row of the *humidity* node's table in Fig. 9.2), observe from Table 1.2 that there are three instances with this combination of attribute values in the weather data, and no instances with *humidity* = *high* and the same values for *play* and *temperature*. Initializing the counts for the two values of *humidity* to 0.5 yields the probability $(3 + 0.5)/(3 + 0 + 1) = 0.875$ for *humidity* = *normal*.

Let us consider more formally how to estimate the conditional and unconditional probabilities in a Bayesian network. The log-likelihood of a Bayesian network with V variables and N examples of complete assignments to the network is

$$\sum_{i=1}^{N} \log P(\{\tilde{A}_1, \tilde{A}_2, \ldots, \tilde{A}_V\}_i) = \sum_{i-1}^{N} \sum_{v=1}^{V} \log P(\tilde{A}_{v,i} | \text{Parents}(\tilde{A}_{v,i}); \Theta_v),$$

where the parameters of each conditional or unconditional distribution are given by Θ_v, and we use the $\sim$ to indicate actual observations of a variable. We find the maximum likelihood parameter values by taking derivatives. Since the log-likelihood is a double sum over examples i and variables v, when we take the derivative of it with respect to any given set of parameters Θ_v, all the terms of the sum that are independent of Θ_v will be zero. This means that the estimation problem *decouples* into the problem of estimating the parameters for each conditional or unconditional probability distribution separately. For variables with no parents, we need to estimate an unconditional probability. In Appendix A.2 we give a derivation illustrating why estimating a discrete distribution with parameters given by the probabilities π_k for k classes corresponds to the intuitive formula $\pi_k = n_k/N$, where n_k is the number of examples of class k and N is the total number of examples. This can also be written

$$P(A = a) = \frac{1}{N} \sum_{i=1}^{N} \mathbf{1}(\tilde{A}_i = a),$$

where $\mathbf{1}(\tilde{A}_i = a)$ is simply an indicator function that returns 1 when the ith observed value for $\tilde{A}_i = a$ and 0 otherwise. The estimation of the entries of a conditional probability table for $P(B|A)$ can be expressed using a notation similar to the intuitive counting procedures outlined above:

$$P(B = b|A = a) = \frac{P(B = b, A = a)}{P(A = a)} = \frac{\sum_{i=1}^{N} \mathbf{1}(\tilde{A}_i = a, \tilde{B}_i = b)}{\sum_{i=1}^{N} \mathbf{1}(\tilde{A}_i = a)}.$$

This derivation generalizes to the situation where A is a subset of random variables. Note that the above expressions give maximum likelihood estimates, and do not deal with the zero-frequency problem.

The nodes in the network are predetermined, one for each attribute (including the class). Learning the network structure amounts to searching through the space of possible sets of edges, estimating the conditional probability tables for each set, and computing the log-likelihood of the resulting network based on the data as a measure of the network's quality. Bayesian network learning algorithms differ mainly in the way in which they search through the space of network structures. Some algorithms are introduced below.

There is one caveat. If the log-likelihood is maximized based on the training data, it will always be better to add more edges: the resulting network will simply overfit. Various methods can be employed to combat this problem. One possibility is to use cross-validation to estimate the goodness of fit. A second is to add a penalty for the complexity of the network based on the number of parameters, i.e., the total number of independent estimates in all the probability tables. For each table, the number of independent probabilities is the total number of entries minus the number of entries in the last column, which can be determined from the other columns because all rows must sum to 1. Let K be the number of parameters, LL the log-likelihood, and N the number of instances in the data. Two popular measures for evaluating the quality of a network are the *Akaike Information Criterion* (AIC):

$$\text{AIC score} = -LL + K,$$

and the following *MDL metric* based on the MDL principle:

$$\text{MDL score} = -LL + \frac{K}{2}\log N.$$

In both cases the log-likelihood is negated, so the aim is to minimize these scores.

A third possibility is to assign a prior distribution over network structures and find the most likely network by combining its prior probability with the probability accorded to the network by the data. This is the maximum a posteriori approach to network scoring. Depending on the prior distribution used, it can take various forms. However, true Bayesians would average over all possible network structures rather than singling one particular network out for prediction. Unfortunately, this generally requires a great deal of computation. A simplified approach is to average over all network structures that are substructures of a given network. It turns out that this can be implemented very efficiently by changing the method for calculating the conditional probability tables so that the resulting probability estimates implicitly contain information from all subnetworks. The details of this approach are rather complex and will not be described here.

The task of searching for a good network structure can be greatly simplified if the right metric is used for scoring. Recall that the probability of a single instance based on a network is the product of all the individual probabilities from the various conditional probability tables. The overall probability of the data set is the product of these products for all instances. Because terms in a product are interchangeable, the product can be rewritten to group together all factors relating to the same table. The same holds for the log-likelihood, using sums instead of products. This means that the likelihood can be optimized separately for each node of the network. This can be done by adding, or removing, edges from other nodes to the node that is being optimized—the only constraint is that cycles must not be introduced. The same trick also works if a local scoring metric such as AIC or MDL is used instead of plain log-likelihood because the penalty term splits into several components, one for each node, and each node can be optimized independently.

SPECIFIC ALGORITHMS

Now we move on to actual algorithms for learning Bayesian networks. One simple and very fast learning algorithm, called *K2*, starts with a given ordering of the attributes (i.e., nodes). Then it processes each node in turn and greedily considers adding edges from previously processed nodes to the current one. In each step it adds the edge that maximizes the network's score. When there is no further improvement, attention turns to the next node. As an additional mechanism for overfitting avoidance, the number of parents for each node can be restricted to a predefined maximum. Because only edges from previously processed nodes are considered and there is a fixed ordering, this procedure cannot introduce cycles. However, the result depends on the initial ordering, so it makes sense to run the algorithm several times with different random orderings.

The Naïve Bayes classifier is a network with an edge leading from the class attribute to each of the other attributes. When building networks for classification, it sometimes helps to use this network as a starting point for the search. This can be done in *K2* by forcing the class variable to be the first one in the ordering and initializing the set of edges appropriately.

Another potentially helpful trick is to ensure that every attribute in the data is in the *Markov blanket* of the node that represents the class attribute. A node's Markov blanket includes all its parents, children, and children's parents. It can be shown that a node is conditionally independent of all other nodes given values for the nodes in its Markov blanket. Hence, if a node is absent from the class attribute's Markov blanket, its value is completely irrelevant to the classification. We show an example of a Bayesian network and its Markov blanket in Fig. 9.3. Conversely, if *K2* finds a network that does not include a relevant attribute in the

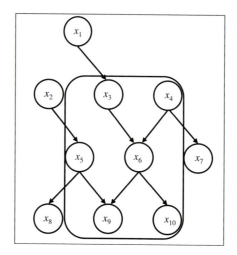

FIGURE 9.3

The Markov blanket for variable x_6 in a 10-variable Bayesian network.

class node's Markov blanket, it might help to add an edge that rectifies this short-coming. A simple way of doing this is to add an edge from the attribute's node to the class node or from the class node to the attribute's node, depending on which option avoids a cycle.

A more sophisticated but slower version of $K2$ is not to order the nodes but to greedily consider adding or deleting edges between arbitrary pairs of nodes (all the while ensuring acyclicity, of course). A further step is to consider inverting the direction of existing edges as well. As with any greedy algorithm, the resulting network only represents a *local* maximum of the scoring function: it is always advisable to run such algorithms several times with different random initial configurations. More sophisticated optimization strategies such as simulated annealing, tabu search, or genetic algorithms can also be used.

Another good learning algorithm for Bayesian network classifiers is called *tree augmented Naïve Bayes* (TAN). As the name implies, it takes the Naïve Bayes classifier and adds edges to it. The class attribute is the single parent of each node of a Naïve Bayes network: TAN considers adding a second parent to each node. If the class node and all corresponding edges are excluded from consideration, and assuming that there is exactly one node to which a second parent is not added, the resulting classifier has a tree structure rooted at the parentless node—i.e., where the name comes from. For this restricted type of network there is an efficient algorithm for finding the set of edges that maximizes the network's likelihood based on computing the network's maximum weighted spanning tree. This algorithm's run-time is linear in the number of instances and quadratic in the number of attributes.

The type of network learned by the TAN algorithm is called a *one-dependence estimator*. An even simpler type of network is the *super-parent one-dependence estimator*. Here, exactly one other node apart from the class node is elevated to parent status, and becomes parent of every other nonclass node. It turns out that a simple ensemble of these one-dependence estimators yields very accurate classifiers: in each of these estimators, a different attribute becomes the extra parent node. Then, at prediction time, class probability estimates from the different one-dependence estimators are simply averaged. This scheme is called AODE, for averaged one-dependence estimator. Normally, only estimators with a certain support in the data are used in the ensemble, but more sophisticated selection schemes are possible. Because no structure learning is involved for each super-parent one-dependence estimator, AODE is a very efficient classifier.

AODE makes strong assumptions, but relaxes the even stronger assumption of Naïve Bayes. The model can be relaxed even further by introducing a set of n super parents instead of a single super-parent attribute and averaging across all possible sets, yielding the AnDE algorithm. Increasing n obviously increases computational complexity. There is good empirical evidence that $n = 2$ (A2DE) yields a useful trade-off between computational complexity and predictive accuracy in practice.

All the scoring metrics that we have described so far are likelihood-based in the sense that they are designed to maximize the joint probability $P(a_1, a_2, \ldots, a_n)$ for each instance. However, in classification, what we really want to maximize is the conditional probability of the class given the values of the other attributes—in other words, the conditional likelihood. Unfortunately, there is no closed-form solution for the maximum *conditional*-likelihood probability estimates that are needed for the tables in a Bayesian network. On the other hand, computing the conditional likelihood for a given network and dataset is straightforward—after all, this is what logistic regression does. Hence it has been proposed to use standard maximum likelihood probability estimates in the network, but the conditional likelihood to evaluate a particular network structure.

Another way of using Bayesian networks for classification is to build a separate network for each class value, based on the data pertaining to that class, and combine their predictions using Bayes' rule. The set of networks is called a *Bayesian multinet*. To obtain a prediction for a particular class value, take the corresponding network's probability and multiply it by the class's prior probability. Do this for each class and normalize the result as we did previously. In this case we would not use the conditional likelihood to learn the network for each class value.

All the network learning algorithms we have introduced are score-based. A different strategy, which we will not explain here, is to piece a network together by testing individual conditional independence assertions based on subsets of the attributes. This is known as *structure learning by conditional independence tests*.

DATA STRUCTURES FOR FAST LEARNING

Learning Bayesian networks involves a lot of counting. For each network structure considered in the search, the data must be scanned afresh to obtain the counts needed to fill out the conditional probability tables. Instead, could they be stored in a data structure that eliminated the need for scanning the data over and over again? An obvious way is to precompute the counts and store the nonzero ones in a table—say, the hash table mentioned in Section 4.5. Even so, any nontrivial data set will have a huge number of nonzero counts.

Again, consider the weather data from Table 1.2. There are five attributes, two with three values and three with two values. This gives $4 \times 4 \times 3 \times 3 \times 3 = 432$ possible counts. Each component of the product corresponds to an attribute, and its contribution to the product is one more than the number of its values because the attribute may be missing from the count. All these counts can be calculated by treating them as item sets, as explained in Section 4.5, and setting the minimum coverage to one. But even without storing counts that are zero, this simple scheme runs into memory problems very quickly. The FP-growth data structure described in Section 6.3 was designed for efficient representation of data in the case of item set mining. In the following, we describe a structure that has been used for Bayesian networks.

It turns out that the counts can be stored effectively in a structure called an *all-dimensions (AD) tree*, which is analogous to the *k*D-trees used for nearest neighbor search described in Section 4.7. For simplicity, we illustrate this using a reduced version of the weather data that only has the attributes *humidity*, *windy*, and *play*. Fig. 9.4A summarizes the data. The number of possible counts is

(A)	Humidity	Windy	Play	Count
	High	True	Yes	1
	High	True	No	2
	High	False	Yes	2
	High	False	No	2
	Normal	True	Yes	2
	Normal	True	No	1
	Normal	False	Yes	4
	Normal	False	No	0

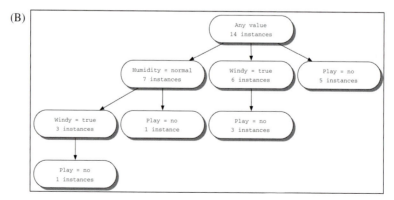

FIGURE 9.4

The weather data: (A) reduced version; (B) corresponding AD tree.

$3 \times 3 \times 3 = 27$, although only 8 of them are shown. For example, the count for *play* = *no* is 5 (count them!).

Fig. 9.4B shows an AD tree for this data. Each node says how many instances exhibit the attribute values that are tested along the path from the root to that node. For example, the leftmost leaf says that there is one instance with values *humidity* = *normal, windy* = *true*, and *play* = *no*, and the rightmost leaf says that there are five instances with *play* = *no*.

It would be trivial to construct a tree that enumerates all 27 counts explicitly. However, that would gain nothing over a plain table and is obviously not what the tree in Fig. 9.4B does, because it contains only 8 counts. There is, e.g., no branch that tests *humidity* = *high*. How was the tree constructed, and how can all counts be obtained from it?

Assume that each attribute in the data has been assigned an index. In the reduced version of the weather data we give *humidity* index 1, *windy* index 2, and *play* index 3. An AD tree is generated by expanding each node corresponding to an attribute i with the values of all attributes that have indices $j > i$, with two important restrictions: the most populous expansion for each attribute is omitted (breaking ties arbitrarily) as are expansions with counts that are zero. The root node is given index 0, so for it all attributes are expanded, subject to the same restrictions.

For example, Fig. 9.4B contains no expansion for *windy* = *false* from the root node because with eight instances it is the most populous expansion: the value *false* occurs more often in the data than the value *true*. Similarly, from the node labeled *humidity* = *normal* there is no expansion for *windy* = *false* because *false* is the most common value for *windy* among all instances with *humidity* = *normal*. In fact, in our example the second restriction—namely that expansions with zero counts are omitted—never kicks in because the first restriction precludes any path that starts with the tests *humidity* = *normal* and *windy* = *false*, which is the only way to reach the solitary zero in Fig. 9.4A.

Each node of the tree represents the occurrence of a particular combination of attribute values. It is straightforward to retrieve the count for a combination that occurs in the tree. However, the tree does not explicitly represent many nonzero counts because the most populous expansion for each attribute is omitted. For example, the combination *humidity* = *high* and *play* = *yes* occurs three times in the data but has no node in the tree. Nevertheless, it turns out that any count can be calculated from those that the tree stores explicitly.

Here's a simple example. Fig. 9.4B contains no node for *humidity* = *normal, windy* = *true*, and *play* = *yes*. However, it shows three instances with *humidity* = *normal* and *windy* = *true*, and one of them has a value for *play* that is different from *yes*. It follows that there must be two instances for *play* = *yes*. Now for a trickier case: how many times does *humidity* = *high, windy* = *true*, and *play* = *no* occur? At first glance it seems impossible to tell because there is no branch for *humidity* = *high*. However, we can deduce the number by calculating the count for *windy* = *true* and *play* = *no* (3) and subtracting the count for *humidity* = *normal, windy* = *true*, and *play* = *no* (1). This gives 2, the correct value.

This idea works for any subset of attributes and any combination of attribute values, but it may have to be applied recursively. For example, to obtain the count for *humidity = high, windy = false*, and *play = no*, we need the count for *windy = false* and *play = no* and the count for *humidity = normal, windy = false*, and *play = no*. We obtain the former by subtracting the count for *windy = true* and *play = no* (3) from the count for *play = no* (5), giving 2, and the latter by subtracting the count for *humidity = normal, windy = true*, and *play = no* (1) from the count for *humidity = normal* and *play = no* (1), giving 0. Thus there must be $2 - 0 = 2$ instances with *humidity = high, windy = false*, and *play = no*, which is correct.

AD trees only pay off if the data contains many thousands of instances. It is pretty obvious that they do not help on the weather data. The fact that they yield no benefit on small data sets means that, in practice, it makes little sense to expand the tree all the way down to the leaf nodes. Usually, a cutoff parameter k is employed, and nodes covering fewer than k instances hold a list of pointers to these instances rather than a list of pointers to other nodes. This makes the trees smaller and more efficient to use.

This section has only skimmed the surface of the subject of learning Bayesian networks. We left open questions of missing values, numeric attributes, and hidden attributes. We did not describe how to use Bayesian networks for regression tasks. Some of these topics are discussed later in this chapter. Bayesian networks are a special case of a wider class of statistical models called *graphical models*, which include networks with undirected edges (called *Markov networks*). Graphical models have attracted a lot of attention in the machine learning community and we will discuss them in Section 9.6.

9.3 CLUSTERING AND PROBABILITY DENSITY ESTIMATION

An incremental heuristic clustering approach was described in Section 4.8. While it works reasonably well in some practical situations, it has shortcomings: the arbitrary division by k in the category utility formula that is necessary to prevent overfitting, the need to supply an artificial minimum value for the standard deviation of clusters, and the ad hoc cutoff value to prevent every single instance from becoming a cluster in its own right. On top of this is the uncertainty inherent in incremental algorithms. To what extent is the result dependent on the order of examples? Are the local restructuring operations of merging and splitting really enough to reverse the effect of bad initial decisions caused by unlucky ordering? Does the final result represent even a *local* maximum of category utility? Add to this the problem that one never knows how far the final configuration is to a *global* maximum—and, of course, the standard trick of repeating the clustering procedure several times and choosing the best will destroy the incremental nature of the algorithm. Finally, does not the hierarchical nature of the result really beg the question of which are the *best* clusters? There are so many clusters in Fig. 4.21 that it is hard to separate the wheat from the chaff.

A more principled statistical approach to the clustering problem can over-come some of these shortcomings. From a probabilistic perspective, the goal of clustering is to find the most likely set of clusters given the data (and, inevitably, prior expectations). Because no finite amount of evidence is enough to make a completely firm decision on the matter, instances—even training instances—should not be placed categorically in one cluster or the other: instead they have a certain probability of belonging to each cluster. This helps to eliminate the brittleness that is often associated with schemes that make hard and fast judgments.

The foundation for statistical clustering is a statistical model called a *finite mixture* model. A *mixture* is a set of k probability distributions, representing k clusters, that govern the attribute values for members of that cluster. In other words, each distribution gives the probability that a particular instance would have a certain set of attribute values if it were *known* to be a member of that cluster. Each cluster has a different distribution. Any particular instance "really" belongs to one and only one of the clusters, but it is not known which one. Finally, the clusters are not equally likely: there is some probability distribution that reflects their relative populations.

THE EXPECTATION MAXIMIZATION ALGORITHM FOR A MIXTURE OF GAUSSIANS

One of the simplest finite mixture situations is when there is only one numeric attribute, which has a Gaussian or normal distribution for each cluster—but with different means and variances. The clustering problem is to take a set of instances—in this case each instance is just a number—and a prespecified number of clusters, and work out each cluster's mean and variance and the population distribution between the clusters. The mixture model combines several normal distributions, and its probability density function looks like a mountain range with a peak for each component.

Fig. 9.5 shows a simple example. There are two clusters A and B, and each has a normal distribution with means and standard deviations μ_A and σ_A for cluster A, and μ_B and σ_B for cluster B. Samples are taken from these distributions, using cluster A with probability p_A and cluster B with probability p_B (where $p_A + p_B = 1$), resulting in a data set like that shown. Now, imagine being given the data set without the classes—just the numbers—and being asked to determine the five parameters that characterize the model: μ_A, σ_A, μ_B, σ_B, and p_A (the parameter p_B can be calculated directly from p_A). That is the finite mixture problem.

If you knew which of the two distributions each instance came from, finding the five parameters would be easy—just estimate the mean and standard deviation for the cluster A samples and the cluster B samples separately, using the formulas

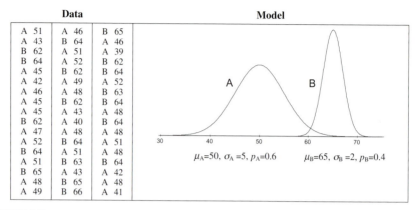

Data				
A	51	A	46	B	65

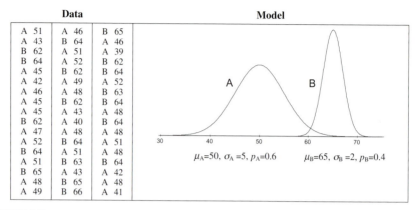

Data		
A 51	A 46	B 65
A 43	B 64	A 46
B 62	A 51	A 39
B 64	A 52	B 62
A 45	B 62	B 64
A 42	A 49	A 52
A 46	A 48	B 63
A 45	B 62	B 64
A 45	A 43	A 48
B 62	A 40	B 64
A 47	A 48	A 48
A 52	B 64	A 51
B 64	A 51	A 48
A 51	B 63	B 64
B 65	A 43	A 42
A 48	B 65	A 48
A 49	B 66	A 41

$\mu_A=50,\ \sigma_A=5,\ p_A=0.6$ $\qquad$ $\mu_B=65,\ \sigma_B=2,\ p_B=0.4$

FIGURE 9.5

A two-class mixture model.

$$\mu = \frac{x_1 + x_2 + \cdots + x_n}{n},$$

$$\sigma^2 = \frac{(x_1-\mu)^2 + (x_2-\mu)^2 + \cdots + (x_n-\mu)^2}{n-1}.$$

(The use of $n-1$ rather than n as the denominator in the second formula ensures an unbiased estimate of the variance, rather than the maximum likelihood estimate: it makes little difference in practice if n is used instead.) Here, $x_1, x_2, \ldots, x_n$ are the samples from the distribution A or B. To estimate the fifth parameter p_A, just take the proportion of the instances that are in the A cluster.

If you knew the five parameters, finding the (posterior) probabilities that a given instance comes from each distribution would be easy. Given an instance x_i, the probability that it belongs to cluster A is

$$P(A|x_i) = \frac{P(x_i|A)\cdot P(A)}{P(x_i)} = \frac{N(x_i; \mu_A, \sigma_A)p_A}{P(x_i)},$$

where $N(x; \mu_A, \sigma_A)$ is the normal or Gaussian distribution function for cluster A, i.e.:

$$N(x; \mu, \sigma) = \frac{1}{\sqrt{2\pi}\sigma} e^{-\frac{(x-\mu)^2}{2\sigma^2}}.$$

In practice we calculate the numerators for both $P(A|x_i)$ and $P(B|x_i)$, then normalize them by dividing by their sum, which is $P(x_i)$. This whole procedure is just the same as the way numeric attributes are treated in the Naïve Bayes learning scheme of Section 4.2. And the caveat explained there applies here too: strictly speaking, $N(x_i; \mu_A, \sigma_A)$ is not the probability $P(x|A)$ because the probability of x being any particular real number x_i is zero. Instead, $N(x_i; \mu_A, \sigma_A)$ is a probability density, which is turned into a probability by the normalization

process used to compute the posterior. Note that the final outcome is not a particular cluster but rather the (posterior) *probability* with which x_i belongs to cluster
A or cluster B.

The problem is that we know neither of these things: not the distribution that
each training instance came from nor the five parameters of the mixture model.
So we adopt the procedure used for the k-means clustering algorithm and iterate.
Start with initial guesses for the five parameters, use them to calculate the cluster
probabilities for each instance, use these probabilities to re-estimate the parameters, and repeat. (If you prefer, you can start with guesses for the classes of the
instances instead.) This is an instance of the *expectation–maximization* or *EM*
algorithm. The first step, calculation of the cluster probabilities (which are the
"expected" class values) is the "expectation"; the second, calculation of the distribution parameters, is our "maximization" of the likelihood of the distributions
given the data.

A slight adjustment must be made to the parameter estimation equations to
account for the fact that it is only cluster probabilities, not the clusters themselves, that are known for each instance. These probabilities just act like weights.
If w_i is the probability that instance i belongs to cluster A, the mean and standard
deviation for cluster A are

$$\mu_A = \frac{w_1 x_1 + w_2 x_2 + \cdots + w_n x_n}{w_1 + w_2 + \cdots + w_n}$$

$$\sigma_A^2 = \frac{w_1(x_1-\mu)^2 + w_2(x_2-\mu)^2 + \cdots + w_n(x_n-\mu)^2}{w_1 + w_2 + \cdots + w_n}$$

where now the x_i are *all* the instances, not just those belonging to cluster A. (This
differs in a small detail from the estimate for the standard deviation given above:
if all weights are equal the denominator is n rather than $n-1$, which uses the maximum likelihood estimator rather than the unbiased estimator.)

Now consider how to terminate the iteration. The k-means algorithm stops
when the classes of the instances do not change from one iteration to the next—a
"fixed point" has been reached. In the EM algorithm things are not quite so easy:
the algorithm converges toward a fixed point but never actually gets there. We
can see how close it is getting by calculating the overall (marginal) *likelihood*
that the data came from this model, given the values for the five parameters. The
marginal likelihood is obtained by summing (or marginalizing) over the two components of the Gaussian mixture, i,e,

$$\prod_{i=1}^{n} P(x_i) = \prod_{i=1}^{n} \sum_{c_i} P(x_i|c_i) \cdot P(c_i)$$
$$= \prod_{i=1}^{n} (N(x_i; \mu_A, \sigma_A)p_A + N(x_i; \mu_B, \sigma_B)p_B).$$

This is the product of the marginal probability densities of the individual
instances, which are obtained from the sum of the probability density under each

normal distribution $N(x; \mu, \sigma)$, weighted by the appropriate (prior) class probability. The cluster membership variable c is a so-called hidden (or latent) variable; we sum it out to obtain the marginal probability density of an instance.

This overall likelihood is a measure of the "goodness" of the clustering and increases at each iteration of the EM algorithm. The above equation and the expressions $N(x_i; \mu_A, \sigma_A)$ and $N(x_i; \mu_B, \sigma_B)$ are probability densities and not probabilities, so they do not necessarily lie between 0 and 1: nevertheless, the resulting magnitude still reflects the quality of the clustering. In practical implementations the log-likelihood is calculated instead: this is done by summing the logarithms of the individual components, avoiding multiplications. But the overall conclusion still holds: you should iterate until the increase in log-likelihood becomes negligible. For example, a practical implementation might iterate until the difference between successive values of log-likelihood is less than 10^{-10} for 10 successive iterations. Typically, the log-likelihood will increase very sharply over the first few iterations and then converge rather quickly to a point that is virtually stationary.

Although the EM algorithm is guaranteed to converge to a maximum, this is a *local* maximum and may not necessarily be the same as the global maximum. For a better chance of obtaining the global maximum, the whole procedure should be repeated several times, with different initial guesses for the parameter values. The overall log-likelihood figure can be used to compare the different final configurations obtained: just choose the largest of the local maxima.

EXTENDING THE MIXTURE MODEL

Now that we have seen the Gaussian mixture model for two distributions, let us consider how to extend it to more realistic situations. The basic method is just the same, but because the mathematical notation becomes formidable we will not develop it in full detail.

Changing the algorithm from two-cluster problems to situations with multiple clusters is completely straightforward, so long as the number k of normal distributions is given in advance.

The model can easily be extended from a single numeric attribute per instance to multiple attributes as long as independence between attributes is assumed. The probabilities for each attribute are multiplied together to obtain the joint probability (density) for the instance, just as in the Naïve Bayes method.

When the dataset is known in advance to contain correlated attributes, the independence assumption no longer holds. Instead, two attributes can be modeled jointly by a bivariate normal distribution, in which each has its own mean value but the two standard deviations are replaced by a "covariance matrix" with four numeric parameters. In Appendix A.2 we show the mathematics for the multivariate Gaussian distribution; the special case of a diagonal covariance model leads to a Naïve Bayesian interpretation. Several correlated attributes can be handled using a multivariate distribution. The number of parameters increases with the square of the number of jointly varying attributes. With n independent attributes, there are $2n$ parameters, a mean and a standard deviation for each. With n covariant attributes, there are $n + n(n + 1)/2$ parameters, a mean for each, and an $n \times n$ covariance matrix that is symmetric and therefore involves $n(n + 1)/2$ different quantities. This escalation in the number of parameters has serious consequences for overfitting, as we will explain later.

To cater for nominal attributes, the normal distribution must be abandoned. Instead, a nominal attribute with v possible values is characterized by v numbers representing the probability of each one. A different set of numbers is needed for every cluster; kv parameters in all. The situation is very similar to the Naïve Bayes method. The two steps of expectation and maximization correspond exactly to operations we have studied before. Expectation—estimating the cluster to which each instance belongs given the distribution parameters—is just like determining the class of an unknown instance. Maximization—estimating the parameters from the classified instances—is just like determining the attribute–value probabilities from the training instances, with the small difference that in the EM algorithm instances are assigned to classes probabilistically rather than categorically. In Section 4.2 we encountered the problem that probability estimates can turn out to be zero, and the same problem occurs here too. Fortunately, the solution is just as simple—use the Laplace estimator.

Naïve Bayes assumes that attributes are independent—i.e., why it is called "naïve." A pair of correlated nominal attributes with v_1 and v_2 possible values, respectively, can be replaced by a single covariant attribute with $v_1 v_2$ possible values. Again, the number of parameters escalates as the number of dependent attributes increases, and this has implications for probability estimates and overfitting.

The presence of both numeric and nominal attributes in the data to be clustered presents no particular problem. Covariant numeric and nominal attributes are more difficult to handle, and we will not describe them here.

Missing values can be accommodated in various different ways. In principle, they should be treated as unknown and the EM process adapted to estimate them as well as the cluster means and variances. A simple way is to replace them by means or modes in a preprocessing step.

With all these enhancements, probabilistic clustering becomes quite sophisticated. The EM algorithm is used throughout to do the basic work. The user must specify the number of clusters to be sought, the type of each attribute (numeric or nominal), which attributes are to modeled as covarying, and what to do about missing values. Moreover, different distributions can be used. Although the normal distribution is usually a good choice for numeric attributes, it is not suitable for attributes (such as weight) that have a predetermined minimum (zero, in the case of weight) but no upper bound; in this case a "log-normal" distribution is more appropriate. Numeric attributes that are bounded above and below can be modeled by a "log-odds" distribution. Attributes that are integer counts rather than real values are best modeled by the "Poisson" distribution. A comprehensive system might allow these distributions to be specified individually for each attribute. In each case, the distribution involves numeric parameters—probabilities of all possible values for discrete attributes and mean and standard deviation for continuous ones.

In this section we have been talking about clustering. But you may be thinking that these enhancements could be applied just as well to the Naïve Bayes algorithm too—and you could be right. A comprehensive probabilistic modeler could accommodate both clustering and classification learning, nominal and numeric attributes with a variety of distributions, various possibilities of covariation, and different ways of dealing with missing values. The user would specify, as part of the domain knowledge, which distributions to use for which attributes.

CLUSTERING USING PRIOR DISTRIBUTIONS

However, there is a snag: overfitting. You might say that if we are not sure which attributes are dependent on each other, why not be on the safe side and specify that *all* the attributes are covariant? The answer is that the more parameters there are, the greater the chance that the resulting structure is overfitted to the training data—and covariance increases the number of parameters dramatically. The problem of overfitting occurs throughout machine learning, and probabilistic clustering is no exception. There are two ways that it can occur: through specifying too large a number of clusters and through specifying distributions with too many parameters.

The extreme case of too many clusters occurs when there is one for every data point: clearly, that will be overfitted to the training data. In fact, in the mixture model, problems will occur whenever any one of the normal distributions becomes so narrow that it is centered on just one data point. Consequently, implementations generally insist that clusters contain at least two different data values.

Whenever there are a large number of parameters, the problem of overfitting arises. If you were unsure of which attributes were covariant, you might try out different possibilities and choose the one that maximized the overall probability of the data given the clustering that was found. Unfortunately, the more parameters there are, the larger the overall data probability will tend to be—not necessarily because of better clustering but because of overfitting. The more parameters there are to play with, the easier it is to find a clustering that seems good.

It would be nice if somehow you could penalize the model for introducing new parameters. One principled way of doing this is to adopt a Bayesian approach in which every parameter has a prior probability distribution whose effect is incorporated into the overall likelihood figure. In a sense, the Laplace estimator that we met in Section 4.2, and whose use we advocated earlier to counter the problem of zero probability estimates for nominal values, is just such a device. Whenever there are few observations, it exacts a penalty because it makes probabilities that are zero, or close to zero, greater, and this will decrease the overall likelihood of the data. In fact, the Laplace estimator is tantamount to using a particular prior distribution for the parameter concerned. Making two nominal attributes covariant will exacerbate the problem of sparse data. Instead of $v_1 + v_2$ parameters, where v_1 and

v_2 are the number of possible values, there are now $v_1 v_2$, greatly increasing the chance of a large number of small observed frequencies.

The same technique can be used to penalize the introduction of large numbers of clusters, just by using a prespecified prior distribution that decays sharply as the number of clusters increases.

AutoClass is a comprehensive Bayesian clustering scheme that uses the finite mixture model with prior distributions on all the parameters. It allows both numeric and nominal attributes, and uses the EM algorithm to estimate the parameters of the probability distributions to best fit the data. Because there is no guarantee that the EM algorithm converges to the global optimum, the procedure is repeated for several different sets of initial values. But that is not all. AutoClass considers different numbers of clusters and can consider different amounts of covariance and different underlying probability distribution types for the numeric attributes. This involves an additional, outer level of search. For example, it initially evaluates the log-likelihood for 2, 3, 5, 7, 10, 15, and 25 clusters: after that, it fits a log-normal distribution to the resulting data and randomly selects from it more values to try. As you might imagine, the overall algorithm is extremely computation intensive. In fact, the actual implementation starts with a prespecified time bound and continues to iterate as long as time allows. Give it longer and the results may be better!

A simpler way of selecting an appropriate model—e.g., to choose the number of clusters—is to compute the likelihood on a separate validation set that has not been used to fit the model. This can be repeated with multiple train-validation splits, just as in the case of classification models—e.g., with k-fold cross-validation. In practice, the ability to pick a model in this way is a big advantage of probabilistic clustering approaches compared to heuristic clustering methods.

Rather than showing just the most likely clustering to the user, it may be best to present all of them, weighted by probability. Recently, fully Bayesian techniques for *hierarchical* clustering have been developed that produce as output a probability distribution over possible hierarchical structures representing a dataset. Fig. 9.6 is a visualization, known as a *DensiTree*, that shows the set of all trees for a particular dataset in a triangular shape. The tree is best described in terms of its "clades," a biological term from the Greek *klados*, meaning *branch*, for a group of the same species that includes all ancestors. Here there are five clearly distinguishable clades. The first and fourth correspond to a single leaf, while the fifth has two leaves that are so distinct they might be considered clades in their own right. The second and third clades each have five leaves, and there is large uncertainty in their topology. Such visualizations make it easy for people to grasp the possible hierarchical clusterings of their data, at least in terms of the big picture.

CLUSTERING WITH CORRELATED ATTRIBUTES

Many clustering methods make the assumption of independence among the attributes. An exception is AutoClass, which does allow the user to specify in advance

FIGURE 9.6

DensiTree showing possible hierarchical clusterings of a given data set.

that two or more attributes are dependent and should be modeled with a joint probability distribution. (There are restrictions, however: nominal attributes may vary jointly, as may numeric attributes, but not both together. Moreover, missing values for jointly varying attributes are not catered for.) It may be advantageous to preprocess a data set to make the attributes more independent, using statistical techniques such as the independent component transform described in Section 8.3. Note that joint variation that is specific to particular classes will not be removed by such techniques; they only remove overall joint variation that runs across all classes.

If all attributes are continuous, more advanced clustering methods can help capture joint variation on a per-cluster basis, without having the number of parameters explode when there are many dimensions. As discussed above, if each covariance matrix in a Gaussian mixture model is "full" we need to estimate $n(n+1)/2$ parameters per mixture component. However, as we will see in Section 9.6, principal component analysis can be formulated as a probabilistic model, yielding probabilistic principal component analysis (PPCA), and approaches known as *mixtures of principal component analyzers* or *mixtures of factor analyzers* provide ways of using a much smaller number of parameters to represent large covariance matrices. In fact, the problem of estimating $n(n+1)/2$ parameters in a *full* covariance matrix can be transformed into the problem of estimating as few as $n \times d$ parameters in a *factorized covariance matrix*, where d

can be chosen to be small. The idea is to decompose the covariance matrix $\mathbf{M}$ into the form $\mathbf{M} = (\mathbf{W}\mathbf{W}^{\mathrm{T}} + \mathbf{D})$, where $\mathbf{W}$ is typically a long and skinny matrix of size $n \times d$, with as many rows as there are dimensions n of the input, and as many columns d as there are dimensions in the reduced space. Standard PCA corresponds to setting $\mathbf{D} = 0$; PPCA corresponds to using the form $\mathbf{D} = \sigma^2 \mathbf{I}$, where σ^2 is a scalar parameter and $\mathbf{I}$ is the identity matrix; and factor analysis corresponds to using a diagonal matrix for $\mathbf{D}$. The mixture model versions give each mixture component this type of factorization.

KERNEL DENSITY ESTIMATION

Mixture models can provide compact representations of probability distributions but do not necessarily fit the data well. In Chapter 4, Algorithms: the basic methods, we mentioned that when the form of a probability distribution is unknown, an approach known as *kernel density estimation* can be used to approximate the underlying distribution more accurately. This estimates the underlying true probability distribution $p(\mathbf{x})$ of data $\mathbf{x}_1, \mathbf{x}_2, \ldots, \mathbf{x}_n$ using a kernel density *estimator*, which can be written in the following general form

$$\hat{p}(\mathbf{x}) = \frac{1}{n} \sum_{i=1}^{n} K_{\sigma}(\mathbf{x}, \mathbf{x}_i) = \frac{1}{n\sigma} \sum_{i=1}^{n} K\left[\frac{\mathbf{x} - \mathbf{x}_i}{\sigma}\right],$$

where $K()$ is a nonnegative kernel function that integrates to one. Here, we use the notation $\hat{p}(\mathbf{x})$ to emphasize that this is an estimation of the true (unknown) distribution $p(\mathbf{x})$. The parameter $\sigma > 0$ is the *bandwidth* of the kernel, and serves as a form of smoothing parameter for the approximation. When the kernel function is defined using σ as a subscript it is known as a "scaled" kernel function and is given by $K_{\sigma}(\mathbf{x}) = 1/\sigma\, K(\mathbf{x}/\sigma)$. Estimating densities using kernels is also known as *Parzen window density estimation*.

Popular kernel functions include the Gaussian, box, triangle, and Epanechnikov kernels. The Gaussian kernel is popular because of its simple and attractive mathematical form. The box kernel implements a windowing function, whereas the triangle kernel implements a smoother, but still conceptually simple, window. The Epanechnikov kernel can be shown to be optimal under a mean squared error metric. The bandwidth parameter affects the smoothness of the estimator and the quality of the estimate. There are several methods for coming up with an appropriate bandwidth, ranging from heuristics motivated by theoretical results on known distributions to empirical choices based on validation sets and cross-validation techniques. Many software packages offer the choice between simple heuristic default values, bandwidth selection through cross-validation methods, and the use of plug-in estimators derived from further analytical analysis.

Kernel density estimation is closely related to k-nearest neighbor density estimation, and it can be shown that both techniques converge to the true distribution $p(\mathbf{x})$ as the amount of data grows towards infinity. This result, combined with the fact that they are easy to implement, makes kernel density estimators attractive methods in many situations.

Consider, e.g., the practical problem of finding outliers in data, given only positive or only negative examples (or perhaps with just a handful of examples of the other class). One effective approach is to do the best possible job of modeling the probability distribution of the data for the plentiful class using a kernel density estimator, and considering new data to which the model assigns low probability as outliers.

COMPARING PARAMETRIC, SEMIPARAMETRIC AND NONPARAMETRIC DENSITY MODELS FOR CLASSIFICATION

One might view a mixture model as intermediate between two extreme ways of modeling distributions by estimating probability densities. One extreme is a single simple parametric form such as the Gaussian distribution. It is easy to estimate the relevant parameters. However, data often arises from a far more complex distribution. Mixture models use two or more Gaussians to approximate the distribution. In the limit, at the other extreme, one Gaussian is used for each data point. This is kernel density estimation with a Gaussian kernel function.

Fig. 9.7 shows a visual example of this spectrum of models. A density estimate for each class of a 3-class classification problem has been created using three different techniques. Fig. 9.7A uses a single Gaussian distribution for each class, an approach that is often referred to as a "parametric" technique. Fig. 9.7B uses a Gaussian mixture model with two components per class, a "semiparametric" technique in which the number of Gaussians can be determined using a variety of methods. Fig. 9.7C uses a kernel density estimate with a Gaussian kernel on each example, a "nonparametric" method. Here the model complexity grows in proportion to the volume of data.

All three approaches define density models for each class, so Bayes' rule can be used to compute the posterior probability over all classes for any given input.

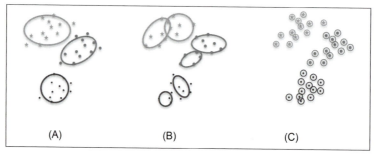

(A)   (B)   (C)

FIGURE 9.7

Probability contours for three types of model, all based on Gaussians.

In this way, density estimators can easily be transformed into classifiers. For simple parametric models, this is quick and easy. Kernel density estimators are guaranteed to converge to the true underlying distribution as the amount of data increases, which means that classifiers constructed from them have attractive properties. They share the computational disadvantages of nearest-neighbor classification, but, just as for nearest-neighbor classification, fast data structures exist that can make them applicable to large datasets.

Mixture models, the intermediate option, give control of model complexity without it growing with the amount of data. For this reason this approach has been standard practice for initial modeling in fields such as in speech recognition, which deal in large datasets. It allows speech recognizers to be created by first clustering data into groups, but in such a way that more complex models of temporal relationships can be added later using a hidden Markov model. (We will consider sequential and temporal probabilistic models, such as hidden Markov models, in Section 9.6.)

9.4 HIDDEN VARIABLE MODELS

We now move on to advanced learning algorithms that can infer new attributes in addition to the ones present in the data—so-called hidden (or latent) variables whose values cannot be observed. As noted in Section 9.3, a quantity called the *marginal likelihood* can be obtained by summing (or integrating) these variables out of the model. It is important not to confuse random variables with observations or hard assignments of random variables. We write $p(x_i = \tilde{x}_i) = p(\tilde{x}_i)$ to denote the probability of the random variable x_i associated with instance i taking the value represented by the observation $\tilde{x}_i$. We use h_i to represent a hidden discrete random variable, and z_i to denote a hidden continuous one. Then, given a model with observations given by $\tilde{x}_i$, the marginal likelihood is

$$L(\theta; \tilde{x}_1, \tilde{x}_2, \ldots, \tilde{x}_n) = \prod_{i=1}^{n} p(\tilde{x}_i; \theta) = \prod_{i=1}^{n} \int_{z_i} \sum_{h_i} p(\tilde{x}_i, z_i, h_i; \theta) dz_i,$$

where the sum is taken over all possible discrete values of h_i and the integral is taken over the entire domain of z_i. The end result of all this integrating and summing is a single number—a scalar quantity—that gives the marginal likelihood for any value of the parameters.

Maximum likelihood based learning for hidden variable models can sometimes be done using marginal likelihood, just as when no hidden variables are present, but the additional variables usually affect the parameterization used to define the model. In fact, these additional variables are often very important: *they are used to represent precisely the things we wish to mine from our data*, be it clusters, topics in a text mining problem, or the factors that underlie variation in the data. By treating parameters as random variables and using functions that are easy to manipulate, marginal likelihoods can also be used to define sophisticated

Bayesian models that involve integrating over parameters. This can create models that are less prone to overfitting.

EXPECTED LOG-LIKELIHOODS AND EXPECTED GRADIENTS

It is not always possible to obtain a form for the marginal likelihood that is easy to optimize. An alternative is to work with another quantity, the *expected log-likelihood*. Writing the set of all observed data as $\tilde{X}$, the set of all discrete hidden variables as H, and the set of all continuous hidden variables as Z, the expected log-likelihood can be expressed as

$$E[\log L(\theta; \tilde{X}, Z, H)]_{P(H,Z|\tilde{X};\theta)} = \sum_{i=1}^{n}\left[\int_{z_i}\sum_{h_i} p(z_i, h_i|\tilde{x}_i; \theta)\log p(\tilde{x}_i, z_i, h_i; \theta)dz_i\right]$$

$$= E\left[\sum_{i=1}^{n}\log p(\tilde{x}_i, z_i, h_i; \theta)\right]_{p(z_i, h_i|\tilde{x}_i;\theta)}.$$

Here, $E[.]_{p(z_i,h_i|\tilde{x}_i;\theta)}$ means that an expectation is performed under the posterior distribution over hidden variables: $p(z_i, h_i|\tilde{x}_i; \theta)$.

It turns out that there is a close relationship between the log marginal likelihood and the expected log-likelihood: the *derivative* of the expected log-likelihood with respect to the parameters of the model equals the *derivative* of the log marginal likelihood. The following derivation, based on applying the chain rule from calculus and considering a single training example for simplicity, demonstrates why this is true:

$$\frac{\partial}{\partial\theta}\log p(\tilde{x}_i; \theta) = \frac{1}{p(\tilde{x}_i; \theta)}\frac{\partial}{\partial\theta}\int_{z_i}\sum_{h_i}p(\tilde{x}_i, z_i, h_i; \theta)dz_i$$

$$= \int_{z_i}\sum_{h_i}\frac{p(\tilde{x}_i, z_i, h_i; \theta)}{p(\tilde{x}_i; \theta)}\frac{\partial}{\partial\theta}\log p(\tilde{x}_i, z_i, h_i; \theta)dz_i$$

$$= \int_{z_i}\sum_{h_i}p(z_i, h_i|\tilde{x}_i; \theta)\frac{\partial}{\partial\theta}\log p(\tilde{x}_i, z_i, h_i; \theta)dz_i$$

$$= E\left[\frac{\partial}{\partial\theta}\log p(\tilde{x}_i, z_i, h_i; \theta)\right]_{p(z_i,h_i|\tilde{x}_i;\theta)}$$

The final expression is the expectation of the derivative of the log joint likelihood. This relationship is with respect to the derivative of the log marginal likelihood and the expected derivative of the log joint likelihood. However, it is also possible to establish a direct relationship between the log marginal and expected log joint probabilities. The variational analysis in Appendix A.2 shows that

$$\log P(\tilde{x}_i; \theta) = E[\log p(\tilde{x}_i, z_i, h_i; \theta)]_{p(z_i,h_i|\tilde{x}_i;\theta)} + H[p(z_i, h_i|\tilde{x}_i; \theta)],$$

where $H[.]$ is the entropy.

As a consequence of this analysis, to perform learning in a probability model with hidden variables, the marginal likelihood can be optimized using gradient ascent by instead computing and following the gradient of the expected log-likelihood, assuming that the posterior distribution over hidden variables can be computed. This prompts a general approach to learning in a hidden variable model based on following the expected gradient. This can be decomposed into three steps: (1) a **P-step**, which computes the posterior over hidden variables; (2) an **E-step**, which computes the expectation of the gradient given the posterior; and (3) a **G-step**, which uses gradient-based optimization to maximize the objective function with respect to the parameters.

THE EXPECTATION MAXIMIZATION ALGORITHM

Using the expected log joint probability as a key quantity for learning in a probability model with hidden variables is better known in the context of the celebrated "expectation maximization" or EM algorithm, which we encountered in "The expectation maximization algorithm for a mixture of Gaussians" section. We discuss the general EM formulation next. Section 9.6 gives a concrete example comparing and contrasting the expected gradient approach and the EM approach, using the probabilistic formulation of principal component analysis.

The EM algorithm follows the expected gradient approach. However, EM is often used with models in which the M-step can be computed *in closed form*—in other words, when exact parameter updates can be found by setting the derivative of the expected log-likelihood with respect to the parameters to 0. These updates often take the same form as the simple maximum likelihood estimates that one would use to compute the parameters of a distribution, and are essentially just modified forms of the equations used for observed data that involve averages weighted over the posterior distribution in place of observed counts.

The EM algorithm consists of two steps: (1) an **E-step** that computes the expectations used in the expected log-likelihood and (2) an **M-step** in which the objective is maximized—typically using a closed-form parameter update.

In the following, we assume that we have only discrete hidden variables **H**. The probability of the observed data $\tilde{X}$ can be maximized by maximizing the log-likelihood $\log P(\tilde{X}; \theta)$ of the parameters θ arising from an underlying latent variable model $P(X, H; \theta)$ as follows. Initialize the parameters as θ^{old} and repeat the following steps, where convergence is measured in terms of either the change to the log-likelihood or the degree of change to the parameters:

1. **E-step**: Compute required expectations involving $P(H|X; \theta^{\text{old}})$
2. **M-step**: Find $\theta^{\text{new}} = \arg\max_\theta \left[\sum_H P(H|X; \theta^{\text{old}}) \log P(X, H; \theta) \right]$
3. If the algorithm has not converged, set $\theta^{\text{old}} = \theta^{\text{new}}$ and return to step 1.

Note that the *M*-step corresponds to maximizing the expected log-likelihood. Although discrete hidden variables are used above, the approach generalizes to continuous ones.

For many latent variable models—Gaussian mixture models, PPCA, and hidden Markov models—the required posterior distributions can be computed exactly, which accounts for their popularity. However, for many other probabilistic models it is simply not possible to compute an exact posterior distribution. This can easily happen with multiple hidden random variables, because the posterior needed in the E-step is the joint posterior of the hidden variables. There is a vast literature on the subject of how to compute approximations to the true posterior distribution over hidden variables in more complex models.

APPLYING THE EXPECTATION MAXIMIZATION ALGORITHM TO BAYESIAN NETWORKS

Bayesian networks capture statistical dependencies between attributes using an intuitive graphical structure, and the EM algorithm can easily be applied to such networks. Consider a Bayesian network with a number of discrete random variables, some of which are observed while others are not. Its marginal probability, in which hidden variables have been integrated out, can be maximized by maximizing the expected log joint probability over the posterior distribution of the hidden variables given the observed data—the expected log-likelihood.

For a network consisting of only discrete variables, this means that the **E-step** involves computing a distribution over hidden variables $\{H\}$ given observed variables $\{\tilde{X}\}$ or $P(\{H\}|\{\tilde{X}\}; \theta^{current})$. If the network is a tree, this can be computed efficiently using the sum-product algorithm, which is explained in Section 9.6. If not, it can be computed efficiently using the junction tree algorithm. However, if the model is large, exact inference algorithms may be intractable, in which case a variational approximation or sampling procedure can be used to approximate the distribution.

The **M-step** seeks

$$\theta^{new} = \arg\max_{\theta} \left[\sum_{\{H\}} P(\{H\}|\{\tilde{X}\}; \theta^{old}) \log P(\{\tilde{X}\}, \{H\}; \theta) \right].$$

Recall that the log joint probability given by a Bayesian network decomposes into a sum over functions of subsets of variables. Notice also that the expression above involves an expectation using the joint conditional distribution or posterior over hidden variables. Using the EM algorithm, taking the derivative with respect to any given parameter leaves just terms that involve the marginal expectation over the distribution of variables that participate in the function for the gradient of the relevant parameter. This means, e.g., that to find the unconditional probability of an unobserved variable A in a network, it is necessary to determine the parameters θ_A of $P(A; \theta_A)$ for which

$$\frac{\partial}{\partial \theta_A} \left[\sum_{A} P(A|\{\tilde{X}\}; \theta^{old}) \log P(A; \theta_A) \right] = 0,$$

along with the further constraint that the probabilities in the discrete distribution sum to 1. This can be achieved using a Lagrange multiplier (Appendix A.2 gives an example of using this technique to estimate a discrete distribution). Setting the derivative of the constrained objective to 0 gives this *closed form* result:

$$\theta_{A=a}^{\text{new}} = P(A = a) = \frac{1}{N} \sum_{i=1}^{N} P(A_i = a | \{\tilde{X}\}_i; \theta^{\text{old}}).$$

In other words, the unconditional probability distribution is estimated in the same way in which it would be computed if the variables A_i had been observed, but with each observation replaced by its probability. Applying this procedure to the entire data set is tantamount to replacing observed counts with expected counts under the current model settings. If many examples have the same configuration, the distribution need only be computed once, and multiplied by the number of times that configuration has been seen.

Estimating entries in the network's conditional probability tables also has an intuitive form. To estimate the conditional probability of unobserved random variable B given unobserved random variable A in a Bayesian network, simply compute their joint (posterior) probability and the marginal (posterior) probability of A for each example. Just as when the data is observed, the update equation is

$$P(B = b | A = a) = \frac{\sum_{i=1}^{N} P(A_i = a, B_i = b | \{\tilde{X}\}_i; \theta^{\text{old}})}{\sum_{i=1}^{N} P(A_i = a | \{\tilde{X}\}_i; \theta^{\text{old}})}.$$

This is just a ratio of the expected numbers of counts. If some of the variables are fully observed, the expression can be adapted by replacing the inferred probabilities by observed values—effectively assigning the observations a probability of 1. Furthermore, if variable B has multiple parents, A can be replaced by the set of parents.

9.5 BAYESIAN ESTIMATION AND PREDICTION

If there is reason to believe that a certain parameter has been drawn from a particular distribution, we can adopt a more Bayesian perspective. A common strategy is to employ a hyperparameter α to represent that distribution. Define the *joint distribution* of data and parameters as

$$p(x_1, x_2, \ldots, x_n, \theta; \alpha) = \prod_{i=1}^{n} p(x_i | \theta) p(\theta; \alpha)$$

Bayesian-style predictions use a quantity known as the *posterior predictive distribution*, which consists of the probability model for a new observation marginalized over the posterior probability inferred for the parameters given the observations so far. Again using a notation that explicitly differentiates variables x_i from their observations $\tilde{x}_i$, the posterior predictive distribution is

$$p(x_{\text{new}}|\tilde{x}_1, \tilde{x}_2, \ldots, \tilde{x}_n; \alpha) = \int_\theta p(x_{\text{new}}|\theta)p(\theta|\tilde{x}_1, \tilde{x}_2, \ldots, \tilde{x}_n; \alpha)d\,\theta.$$

Given a Bayesian model that uses distributions over parameters, so-called "empirical Bayesian" methods can be employed to find a suitable value for the hyperparameter α. One such approach is obtained by maximizing the log marginal likelihood with respect to the model's hyperparameters:

$$\alpha_{\text{MML}} = \arg\max_\alpha \left[\log \int \prod_{i=1}^n p(x_i|\theta)p(\theta; \alpha)d\theta \right].$$

The remainder of this section demonstrates several techniques for creating complex structured probabilistic models.

PROBABILISTIC INFERENCE METHODS

With complex probability models—and even with some seemingly simple ones—computing quantities such as posterior distributions, marginal distributions, and the maximum probability configuration, often require specialized methods to achieve results efficiently—even approximate ones. This is the field of *probabilistic inference*. Below we review some widely used probabilistic inference methods, including probability propagation, sampling and simulated annealing, and variational inference.

Probability propagation

Structured probability models like the Bayesian networks and Markov random fields discussed in Section 9.6 decompose a joint probability distribution into a factorized structure consisting of products of functions over subsets of variables. Then the task of computing marginal probabilities to find a maximum-probability configuration can be computationally demanding using brute force computation. In some cases even a naïve approach is completely infeasible in practice. However, it is sometimes possible to take advantage of the model's structure to perform inference more efficiently. When Bayesian networks and related graphical models have an underlying tree connectivity structure, then *belief propagation* (also known as *probability propagation*) based on the sum-product and max-product algorithms presented in Section 9.6 can be applied to compute exact marginals, and hence the most probable model configuration.

Sampling, simulated annealing, and iterated conditional modes

With fully Bayesian methods that use distributions on parameters, or graphical models with cyclic structures, sampling methods are popular in both statistics and machine learning. Markov chain Monte Carlo methods are widely used to generate random samples from probability distributions that are difficult to compute. For example, as we have seen above, posterior distributions are often needed for expectations required during learning, but in many settings these can be difficult to compute. *Gibbs sampling* is a popular special case of the more general Metropolis–Hastings algorithm that allows one to generate samples from a joint distribution even when the true distribution is a complex continuous function. These samples can then be used to approximate expectations of interest, and also to approximate marginal distributions of subsets of variables by simply ignoring parts pertaining to other variables.

Gibbs sampling is conceptually very simple. Assign an initial set of states to the random variables of interest. With n random variables, this initial assignment or set of samples can be written $x_1 = x_1^{(0)}, \ldots, x_n = x_n^{(0)}$. We then iteratively update each variable by *sampling* from its conditional distribution given the others:

$$x_1^{(i+1)} \sim p(x_1 | x_2 = x_2^{(i)}, \ldots, x_n = x_n^{(i)}),$$
$$\vdots$$
$$x_n^{(i+1)} \sim p(x_n | x_1 = x_1^{(i)}, \ldots, x_{n-1} = x_{n-1}^{(i)}).$$

In practice, these conditional distributions are often easy to compute. Furthermore, the idea of a "Markov blanket" introduced in Section 9.2 can often be used to reduce the number of variables necessary, because conditionals in structured models may depend on a much smaller subset of the variables.

To ensure an unbiased sample it is necessary to cycle through the data discarding samples in a process known as "burn-in." The idea is to allow the Markov chain defined by the sampling procedure to approach its stationary distribution, and it can be shown that in the limit one will indeed obtain a sample from this distribution, and that the distribution corresponds to the underlying joint probability we wish to sample from. There is considerable theory concerning how much burn-in is required, but in practice it is common to discard samples arising from the first 100–1000 cycles. Sometimes, if more than one sample configuration is desired, averages are taken over k additional configurations of the sampler obtained after periods of about 100 cycles. We see how this procedure is used in practice in Section 9.6, under latent Dirichlet allocation.

Simulated annealing is a procedure that seeks an approximate most probable configuration or explanation. It adapts the Gibbs sampling procedure, described above, to include an iteration-dependent "temperature" term t_i. Starting with an initial assignment $x_1 = x_1^{(0)}, \ldots, x_n = x_n^{(0)}$, subsequent samples take the form

$$x_1^{(i+1)} \sim p(x_1 | x_2 = x_2^{(i)}, \ldots, x_n = x_n^{(i)})^{\frac{1}{t_i}},$$
$$\vdots$$
$$x_n^{(i+1)} \sim p(x_n | x_1 = x_1^{(i)}, \ldots, x_{n-1} = x_{n-1}^{(i)})^{\frac{1}{t_i}},$$

Where the temperature is decreased at each iteration: $t_{i+1} < t_i$. If the schedule is slow enough, this process will converge to the true global minimum. But therein lies the catch: the temperature may have to decrease very slowly. However, this is often possible, particularly with an efficient implementation of the sampler.

Another well-known algorithm is the *iterated conditional modes* procedure, consisting of iterations of the form

$$x_1^{(i+1)} \sim \arg\max_{x_1} p(x_1 | x_2 = x_2^{(i)}, \ldots, x_n = x_n^{(i)}),$$

$$\vdots$$

$$x_n^{(i+1)} \sim \arg\max_{x_n} p(x_n | x_1 = x_1^{(i)}, \ldots, x_{n-1} = x_{n-1}^{(i)}).$$

This can be very fast, but prone to local minima. It can be useful when constructing more interesting graphical models and optimizing them quickly in an analogous, greedy way.

Variational inference

Rather than sampling from a distribution that is difficult to manipulate, the distribution can be approximated by a simpler, more tractable, function. Suppose we have a probability model with a set H of hidden variables and a set X of observed variables. Let $p = p(H|\tilde{X}; \theta)$ be the exact posterior distribution of the model and $q = q(H|\tilde{X}; \Phi)$ be an approximation to it, where Φ is a set of so-called "variational parameters." Variational methods for probability models commonly involve defining a simple form for q that makes it easy to optimize Φ in a way that brings q closer to p. The theory of variation EM optimizes latent variable models by maximizing a lower bound on the log marginal likelihood. This so-called "variational bound" is described in Appendix A.2, where we see how the EM algorithm can be viewed through a variational analysis. This allows one to create EM algorithms using either exact or approximate posterior distributions. While statisticians often prefer sampling methods to variational ones, variational methods are popular in machine learning because they can be faster—and can also be combined with sampling methods.

9.6 GRAPHICAL MODELS AND FACTOR GRAPHS

Bayesian networks give an intuitive picture of a probabilistic model that corresponds directly with how we have decided to decompose the joint probability of the random variables representing attributes into a product of conditional and unconditional probability distributions. Mixture models, such as the Gaussian mixture models of Section 9.3, are alternative ways of approximating joint distributions. This section shows how such models can be illustrated using Bayesian networks, and introduces a generalization of Bayesian networks, the so-called "plate notation," that allows one to visualize the result of techniques that treat parameters as random quantities. A further generalization, "factor graphs," can represent and visualize an even wider class of probabilistic graphical models. As before, we view attributes as random variables and instances as observations of them; we also represent things like the label of a cluster by a random variable in a graph.

GRAPHICAL MODELS AND PLATE NOTATION

Consider a simple two-cluster Gaussian mixture model. It can be illustrated in the form of a Bayesian network with a binary random variable C for the cluster membership and a continuous random variable x for the real-valued attribute. In the mixture model, the joint distribution $P(C, x)$ is the product of the prior $P(C)$ and the conditional probability distribution $P(x|C)$. This structure is illustrated by the Bayesian network in Fig. 9.8A, where for each state of C a different Gaussian is used for the conditional distribution of the continuous variable x.

Multiple Bayesian networks can be used to visualize the underlying joint likelihood that results when parameter estimation is performed. The probability model for N observations $x_1 = x_1$, $x_2 = x_2$, and $x_N = x_N$ can be conceptualized as N Bayesian networks, one for each variable x_i observed or instantiated to the value x_i. Fig. 9.8B illustrates this, using shaded nodes to indicate which random variables are observed.

A "plate" is simply a box around a Bayesian network that denotes a certain number of replications of it. The plate in Fig. 9.8C indicates $i = 1,\ldots,N$ networks, each with an observed value for x_i. Plate notation captures a model for the joint probability of the entire data with a simple picture.

Bayesian networks, and more complex models comprising plates of Bayesian networks, are known as *generative models* because the probabilistic definition of the model can be used to randomly generate data governed by the probability distribution that the model represents. Bayesian hierarchical modeling involves defining a hierarchy of levels for the *parameters* of a model and using the rules of probability arising from the application of Bayesian methods to infer the parameter values given observed data. These can be drawn with graphical models in which both random variables and parameters are treated as random quantities. The section on latent Dirichlet allocation below gives an example of this technique.

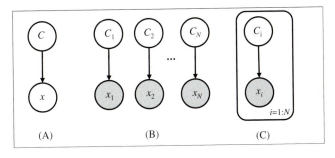

(A)   (B)   (C)

FIGURE 9.8

(A) Bayesian network for a mixture model; (B) multiple copies of the Bayesian network, one for each observation; (C) plate notation version of (B).

PROBABILISTIC PRINCIPAL COMPONENT ANALYSIS

Principal component analysis can be viewed as the consequence of performing parameter estimation in a special type of linear Gaussian hidden variable model. This connects the traditional view of this standard technique, presented in Chapter 8, Data transformations, with the probabilistic formulation discussed here, and leads to more advanced methods based on Boltzmann machines and autoencoders that are introduced in Chapter 10, Deep learning. The probabilistic formulation also helps deal with missing values. The underlying idea is to represent data as being generated by a Gaussian distributed continuous hidden latent variable that is linearly transformed under a Gaussian model. As a result, the principal components of a given data set correspond to an underlying factorized covariance model for a corresponding multivariate Gaussian distribution model for the data. This factorized model becomes apparent when the hidden variables of the underlying latent variable model are integrated out.

More specifically, a set of hidden variables is used to represent the input data in a space of reduced dimensionality. Each dimension corresponds to an independent random variable drawn from a Gaussian distribution with zero mean and unit variance. Let $\mathbf{x}$ be a random variable corresponding to the d-dimensional vectors of observed data, and $\mathbf{h}$ be a k-dimensional vector of hidden random variables. k is typically smaller than d (but need not be). Then the underlying joint probability model has this linear Gaussian form:

$$p(\mathbf{x}, \mathbf{h}) = p(\mathbf{x}|\mathbf{h})p(\mathbf{h})$$
$$= N(\mathbf{x}; \mathbf{Wh} + \boldsymbol{\mu}, \mathbf{D})N(\mathbf{h}; \mathbf{0}, \mathbf{I}),$$

where the zero vector $\mathbf{0}$ and identity matrix $\mathbf{I}$ denote the mean and covariance matrix for the Gaussian distribution used for $p(\mathbf{h})$, and $p(\mathbf{x}|\mathbf{h})$ is Gaussian with mean $\mathbf{Wh} + \boldsymbol{\mu}$ and a diagonal covariance matrix $\mathbf{D}$. (The expression for the mean is where the term "linear" in "linear Gaussian" comes from.) The mean $\boldsymbol{\mu}$ is included as a parameter, but it would be zero if we first mean-centered the data. Fig. 9.9A shows a Bayesian network for PPCA; it reveals intuitions about the

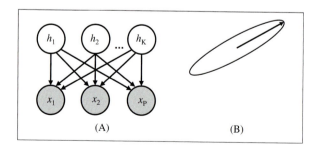

(A)   (B)

FIGURE 9.9

(A) Bayesian network for probabilistic PCA; (B) equal-probability contour for a Gaussian distribution along with its covariance matrix's principal eigenvector.

probabilistic interpretation of principal component analysis based on hidden variables that will help in understanding other models discussed later.

Probabilistic PCA is a form of generative model, and Fig. 9.9A visualizes the associated underlying generative process. Data is generated by sampling each dimension of **h** from an independent Gaussian distribution and using the matrix $\mathbf{Wh} + \boldsymbol{\mu}$ to project this lower dimensional representation of the data into the observed, higher dimensional representation. Noise, specified by the diagonal covariance matrix **D**, is added separately to each dimension of the higher dimensional representation.

If the noise associated with the conditional distribution of **x** given **h** is the same in each dimension (i.e., isotropic) and infinitesimally small (such that $\mathbf{D} = \lim_{\sigma^2 \to 0} \sigma^2 \mathbf{I}$), a set of estimation equations can be derived that give the same principal components as those obtained by conventional principal component analysis. Restricting the covariance matrix **D** to be diagonal produces a model known as *factor analysis*). If **D** is isotropic (i.e., has the form $\mathbf{D} = \sigma^2 \mathbf{I}$), then after optimizing the model and learning σ^2 the columns of **W** will be scaled and rotated principal eigenvectors of the covariance matrix of the data. The contours of equal probability for a multivariate Gaussian distribution can be drawn with an ellipse whose principal axis corresponds to the principal eigenvector of the covariance matrix, as illustrated in Fig. 9.9B.

Because of the nice properties of Gaussian distributions, the marginal distributions of **x** in these models are also Gaussian, with parameters that can be computed *analytically* using simple algebraic expressions. For example, a model with $\mathbf{D} = \sigma^2 \mathbf{I}$ has $p(\mathbf{x}) = N(\mathbf{x}; \boldsymbol{\mu}, \mathbf{WW}^{\mathsf{T}} + \sigma^2 \mathbf{I})$, which is the marginal distribution of **x** under the joint probability model, obtained by integrating out the uncertainty associated with **h** from the joint distribution $p(\mathbf{x}, \mathbf{h})$ defined earlier. Integrating out the hidden variables **h** from a PPCA model defines a Gaussian distribution whose covariance matrix **M** has the special form $\mathbf{WW}^{\mathsf{T}} + \mathbf{D}$. Appendix A.2 relates this factorization to an eigenvector analysis of the covariance matrix, resulting in the standard matrix factorization view of principal component analysis.

Inference with PPCA

As a result of the underlying linear Gaussian formulation, various other quantities needed for making inferences and performing parameter estimation can also be obtained analytically. For example, given $\mathbf{M} = (\mathbf{WW}^{T} + \sigma^2 \mathbf{I})$, the *posterior distribution* for **h** can be obtained from Bayes' rule, along with some Gaussian identities given in Appendix A.2. The posterior can be written

$$p(\mathbf{h}|\mathbf{x}) = N(\mathbf{h}; \mathbf{M}^{-1}\mathbf{W}^{\mathsf{T}}(\mathbf{x} - \boldsymbol{\mu}), \sigma^2 \mathbf{M}^{-1}). \qquad (9.1)$$

Once the model parameters have been estimated, the mean of the posterior for a new example can be calculated, which can then serve as a reduced dimensional representation for it. The mathematics (though still perhaps daunting) is greatly simplified by the fact that marginalizing, multiplying and dividing

Gaussians distributions produces other Gaussian distributions that are functions of observed values, mean vectors, and covariance matrices. In fact, many more sophisticated methods and models for data analysis rely on the ease with which key quantities can be computed when the underlying model is based on linear Gaussian forms.

Marginal log-likelihood for PPCA

Given a probabilistic model with hidden variables, the Bayesian philosophy is to integrate out the uncertainly associated with them. As we have just seen, linear Gaussian models make it possible to obtain the marginal probability of the data, $p(\mathbf{x})$, which takes the form of a Gaussian distribution. Then, the learning problem is tantamount to maximizing the probability of the given data under the model. The probability that variable $\mathbf{x}$ is observed to be $\tilde{\mathbf{x}}$ is indicated by $p(\tilde{\mathbf{x}}) = p(\mathbf{x} = \tilde{\mathbf{x}})$. The log (marginal) likelihood of the parameters given all the observed data $\tilde{\mathbf{X}}$ can be maximized using this objective function:

$$L(\tilde{\mathbf{X}}; \theta) = \log \left[\prod_{i=1}^{N} P(\tilde{\mathbf{x}}_i; \theta) \right] = \sum_{i=1}^{N} \log[N(\tilde{\mathbf{x}}_i; \mu, \mathbf{W}\mathbf{W}^{\mathsf{T}} + \sigma^2 \mathbf{I})],$$

where the parameters $\theta = \{\mathbf{W}, \mu, \sigma^2\}$, consist of a matrix, a vector, and a scalar. We will assume henceforth that the data has been mean-centered: $\mu = \mathbf{0}$. (However, when creating generalizations of this approach there can be advantages to retaining the mean as an explicit parameter of the model.)

Expected log-likelihood for PPCA

Section 9.4 showed that the derivative of the log marginal likelihood of a hidden variable model with respect to its parameters equals the derivative of the expected log joint likelihood, where the expectation is taken with respect to the exact posterior distribution over the model's hidden variables. The underlying Gaussian formulation of PPCA means that an exact posterior can be computed, which provides an alternative way to optimize the model based on the expected log-likelihood. The log joint probability of all data and all hidden variables $\mathbf{H}$ under the model is

$$L(\tilde{\mathbf{X}}, \mathbf{H}; \theta) = \log \left[\prod_{i=1}^{N} p(\tilde{\mathbf{x}}_i, \mathbf{h}_i; \theta) \right] = \sum_{i=1}^{N} \log[p(\tilde{\mathbf{x}}_i | \mathbf{h}_i; \mathbf{W}) p(\mathbf{h}_i; \sigma^2)].$$

Notice that while the data $\tilde{\mathbf{X}}$ is observed, the hidden variables $\mathbf{h}_i$ are unknown, so for a given parameter value $\theta = \tilde{\theta}$ this expression does not evaluate to a scalar quantity. It can be converted into a scalar-valued function using the expected log-likelihood, which can then be optimized. As we saw in Section 9.4, the expected log-likelihood of the data using the posterior distribution of each example for the expectations is given by

$$E[L(\tilde{\mathbf{X}}, \mathbf{H}; \theta)]_{p(\mathbf{H}|\tilde{\mathbf{X}})} = \sum_{i=1}^{N} E[\log[p(\tilde{\mathbf{x}}_i, \mathbf{h}_i; \theta)]]_{p(\mathbf{h}_i|\tilde{\mathbf{X}}_i)}.$$

Expected gradient for PPCA

Gradient descent can be used to learn the parameter matrix $\mathbf{W}$ using the expected log-likelihood as the objective, an example of the expected gradient approach discussed in Section 9.4. The gradient is a sum over examples, and a fairly lengthy derivation shows that each example contributes the following term to this sum:

$$\frac{\partial}{\partial \mathbf{W}} E[L(\tilde{\mathbf{x}}, \mathbf{h})] = E[\mathbf{W}\mathbf{h}\mathbf{h}^{\mathrm{T}}] - E[\tilde{\mathbf{x}}\mathbf{h}^{T}] \tag{9.2}$$

$$= \mathbf{W}E[\mathbf{h}\mathbf{h}^{\mathrm{T}}] - \tilde{\mathbf{x}}E[\mathbf{h}]^{T},$$

where in all cases the expectations are taken with respect to the posterior, $p(\mathbf{h}|\tilde{\mathbf{x}})$, using the current settings of the model parameters. This partial derivative has a natural interpretation as a difference between two expectations. The second term creates a matrix the same size as $\mathbf{W}$, consisting of an observation and the hidden variable representation. The first term simply replaces the observation with a similar $\mathbf{W}\mathbf{h}$ factor, which could be thought of as the model's prediction of the input. (We will revisit this interpretation when we examine conditional probability models in Section 9.7 and restricted Boltzmann machines in Section 10.5.)

This shows that the model reconstructs the data as it ascends the gradient. If the optimization converges to a model that perfectly reconstructs the data, the derivative in (9.2) will be zero. Other probabilistic models examined show similar forms for the gradients for key parameters, consisting of differences of expectations—but different types of expectation are involved.

To compute these quantities, note that the expected value $E[\mathbf{h}] = \mathbf{M}^{-1}\mathbf{W}^{\mathrm{T}}(\mathbf{x} - \boldsymbol{\mu})$ can be obtained from the mean of the posterior distribution for each example given by (9.1). The $E[\mathbf{h}\mathbf{h}^{\mathrm{T}}]$ term can be found using the fact that $E[\mathbf{h}\mathbf{h}^{\mathrm{T}}] = \text{cov}[\mathbf{h}] + E[\mathbf{h}]E[\mathbf{h}]^{\mathrm{T}}$, where $\text{cov}[\mathbf{h}]$ is the posterior covariance matrix, which we also know from (9.1) is $\sigma^2\mathbf{M}^{-1}$.

EM for PPCA

An alternative to gradient ascent using the expected log-likelihood is to formulate the model as an expected gradient-based learning procedure using the classical EM algorithm. The M-step update can be obtained by setting the derivative in (9.2) to zero and solving for $\mathbf{W}$. This can be expressed in closed form: $\mathbf{W}$ in the first term is independent of the expectation and can therefore be moved out of the expectation and terms re-arranged into a closed-form M-step. In a zero mean model with $\mathbf{D} = \sigma^2\mathbf{I}$ and some small value for σ^2, the E and M steps of the PPCA EM algorithm can be rewritten

E-Step: $E[\mathbf{h}_i] = \mathbf{M}^{-1}\mathbf{W}^{\mathrm{T}}\tilde{\mathbf{x}}_i$, $E[\mathbf{h}_i\mathbf{h}_i^{T}] = \sigma^2\mathbf{M}^{-1} + E[\mathbf{h}_i]E[\mathbf{h}_i^{T}]$,

M-Step: $\mathbf{W}^{\text{New}} = \left[\sum_{i=1}^{N} \tilde{\mathbf{x}}_i \, E[\mathbf{h}_i]^{\mathrm{T}}\right]\left[\sum_{i=1}^{N} E[\mathbf{h}_i\mathbf{h}_i^{\mathrm{T}}]\right]^{-1}$,

where all expectations are taken with respect to each example's posterior distribution, $p(\mathbf{h}_i|\tilde{\mathbf{x}}_i)$, and, as above, $\mathbf{M} = (\mathbf{W}\mathbf{W}^{T} + \sigma^2\mathbf{I})$.

The EM algorithm can be further simplified by taking the limit as σ^2 approaches zero. This is the *zero input noise* case, and it implies $\mathbf{M} = \mathbf{W}\mathbf{W}^T$. Define the matrix $\mathbf{Z} = E[\mathbf{H}]$, each column of which contains the expected vector from $P(\mathbf{h}_i|\tilde{\mathbf{x}}_i)$ for one of the hidden variables $\mathbf{h}_i$, so that $E[\mathbf{H}\mathbf{H}^T] = E[\mathbf{H}]E[\mathbf{H}^T] = \mathbf{Z}\mathbf{Z}^T$. This yields simple and elegant equations for the E and M steps:

E-Step: $\mathbf{Z} = E[\mathbf{H}] = (\mathbf{W}^T\mathbf{W})^{-1}\mathbf{W}^T\tilde{\mathbf{X}}$,
M-Step: $\mathbf{W}^{\text{New}} = \tilde{\mathbf{X}}\mathbf{Z}^T[\mathbf{Z}\mathbf{Z}^T]^{-1}$.

where both equations operate on the entire data matrix $\tilde{\mathbf{X}}$.

The probabilistic formulation of principal component analysis permits traditional likelihoods to be defined, which supports maximum likelihood based learning and probabilistic inference. This in turn leads to natural methods for dealing with missing data. It also leads on to the other models discussed below.

LATENT SEMANTIC ANALYSIS

Chapter 8, Data transformations, introduced principal component analysis, which, as we have seen above, can be viewed as a form of linear Gaussian latent variable model. We now discuss an influential early form of data driven document analysis known as "latent semantic analysis" (LSA), which uses singular value decomposition to decompose each document in a collection into *topics*. If documents and terms are projected into the topic space, comparisons can be made that capture semantic structure in the documents resulting from the cooccurrence of words across the collection. Characterizing documents in this way is called "latent semantic indexing." Probabilistic LSA (pLSA) addresses similar goals but applies a statistical model based on multinomial distributions. Latent Dirichlet allocation is a related model that uses a hierarchical Bayesian approach in which Dirichlet priors are placed on the underlying multinomial distributions.

To motivate the introduction of these techniques, let us examine the relationship between the original LSA method and singular value decomposition. Imagine a term by document matrix $\mathbf{X}$, with t rows and d columns, each element of which contains the number of times the word associated with its row occurs in the document associated with its column. LSA decomposes $\mathbf{X}$ into a product $\mathbf{X} = \mathbf{U}\mathbf{S}\mathbf{V}^T$, where $\mathbf{U}$ and $\mathbf{V}$ have orthogonal columns and $\mathbf{S}$ is a diagonal matrix containing the singular values, which are conventionally sorted in decreasing order. This factorization is known as the singular value decomposition, and has the property that for every value k, if all but the k largest singular values are discarded the data matrix can be reconstructed in a way that is optimal in a least squares sense. For any given approximation level k, we can write $\mathbf{X} \approx \tilde{\mathbf{X}} = \mathbf{U}_k\mathbf{S}_k\mathbf{V}_k^T$.

Fig. 9.10 illustrates how this works. The $\mathbf{U}_k$ matrix can be thought of as k orthogonal "topics" that are combined according to the appropriate proportions for each document, encoded in the $k \times d$ matrix $\mathbf{V}_k^T$. The matrix $\mathbf{A} = \mathbf{S}_k\mathbf{V}_k^T$ represents

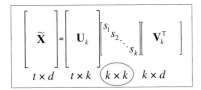

FIGURE 9.10

The singular value decomposition of a t by d matrix.

the activity level of the topics associated with each document. Thus the learning phase of LSA simply performs singular value decomposition on the data matrix.

The dot (or scalar) product of any two columns of the approximated data matrix $\tilde{\mathbf{X}}$ provides a measure of the similarity of term usage in the two documents. The dot products between all pairs of documents used to compute the singular value decomposition are

$$\tilde{\mathbf{X}}^T \tilde{\mathbf{X}} = \mathbf{V}_k \mathbf{S}_k^2 \mathbf{V}_k^T.$$

To analyze a new document (or query) $\mathbf{x}_q$ that is not in the original collection used for the decomposition, it can be projected into the semantic space of topic activity defined by the model using

$$\mathbf{a}_q = \mathbf{S}_k^{-1} \mathbf{U}_k^T \mathbf{x}_q. \tag{9.3}$$

USING PRINCIPAL COMPONENT ANALYSIS FOR DIMENSIONALITY REDUCTION

The singular value decomposition is widely used to project data into a space of reduced dimensions, often before applying other analysis techniques. For instance, data can be projected into a lower dimensional space in order to effectively apply nearest neighbor techniques, which tend to break down in high dimensional spaces.

LSA is in fact a form of principal component analysis. When viewed as a probability model, the projection of a document into a lower dimensional semantic space is, in effect, a *latent variable representation for the document*. The equivalent quantity in PPCA is given by the expected value of the posterior distribution over the hidden variables. This gives an intuitive view of what it means to project a document or query vector into a lower dimensional space.

For a PPCA model with no noise in the observed variables $\mathbf{x}$, we have seen that an input vector $\mathbf{x}$ can be projected into a reduced dimensional random vector $\mathbf{z}$ by computing the mean value of the posterior for the latent variables using $\mathbf{z} = E[\mathbf{h}] = (\mathbf{W}^T \mathbf{W})^{-1} \mathbf{W}^T \mathbf{x}$. Appendix A.2 details the relationships between PCA, PPCA, the singular value decomposition and eigendecompositions, and shows that for mean-centered data the $\mathbf{U}$ matrix in (9.3) equals the matrix of eigenvectors $\mathbf{\Phi}$ of the eigendecomposition of the corresponding covariance matrix of the data, i.e. $\mathbf{U} = \mathbf{\Phi}$. The diagonal matrix $\mathbf{S}$ in (9.3) is related to the diagonal matrix of eigenvalues $\mathbf{\Lambda}$ by $\mathbf{S} = \mathbf{\Lambda}^{\frac{1}{2}}$. Furthermore, the eigendecomposition of the covariance matrix implies that $\mathbf{W} = \mathbf{\Phi}\mathbf{\Lambda}^{\frac{1}{2}}$ in the corresponding PPCA. Thus, under the probabilistic interpretation of principal component analysis with no noise for observed variables, $\mathbf{W} = \mathbf{US}$. Using the fact that $\mathbf{U}$ is orthogonal and $\mathbf{S}$ is diagonal, this means that computing a principal component analysis of mean-centered data using the singular value decomposition and interpreting the result as a linear Gaussian hidden variable model yields the following expression for projecting results into the reduced dimensional space based on the mean of the posterior:

$$\begin{aligned}
\mathbf{z} &= (\mathbf{W}^T\mathbf{W})^{-1}\mathbf{W}^T\mathbf{x} \\
&= (\mathbf{SU}^T\mathbf{US})^{-1}\mathbf{SU}^T\mathbf{x} \\
&= (\mathbf{S}^2)^{-1}\mathbf{SU}^T\mathbf{x} \\
&= \mathbf{S}^{-1}\mathbf{U}^T\mathbf{x}.
\end{aligned}$$

This is the same expression as the LSA projection in (9.3) to compute $\mathbf{a}_q$, the semantic representation of a document, and it represents a general expression for dimensionality reduction using principal component analysis. This means that principal component analysis can be performed using the singular value decomposition of the data matrix, or an eigendecomposition of the covariance matrix, the EM algorithm, or even expected gradient descent. When working with large datasets or data with missing values there are advantages and disadvantages to each method.

The input data $\mathbf{X}$ need not arise from documents: LSA is just a concrete example of applying singular value decomposition to a real problem. Indeed, the general idea of computing such projections is widely used across machine learning and data mining. Because of the relationships discussed above the methods are often discussed using different terminology, even when they refer to the same underlying analysis.

PROBABILISTIC LSA

PPCA is based on continuous valued representations of data and an underlying Gaussian model. In contrast, the pLSA approach, also known as an "aspect model," is based on a formulation using the multinomial distribution; it was originally applied to the cooccurrences of words and documents. The multinomial distribution is a natural distribution for modeling word occurrence counts. In the pLSA framework one considers the index of each document as being encoded using observations of discrete random variables d_i for $i = 1,\ldots,n$ documents. Each variable d_i has n states, and over the document corpus there is one observation of the variable for each state. Topics are represented with discrete variables z_{ij}, while words are represented with random variables w_{ij}, where m_i words are associated

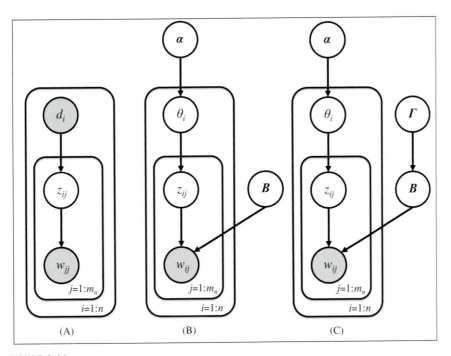

FIGURE 9.11

Graphical models for (A) pLSA, (B) LDA^b, and (C) smoothed LDA^b.

with each document and each word is associated with a topic. There are two variants: an asymmetric and a symmetric formulation.

Fig. 9.11A illustrates the asymmetric formulation; the symmetric formulation reverses the arrow from d to z. D is a set of random variables for the document index observations, and W is a set of random variables for all the words observed across the documents. The asymmetric formulation corresponds to

$$P(W, D) = \prod_{i=1}^{n} P(d_i) \prod_{j=1}^{m_n} \sum_{z_{ij}} P(z_{ij}|d_i)P(w_{ij}|z_{ij}).$$

Because d, an index over the training documents, is a random variable in the graph, pLSA is not a generative model for new documents. However, it does correspond to a valid probabilistic model with hidden variables, so the EM algorithm can be used to estimate parameters and obtain a representation of each document in a corpus in terms of its distribution over the topic variables.

LATENT DIRICHLET ALLOCATION

pLSA can be extended into a hierarchical Bayesian model with three levels, known as *latent Dirichlet allocation*. We refer to this as LDA^b ("b" for Bayesian) to distinguish it from linear discriminant analysis which is commonly referred to as LDA. LDA[b] was proposed in part to reduce the overfitting that has been observed with pLSA, and has been extended in many ways. Extensions of LDA[b] can be used to determine trends over time and identify "hot" and "cold" topics. Such analyses are particularly interesting today, with the recent explosion of social media and the interest in analyzing it.

Latent Dirichlet allocation is a hierarchical Bayesian model that reformulates pLSA by replacing the document index variables d_i with the random parameter θ_i, a vector of multinomial parameters for the documents. The distribution of θ_i is influenced by a Dirichlet prior with hyperparameter α, which is also a vector. (Appendix A.2 explains Dirichlet distributions and their use as priors for the parameters of the discrete distribution.) Finally, the relationship between the discrete topic variables z_{ij} and the words w_{ij} is also given an explicit dependence on a hyperparameter, namely, the matrix $\mathbf{B}$. Fig. 9.11B shows the corresponding graphical model. The probability model for the set of all observed words W is

$$P(W|\alpha, \mathbf{B}) = \prod_{i=1}^{n} \int P(\theta_i|\alpha) \left[\prod_{j=1}^{m_n} \sum_{z_{ij}} P(z_{ij}|\theta_i)P(w_{ij}|z_{ij}, \mathbf{B}) \right] d\theta_i$$

$$= \prod_{i=1}^{n} \int P(\theta_i|\alpha) \left[\prod_{j=1}^{m_n} P(w_{ij}|\theta_i, \mathbf{B}) \right] d\theta_i,$$

which marginalizes out the uncertainty associated with each θ_i and z_{ij}. $P(\theta_i|\alpha)$ is given by a k-dimensional Dirichlet distribution, which also leads to k-dimensional topic variables z_{ij}. For a vocabulary of size V, $P(w_{ij}|z_{ij}, \mathbf{B})$ encodes the probability of each word given each topic, and prior information is therefore captured by the $k \times V$ dimensional matrix $\mathbf{B}$.

The marginal log-likelihood of the model can be optimized using an empirical Bayesian method by adjusting the hyperparameters α and $\mathbf{B}$ via the variational EM procedure. To perform the E-step of EM, the posterior distribution over the unobserved random quantities is needed. For the model defined by the above equation, with a random θ for each document, word observations $\mathbf{w}$, and hidden topic variables $\mathbf{z}$, the posterior distribution is

$$P(\theta, z|\mathbf{w}, \alpha, \mathbf{B}) = \frac{P(\theta, z, \mathbf{w}|\alpha, \mathbf{B})}{P(\mathbf{w}|\alpha, \mathbf{B})}$$

which, unfortunately, is intractable. For the M-step it is necessary to update hyperparameters α and $\mathbf{B}$, which can be done by computing the maximum likelihood estimates using the expected sufficient statistics from the E-step. The variational EM procedure amounts to computing and using a separate approximate posterior for each θ_i and each z_{ij}.

A method called "collapsed Gibbs sampling" turns out to be a particularly effective alternative to variational methods for performing LDA[b]. Consider first that the model in Fig. 9.11B can be expanded to that shown in Fig. 9.11C,

Table 9.1 Highest Probability Words and User Tags From a Sample of Topics Extracted From a Collection of Scientific Articles

Topic 2	Topic 39	Topic 102	Topic 201	Topic 210
Species	Theory	Tumor	Resistance	Synaptic
Global	Time	Cancer	Resistant	Neurons
Climate	Space	Tumors	Drug	Postsynaptic
CO_2	Given	Human	Drugs	Hippocampal
Water	Problem	Cells	Sensitive	Synapses
Geophysics, geology, ecology	Physics, math, applied math	Medical sciences	Pharmacology	Neurobiology

which was originally cast as the smoothed version of LDA[b]. Then add another Dirichlet prior with parameters given by Γ on the topic parameters of **B**, a formulation that further reduces the effects of overfitting. Standard Gibbs sampling involves iteratively sampling the hidden random variables z_{ij}, the θ_i's and the elements of matrix **B**. Collapsed Gibbs sampling is obtained by integrating out the θ_i's and **B** analytically, which deals with these distributions exactly. Consequently, conditioned by the current estimates of Γ, α, and the observed words of a document corpus, the Gibbs sampler proceeds by simply iteratively updating each z_{ij} to compute the required approximate posterior. Using either samples or variational approximations it is then relatively straightforward to obtain estimates for the θ_i's and **B**.

The overall approach of using a smoothed, collapsed LDA[b] model to extract topics from a document collection can be summarized as follows: first define a hierarchical Bayesian model for the joint distribution of documents and words following the structure of Fig. 9.11C. We could think of there being a Bayesian **E-step** that performs approximate inference using Gibbs' sampling to sample from the *joint posterior* over *all* topics for all documents in the model, or $P(z_{ij}|w_{ij}, \Gamma, \alpha)$, where the θ_i's and **B** have been integrated out. This is followed by an **M-step** that uses these samples to update the estimates of the θ_i's and **B**, using update equations that are functions of Γ, α, and the samples. This procedure is performed within a hierarchical Bayesian model, so the updated parameters can be used to create a Bayesian predictive distribution over new words and new topics given the observed words.

Table 9.1 shows the highest probability words from a sampling of topics mined by Griffiths and Steyvers (2004) through applying LDA[b] to 28,154 abstracts of papers published in the *Proceedings of the National Academy of Science* from 1991 to 2001 and tagged by authors with subcategory information. Analyzing the distribution over these tags identifies the highest probability user tags for each topic, which are shown at the bottom of Table 9.1. Note that the user tags were not used to create the topics, but we can see how well the extracted topics match with human labels.

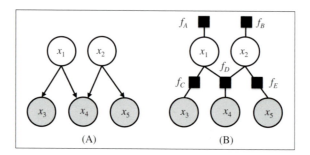

FIGURE 9.12

(A) Bayesian network and (B) corresponding factor graph.

FACTOR GRAPHS

Bayesian networks are a special kind of probability model that factorize a joint probability distribution into the product of conditional and unconditional distributions. Factor graphs provide an even more general framework for representing general functions by factoring them into the product of local functions, each of which acts on a subset of the full argument set:

$$F(x_1,\ldots,x_n) = \prod_{j=1}^{S} f_j(X_j),$$

where X_j is a subset of the original set of arguments $\{x_1,\ldots,x_n\}$, $f_j(X_j)$ is a function of X_j, and $j = 1,\ldots,S$ enumerates the argument subsets. A *factor graph* consists of variable nodes—circles—for each variable x_k and factor nodes—rectangles—for each function, with edges that connect each factor node to its variables.

Fig. 9.12A and B shows a Bayesian network and its factor graph corresponding to the factorization

$$F(x_1,\ldots,x_5) = f_A(x_1)f_B(x_2)f_C(x_3,x_1)f_D(x_4,x_1,x_2)f_E(x_5,x_2)$$
$$= P(x_1)P(x_2)P(x_3|x_1)P(x_4|x_1,x_2)P(x_5|x_2).$$

Factor graphs make concepts such as the Markov blanket for a given variable in a Bayesian network easy to identify. For example, Fig. 9.13 shows the Markov blanket for variable x_6 in a factor graph that corresponds to the Bayesian network in Fig. 9.3: it consists of all nodes that are connected to it through a factor. Factor graphs are more powerful than Bayesian networks because they can represent a wider class of factorizations and models. These include Markov random fields, which we will meet shortly.

Factor graphs, Bayesian networks, and the logistic regression model

It is instructive to compare the factor graph for a naïvely constructed Bayesian model with the factor graph for a Naïve Bayes model of the same set of variables (and, later, with the factor graph for a logistic regression formulation of the same

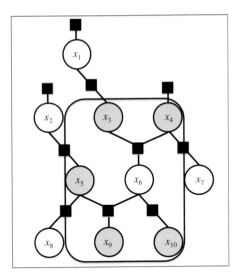

FIGURE 9.13

The Markov blanket for variable x_6 in a 10-variable factor graph.

problem). Fig. 9.14A and B shows the Bayesian network and its factor graph for a network with a child node y that has several parents x_i, $i = 1,\ldots,n$. Fig. 9.14B involves a large conditional probability table for $P(y|x_1,\ldots,x_n)$, with many parameters that must be estimated or specified, because in

$$P(y, x_1,\ldots,x_n) = P(y|x_1,\ldots,x_n)\prod_{i-1}^{n} P(x_i)$$

the number of parameters increases exponentially with the number of parent variables. In contrast, Fig. 9.14C and D shows the Bayesian network and its factor graph for the Naïve Bayes model. Here the number of parameters is linear in the number of children because the model breaks down into the product of functions involving y and just one x_i, because the underlying factorization is

$$P(y, x_1,\ldots,x_n) = P(y)\prod_{i-1}^{n} P(x_i|y).$$

The factor graphs show the different complexities very clearly. The graph in Fig. 9.14B has a factor involving $n + 1$ variables, while the factors in Fig. 9.14D involve no more than two variables.

Factor graphs can be extended to clarify an important distinction for conditional models. The Bayesian network of Fig. 9.15A involves a large table for the conditional distribution of y given many x_i's, but a logistic regression model could be used to reduce the number of parameters for $P(y|x_1,\ldots,x_n)$ from exponential to linear, depicted in Fig. 9.15B.

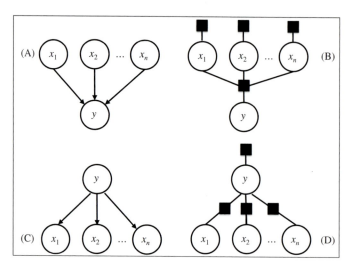

FIGURE 9.14

(A) and (B) Bayesian network and corresponding factor graph; (C) and (D) Naïve Bayes model and corresponding factor graph.

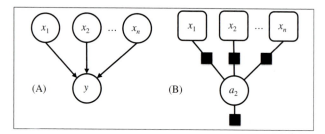

FIGURE 9.15

(A) Bayesian network representing the joint distribution of y and its parents; (B) factor graph for a logistic regression for the conditional distribution of y given its parents.

Let us assume that all variables are binary. Given a separate function $f_i(y, x_i)$ for each binary variable x_i, the conditional distribution defined by a logistic regression model has the form

$$P(y|x_1, \ldots, x_n) = \frac{1}{Z(x_1, \ldots, x_n)} \exp\left(\sum_{i=1}^{n} w_i f_i(y, x_i)\right)$$

$$= \frac{1}{Z(x_1, \ldots, x_n)} \prod_{i=1}^{n} \phi_i(x_i, y).$$

where the denominator Z is a data-dependent normalization term that makes the conditional distribution sum to 1, and $\phi_i(x_i, y) = \exp(w_i f_i(y, x_i))$. This corresponds to a factor graph that resembles the Naïve Bayes model, but with the factorized conditional distribution shown in Fig. 9.15B. Here, curved rectangles represent variables that are not explicitly defined as random variables. This graph represents the conditional probability function $P(y|x_1, \ldots, x_n)$, and the number of parameters scales linearly because each function is connected to just a pair of variables.

MARKOV RANDOM FIELDS

Markov random fields define another factorized model for a set of random variables X, where these variables are divided into so-called "cliques" X_c and a factor $\Psi_c(X_c)$ is defined for each clique:

$$P(X) = \frac{1}{Z} \prod_{c=1}^{C} \Psi_c(X_c),$$

A clique is a group of nodes in an undirected graph that all connect to every other node in the clique. Z, known as the partition function, normalizes the model to ensure that it is a probability distribution, and consists of a sum over all possible values for all variables in the model. It could be written

$$Z = \sum_{x \in X} \prod_{c=1}^{C} \Psi_c(X_c).$$

Fig. 9.16A and B shows an undirected graph corresponding to a Markov random field, and its factor graph. Again the factor graph makes explicit the nature of the underlying functions used to create the model. For example, it shows that functions are associated with each node, which is not clear from the undirected graph notation. The Markov random field structure in Fig. 9.16 has been widely used for images: this general structure is typically repeated over an entire image, with each node representing a property of a pixel—e.g., a label, or its depth.

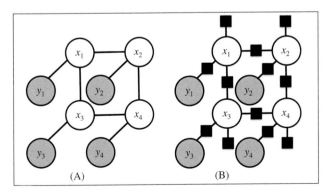

(A)   (B)

FIGURE 9.16

(A) Undirected graph representing a Markov random field structure; (B) corresponding factor graph.

Fig. 9.16 factorizes the joint probability for four variables as follows:

$$P(x_1, x_2, x_3, x_4) = \frac{1}{Z} f_A(x_1) f_B(x_2) f_C(x_1) f_D(x_2) f_E(x_1, x_2) f_F(x_2, x_3) f_G(x_3, x_4) f_H(x_4, x_1)$$

$$= \frac{1}{Z} \prod_{u=1}^{U} \phi_u(X_u) \prod_{v=1}^{V} \Psi_v(X_v),$$

where $\phi_u(X_u) = \phi_u(x_i)$ represents a set of unary functions of just one variable, while $\Psi_v(X_v) = \Psi_v(x_i, x_j)$ represents a set of pairwise functions of two variables. Subscripts u and v index both the functions and the sets of single variables $X_u = \{x_i\}_u$ and variable pairs $X_v = \{x_i, x_j\}_v$ that serve as their arguments.

This representation can equivalently be expressed using an energy function $F(X)$ of this form:

$$F(X) = \sum_{u=1}^{U} U(X_u) + \sum_{v=1}^{V} V(X_v).$$

Then a Markov random field can be written

$$P(X) = \frac{1}{Z} \exp(-F(X)) = \frac{1}{Z} \exp\left(-\sum_{u=1}^{U} U(X_u) - \sum_{v=1}^{V} V(X_v) \right).$$

Since Z is constant for any assignment of the variables X, the negative log probability under the model can be written

$$-\log P(x_1, x_2, x_3, x_4) = -\log \left[\prod_{u=1}^{U} \phi_u(X_u) \prod_{v=1}^{V} \psi_v(X_V) \right] - \log Z$$

$$\alpha \sum_{u=1}^{U} U(X_u) + \sum_{V=1}^{V} V(X_V),$$

This leads to the commonly used strategy of minimizing an energy function in this form to perform tasks such as image segmentation and entity resolution in text documents. When such minimization tasks are "submodular," a term that denotes a particular category of optimization problems, an exact minimum can be found using algorithms based on graph-cuts; otherwise methods such as tree-reweighted message passing are used.

COMPUTING USING THE SUM-PRODUCT AND MAX-PRODUCT ALGORITHMS

Key quantities of interest for any probability model are the marginal probabilities and the most probable explanation of the model. For tree-structured graphical models, exact solutions for these can be found efficiently by the sum-product and max-product algorithms. When applied to the hidden Markov models discussed in Section 9.8, these are known as the *forwards-backwards* and *Viterbi* algorithms, respectively. We begin with some simple examples for motivation, and then present the algorithms themselves.

Marginal probabilities

Given a Bayesian network, an initial step is to determine the marginal probability of each node given no observations whatsoever. These *single node marginals* differ from the conditional and unconditional probabilities that were used to specify the network. Indeed, software packages for manipulating Bayesian networks often take the definition of a network in terms of the underlying conditional and unconditional probabilities and show the user the single node marginals for each node in a visual interface. The marginal for variable x_i is

$$P(x_i) = \sum_{x_{j\neq i}} P(x_1, \ldots, x_n),$$

where the sum is over the states of all variables $x_j \neq x_i$, and can be computed by the sum-product algorithm. In fact, the same algorithm serves in many other situations, such as when some variables are observed and we wish to compute the belief of others, and also for finding the posterior distributions needed for learning—e.g., using the EM algorithm.

Consider the task of computing the marginal probability of variable x_3 given the observation $x_4 = \tilde{x}_4$ from the Bayesian network in Fig. 9.12A. Since we are conditioning on a variable, we need to compute a marginal *conditional* probability. This corresponds to the practical notion of posing a query, where the model is used to infer an updated belief about x_3 given the state of variable x_4.

Since other variables in the graph have not been observed, they should be integrated out of the graphical model to obtain the desired result:

$$P(x_3|\tilde{x}_4) = \frac{P(x_3, \tilde{x}_4)}{P(\tilde{x}_4)} = \frac{P(x_3, \tilde{x}_4)}{\sum_{x_3}(x_3, \tilde{x}_4)},$$

Here the key probability of interest is

$$P(x_3, \tilde{x}_4) = \sum_{x_1}\sum_{x_2}\sum_{x_5} P(x_1, x_2, x_3, \tilde{x}_4, x_5)$$

$$= \sum_{x_1}\sum_{x_2}\sum_{x_5} P(x_1)P(x_2)P(x_3|x_1)P(\tilde{x}_4|x_1, x_2)P(x_5|x_2).$$

However, this sum involves a large data structure containing the joint probability, composed of the products over the individual probabilities. The *sum-product algorithm* refers to a much better solution: simply *push the sums as far as possible to the right* before computing products of probabilities. Here, the required marginalization can be computed by

$$P(x_3, \tilde{x}_4) = \sum_{x_1} P(x_3|x_1)P(x_1) \sum_{x_2} P(\tilde{x}_4|x_1, x_2)P(x_2) \sum_{x_5} P(x_5|x_2)$$

$$= \sum_{x_1} P(x_3|x_1)P(x_1)P(\tilde{x}_4|x_1)$$

$$= \sum_{x_1} P(x_1, x_3, \tilde{x}_4).$$

The sum-product algorithm

The approach illustrated by this simple example can be generalized into an algorithm for computing marginals that can be transformed into conditional marginals if desired. Conceptually, it is based on sending messages between the variables and functions defined by a factor graph.

Begin with variable or function nodes that have only one connection. Function nodes send the message $\mu_{f \to x}(x) = f(x)$ to the variable connected to them, while variable nodes send $\mu_{x \to f}(x) = 1$. Each node waits until it has received a message from all neighbors except the one it sent its message to. Then function nodes send messages of the following form to variable x:

$$\mu_{f \to x}(x) = \sum_{x_1,\dots,x_K} f(x, x_1, \dots, x_K) \prod_{k \in N(f) \, x} \mu_{x_k \to f}(x_k),$$

where $N(f)\backslash x$ represents the set of the function node f's neighbors, excluding the recipient variable x; we write these variables of the K other neighboring nodes as $x_1,\dots,x_K$. If a variable is observed, messages for functions involving it no longer need a sum over the states of the variable, the function is evaluated with the observed state. One could think of the associated variable node as being transformed into the new modified function. There is then no variable to function message for the observed variable.

Variable nodes send messages of this form to functions:

$$\mu_{x \to f}(x) = \mu_{f_1 \to x}(x) \dots \mu_{f_K \to x}(x) = \prod_{k \in N(x) \, f} \mu_{f_k \to x}(x),$$

where the product is over the messages from all neighboring functions $N(x)$ other than the recipient function f; i.e., $fk \in N(x) \, f$. When the algorithm terminates, the marginal probability of each node is the product over all incoming messages from all functions connected to the variable:

$$P(x_i) = \mu_{f_1 \to x}(x) \dots \mu_{f_K \to x}(x)\mu_{f_{K+1} \to x}(x) = \prod_{k=1}^{K+1} \mu_{f_k \to x}(x),$$

This is written as a product over $K + 1$ function messages to emphasize its similarity to the variable-to-function-node messages. After sending a message to any given function f consisting of the product of K messages, the variable simply needs to receive one more incoming message back from f to compute its marginal.

If some of the variables in the graph are observed, the algorithm yields the marginal probability of each variable *and* the observations. The marginal conditional distribution for each variable can be obtained by normalizing the result by the probability of the observation, obtainable from any node by summing over x_i in the resulting distributions, which have the form $P(x_i, \{\tilde{x}_{j \in O}\})$ where O is the set of indices of the observed variables.

As is often the case with probability models, multiplying many probabilities quickly leads to very small numbers. The sum-product algorithm is often implemented with rescaling. Alternatively, the computations can be performed in log space (as they are in the max-product algorithm; see below), leading to computations of the form $c = \log(\exp(a) + \exp(b))$. To help prevent loss of precision when computing the exponents, note that

$$c = \log(e^a + e^b) = a + \log(1 + e^{b-a}) = b + \log(1 + e^{a-b}),$$

and pick the expression with the smaller exponent.

Sum-product algorithm example

The idea behind the sum-product algorithm is to push sums as far to the right as possible, and this is done efficiently for all variables simultaneously. When the algorithm is used to compute $P(x_3, \tilde{x}_4)$ from the Bayesian network in Fig. 9.12A and the corresponding factor graph in Fig. 9.17, the key messages involved are:

$$P(x_3, \tilde{x}_4) = \sum_{x_1} P(x_3|x_1) \underbrace{P(x_1)}_{1d} \sum_{x_2} P(\tilde{x}_4|x_1, x_2) \underbrace{P(x_2)}_{1c} \sum_{x_5} P(x_5|x_2) \cdot \underbrace{1}_{1a}$$

These numbered messages can be written

1a: $\mu_{x_5 \to f_E}(x_5) = 1$, 1c: $\mu_{f_B \to x_2}(x_2) = f_B(x_2)$, 1d: $\mu_{f_A \to x_1}(x_1) = f_A(x_1)$
2a: $\mu_{f_E \to x_2}(x_2) = \sum_{x_5} f_E(x_5, x_2)$
3a: $\mu_{x_2 \to f_D}(x_5) = \mu_{f_B \to x_2}(x_2)\mu_{f_E \to x_2}(x_2)$
4a: $\mu_{f_D \to x_1}(x_1) = \sum_{x_2} f_D(\tilde{x}_4|x_1, x_2)\mu_{x_2 \to f_D}(x_5)$
5a: $\mu_{x_1 \to f_C}(x_1) = \mu_{f_A \to x_1}(x_1)\mu_{f_D \to x_1}(x_1)$
6a: $\mu_{f_C \to x_3}(x_3) = \sum_{x_1} f_C(x_3, x_1)\mu_{x_1 \to f_C}(x_1)$

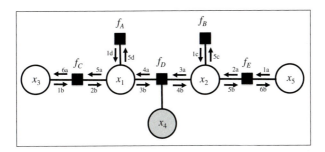

FIGURE 9.17

Message sequence in an example factor graph.

Keep in mind that the complete algorithm will yield all single-variable marginals in the graph using the other messages shown in Fig. 9.17, but not enumerated above. This simple example is based on a Bayesian network, which transforms into a chain-structured factor graph when $\tilde{x}_4$ is observed, and the message passing structure resembles the computations used for the hidden Markov models and conditional random fields discussed below. For long chains or large tree-structured networks, such computations are essential for computing the necessary quantities efficiently, without recourse to approximate methods.

Most probable explanation example

Finding the most probable configuration of all other variables in our example given $x_4 = \tilde{x}_4$ involves searching for

$$\left\{x_1^*, x_2^*, x_3^*, x_5^*\right\} = \arg\max_{x_1, x_2, x_3, x_5} P(x_1, x_2, x_3, x_5 | \tilde{x}_4),$$

for which

$$P(x_1^*, x_2^*, x_3^*, x_5^* | \tilde{x}_4) = \max_{x_1, x_2, x_3, x_5} P(x_1, x_2, x_3, x_5 | \tilde{x}_4).$$

The joint probability is related to the conditional by a constant, so one could equally well find the maximum of $P(x_1, x_2, x_3, \tilde{x}_4, x_5)$. Because max behaves in a similar way to sum, we can take a tip from the sum-product and push the max operations as far to the right as possible, noting that $\max(ab, ac) = a \max(b, c)$. Here,

$$\max_{x_1} \max_{x_2} \max_{x_3} \max_{x_5} P(x_1, x_2, x_3, \tilde{x}_4, x_5)$$
$$= \max_{x_3} \max_{x_1} P(x_1)P(x_3|x_1) \max_{x_2} P(x_2)P(\tilde{x}_4|x_1, x_2) \max_{x_5} P(x_5|x_2).$$

Consider the max over x_5 at the far right, which seeks the greatest probability among the possible states of x_5 for each of the possible states of x_2. This involves creating a table giving the maximum values of x_5 for each configuration of x_2. The next operation to the left, the max over x_2, involves multiplying the current maximum values in the table for x_2 by the corresponding probabilities for $P(x_2)P(\tilde{x}_4|x_1, x_2)$. We thus need to find the maximum for each state of x_2 for each state of x_1, which can be modeled by producing a message over the states of x_1 with the greatest values obtained for each possible state based on all information propagated so far from the right.

This process continues until eventually we have a final max over x_3. This gives a single value, the probability of the most probable explanation, which corresponds to the entry in the data structure with scores for each state of x_3. By changing which variable is used to compute the final max, we can extract it from any variable, because this will lead to the same maximum value. However, taking the *arg max* for each variable will yield the desired most probable explanation $x_1^*, x_2^*, x_3^*, x_5^*$—the configuration of all variables which has the greatest probability. Generalizing these ideas and performing them efficiently leads to the max-product algorithm, a general template for performing such computations exactly in arbitrary tree-structured graphs.

The max-product or max-sum algorithm

The max-product algorithm can be used to find the most probable explanation in a tree-structured probability model. It is generally implemented in logarithmic space to alleviate problems with numerical stability, where it is better characterized as the max-sum algorithm. Since the log function increases monotonically, $\log(\max_x p(x)) = \max_x \log p(x)$, and, as mentioned above, $\max(c + a, c + b) = c + \max(a, b)$. These properties allow the maximum probability configuration in a tree-structured probability model to be computed as follows.

As in the sum-product algorithm, variables or factors that have only one connection in the graph begin by sending either a function-to-variable message consisting of $\mu_{x \to f}(x) = 0$, or a variable-to-function message consisting of $\mu_{f \to x}(x) = \log f(x)$. Each function and variable node in the graph waits until it has received a message from all neighbors other than the node that will receive its message. Then function nodes send messages of the following form to variable x

$$\mu_{f \to x}(x) = \max_{x_1, \ldots, x_K} \left[\log f(x, x_1, \ldots, x_K) + \sum_{k \in N(f) \, x} \mu_{x_k \to f}(x_k) \right],$$

where the notation $N(f) \backslash x$ is the same as for the sum-product algorithm above. Likewise, variables send messages of this form to functions:

$$\mu_{x \to f}(x) = \sum_{k \in N(x) \, f} \mu_{f_k \to x}(x),$$

where the sum is over the messages from all functions other than the recipient function. When the algorithm terminates, the probability of the most probable configuration can be extracted from any node using

$$p^* = \max_x \left[\sum_{k \in N(x)} \mu_{f_k \to x}(x) \right].$$

The most probable configuration itself can be obtained by applying this computation to each variable:

$$x^* = \arg \max_x \left[\sum_{k \in N(x)} \mu_{f_k \to x}(x) \right].$$

To understand how this works for a concrete example, follow the sequence of messages illustrated in Fig. 9.17, but use the max-product messages defined above and the final computations for the max and arg max in place of the sum-product messages we examined earlier.

The max-product algorithm is widely used to make final predictions for tree-structured Bayesian networks, as well as for sequences of labels in conditional random fields and hidden Markov models, discussed in Sections 9.7 and 9.8, respectively.

9.7 CONDITIONAL PROBABILITY MODELS

You may be surprised to learn that the regression models of Section 4.6 correspond to the simplest and most popular types of conditional probability model. The Linear and Polynomial Regression as Probability Models section views linear regression through the lens of probability, and we go on to examine the multiclass extension to logistic regression, expressing this in both scalar and matrix-vector forms. The leap to the matrix-vector form reveals that key aspects of modeling and learning can be expressed in compact and elegant ways. This allows computer implementations to be accelerated by using libraries—or hardware—for matrix-vector manipulation, which are highly optimized and exploit modern computing hardware. Graphics processing units (GPUs) can yield execution speeds that are orders of magnitude faster than standard implementations.

LINEAR AND POLYNOMIAL REGRESSION AS PROBABILITY MODELS

Suppose the conditional probability distribution for the observations of a continuous variable y_i given observations of another variable x_i is a linear Gaussian:

$$p(y_i|x_i) = \frac{1}{\sqrt{2\pi}\sigma} \exp\left[-\frac{\{y_i - (\theta_0 + \theta_1 x_i)\}^2}{2\sigma^2} \right],$$

where the parameters θ_0 and θ_1 represent the slope and intercept. The conditional distribution for the observed y_i's given the corresponding observed x_i's can be defined as

$$p(y_1, \ldots, y_N | x_1, \ldots, x_N) = \prod_{i=1}^{N} p(y_i|x_i).$$

As usual, we work with the log-likelihood instead:

$$L_{y|x} = \log \prod_{i=1}^{N} p(y_i|x_i) = \sum_{i=1}^{N} \log p(y_i|x_i).$$

This simplifies to

$$L_{y|x} = \sum_{i=1}^{N} \log \left\{ \frac{1}{\sigma\sqrt{2\pi}} \exp\left[-\frac{\{y_i - (\theta_0 + \theta_1 x_i)\}^2}{2\sigma^2} \right] \right\}$$

$$= -N \log\left[\sigma\sqrt{2\pi} \right] - \sum_{i=1}^{N} \frac{\{y_i - (\theta_0 + \theta_1 x_i)\}^2}{2\sigma^2}.$$

The first term is independent of the data. Thus to find the parameters that maximize the log-likelihood, it suffices to find the parameters that minimize the squared error:

$$\arg\max_{\theta_0,\theta_1}(L_{y|x}) = \arg\min_{\theta_0,\theta_1}\left(\sum_{i=1}^{N}\{y_i - (\theta_0 + \theta_1 x_i)\}^2\right).$$

This is ordinary linear regression!

Although x_i is a scalar here, the method generalizes to a vector $\mathbf{x}_i$. Categorical variables can be encoded into a subset of the dimensions of $\mathbf{x}$ using the so-called "one-hot" method, placing a 1 in the dimension corresponding to the category label and 0s in all other dimensions allocated to the variable. If all input variables are categorical, this corresponds to the classic *analysis of variance* (ANOVA) method.

USING PRIORS ON PARAMETERS

Placing a Gaussian prior on the parameters $\mathbf{w}$ leads to the method of ridge regression (Section 7.2)— also called "weight decay." Consider a regression that uses a D-dimensional vector $\mathbf{x}$ to make predictions. The regression's bias term can be represented by defining the first dimension of $\mathbf{x}$ as the constant 1 for every example. Defining $[\theta_1 \ldots \theta_D] = \mathbf{w}^T$ and using the usual $N(x; \mu, \sigma)$ notation for scalar Gaussians, the underlying probability model is

$$\prod_{i=1}^{N} p(y_i|x_i; \theta)p(\theta; \tau) = \left[\prod_{i=1}^{N} N(y_i; \mathbf{w}^T x_i, \sigma^2)\right]\left[\prod_{d=1}^{D} N(w_d; 0, \tau^2)\right],$$

where τ is the hyperparameter specifying the prior. Setting $\lambda \equiv \sigma^2/\tau^2$, it is possible to show that maximum a posteriori parameter estimation based on the log conditional likelihood is equivalent to minimizing the squared error loss function

$$F(\mathbf{w}) = \sum_{i=1}^{N}\{y_i - \mathbf{w}^T x_i\}^2 + \lambda\mathbf{w}^T\mathbf{w}, \tag{9.4}$$

which includes an L_2-based regularization term given by $R_{L_2}(\mathbf{w}) = \mathbf{w}^T\mathbf{w} = ||\mathbf{w}||_2^2$. ("Regularization" is another term for overfitting avoidance.)

Using a Laplace prior for the distribution over weights and taking the log of the likelihood function yields an L_1-based regularization term $R_{L_1}(\mathbf{w}) = ||\mathbf{w}||_1$. To see why, note that the Laplace distribution has the form

$$P(w; \mu, b) = L(w; \mu, b) = \frac{1}{2b}\exp\left(-\frac{|w - \mu|}{b}\right),$$

where μ and b are parameters. Modeling the prior probability for each weight by a Laplace distribution with $\mu_j = 0$ yields

$$-\log\left[\prod_{d=1}^{D} L(w_d; 0, b)\right] = \log(2b) + \frac{1}{b}\sum_{d=1}^{D} |w_d| \propto ||\mathbf{w}||_1.$$

Since the Laplace distribution places more probability at zero than the Gaussian distribution does, it can provide both regularization and variable selection in regression problems. This technique has been popularized as a regression approach known as the LASSO, "Least Absolute Shrinkage and Selection Operator."

An alternative approach known as the "elastic net" combines L_1 and L_2 regularization techniques using

$$\lambda_1 R_{L_1}(\boldsymbol{\theta}) + \lambda_2 R_{L_2}(\boldsymbol{\theta}) = \lambda_1 ||\mathbf{w}||_1 + \lambda_2 ||\mathbf{w}||_2^2.$$

This corresponds to a prior distribution that consist of the product of a Gaussian and a Laplacian distribution. The result leads to convex optimization problems—i.e., problems where any local minimum must be a global minimum—if the loss is convex, which applies to models like logistic or linear regression.

Matrix vector formulations of linear and polynomial regression

This section formulates linear regression using matrix operations. Observe that the loss in (9.4)—without the penalty term—can be written

$$\sum_{i=1}^{N}\{y_i - (\theta_0 + \theta_1 x_{1i} + \theta_2 x_{2i} + \ldots + \theta_D x_{Di})\}^2$$

$$= \left(\begin{bmatrix} y_1 \\ \vdots \\ y_N \end{bmatrix} - \begin{bmatrix} 1 & x_{11} & x_{21} & \cdots & x_{D1} \\ \vdots & \vdots & \vdots & & \vdots \\ 1 & x_{1N} & x_{2N} & & x_{DN} \end{bmatrix}\begin{bmatrix} \theta_0 \\ \vdots \\ \theta_D \end{bmatrix}\right)^T \left(\begin{bmatrix} y_1 \\ \vdots \\ y_N \end{bmatrix} - \begin{bmatrix} 1 & x_{11} & x_{21} & \cdots & x_{D1} \\ \vdots & \vdots & \vdots & & \vdots \\ 1 & x_{1N} & x_{2N} & & x_{DN} \end{bmatrix}\begin{bmatrix} \theta_0 \\ \vdots \\ \theta_D \end{bmatrix}\right)$$

$$= (\mathbf{y} - \mathbf{A}\mathbf{w})^T(\mathbf{y} - \mathbf{A}\mathbf{w}).$$

where the vector $\mathbf{y}$ is just the individual y_i's stacked up, and $\mathbf{w}$ is the vector of parameters (or weights) for the model. Taking the partial derivative with respect to $\mathbf{w}$ and setting the result to zero yields a closed form expression for the parameters:

$$\frac{\partial}{\partial \mathbf{w}}(\mathbf{y} - \mathbf{A}\mathbf{w})^T(\mathbf{y} - \mathbf{A}\mathbf{w}) = 0$$

$$\Rightarrow \mathbf{A}^T \mathbf{A}\mathbf{w} = \mathbf{A}^T\mathbf{y} \tag{9.5}$$

$$\mathbf{w} = (\mathbf{A}^T \mathbf{A})^{-1}\mathbf{A}^T\mathbf{y}.$$

These are famous equations. $\mathbf{A}^T \mathbf{A}\mathbf{w} = \mathbf{A}^T\mathbf{y}$ is known as the *normal equations*, and the quantity $\mathbf{A}^+ = (\mathbf{A}^T \mathbf{A})^{-1}\mathbf{A}^T$ is known as the *pseudoinverse*. Note that $\mathbf{A}^T \mathbf{A}$ is not always invertible, but this problem can be addressed using regularization.

For ridge regression, a prior is added to make the objective function

$$F(\mathbf{w}) = (\mathbf{y} - \mathbf{A}\mathbf{w})^T(\mathbf{y} - \mathbf{A}\mathbf{w}) + \lambda \mathbf{w}^T \mathbf{w}, \tag{9.6}$$

for a suitably defined matrix $\mathbf{A}$ with vectors $\mathbf{x}_i$ in the rows, and λ as defined above. Again, setting the partial derivative of $F(\mathbf{w})$ to zero yields a closed form solution:

$$\frac{\partial}{\partial \mathbf{w}} F(\mathbf{w}) = 0$$

$$\Rightarrow \mathbf{A}^T \mathbf{A}\mathbf{w} + \lambda \mathbf{w} = \mathbf{A}^T \mathbf{y}$$
$$\mathbf{w} = (\mathbf{A}^T \mathbf{A} + \lambda \mathbf{I})^{-1} \mathbf{A}^T \mathbf{y}.$$

This modification to the pseudoinverse equation allows solutions to be found that would otherwise not exist, often using a very small λ. It is often presented as a regularization method that avoids numerical instability, but the analysis in terms of a prior on parameters gives more insight. For example, it may be appropriate to use Gaussian priors of different strengths for different terms. In fact, it is common practice to impose no penalty at all on the bias weight. This could be implemented by replacing the $\lambda \mathbf{w}^T \mathbf{w}$ term in (9.6) by $\mathbf{w}^T \mathbf{D} \mathbf{w}$, where $\mathbf{D}$ is a diagonal matrix containing the λ_i's to be used for each weight, transforming the solution into $\mathbf{w} = (\mathbf{A}^T \mathbf{A} + \mathbf{D})^{-1} \mathbf{A}^T \mathbf{y}$. While the above expression for the partial derivative is fairly simple, care must still be taken during implementation to avoid numerically instable results.

The linear regression model can be transformed into a nonlinear polynomial model. Although the polynomial regression model yields nonlinear predictions, the estimation problem is linear in the parameters. To see this, express the problem in matrix form, using a suitably defined matrix $\mathbf{A}$ to encode the polynomial's higher order terms and a vector $\mathbf{c}$ to encode the coefficients, including those used for the higher order terms:

$$\sum_{i=1}^{N} \{y_i - (\theta_0 + \theta_1 x_i + \theta_2 x_i^2 + \cdots + \theta_K x_i^K)\}^2$$

$$= \left(\begin{bmatrix} y_1 \\ \vdots \\ y_N \end{bmatrix} - \begin{bmatrix} 1 & x_1 & x_1^2 & \cdots & x_1^K \\ \vdots & \vdots & \vdots & & \vdots \\ 1 & x_N & x_N^2 & \cdots & x_N^K \end{bmatrix} \begin{bmatrix} \theta_0 \\ \vdots \\ \theta_K \end{bmatrix} \right)^T \left(\begin{bmatrix} y_1 \\ \vdots \\ y_N \end{bmatrix} - \begin{bmatrix} 1 & x_1 & x_1^2 & \cdots & x_1^K \\ \vdots & \vdots & \vdots & & \vdots \\ 1 & x_N & x_N^2 & \cdots & x_N^K \end{bmatrix} \begin{bmatrix} \theta_0 \\ \vdots \\ \theta_K \end{bmatrix} \right)$$

$$= (\mathbf{y} - \mathbf{A}\mathbf{c})^T (\mathbf{y} - \mathbf{A}\mathbf{c}).$$

Eq. (9.5) can be used to solve for the parameters in closed form.

This trick of transforming a linear prediction method into a nonlinear one while keeping the underlying estimation problem linear can be generalized. The general approach goes by the name of *basis function expansion*. For polynomial regression, the polynomial basis given by the rows of the matrix $\mathbf{A}$ (the powers of x) is used. However, any nonlinear function of the inputs $\phi(\mathbf{x})$ could be used to define models of the form

$$p(y|\mathbf{x}) = N(y; \mathbf{w}^T \phi(\mathbf{x}), \sigma^2),$$

which also give closed form solutions for a linear parameter estimation problem. We will return to this when discussing kernelizing probabilistic models below.

MULTICLASS LOGISTIC REGRESSION

Binary logistic regression was introduced in Section 4.6. Consider now a *multi-class classification problem* where class values are encoded as instances of the random variable $y \in \{1, \ldots, N\}$, and, as before, feature vectors are instances of a variable $\mathbf{x}$. Assume there is no significance to the order of the classes.

A simple linear probabilistic classifier can be created using this parametric form:

$$p(y|\mathbf{x}) = \frac{\exp\left(\sum_{k=1}^{K} w_k f_k(y, \mathbf{x})\right)}{\sum_y \exp\left(\sum_{k=1}^{K} w_k f_k(y, \mathbf{x})\right)} = \frac{1}{Z(\mathbf{x})} \exp\left(\sum_{k=1}^{K} w_k f_k(y, \mathbf{x})\right), \qquad (9.7)$$

which employs K *feature functions* $f_k(y, \mathbf{x})$ and K weights, w_k as the parameters of the model. This is one way of formulating *multinomial logistic regression*. The feature functions could encode complex features extracted from the input vector $\mathbf{x}$. To perform learning using maximum conditional likelihood and observations that are instances of y and $\mathbf{x}$, $\{\tilde{y}_1, \ldots, \tilde{y}_N, \tilde{\mathbf{x}}_1, \ldots, \tilde{\mathbf{x}}_N\}$, write the objective function as

$$L_{y|x} = \log \prod_{i=1}^{N} p(\tilde{y}_i | \tilde{\mathbf{x}}_i) = \sum_{i=1}^{N} \log p(\tilde{y}_i | \tilde{\mathbf{x}}_i).$$

Unfortunately there is no closed form solution for the parameter values that maximize this conditional likelihood, and optimization is usually performed using a gradient based procedure. On taking the partial derivative with respect to one of the weights of the log conditional probability for just one observation we have

$$\frac{\partial}{\partial w_j} p(\tilde{y}|\tilde{\mathbf{x}}) = \frac{\partial}{\partial w_j} \left\{ \log\left(\frac{1}{Z(\tilde{\mathbf{x}})} \exp\left(\sum_{k=1}^{K} w_k f_k(\tilde{y}, \tilde{\mathbf{x}})\right)\right) \right\}$$

$$= \frac{\partial}{\partial w_j} \left\{ \left[\sum_{k=1}^{K} \underbrace{w_k f_k(\tilde{y}, \tilde{\mathbf{x}})}_{\text{easy part}}\right] - \underbrace{\log Z(\tilde{\mathbf{x}})}_{\text{cool part}} \right\}$$

$$= f_{k=j}(\tilde{y}, \tilde{\mathbf{x}}) - \frac{\partial}{\partial w_j} \left\{ \sum_y \exp\left(\sum_{k=1}^{K} w_k f_k(y, \tilde{\mathbf{x}})\right) \right\}.$$

The derivative breaks apart into two terms. The first is easy because all terms involving weights where $w_k \neq w_j$ are 0, leaving the sum with just one term. The second, while seemingly daunting, has a derivative that yields an intuitive and interpretable result:

$$\frac{\partial}{\partial w_j} - \log Z(\tilde{\mathbf{x}}) = -\frac{\partial}{\partial w_j}\left\{\sum_y \exp\left(\sum_{k=1}^{K} w_k f_k(y, \tilde{\mathbf{x}})\right)\right\}$$

$$= -\frac{\sum_y \exp\left(\sum_{k=1}^{K} w_k f_k(y, \tilde{\mathbf{x}})\right) f_j(y, \tilde{\mathbf{x}})}{\sum_y \exp\left(\sum_{k=1}^{K} w_k f_k(y, \tilde{\mathbf{x}})\right)}$$

$$= -\sum_y p(y|\tilde{\mathbf{x}}) f_j(y, \tilde{\mathbf{x}}) = -\text{E}[f_j(y, \tilde{\mathbf{x}})]_{p(y|\tilde{\mathbf{x}})},$$

which corresponds to the expectation $\text{E}[.]_{P(y|\tilde{\mathbf{x}})}$ of the feature function $f_j(y|\tilde{\mathbf{x}})$ under the probability distribution $p(y|\tilde{\mathbf{x}})$ given by the model with the current parameter settings. Write the feature functions as a function $\mathbf{f}(\tilde{y}|\tilde{\mathbf{x}})$ in vector form. Then for a vector of weights $\mathbf{w}$, the partial derivative of the conditional log-likelihood for the entire dataset with respect to $\mathbf{w}$ is

$$\frac{\partial}{\partial \mathbf{w}} L_{y|x} = \sum_{i=1}^{N} [\mathbf{f}(\tilde{y}_i|\tilde{\mathbf{x}}_i) - E[\mathbf{f}(y_i|\tilde{\mathbf{x}}_i)]_{P(y_i|\tilde{\mathbf{x}}_i)}].$$

This consists of the sum of the differences between the observed feature vector for a given example and the expected value of the feature vector under the current model settings. If the model were perfect, classifying each example correctly with probability 1, the partial derivative would be zero. Intuitively, the learning procedure adjusts the model parameters so as to produce predictions that are closer to the observed data.

Matrix vector formulation of multiclass logistic regression

The model in (9.7) for a multiclass linear probabilistic classifier using vectors $\mathbf{w}_c$ for the weights associated with each class can be written

$$p(y = c|\mathbf{x}) = \frac{\exp(\mathbf{w}_c^T \mathbf{x})}{\sum_y \exp(\mathbf{w}_y^T \mathbf{x})},$$

where y is an index, the weights are encoded into a vector of length K, and the features $\mathbf{x}$ have been re-defined as the result of evaluating the feature functions $f_k(y,\mathbf{x})$ in such a way that there is no difference between the features given by $f_k(y = i,\mathbf{x})$ and $f_k(y = j,\mathbf{x})$. This form is widely used for the last layer in neural network models, where it is referred to as the *softmax* function.

The information concerning class labels can be encoded into a *multinomial vector* $\mathbf{y}$, which is all 0s except for a single 1 in the dimension that represents the correct class label—e.g., $\mathbf{y} = \begin{bmatrix} 0 & 1 & 0 \dots & 0 \end{bmatrix}^T$ for the second class. The weights form a matrix $\mathbf{W} = \begin{bmatrix} \mathbf{w}_1 & \mathbf{w}_2 & \dots & \mathbf{w}_K \end{bmatrix}^T$, and the biases form a vector $\mathbf{b} = \begin{bmatrix} b_1 & b_2 & \dots & b_K \end{bmatrix}^T$. Then the model yields *vectors of probabilities*

$$p(\mathbf{y}|\mathbf{x}) = \frac{\exp(\mathbf{y}^T \mathbf{W}^T \mathbf{x} + \mathbf{y}^T \mathbf{b})}{\sum_{\mathbf{y} \in Y} \exp(\mathbf{y}^T \mathbf{W}^T \mathbf{x} + \mathbf{y}^T \mathbf{b})},$$

where the denominator sums over each possible label $\mathbf{y} \in Y$, which is $Y = \{[1 \ \ 0 \ \ 0 \ \ \ldots \ \ 0]^T, [0 \ \ 1 \ \ 0 \ \ \ldots \ \ 0]^T, \ldots, [0 \ \ 0 \ \ 0 \ \ \ldots \ \ 1]^T\}$. Redefining $\mathbf{x}$ as $\mathbf{x} = [\mathbf{x}^T \ 1]^T$ and the parameters as a matrix of the form

$$\theta = [\mathbf{W} \ \mathbf{b}] = \begin{bmatrix} \mathbf{w}_1^T & b_1 \\ \mathbf{w}_2^T & b_2 \\ \vdots & \vdots \\ \mathbf{w}_k^T & b_k \end{bmatrix},$$

the conditional model can be written in this compact matrix-vector form:

$$p(\mathbf{y}|\mathbf{x}) = \frac{\exp(\mathbf{y}^T \theta \mathbf{x})}{\sum_{\mathbf{y} \in Y} \exp(\mathbf{y}^T \theta \mathbf{x})} = \frac{1}{Z(\mathbf{x})} \exp(\mathbf{y}^T \theta \mathbf{x}).$$

Then the gradient of the log-conditional-likelihood with respect to the parameter matrix θ can be expressed as

$$\frac{\partial}{\partial \theta} \log \prod_i p(\tilde{\mathbf{y}}_i | \tilde{\mathbf{x}}_i; \theta) = \sum_{i=1}^{N} \left[\frac{\partial}{\partial \theta} (\tilde{\mathbf{y}}_i^T \theta \tilde{\mathbf{x}}_i) - \frac{\partial}{\partial \theta} \log Z(\tilde{\mathbf{x}}_i) \right]$$

$$= \sum_{i=1}^{N} \tilde{\mathbf{y}}_i \tilde{\mathbf{x}}_i^T - \sum_{i=1}^{N} \sum_{\mathbf{y} \in Y} P(\mathbf{y}|\tilde{\mathbf{x}}_i) \mathbf{y} \tilde{\mathbf{x}}_i^T$$

$$= \sum_{i=1}^{N} \tilde{\mathbf{y}}_i \tilde{\mathbf{x}}_i^T - \sum_{i=1}^{N} E[\mathbf{y}\tilde{\mathbf{x}}_i^T]_{P(\mathbf{y}|\tilde{\mathbf{x}}_i)},$$

where the notation $E[\mathbf{y}\tilde{\mathbf{x}}_i^T]_{P(\mathbf{y}|\tilde{\mathbf{x}}_i)}$ denotes the expectation of the random vector $\mathbf{y}$ under $P(\mathbf{y}|\tilde{\mathbf{x}}_i)$, the vector of conditional probabilities that the model yields for the observed input $\tilde{\mathbf{x}}_i$ under the current parameter settings. The first term corresponds to a matrix that is computed just once, when the procedure commences. The second corresponds to a matrix that approaches the first term more closely as the model learns to make predictions that match the observed data.

Formulating these equations as vector and matrix operations allows highly optimized numerical libraries to be applied. Fast libraries for vector and matrix operations are key facilitators of big data techniques. In particular, state-of-the-art methods for deep learning with large datasets rely heavily on the dramatic performance improvements enabled by GPUs.

Note that we have not taken account of the fact that the final prediction need only yield probabilities for $N-1$ of the N classes, the remaining one being inferred from the fact that they must all sum to 1. Multinomial logistic regression models can be formulated that exploit this fact and involve fewer parameters.

Priors on parameters, and the regularized loss function

Logistic regression is frequently performed with some regularizer or prior on the parameters to combat overfitting. From a probabilistic perspective, this means that the conditional probability for the set of all labels Y given the set of all input vectors X can be rewritten

$$p(Y, \theta|X) = p(\theta; \sigma) \prod_{i=1}^{N} p(y_i|\mathbf{x}_i, \theta),$$

where $p(\theta; \sigma)$ is a prior distribution for the parameters. Given observed data $\tilde{Y}, \tilde{X}$, finding the value of θ that maximizes this expression is an instance of maximum a posteriori parameter estimation with a conditional probability model. The goal, then, is to minimize

$$-\log p(\tilde{Y}, \theta|\tilde{X}) = -\sum_{i=1}^{N} \log p(\tilde{y}_i|\tilde{\mathbf{x}}_i) - \log p(\theta; \lambda)$$

The first term is the negative log-likelihood, corresponding to the loss function, and the second is the negative log of the prior for the parameters, also known as the "regularization" term. L_2 regularization is often used for the weights in a logistic regression model. A prior could be applied to the bias too; but in practice it is often better not to do this (or, equivalently, to use a uniform distribution as the prior).

So-called "L_2 regularization" is based on the L_2 norm, which is just the Euclidean distance $||\mathbf{w}||_2 = \sqrt{\mathbf{w}^T\mathbf{w}}$. If a Gaussian distribution with zero mean and a common variance for each weight is used as the prior for the weights, the corresponding regularization term is the squared L_2 distance weighted by λ, plus a constant:

$$-\log p(\theta; \sigma) = \lambda||\mathbf{w}||_2^2 + const.$$

The constant can be ignored during the optimization and is often omitted from the regularized loss function. However, using $\lambda/2$ or $1/2\,\sigma^2$ as the regularization term gives a more direct correspondence with the σ^2 parameter of the Gaussian distribution.

Solving a regularized multiclass logistic regression with M weight parameters corresponds to finding the weights and biases that minimize

$$-\sum_{i=1}^{N} \log p(\tilde{y}_i|\tilde{\mathbf{x}}_i; \mathbf{W}, \mathbf{b}) + \lambda \sum_{j=1}^{M} w_j^2,$$

the regularization term will encourage the weights to be small. In the context of multilayer perceptrons, this sort of regularization is known as weight decay; in statistics it is known as ridge regression.

In regression, the elastic net regularization introduced earlier combines L_1 and L_2 regularization using $\lambda_2 R_{L_2}(\theta) + \lambda_1 R_{L_1}(\theta)$, which corresponds to a prior on weights consisting of the product of Laplacian and Gaussian distributions. In terms of a matrix representation, given a weight matrix $\mathbf{W}$ with row and column entries given by $w_{r,c}$, this can be written

$$R_{L_2}(\theta) = \sum_r \sum_c (w_{r,c})^2, \frac{\partial}{\partial \mathbf{W}} R_{L_2}(\theta) = 2\mathbf{W},$$

$$R_{L_1}(\theta) = \sum_r \sum_c |w_{r,c}|, \frac{\partial}{\partial w_{r,c}} R_{L_1}(\theta) = \begin{cases} 1, & w_{r,c} > 0 \\ 0, & w_{r,c} = 0, \\ -1, & w_{r,c} < 0 \end{cases}$$

where we have set the derivative of the L_1 prior to zero at zero despite the fact that it is technically undefined at this point. This is common practice, since the goal of this type of regularization is to induce sparsity: once a weight is zero the gradient will be zero. Notice that regularization has not been applied to the bias terms. This regularizer leads to convex optimization problems if the loss is convex, which is the case for logistic regression and linear regression.

GRADIENT DESCENT AND SECOND-ORDER METHODS

By formulating maximum likelihood learning with a prior on parameters as the problem of minimizing the negative log probability, gradient descent can be used to optimize the model's parameters. Given a conditional probability model $p(y|\mathbf{x}; \theta)$ with parameter vector θ and data $\tilde{y}_i, \tilde{\mathbf{x}}_i, i = 1, \ldots, N$, along with a prior on parameters given by $p(\theta; \lambda)$, with hyperparameter λ, the gradient descent procedure with learning rate η is:

$$\theta = \theta_o // \text{initialize parameters}$$
$$\text{while converged} == \text{FALSE}$$
$$\mathbf{g} = \frac{\partial}{\partial \theta} \left[-\sum_{i=1}^{N} \log p(\tilde{y}_i|\tilde{\mathbf{x}}_i; \theta) - \log p(\theta; \lambda) \right]$$
$$\theta \leftarrow \theta - \eta \mathbf{g}$$

Convergence is usually determined by monitoring the change in the loss or the parameters and terminating when one of them stabilizes. Appendix A.1 shows how a Taylor series expansion can be used to interpret and justify the learning rate parameter η.

Alternatively, gradient descent can be based on the second derivative by computing the Hessian matrix $\mathbf{H}$ at each iteration and replacing the above update by

$$\mathbf{H} = \frac{\partial^2}{\partial \theta^2} \left[-\sum_{i=1}^{N} \log p(\tilde{y}_i|\tilde{\mathbf{x}}_i; \theta) - \log p(\theta; \lambda) \right],$$
$$\theta \leftarrow \theta - \mathbf{H}^{-1} \mathbf{g}.$$

GENERALIZED LINEAR MODELS

Linear regression and logistic regression are special cases of a family of conditional probability models known in statistics as "generalized linear models," which were proposed to unify and generalize linear and logistic regression. In this formulation, linear models may be related to a response variable using distributions other than the Gaussian distribution used for linear regression. Generalized linear models can be created for any distribution in the exponential family (Appendix A.2 introduces exponential-family distributions).

In this context, the data can be thought of in terms of response variables y_i and explanatory variables organized as p-dimensional vectors $\mathbf{x}_i$, $i = 1, \ldots, n$. Response variables can be expressed in different ways, ranging from binary to categorical or ordinal data. A model is then defined where the expected value $E[y]$ of the distribution used for the response variable consists of an initial linear prediction $\eta_i = \beta^T \mathbf{x}_i$ using a parameter vector β, which is then subjected to a smooth, invertible, and potentially nonlinear transformation using the *mean function* g^{-1}:

$$\mu_i = E[y_i] = g^{-1}(\beta^T \mathbf{x}_i).$$

The mean function is the inverse of the *link function g*. In generalized linear modeling the entire set of explanatory variables for all the observations is arranged as an $n \times p$ matrix $\mathbf{X}$, so that a vector of linear predictions for the entire data set is $\eta = \mathbf{X}\beta$. The variance of the underlying distribution can also be modeled; typically as a function of the mean. Different distributions, link functions, and corresponding mean functions give a great deal of flexibility in defining probabilistic models; Table 9.2 shows some examples.

The multiclass extension of logistic regression discussed above is another example of a generalized linear model that uses the multinomial distribution for the response variable y. Because this model is defined in terms of probability distributions, the parameters can be estimated using maximum likelihood techniques.

Since these models are fairly simple, the coefficients β_j are interpretable. Applied statisticians are often interested not only in the estimated values but in other information such as the standard error of the estimates and statistical significance tests.

Table 9.2 Link Functions, Mean Functions, and Distributions Used in Generalized Linear Models

Link Name	Link Function $\eta = \beta^T \mathbf{x} = g(\mu)$	Mean Function $\mu = g^{-1}(\beta^T \mathbf{x}) = g^{-1}(\eta)$	Typical Distribution
Identity	$\eta = \mu$	$\mu = \eta$	Gaussian
Inverse	$\eta = \mu^{-1}$	$\mu = \eta^{-1}$	Exponential
Log	$\eta = \log_e \mu$	$\mu = \exp(\eta)$	Poisson
Log-log	$\eta = -\log(-\log_e \mu)$	$\mu = \exp(-\exp(-\eta))$	Bernoulli
Logit	$\eta = \log_e \frac{\mu}{1-\mu}$	$\mu = \frac{1}{1 + \exp(-\eta)}$	Bernoulli
Probit	$\eta = \Phi^{-1}(\mu)$	$\mu = \Phi(\eta)$	Bernoulli

Note: $\Phi(\cdot)$ is the cumulative normal distribution.

MAKING PREDICTIONS FOR ORDERED CLASSES

In many situations class values are categorical but possess a natural ordering. To deal with ordinal class attributes, the class probabilities can be expressed in terms of cumulative distributions, which are then modeled to construct an underlying probability distribution function for each class. To define a model with M ordinal categories, $M-1$ cumulative probability models of the form $P(Y_i \leq j)$ are used for the random variable Y_i that represents the category of a given instance i. Models for $P(Y_i = j)$ are then obtained using differences between the cumulative distribution models. Here we will use complementary cumulative probabilities, known as *survival functions*, of the form $P(Y_i > j) = 1 - P(Y_i \leq j)$, because this sometimes simplifies the interpretation of parameters. Then the class probabilities are obtained by:

$$P(Y_i = 1) = 1 - P(Y_i > 1)$$
$$P(Y_i = j) = P(Y_i > j - 1) - P(Y_i > j)$$
$$P(Y_i = M) = P(Y_i > M - 1).$$

The generalized linear models discussed above can be further generalized to ordinal categorical data. In fact, the general approach can be applied to various model classes by modeling complementary cumulative probabilities with a smooth and invertible link function that transforms them nonlinearly and equates the result to a linear predictor. For binary predictions, the models often take this form:

$$\text{logit}(\gamma_{ij}) = \log \frac{\gamma_{ij}}{1 - \gamma_{ij}} = b_j + \mathbf{w}^T \mathbf{x}_i,$$

where $\mathbf{w}$ is a vector of weights, $\mathbf{x}_i$ are vectors of features, and γ_{ij} represent the probability that example i is greater than the discretized, ordinal category j. Such models are called "proportional odds" models, or "ordered logit" models. The model above uses a different bias for each inequality, but the same set of weights. This guarantees a consistent set of probabilities.

CONDITIONAL PROBABILISTIC MODELS USING KERNELS

Linear models can be transformed into nonlinear ones by applying the "kernel trick" mentioned in Section 7.2 under kernel regression, or, alternatively, through basis expansion as mentioned in the section above on matrix formulations of linear and polynomial regression. This can be applied to both kernel regression and kernel logistic regression.

Suppose the features $\mathbf{x}$ are replaced by the vector $\mathbf{k}(\mathbf{x})$ whose elements are determined using a kernel function $k(\mathbf{x}, \mathbf{x}_j)$ for every training example (or for some subset of training vectors):

$$\mathbf{k}(\mathbf{x}) = \begin{bmatrix} k(\mathbf{x}, \mathbf{x}_1) \\ \vdots \\ k(\mathbf{x}, \mathbf{x}_V) \\ 1 \end{bmatrix}$$

A "1" has been appended to this vector to implement the bias term in the parameter matrix. A kernel regression is then

$$p(y|\mathbf{x}) = N(y; \mathbf{w}^T \mathbf{k}(\mathbf{x}), \sigma^2).$$

For classification, an analogous kernel logistic regression is

$$p(\mathbf{y}|\mathbf{x}) = \frac{\exp(\mathbf{y}^T \theta \mathbf{k}(\mathbf{x}))}{\sum_{\mathbf{y}} \exp(\mathbf{y}^T \theta \mathbf{k}(\mathbf{x}))} = \frac{1}{Z(\mathbf{k}(\mathbf{x}))} \exp(\mathbf{y}^T \theta \mathbf{k}(\mathbf{x})).$$

Since every example in the training set can have a different kernel vector, it is necessary to compute a *kernel matrix* $\mathbf{K}$ with entries given by $\mathbf{K}_{ij} = k(\mathbf{x}_i, \mathbf{x}_j)$. For large datasets this operation can be time- and memory-intensive.

Support vector machines have a similar form, although they are not formulated probabilistically, and multiclass support vector machines are not as easily formulated as multiclass kernel logistic regression. Because they use an underlying hinge loss and weight regularization term, support vector machines often assign zero weights to many of the terms; they also have the appealing feature of placing nonzero weights only on vectors that reside at the boundary of the decision surface. In many applications this results in a significant reduction in the number of kernel evaluations needed at test time. Neither kernel logistic regression nor kernel ridge regression produce such sparse solutions, even when a Gaussian or (squared) L_2 regularization is used: in general there is a nonzero weight for every exemplar. However, kernel logistic regression can outperform support vector machines, and several techniques have been proposed to make these methods sparse. They are mentioned in the *Further Reading* section at the end of the chapter.

9.8 SEQUENTIAL AND TEMPORAL MODELS

Consider the task of creating a probability model for a sequence of observations. If they correspond to words, random variables could be defined with as many states as there are words in the vocabulary. If they are continuous, some parametric form is needed to create suitable continuous distributions.

MARKOV MODELS AND *N*-GRAM METHODS

One simple and effective probabilistic model for discrete sequential data is known as a "Markov model." A first-order Markov model assumes that each symbol in a sequence can be predicted using its conditional probability given the preceding symbol. (For the very first symbol, an unconditional probability is used.) Given observation variables $O = \{O_1, \ldots, O_T\}$, this can be written

$$P(O) = P(O_1) \prod_{t=1}^{T} P(O_{t+1}|O_t).$$

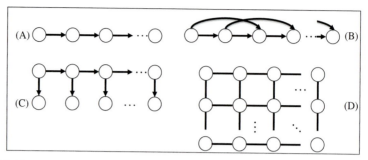

FIGURE 9.18

(A) and (B) First- and second-order Markov models for a sequence of variables;
(C) Hidden Markov model; (D) Markov random field.

Usually, every conditional probability used in such models is the same. The corresponding Bayesian networks consist simply of a linear chain of variables with directed edges between each successive pair; Fig. 9.18A shows an example. The method generalizes naturally to second-order models (Fig. 9.18B), and to higher orders. N-gram models correspond to the use of an $(N-1)$-th order Markov model. For example, first-order models involve the use of 2-grams (or "bigrams"); third-order models use trigrams, and zero-th order models correspond to single observations or "unigrams." Such models are widely used for modeling biological sequences such as DNA, as well as for text mining and computational linguistics applications.

All probabilistic models raise the issue of what to do when there is no data for certain configurations of variables. Zero-valued parameters cause problems, as we saw in Section 4.2. This is particularly severe with high-order Markov models, and smoothing techniques—such as Laplace or Dirichlet smoothing, which can be derived from a Bayesian analysis—become critical. See the *Further Reading* section for some pointers to some specialized methods for smoothing n-grams.

Large n-gram models are extremely useful for applications ranging from machine translation and speech recognition to spelling correction and information extraction. Indeed, Google has made available English language word counts for a billion five-word sequences that appear at least 40 times in a trillion-word corpus After discarding words that appear less than 200 times, there remain 13 million unique words (unigrams), 300 million bigrams; and around a billion each of trigrams, four-grams, and five-grams.

HIDDEN MARKOV MODELS

Hidden Markov models have been widely used for pattern recognition since at least the 1980s. Until recently most of the major speech recognition systems have consisted of large Gaussian mixture models combined with hidden Markov models. Many problems in biological sequence analysis can also be formulated in terms of hidden Markov models, with various extensions and generalizations.

A hidden Markov model is a joint probability model of a set of discrete observed variables $O = \{O_1,\ldots,O_T\}$ and discrete hidden variables $H = \{H_1,\ldots, H_T\}$ for T observations that factors the joint distribution as follows:

$$P(O, H) = P(H_1) \prod_{t=1}^{T} P(H_{t+1}|H_t) \prod_{t=1}^{T} P(O_t|H_t),$$

Each O_t is a discrete random variable with N possible values, and each H_t is a discrete random variable with M possible values. Fig. 9.18C illustrates a hidden Markov model as a type of Bayesian network that is known as a "dynamic" Bayesian network because variables are replicated dynamically over the appropriate number of time steps. They are an obvious extension of first-order Markov models, and it is common to use "time-homogeneous" models where the transition matrix $P(H_{t+1}|H_t)$ is the same at each time step. Define $\mathbf{A}$ to be a transition matrix whose elements encode $P(H_{t+1} = j|H_t = i)$, and $\mathbf{B}$ to be an emission matrix $\mathbf{B}$ whose elements b_{ij} correspond to $P(O_t = j|H_t = i)$. For the special $t = 1$ the initial state probability distribution is encoded in a vector π with elements $\pi_i = P (H_t = i)$. The complete set of parameters is $\theta = \{\mathbf{A}, \mathbf{B}, \pi\}$, a set containing two matrices and one vector. We write a particular observation sequence as a set of observations $\tilde{O} = \{O_1 = o_1, \ldots, O_T = o_T\}$.

Hidden Markov models pose three key problems:

1. Compute $P(\tilde{O}; \theta)$, the probability of a sequence under the model with parameters θ.
2. Find the most probable explanation—the best sequence of states $H^* = \{H_1 = h_1, \ldots, H_T = h_T\}$ that explains an observation.
3. Find the best parameters θ for the model given a data set of observed sequences.

The first problem can be solved using the sum-product algorithm, the second using the max-product algorithm, and the third using the EM algorithm for which the required expectations are computed using the sum-product algorithm. If there is labeled data for the sequences of hidden variables that correspond to observed sequences, the required conditional probability distributions can be computed from the corresponding counts in the same way as we did with Bayesian networks.

The only difference between the parameter estimation task when using an hidden Markov model viewed as a dynamic Bayesian network and the updates used for learning the conditional probability tables in a Bayesian network is that one can average over the statistics obtained at each time step, because the same emission and transition matrices are used at each step. The basic hidden Markov model formulation serves as a point of reference when coupling more complex probabilistic models over time using more general dynamic Bayesian network models.

Meeting Record	
Date	Tuesday, March 1, 2016
Time	12:00pm
Where	AA3195
Duration	unknown

Hello Pascal,
How about we meet next Tuesday at noon?
I will reserve room AA3195. If you cannot
make it call me on my cell phone at:
514-555-5555.
Cheers,
Chris

Christopher Pal
Associate Professor
Dept. of Computer and Software Engineering
Polytechnique Montréal
University of Montréal, Pavillon Lassonde
Montréal, Québec, Canada, H3T 1J4
Telephone : (514) 340-5121, ext. 7174

Contact Record	
Last Name	Christopher
First Name	Pal
Cell Phone	(514) 555-5555
Office Phone	(514) 340-5121 ext. 7174
Organization	Polytechnique Montréal
Address	University of Montréal, Pavillon Lassonde Montréal, Québec, Canada, H3T 1J4

FIGURE 9.19

Mining emails for meeting details.

CONDITIONAL RANDOM FIELDS

Hidden Markov models are not the only models that are useful when working with sequence data. *Conditional random fields* are a statistical modeling technique that takes context into account, and are often structured as linear chains. They are widely used for sequence processing tasks in data mining, but are also popular in image processing and computer vision. Fig. 9.19 illustrates the problem of extracting locations and dates of meetings from email text, which can be addressed using chain-structured conditional random fields. A major advantage is that these models can be given arbitrarily complex features of the input sequence to be used for making predictions—e.g., matching words to lists of organizations and processing variations of known abbreviations.

Inference for chain-structured conditional random fields can be performed efficiently using the sum- and max-product algorithms discussed above. The sum-product algorithm can be used to compute the expected gradients needed to learn them, and the max-product algorithm serves to label new sequences—with tags such as "where" indicating the location or room and "time" labels associated with a meeting.

We begin with a general definition, and then focus on the simpler case of linear conditional random fields. Fig. 9.20D shows a chain-structured conditional

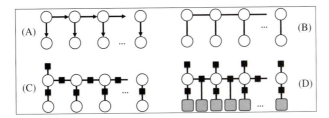

FIGURE 9.20

(A) Dynamic Bayesian network representation of a hidden Markov model; (B) similarly structured Markov random field; (C) factor graph for (A); and (D) factor graph for a linear chain conditional random field.

random field, illustrated as a factor graph, which can be contrasted with the Markov random field depicted in Fig. 9.20B and the hidden Markov model in Fig. 9.20C, also shown as a factor graph. Circles are not used to represent the observed variables in Fig. 9.20D because the underlying conditional random field model does not explicitly encode these as random variables in the graph.

From Markov random fields to conditional random fields

Whereas both Bayesian networks and Markov random fields define a joint probability model for data, conditional random fields (also known as "structured prediction" techniques) define a joint *conditional* distribution for multiple predictions. For a set X of random variables, we have already seen how a Markov random field factorizes the joint distribution for X using an exponentiated energy function $F(X)$:

$$P(X) = \frac{1}{Z}\exp(-F(X)),$$

$$Z = \sum_X \exp(-F(X)),$$

where the sum is over all states of all variables in X. Conditional random fields condition on some observations, yielding a conditional distribution:

$$P(Y|X) = \frac{1}{Z(X)}\exp(-F(Y,X)),$$

$$Z(X) = \sum_Y \exp(-F(Y,X)),$$

where the sum is over all states of all variables in Y. Both Markov and conditional random fields can be defined for general model structures, but the energy functions usually include just one or two variables—unary and pairwise potentials. Conceptually, to create a conditional random field for $P(Y|X)$ based on U unary and V pairwise functions of variables in Y, the energy function takes the form

$$F(Y,\tilde{X}) = \sum_{u=1}^{U} U(Y_u,\tilde{X}) + \sum_{v=1}^{V} V(Y_v,\tilde{X}).$$

Such energy functions can be transformed into so-called potential functions by negation, exponentiation, and normalization. The conditional probability model takes this form:

$$P(Y|\tilde{X}) = \frac{1}{Z(\tilde{X})} \exp\left[\sum_{u=1}^{U} U(Y_u, \tilde{X}) + \sum_{v=1}^{V} V(Y_v, \tilde{X}) \right]$$

$$= \frac{1}{Z(\tilde{X})} \prod_{u=1}^{U} \phi_u(Y_u, \tilde{X}) \prod_{v=1}^{V} \Psi_v(Y_v, \tilde{X}).$$

(9.8)

Lattice-structured models like this are used in image processing applications, as mentioned earlier. Processing sequences with chain-structured conditional random fields is even simpler. Note that logistic regression could be thought of as a simple conditional random field, one that arises naturally from a conditional version of a Markov random field with a factorization shown in Fig. 9.15B.

Linear chain conditional random fields

Consider observations $\tilde{Y} = \{y_1 = \tilde{y}_1, \ldots, y_N = \tilde{y}_N\}$ of a sequence of discrete random variables $Y = \{y_1, \ldots, y_N\}$, using integers to encode the relevant states, and an observed input sequence $\tilde{X} = \{\tilde{x}_1, \ldots, \tilde{x}_N\}$, which can be of any data type. A conditional random field defines the conditional probability $P(Y|X)$ of a label sequence given an input sequence. This contrasts with hidden Markov models, which treat both Y and X as random variables and defines a joint probability model for $P(Y, X)$. Note that X above was intentionally not defined as a sequence of random variables because we will define the conditional distribution of Y given X and need not have an explicit model for $P(X)$. Of course, an *implicit* model for $P(X)$ could be defined as the empirical distribution of the data, or the distribution produced by placing a Dirac or Kronecker delta function on each observation and normalizing by the number of examples. Not defining X as a sequence leaves open what type of variables these are, and whether it is just a set of variables or a set of formally defined *random* variables. Fig. 9.20D uses shaded rectangles to emphasize this point. In this chain model, for a given sequence of length N, Eq. (9.8) could be re-written

$$P(Y|\tilde{X}) = \frac{1}{Z(\tilde{X})} \prod_{u=1}^{N} \phi_u(y_u, \tilde{X}) \prod_{v=1}^{N} \Psi_v(y_v, y_{v+1}, \tilde{X}).$$

Focusing on a linear chain structure reveals some analogies with the emission and transition matrices of hidden Markov models. There are two types of features: a set of J *single variable* (state) features $u_j(y_i, X, i)$ that are a function of a single y_i, and which are computed for each y_i in the sequence $i = 1, \ldots, N$; and a set of K *pairwise* (transition) features $v_k(y_{i-1}, y_i, X, i)$ for $i > 1$. Each type has associated unary weights θ_j^u and pairwise weights θ_k^v. Note that these features can be a function of the entire observed sequence $\tilde{X}$, or of some subset. This global dependence on the input is a major advantage of conditional random fields over hidden Markov models. The analog of the Markov model transition matrix are the *per-position pairwise potential functions*: these can be written as a set of matrices that depend upon the observation sequence and consist of a sum over the product of pairwise weights θ_k^v and pairwise features

$$\Psi_i[y_i, y_{i+1}] = \exp\left[\sum_{k=1}^{K} \theta_k^v v_k(y_i, y_{i+1}, \tilde{X}, i)\right].$$

The unary potential functions play a similar role to the terms arising from the hidden Markov model emission matrices, and can be written as the following set of vectors that involve exponentiated weighted combinations of unary features

$$\phi_i[y_i] = \exp\left[\sum_{j=1}^{J} \theta_j^u u_j(y_i, \tilde{X}, i)\right].$$

Sometimes, rather than keeping the unary and pairwise features and their parameters separate, it is useful to work with all features for a given position i. To do this, define $\mathbf{f}(y_i, y_{i+1}, X, i)$ as a length-L vector containing all single-variable and pairwise features, and define the global feature vector to be the sum over each of these position dependent feature vectors:

$$\mathbf{g}(Y, X) = \sum_{i=1}^{N} \mathbf{f}(y_i, y_{i+1}, X, i).$$

Now a conditional random field can be written in a particularly compact form

$$P(Y|X) = \frac{\exp(\theta^T \mathbf{g}(Y, X))}{\sum_Y \exp(\theta^T \mathbf{g}(Y, X))}.$$

If we turn to the problem of learning based on maximizing the conditional likelihood for this model, an analogy can be drawn to the simpler case of logistic regression. The gradient of the log-likelihood of a conditional random field for a set of M input sequences $A = \{\tilde{X}_1, \ldots, \tilde{X}_M\}$ and corresponding output sequences $B = \{\tilde{Y}_1, \ldots, \tilde{Y}_M\}$, is

$$\frac{\partial}{\partial \theta} \log P(B|A) = \sum_{m=1}^{M} [\mathbf{g}(\tilde{Y}_m, \tilde{X}_m) - E_m[\mathbf{g}(Y_m, \tilde{X}_m)]].$$

Here, $E_m[.]$ is an expectation taken with respect to $P(Y_m|\tilde{X}_m)$. It is standard practice to include a Gaussian prior or L_2 regularization on parameters by adding a regularization term to this expression. Unlike logistic regression, this expectation involves the joint distribution of the label sequence and not just the distribution for a single label variable. However, in chain-structured graphs it can be computed efficiently and exactly using the sum-product algorithm.

Learning for chain-structured conditional random fields

To compute the gradient for a linear chain conditional random field, it is useful to expose each parameter in the L_2 regularized log-likelihood in scalar form:

$$\log P(B|A) = \sum_{m=1}^{M}\sum_{i=1}^{N_m}\sum_{l=1}^{L}\theta_l g_l(\tilde{y}_{m,i}, \tilde{y}_{m,i+1}, \tilde{X}_m) - \sum_{m=1}^{M}\log Z(\tilde{X}_m) - \sum_{l=1}^{L}\frac{\theta_l^2}{2\sigma^2}.$$

where σ is the regularization parameter. Taking the derivative with respect to a single parameter and training example, the contribution to the gradient of each example is

$$\frac{\partial}{\partial\theta_l}\log P(\tilde{Y}_m|\tilde{X}_m) = \sum_{i=1}^{N_m} g_l(\tilde{y}_i, \tilde{y}_{i+1}, \tilde{X}) - \sum_{i=1}^{N_m}\sum_{y_i}\sum_{y_{i+1}} g_l(y_i, y_{i+1}, \tilde{X})P(y_i, y_{i+1}|\tilde{X}) - \frac{\theta_l}{\sigma^2}.$$

This is simply the difference between the observed occurrence of the feature and its expectation under the current prediction of the model, taken with respect to $P(y_i, y_{i+1}|\tilde{X})$, minus the partial derivative of the regularization term. Similar terms arise for unary functions, but the expectation is taken with respect to $P(y_i|\tilde{X})$. These distributions are the single- and pairwise-variable marginal conditional distributions, and can be computed efficiently using the sum-product algorithm.

Using conditional random fields for text mining

The text information extraction scenario in Fig. 9.19 is just one example of applying data mining to extract information from natural language. Such information might be other *named entities* such as *locations, personal names, organizations, money, percentages, dates,* and *times*; or fields in a seminar announcement such as *speaker name, seminar room, start time,* and *end time.* In such tasks, input features often consist of current, previous, and next word; character *n*-grams; part-of-speech tag sequences; the presence of certain key words in windows to the left or right of the current position. Other features can be defined using lists of known words, such as first and last names and honorifics; locations and organizations. Features such as capitalization and alphanumeric characters can be defined using regular expressions and integrated into an underlying probabilistic model based on conditional random fields.

9.9 FURTHER READING AND BIBLIOGRAPHIC NOTES

The field of probabilistic machine learning and data mining is enormous: it essentially subsumes all classical and modern statistical techniques. This chapter has focused on foundational concepts and some widely used probabilistic techniques in data mining and machine learning. Excellent books that focus on statistical and probabilistic methods include Hastie, Tibshirani, and Friedman (2009), and

Murphy (2012). Koller and Friedman (2009)'s excellent book specializes in advanced techniques and principles of probabilistic graphical models.

The *K*2 algorithm for learning Bayesian networks was introduced by Cooper and Herskovits (1992). Bayesian scoring metrics are covered by Heckerman et al. (1995). Friedman, Geiger, and Goldszmidt (1997) introduced the tree augmented Naïve Bayes algorithm, and also describe multinets. Grossman and Domingos (2004) show how to use the conditional likelihood for scoring networks. Guo and Greiner (2004) present an extensive comparison of scoring metrics for Bayesian network classifiers. Bouckaert (1995) describes averaging over subnetworks. AODEs are described by Webb, Boughton, and Wang (2005), and AnDEs by Webb et al. (2012). AD trees were introduced and analyzed by Moore and Lee (1998)—the same Andrew Moore whose work on *k*D-trees and ball trees was mentioned in Section 4.10. Komarek and Moore (2000) introduce AD trees for incremental learning that are also more efficient for data sets with many attributes.

The AutoClass program is described by Cheeseman and Stutz (1995). Two implementations have been produced: the original research implementation, written in LISP, and a follow-up public implementation in C that is 10 or 20 times faster but somewhat more restricted—e.g., only the normal distribution model is implemented for numeric attributes. DensiTrees were developed by Bouckaert (2010).

Kernel density estimation is an effective and conceptually simple probabilistic model. Epanechnikov (1969) showed the optimality of the Epanechnikov kernel under the mean-squared error metric. Jones, Marron, and Sheather (1996) recommends using a so-called "plug-in" estimate to select the kernel bandwidth. Duda and Hart (1973) and Bishop (2006) show theoretically that kernel density estimation converges to the true distribution as the amount of data grows.

The EM algorithm, which originates in the work of Dempster, Laird, and Rubin (1977), is the key to learning in hidden or latent variable models. The modern variational view provides a solid theoretical justification for the use of approximate posterior distributions, as discussed in Appendix A.2 and in Bishop (2006). This perspective originated in the 1990s with work by Neal and Hinton (1998), Jordan, Ghahramani, Jaakkola, and Saul (1998), and others. Salakhutdinov, Roweis and Ghahramani (2003) explore the EM approach and compare it with the expected gradient, including the more sophisticated expected conjugate gradient based optimization.

Markov chain Monte Carlo methods are popular in Bayesian statistical modeling; see, e.g., Gilks (2005). Geman and Geman (1984) first described the Gibbs sampling procedure, naming it after the physicist Josiah Gibbs because of the analogy between sampling, the underlying functional forms of random fields and statistical physics. Hastings' (1970) generalization of the Metropolis, Rosenbluth, Rosenbluth, Teller, and Teller (1953) algorithm has been influential in laying the foundation for present-day methods. The *iterated conditional modes* approach for finding an approximate most probable explanation was proposed by Besag (1986).

Plate notation has been widely used in artificial intelligence (Buntine, 1994), machine learning (Blei, Ng, & Jordan, 2003) and computational statistics (Lunn, Thomas, Best, & Spiegelhalter, 2000) to define complex probabilistic graphical models, and forms the basis of the BUGS (Bayesian inference Using Gibbs Sampling) software project (Lunn et al., 2000). Our presentation of factor graphs and the sum-product algorithm follows their origins in Kschischang, Frey, and Loeliger (2001) and Frey (1998). The sum- and max-product algorithms only apply to trees. However, Bayesian networks and other models that contain cycles can be manipulated into a structure known as a *junction tree* by clustering variables, and Lauritzen and Spiegelhalter (1988)'s junction tree algorithm permits exact inference. Ripley (1996) covers the junction tree algorithm, with practical examples; Huang and Darwiche (1996)'s procedural guide is an excellent resource for those who need to implement the algorithm. Probability propagation in a junction tree yields exact results, but is sometimes infeasible because the clusters become too large—in which case one must resort to sampling or variational methods.

Roweis (1998) gives an early EM formulation for PPCA: he examines the zero input noise case and provides the elegant mathematics for the simplified EM algorithm presented above. Tipping and Bishop (1999a, 1999b) give further analysis, and show that after optimizing the model and learning the variance of the observation noise the columns of the matrix $\mathbf{W}$ are scaled and rotated principal eigenvectors of the covariance matrix of the data. The probabilistic formulation of principal component analysis opens the door to probabilistic formulations of further generalizations, such as mixtures of principal component analyzers (Dony & Haykin, 1995; Tipping & Bishop, 1999a, 1999b) and mixtures of factor analyzers (Ghahramani & Hinton, 1996). Of particular utility is the ability of PPCA and factor analysis to easily deal with missing data: providing the data is missing at random one can marginalize over the distribution associated with unobserved values, as detailed by Ilin and Raiko (2010).

PPCA corresponds to factorizing a covariance matrix. Another way to reduce the number of parameters in a continuous Gaussian model is to use sparse inverse covariance models, which, when combined with mixture models and EM, yield another form of clustering with correlated attributes. Edwards (2012) provides a nice introduction to graphical modeling, including mixed models with discrete and continuous components. Unlike any other treatments, he also examines graphical Gaussian models and delves further into the correspondence between a graphical model and the sparsity structure of an inverse covariance matrix. These concepts are better grasped using the "canonical" parameterization of the Gaussian distribution in terms of $\beta = \Sigma^{-1}\mu$, and $\Omega = \Sigma^{-1}$, rather than the usual "moment" parameterization that uses the mean μ and covariance matrix Σ.

LSA was introduced by Deerwester, Dumais, Landauer, Furnas, and Harshman (1990). pLSA has its origins in Hofmann (1999). Latent Dirichlet allocation (LDA[b]) was proposed in Blei et al (2003). The highly effective "collapsed Gibbs sampling" approach for LDA[b] was proposed by Teh et al.

(2006), who also extended the concept to variational methods. Rather than applying LDA[b] naïvely when looking for trends over time, Blei and Lafferty (2006)'s *dynamic topic models* treat the temporal evolution of topics explicitly; they examined topical trends in the journal *Science*. Griffiths and Steyvers (2004) used Bayesian model selection to determine the number of topics in their LDA[b] analysis of *Proceedings of the National Academy of Science* abstracts. Griffiths and Steyvers (2004) and Teh et al. (2006) give more details on the collapsed Gibbs sampling and variational approaches to LDA[b]. Hierarchical Dirichlet processes (Teh et al., 2006) and related techniques offer alternatives to the problem of determining the number of topics or clusters in hierarchical Bayesian models. These technically sophisticated methods are quite popular, and high-quality implementations are available online.

Logistic regression is sometimes referred to as the workhorse of applied statistics; Hosmer and Lemeshow (2004) is a useful resource. Nelder and Wedderburn (1972)'s work led to the generalized linear modeling framework. McCullagh (1980) developed proportional odds models for ordinal regression, which are sometimes called ordered logit models because they use the generalized logit function. Frank and Hall (2001) showed how to adapt arbitrary machine learning techniques to ordered predictions. McCullagh and Nelder (1989)'s widely cited monograph is another good source for additional details on the framework of generalized linear models.

Tibshirani (1996) developed the famous "Least Absolute Shrinkage and Selection Operator," also known as the LASSO; while Zou and Hastie (2005) developed the "elastic net" regularization approach.

Kernel logistic regression transforms a linear classifier into a nonlinear one, and probabilistic sparse kernel techniques are attractive alternatives to support vector machines. Tipping (2001) proposed a "relevance vector machine" that manipulates priors on parameters in a way that encourages kernel weights to become zero during learning. Lawrence, Seeger, and Herbrich (2003) proposed an "informative vector machine," which tackles the problem with a fast, sparse Gaussian process method in the sense of Williams and Rasmussen (2006). Zhu and Hastie (2005) formulated sparse kernel logistic regression as an "import vector machine" that uses greedy search methods. However, none of these approach the popularity of Cortes and Vapnik (1995)'s support vector machines, perhaps because their objective functions are not convex, in contrast to that of an SVM (and L_2 regularized kernel logistic regression). Convex optimization problems have a single minimum in the loss function (maximum in the likelihood). When probabilities are needed from an SVM, Platt (1999) shows how to fit a logistic regression to the classification scores.

Some techniques for smoothing *n*-grams arise from applying prior distributions to the parameters of the model's conditional probabilities. Others come from different perspectives—such as interpolation techniques, where weighted combinations of lower order *n*-grams are used. Good-Turing discounting (Good, 1953) (coinvented by Alan Turing, one of the fathers of computing), and Witten−Bell smoothing (Witten & Bell, 1991) are based on these ideas. Brants and Franz (2006) discuss the massive Google *n*-gram collections mentioned in Section 9.8; they are available as a 24 GB compressed text file from the Linguistic Data Consortium.

Rabiner and Juang (1986) and Rabiner (1989) give a classic introduction and tutorial respectively on Hidden Markov Models. They have been used extensively for decades in speech recognition systems, and are widely applicable to many other problems. The human genome sequencing project stretched from around 1990 to the early 2000s (International Human Genome Sequencing Consortium, 2001; Venter et al., 2001), and spawned a surge of activity in recognizing and modeling genes in genomes using hidden Markov models (Burge & Karlin, 1997; Kulp, Haussler, Rees, & Eeckman, 1996)—a particularly impressive and important application of data mining. Murphy (2002) is an excellent source for details on how dynamic Bayesian networks extend hidden Markov models.

Lafferty, McCallum, and Pereira (2001) is a seminal paper on conditional random fields; Sutton and McCallum (2006) is an excellent source of further details. Sha and Pereira (2003) present the global feature vector view of conditional random fields. Our presentation synthesizes these perspectives. The original application was to sequence labeling problems, but they have since become widely used for many sequence processing tasks in data mining. Kristjansson, Culotta, Viola, and McCallum (2004) examined the specific problem of extracting information from email text. The Stanford Named Entity Recognizer is based on conditional random fields; Finkel, Grenager, and Manning (2005) give details of the implementation.

Markov logic networks (Richardson & Domingos, 2006) provide a way to create dynamically instantiated Markov random fields from programs encoded using weighted clauses in first-order logic. This approach has been used for collective or structured classification, link or relationship prediction, entity and identity disambiguation, among many others, as described in Domingos and Lowd (2009)'s textbook.

SOFTWARE PACKAGES AND IMPLEMENTATIONS

Implementations of principal component analysis, Gaussian mixture models, and hidden Markov models are widely available in many software packages. MatLab's statistics toolbox, e.g., has implementations of principal component analysis and its probabilistic variant based on the methods we have discussed, and also contains implementations of Gaussian mixture models and all the canonical hidden Markov model manipulations.

Kevin Murphy's MatLab-based Probabilistic Modeling Toolkit is a large, open source collection of MatLab functions and tools. The software contains implementations for many of the methods we have discussed here, including code for Bayesian network manipulation and inference methods.

The Hugin software package from Hugin Expert A/S and the Netica software from Norsys are well-known commercial software implementations for manipulating Bayesian networks. They contain excellent graphical user interfaces for interacting with these networks.

The BUGS (Bayesian inference Using Gibbs Sampling) project has created a variety of software packages for the Bayesian analysis of complex statistical models using Markov chain Monte Carlo methods. WinBUGS (Lunn et al., 2000) is a stable version of the software, but the more recent OpenBUGS project is an open source version of the core BUGS implementation (Lunn, Spiegelhalter, Thomas, & Best, 2009).

The VIBES software package (Bishop, Spiegelhalter, & Winn, 2002) allows inference in graphical models using variational methods. Microsoft Research has created a programming language known as infer.net that allows one to define graphical models and perform inference in them using variational methods, Gibbs sampling or another message passing method known as expectation propagation (Minka, 2001). Expectation propagation generalizes belief propagation to distributions and models beyond the typical discrete and binary models used to create Bayesian networks. John Winn and Tom Minka at Microsoft Research have been leading the infer.net project.

The R programming language and software environment was created for statistical computing and visualization (Ihaka & Gentleman, 1996). It has its origins at the University of Auckland, and provides an open source implementation of the S programming language from Bell Labs. It is comparable to well known commercial packages such as SAS, SPSS, and Stata, and contains implementations of many classical statistical methods such as generalized linear models and other regression techniques. Since it is a general purpose programming language there are many extensions and implementations of the models discussed in this chapter available online. Historically Brian D. Ripley has overseen the development of R. Ripley is now retired from Oxford University where he was a statistic Professor. He is the coauthor of a number of books on S programming (Venables & Ripley, 2000, 2002) and an older but very high-quality textbook on pattern recognition and neural networks (Ripley, 1996).

The MALLET Machine Learning for Language Toolkit (McCallum, 2002) provides excellent Java implementations of latent Dirichlet allocation and conditional random fields. It also provides many other statistical natural language-processing methods ranging from document classification and clustering to topic modeling, information extraction, and other machine learning techniques frequently used for text processing.

The open source Alchemy software package is widely used for Markov logic networks (Richardson & Domingos, 2006).

Scikit-learn (Pedregosa et al., 2011) is a rapidly growing Python-based set of implementations of many machine learning methods. It contains implementations of many probabilistic and statistical methods for classification, regression, clustering, dimensionality reduction (including factor analysis and PPCA), model selection and preprocessing.

9.10 WEKA IMPLEMENTATIONS

- Bayesian networks

  BayesNet (Bayesian networks without hidden variables for classification)

  A1DE and *A2DE* (in the *AnDE* package)
- Conditional probability models

  LatentSemanticAnalysis (in the *latentSemanticAnalysis* package)

  ElasticNet (in the *elasticNet* package)

  KernelLogisticRegression (in the *kernelLogisticRegression* package)
- Clustering

  EM (clustering and density estimation using the EM algorithm)

Deep learning

CHAPTER OUTLINE

10.1 Deep Feedforward Networks...420
    The MNIST Evaluation 421
    Losses and Regularization 422
    Deep Layered Network Architecture...423
    Activation Functions 424
    Backpropagation Revisited 426
    Computation Graphs and Complex Network Structures...............................429
    Checking Backpropagation Implementations 430
10.2 Training and Evaluating Deep Networks...431
    Early Stopping 431
    Validation, Cross-Validation, and Hyperparameter Tuning 432
    Mini-Batch-Based Stochastic Gradient Descent..433
    Pseudocode for Mini-Batch Based Stochastic Gradient Descent....................434
    Learning Rates and Schedules..434
    Regularization With Priors on Parameters 435
    Dropout 436
    Batch Normalization 436
    Parameter Initialization...436
    Unsupervised Pretraining 437
    Data Augmentation and Synthetic Transformations 437
10.3 Convolutional Neural Networks 437
    The ImageNet Evaluation and Very Deep Convolutional Networks...............438
    From Image Filtering to Learnable Convolutional Layers............................439
    Convolutional Layers and Gradients..443
    Pooling and Subsampling Layers and Gradients 444
    Implementation..445
10.4 Autoencoders..445
    Pretraining Deep Autoencoders With RBMs..448
    Denoising Autoencoders and Layerwise Training 448
    Combining Reconstructive and Discriminative Learning 449
10.5 Stochastic Deep Networks 449
    Boltzmann Machines 449
    Restricted Boltzmann Machines..451

Data Mining.
© 2017 Elsevier Inc. All rights reserved.

Contrastive Divergence..452
Categorical and Continuous Variables 452
Deep Boltzmann Machines..453
Deep Belief Networks 455
10.6 **Recurrent Neural Networks** 456
Exploding and Vanishing Gradients 457
Other Recurrent Network Architectures..................................459
10.7 **Further Reading and Bibliographic Notes** 461
10.8 **Deep Learning Software and Network Implementations** 464
Theano 464
Tensor Flow..464
Torch..465
Computational Network Toolkit 465
Caffe 465
Deeplearning4j...465
Other Packages: Lasagne, Keras, and cuDNN............................465
10.9 **WEKA Implementations**...466

In recent years, so-called "deep learning" approaches to machine learning have had a major impact on speech recognition and computer vision. Other disciplines, such as natural language processing, are also starting to see benefits. A critical ingredient is the use of much larger quantities of data than has heretofore been possible. Recent successes have arisen in settings involving *high-capacity* models—ones with many parameters. These flexible models exploit information buried in massive data sets more effectively than traditional machine learning techniques using hand-engineered features.

This chapter begins by discussing the notion of deep learning and why it is effective. We then introduce key innovations, along with some specific results and experiments. We present the main approaches associated with deep learning, and also discuss common practical issues and aspects of training contemporary deep network architectures.

There are three approaches to making predictions from data based on machine learning:

- *Classical machine learning* techniques, which make predictions directly from a set of features that have been prespecified by the user,
- *Representation learning* techniques, which transform features into some intermediate representation prior to mapping them to final predictions, and
- *Deep learning* techniques, a form of representation learning that uses multiple transformation steps to create very complex features.

We have seen many ways of transforming features into an intermediate representation before applying machine learning. A classic example is principal component analysis followed by nearest-neighbor learning. Fisher's linear discriminant analysis is another example of representation learning: a discriminative objective is used to adapt the learned representation using labeled data. The result can be used to make classifications directly, or serve as input to a more flexible, nonlinear classifier.

In contrast, a simple three-layer perceptron learns a representation by adapting the hidden layer to the task of interest, jointly training it and the output layer so that the hidden-layer parameters coadapt to the output-layer parameters. Making a network "deep" by adding further hidden layers subject features to a sequence of transformations. Each layer's transformation is a form of inference, and one can imagine how complex inferences might be more easily modeled as a sequence of computational steps. Deep *recurrent* neural networks, which we will also discuss, include feedback loops, and their depth is related to the complexity of the underlying algorithm being learned, as opposed to an iterative procedure of feature aggregation and abstraction.

Deep multilayer perceptrons, deep convolutional neural networks (CNNs), and recurrent neural networks are central to the current wave of interest in deep learning. However, other methods can also be characterized as instances of deep learning, as we will see below. Most deep learning methods use multilayer perceptrons as building blocks.

This chapter highlights some notable empirical successes where deep learning methods have out-performed state-of-the-art alternatives. The main reason for using deep learning is its empirical effectiveness compared to alternative approaches. But there are other, more theoretical, motivations. There are analogies at a conceptual level between neural networks and circuit analysis that lead to theoretical results in complexity theory. Some neural networks implement soft variants of logical functions, and under certain parameter settings they can behave exactly like logic gates, as we saw in Section 7.2. Functions that can be compactly represented by multilevel networks may require far more elements when expressed as shallower architectures.

Deep learning formulates the underlying problem as a network architecture whose output layer defines a loss function needed for learning. The output units can be formulated as probabilistic predictions, and if these predictions are parameterized, one can simply define the loss to be the negative log-likelihood under the model. Parameters are typically regularized using the techniques introduced in Section 9.7, either by placing priors on parameters or (equivalently) by adding regularization terms to the loss function. We also discuss some newer approaches to regularization.

Deep learning methods are frequently based upon networks for which the backpropagation algorithm serves to compute the gradients required for learning. A variation of stochastic gradient descent is used that computes gradients and updates model parameters from small "mini-batches" of examples—subsets of the training set.

Deep learning has sparked a renaissance of neural network research and applications. Many high-profile media (e.g., *The New York Times*) have documented striking successes of deep learning techniques on key benchmark problems. Starting around 2012, impressive results were achieved on long-standing problems in speech recognition and computer vision, and in competitive challenges such as the ImageNet *Large Scale Visual Recognition Challenge* and the *Labeled Faces in the Wild* evaluation. In speech processing, computer vision, and even in the neural networks community itself the impact was substantial. For more information, see the *Further Reading* section at the end of the chapter.

The easy availability of high-speed computation in the form of graphics processing units has been critical to the success of deep learning techniques. When formulated in matrix-vector form, computation can be accelerated using optimized graphics libraries and hardware. As network models become more complex, some quantities can only be represented using multidimensional arrays of numbers—sometimes referred to as tensors, a generalization of matrices that permit an arbitrary number of indices. Software for deep learning supporting tensors is invaluable for accelerating the creation of complex network structures and making it easier to learn them. We introduce some software packages at the end of this chapter.

This chapter gives equations for implementing backpropagation in matrix-vector form. For readers unfamiliar with manipulating functions that have matrix arguments, and their derivatives, Appendix A.1 summarizes some useful background.

10.1 DEEP FEEDFORWARD NETWORKS

While neural networks have been considered standard machine learning techniques for decades, four key developments have played a crucial role in their resurgence:

- proper evaluation of machine learning methods;
- vastly increased amounts of data;
- deeper and larger network architectures;
- accelerated training using GPU techniques.

With regard to the first point, evaluation, it has been standard practice in the past for different groups to compare results using the same data sets. However, even when the data was public, results were often difficult to compare because researchers used different protocols for their experiments—such as different testing and training splits. Moreover, significant time was spent reimplementing other methods—which often leads to weak baselines. The rise of machine learning challenges with large common test sets ensures that results are more directly comparable, and motivates teams to spend their time and energy on their own method. As the volume of evaluation data increases, deeper, more complex, and flexible models become feasible. The use of high-capacity models, which require extra care to prevent overfitting, makes it even more important to ensure that test sets are

Table 10.1 Summary of Performance on the MNIST Evaluation

Classifier	Test Error Rate (%)	References
Linear classifier (1-layer neural net)	12.0	LeCun et al. (1998)
K-nearest-neighbors, Euclidean (L2)	5.0	LeCun et al. (1998)
2-Layer neural net, 300 hidden units, mean square error	4.7	LeCun et al. (1998)
Support vector machine, Gaussian kernel	1.4	MNIST Website
Convolutional net, LeNet-5 (no distortions)	**0.95**	LeCun et al. (1998)
Methods using distortions		
Virtual support vector machine, deg-9 polynomial, (2-pixel jittered and deskewing)	0.56	DeCoste and Scholkopf (2002)
Convolutional neural net (elastic distortions)	0.4	Simard, Steinkraus, and Platt (2003)
6-Layer feedforward neural net (on GPU) (elastic distortions)	**0.35**	Ciresan, Meier, Gambardella, and Schmidhuber (2010)
Large/deep convolutional neural net (elastic distortions)	**0.35**	Ciresan, Meier, Masci, Maria Gambardella, and Schmidhuber (2011)
Committee of 35 convolutional networks (elastic distortions)	0.23	Ciresan, Meier, and Schmidhuber (2012)

reserved for final tests only. For these and other reasons, some competitive challenges have been organized in which the labels for test data are hidden and results must be submitted to a remote server for evaluation. In some cases the test data itself is also hidden, in which case participants must submit executable code.

THE MNIST EVALUATION

To underscore the importance of large benchmark evaluations, consider the Mixed National Institute of Standards and Technology (MNIST) database of handwritten digits. It contains 60,000 training and 10,000 test instances of hand-written digits, encoded as 28×28 pixel grayscale images. The data is a remix of an earlier NIST data set in which adults generated the training data and high school students generated the test set. Table 10.1 gives some results on this data. Note that the LeNet convolutional network (row 5), a deep architecture discussed in Section 10.3, outperformed many standard machine learning techniques, even in 1998.

The lower half of the table shows the results of methods that augment the training set with synthetic distortions of the input images. The use of transformations to further extend the size of an already large data set is an important technique in deep learning. Large networks, with more parameters, have high representational capacity. Plausible synthetic distortion of the data multiplies the amount of data available, preventing overfitting and helping the network to generalize. Of course, other methods such as support vector machines can also scale up model complexity with additional data. Simply adding more support vectors can allow SVM-based methods to outperform classical network architectures. However, as Table 10.1 shows, training deep feedforward networks or CNN with synthetic elastically transformed imagery yields even better results. Because of the large test set, differences in the error rate of more than 0.01 are statistically significant.

The last four entries illustrate the effectiveness of deep networks. Interestingly, a standard multilayer perceptron with six layers using synthetic transformations and trained on a graphics processing unit matches the performance of a large and deep CNN. This shows that plain neural networks can be effective when they are deep and data augmentation is used, because training such a network with synthetically transformed data encourages robustness with respect to plausible distortions. In contrast, CNNs embed translational invariances within the network design itself (see Section 10.3). The best result in Table 10.1 is based on an ensemble of convolutional networks. Ensembles are used to obtain the top performance in many settings.

LOSSES AND REGULARIZATION

Section 7.2 noted that different activation functions can be used for multilayer perceptrons. We distinguish the final-layer parameterization, from which the loss function is computed, from the intermediate-layer activation functions. In the past, it was common practice to use sigmoids as output activation functions and base final-layer loss functions on squared errors—sometimes even when classification labels were constrained to be 0 or 1. Later designs, however, embrace the natural probabilistic encoding for any given data type by defining output activation functions as the negative log of the distribution functions used to make probabilistic predictions, whether these distributions are binary, categorical, or continuous. Then predictions can correspond precisely to the underlying probability models defined by Bernoulli, discrete or Gaussian distributions—as in linear and logistic regression, but with greater flexibility.

Viewed in this way, logistic regression is a simple neural network with no hidden units. The underlying optimization criterion for predicting $i = 1, \ldots, N$ labels y_i from features $\mathbf{x}_i$ with parameters θ consisting of a matrix of weights $\mathbf{W}$ and a vector of biases $\mathbf{b}$ is

$$\sum_{i=1}^{N} -\log p(y_i|\mathbf{x}_i; \mathbf{W}, \mathbf{b}) + \lambda \sum_{j=1}^{M} w_j^2 = \sum_{i=1}^{N} L(f_i(\mathbf{x}_i; \theta), y_i) + \lambda R(\theta)$$

where the first term, $L(f_i(\mathbf{x}_i; \theta), y_i)$, is the negative conditional log-likelihood or loss, and the second, $\lambda R(\theta)$, is a weighted regularizer used to prevent overfitting.

This formulation as a loss- and regularizer-based objective function gives us the freedom to choose either probabilistic losses or other loss functions dictated by the needs of the application. Using the average loss over the training data, called the *empirical risk*, leads to the following formulation of the fundamental optimization problem posed by training a deep model: minimize the empirical risk plus a regularization term, i.e.,

$$\arg\min_{\theta} \left[\frac{1}{N} \sum_{i=1}^{N} L(f_i(\mathbf{x}_i; \theta), \mathbf{y}_i) + \lambda R(\theta) \right].$$

Note that the factor N must be accounted for if one relates the regularization weight λ here to the corresponding parameter derived from a formal probabilistic model for the distribution. In deep learning we are often interested in examining learning curves that show the loss or some other performance metric on a graph as a function of the number of passes that an algorithm has taken over the data. It is much easier to compare the *average* loss over a training set with the *average* loss over a validation set on the same graph, because dividing by N gives them the same scale.

To see how deep networks learn, consider composing the final output function of a network in which $f_k(\mathbf{x}) = f_k(a_k(\mathbf{x}))$. This function is applied to an input activation consisting of $a_k(\mathbf{x})$. The input frequently comprises a computation of the form $\mathbf{a}(\mathbf{x}) = \mathbf{W}\mathbf{h}(\mathbf{x}) + \mathbf{b}$, where function $\mathbf{a}(\mathbf{x})$ takes a vector argument and returns a vector as its result, so that $a_k(\mathbf{x})$ is just one of the elements of $\mathbf{a}(\mathbf{x})$. Table 10.2 gives commonly used output loss functions, output activation functions, and underlying distributions from which they derive.

DEEP LAYERED NETWORK ARCHITECTURE

Deep neural networks compose computations performed by many layers. Denoting the output of hidden layers by $\mathbf{h}^{(l)}(\mathbf{x})$, the computation for a network with L hidden layers is:

$$\mathbf{f}(\mathbf{x}) = \mathbf{f}\left[\mathbf{a}^{(L+1)}\left(\mathbf{h}^{(L)}\left(\mathbf{a}^{(L)}\left(\ldots\left(\mathbf{h}^{(2)}\left(\mathbf{a}^{(2)}\left(\mathbf{h}^{(1)}\left(\mathbf{a}^{(1)}(\mathbf{x})\right)\right)\right)\right)\right)\right)\right)\right].$$

Table 10.2 Loss Functions, Corresponding Distributions, and Activation Functions

Loss Name, $L(f_i(\mathbf{x}_i; \theta), \mathbf{y}_i) =$	Distribution Name, $P(f_i(\mathbf{x}_i; \theta), \mathbf{y}_i) =$	Output Activation Function, $f_k(a_k(\mathbf{x})) =$
Squared error, $\sum_{k=1}^{K} (f_k(\mathbf{x}) - y_k)^2$	Gaussian, $N(\mathbf{y}; \mathbf{f}(\mathbf{x}; \theta), \mathbf{I})$	$\dfrac{1}{(1 + \exp(-a_k(\mathbf{x})))}$
Cross entropy, $-\sum_{k=1}^{K} [y_k \log f_k(\mathbf{x}) + (1 - y_k) \log(1 - f_k(\mathbf{x}))]$	Bernoulli, $\mathrm{Bern}(\mathbf{y}; \mathbf{f}(\mathbf{x}; \theta))$	$\dfrac{1}{(1 + \exp(-a_k(\mathbf{x})))}$
Softmax, $-\sum_{k=1}^{K} y_k \log f_k(\mathbf{x})$	Discrete or Categorical, $\mathrm{Cat}(\mathbf{y}; \mathbf{f}(\mathbf{x}; \theta))$	$\dfrac{\exp(a_k(\mathbf{x}))}{\sum_{j=1}^{K} \exp(a_j(\mathbf{x}))}$

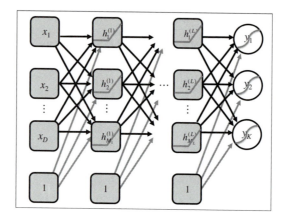

FIGURE 10.1

A feedforward neural network.

Each *preactivation function* $\mathbf{a}^{(l)}(\mathbf{x})$ is typically a linear operation with matrix $\mathbf{W}^{(l)}$ and bias $\mathbf{b}^{(l)}$, which can be combined into a parameter θ:

$$\mathbf{a}^{(l)}(\mathbf{x}) = \mathbf{W}^{(l)}\mathbf{x} + \mathbf{b}^{(l)},$$
$$\mathbf{a}^{(l)}(\hat{\mathbf{x}}) = \theta^{(l)}\hat{\mathbf{x}} \quad , \, l = 1$$
$$\mathbf{a}^{(l)}(\hat{\mathbf{h}}^{(l-1)}) = \theta^{(l)}\hat{\mathbf{h}}^{(l-1)} \quad , \, l > 1$$

The "hat" notation $\hat{\mathbf{x}}$ indicates that 1 has been appended to the vector $\mathbf{x}$. Hidden-layer activation functions $\mathbf{h}^{(l)}(\mathbf{x})$ often have the same form at each level, but this is not a requirement.

Fig. 10.1 shows an example network. In contrast to graphical models such as Bayesian networks where hidden variables are random variables, the hidden units here are intermediate deterministic computations, which is why they are not represented as circles. However, the output variables y_k are drawn as circles because they can be formulated probabilistically.

ACTIVATION FUNCTIONS

Activation functions generally operate on the preactivation vectors in an element-wise fashion.

Table 10.3 depicts common hidden-layer activation functions, along with their functional forms and derivatives.

While sigmoid functions have been popular, the hyperbolic tangent function is sometimes preferred, partly because it has a steady state at 0. However, more recently the *rectify()* function or rectified linear units (ReLUs) have been found to

Table 10.3 Activation Functions and Their Derivatives

Name and Graph	Function	Derivative
sigmoid(x)	$h(x) = \dfrac{1}{1 + \exp(-x)}$	$h'(x) = h(x)[1 - h(x)]$
tanh(x)	$h(x) = \dfrac{\exp(x) - \exp(-x)}{\exp(x) + \exp(-x)}$	$h'(x) = 1 - h(x)^2$
softplus(x)	$h(x) = \log(1 + \exp(x))$	$h'(x) = \dfrac{1}{1 + \exp(-x)}$
rectify(x)	$h(x) = \max(0, x)$	$h'(x) = \begin{cases} 1 \text{ if } x \geq 0 \\ 0 \text{ if } x < 0 \end{cases}$
pw_linear(x)	$h(x) = \begin{cases} x \text{ if } x \geq 0 \\ ax \text{ if } x < 0 \end{cases}$	$h'(x) = \begin{cases} 1 \text{ if } x \geq 0 \\ a \text{ if } x < 0 \end{cases}$

yield superior results in many different settings. Since this function is 0 for negative argument values, some units in the model will yield activations that are 0, giving a "sparseness" property that is useful in many contexts. Moreover, the gradient is particularly simple—either 0 or 1. The fact that when activated, the activation function has a gradient of exactly 1 helps address the *vanishing or exploding gradient problem*—we discuss this in more detail below, under recurrent networks. ReLUs are a popular choice for $\mathbf{h}^{(l)}(\mathbf{x})$, while piecewise linear functions (the last entry of Table 10.3) have also grown in popularity for deep learning systems. Like ReLUs, these are not differentiable at 0, but gradient descent can be applied by using a subgradient instead, which means that $h'(0)$ can be set to a (e.g.).

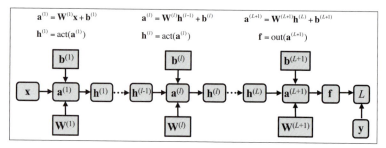

FIGURE 10.2

Computation graph showing forward propagation in a deep network.

Many deep learning software packages make it easy to use a variety of activation functions, including piecewise-linear ones. Some determine the gradients needed for the backpropagation algorithm automatically, using symbolic computations built into the software.

Fig. 10.2 is a computation graph that shows the general form of a canonical deep network architecture with several hidden layers. It illustrates how predictions are computed, how the loss L is obtained, and how the forward pass of the backpropagation algorithm is computed. Hidden-layer activation functions are given by act $(\mathbf{a}^{(l)})$, and the final layer activation function is given by out $(\mathbf{a}^{(L+1)})$.

BACKPROPAGATION REVISITED

Backpropagation is based on the chain rule of calculus. Consider the loss $L(\mathbf{f}(\mathbf{x}; \theta), \mathbf{y})$ for a single-layer network with a softmax output that corresponds exactly to the model for multinomial logistic regression. We use multinomial vectors $\mathbf{y}$, with a single dimension $y_k = 1$ for the corresponding class label and whose other dimensions are 0. Define $\mathbf{f} = \begin{bmatrix} f_1(\mathbf{a}), & \dots, & f_K(\mathbf{a}) \end{bmatrix}$, and $\mathbf{a}(\mathbf{x}; \theta) = \begin{bmatrix} a_1(\mathbf{x}; \theta_1), & \dots, & a_K(\mathbf{x}; \theta_K) \end{bmatrix}$ with $a_k(\mathbf{x}; \theta_k) = \theta_k^T \mathbf{x}$, where θ_k is a column vector containing the kth row of the parameter matrix θ. A softmax loss for $\mathbf{f}(\mathbf{a}(\mathbf{x}))$ is given by

$$L = -\sum_{k=1}^{K} y_k \log f_k(\mathbf{x}), \quad f_k(\mathbf{x}) = \frac{\exp(a_k(\mathbf{x}))}{\sum_{c=1}^{K} \exp(a_c(\mathbf{x}))}.$$

To replicate a model of the form $a_k(\mathbf{x}; \mathbf{w}_k, \mathbf{b}) = \mathbf{w}_k^T \mathbf{x} + \mathbf{b}$, define $\mathbf{x}$ to include a 1 at the end, so that the bias parameter $\mathbf{b}$ is the last element of each parameter vector θ_k. The chain rule in vector form gives the partial derivative with respect to any given parameter vector θ_k as

$$\frac{\partial L}{\partial \theta_k} = \frac{\partial \mathbf{a}}{\partial \theta_k} \frac{\partial \mathbf{f}}{\partial \mathbf{a}} \frac{\partial L}{\partial \mathbf{f}} = \frac{\partial \mathbf{a}}{\partial \theta_k} \frac{\partial L}{\partial \mathbf{a}}.$$

(Note that the order of terms is reversed compared to earlier applications of the chain rule in this book.)

For each component of the partial derivative of the loss with respect to **a**,

$$\frac{\partial L}{\partial a_j} = \frac{\partial}{\partial a_j}\left[-\sum_{k=1}^{K} y_k \left[a_k - \log\left[\sum_{c=1}^{K}\exp(a_c)\right]\right]\right]$$

$$= -\left[y_{k=j} - \frac{\exp(a_{k=j})}{\sum_{c=1}^{K}\exp(a_c)}\right]$$

$$= -\left[y_j - p(y_j|\mathbf{x})\right]$$

$$= -\left[y_j - f_j(\mathbf{x})\right],$$

which implies that the vector form can be written

$$\frac{\partial L}{\partial \mathbf{a}} = -[\mathbf{y} - \mathbf{f}(\mathbf{x})],$$

where $\Delta = [\mathbf{y} - \mathbf{f}(\mathbf{x})]$ is often referred to as the error.
    Next, since

$$\frac{\partial a_j}{\partial \theta_k} = \begin{cases} \dfrac{\partial}{\partial \theta_k}\theta_k^T\mathbf{x} = \mathbf{x} & ,j = k \\ 0 & ,j \neq k \end{cases}$$

this implies that

$$\frac{\partial \mathbf{a}}{\partial \theta_k} = \mathbf{H}_k = \begin{bmatrix} 0 & x_1 & 0 \\ \vdots & \vdots & \vdots \\ 0 & x_n & 0 \end{bmatrix}$$

where the vector **x** is stored in the kth column of the matrix. Notice that we avoid working with the partial derivative of the vector **a** with respect to the matrix θ, because it cannot be represented as a matrix—it is a multidimensional array of numbers (a tensor).
    Using the quantities derived above, we can compute

$$\frac{\partial L}{\partial \theta_k} = \frac{\partial \mathbf{a}}{\partial \theta_k}\frac{\partial L}{\partial \mathbf{a}} = -\begin{bmatrix} 0 & x_1 & 0 \\ \vdots & \vdots & \vdots \\ 0 & x_n & 0 \end{bmatrix}[\mathbf{y} - \mathbf{f}(\mathbf{x})]$$

$$= -\mathbf{x}(y_k - f_k(\mathbf{x})).$$

This gives the gradient (as a column vector) for the vector in the kth row of the parameter matrix. However, with a little rearrangement the gradient for the entire matrix of parameters θ can be written compactly:

$$\frac{\partial L}{\partial \theta} = -[\mathbf{y} - \mathbf{f}(\mathbf{x})]\mathbf{x}^T$$

$$= -\Delta\mathbf{x}^T.$$

This formulates the computation of the gradient matrix as the error $\Delta = [\mathbf{y} - \mathbf{f}(\mathbf{x})]$ times $\mathbf{x}^T$.

Consider now a network using the same activation function for all L hidden layers, and a softmax output layer. The gradient of the kth parameter vector of the $(L+1)$th matrix of parameters is

$$\frac{\partial L}{\partial \boldsymbol{\theta}_k^{(L+1)}} = \frac{\partial \mathbf{a}^{(L+1)}}{\partial \boldsymbol{\theta}_k^{(L+1)}} \frac{\partial L}{\partial \mathbf{a}^{(L+1)}}, \qquad \frac{\partial L}{\partial \mathbf{a}^{(L+1)}} = -\Delta^{(L+1)}$$

$$= -\frac{\partial \mathbf{a}^{(L+1)}}{\partial \boldsymbol{\theta}_k^{(L+1)}} \Delta^{(L+1)}$$

$$= -\mathbf{H}_k^L \Delta^{(L+1)},$$

where $\mathbf{H}_k^L$ is a matrix containing the activations of the corresponding hidden layer, in column k, and $\Delta^{(L+1)} = [\mathbf{y} - \mathbf{f}(\mathbf{x})]$, the error term of the output layer. The entire matrix parameter update can be restructured as

$$\frac{\partial L}{\partial \boldsymbol{\theta}^{(L+1)}} = -\Delta^{(L+1)} \tilde{\mathbf{h}}_{(L)}^T.$$

This error term is backpropagated. Consider the gradient of the kth row of the Lth matrix of parameters. Since the bias terms are constant, it is unnecessary to back-propagate through them, so

$$\frac{\partial L}{\partial \boldsymbol{\theta}_k^{(L)}} = \frac{\partial \mathbf{a}^{(L)}}{\partial \boldsymbol{\theta}_k^{(L)}} \frac{\partial \mathbf{h}^{(L)}}{\partial \mathbf{a}^{(L)}} \frac{\partial \mathbf{a}^{(L+1)}}{\partial \mathbf{h}^{(L)}} \frac{\partial L}{\partial \mathbf{a}^{(L+1)}}$$

$$= -\frac{\partial \mathbf{a}^{(L)}}{\partial \boldsymbol{\theta}_k^{(L)}} \frac{\partial \mathbf{h}^{(L)}}{\partial \mathbf{a}^{(L)}} \frac{\partial \mathbf{a}^{(L+1)}}{\partial \mathbf{h}^{(L)}} \Delta^{(L+1)}, \qquad \Delta^{(L)} \equiv \frac{\partial \mathbf{h}^{(L)}}{\partial \mathbf{a}^{(L)}} \frac{\partial \mathbf{a}^{(L+1)}}{\partial \mathbf{h}^{(L)}} \Delta^{(L+1)}$$

$$= -\frac{\partial \mathbf{a}^{(L)}}{\partial \boldsymbol{\theta}_k^{(L)}} \Delta^{(L)},$$

where $\Delta^{(L)}$ is defined in terms of $\Delta^{(L+1)}$. Similarly, for $l \leq L$ the other $\Delta^{(l)}$s can be defined recursively in terms of $\Delta^{(l+1)}$ as follows:

$$\Delta^{(l)} = \frac{\partial \mathbf{h}^{(l)}}{\partial \mathbf{a}^{(l)}} \frac{\partial \mathbf{a}^{(l+1)}}{\partial \mathbf{h}^{(l)}} \Delta^{(l+1)}$$

$$\Delta^{(l)} = \mathbf{D}^{(l)} \mathbf{W}^{T(l+1)} \Delta^{(l+1)}.$$

The last simplification uses the fact that the partial derivatives involved correspond to matrices that can be written

$$\frac{\partial \mathbf{h}^{(l)}}{\partial \mathbf{a}^{(l)}} = \mathbf{D}^{(l)}, \qquad \frac{\partial \mathbf{a}^{(l+1)}}{\partial \mathbf{h}^{(l)}} = \mathbf{W}^{T(l+1)},$$

where $\mathbf{D}^{(l)}$ contains the partial derivatives of the hidden-layer activation function with respect to the preactivation input. This matrix is generally diagonal, because activation functions usually operate on an elementwise basis. The $\mathbf{W}^{T(l+1)}$ term results from the fact that $\mathbf{a}^{(l+1)}(\mathbf{h}^{(l)}) = \mathbf{W}^{(l+1)}\mathbf{h}^{(l)} + \mathbf{b}^{(l+1)}$. The gradients for the kth

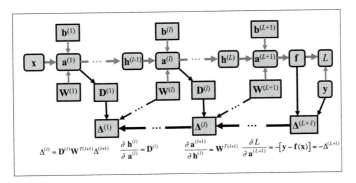

FIGURE 10.3

Backpropagation in a deep network (the forward computation is shown with gray arrows).

vector of parameters of the lth network layer can therefore be computed using products of matrices of the following form

$$\frac{\partial L}{\partial \theta_k^{(l)}} = -\mathbf{H}_k^{(l-1)}\mathbf{D}^{(l)}\mathbf{W}^{T(l+1)}\dots\mathbf{D}^{(L)}\mathbf{W}^{T(L+1)}\Delta^{(L+1)}. \qquad (10.1)$$

Given these equations, the definition of $\mathbf{f}(\mathbf{x})$, a loss function, and any regularization terms, deep networks formulated in this general way can be optimized using gradient descent. The recursive definitions for $\Delta^{(l)}$ reflect how the algorithm propagates information back from the loss.

The above equations are amenable to numerical optimizations. For example, matrix–matrix multiplications can be avoided in favor of matrix–vector multiplications by computing $\Delta^{(l)} = \mathbf{D}^{(l)}(\mathbf{W}^{T(l+1)}\Delta^{(l+1)})$. Observing that most hidden-layer activation functions give a diagonal form for $\mathbf{D}^{(l)}$, the matrix–vector multiply can be transformed into an elementwise product, $\Delta^{(l)} = \mathbf{d}^{(l)} \odot (\mathbf{W}^{T(l+1)}\Delta^{(l+1)})$, where $\odot$ is elementwise and vector $\mathbf{d}^{(l)}$ is created by extracting the elements from the diagonal of $\mathbf{D}^{(l)}$. Using our observations above we can see here that the entire parameter matrix update at each level has the following simple form:

$$\frac{\partial L}{\partial \theta^{(l)}} = -\Delta^{(l)}\hat{\mathbf{h}}_{(l-1)}^T.$$

When $l = 1$, $\hat{\mathbf{h}}_{(0)} = \hat{\mathbf{x}}$, the input data with a 1 appended.

Fig. 10.3 shows the backward computation or error "propagation" step, while Fig. 10.4 shows the final computations required for gradient-based learning.

COMPUTATION GRAPHS AND COMPLEX NETWORK STRUCTURES

For a simple feedforward network learning takes place in two phases: a forward pass and a backward pass. Furthermore, using vector notation, we saw above that the gradient computations decompose into a simple chain of matrix products.

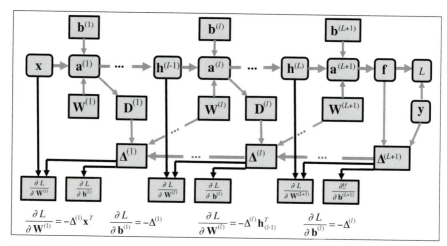

FIGURE 10.4

Parameter updates that follow the forward and backward propagation steps (shown with gray arrows).

But what if the graph does not have a simple layered structure? It turns out that more complex computations consisting of applying functions to intermediate results can also be represented by computation graphs. The *Computation Graphs and Backpropagation* subsection of Appendix A.1 gives an example of a more advanced computation for which finding the gradients needed for backpropagation can be understood and visualized using a computation graph.

Implementing general mechanisms for backpropagation efficiently can become quite complex. Using the concept of a computation graph, gradient information "simply" needs to be propagated along the path found by reversing the arrows in the graph used to define the steps of the forward-propagation of information. Many software packages use interleaved forward propagation and backward propagation phases within computation graphs. Some allow users to define complex network structures in such a way that the system can obtain the required derivatives automatically, and perform computations efficiently using libraries that call graphics processing units.

In principle, learning in a deep network could be by gradient descent or more sophisticated methods that exploit higher-order derivatives. However, in practice a variation of stochastic gradient descent based on "mini-batches" is by far the most popular method, such that software packages and implementations are often optimized assuming that this will be used. We discuss this method, and other key practical aspects of training deep networks, in Section 10.2.

CHECKING BACKPROPAGATION IMPLEMENTATIONS

An implementation of the backpropagation algorithm can be checked for correctness by comparing the analytic values of gradients with those computed numerically. For example, one could add and subtract a small perturbation ε to each parameter θ and then compute the symmetric finite difference approximation to the derivative of the loss:

$$\frac{\partial L}{\partial \theta} \approx \frac{L(\theta + \varepsilon) - L(\theta - \varepsilon)}{2\varepsilon},$$

where the error in the approximation is $O(\varepsilon^2)$.

10.2 TRAINING AND EVALUATING DEEP NETWORKS

When working with deep learning, it is vital to have separate training, test, and validation sets. The validation set is used to tune a model's hyperparameters, for model selection, and also to prevent overfitting by performing early stopping.

EARLY STOPPING

Chapter 7, Extending instance-based and linear models, mentioned that "early stopping" is a simple way of alleviating overfitting during training. Deep learning utilizes high-capacity architectures, which are susceptible to overfitting even when data is plentiful, and early stopping is standard practice even when other methods to reduce overfitting are employed, such as regularization and dropout (discussed below). This is done by monitoring learning curves that plot the *average* loss for the training and validation sets as a function of epoch. The key is to find the point at which the validation set average loss begins to deteriorate.

Fig. 10.5 plots a pair of training set and validation set curves, although with mini-batch-based stochastic gradient descent they are usually noisier. To combat this, model parameters can be retained over a window of recent updates in order to select the final version to be applied to the test set.

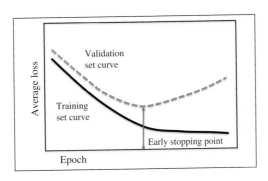

FIGURE 10.5

Typical learning curves for the training and validation sets.

People often use one of the standard loss function formulations for neural network outputs simply because it is already integrated into software tools. However, the underlying goal of learning may be different: to minimize the classification error, or perhaps to optimize some combination of precision and recall. In these cases it is important to monitor the true evaluation metric as well as the average loss, to gain a clearer idea as to whether the model is overfitting the training set. Furthermore, it can be instructive to determine whether the model can classify the data perfectly by adding more capacity and stopping at the appropriate point.

VALIDATION, CROSS-VALIDATION, AND HYPERPARAMETER TUNING

Hyperparameters are tuned by identifying what settings lead to best performance on the validation set, with early stopping. Common hyperparameters include the strength of parameter regularization, model complexity in terms of the number of hidden units and layers and their connectivity, the form of activation functions, and parameters of the learning algorithm itself. Because of the many choices involved, performance monitoring on validation sets assumes an even more central role than it does with traditional machine learning methods.

As usual, the test set should be set aside for a truly final evaluation, because repeated rounds of experiments using test set data would give misleading estimates of performance on fresh data. For this reason, the research community has come to favor public challenges with hidden test-set labels, a development that has undoubtedly helped gauge progress in the field. However, controversy arises when participants submit multiple entries, and some favor a model where participants submit code to a competition server, so that the test data itself is hidden.

The use of a validation set is different from using k-fold cross-validation to evaluate a learning technique or to select hyperparameters. As Section 5.3 explained, cross-validation involves creating multiple training and testing partitions. But data sets for deep learning tend to be so massive that a single large test set adequately represents a model's performance, reducing the need for cross-validation—and since training often takes days or weeks, even using graphics processing units, cross-validation is impractical anyway.

To obtain the best possible results, one needs to tune hyperparameters, usually with a single validation set extracted from the training set. However, there is a dilemma: omitting the validation set from final training can reduce performance in the test. It is advantageous to train on the combined training and validation data, but this risks overfitting. One solution is to stop training after the same number of epochs that led to the best validation set performance; another is to monitor the average loss over the combined training set and stop when it reaches the level it was at when early stopping was performed using the validation set.

Hyperparameters in deep learning are often tuned heuristically by hand, or using grid search. An alternative is random search, where instead of placing a regular grid over hyperparameter space, probability distributions are specified from which samples are taken. Another approach is to use machine learning and

Bayesian techniques to infer the next hyperparameter configuration to try in a sequence of experimental runs.

We have been talking about tuning model hyperparameters, such as the weight used for the regularization term. However, many of the parameters and choices that arise below can be viewed as learning algorithm hyperparameters that could also be tuned. In practice, they are often chosen during informal manual trials, but they could be determined by automated searching using validation sets as a guide.

MINI-BATCH-BASED STOCHASTIC GRADIENT DESCENT

Section 7.2 introduced the method of stochastic gradient descent. For convex functions such as the one used in logistic regression with L_2 regularization, and a learning rate that decays over time t, it can be shown that the approximate gradients converge at a rate that is of the order $1/t$. Earlier in this chapter we remarked on the fact that deep learning architectures are often optimized using mini-batch-based stochastic gradient descent. We now explain this technique.

Stochastic gradient descent updates the model parameters according to the gradient computed from one example. The mini-batch variant uses a small subset of the data and bases updates to parameters on the average gradient over the examples in the batch. This operates just like the regular procedure: initialize the parameters, enter a parameter update loop, and terminate by monitoring a validation set. However, in contrast to standard stochastic gradient descent the main loop iterates over mini-batches that have been obtained from the training set, and updates the parameters after processing each batch. Normally these batches are randomly selected disjoint subsets of the training set, perhaps shuffled after each epoch, depending on the time required to do so.

Each pass through a set of mini-batches that represent the complete training set is an epoch. Using the empirical risk plus a regularization term as the objective function, after processing a mini-batch the parameters are updated by

$$\theta^{\text{new}} \leftarrow \theta - \eta_t \left[\frac{1}{B_k} \sum_{i \in I} \left[\frac{\partial}{\partial \theta} L(f(\mathbf{x}_i; \theta), \mathbf{y}_i) \right] + \frac{B_k}{N} \lambda \frac{\partial}{\partial \theta} R(\theta) \right],$$

where η_t is the learning rate (which may depend on the epoch t); the kth batch has B_k examples and is represented by a set $I = I(t, k)$ of indices into the original data; N is the size of the training set; $L(f(\mathbf{x}_i; \theta), \mathbf{y}_i)$ is the loss for example $\mathbf{x}_i$, label $\mathbf{y}_i$ and parameters θ; and $R(\theta)$ is the regularizer, with weight λ. At one extreme, where a single mini-batch contains the whole training set, is the standard update for batch gradient descent; while at the other, with a batch size of 1, is the standard single-example stochastic gradient descent update.

Mini-batches typically contain two to several hundred examples, although for large models the choice may be constrained by computational resources. The batch size often influences the stability and speed of learning; some sizes work particularly well for a given model and data set. Sometimes a search is performed over a set of potential batch sizes to find one that works well, before launching a lengthy optimization.

The mix of class labels in the batches can influence the result. For unbalanced data there may be an advantage in pretraining the model using mini-batches in which the labels are balanced, and then fine-tuning the upper layer or layers using the unbalanced label statistics. This can involve implementing a sampling scheme that ensures that as one cycles through examples they are presented to the learning procedure in an unbiased way.

As with regular gradient descent, invoking momentum can help the optimization escape plateaus in the loss function. If the current gradient of the loss is $\nabla_\theta L(\theta)$, momentum is implemented by computing a moving average, and updating the parameters by $\Delta\theta = -\eta\nabla_\theta L(\theta) + \alpha\Delta\theta^{old}$, where $\alpha \in [0, 1]$. Since the mini-batch approach operates on a small subset of the data, this averaging can allow information from other recently seen mini-batches to contribute to the current parameter update. A momentum value of 0.9 is often used as a starting point, but it is common to hand-tune it, the learning rate, and the schedule used to modify the learning rate during the training process.

PSEUDOCODE FOR MINI-BATCH BASED STOCHASTIC GRADIENT DESCENT

Given data $\mathbf{x}_i, \mathbf{y}_i$, $i = 1,\ldots, N$, loss function $L(f(\mathbf{x}_i; \theta), \mathbf{y}_i)$ with parameters θ, and a parameter regularization term $R(\theta)$ weighted by λ, we wish to optimize the empirical risk plus regularization term, i.e.,

$$1/N \sum_{i=1}^{N} L(f(\mathbf{x}_i; \theta), \mathbf{y}_i) + \lambda R(\theta).$$

The pseudocode in Fig. 10.6 accomplishes this. It uses K mini-batches indexed by the sets I_k, each of which contain B_k examples. The learning rate η_t may depend on time t. The gradient vector is $\mathbf{g}$, and the update $\Delta\theta$ incorporates a momentum term. Mini-batches are often created before entering the *while* loop; however, in some cases shuffling within the loop yields an improvement.

LEARNING RATES AND SCHEDULES

The learning rate η is a critical choice when using mini-batch based stochastic gradient descent. Small values such as 0.001 often work well, but it is common to perform a logarithmically spaced search, say in the interval $[10^{-8}, 1]$, followed by a finer grid or binary search.

The learning rate may be adapted over epochs t to give a learning rate schedule η_t. A fixed learning rate is often used in the first few epochs, followed by a decreasing schedule such as

```
θ = θ₀   // initialize parameters
Δθ = 0
t = 0
while converged == FALSE
    {I₁,...,I_K} = shuffle(X)   // create K mini-batches
    for k = 1...K
```

$$\mathbf{g} = \frac{1}{B_k} \sum_{i \in I_k} \left[\frac{\partial}{\partial \theta} L(f(\mathbf{x}_i; \theta), \mathbf{y}_i) \right] + \frac{B_k}{N} \lambda \frac{\partial}{\partial \theta} R(\theta)$$

```
        Δθ ← −η_t g + αΔθ
        θ ← θ + Δθ
    end
    t = t + 1
end
```

FIGURE 10.6

Pseudocode for mini-batch based stochastic gradient descent.

$$\eta_t = \frac{\eta_0}{1 + \varepsilon t}, \quad \text{or } \eta_t = \frac{\eta_0}{t^\varepsilon}, \quad (0.5 < \varepsilon \le 1).$$

There are however many heuristics for adapting learning rates by hand during training. For example, the AlexNet model that won the ImageNet 2012 challenge divides the rate by 10 when the validation error rate ceases to improve. The intuition is that a model may make good progress with a given learning rate but eventually become stuck, jumping around a local minimum in the loss function because the parameter steps are too large. Monitoring performance on the validation set is a good guide as to when the learning rate should be changed.

Second-order analysis based on a Taylor expansion of the loss to higher-order terms can also help explain why smaller rates may be desirable in the final stages of learning. If stochastic gradient descent is used it can be shown that the learning rate must be reduced for the approach to yield results consistent with batch gradient descent.

REGULARIZATION WITH PRIORS ON PARAMETERS

Many standard techniques for parameter regularization are applicable to deep networks. We mentioned earlier that L_2 regularization corresponding to a Gaussian prior on parameters has been used for neural networks under the name "weight decay." As with logistic regression, such regularization is usually applied just to the weights in a network, not to the biases. Alternatively, a weighted combination of L_2 and L_1 regularization, $\lambda_2 R_{L_2}(\theta) + \lambda_1 R_{L_1}(\theta)$, can be applied to the weights in a network, as in the elastic net model discussed in Chapter 9, Probabilistic methods. Although the loss functions used in deep learning may not generally be convex, such regularizers can nevertheless be implemented.

DROPOUT

Dropout is a form of regularization that randomly deletes units and their connections during training, with the intention of reducing the degree to which hidden units coadapt and thus combat overfitting. It has been argued that this corresponds to sampling from an exponential number of networks with shared parameters from which some connections are missing. One then averages over them at test time by using the original network without any dropped-out connections but with scaled-down weights. If a unit is retained with probability p during training, its outgoing weights are rescaled or multiplied by a factor of p at test time. In effect, by performing dropout a neural network with n units can be made to behave like an ensemble of 2^n smaller networks.

One way to implement dropout is with a binary mask vector $\mathbf{m}^{(l)}$ for each hidden layer l in the network: the dropped out version of $\mathbf{h}^{(l)}$ masks out units from the original version using elementwise multiplication, $\mathbf{h}_d^{(l)} = \mathbf{h}^{(l)} \odot \mathbf{m}^{(l)}$. If the activation functions lead to diagonal gradient matrices, the backpropagation update is $\Delta^{(l)} = \mathbf{d}^{(l)} \odot \mathbf{m}^{(l)} \odot (\mathbf{W}^{(l+1)} \Delta^{(l+1)})$.

BATCH NORMALIZATION

Batch normalization is a way of accelerating training and many studies have found it to be important to use to obtain state-of-the-art results on benchmark problems. With batch normalization each element of a layer in a neural network is normalized to zero mean and unit variance, based on its statistics within a mini-batch. This can change the network's representational power, so each activation is given a learned scaling and shifting parameter. Mini-batch-based stochastic gradient descent is modified by calculating the mean μ_j and variance σ_j^2 over the batch for each hidden unit h_j in each layer and then normalizing the units, scaling them using the learned scaling parameter γ_j and shifting them by the learned shifting parameter β_j:

$$\hat{h}_j \leftarrow \gamma_j \frac{h_j - \mu_j}{\sqrt{\sigma_j^2 + \varepsilon}} + \beta_j.$$

Of course, to update the scaling and shifting parameters one needs to backpropagate the gradient of the loss through these additional parameters.

PARAMETER INITIALIZATION

The strategy used to initialize parameters before training commences can be deceptively important. Bias terms are often initialized to 0, but initializing the weight matrices can be tricky. For example, if they are initialized to all 0s, it can be shown that the tanh activation function will yield zero gradients. If the weights are all the same, the hidden units will produce the same gradients and behave the same as each other, wasting the model's capacity.

One solution is to initialize all elements of the weight matrix from a uniform distribution over the interval $[-b, b]$. Different methods have been proposed for selecting the value of b, often motivated by the idea that units with more inputs should have smaller weights. For example, for a given layer l one might scale b by the inverse of the square root of the dimensionality of $\mathbf{h}^{(l-1)}(\mathbf{x})$, known as the "fan-in size." Or one might incorporate the fan-out size as well.

The weight matrices of ReLUs have been successfully initialized using a zero-mean isotropic Gaussian distribution with standard deviation of 0.01. This strategy has also been used for training Gaussian restricted Boltzmann machines (RBMs), which are discussed later in this chapter.

UNSUPERVISED PRETRAINING

Unsupervised pretraining can be an effective way to both initialize and regularize a feedforward network, especially when the volume of labeled data is small relative to the model's capacity. The general idea is to model the distribution of unlabeled data using a method that allows the parameters of the learned model to be somehow transferred to the network, or used to initialize or regularize it. We will return to the subject of unsupervised learning in Section 10.4 and Section 10.5. However, the use of activation functions such as ReLUs that improve gradient flow in deep networks, along with good parameter initialization techniques, mitigates the need for sophisticated pretraining methods.

DATA AUGMENTATION AND SYNTHETIC TRANSFORMATIONS

Data augmentation can be critical for best results. As Table 10.1 illustrates, augmenting even a large data set with transformed training data can increase performance significantly—and not just for deep architectures. A simple transformation for visual problems is simply to jiggle the image. If the object to be classified can be cropped out of a larger image, random bounding boxes can be placed around it, adding small translations in the vertical and horizontal directions. By reducing the cropped image, larger displacements can be applied. Other translations such as rotation, scale change, and shearing are appropriate too. In fact, there is a hierarchy of rigid transformations that increase in complexity as parameters are added. One augmentation strategy is to apply them to the original image, then crop a patch of given size out of the distorted result.

10.3 CONVOLUTIONAL NEURAL NETWORKS

CNNs are a special kind of feedforward network that has proven extremely successful for image analysis. When classifying images, filtering them—e.g., by applying a filter for edge detection—can provide a useful set of spatially organized features. Imagine now if one could learn many such filters jointly, along with the other parameters of the neural network. Each filter can be implemented by multiplying a relatively small spatial zone of the image by a set of weights and feeding the result to an activation function like those discussed above for vanilla feedforward networks. Because this filtering operation is simply repeated around the image using the same weights, it can be implemented using so-called convolution operations. The result is a CNN, for which it is possible to learn both the filters and the classifier using gradient descent and the backpropagation algorithm.

In a CNN, once an image has been filtered by several learnable filters, each filter bank's output is often aggregated across a small spatial region, using the average or maximum value. Aggregation can be performed within nonoverlapping regions, or using subsampling, yielding a lower-resolution layer of spatially organized features—a process that is sometimes referred to as "decimation." This gives the model a degree of invariance to small differences as to exactly where a feature has been detected. For example, if aggregation uses the max operation, a feature is activated if it is detected anywhere in the pooling zone.

We have seen how synthetic transformations allowed deep feedforward networks to yield state-of-the-art performance in the MNIST evaluation, and that cropping small regions of an image can be a useful, easy-to-implement transformation. Although this can be applied to any classification technique, it is particularly effective for training CNNs. Random cropping positions can be used, or deterministic strategies such as cropping from the corners and center of the image. The same strategy can be used at test time, where the model's predictions are averaged over crops from the test image. These networks are designed to have a certain degree of translational invariance, but augmenting data through such global transformations can increase performance significantly.

Fig. 10.7 shows a typical network structure. A smaller part of the original image is subjected to repeated phases of convolutional filtering, pooling, and decimation before being passed to a fully connected, nonconvolutional multilayer perceptron, which may have a number of hidden layers prior to making a final prediction.

CNNs are usually optimized using mini-batch-based stochastic gradient descent, and the practical discussion above about learning deep networks applies here too. Resource issues related to the amount of CPU versus GPU memory available are often important to consider, particularly when processing videos.

THE IMAGENET EVALUATION AND VERY DEEP CONVOLUTIONAL NETWORKS

The ImageNet challenge has been crucial in demonstrating the effectiveness of deep CNNs. The problem is to recognize object categories in typical imagery that one might find on the Internet. The 2012 ImageNet Large Scale Visual

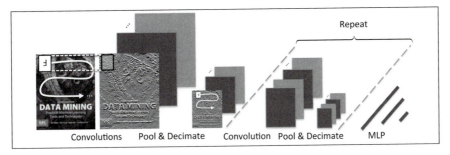

FIGURE 10.7

Typical convolutional neural network architecture.

Table 10.4 Convolutional Neural Network Performance on the ImageNet Challenge

Name	Layers	Top-5 Error (%)	References
AlexNet	8	15.3	Krizhevsky et al. (2012)
VGG Net	19	7.3	Simonyan and Zisserman (2014)
ResNet	152	3.6	He et al. (2016)

Recognition Challenge (ILSVRC) classification task is to classify imagery obtained from Flickr and other search engines into the correct one of 1000 possible object category classes. This task serves as a standard benchmark for deep learning. The imagery was hand-labeled based on the presence or absence of an object belonging to these categories. There are 1.2 *million* images in the training set with 732–1300 training images available per class. A random subset of 50,000 images was used as the validation set and 100,000 images were used for the test set, with 50 and 100 images per class, respectively.

Visual recognition methods not based on deep CNNs hit a plateau in performance on this benchmark. The "top-5 error" is the percentage of times that the target label does not appear among the 5 highest-probability predictions, and many methods cannot get below 25%. Table 10.4 summarizes the performance of different CNN architectures as a function of network depth for the ImageNet challenge. Note that CNNs dramatically outperform the 25% plateau, and that increasing network depth can further improve performance. Smaller filters have been found to lead to superior results in deep networks: the ones with 19 and 152 layers use filters of size 3 × 3. The performance for human agreement has been measured at 5.1% top-5 error for ImageNet, so deep CNNs are able to outperform people on this task.

FROM IMAGE FILTERING TO LEARNABLE CONVOLUTIONAL LAYERS

When an image is filtered, the output is another image that contains the filter's response at each spatial location, e.g., one with its edges emphasized. We could also think of such an image as a *feature map* that indicates where certain features were detected in the image—e.g., edges. However, in a deep network the initial filtered images or feature maps are subjected to many further levels of filtering. Over many successive filter applications this produces spatially organized neurons that respond to much more complex inputs, and the term "feature map" becomes more descriptive.

When viewed as layers in a neural network that takes an image as input, these filtering operations can be viewed as constraining spatially organized neurons to respond only to features that are within a limited region of the input known as the neuron's *receptive field*. When groups of such neurons respond in the same way to the same types of input we say they have shared parameters—but each neuron forming the feature map responds only when certain inputs are detected at corresponding spatially restricted receptive fields in the image.

Consider a simple example with a 1D vector $\mathbf{x}$. A filtering operation can be implemented by multiplying it by a matrix $\mathbf{W}$ that has a special structure, such as

$$\mathbf{y} = \mathbf{W}\mathbf{x}$$

$$= \begin{bmatrix} w_1 & w_2 & w_3 & & & \\ & w_1 & w_2 & w_3 & & \\ & & & \ddots & & \\ & & & w_1 & w_2 & w_3 \end{bmatrix},$$

where the blank elements are zero. This matrix corresponds to a simple filter having only three nonzero coefficients and a "stride" of one. To account for samples at the beginning and end of the input, or pixels at the edge of the image in the 2D case, zeros can be placed before the start and end, or around the image boundary—e.g., a zero could be added to the start and end of $\mathbf{x}$ above, in which case the output would have the same size as the input. If we dispensed with zero-padding, the valid part of the convolution would be restricted to filter responses computed from input data.

If the rows of a 2D image were packed into one long column vector, a version of this same 3×3 filter could be achieved by a much larger matrix $\mathbf{W}$, having two other sets of three coefficients further along each row. The result would implement the multiplication and additions performed by the matrix encoding of a 2D filter. This could be thought of in another way, as an operation known in signal processing as the *cross-correlation* or *sliding dot product*, which is closely related to a computation known as *convolution*.

Suppose the filter above is centered by giving the first vector element an index of -1, or, in general, an index of $-K$, where K is the "radius" of the filter. The 1D filtering is then

$$\mathbf{y}[n] = \sum_{k=-K}^{K} \mathbf{w}[k]\mathbf{x}[n+k].$$

FIGURE 10.8

Original image; filtered with the two Sobel operators; magnitude of the result.

Directly generalizing this filtering to a 2D image $\mathbf{X}$ and filter $\mathbf{W}$ gives the *cross-correlation*, $\mathbf{Y} = \mathbf{W} * \mathbf{X}$, for which the result for row r and column c is

$$\mathbf{Y}[r, c] = \sum_{j=-J}^{J} \sum_{k=-K}^{K} \mathbf{W}[j, k]\mathbf{X}[r + j, c + k].$$

The *convolution* of an image with a filter, $\mathbf{Y} = \mathbf{W} * \mathbf{X}$, is obtained by flipping the sense of the filter,

$$\mathbf{Y}[r, c] = \sum_{j=-J}^{J} \sum_{k=-K}^{K} \mathbf{W}[-j, -k]\mathbf{X}[r + j, c + k].$$

As an example, consider the task of detecting edges in an image. A well-known technique is to filter it with so-called "Sobel" filters, which involve cross-correlating or convolving it with:

$$\mathbf{G}_x = \begin{bmatrix} -1 & 0 & 1 \\ -2 & 0 & 2 \\ -1 & 0 & 1 \end{bmatrix}, \quad \mathbf{G}_y = \begin{bmatrix} -1 & -2 & -1 \\ 0 & 0 & 0 \\ 1 & 2 & 1 \end{bmatrix}.$$

These particular filters behave much like derivatives of the image. Fig. 10.8 shows the result: a photograph; a version filtered with the Sobel operator $\mathbf{G}_x$, which emphasizes vertical edges; a version filtered with the Sobel operator $\mathbf{G}_y$, which emphasizes horizontal edges; and the result of computing $\mathbf{G} = \sqrt{\mathbf{G}_x^2 + \mathbf{G}_y^2}$. The center two images have been scaled so that midgray corresponds to zero, while the intensity is flipped in the last one to make large values darker and white zero.

Rather than using predetermined filters, convolutional networks jointly learn sets of convolutional filters and a classifier that takes them as input, everything being learned together by backpropagation. By convolving the image with filters successively within the layers of a neural network spatially organized hidden layers can be created, which, as discussed above, could be thought of as feature activity maps indicating where a given feature type has been detected within the

First Layer

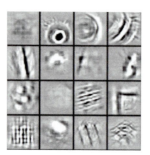

Second Layer

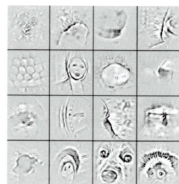

Third Layer

FIGURE 10.9

Examples of what random neurons detect in different layers of a convolutional neural network using the visualization approach of Zeiler and Fergus (2013). Underlying imagery kindly provided by Matthew Zeiler.

image. While filters and activation functions are not specifically constructed as shown in Fig. 10.8, edge-like filters and texture-like filters are frequently observed in the early layers of CNNs that have been trained using natural images. Since each layer in a CNN involves filtering the feature map produced by the layer below, as one moves upwards the receptive field of any given neuron or feature detector becomes larger. As a result, after learning, higher-level layers detect larger features, which often correspond to small pieces of objects in midlevel layers, and quite large pieces of objects toward the top of the network. Fig. 10.9 shows examples of the strongest activation of some random neurons in each layer, projecting the activation back into image space using deconvolution.

Spatial pooling operations applied to the result of a convolutional network are frequently used to impart a degree of local spatial invariance to the precise locations where features have been detected. If pooling is done by averaging, it can be implemented using convolutions. CNNs often apply multiple layers of convolution, followed by pooling and decimation layers. It is common to have about three phases of pooling and decimation. After the last pooling and decimation layer the resulting feature maps are typically fed into a multilayer perceptron. Since decimation reduces the size of feature maps, each such operation reduces the size of subsequent activity maps. Extremely deep convolutional network architectures (having more than 8 layers) typically repeat convolutional layers many times before applying the pooling and decimation operations.

Fig. 10.10 shows a numerical example of the key operations of convolution, pooling, and decimation. First, an image is convolved with the (flipped) filter

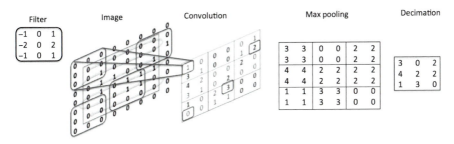

FIGURE 10.10

Example of the convolution, pooling, and decimation operations used in convolutional neural networks.

shown on the left. The curved rectangular regions in the image matrix depict a random set of image locations. The next matrix shows the result of the convolution operation, and here the maximum values within small 2×2 regions are indicated in bold. Next the result is pooled, using max-pooling in this case; and then the pooled matrix is decimated by a factor of two to yield the final result.

CONVOLUTIONAL LAYERS AND GRADIENTS

Let us consider how to compute the gradients needed to optimize a convolutional network. At a given layer we have $i = 1, \ldots, N^{(l)}$ feature filters and corresponding feature maps. The convolutional kernel matrices $\mathbf{K}_i$ contain flipped weights with respect to kernel weight matrices $\mathbf{W}_i$. With activation function act(), and for each feature type i a scaling factor g_i and bias matrix $\mathbf{B}_i$, the feature maps are matrices $\mathbf{H}_i(\mathbf{A}_i(\mathbf{X}))$ and can be visualized as a set of feature map images given by

$$\mathbf{H}_i = g_i \, \text{act}[\mathbf{K}_i^* \mathbf{X} + \mathbf{B}_i] = g_i \, \text{act}[\mathbf{A}_i(\mathbf{X})].$$

The loss $L = L(\mathbf{H}_1^{(l)}, \cdots, \mathbf{H}_{N^{(l)}}^{(l)})$ is a function of the $N^{(l)}$ feature maps for a given layer. Define $\mathbf{h} = \text{vec}(\mathbf{H})$, $\mathbf{x} = \text{vec}(\mathbf{X})$, $\mathbf{a} = \text{vec}(\mathbf{A})$, where the vec() function returns a vector with stacked columns of the given matrix argument. Choose an act() function that operates elementwise on an input matrix of preactivations and has scale parameters of 1 and biases of 0. The partial derivatives of the hidden layer output with respect to $\mathbf{X}$ of the convolutional units are

$$\frac{\partial L}{\partial \mathbf{X}} = \sum_i \sum_j \sum_k \frac{\partial a_{ijk}}{\partial \mathbf{X}} \frac{\partial \mathbf{H}_i}{\partial a_{ijk}} \frac{\partial L}{\partial \mathbf{H}_i} = \sum_i \frac{\partial \mathbf{a}_i}{\partial \mathbf{x}} \frac{\partial \mathbf{h}_i}{\partial \mathbf{a}_i} \frac{\partial L}{\partial \mathbf{h}_i} = \sum_i [\mathbf{W}_i^* \mathbf{D}_i],$$

where $\mathbf{D}_i = dL/\partial \mathbf{A}_i$ is a matrix containing the partial derivative of the elementwise act() function's input with respect to its preactivation value for the ith feature type, organized according to spatial positions given by row j and column k. Intuitively, the result is a sum of the convolution of each of the (zero padded) filters $\mathbf{W}_i$ with an image-like matrix of derivatives $\mathbf{D}_i$. The partial derivatives of the hidden layer output are

$$\frac{\partial L}{\partial \mathbf{W}_i} = \sum_j \sum_k \frac{\partial a_{ijk}}{\partial \mathbf{W}_i} \frac{\partial \mathbf{H}_i}{\partial a_{ijk}} \frac{\partial L}{\partial \mathbf{H}_i} = \left[\mathbf{X}^\dagger * \mathbf{D}_i \right],$$

where $\mathbf{X}^\dagger$ is the row- and column-flipped version of the input $\mathbf{X}$ (if the convolution is written as a linear matrix operation, this will involve just a matrix transpose).

POOLING AND SUBSAMPLING LAYERS AND GRADIENTS

Consider applying a pooling operation to a spatially organized feature map. The input consists of matrices $\mathbf{H}_i$ for each feature map, with elements h_{ijk}. The max pooled and average pooled feature maps are matrices $\mathbf{P}_i$ with elements p_{ijk} given by

$$p_{i,j,k} = \max_{\substack{r \in R_{j,k}, \\ c \in C_{j,k}}} h_{i,r,c}, \quad p_{i,j,k} = \frac{1}{m} \sum_{\substack{r \in R_{j,k}, \\ c \in C_{j,k}}} h_{i,r,c},$$

respectively, where $R_{j,k}$ and $C_{j,k}$ are sets of indices that encode the pooling regions for each location j, k, and m is the number of elements in the pooling region. Although these pooling operations do not include a subsampling step, they typically account for boundary effects either by creating a matrix $\mathbf{P}_i$ that is slightly smaller than the input matrix $\mathbf{H}_i$, or by padding with zeros. The subsampling step either samples every nth output, or avoids needless computation by only evaluating every nth pooling computation.

What are the consequences of backpropagating gradients through layers consisting of max or average pooling? In the former case, the units that are responsible for the maximum within each zone j, k —the "winning units"—are given by

$$\{r^*, c^*\}_{j,k} = \arg\max_{r \in R_{j,k}, \ c \in C_{j,k}} h_{i,r,c}.$$

For nonoverlapping zones, the gradient is propagated back from the pooled layer $\mathbf{P}_i$ to the original spatial feature layer $\mathbf{H}_i$, flowing from each p_{ijk} to just the winning unit in each zone. This can be written

$$\frac{\partial L}{\partial h_{i,r_j,c_k}} = \begin{cases} 0 & r_j \neq r_j^*, c_k \neq c_k^* \\ \dfrac{\partial L}{\partial p_{i,j,k}} & r_j = r_j^*, c_k = c_k^* \end{cases}.$$

In the latter case, average pooling, the averaging operation is simply a special type of convolution with a fixed kernel that computes the (possibly weighted) average of pixels in a zone, so the required gradients are computed using the result above. These various pieces are the building blocks that allow for the implementation of a CNN according to a given architecture.

IMPLEMENTATION

Convolutions are particularly well suited to implementation on graphics hardware. Since graphics hardware can accelerate convolutions by an order of magnitude or more over CPU implementations, it plays an important role in training CNNs. An experimental turn-around time of days rather than weeks makes a huge difference to model development times.

It can also be challenging to construct software for learning a CNN in such a way that alternative architectures can be explored. Although early GPU implementations were hard to extend, newer tools allow for both fast computation and flexible high-level programming primitives. Some of these tools are discussed at the end of this chapter; many of them allow gradient computations and the back-propagation algorithm for large networks to be almost completely automated.

10.4 AUTOENCODERS

Neural networks can also be used for unsupervised learning. An "autoencoder" is a network that learns an efficient coding of its input. The objective is simply to reconstruct the input, but through the intermediary of a compressed or reduced-dimensional representation. If the output is formulated using probability, the objective function is to optimize $p(\mathbf{x} = \hat{\mathbf{x}}|\tilde{\mathbf{x}})$, i.e., the probability that the model gives a random variable $\mathbf{x}$ the value $\hat{\mathbf{x}}$ given the observation $\tilde{\mathbf{x}}$, where $\hat{\mathbf{x}} = \tilde{\mathbf{x}}$. In other words, the model is trained to predict its own input—but it must map it through a representation created by the hidden units of a network.

Fig. 10.11 shows a simple autoencoder, where $p(\hat{\mathbf{x}}|\tilde{\mathbf{x}}) = p(\mathbf{x} = \hat{\mathbf{x}}|\tilde{\mathbf{x}}; \mathbf{f}(\tilde{\mathbf{x}}))$. The parameters of the final probabilistic prediction are given by the last layer's

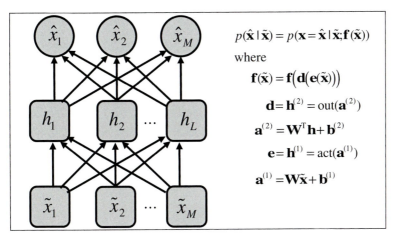

$$p(\hat{\mathbf{x}}|\tilde{\mathbf{x}}) = p(\mathbf{x} = \hat{\mathbf{x}}|\tilde{\mathbf{x}}; \mathbf{f}(\tilde{\mathbf{x}}))$$

where

$$\mathbf{f}(\tilde{\mathbf{x}}) = \mathbf{f}\big(\mathbf{d}(\mathbf{e}(\tilde{\mathbf{x}}))\big)$$

$$\mathbf{d} = \mathbf{h}^{(2)} = \text{out}(\mathbf{a}^{(2)})$$

$$\mathbf{a}^{(2)} = \mathbf{W}^{\mathsf{T}}\mathbf{h} + \mathbf{b}^{(2)}$$

$$\mathbf{e} = \mathbf{h}^{(1)} = \text{act}(\mathbf{a}^{(1)})$$

$$\mathbf{a}^{(1)} = \mathbf{W}\tilde{\mathbf{x}} + \mathbf{b}^{(1)}$$

FIGURE 10.11

A simple autoencoder.

activation function $\mathbf{f}(\tilde{\mathbf{x}}) = \mathbf{f}(\mathbf{d}(\mathbf{e}(\tilde{\mathbf{x}})))$, which is created using a neural network consisting of an encoding step $\mathbf{e}(\tilde{\mathbf{x}}) = \text{act}(\mathbf{W}\tilde{\mathbf{x}} + \mathbf{b}^{(1)})$ followed by a decoding step $\mathbf{d} = \text{out}(\mathbf{W}^T \mathbf{e} + \mathbf{b}^{(2)})$, using the same matrix $\mathbf{W}$ in both steps. Each function has its own bias vector $\mathbf{b}^{(i)}$. Since the idea of an autoencoder is to compress the data into a lower-dimensional representation, the number L of hidden units used for encoding is less than the number M in the input and output layers. Optimizing the autoencoder using the negative log probability over a data set as the objective function leads to the usual forms. Like other neural networks it is typical to optimize autoencoders using backpropagation with mini-batch based stochastic gradient descent.

Both the encoder activation function act() and the output activation function out() in Fig. 10.11 could be defined as the sigmoid function. It can be shown that with no activation function, $\mathbf{h}^{(i)} = \mathbf{a}^{(i)}$, the resulting "linear autoencoder" will find the same subspace as principal component analysis, assuming a squared-error loss function and normalizing the data using mean centering. This autoencoder can be shown to be optimal in the sense that any model with a nonlinear activation function would require a weight matrix with more parameters to achieve the same reconstruction error. It is known that even with a nonlinear activation function such as the sigmoid function, optimization will tend toward solutions where the network operates in the linear regime of the sigmoid, replicating the behavior of principal component analysis.

This might seem discouraging: linear autoencoders are no better than principal component analysis. However, using a neural network with even one hidden layer to create an encoding can construct much more flexible transformations, and there is growing evidence that deeper models can learn more useful representations. When building autoencoders from more flexible models, it is common to use a bottleneck in the network to produce an under-complete representation, providing a mechanism to obtain an encoding of lower dimension than the input.

Deep autoencoders are able to learn low-dimensional representations with smaller reconstruction error than principal component analysis using the same number of dimensions. They are constructed by using L layers to create a hidden layer representation $\mathbf{h}_c^{(L)}$ of the data, and following this with a further L layers $\mathbf{h}_d^{(L+1)} \ldots \mathbf{h}_d^{(2L)}$ to decode the representation back into its original form, as shown in Fig. 10.12. The $j = 1,\ldots, 2L$ weight matrices for each of the $i = 1,\ldots, L$ encoding and decoding layers are constrained by $\mathbf{W}_{L+i} = \mathbf{W}_{L+1-i}^T$.

A deep encoder for $p(\mathbf{x} = \hat{\mathbf{x}}|\tilde{\mathbf{x}}) = p(\hat{\mathbf{x}}; \mathbf{f}_d(\tilde{\mathbf{x}}))$ has the form

$$\mathbf{f}(\mathbf{x}) = \mathbf{f}_d(\mathbf{a}_d^{(2L)}(\ldots \mathbf{h}_d^{(L+1)}(\mathbf{a}_d^{(L+1)}(\mathbf{h}_c^{(L)}(\mathbf{a}_e^{(L)}(\ldots \mathbf{h}_e^{(1)}(\mathbf{a}_e^{(1)}(\mathbf{x})))))))).$$

Fig. 10.13 compares data projected into a 2D space learned in this way with 2D principal component analysis for a particular data set. Since the underlying autoencoder is nonlinear, the network can arrange the learned space in such a way that it better separates natural groupings of the data.

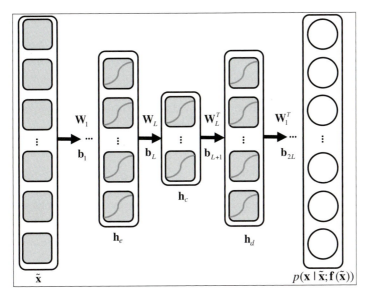

FIGURE 10.12

A deep autoencoder with multiple layers of transformation.

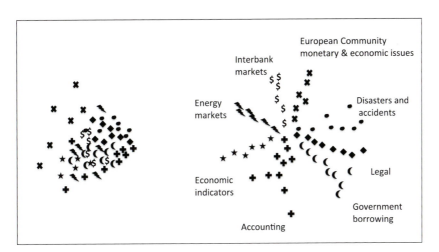

FIGURE 10.13

Low-dimensional principal component space (left) compared with one learned by a deep autoencoder (right).

Adapted from Hinton and Salakhutdinov, (2006).

PRETRAINING DEEP AUTOENCODERS WITH RBMs

Deep autoencoders are an effective framework for nonlinear dimensionality reduction. Once such a network has been built, the top-most layer of the encoder, the code layer $\mathbf{h}_c$, can be input to a supervised classification procedure. If a neural network classifier is used, the entire deep autoencoder network can be discriminatively fine-tuned using gradient descent. In effect, the autoencoder approach is used to pretrain a neural network classifier.

However, it is difficult to optimize autoencoders with multiple hidden layers in both encoder and decoder. It is well known that initializing any deep neural network with weights that are too large leads to poor local minima; while initialization with weights that are too small can lead to small gradients that make learning slow. One approach is to be very careful about the choices of activation function and initialization. However, this has been found difficult in practice.

Another approach is based on pretraining by stacking two-layered RBMs. RBMs are a generalized form of probabilistic PCA with binary hidden variables and binary or continuous observed variables that can perform unsupervised learning; they are discussed further in Section 10.5; To use them for pretraining, start by learning a 2-layer RBM from the data, project the data into its hidden-layer representation, use that to train another RBM, and repeat the process until the encoding layer is reached. The details of how this is done is described in Section 10.5. The parameters of each two-layer network are then used to initialize the parameters of an autoencoder with a similar structure that has nonstochastic sigmoid hidden units.

DENOISING AUTOENCODERS AND LAYERWISE TRAINING

One can also use greedy layerwise training strategies involving plain autoencoders to train deep autoencoders, but attempts to do this for networks of even moderate depth have encountered difficulties. Procedures based on stacking denoising autoencoders have been found to work better. Denoising autoencoders are trained to remove different types of noise that has been added synthetically to their inputs. Autoencoder inputs can be corrupted with noise such as: Gaussian noise; masking noise, where some elements are set to 0; and salt-and-pepper noise, where some elements are set to minimum and maximum input values (such as 0 and 1).

Using autoencoders with stochastic hidden units involves fairly minor modifications to backpropagation based learning. In essence, these procedures resemble dropout. In contrast, more general stochastic models like RBMs rely on approximate probabilistic inference techniques, and the procedures for learning deep stochastic models tend to be quite elaborate (see Section 10.5).

COMBINING RECONSTRUCTIVE AND DISCRIMINATIVE LEARNING

When an autoencoder is used to learn a feature representation intended for classification or regression, a model can be defined that both reconstructs inputs and classifies inputs. This hybrid model has a composite loss that consists of a reconstructive (unsupervised) and a discriminative (supervised) criterion, $L(\theta) = (1 - \lambda)L_{sup}(\theta) + \lambda L_{unsup}(\theta)$, where the hyperparameter $\lambda \in [0, 1]$ controls the balance between the two objectives. In the extreme cases, $\lambda = 0$ yields a purely supervised training procedure, while $\lambda = 1$ yields a purely unsupervised training procedure. If some data is only available without labels, one can optimize just a reconstructive loss. For the hybrid model, one could imagine augmenting the deep autoencoder of Fig. 10.12 to make predictions using $\mathbf{h}_c$ as input, either with a single set of weights leading to an activation function and final prediction, or with multiple layers prior to making a prediction. Training with a combined objective function appears to provide a form of regularization that can lead to increased performance on the discriminative task. When combined with more numerically well-behaved activation functions like ReLUs this procedure has been found to allow deeper models to be learned with fewer problems. Of course, one must be careful to tune λ on a validation set. Some similar approaches can be taken with the stochastic methods below, which can be defined in both generative and discriminative forms.

10.5 STOCHASTIC DEEP NETWORKS

The networks considered so far are constructed from deterministic components. We now look at stochastic networks, beginning with a model for unsupervised learning known as a Boltzmann machine. This stochastic neural network model is a type of Markov random field (see Section 9.6). Unlike the units of a feedforward neural network, the units in Boltzmann machines correspond to random variables, such as are used in Bayesian networks. Older variants of Boltzmann machines were defined using exclusively binary variables, but models with continuous and discrete variables are also possible. They became popular prior to the impressive results of CNNs on the ImageNet challenge, but have since waned in popularity because they are more difficult to work with. However, stochastic methods have certain advantages, such as the ability to capture multimodal distributions.

BOLTZMANN MACHINES

To create a Boltzmann machine we begin by partitioning variables into ones that are visible, defined by a D-dimensional binary vector $\mathbf{v} \in \{0, 1\}^D$, and ones that are hidden, defined by a K-dimensional binary vector $\mathbf{h} \in \{0, 1\}^K$. Then a Boltzmann machine is a joint probability model of the form

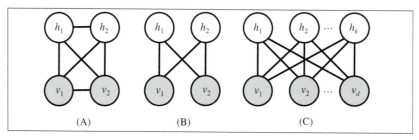

FIGURE 10.14

Boltzmann machines: (A) fully connected; (B) restricted; (C) more general form of (B).

$$p(\mathbf{v}, \mathbf{h}; \theta) = \frac{1}{Z(\theta)} \exp(-E(\mathbf{v}, \mathbf{h}; \theta)),$$

$$Z(\theta) = \sum_{\mathbf{v}} \sum_{\mathbf{h}} \exp(-E(\mathbf{v}, \mathbf{h}; \theta)),$$

$$E(\mathbf{v}, \mathbf{h}; \theta) = -\frac{1}{2}\mathbf{v}^T \mathbf{A}\mathbf{v} - \frac{1}{2}\mathbf{h}^T \mathbf{B}\mathbf{h} - \mathbf{v}^T \mathbf{W}\mathbf{h} - \mathbf{a}^T \mathbf{v} - \mathbf{b}^T \mathbf{h},$$

where $E(\mathbf{v}, \mathbf{h}; \theta)$ is the energy function, $Z(\theta)$ normalizes E so that it defines a valid joint probability, the matrices $\mathbf{A}$, $\mathbf{B}$, and $\mathbf{W}$ encode the visible-to-visible, hidden-to-hidden, and visible-to-hidden variable interactions, respectively, and vectors $\mathbf{a}$ and $\mathbf{b}$ encode the biases associated with each variable. Matrices $\mathbf{A}$ and $\mathbf{B}$ are symmetric, and their diagonal elements are 0. This structure is effectively a binary Markov random field with pairwise connections between all variables, illustrated in Fig. 10.14A.

A key feature of Boltzmann machines (and binary Markov random fields in general) is that the conditional distribution of one variable given the others is a sigmoid function whose argument is a weighted linear combination of the states of the other variables:

$$p(h_j = 1 | \mathbf{v}, \mathbf{h}_{-j}; \theta) = \text{sigmoid}\left(\sum_{i=1}^{D} W_{ij} v_i + \sum_{k=1}^{K} B_{jk} h_k + b_j \right),$$

$$p(v_i = 1 | \mathbf{h}, \mathbf{v}_{-i}; \theta) = \text{sigmoid}\left(\sum_{j=1}^{K} W_{ij} h_j + \sum_{d=1}^{D} A_{id} v_d + c_i \right),$$

where the notation $\neg i$ indicates all elements with subscript other than i. The diagonal elements of A and B are zero, so there is no need for the sum to skip terms involving $h_{k=j}$ and $v_{d=i}$, since they are zero anyway. The fact that these equations are separate sigmoid functions for each variable makes it easy to construct a Gibbs' sampler (Section 9.5), which can be used to compute approximations to the conditional probability $p(\mathbf{h}|\tilde{\mathbf{v}})$ and the joint probability $p(\mathbf{h}, \mathbf{v})$.

Define the loss as the negative log-likelihood of the marginal probability for a single example $\tilde{\mathbf{v}}$ under the Boltzmann machine model: $L = -\log p(\tilde{\mathbf{v}}; \theta) = -\log \sum_{\mathbf{h}} p(\tilde{\mathbf{v}}, \mathbf{h}; \theta)$. Then, based on some calculus, the partial derivatives can be shown to be

$$\frac{\partial L}{\partial \mathbf{W}} = - \left[E[\tilde{\mathbf{v}} \mathbf{h}^T]_{P(\mathbf{h}|\tilde{\mathbf{v}})} - E[\mathbf{v} \mathbf{h}^T]_{P(\mathbf{h},\mathbf{v})} \right],$$

$$\frac{\partial L}{\partial \mathbf{A}} = - \left[\tilde{\mathbf{v}} \tilde{\mathbf{v}}^T - E[\mathbf{v} \mathbf{v}^T]_{P(\mathbf{h},\mathbf{v})} \right],$$

$$\frac{\partial L}{\partial \mathbf{B}} = - \left[E[\mathbf{h} \mathbf{h}^T]_{P(\mathbf{h}|\tilde{\mathbf{v}})} - E[\mathbf{h} \mathbf{h}^T]_{P(\mathbf{h},\mathbf{v})} \right],$$

$$\frac{\partial L}{\partial \mathbf{a}} = - \left[\tilde{\mathbf{v}} - E[\mathbf{v}]_{P(\mathbf{h},\mathbf{v})} \right],$$

$$\frac{\partial L}{\partial \mathbf{b}} = - \left[E[\mathbf{h}]_{P(\mathbf{h}|\tilde{\mathbf{v}})} - E[\mathbf{h}]_{P(\mathbf{h},\mathbf{v})} \right].$$

The distributions $p(\mathbf{h}|\tilde{\mathbf{v}})$ and $p(\mathbf{h},\mathbf{v})$ needed to compute the expectations in these derivatives are not available in analytic form, but samples approximating them can be used instead. To compute the gradient of the negative log-likelihood over an entire training set with N examples, the sum of the terms is N times a single expectation using the empirical distribution of the data $P_{data}(\tilde{\mathbf{v}})$, or the distribution obtained by placing a delta function on each example and dividing by N. A sum over a training set involving expectations of the form $p(\mathbf{h}|\tilde{\mathbf{v}})$ is sometimes written as a single expectation and referred to as the *data-dependent expectation*, whereas the expectations involving $p(\mathbf{h},\mathbf{v})$ do not depend on the data and are referred to as the *model's expectation*.

Using these equations and approximations for the distributions, one can implement optimization via gradient descent. Gradients in probabilistic models often come down to computing differences of expectations, as in models such as logistic regression, conditional random fields, and even probabilistic principal component analysis, as we saw in Chapter 9, Probabilistic methods.

RESTRICTED BOLTZMANN MACHINES

Eliminating connections between hidden variables, and connections between visible variables, yields a *restricted* Boltzmann machine (RBM), with the same distribution $p(\mathbf{v},\mathbf{h};\theta) = Z^{-1}(\theta) \exp(-E(\mathbf{v},\mathbf{h};\theta))$ but this energy function:

$$E(\mathbf{v},\mathbf{h};\theta) = - \mathbf{v}^T \mathbf{W} \mathbf{h} - \mathbf{a}^T \mathbf{v} - \mathbf{b}^T \mathbf{h}.$$

Fig. 10.14B shows the result of this transformation on Fig. 10.14A; while Fig. 10.14C shows a more general form.

Eliminating the coupling matrices $\mathbf{A}$ and $\mathbf{B}$ means that that the exact inference step for $\mathbf{h}$, the entire vector of hidden variables, can be performed in one shot. $p(\mathbf{h}|\mathbf{v})$ becomes the product of a different sigmoid for each dimension, each sigmoid depending only on the observed input vector $\mathbf{v}$. $p(\mathbf{v}|\mathbf{h})$ has a similar form.

$$p(\mathbf{h}|\mathbf{v}) = \prod_{k=1}^{K} p(h_k|\mathbf{v}) = \prod_{k=1}^{K} \mathrm{Bern}(h_k; \mathrm{sigmoid}(b_k + \mathbf{W}_{\cdot k}^T \mathbf{v})),$$

$$p(\mathbf{v}|\mathbf{h}) = \prod_{i=1}^{D} p(v_i|\mathbf{h}) = \prod_{i=1}^{D} \mathrm{Bern}(v_i; \mathrm{sigmoid}(a_i + \mathbf{W}_{i\cdot} \mathbf{h})),$$

where $\mathbf{W}_{\cdot k}^T$ is a vector consisting of the transpose of the kth column of the weight matrix $\mathbf{W}$, while $\mathbf{W}_{i\cdot}$ is the ith row of $\mathbf{W}$. These are conditional distributions that are derived from the underlying joint model, and the equations can be used to compute the gradient of the loss with respect to $\mathbf{W}$, $\mathbf{a}$, and $\mathbf{b}$. The expectations needed for learning are easier to compute than for an unrestricted model: an exact expression can be obtained for $p(\mathbf{h}|\tilde{\mathbf{v}})$, but $p(\mathbf{h}, \mathbf{v})$ remains intractable and must be approximated.

CONTRASTIVE DIVERGENCE

Running a Gibbs sampler for a Boltzmann machine often requires many iterations, and a technique called "contrastive divergence" is a popular alternative that initializes the sampler to the observed data instead of randomly and performs a limited number of Gibbs updates. In an RBM, a sample $\hat{\mathbf{h}}^{(0)}$ can be generated from the distribution $p(\mathbf{h}|\hat{\mathbf{v}}^{(0)} = \tilde{\mathbf{v}})$ followed by a sample for $\hat{\mathbf{v}}^{(1)}$ from $p(\mathbf{v}|\hat{\mathbf{h}}^{(1)})$. This single step often works well in practice, although the process of alternating the sampling of hidden and visible units can be continued for multiple steps.

CATEGORICAL AND CONTINUOUS VARIABLES

The RBMs discussed so far have been composed of binary variables. However, they can be extended to categorical or continuous attributes by encoding $r = 1,\ldots, R$ visible categorical variables using one-hot vectors $\mathbf{v}_{(r)}$ and defining hidden binary variables $\mathbf{h}$ with the following energy function

$$E(\mathbf{v}, \mathbf{h}; \theta) = - \sum_{r=1}^{R} \left[\mathbf{v}_{(r)}^T \mathbf{W}_{(r)} \mathbf{h} + \mathbf{a}_{(r)}^T \mathbf{v}_{(r)} \right] - \mathbf{b}^T \mathbf{h}.$$

The joint distribution defined by this model is complex, but as for binary RBMs the conditional distributions under the model for one layer given the other have simple forms:

$$p(\mathbf{h}|\mathbf{v}_{(r=1,\ldots,R)}) = \prod_{k=1}^{K} \mathrm{Bern}\left(h_k; \mathrm{sigmoid}\left(b_k + \sum_{r=1}^{R} \mathbf{W}_{(r)\cdot k}^T \mathbf{v}_{(r)} \right) \right),$$

$$p(\mathbf{v}_{(r=1,\ldots,R)}|\mathbf{h}) = \prod_{r=1}^{R} \mathrm{Cat}\left(\mathbf{v}_{(r)}; \mathrm{softmax}(\mathbf{a}_{(r)} + \mathbf{W}_{(r)\cdot} \mathbf{h}) \right),$$

A model with a layer of continuous observed variables $\mathbf{v}$ and a layer of hidden binary variables $\mathbf{h}$ can be constructed using this energy function:

$$E(\mathbf{v}, \mathbf{h}; \theta) = -\mathbf{v}^T \mathbf{W}\mathbf{h} - \frac{1}{2}(\mathbf{v} - \mathbf{a})^2 - \mathbf{b}^T \mathbf{h}.$$

The conditional distributions are

$$p(\mathbf{h}|\mathbf{v}) = \prod_{k=1}^{K} \text{Bern}\left(h_k; \text{sigmoid}(b_k + \mathbf{W}_{:k}^T \mathbf{v})\right),$$

$$p(\mathbf{v}|\mathbf{h}) = \prod_{i=1}^{D} N(v_i; a_i + \mathbf{W}_{i \cdot} \mathbf{h}, 1) = N(\mathbf{v}; \mathbf{a} + \mathbf{W}\mathbf{h}, \mathbf{I}),$$

where the conditional distribution of the observed variables given the hidden is a Gaussian whose mean depends on a bias term plus a linear transformation of the binary hidden variable. This Gaussian has an identity covariance matrix and can therefore be written as a product of independent Gaussians for each dimension.

DEEP BOLTZMANN MACHINES

Deep Boltzmann machines involve coupling layers of random variables using RBM connectivity, as illustrated in Fig. 10.15A. Assuming Bernoulli random variables, the energy function is

$$E(\mathbf{v}, \mathbf{h}^{(1)}, \ldots, \mathbf{h}^{(L)}; \theta) = -\mathbf{v}^T \mathbf{W}^{(1)} \mathbf{h}^{(1)} - \mathbf{a}^T \mathbf{v} - \mathbf{b}^{(1)T} \mathbf{h}^{(1)}$$

$$- \left[\sum_{l=2}^{L} \left[\mathbf{h}^{(l-1)T} \mathbf{W}^{(l)} \mathbf{h}^{(l)} + \mathbf{b}^{(l)T} \mathbf{h}^{(l)} \right] \right],$$

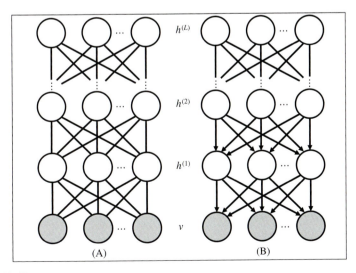

FIGURE 10.15

(A) Deep Boltzmann machine and (B) deep belief network.

where the layers are coupled with matrices $\mathbf{W}^{(l)}$, and $\mathbf{a}$ and $\mathbf{b}^{(l)}$ are the biases for the visible layer and each hidden layer. The gradients for the intermediate layer matrices are

$$\frac{\partial L}{\partial \mathbf{W}^{(l)}} = -\left[E[\mathbf{h}^{(l-1)} \, \mathbf{h}^{(l)T}]_{P(\mathbf{h}^{(l-1)}, \, \mathbf{h}^{(l)T}|\tilde{\mathbf{v}})} - E[\mathbf{h}^{(l-1)} \, \mathbf{h}^{(l)T}]_{P(\mathbf{h}^{(l-1)}, \, \mathbf{h}^{(l)T}, \mathbf{v})} \right],$$

$$\frac{\partial L}{\partial \mathbf{b}^{(l)}} = -\left[E[\mathbf{h}^{(l)}]_{P(\mathbf{h}^{(l)}|\tilde{\mathbf{v}})} - E[\mathbf{h}^{(l)}]_{P(\mathbf{h}^{(l)},\mathbf{v})} \right],$$

where the probability distributions needed for the expectations can be computed using approximate inference techniques such as Gibbs sampling or variational methods.

Examining the Markov blanket of a layer in this network shows that, given the layers above and below, variables in a given layer are independent of other layers. The conditional distribution is

$$p(\mathbf{h}^{(l)}|\mathbf{h}^{(l-1)}, \mathbf{h}^{(l+1)}) = \prod_{k_l=1}^{K_l} p(h_k^l|\mathbf{h}^{(l-1)}, \mathbf{h}^{(l+1)})$$

$$= \prod_{k=1}^{K_l} \text{Bern}\left(h_k^l; \text{sigmoid}(b_k^l + \mathbf{W}_{\cdot k}^{(l)T} \mathbf{h}^{(l-1)} + \mathbf{W}_{k\cdot}^{(l+1)} \mathbf{h}^{(l+1)}) \right).$$

This enables all variables in a layer to be updated in parallel using a method known as "block Gibbs sampling." This is quicker than standard Gibbs sampling, but yields samples of sufficient quality for fast learning.

The overall learning procedure in deep Boltzmann machines using sampling or variational methods can be slow, and consequently greedy, incremental approaches are often used to initialize weights prior to learning. Deep Boltzmann machines can be trained incrementally by stacking two-layer Boltzmann machines, and learning the two-layer models using gradient descent and the contrastive divergence-based sampling procedure.

When training a deep RBM incrementally by stacking, to deal with the lack of top-down connections in the model, one can double the input variables of the lower-level model and constrain the associated matrix to be the same as the original; double the output variables of the higher-level model and constrain its matrix in the same way. Once the first Boltzmann machine has been learned, the next can be learned using either a sample from independent Bernoulli distributions for the dimensions of $p(\mathbf{h}^{(1)}|\mathbf{v})$ based on the sigmoid models of the rewritten Boltzmann machine, or using the value of the sigmoid activations. In both cases a fast approximate inference upward pass can be performed using a doubled weight matrix to compensate for the fact that the top-down influence of the model is not captured. When generating a sampler or sigmoid activity for the final layer, it is not necessary to double the weights. Subsequent levels can be learned similarly.

DEEP BELIEF NETWORKS

While any deep Bayesian network is technically a deep belief network, the term "deep belief network" has become strongly associated with a particular type of deep architecture that can be constructed by training RBMs incrementally. The procedure is based on converting the lower part of a growing model into a Bayesian belief network, adding an RBM for the upper part of the model, then continuing the training, conversion, and stacking process. As we have seen above, an RBM is a two-layer joint model for which we can use some algebra to write conditional models of observed given hidden, or hidden given observed layers that are consistent with the underlying joint distribution. It therefore follows that a deep belief network can be obtained through a procedure of learning a joint RBM model for two layers, converting the model into its conditional formulation for the layer below given the layer above, then adding a new layer on top to the model, parameterizing the top two layers as a new joint RBM model, then learning the new parameters. Fig. 10.15B illustrates the general form, which can be written

$$P(\mathbf{v}, \mathbf{h}^{(1)}, \ldots, \mathbf{h}^{(L)}; \theta) = P(\mathbf{v}|\mathbf{h}^{(1)}) \left[\prod_{l=1}^{L-2} P(\mathbf{h}^{(l)}|\mathbf{h}^{(l+1)}) \right] P(\mathbf{h}^{(L-1)}, \mathbf{h}^{(L)}),$$

where as before the model is defined in terms of a visible layer $\mathbf{v}$ and $l = 1, \ldots, L$ hidden layers $\mathbf{h}^{(l)}$. The conditional distributions are all products of Bernoulli distributions with sigmoidal parameterizations.

The top *two* layers are parameterized as an RBM. If they have directed rather than undirected connections, they can be decomposed into the form $P(\mathbf{h}^{(L-1)}, \mathbf{h}^{(L)}) = P(\mathbf{h}^{(L-1)}|\mathbf{h}^{(L)})P(\mathbf{h}^{(L)})$, where the conditional distribution is another sigmoidally parameterized Bernoulli product and $P(\mathbf{h}^{(L)})$ is the product over a separate distribution for each $P(\mathbf{h}^{(L)})$. The result is known as a deep sigmoidal belief network.

The network shown in Fig. 10.15B can be constructed and trained in a layer-by-layer manner. To see this, consider a RBM with visible variables $\mathbf{v}$ and two layers of hidden variables $\mathbf{h}^{(1)}$ followed by $\mathbf{h}^{(2)}$ on top. A joint model for $P(\mathbf{v}, \mathbf{h}^{(1)}, \mathbf{h}^{(2)})$ can be defined as either a 3-layer Boltzmann machine, or, by restructuring the parameterization of the lower two layers, as a belief network with an RBM at the top using

$$P(\mathbf{v}, \mathbf{h}^{(1)}, \mathbf{h}^{(2)}) = P(\mathbf{v}|\mathbf{h}^{(1)})P(\mathbf{h}^{(1)}, \mathbf{h}^{(2)})$$
$$= \prod_{i=1}^{D} \mathrm{Bern}\left(v_i; \mathrm{sigmoid}(a_i + \mathbf{W}_i^{(1)}\mathbf{h}) \right) \cdot \frac{1}{Z(\theta)} \exp(-E(\mathbf{h}^{(1)}, \mathbf{h}^{(2)}; \theta)), \quad (10.2)$$

where $P(\mathbf{h}^{(1)}, \mathbf{h}^{(2)})$ has the usual form

$$Z(\theta) = \sum_{\mathbf{h}^{(1)}} \sum_{\mathbf{h}^{(2)}} \exp(-E(\mathbf{h}^{(1)}, \mathbf{h}^{(2)}; \theta)),$$

$$-E(\mathbf{h}^{(1)}, \mathbf{h}^{(2)}; \theta) = \mathbf{h}^{(1)\mathrm{T}}\mathbf{W}^{(2)}\mathbf{h}^{(2)} + \mathbf{b}^{(1)T}\mathbf{h}^{(1)} + \mathbf{b}^{(2)T}\mathbf{h}^{(2)},$$

and the parameters $\mathbf{W}^{(1)}$ and $\mathbf{a}$ of $P(\mathbf{v}|\mathbf{h}^{(1)})$ are independent of the parameters $\mathbf{W}^{(1)}$, $\mathbf{b}^{(1)}$, and $\mathbf{b}^{(2)}$ of $P(\mathbf{h}^{(1)}, \mathbf{h}^{(2)})$.

Such networks can be trained as follows: first train a 2-layer Boltzmann machine using the observed data. Then add a layer on top, and initialize its weights to the transpose of the weights learned in the layer below. To train the next layer, compute the conditional distribution for the layer above given the layer below, and either generate a sample or use the activation of the sigmoid function to transform each example of the training data into the first hidden layer representation. The properties of a RBM can be further exploited to obtain the conditional distribution of the lower layer given the upper layer, and the parameters of the conditional model in this direction can be fixed. Once the second Boltzmann machine has been trained, the model has the form (Eq. 10.2), and the process of transforming the data, transforming the top-level Boltzmann machine into a conditional model, adding a layer, and training a top layer Boltzmann machine can be repeated as desired.

If the layer above has a different number of units, the transpose of the matrix below cannot be used for initialization and certain theoretical guarantees no longer apply. However, in practice the procedure is known to work well with random initialization.

10.6 RECURRENT NEURAL NETWORKS

Recurrent neural networks are networks with connections that form directed cycles. As a result, they have an internal state, which makes them prime candidates for tackling learning problems involving sequences of data—such as handwriting recognition, speech recognition, and machine translation. Fig. 10.16A shows how a feedforward network can be transformed into a recurrent network by

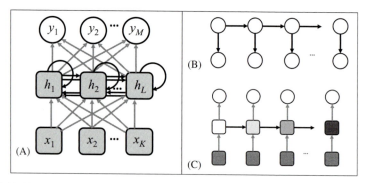

FIGURE 10.16

(A) Feedforward network transformed into a recurrent network; (B) hidden Markov model; and (C) recurrent network obtained by unwrapping (A).

adding connections from all hidden units h_i to h_j. Each hidden unit has connections to both itself and other hidden units.

Imagine unfolding a recurrent network over time by following the sequence of steps that perform the underlying computation. Like a hidden Markov model, a recurrent network can be unwrapped and implemented using the same weights and biases at each step to link units over time. Fig. 10.16B shows a hidden Markov model unfolded in time and written as a dynamic Bayesian network, while Fig. 10.16C shows a recurrent network obtained by unwrapping Fig. 10.16A. Recurrent neural networks operate in a deterministic continuous space, in contrast to hidden Markov models, which generally utilize discrete random variables. Whereas it is common to think of deep feedforward networks as computing more abstract features as one progresses up the network, information processing in recurrent networks proceeds more like steps in the execution of a more general algorithm.

Recurrent neural networks, and the particular discussed below—known as "long short-term memory" (LSTM) recurrent neural networks—have been particularly successful for many tasks, from unconstrained handwriting recognition to speech recognition and machine translation.

These networks apply linear matrix operations to the current observation and the hidden units from the previous time step, and the resulting linear terms serve as arguments of activation functions act():

$$\mathbf{h}_t = \text{act}(\mathbf{W}_h\mathbf{x}_t + \mathbf{U}_h\mathbf{h}_{t-1} + \mathbf{b}_h)$$
$$\mathbf{o}_t = \text{act}(\mathbf{W}_o\mathbf{h}_t + \mathbf{b}_o) \qquad (10.3)$$

The same matrix $\mathbf{U}_h$ is used at each time step. Through it, the hidden units in the previous step $\mathbf{h}_{t-1}$ influence the computation of $\mathbf{h}_t$, while the current observation contributes a term $\mathbf{W}_h\mathbf{x}$ term that is summed with $\mathbf{U}_h\mathbf{h}_{t-1}$ and a bias term $\mathbf{b}_h$. Both $\mathbf{W}_h$ and $\mathbf{b}_h$ are typically replicated over time. The output layer is modeled by a classical neural network activation function applied to a linear transformation of the hidden units, and the operation is replicated at each time step.

The loss for a particular sequence in the training data can be computed either at each time step or just once, at the end of the sequence. In either case, predictions will be made after many processing steps. This brings us to an important problem. Eq. (10.1) for feedforward networks decomposes the gradient of parameters at layer l into a product of matrix multiplications of the form $\mathbf{D}^{(l)}\mathbf{W}^{T(l+1)}$. A recurrent network uses the same matrix at each time step, and over many steps the gradient can very easily either diminish to zero or explode to infinity—just as the magnitude of any number (other than one) taken to a large power either approaches zero or increases indefinitely.

EXPLODING AND VANISHING GRADIENTS

The use of L_1 or L_2 regularization can mitigate the problem of exploding gradients by encouraging weights to be small. Another strategy is to simply detect if the norm of the gradient exceeds some threshold and, if so, scale it down. This is sometimes called gradient (norm) clipping. That is, for a gradient vector $\mathbf{g} = \partial L / \partial \theta$ and threshold T,

$$\text{if } \|\mathbf{g}\| \geq T \text{ then}$$
$$\mathbf{g} \leftarrow \frac{T}{\|\mathbf{g}\|} \mathbf{g}$$

T is a hyperparameter, which can be set to the average norm over several previous updates where clipping was not used.

The so-called "LSTM" recurrent neural network architecture was specifically created to address the vanishing gradient problem. It uses a special combination of hidden units, elementwise products and sums between units to implement gates that control "memory cells." These cells are designed to retain information without modification for long periods of time. They have their own input and output gates, which are controlled by learnable weights that are a function of the current observation and the hidden units at the previous time step. As a result, backpropagated error terms from gradient computations can be stored and propagated backwards without degradation. The original LSTM formulation consisted of *input gates* and *output gates*, but *forget gates* and "peephole weights" were added later. The architecture is complex, but has produced state-of-the-art results on a wide variety of problems. Below we present the most popular variant of LSTM RNNs, which does not include peephole weights but does use forget gates.

LSTM RNNs work as follows: at each time step there are three types of gate, input $\mathbf{i}_t$, forget $\mathbf{f}_t$, and output $\mathbf{o}_t$, each being a function of the underlying input $\mathbf{x}_t$ at time t and the hidden units at time $t-1$, $\mathbf{h}_{t-1}$. Gates multiply $\mathbf{x}_t$ by their own gate-specific $\mathbf{W}$ matrix $\mathbf{h}_{t-1}$, by their own $\mathbf{U}$ matrix, and add their own bias vector $\mathbf{b}$, followed by the application of a sigmoidal elementwise nonlinearity.

At each time step t, input gates $\mathbf{i}_t = \text{sigmoid}(\mathbf{W}_i \mathbf{x}_t + \mathbf{U}_i \mathbf{h}_{t-1} + \mathbf{b}_i)$ are used to determine whether a potential input given by $\mathbf{s}_t = \tanh(\mathbf{W}_c \mathbf{x}_t + \mathbf{U}_c \mathbf{h}_{t-1} + \mathbf{b}_c)$ is sufficiently important to be placed into the memory unit $\mathbf{c}_t$. The computation of $\mathbf{s}_t$ itself is a linear combination of the current input value $\mathbf{x}_t$ and the previous hidden unit vector $\mathbf{h}_{t-1}$, using weight matrices $\mathbf{W}_c$ and $\mathbf{U}_c$ along with a bias vector $\mathbf{b}_c$. Forget gates $\mathbf{f}_t$ allow the content of memory units to be erased using $\mathbf{f}_t = \text{sigmoid}(\mathbf{W}_f \mathbf{x}_t + \mathbf{U}_f \mathbf{h}_{t-1} + \mathbf{b}_f)$, involving a similar linear input based on $\mathbf{W}_f$ and $\mathbf{U}_f$ matrices, plus a bias $\mathbf{b}_f$. Output gates $\mathbf{o}_t$ determine whether $\mathbf{y}_t$, the content of the memory units transformed by activation functions, should be placed in the hidden units $\mathbf{h}_t$. They are typically controlled by a sigmoidal activation function $\mathbf{o}_t = \text{sigmoid}(\mathbf{W}_o \mathbf{x}_t + \mathbf{U}_o \mathbf{h}_{t-1} + \mathbf{b}_o)$ applied to a linear combination of the current input value $\mathbf{x}_t$ and the previous hidden unit vector $\mathbf{h}_{t-1}$, using weight matrices $\mathbf{W}_o$ and $\mathbf{U}_o$ along with a bias vector $\mathbf{b}_o$.

This final gating is implemented as an elementwise product between the output gate and the transformed memory contents, $\mathbf{h}_t = \mathbf{o}_t \circ \mathbf{y}_t$, where memory units are typically transformed by the tanh function prior to the gated output:

Table 10.5 Components of a "Long Short-Term Memory" Recurrent Neural Network

LSTM unit output	$h_t = o_t {\circ} y_t$
Output gate units	$o_t = \text{sigmoid}(W_o x_t + U_o h_{t-1} + b_o)$
Transformed memory cell contents	$y_t = \text{tanh}(c_t)$
Gated update to memory cell units	$c_t = f_t {\circ} c_{t-1} + i_t {\circ} s_t$
Forget gate units	$f_t = \text{sigmoid}(W_f x_t + U_f h_{t-1} + b_f)$
Input gate units	$i_t = \text{sigmoid}(W_i x_t + U_i h_{t-1} + b_i)$
Potential input to memory cell	$s_t = \text{tanh}(W_c x_t + U_c h_{t-1} + b_c)$

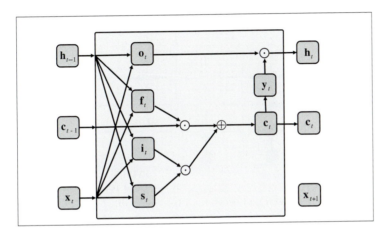

FIGURE 10.17

Structure of a "long short-term memory" unit.

$y_t = \text{tanh}(c_t)$. Memory units are updated by $c_t = f_t {\circ} c_{t-1} + i_t {\circ} s_t$, an elementwise product between the forget gates f_t and the previous contents of the memory units c_{t-1}, plus the elementwise product of the input gates i_t, and the new potential inputs s_t. Table 10.5 defines these components, and Fig. 10.17 shows a computation graph for the intermediate quantities.

OTHER RECURRENT NETWORK ARCHITECTURES

A wide variety of other recurrent network architectures have been proposed. For example, the network given by Eq. (10.3) can be used with rectified linear activation functions, using scaled versions of the identity matrix to initialize the recurrent weight matrix, and initializing biases to zero. The identity initialization means that error derivatives flow through the network unmodified. Initializing with smaller, scaled versions of the identity matrix has the effect of causing the model to forget longer range dependencies. This approach is known as an IRNN. Another

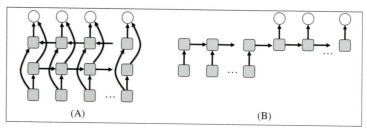

FIGURE 10.18

Recurrent neural networks: (A) bidirectional, (B) encoder-decoder.

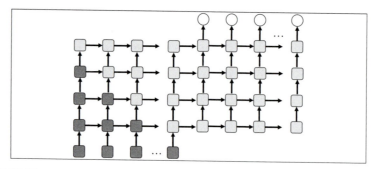

FIGURE 10.19

A deep encoder-decoder recurrent network.

possibility is to simplify LSTM networks by dispensing with separate memory cells and using gated recurrent units or GRUs. For some problems GRUs can provide performance comparable with LSTMs, but with a lower memory requirement.

Recurrent networks can be made bidirectional, propagating information in both directions: Fig. 10.18A shows the general structure. Bidirectional networks have been used for a wide variety of applications, including protein secondary structure prediction and handwriting recognition. Modern software tools determine the gradients required for learning via backpropagation automatically, by manipulating computation graphs.

Fig. 10.18B shows an "encoder-decoder" network. Such networks allow the creation of fixed-length vector representations for variable-length inputs, and can use the fixed-length encoding to generate another variable-length sequence as the output. This is particularly useful for machine translation, where the input is a string in one language and the output is the corresponding string in another language. Given enough data, a deep encoder-decoder architecture such as that of Fig. 10.19 can yield results that compete with those of systems that have been hand-engineered over decades of research. The connectivity structure means that partial computations in the model can flow through the graph in a wave, illustrated by the darker nodes in the figure.

10.7 FURTHER READING AND BIBLIOGRAPHIC NOTES

The backpropagation algorithm has been known in close to its current form since Werbos' (1974) PhD thesis; in his extensive literature review of deep learning, Schmidhuber (2015) traces key elements of the algorithm back even further. He also traces the idea of "deep networks" back to the work of Ivakhnenko and Lapa (1965). Modern CNNs are widely acknowledged as having their roots with the "neocognitron" proposed by Fukushima (1980). However, the work of LeCun, Bottou, Bengio, and Haffner (1998) on the LeNet convolutional network architecture has been extremely influential.

The popularity of neural network techniques has gone through several cycles. While some factors are social, there are important technical reasons behind the trends. A single-layer neural network cannot solve the XOR problem, a failing that was derided by Minsky and Papert (1969) which, as mentioned in Section 4.10, stymied neural network development until the mid-1980s. However, it is well known that networks with one additional layer can approximate any function (Cybenko, 1989; Hornik, 1991), and Rumelhart, Hinton, and Williams' (1986) influential work repopularized neural network methods for a while. However, by the early 2000s they had fallen out of favor again. Indeed, the organizers of NIPS, the *Neural Information Processing Systems* conference, which was (and still is) widely considered to be the premier forum for neural network research, found that the presence of the term "neural networks" in the title was highly correlated with the paper's rejection!—a fact that is underscored by citation analysis of key neural network papers during this period. The recent resurgence of interest in deep learning really does feel like a "revolution."

It is known that most complex Boolean functions require an exponential number of two-step logic gates for their representation (Wegener, 1987). The solution appears to be greater depth: according to Bengio (2009), the evidence strongly suggests that "functions that can be compactly represented with a depth-k architecture could require a very large number of elements in order to be represented by a shallower architecture."

Many neural network books (Haykin, 1994; Bishop, 1995; Ripley, 1996) do not formulate backpropagation in vector-matrix terms. However, recent online courses (e.g., by Hugo Larochelle), and Rojas' (1996) text, do adopt this formulation, as we have done in this chapter.

Stochastic gradient descent methods go back at least as far as Robbins and Monro (1951). Bottou (2012) is an excellent source of tips and tricks for learning with stochastic gradient descent, while Bengio (2012) gives further practical recommendations for training deep networks. Bergstra and Bengio (2012) give empirical and theoretical justification for the use of random search for hyperparameter settings. Snoek, Larochelle, and Adams (2012) propose the use of Bayesian learning methods to infer the next hyperparameter setting to explore, and their Spearmint software package performs Bayesian optimizations of both deep network hyperparameters and general machine learning algorithm hyperparameters.

Good parameter initialization can be critical for the success of neural networks, as discussed in LeCun et al.'s (1998) classic work and the more recent work of Glorot and Bengio (2010). Krizhevsky et al.'s (2012) convolutional network of ReLUs initialized weights using 0-mean isotropic Gaussian distributions with a standard deviation of 0.01, and initialized the biases to 1 for most hidden convolutional layers as well as the model's hidden fully connected layers. They observed that this initialization accelerated the early phase of learning by providing ReLUs with positive inputs.

The origins of dropout and more details about it can be found in Srivastava, Hinton, Krizhevsky, Sutskever, and Salakhutdinov (2014). Ioffe and Szegedy (2015) proposed batch normalization and give more details on its implementation. Glorot and Bengio (2010) cover various weight matrix initialization heuristics, and how the concepts of fan-in and fan-out can be used to justify them for networks with different kinds of activation functions.

The MNIST data set containing 28×28 pixel images of handwritten digits has been popular for exploring ideas in the deep learning research community. However, it was the ImageNet challenge, with a variety of much higher resolutions, that catapulted deep learning into the spotlight in 2012 (Russakovsky et al., 2015). The winning entry from the University of Toronto processed the images at a resolution of 256×256 pixels. Up till then, CNNs were simply incapable of processing such large volumes of imagery at such high resolutions in a reasonable amount of time. Krizhevsky et al.'s (2012) dramatic win used a GPU-accelerated CNNs. This spurred a great deal of development, reflected in rapid subsequent advances in visual recognition performance on the ImageNet benchmark.

In the 2014 challenge, the Oxford Visual Geometry Group and a team from Google pushed performance even further using much deeper architectures: 16−19 weight layers for the Oxford group, using tiny 3×3 convolutional filters (Simonyan and Zisserman, 2014); 22 layers, with filters up to 5×5 for the Google team (Szegedy et al., 2015). The 2015 ImageNet challenge was won by a team from Microsoft Research Asia using an architecture with 152 layers (He et al., 2015), using tiny 3×3 filters combined with shortcut connections that skip over layers, they also perform pooling and decimation after multiple layers of convolution have been applied.

Hinton and Salakhutdinov (2006) noted that it has been known since the 1980s that deep autoencoders, optimized through backpropagation, could be effective for nonlinear dimensionality reduction. The key limiting factors were the small size of the data sets used to train them, coupled with low computation speeds: plus the old problem of local minima. By 2006, data sets such as the MNIST digits and the 20 Newsgroups collection were large enough, and computers were fast enough, for Hinton and Salakhutdinov to present compelling results illustrating the advantages of deep autoencoders over principal component analysis. Their experimental work used generative pretraining to initialize weights to avoid problems with local minima.

Bourlard and Kamp (1988) provide a deep analysis of the relationships between autoencoders and principal component analysis. Vincent, Larochelle,

Lajoie, Bengio, and Manzagol (2010) proposed stacked denoising autoencoders and found that they outperform both stacked standard autoencoders and models based on stacking RBMs. Cho and Chen (2014) produced state-of-the-art results on motion capture sequences by training deep autoencoders with rectified linear units using hybrid unsupervised and supervised learning.

The history of Markov random fields has roots in statistical physics in the 1920s with so-called "Ising models" of ferromagnetism. Our presentation of Boltzmann machines follows Hinton and Sejnowski (1983), but we use matrix-vector notation and our exposition more closely resembles formulations such as that of Salakhutdinov and Hinton (2009). Harmonium networks proposed in Smolensky (1986) are essentially equivalent to what are now commonly referred to as RBMs.

Contrastive divergence was proposed by Hinton (2002). The idea of using unsupervised pretraining to initialize deep networks using stacks of RBMs was popularized by Hinton and Salakhutdinov (2006); Salakhutdinov and Hinton (2009) give further details on the use of deep Boltzmann machines and training procedures for deep belief networks, including the variable doubling procedure and other nuances discussed above for greedy training of deep restricted Boltzmann machines. Neal (1992) introduced sigmoidal belief networks. Welling, Rosen-Zvi, and Hinton (2004) showed how to extend Boltzmann machines to categorical and continuous variables using exponential-family models. The greedy layerwise training procedure for deep Boltzmann machines in Section 10.4 is based on a procedure proposed by Hinton and Salakhutdinov (2006) and refined by Murphy (2012).

Hybrid supervised and unsupervised learning procedures for restricted Boltzmann machines were proposed by McCallum, Pal, Druck, and Wang (2006) and further explored by Larochelle and Bengio (2008). Vincent et al. (2010) proposed the autoencoder approach to unsupervised pretraining; they also explored various layerwise stacking and training strategies and compared stacked RBMs with stacked autoencoders.

Graves et al. (2009) demonstrate how recurrent neural networks are particularly effective at handwriting recognition, while Graves, Mohamed, and Hinton (2013) apply recurrent neural networks to speech. The form of gradient clipping presented in Section 10.6 was proposed by Pascanu, Mikolov, and Bengio (2013).

The vanishing gradient problem was formally identified as a key issue for learning in deep networks by Sepp Hochreiter in his diploma thesis (Hochreiter, 1991). The impact in terms of the difficulty of learning long-term dependencies is discussed by Bengio, Simard, and Frasconi (1994). Further analysis of the issue is given by Hochreiter, Bengio, Frasconi, and Schmidhuber (2001).

Hochreiter and Schmidhuber (1997) is the seminal paper on the "long short-term memory" architecture for recurrent neural networks; our explanation follows Graves and Schmidhuber (2005)'s formulation. Greff, Srivastava, Koutník, Steunebrink, and Schmidhuber's (2015) paper "LSTM: A search space odyssey" explored a wide variety of variants and finds that: (1) none of them significantly outperformed the standard LSTM architecture; and (2) forget gates and the output activation function were the most critical components. Forget gates were added by Gers, Schmidhuber, and Cummins (2000).

IRNNs were proposed by Le, Jaitly, and Hinton (2015), while Chung, Gulcehre, Cho, and Bengio (2014) proposed gated recurrent units and Schuster and Paliwal (1997) proposed bidirectional recurrent neural networks. Chen and Chaudhari (2004) used bidirectional networks for protein structure prediction, while Graves et al. (2009) used them for handwriting recognition. Cho et al. (2014) used encoder-decoder networks for machine translation, while Sutskever, Vinyals, and Le (2014) proposed deep encoder-decoder networks and used them with massive quantities of data.

For further accounts of advances in deep learning and a more extensive history of the field, consult the reviews of LeCun, Bengio, and Hinton (2015), Bengio (2009), and Schmidhuber (2015).

10.8 DEEP LEARNING SOFTWARE AND NETWORK IMPLEMENTATIONS

THEANO

Theano is a library in the Python programming language that has been developed with the specific goal of facilitating research in deep learning (Bergstra et al., 2010; Theano Development Team, 2016). It is also a powerful general purpose tool for mathematical programming. Theano extends NumPy (the fundamental Python package for scientific computing) by adding symbolic differentiation and GPU support, among various other functions. It provides a high-level language for creating the mathematical expressions that underlie deep learning models, and a compiler that takes advantage of deep learning techniques, and calls to GPU libraries, to produce code that executes quickly. Theano supports execution on multiple GPUs. It allows the user to declare symbolic variables for inputs and targets, and supply numerical values only when they are used. Shared variables such as weights and biases are associated with numerical values stored in NumPy arrays. Theano creates symbolic graphs as a result of defining mathematical expressions involving the application of operations to variables. These graphs consist of *variable*, *constant*, *apply*, and *operation* nodes. Constants, and constant nodes, are a subclass of variables, and variable nodes, which hold data that will remain constant—and can therefore be subjected to various optimizations by the compiler. Theano is an open-source project using a BSD license.

TENSOR FLOW

Tensor Flow is a C++ and Python-based software library for the types of numerical computation typically associated with deep learning (Abadi et al., 2016). It is heavily inspired by Theano and, like it, uses dataflow graphs to represent the ways in which multidimensional data arrays communicate between one another. These multidimensional arrays are referred to as "tensors." Tensor Flow also supports symbolic differentiation and execution on multiple GPUs. It was released in 2015 and is available under the Apache 2.0 license.

TORCH

Torch is an open-source machine learning library built using C and a high-level scripting language known as Lua (Collobert, Kavukcuoglu, & Farabet, 2011). It uses multidimensional array data structures, and supports various basic numerical linear algebra manipulations. It has a neural network package with modules that permit the typical forward and backward methods needed for training neural networks. It also supports automatic differentiation.

COMPUTATIONAL NETWORK TOOLKIT

The Computational Network Toolkit (CNTK) is a C++ library for manipulating computational networks (Yu et al., 2014). It was produced by Microsoft Research, but has been released under a permissive license. It has been popular for speech and language processing, but also supports convolutional networks of the type used for images. It supports execution on multiple machines and using multiple GPUs.

CAFFE

Caffe is a C++ and Python-based BSD-licensed CNN library (Jia et al., 2014). It has a clean and extensible design that makes it a popular alternative to the original open-source implementation of Krizhevsky et al.'s (2012) famous AlexNet that won the 2012 ImageNet challenge.

DEEPLEARNING4J

Deeplearning4j is a Java-based open-source deep learning library available under the Apache 2.0 license. It uses an multidimensional array class and provides linear algebra and matrix manipulation support similar to that provided by Numpy.

OTHER PACKAGES: LASAGNE, KERAS, AND CUDNN

Lasagne is a lightweight Python library built on top of Theano that simplifies the creation of neural network layers. Similarly, Keras is a Python library that runs on top of either Theano or TensorFlow (Chollet, 2015). It allows one to quickly define a network architecture in terms of layers and also includes functionality for image and text preprocessing. cuDNN is a highly optimized GPU library for

NVIDIA units that allows deep networks to be trained more quickly. It can dramatically accelerate the performance of a deep network and is often called by the other packages above.

10.9 WEKA IMPLEMENTATIONS

Deep learning can be implemented in WEKA using three methods:

- With the wrapper classifier for the third-party *DeepLearningForJ* package that is available in the *deepLearningForJ* package.
- Using the MLRClassifier from the *RPlugin* package to exploit deep learning implementations in R.
- By accessing Python-based deep learning libraries using the *PyScript* package.

Beyond supervised and unsupervised learning

11

CHAPTER OUTLINE

11.1 Semisupervised Learning...468
    Clustering for Classification...468
    Cotraining...470
    EM and Cotraining..471
    Neural Network Approaches 471
11.2 Multi-instance Learning...472
    Converting to Single-Instance Learning...472
    Upgrading Learning Algorithms...475
    Dedicated Multi-instance Methods...475
11.3 Further Reading and Bibliographic Notes 477
11.4 WEKA Implementations...478

Modern machine learning embraces scenarios that transcend the classic dichotomy of supervised versus unsupervised learning. For example, in many practical applications labeled data is very scarce but unlabeled data is plentiful. "Semisupervised" learning attempts to improve the accuracy of supervised learning by exploiting information in unlabeled data. This sounds like magic, but it can work! This chapter reviews several well-established approaches to semisupervised learning: applying EM-style clustering to classification, combining generative and discriminative methods, and cotraining. We will also see how cotraining and EM-based semisupervised learning can be merged into a single algorithm.

Another nonstandard scenario with many practical applications is multi-instance learning. Here, each example is a bag of instances, each of which describes an aspect of the object to be classified—but there is still only one label for the entire example. Learning from such data poses serious algorithmic challenges, and some heuristic ingenuity may be necessary to make it practical. We will look at three different approaches: converting multi-instance data to single-instance data by aggregating the information in each bag of instances into a single instance, upgrading single-instance algorithms to be able to deal with bags of data, and dedicated approaches to multi-instance learning that do not have a single-instance equivalent.

Data Mining.
© 2017 Elsevier Inc. All rights reserved.

11.1 SEMISUPERVISED LEARNING

When introducing the machine learning process in Chapter 2, Input: concepts, instances, attributes, we drew a sharp distinction between supervised and unsupervised learning. Recently researchers have begun to explore territory between the two, sometimes called *semisupervised learning*, in which the goal is classification but the input contains both unlabeled and labeled data. You cannot do classification without labeled data, of course, because only the labels tell what the classes are. But it is sometimes attractive to augment a small amount of labeled data with a large pool of unlabeled data. It turns out that the unlabeled data can help you learn the classes. How can this be?

First, why would you want it? Many situations present huge volumes of raw data, but assigning classes is expensive because it requires human insight. Text mining provides some classic examples. Suppose you want to classify Web pages into predefined groups. In an academic setting you might be interested in faculty pages, graduate student pages, course information pages, research group pages, and department pages. You can easily download thousands, or millions, of relevant pages from university Web sites. But labeling the training data is a laborious manual process. Or suppose your job is to use machine learning to spot names in text, differentiating between personal names, company names, and place names. You can easily download megabytes, or gigabytes, of text, but making this into training data by picking out the names and categorizing them can only be done manually. Cataloging news articles, sorting electronic mail, learning users' reading interests—applications are legion. Leaving text aside, suppose you want to learn to recognize certain famous people in television broadcast news. You can easily record hundreds or thousands of hours of newscasts, but again labeling is manual. In any of these scenarios it would be enormously attractive to be able to leverage a large pool of unlabeled data to obtain excellent performance from just a few labeled examples—particularly if you were the graduate student who had to do the labeling!

CLUSTERING FOR CLASSIFICATION

How can unlabeled data be used to improve classification? Here is a simple idea. Use Naïve Bayes to learn classes from a small labeled data set and then extend it to a large unlabeled data set using the EM (expectation–maximization) iterative clustering algorithm of Section 9.3. The procedure is this. First, train a classifier using the labeled data. Second, apply it to the unlabeled data to label it with class probabilities (the "expectation" step). Third, train a new classifier using the labels for all the data (the "maximization" step). Fourth, iterate until convergence. You could think of this as iterative clustering, where starting points and cluster labels are gleaned from the labeled data. The EM procedure guarantees to find model parameters that have equal or greater likelihood at each iteration. The key question, which can only be answered empirically, is whether these higher likelihood parameter estimates will improve classification accuracy.

Intuitively, this might work well, particularly if the data has many attributes and there are strong relationships between them. Consider document classification. Certain phrases are indicative of the classes. Some occur in labeled documents, whereas others only occur in unlabeled ones. But there are probably some documents that contain both, and the EM procedure uses these to generalize the learned model to utilize phrases that do not appear in the labeled data set. For example, both *supervisor* and *PhD topic* might indicate a graduate student's home page. Suppose that only the former phrase occurs in the labeled documents. EM iteratively generalizes the model to correctly classify documents that contain just the latter.

This might work with any classifier and any iterative clustering algorithm. But it is basically a bootstrapping procedure, and you must take care to ensure that the feedback loop is a positive one. Using probabilities rather than hard decisions seems beneficial because it allows the procedure to converge slowly instead of jumping to conclusions that may be wrong. Naïve Bayes together with the basic probabilistic EM-based clustering procedure described in Section 9.3 are a particularly apt choice because they share the same fundamental assumption: independence between attributes or, more precisely, conditional independence between attributes given the class.

Of course, the independence assumption is universally violated. Even our little example used the two-word phrase *PhD topic*, whereas actual implementations would likely use individual words as attributes—and the example would have been far less compelling if we had substituted either of the single terms *PhD* or *topic*. The phrase *PhD students* is probably more indicative of faculty rather than graduate student home pages; the phrase *research topic* is probably less discriminating. It is the very fact that *PhD* and *topic* are *not* conditionally independent given the class that makes the example work: it is their combination that characterizes graduate student pages.

Nevertheless, coupling Naïve Bayes and EM in this manner works well in the domain of document classification. In a particular classification task it attained the performance of a traditional learner using fewer than one-third of the labeled training instances, as well as five times as many unlabeled ones. This is a good tradeoff when labeled instances are expensive but unlabeled ones are virtually free. With a small number of labeled documents, classification accuracy can be improved dramatically by incorporating many unlabeled ones.

Two refinements to the procedure have been shown to improve performance. The first is motivated by experimental evidence that when there are many labeled documents the incorporation of unlabeled data may reduce rather than increase accuracy. Hand-labeled data is (or should be) inherently less noisy than automatically labeled data. The solution is to introduce a weighting parameter that reduces the contribution of the unlabeled data. This can be incorporated into the maximization step of EM by maximizing the weighted likelihood of the labeled and unlabeled instances. When the parameter is close to zero, unlabeled documents have little influence on the shape of EM's hill-climbing surface; when it is close to one, the algorithm reverts to the original version in which the surface is equally affected by both kinds of document.

The second refinement is to allow each class to have several clusters. As explained in Section 9.3, the EM clustering algorithm assumes that the data is generated randomly from a mixture of different probability distributions, one per cluster. Until now, a one-to-one correspondence between mixture components and classes has been assumed. In many circumstances this is unrealistic—including document classification, because most documents address multiple topics. With several clusters per class, each labeled document is initially assigned randomly to each of its components in a probabilistic fashion. The maximization step of the EM algorithm remains as before, but the expectation step is modified to not only probabilistically label each example with the classes, but to probabilistically assign it to the components within the class. The number of clusters per class is a parameter that depends on the domain and can be set by cross-validation.

COTRAINING

Another situation in which unlabeled data can improve classification performance is when there are two different and independent perspectives on the classification task. The classic example again involves documents, this time Web documents, where the two perspectives are the *content* of a Web page and the *links* to it from other pages. These two perspectives are well known to be both useful and different: successful Web search engines capitalize on them both, using secret recipes. The text that labels a link to another Web page gives a revealing clue as to what that page is about—perhaps even more revealing than the page's own content, particularly if the link is an independent one. Intuitively, a link labeled *my advisor* is strong evidence that the target page is a faculty member's home page.

The idea, called *cotraining*, is this. Given a few labeled examples, first learn a different model for each perspective—in this case a content-based and a hyperlink-based model. Then use each one separately to label the unlabeled examples. For each model, select the example that it most confidently labels as positive and the one it most confidently labels as negative, and add these to the pool of labeled examples. Better yet, maintain the ratio of positive and negative examples in the labeled pool by choosing more of one kind than the other. In either case, repeat the whole procedure, training both models on the augmented pool of labeled examples, until the unlabeled pool is exhausted.

There is some experimental evidence, using Naïve Bayes throughout as the learner, that this bootstrapping procedure outperforms one that employs all the features from both perspectives to learn a single model from the labeled data. It relies on having two different views of an instance that are redundant but not completely correlated. Various domains have been proposed, from spotting celebrities in televised newscasts using video and audio separately to mobile robots with vision, sonar, and range sensors. The independence of the views reduces the likelihood of both hypotheses agreeing on an erroneous label.

EM AND COTRAINING

On data sets with two feature sets that are truly independent, experiments have shown that cotraining gives better results than using EM as described previously. Even better performance, however, can be achieved by combining the two into a modified version of cotraining called *co-EM*. Cotraining trains two classifiers representing different perspectives A and B, and uses both to add new examples to the training pool by choosing whichever unlabeled examples they classify most positively or negatively. The new examples are few in number and deterministically labeled. Co-EM, on the other hand, trains classifier A on the labeled data and uses it to *probabilistically* label *all* the unlabeled data. Next it trains classifier B on both the labeled data and the unlabeled data with classifier A's tentative labels, and then it probabilistically relabels all the data for use by classifier A. The process iterates until the classifiers converge. This procedure seems to perform consistently better than cotraining because it does not commit to the class labels that are generated by classifiers A and B but rather reestimates their probabilities at each iteration.

The range of applicability of co-EM, like cotraining, is still limited by the requirement for multiple independent perspectives. But there is some experimental evidence to suggest that even when there is no natural split of features into independent perspectives, benefits can be achieved by manufacturing such a split and using cotraining—or, better yet, co-EM—on the split data. This seems to work even when the split is made randomly; performance could surely be improved by engineering the split so that the feature sets are maximally independent. Why does this work? Researchers have hypothesized that these algorithms succeed in part because the split makes them more robust to the assumptions that their underlying classifiers make.

There is no particular reason to restrict the base classifier to Naïve Bayes. Support vector machines (SVMs) are particularly useful for text categorization. However, for the EM iteration to work it is necessary that the classifier labels the data probabilistically; it must also be able to use probabilistically weighted examples for training. SVMs can easily be adapted to do both. We explained how to adapt learning algorithms to deal with weighted instances in Section 7.3 under *Locally weighted linear regression*. One way of obtaining probability estimates from SVMs is to fit a one-dimensional logistic model to the output, effectively performing logistic regression as described in Section 4.6 on the output. Excellent results have been reported for text classification using co-EM with the SVM classifier. It outperforms other variants of SVM and seems quite robust to varying proportions of labeled and unlabeled data.

NEURAL NETWORK APPROACHES

Chapter 10, Deep learning, introduced the idea of using unsupervised pretraining to initialize deep networks. For very large labeled data sets, the use of rectified linear activation functions in purely supervised models has reduced the need for unsupervised pretraining. However, when the amount of labeled data is small relative to a larger source of unlabeled data, unsupervised pretraining methods can be effective.

Chapter 10, Deep learning, also showed how a network can be trained to predict its own input—an autoencoder. When labeled data is available, autoencoders can be augmented with another branch that makes predictions using the labeled data. There is evidence that this can make it easier to learn the reconstructive autoencoding part of the network, and also boost discriminative performance. Evidence suggests that unlabeled data can serve as a form of regularization, allowing higher capacity networks to be used. It may be important to weight the relative importance of the composite loss function, and one must take care to use validation sets to find the best model complexity (number of layers and units, etc.) to ensure that the model generalizes well to new data.

Designing networks that use the same representation to make multiple kinds of prediction is another way to leverage data from one task to help with another. If one of the tasks is to predict some other feature or set of features that are normally used as input, we can create network configurations that use both supervised and unsupervised learning.

11.2 MULTI-INSTANCE LEARNING

We have already encountered another nonstandard learning scenario in Section 4.9: multi-instance learning. This can be viewed as a form of supervised learning where examples are *bags* of feature vectors rather than individual vectors. It can also be viewed as a form of weakly supervised learning where the "teacher" provides labels for bags of instances, rather than for each individual one. This section describes approaches to multi-instance learning that are more advanced than the simple techniques discussed earlier. First, we consider how to convert multi-instance learning to single-instance learning by transforming the data. Then we discuss how to upgrade single-instance learning algorithms to the multi-instance case. Finally we look at some methods that have no direct equivalent in single-instance learning.

CONVERTING TO SINGLE-INSTANCE LEARNING

Section 4.9 presented some ways of applying standard single-instance learning algorithms to multi-instance data by aggregating the input or the output. Despite their simplicity, these techniques often work surprisingly well in practice. Nevertheless, there are clearly situations in which they will fail. Consider the method of aggregating the input by computing the minimum and maximum values of numeric attributes present in a bag and treating the result as a single instance. This will yield a huge loss of information because attributes are condensed to summary statistics individually and independently. Can a bag be converted to a single instance without discarding quite so much information?

The answer is yes, although the number of attributes that are present in the so-called "condensed" representation may increase substantially. The basic idea is to partition the instance space into regions and create one attribute per region in the single-instance representation. In the simplest case, attributes can be Boolean: if a bag has at least one instance in the region corresponding to a particular attribute the value of the attribute is set to true, otherwise, it is set to false. However, to preserve more information the condensed representation could instead contain numeric attributes whose values are counts that indicate how many instances of the bag lie in the corresponding region.

Regardless of the exact types of attributes that are generated, the main problem is to come up with a partitioning of the input space. A simple approach is to partition it into hypercubes of equal size. Unfortunately, this only works when the space has very few dimensions (i.e., attributes): the number of cubes required to achieve a given granularity grows exponentially with the dimension of the space. One way to make this approach more practical is to use unsupervised learning. Simply take all the instances from all the bags in the training data, discard their class labels, and form a big single-instance data set; then process it with a clustering technique such as k-means. This will create regions corresponding to the different clusters (k regions, in the case of k-means). Then, for each bag, create one attribute per region in the condensed representation and use it as described previously.

Clustering is a rather heavy-handed way to infer a set of regions from the training data because it ignores information about class membership. An alternative approach that often yields better results is to partition the instance space using decision tree learning. Each leaf of a tree corresponds to one region of instance space. But how can a decision tree be learned when the class labels apply to entire bags of instances, rather than to individual instances? The approach described under *Aggregating the Output* in Section 4.9 can be used: take the bag's class label and attach it to each of its instances. This yields a single-instance data set, ready for decision tree learning. Many of the class labels will be incorrect—the whole point of multi-instance learning is that it is not clear how bag-level labels relate to instance-level ones. However, these class labels are only being used to obtain a partition of instance space. The next step is to transform the multi-instance data set into a single-instance one that represents how instances from each bag are distributed throughout the space. Then another single-instance learning method is applied—perhaps, again, decision tree learning—that determines the importance of individual attributes in the condensed representation, which correspond to regions in the original space.

Using decision trees and clustering yields "hard" partition boundaries, where an instance either does or does not belong to a region. Such partitions can also be obtained using a distance function, combined with some reference points, by assigning instances to their closest reference point. This implicitly divides the space into regions, each corresponding to one reference point. (In fact, this is exactly what happens in k-means clustering: the cluster centers are the reference points.) But there is no fundamental reason to restrict attention to hard boundaries: we can make the region membership function "soft" by using distance—transformed into a similarity score—to compute attribute values in the condensed representation of a bag. All that is needed is some way of aggregating the similarity scores between each bag and reference point into a single value—e.g., by taking the maximum similarity between each instance in that bag and the reference point.

In the simplest case, each instance in the training data can be used as a reference point. That creates a large number of attributes in the condensed representation, but it preserves much of the information from a bag of instances in its corresponding single-instance representation. This method has been successfully applied to multi-instance problems.

Regardless of how the approach is implemented, the basic idea is to convert a bag of instances into a single one by describing the distribution of instances from this bag in instance space. Alternatively, ordinary learning methods can be applied to multi-instance data by aggregating the output rather than the input. Section 4.9 described a simple way: join instances of bags in the training data into a single data set by attaching bag-level class labels to them, perhaps weighting instances to give each bag the same total weight. A single-instance classification model can then be built. At classification time, predictions for individual instances are combined—e.g., by averaging predicted class probabilities.

Although this approach often works well in practice, attaching bag-level class labels to instances is simplistic. Generally, the assumption in multi-instance learning is that only some of the instances—perhaps just one—are responsible for the class label of the associated bag. How can the class labels be corrected to yield a more accurate representation of the true underlying situation? This is obviously a difficult problem; if it were solved, it would make little sense to investigate other approaches to multi-instance learning. One method that has been applied is iterative: start by assigning each instance its bag's class label and learn a single-instance classification model; then replace the instances' class labels by the predicted labels of this single-instance classification model for these instances. Repeat the whole procedure until the class labels remain unchanged from one iteration to the next.

Some care is needed to obtain sensible results. For example, suppose every instance in a bag were to receive a class label that differs from the bag's label. Such a situation should be prevented by forcing the bag's label on at least one instance—e.g., the one with the largest predicted probability for this class.

This iterative approach has been investigated for the original multi-instance scenario with two-class values, where a bag is positive if and only if one of its instances is positive. In that case it makes sense to assume that all instances from negative bags are truly negative and modify only the class labels of instances from positive bags. At prediction time, bags are classified as positive if one of their instances is classified as positive.

UPGRADING LEARNING ALGORITHMS

Tackling multi-instance learning by modifying the input or output so that single-instance schemes can be applied is appealing because there is a large battery of such techniques that can then be used directly, without any modification. However, it may not be the most efficient approach. An alternative is to adapt the internals of a single-instance algorithm to the multi-instance setting. This can be done in a particularly elegant fashion if the algorithm in question only considers the data through application of a distance (or similarity) function, as with nearest-neighbor classifiers or SVMs. These can be adapted by providing a distance (or similarity) function for multi-instance data that computes a score between two bags of instances.

In the case of kernel-based methods such as SVMs, the similarity must be a proper kernel function that satisfies certain mathematical properties. One that has been used for multi-instance data is the so-called *set kernel*. Given a kernel function for pairs of instances that SVMs can apply to single-instance data—e.g., one of the functions considered in Section 7.2—the set kernel sums it over all pairs of instances from the two bags being compared. This idea is generic and can be applied with any single-instance kernel function.

Nearest-neighbor learning has been adapted to multi-instance data by applying variants of the Hausdorff distance, which is defined for sets of points. Given two bags and a distance function between pairs of instances—e.g., the Euclidean distance—the Hausdorff distance between the bags is the largest distance from any instance in one bag to its closest instance in the other bag. It can be made more robust to outliers by using the nth-largest distance rather than the maximum.

For learning algorithms that are not based on similarity scores, more work is required to upgrade them to multi-instance data. There are multi-instance algorithms for rule learning and for decision tree learning, but we will not describe them here. Adapting algorithms to the multi-instance case is more straightforward if the algorithm concerned is essentially a numerical optimization strategy that is applied to the parameters of some function by minimizing a loss function on the training data. Logistic regression and multilayer perceptrons fall into this category; both have been adapted to multi-instance learning by augmenting them with a function that aggregates instance-level predictions. The so-called "soft maximum" is a differentiable function that is suitable for this purpose: it aggregates instance-level predictions by taking their (soft) maximum as the bag-level prediction.

DEDICATED MULTI-INSTANCE METHODS

Some multi-instance learning schemes are not based directly on single-instance algorithms. Here is an early technique that was specifically developed for the drug activity prediction problem mentioned in Section 2.2, in which instances are conformations—shapes—of a molecule and a molecule (i.e., a bag) is considered positive if and only if it has at least one active conformation. The basic idea is to learn a single hyperrectangle that contains at least one instance from each positive bag in the training data and no instances from any negative bags. Such a rectangle encloses an area of instance space where all positive bags overlap but contains no negative instances—an area that is common to all active molecules but not represented in any inactive ones. The particular drug activity data originally considered was high-dimensional, with 166 attributes describing each instance, in which case it is computationally difficult to find a suitable hyperrectangle. Consequently a heuristic approach was developed that is tuned to this particular problem.

Other geometric shapes can be used instead of hyperrectangles. Indeed, the same basic idea has been applied using hyperspheres (balls). Training instances are treated as potential ball centers. For each one, a radius is found that yields the smallest number of errors for the bags in the training data. The original multi-instance assumption is used to make predictions: a bag is classified as positive if and only if it has at least one instance inside the ball. A single ball is generally not powerful enough to yield good classification performance. However, this method is not intended as a standalone algorithm. Rather, it is advocated as a "weak" learner to be used in conjunction with boosting algorithms (see Section 12.4) to obtain a powerful ensemble classifier—an ensemble of balls.

The dedicated multi-instance methods discussed so far have hard decision boundaries: an instance either falls inside or outside a ball or hyperrectangle. Other multi-instance algorithms use soft concept descriptions couched in terms of probability theory. The so-called *diverse density* method is a classic example, again designed with the original multi-instance assumption in mind. Its basic and most commonly used form learns a single reference point in instance space. The probability that an instance is positive is computed from its distance to this point: it is 1 if the instance coincides with the reference point and decreases with increasing distance from this point, usually based on a bell-shaped function.

The probability that a bag is positive is obtained by combining the individual probabilities of the instances it contains, generally using the "noisy-OR" function. This is a probabilistic version of the logical OR. If all instance-level probabilities are 0, the noisy-OR value—and thus the bag-level probability—is 0; if at least one instance-level probability is 1, the value is 1; otherwise the value falls somewhere in between.

The diverse density is defined as the probability of the class labels of the bags in the training data, computed based on this probabilistic model. It is maximized when the reference point is located in an area where positive bags overlap and no negative bags are present, just as for the two geometric methods discussed previously. A numerical optimization routine such as gradient ascent can be used to find the reference point that maximizes the diverse density measure. In addition to the location of the reference point, implementations of diverse density also optimize the scale of the distance function in each dimension, because generally not all attributes are equally important. This can improve predictive performance significantly.

11.3 FURTHER READING AND BIBLIOGRAPHIC NOTES

Nigam, McCallum, Thrun, and Mitchell (2000) thoroughly explored the idea of clustering for classification, showing how the EM clustering algorithm can use unlabeled data to improve an initial classifier built by Naïve Bayes. The idea of cotraining is older: Blum and Mitchell (1998) pioneered it and developed a theoretical model for the use of labeled and unlabeled data from different independent perspectives. Nigam and Ghani (2000) analyzed the effectiveness and applicability of cotraining, relating it to the traditional use of standard EM to fill in missing values; they also introduced the co-EM algorithm. Up to this point, cotraining and co-EM were applied mainly to small two-class problems. Ghani (2002) used error-correcting output codes to address multiclass situations with many classes. Brefeld and Scheffer (2004) extended co-EM to use a SVM rather than Naïve Bayes.

Condensing the input data by aggregating information into simple summary statistics is a well-known technique in multirelational learning, used in the RELAGGS system by Krogel and Wrobel (2002), and multi-instance learning can be viewed as a special case of this more general setting (de Raedt, 2008). The idea of replacing simple summary statistics by region-based attributes, derived from partitioning the instance space, was explored by Weidmann, Frank, and Pfahringer (2003), Zhou and Zhang (2007), and Frank and Pfahringer (2013). Using reference points to condense bags was investigated by Chen, Bi, and Wang (2006) and evaluated in a broader context by Foulds and Frank (2008). Andrews et al. (2002) proposed manipulating the class labels of individual instances using an iterative learning process for learning SVM classifiers based on the original multi-instance assumption.

Nearest-neighbor learning based on variants of the Hausdorff distance was investigated by Wang and Zucker (2000). Gärtner et al. (2002) experimented with the set kernel to learn SVM classifiers for multi-instance data. Multi-instance algorithms for rule and decision tree learning, which are not covered here, have been described by Chevaleyre and Zucker (2001), Blockeel, Page, and Srinivasan (2005), and Bjerring and Frank (2011). Logistic regression has been adapted for multi-instance learning by Xu and Frank (2004) and Ray and Craven (2005); multilayer perceptrons have been adapted by Ramon and de Raedt (2000).

Hyperrectangles and spheres were considered as concept descriptions for multi-instance learning by Dietterich et al. (1997) and Auer and Ortner (2004), respectively. The diverse density method is the subject of Maron's (1998) PhD thesis, and is also described in (Maron and Lozano-Peréz, 1997). A quicker, heuristic variant is evaluated by Foulds and Frank (2010b).

The multi-instance literature makes many different assumptions regarding the type of concept to be learned, defining, e.g., how the bag-level and instance-level class labels are connected, starting with the original assumption that a bag is labeled positive if and only if one of its instances is positive. A review of assumptions in multi-instance learning can be found in Foulds and Frank (2010a).

11.4 WEKA IMPLEMENTATIONS

- Multi-instance learning methods (in the *multiInstanceLearning* package, unless otherwise mentioned)
    - *TLC* (creates single-instance representations using partitioning methods)
    - *MILES* (single-instance representation using soft memberships, in the *multiInstanceFilters* package)
    - *MISVM* (iterative method for learning an SVM by relabeling instances)
    - *MISMO* (SVM with multi-instance kernel)
    - *CitationKNN* (nearest-neighbor method with Hausdorff distance)
    - *MITI* (learns a decision tree from multi-instance data)
    - *MIRI* (learns rule sets for multi-instance data)
    - *MILR* (logistic regression for multi-instance data)
    - *MIOptimalBall* (learning balls for multi-instance classification)
    - *MIDD* (the diverse density method using the noisy-or function)
    - *QuickDDIterative* (a heuristic, faster version of *MIDD*)

Ensemble learning

12

CHAPTER OUTLINE

12.1 Combining Multiple Models 480
12.2 Bagging 481
    Bias—Variance Decomposition 482
    Bagging With Costs...483
12.3 Randomization 484
    Randomization Versus Bagging 485
    Rotation Forests 486
12.4 Boosting 486
    AdaBoost...487
    The Power of Boosting 489
12.5 Additive Regression 490
    Numeric Prediction 491
    Additive Logistic Regression..492
12.6 Interpretable Ensembles 493
    Option Trees..494
    Logistic Model Trees 496
12.7 Stacking 497
12.8 Further Reading and Bibliographic Notes 499
12.9 WEKA Implementations...501

To maximize accuracy, it is often necessary to combine the predictions of several models learned from the same data, and we now turn to techniques for accomplishing this. There are some surprises in store. For example, it is often advantageous to take the training data and derive several different training sets from it, learn a model from each, and combine them to produce an ensemble of learned models. Indeed, techniques for doing this can be very powerful. It is, e.g., possible to transform a relatively weak learning scheme into an extremely strong one (in a precise sense that we will explain). Loss of interpretability is a drawback when applying ensemble learning, but there are ways to derive intelligible structured descriptions based on what these methods learn. Finally, if several learning schemes are available, it may be advantageous not to choose the best-performing one for your dataset (using cross-validation) but to use them all and combine the results.

Many of these results are quite counterintuitive, at least at first blush. How can it be a good idea to use many different models together? How can you possibly do better than choose the model that performs best? Surely all this runs counter to Occam's razor, which advocates simplicity? How can you possibly obtain first-class performance by combining indifferent models, as one of these techniques appears to do? But consider committees of humans, which often come up with wiser decisions than individual experts. Recall Epicurus's view that, faced with alternative explanations, one should retain them all. Imagine a group of specialists each of whom excels in a limited domain even though none is competent across the board. In struggling to understand how these methods work, researchers have exposed all sorts of connections and links that have led to even greater improvements.

12.1 COMBINING MULTIPLE MODELS

When wise people make critical decisions, they usually take into account the opinions of several experts rather than relying on their own judgment or that of a solitary trusted advisor. For example, before choosing an important new policy direction, a benign dictator consults widely: he or she would be ill advised to follow just one expert's opinion blindly. In a democratic setting, discussion of different viewpoints may produce a consensus; if not, a vote may be called for. In either case, different expert opinions are being combined.

In data mining, a model generated by machine learning can be regarded as an expert. *Expert* is probably too strong a word!—depending on the amount and quality of the training data, and whether the learning algorithm is appropriate to the problem at hand, the expert may in truth be regrettably ignorant—but we use the term nevertheless. An obvious approach to making decisions more reliable is to combine the output of several different models. Several machine learning techniques do this by learning an ensemble of models and using them in combination: prominent among these are schemes called *bagging*, *boosting*, and *stacking*. They can all, more often than not, increase predictive performance over a single model. And they are general techniques that can be applied to classification tasks and numeric prediction problems.

Bagging, boosting, and stacking have been developed over the last couple of decades, and their performance is often astonishingly good. Machine learning researchers have struggled to understand why. And during that struggle, new methods have emerged that are sometimes even better. For example, whereas human committees rarely benefit from noisy distractions, shaking up bagging by adding random variants of classifiers can improve performance. Closer analysis revealed that boosting—perhaps the most powerful of the three methods—is closely related to the established statistical technique of additive models, and this realization has led to improved procedures.

These combined models share the disadvantage of being rather hard to analyze: they can comprise dozens or even hundreds of individual models, and although they perform well it is not easy to understand in intuitive terms what factors are contributing to the improved decisions. However, methods have been developed that combine the performance benefits of committees with comprehensible models. Some produce decision tree models; others introduce new variants of trees that provide optional paths.

12.2 BAGGING

Combining the decisions of different models means amalgamating the various outputs into a single prediction. The simplest way to do this in the case of classification is to take a vote (perhaps a weighted vote); in the case of numeric prediction it is to calculate the average (perhaps a weighted average). Bagging and boosting both adopt this approach, but they derive the individual models in different ways. In bagging, the models receive equal weight, whereas in boosting, weighting is used to give more influence to the more successful ones—just as an executive might place different values on the advice of different experts depending on how successful their predictions were in the past.

To introduce bagging, suppose that several training datasets of the same size are chosen at random from the problem domain. Imagine using a particular machine learning technique to build a decision tree for each dataset. You might expect these trees to be practically identical and to make the same prediction for each new test instance. But, surprisingly, this assumption is usually quite wrong, particularly if the training datasets are fairly small. This is a rather disturbing fact and seems to cast a shadow over the whole enterprise! The reason for it is that decision tree induction (at least, the standard top-down method described in chapter: Algorithms: the basic methods) is an unstable process: slight changes to the training data may easily result in a different attribute being chosen at a particular node, with significant ramifications for the structure of the subtree beneath that node. This automatically implies that there are test instances for which some of the decision trees produce correct predictions and others do not.

Returning to the preceding experts analogy, consider the experts to be the individual decision trees. We can combine the trees by having them vote on each test instance. If one class receives more votes than any other, it is taken as the correct one. Generally, the more the merrier: predictions made by voting become more reliable as more votes are taken into account. Decisions rarely deteriorate if new training sets are discovered, trees are built for them, and their predictions participate in the vote as well. In particular, the combined classifier will seldom be less accurate than a decision tree constructed from just one of the datasets. (Improvement is not guaranteed, however. It can be shown theoretically that pathological situations exist in which the combined decisions are worse.)

BIAS–VARIANCE DECOMPOSITION

The effect of combining multiple hypotheses can be viewed through a theoretical device known as the *bias–variance decomposition*. Suppose we could have an infinite number of independent training sets of the same size and use them to make an infinite number of classifiers. A test instance is processed by all classifiers, and a single answer is determined by majority vote. In this idealized situation, errors will still occur because no learning scheme is perfect: the error rate will depend on how well the machine learning method matches the problem at hand, and there is also the effect of noise in the data, which cannot possibly be learned. Suppose the expected error rate were evaluated by averaging the error of the combined classifier over an infinite number of independently chosen test examples. The error rate for a particular learning algorithm is called its *bias* for the learning problem and measures how well the learning method matches the problem. (We include the "noise" component in the bias term because it is generally unknown in practice anyway.) This technical definition is a way of quantifying the vaguer notion of bias that was introduced in Section 1.5: it measures the "persistent" error of a learning algorithm that can't be eliminated even by taking an infinite number of training sets into account. Of course, it cannot be calculated exactly in practical situations; it can only be approximated.

A second source of error in a learned model, in a practical situation, stems from the particular training set used, which is inevitably finite and therefore not fully representative of the actual population of instances. The expected value of this component of the error, over all possible training sets of the given size and all possible test sets, is called the *variance* of the learning method for that problem. The total expected error of a classifier is made up of the sum of bias and variance: this is the bias–variance decomposition.

Note that we are glossing over the details here. The bias–variance decomposition was introduced in the context of numeric prediction based on squared error, where there is a widely accepted way of performing it. However, the situation is not so clear for classification, and several competing decompositions have been proposed. Regardless of the specific decomposition used to analyze the error, combining multiple classifiers generally decreases the expected error by reducing the variance component. The more classifiers that are included, the greater the reduction in variance. Of course, a difficulty arises when putting this voting scheme into practice: usually there is only one training set, and obtaining more data is either impossible or expensive.

Bagging attempts to neutralize the instability of learning methods by simulating the process described previously using a given training set. Instead of sampling a fresh, independent training dataset each time, the original training data is altered by deleting some instances and replicating others. Instances are randomly sampled, with replacement, from the original dataset to create a new one of the same size. This sampling procedure inevitably replicates some of the instances and deletes others. If this idea strikes a chord, it is because we encountered it in

Model generation

```
Let n be the number of instances in the training data.
For each of t iterations:
  Sample n instances with replacement from training data.
  Apply the learning algorithm to the sample.
  Store the resulting model.
```

Classification

```
For each of the t models:
  Predict class of instance using model.
Return class that has been predicted most often.
```

FIGURE 12.1

Algorithm for bagging.

Chapter 5, Credibility: evaluating what's been learned, when explaining the bootstrap method for estimating the generalization error of a learning method (Section 5.4): indeed, the term *bagging* stands for *bootstrap aggregating*. Bagging applies the learning scheme—e.g., a decision tree inducer—to each one of these artificially derived datasets, and the classifiers generated from them vote for the class to be predicted. The algorithm is summarized in Fig. 12.1.

The difference between bagging and the idealized procedure described above is the way in which the training datasets are derived. Instead of obtaining independent datasets from the domain, bagging just resamples the original training data. The datasets generated by resampling are different from one another but are certainly not independent because they are all based on one dataset. However, it turns out that bagging produces a combined model that often performs significantly better than the single model built from the original training data, and is never substantially worse.

Bagging can also be applied to learning schemes for numeric prediction—e.g., model trees. The only difference is that, instead of voting on the outcome, the individual predictions, being real numbers, are averaged. The bias–variance decomposition is applied to numeric prediction by decomposing the expected value of the mean-squared error of the predictions on fresh data. Bias is defined as the mean-squared error expected when averaging over models built from all possible training datasets of the same size, and variance is the component of the expected error of a single model that is due to the particular training data it was built from. It can be shown theoretically that averaging over infinitely many models built from independent training sets always reduces the expected value of the mean-squared error. (As we mentioned earlier, the analogous result is not true for classification.)

BAGGING WITH COSTS

Bagging helps most if the underlying learning scheme is unstable in that small changes in the input data can lead to quite different classifiers. Indeed results can be improved by increasing the diversity in the ensemble of classifiers by making the learning scheme as unstable as possible, while maintaining some level of accuracy. For example, when bagging decision trees, which are already unstable, better performance is often achieved by switching pruning off, which makes them even more unstable. Another improvement can be obtained by changing the way that predictions are combined for classification. As originally formulated, bagging uses voting. But when the models can output probability estimates and not just plain classifications, it makes intuitive sense to average these probabilities instead. Not only does this often improve classification slightly, but the bagged classifier also generates probability estimates—ones that are often more accurate than those produced by the individual models. Implementations of bagging commonly use this method of combining predictions.

In Section 5.8 we showed how to make a classifier cost sensitive by minimizing the expected cost of predictions. Accurate probability estimates are necessary because they are used to obtain the expected cost of each prediction. Bagging is a prime candidate for cost-sensitive classification because it produces very accurate probability estimates from decision trees and other powerful, yet unstable, classifiers. However, a disadvantage is that bagged classifiers are hard to analyze.

A method called *MetaCost* combines the predictive benefits of bagging with a comprehensible model for cost-sensitive prediction. It builds an ensemble classifier using bagging and deploys it to relabel the training data by giving every training instance the prediction that minimizes the expected cost, based on the probability estimates obtained from bagging. MetaCost then discards the original class labels and learns a single new classifier—e.g., a single pruned decision tree—from the relabeled data. This new model automatically takes costs into account because they have been built into the class labels! The result is a single cost-sensitive classifier that can be analyzed to see how predictions are made.

In addition to the cost-sensitive *classification* technique just mentioned, Section 5.8 also described a cost-sensitive *learning* method that learns a cost-sensitive classifier by changing the proportion of each class in the training data to reflect the cost matrix. MetaCost seems to produce more accurate results than this method, but it requires more computation. If there is no need for a comprehensible model, MetaCost's postprocessing step is superfluous: it is better to use the bagged classifier directly in conjunction with the minimum expected cost method.

12.3 RANDOMIZATION

Bagging generates a diverse ensemble of classifiers by introducing randomness into the learning algorithm's input, often with excellent results. But there are other ways of creating diversity by introducing randomization. Some learning algorithms already have a built-in random component. For example, when learning multilayer perceptrons using the backpropagation algorithm the network weights are set to small randomly chosen values. The learned classifier depends on the random numbers because the algorithm may find a different local minimum of the error function. One way to make the outcome of classification more stable is to run the learner several times with different random number seeds and combine the classifiers' predictions by voting or averaging.

Almost every learning method is amenable to some kind of randomization. Consider an algorithm that greedily picks the best option at every step—such as a decision tree learner that picks the best attribute to split on at each node. It could be randomized by picking one of the N best options at random instead of a single winner, or by choosing a random subset of options and picking the best from that. Of course, there is a tradeoff: more randomness generates more variety in the learner but makes less use of the data, probably decreasing the accuracy of each individual model. The best dose of randomness can only be prescribed by experiment.

Although bagging and randomization yield similar results, it sometimes pays to combine them because they introduce randomness in different, perhaps complementary, ways. A popular algorithm for learning random forests builds a randomized decision tree in each iteration of the bagging algorithm, and often produces excellent predictors.

RANDOMIZATION VERSUS BAGGING

Randomization demands more work than bagging because the learning algorithm must be modified, but it can profitably be applied to a greater variety of learners. We noted earlier that bagging fails with stable learning algorithms whose output is insensitive to small changes in the input. For example, it is pointless to bag nearest-neighbor classifiers because their output changes very little if the training data is perturbed by sampling. But randomization can be applied even to stable learners: the trick is to randomize in a way that makes the classifiers diverse without sacrificing too much performance. A nearest-neighbor classifier's predictions depend on the distances between instances, which in turn depend heavily on which attributes are used to compute them, so nearest-neighbor classifiers can be randomized by using different, randomly chosen subsets of attributes. In fact, this approach is called the *random subspaces* method for constructing an ensemble of classifiers and was proposed as a method for learning a random forest. As with bagging, it does not require any modification to the learning algorithm. Of course, random subspaces can be used in conjunction with bagging in order to introduce randomness to the learning process in terms of both instances and attributes.

Returning to plain bagging, the idea is to exploit instability in the learning algorithm in order to create diversity amongst the ensemble members—but the degree of diversity achieved is less than that of other ensemble learning methods such as random forests, because of randomization built in to the learning algorithm, or boosting (discussed in Section 12.4). This is because bootstrap sampling creates training datasets whose distribution resembles that of the original data. Consequently, the classifiers learned by bagging are individually quite accurate, but their low diversity can detract from the overall accuracy of the ensemble.

Introducing randomness in the learning algorithm increases diversity but sacrifices accuracy of the individual classifiers. If it were possible for ensemble members to be both diverse and individually accurate, smaller ensembles could be used. Of course, this would have computational benefits.

ROTATION FORESTS

An ensemble learning method called *rotation forests* has the specific goal of creating diverse yet accurate classifiers. It combines the random subspace and bagging approaches with principal component feature generation to construct an ensemble of decision trees. In each iteration, the input attributes are randomly divided into k disjoint subsets. Principal component analysis is applied to each subset in turn in order to create linear combinations of the attributes in the subset that are rotations of the original axes. The k sets of principal components are used to compute values for the derived attributes; these comprise the input to the tree learner at each iteration. Because all the components obtained on each subset are retained, there are as many derived attributes as there are original ones. To discourage the generation of identical coefficients if the same feature subset is chosen in different iterations, principal component analysis is applied to training instances from a randomly chosen subset of the class values (however, the values of the derived attributes that are input to the tree learner are computed from all the instances in the training data). To further increase diversity, a bootstrap sample of the data can be created in each iteration before the principal component transformations are applied.

Experiments indicate that rotation forests can give similar performance to random forests, with far fewer trees. An analysis of diversity (measured by the Kappa statistic, introduced in Section 5.8 to measure agreement between classifiers) versus error for pairs of ensemble members shows a minimal increase in diversity and reduction in error for rotation forests when compared to bagging. However, this appears to translate into significantly better performance for the ensemble as a whole.

12.4 BOOSTING

We have explained that bagging exploits the instability inherent in learning algorithms. Intuitively, combining multiple models only helps when these models are significantly different from one another and each one treats a reasonable percentage of the data correctly. Ideally the models complement one another, each being a specialist in a part of the domain where the other models don't perform very well—just as human executives seek advisors whose skills and experience complement, rather than duplicate, one another.

The boosting method for combining multiple models exploits this insight by explicitly seeking models that complement one another. First, the similarities: like bagging, boosting uses voting (for classification) or averaging (for prediction) to combine the output of individual models. Again, like bagging, it combines models of the same type—e.g., decision trees. However, boosting is iterative. Whereas in bagging individual models are built separately, in boosting each new model is influenced by the performance of those built previously. Boosting encourages new models to become experts for instances handled incorrectly by earlier ones. A final difference is that boosting weights a model's contribution by its performance, rather than giving equal weight to all models.

ADABOOST

There are many variants on the idea of boosting. We describe a widely used method called *AdaBoost.M1* that is designed specifically for classification. Like bagging, it can be applied to any classification learning algorithm. To simplify matters we assume that the learning algorithm can handle weighted instances, where the weight of an instance is a positive number. (We revisit this assumption later.) The presence of instance weights changes the way in which a classifier's error is calculated: it is the sum of the weights of the misclassified instances divided by the total weight of all instances, instead of the fraction of instances that are misclassified. By weighting instances, the learning algorithm can be forced to concentrate on a particular set of instances, namely, those with high weight. Such instances become particularly important because there is a greater incentive to classify them correctly. The C4.5 algorithm, described in Section 6.1, is an example of a learning method that can accommodate weighted instances without modification because it already uses the notion of fractional instances to handle missing values.

The boosting algorithm, summarized in Fig. 12.2, begins by assigning equal weight to all instances in the training data. It then calls the learning algorithm to form a classifier for this data and reweights each instance according to the classifier's output. The weight of correctly classified instances is decreased, and that of misclassified ones is increased. This produces a set of "easy" instances with low weight and a set of "hard" ones with high weight. In the next iteration—and all subsequent ones—a classifier is built for the reweighted data, which consequently focuses on classifying the hard instances correctly. Then the instances' weights are increased or decreased according to the output of this new classifier. As a result, some hard instances might become even harder and easier ones even easier; on the other hand, other hard instances might become easier, and easier ones harder—all possibilities can occur in practice. After each iteration, the weights reflect how often the instances have been misclassified by the classifiers produced so far. By maintaining a measure of "hardness" with each instance, this procedure provides an elegant way of generating a series of experts that complement one another.

Model generation

```
Assign equal weight to each training instance.
For each of t iterations:
  Apply learning algorithm to weighted dataset and store resulting model.
  Compute error e of model on weighted dataset and store error.
  If e equal to zero, or e greater or equal to 0.5:
    Terminate model generation.
  For each instance in dataset:
    If instance classified correctly by model:
      Multiply weight of instance by e / (1 - e).
  Normalize weight of all instances.
```

Classification

```
Assign weight of zero to all classes.
For each of the t (or less) models:
  Add -log(e / (1 - e)) to weight of class predicted by model.
Return class with highest weight.
```

FIGURE 12.2

Algorithm for boosting.

How much should the weights be altered after each iteration? The answer depends on the current classifier's overall error. More specifically, if e denotes the classifier's error on the weighted data (a fraction between 0 and 1), then weights are updated by

$$\text{Weight} \leftarrow \text{Weight} \times e/(1-e)$$

for correctly classified instances, and the weights remain unchanged for misclassified ones. Of course, this does not increase the weight of misclassified instances as claimed earlier. However, after all weights have been updated they are renormalized so that their sum remains the same as it was before. Each instance's weight is divided by the sum of the new weights and multiplied by the sum of the old ones. This automatically increases the weight of each misclassified instance and reduces that of each correctly classified one.

Whenever the error on the weighted training data exceeds or equals 0.5, the boosting procedure deletes the current classifier and does not perform any more iterations. The same thing happens when the error is 0, because then all instance weights become 0.

We have explained how the boosting method generates a series of classifiers. To form a prediction, their output is combined using a weighted vote. To determine the weights, note that a classifier that performs well on the weighted training data from which it was built (e close to 0) should receive a high weight, and a classifier that performs badly (e close to 0.5) should receive a low one. The AdaBoost.M1 algorithm uses

$$\text{Weight} = -\log\frac{e}{1-e},$$

which is a positive number between 0 and infinity. Incidentally, this formula explains why classifiers that perform perfectly on the training data must be deleted, because when *e* is 0 the weight is undefined. To make a prediction, the weights of all classifiers that vote for a particular class are summed, and the class with the greatest total is chosen.

We began by assuming that the learning algorithm can cope with weighted instances. Any algorithm can be adapted to deal with weighted instances; we explained how at the end of Section 7.3 under *Locally weighted linear regression*. Instead of changing the learning algorithm, it is possible to generate an unweighted dataset from the weighted data by resampling—the same technique that bagging uses. Whereas for bagging each instance is chosen with equal probability, for boosting instances are chosen with probability proportional to their weight. As a result, instances with high weight are replicated frequently, and ones with low weight may never be selected. Once the new dataset becomes as large as the original one, it is fed into the learning scheme instead of the weighted data. It's as simple as that.

A disadvantage of this procedure is that some instances with low weight do not make it into the resampled dataset, so information is lost before the learning scheme is applied. However, this can be turned into an advantage. If the learning scheme produces a classifier whose error exceeds 0.5, boosting must terminate if the weighted data is used directly, whereas with resampling it might be possible to produce a classifier with error below 0.5 by discarding the resampled dataset and generating a new one from a different random seed. Sometimes more boosting iterations can be performed by resampling than when using the original weighted version of the algorithm.

THE POWER OF BOOSTING

The idea of boosting originated in a branch of machine learning research known as *computational learning theory*. Theoreticians are interested in boosting because it is possible to derive performance guarantees. For example, it can be shown that the error of the combined classifier on the training data approaches zero very quickly as more iterations are performed (exponentially quickly in the number of iterations). Unfortunately, as explained in Section 5.1, guarantees for the training error are not very interesting because they do not necessarily indicate good performance on fresh data. However, it can be shown theoretically that boosting only fails on fresh data if the individual classifiers are too "complex" for the amount of training data present or their training errors become too large too quickly. As usual, the problem lies in finding the right balance between the individual models' complexity and their fit to the data.

If boosting does succeed in reducing the error on fresh test data, it often does so in a spectacular way. One very surprising finding is that performing more boosting iterations can reduce the error on new data long after the classification error of the combined classifier on the training data has dropped to zero. Researchers were puzzled by this result because it seems to contradict Occam's razor, which declares that, of two hypotheses that explain the empirical evidence

equally well the simpler one is to be preferred. Performing more boosting iterations without reducing training error does not explain the training data any better,
and it certainly adds complexity to the combined classifier. The contradiction can
be resolved by considering the classifier's confidence in its predictions. More specifically, we measure confidence by the difference between the estimated confidence for the true class and that of the most likely predicted class other than the
true class—a quantity known as the *margin*. The larger the margin, the more confident the classifier is in predicting the true class. It turns out that boosting can
increase the margin long after the training error has dropped to zero. The effect
can be visualized by plotting the cumulative distribution of the margin values of
all the training instances for different numbers of boosting iterations, giving a
graph known as the *margin curve*. Hence, if the explanation of empirical evidence
takes the margin into account, Occam's razor remains as sharp as ever.

The beautiful thing about boosting is that a powerful combined classifier can
be built from very simple ones as long as they achieve less than 50% error on the
reweighted data. Usually, this is easy—certainly for learning problems with two
classes! Simple learning schemes are called *weak* learners, and boosting converts
weak learners into strong ones. For example, good results for two-class problems
can be obtained by boosting extremely simple decision trees that have only one
level—called *decision stumps*. Another possibility is to apply boosting to an algorithm that learns a single conjunctive rule—such as a single path in a decision
tree—and classifies instances based on whether or not the rule covers them. Of
course, multiclass datasets make it more difficult to achieve error rates below 0.5.
Decision trees can still be boosted, but they usually need to be more complex
than decision stumps. More sophisticated algorithms have been developed that
allow very simple models to be boosted successfully in multiclass situations.

Boosting often produces classifiers that are significantly more accurate on
fresh data than ones generated by bagging. However, unlike bagging, boosting
sometimes fails in practical situations: it can generate a classifier that is significantly less accurate than a single classifier built from the same data. This indicates that the combined classifier overfits the data.

12.5 ADDITIVE REGRESSION

When boosting was first investigated it sparked intense interest among researchers
because it could coax first-class performance from indifferent learners.
Statisticians soon discovered that it could be recast as a greedy algorithm for fitting an additive model. Additive models have a long history in statistics. Broadly,
the term refers to any way of generating predictions by summing up contributions
obtained from other models. Most learning algorithms for additive models do not
build the base models independently but ensure that they complement one another
and try to form an ensemble of base models that optimizes predictive performance
according to some specified criterion.

Boosting implements *forward stagewise additive modeling*. This class of algorithms starts with an empty ensemble and incorporates new members sequentially. At each stage the model that maximizes the predictive performance of the ensemble as a whole is added, without altering those already in the ensemble. Optimizing the ensemble's performance implies that the next model should focus on those training instances on which the ensemble performs poorly. This is exactly what boosting does by giving those instances larger weights.

NUMERIC PREDICTION

Here is a well-known forward stagewise additive modeling method for numeric prediction. First, build a standard regression model, e.g., a regression tree. The errors it exhibits on the training data—the differences between predicted and observed values—are called *residuals*. Then correct for these errors by learning a second model—perhaps another regression tree—that tries to predict the observed residuals. To do this, simply replace the original class values by their residuals before learning the second model. Adding the predictions made by the second model to those of the first one automatically yields lower error on the training data. Usually some residuals still remain, because the second model is not a perfect one, so we continue with a third model that learns to predict the residuals of the residuals, and so on. The procedure is reminiscent of the use of rules with exceptions for classification that we met in Section 3.4.

If the individual models minimize the squared error of the predictions, as linear regression models do, this algorithm minimizes the squared error of the ensemble as a whole. In practice it also works well when the base learner uses a heuristic approximation instead, such as the regression and model tree learners described in Section 7.3. In fact, there is no point in using standard linear regression as the base learner for additive regression, because the sum of linear regression models is again a linear regression model and the regression algorithm itself minimizes the squared error. However, it is a different story if the base learner is a regression model based on a single attribute, the one that minimizes the squared error. Statisticians call this *simple* linear regression, in contrast to the standard multiattribute method, properly called *multiple* linear regression. In fact, using additive regression in conjunction with simple linear regression and iterating until the squared error of the ensemble decreases no further yields an additive model identical to the least-squares multiple linear regression function.

Forward stagewise additive regression is prone to overfitting because each model added fits the training data closer and closer. To decide when to stop, use cross-validation. For example, perform a cross-validation for every number of iterations up to a user-specified maximum and choose the one that minimizes the cross-validated estimate of squared error. This is a good stopping criterion because cross-validation yields a fairly reliable estimate of the error on future data. Incidentally, using this method in conjunction with simple linear regression as the base learner effectively combines multiple linear regression with built-in attribute selection, because the next most important attribute's contribution is only included if it decreases the cross-validated error.

For implementation convenience, forward stagewise additive regression usually begins with a level-0 model that simply predicts the mean of the class on the training data so that every subsequent model fits residuals. This suggests another possibility for preventing overfitting: instead of subtracting a model's entire prediction to generate target values for the next model, shrink the predictions by multiplying them by a user-specified constant factor between 0 and 1 before subtracting. This reduces the model's fit to the residuals, and consequently reduces the chance of overfitting. Of course, it may increase the number of iterations needed to arrive at a good additive model. Reducing the multiplier effectively damps down the learning process, increasing the chance of stopping at just the right moment—but also increasing run time.

ADDITIVE LOGISTIC REGRESSION

Additive regression can also be applied to classification just as linear regression can. But we know from Section 4.6 that logistic regression is more suitable than linear regression for classification. It turns out that a similar adaptation can be made to additive models by modifying the forward stagewise modeling method to perform additive *logistic* regression. Use the logit transform to translate the probability estimation problem into a regression problem, as we did in Section 4.6, and solve the regression task using an ensemble of models—e.g., regression trees—just as for additive regression. At each stage, add the model that maximizes the probability of the data given the ensemble classifier.

Suppose f_j is the jth regression model in the ensemble and $f_j(\mathbf{a})$ is its prediction for instance $\mathbf{a}$. Assuming a two-class problem, use the additive model $\sum f_j(\mathbf{a})$ to obtain a probability estimate for the first class:

$$p(1|\mathbf{a}) = \frac{1}{1 + e^{-\sum f_j(\mathbf{a})}}.$$

This closely resembles the expression used in Section 4.6, except that here it is abbreviated by using vector notation for the instance $\mathbf{a}$ and the original weighted sum of attributes values is replaced by a sum of arbitrarily complex regression models f.

Fig. 12.3 shows the two-class version of the so-called *LogitBoost* algorithm, which performs additive logistic regression and generates the individual models f_j. Here, y_i is 1 for an instance in the first class and 0 for an instance in the second. In each iteration this algorithm fits a regression model f_j to a weighted version of the original dataset based on dummy class values z_i and weights w_i. We assume that $p(1|\mathbf{a})$ is computed using the f_j that were built in previous iterations.

The derivation of this algorithm is beyond the scope of this book, but it can be shown that the algorithm maximizes the probability of the data with respect to

Model generation

```
for j = 1 to t iterations:
  for each instance a[i]:
    set the target value for the regression to
      z[i] = (y[i] - p(1|a[i])) / [p(1|a[i]) * (1 - p(1|a[i]))]
    set the weight of instance a[i] to p(1|a[i]) * (1 - p(1|a[i]))
  fit a regression model f[j] to the data with class values z[i] and weights w[i]
```

Classification

```
predict class 1 if p(1 | a) > 0.5, otherwise predict class 0
```

FIGURE 12.3

Algorithm for additive logistic regression.

the ensemble if each model f_j is determined by minimizing the squared error on the corresponding regression problem. In fact, if multiple linear regression is used to form the f_j, the algorithm converges to the maximum likelihood linear-logistic regression model: it is an incarnation of the iteratively reweighted least-squares method mentioned in Section 4.6.

Superficially, LogitBoost looks quite different to AdaBoost, but the predictors they produce differ mainly in that the former optimizes the likelihood directly whereas the latter optimizes an exponential loss function that can be regarded as an approximation to it. From a practical perspective, the difference is that LogitBoost uses a regression scheme as the base learner whereas AdaBoost works with classification algorithms.

We have only shown the two-class version of LogitBoost, but the algorithm can be generalized to multiclass problems. As with additive regression, the danger of overfitting can be reduced by shrinking the predictions of the individual f_j by a predetermined multiplier and using cross-validation to determine an appropriate number of iterations.

12.6 INTERPRETABLE ENSEMBLES

Bagging, boosting, and randomization all produce ensembles of classifiers. This makes it very difficult to analyze what kind of information has been extracted from the data. It would be nice to have a single model with the same predictive performance. One possibility is to generate an artificial dataset, by randomly sampling points from the instance space and assigning them the class labels predicted by the ensemble classifier, and then learn a decision tree or rule set from this new dataset. To obtain similar predictive performance from the tree as from the ensemble a huge dataset may be required, but in the limit this strategy should be able to replicate the performance of the ensemble classifier—and it certainly will if the ensemble itself consists of decision trees.

OPTION TREES

Another approach is to derive a single structure that can represent an ensemble of classifiers compactly. This can be done if the ensemble consists of decision trees; the result is called an *option tree*. Option trees differ from decision trees in that they contain two types of node: decision nodes and option nodes. Fig. 12.4 shows a simple example for the weather data, with only one option node. To classify an instance, filter it down through the tree. At a decision node take just one of the branches, as usual, but at an option node take *all* the branches. This means that the instance ends up in more than one leaf, and the classifications obtained from those leaves must somehow be combined into an overall classification. This can be done simply by voting, taking the majority vote at an option node to be the prediction of the node. In that case it makes little sense to have option nodes with only two options (as in Fig. 12.4) because there will only be a majority if both branches agree. Another possibility is to average the probability estimates obtained from the different paths, using either an unweighted average or a more sophisticated Bayesian approach.

Option trees can be generated by modifying an existing decision tree learner to create an option node if there are several splits that look similarly useful according to their information gain. All choices within a certain user-specified

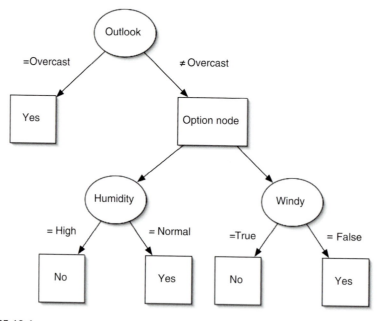

FIGURE 12.4

Simple option tree for the weather data.

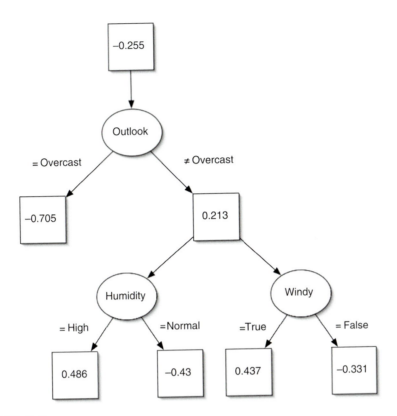

FIGURE 12.5

Alternating decision tree for the weather data.

tolerance of the best one can be made into options. During pruning, the error of an option node is the average error of its options.

Another possibility is to grow an option tree by incrementally adding nodes to it. This is commonly done using a boosting algorithm, and the resulting trees are usually called *alternating decision trees* instead of option trees. In this context the decision nodes are called *splitter nodes* and the option nodes are called *prediction nodes*. Prediction nodes are leaves if no splitter nodes have been added to them yet. The standard alternating decision tree applies to two-class problems, and with each prediction node is associated a positive or negative numeric value. To obtain a prediction for an instance, filter down all applicable branches and sum up the values from any prediction nodes that are encountered; predict one class or the other depending on whether the sum is positive or negative.

A simple example tree for the weather data is shown in Fig. 12.5, where a positive value corresponds to class *play* = *no* and a negative one to *play* = *yes*. To classify an instance with *outlook* = *sunny*, *temperature* = *hot*, *humidity* = *normal*, and *windy = false*, filter it down to the corresponding leaves, obtaining values −0.255, 0.213, −0.430, and −0.331. The sum of these values is negative; hence predict *play = yes*. Alternating decision trees always have a prediction node at the root, as in this example.

The alternating tree is grown using a boosting algorithm—e.g., a boosting algorithm that employs a base learner for numeric prediction, such as the LogitBoost method described previously. Assume that the base learner produces a single conjunctive rule in each boosting iteration. Then an alternating decision tree can be generated by simply adding each rule into the tree. The numeric scores associated with the prediction nodes are obtained from the consequents of the rules. However, the resulting tree will grow large very quickly because the rules from different boosting iterations are likely to be different. Hence, learning algorithms for alternating decision trees consider only those rules that extend one of the *existing* paths in the tree by adding a splitter node and two corresponding prediction nodes (assuming binary splits). In the standard version of the algorithm, every possible location in the tree is considered for addition, and a node is added according to a performance measure that depends on the particular boosting algorithm employed. However, heuristics can be used instead of an exhaustive search to speed up the learning process.

LOGISTIC MODEL TREES

Option trees and alternating trees yield very good classification performance based on a single structure, but they may still be difficult to interpret when there are many options nodes because it becomes difficult to see how a particular prediction is derived. However, it turns out that boosting can also be used to build very effective decision trees that do not include any options at all. For example, the LogitBoost algorithm has been used to induce trees with linear-logistic regression models at the leaves. These are called *logistic model trees* and are interpreted in the same way as the model trees for regression described in Section 7.3.

LogitBoost performs additive logistic regression. Suppose that each iteration of the boosting algorithm fits a simple regression function by going through all the attributes, finding the simple regression function with the smallest error, and adding it into the additive model. If the LogitBoost algorithm is run until convergence, the result is a maximum likelihood multiple-logistic regression model. However, for optimum performance on future data it is usually unnecessary to wait for convergence—and to do so is often detrimental. An appropriate number of boosting iterations can be determined by estimating the expected performance for a given number of iterations using cross-validation and stopping the process when performance ceases to increase.

A simple extension of this algorithm leads to logistic model trees. The boosting process terminates when there is no further structure in the data that can be modeled using a linear-logistic regression function. However, there may still be structure that linear models can fit if attention is restricted to subsets of the data, obtained, e.g., by splitting the data using a standard decision tree criterion such as information gain. Thus, once no further improvement can be obtained by adding more simple linear models, the data is split and boosting resumed separately in each subset. This process takes the logistic model generated so far and refines it separately for the data in each subset. Again, cross-validation is run in each subset to determine an appropriate number of iterations to perform in that subset.

The process is applied recursively until the subsets become too small. The resulting tree will surely overfit the training data, and one of the standard methods of decision tree learning can be used to prune it. Experiments indicate that the pruning operation is very important. Using the cost-complexity pruning method discussed in Section 6.1, which chooses the right tree size using cross-validation, the algorithm produces small but very accurate trees with linear-logistic models at the leaves.

12.7 STACKING

Stacked generalization, or *stacking* for short, is a different way of combining multiple models. Although developed some years ago, it is less widely mentioned in the machine learning literature than bagging and boosting, partly because it is difficult to analyze theoretically and partly because there is no generally accepted best way of doing it—the basic idea can be applied in many different variations.

Unlike bagging and boosting, stacking is not normally used to combine models of the same type—e.g., a set of decision trees. Instead it is applied to models built by different learning algorithms. Suppose you have a decision tree inducer, a Naïve Bayes learner, and an instance-based learning scheme and you want to form a classifier for a given dataset. The usual procedure would be to estimate the expected error of each algorithm by cross-validation and to choose the best one to form a model for prediction on future data. But is not there a better way? With three learning algorithms available, cannot we use all three for prediction and combine the outputs together?

One way to combine outputs is by voting—the same mechanism used in bagging. However, (unweighted) voting only makes sense if the learning schemes perform comparably well. If two of the three classifiers make predictions that are grossly incorrect, we will be in trouble! Instead, stacking introduces the concept of a *metalearner*, which replaces the voting procedure. The problem with voting is that it is not clear which classifier to trust. Stacking tries to *learn* which classifiers are the reliable ones, using another learning algorithm—the metalearner—to discover how best to combine the output of the base learners.

The input to the metamodel—also called the *level-1 model*—are the predictions of the base models, or *level-0 models*. A level-1 instance has as many attributes as there are level-0 learners, and the attribute values give the predictions of these learners on the corresponding level-0 instance. When the stacked learner is used for classification, an instance is first fed into the level-0 models, and each one guesses a class value. These guesses are fed into the level-1 model, which combines them into the final prediction.

There remains the problem of training the level-1 learner. To do this, we need to find a way of transforming the level-0 training data (used for training the level-0 learners) into level-1 training data (used for training the level-1 learner). This seems straightforward: let each level-0 model classify a training instance, and attach to their predictions the instance's actual class value to yield a level-1 training instance. Unfortunately, this does not work well. It would allow rules to be learned such as *always believe the output of classifier A, and ignore B and C.* This rule may well be appropriate for particular base classifiers A, B, and C; and if so it will probably be learned. But just because it seems appropriate on the training data does not necessarily mean that it will work well on the test data— because it will inevitably learn to prefer classifiers that overfit the training data over ones that make decisions more realistically.

Consequently, stacking does not simply transform the level-0 training data into level-1 data in this manner. Recall from Chapter 5, Credibility: evaluating what's been learned, that there are better methods of estimating a classifier's performance than using the error on the training set. One is to hold out some instances and use them for an independent evaluation. Applying this to stacking, we reserve some instances to form the training data for the level-1 learner and build level-0 classifiers from the remaining data. Once the level-0 classifiers have been built they are used to classify the instances in the holdout set, forming the level-1 training data. Because the level-0 classifiers have not been trained on these instances, their predictions are unbiased; therefore the level-1 training data accurately reflects the true performance of the level-0 learning algorithms. Once the level-1 data has been generated by this holdout procedure, the level-0 learners can be reapplied to generate classifiers from the full training set, making slightly better use of the data and leading to better predictions.

The holdout method inevitably deprives the level-1 model of some of the training data. In Chapter 5, Credibility: evaluating what's been learned, cross-validation was introduced as a means of circumventing this problem for error estimation. This can be applied in conjunction with stacking by performing a cross-validation for every level-0 learner. Each instance in the training data occurs in exactly one of the test folds of the cross-validation, and the predictions of the level-0 inducers built from the corresponding training fold are used to build a level-1 training instance from it. This generates a level-1 training instance for each level-0 training instance. Of course, it is slow because a level-0 classifier has to be trained for each fold of the cross-validation, but it does allow the level-1 classifier to make full use of the training data.

Given a test instance, most learning schemes are able to output probabilities for every class label instead of making a single categorical prediction. This can be exploited to improve the performance of stacking by using the probabilities to form the level-1 data. The only difference to the standard procedure is that each nominal level-1 attribute—representing the class predicted by a level-0 learner—is replaced by several numeric attributes, each representing a class probability output by the level-0 learner. In other words, the number of attributes in the level-1 data is multiplied by the number of classes. This procedure has the advantage that the level-1 learner is privy to the confidence that each level-0 learner associates with its predictions, thereby amplifying communication between the two levels of learning.

An outstanding question remains: What algorithms are suitable for the level-1 learner? In principle, any learning scheme can be applied. However, because most of the work is already done by the level-0 learners, the level-1 classifier is basically just an arbiter and it makes sense to choose a rather simple algorithm for this purpose. In the words of David Wolpert, the inventor of stacking, it is reasonable that "relatively global, smooth" level-1 generalizers should perform well. Simple linear models or trees with linear models at the leaves usually work well.

Stacking can also be applied to numeric prediction. In that case, the level-0 models and the level-1 model all predict numeric values. The basic mechanism remains the same; the only difference lies in the nature of the level-1 data. In the numeric case, each level-1 attribute represents the numeric prediction made by one of the level-0 models, and instead of a class value the numeric target value is attached to level-1 training instances.

12.8 FURTHER READING AND BIBLIOGRAPHIC NOTES

Ensemble learning is a popular research topic in machine learning research, with many related publications. The term *bagging* (for "bootstrap aggregating") was coined by Breiman (1996b), who investigated the properties of bagging theoretically and empirically for both classification and numeric prediction.

The bias—variance decomposition for classification presented in Section 12.2 is due to Dietterich and Kong (1995). We chose this version because it is both accessible and elegant. However, the variance can turn out to be negative, because, as we mentioned, aggregating models from independent training sets by voting may in pathological situations actually *increase* the overall classification error compared to a model from a single training set. This is a serious disadvantage because variances are normally squared quantities—the square of the standard deviation—and therefore cannot become negative. Breiman, in the technical report Breiman (1996c), proposed a different bias—variance decomposition for classification. This has caused some confusion in the literature, because three different versions of this report can be located on the Web. The official version, entitled "Arcing classifiers," describes a more complex decomposition that cannot, by construction, produce negative variance. However, the original version, entitled "Bias, variance, and arcing classifiers," follows Dietterich and Kong's formulation (except that Breiman splits the bias term into bias plus noise), and there is also an intermediate version with the original title but the new decomposition that includes an appendix in which Breiman explains that he abandoned the old definition because it can produce negative variance. However, in the new version (and in decompositions proposed by other authors) the bias of the aggregated classifier can exceed the bias of a classifier built from a single training set, which also seems counterintuitive.

We discussed the fact that bagging can yield excellent results when used for cost-sensitive classification. The MetaCost algorithm was introduced by Domingos (1999).

The random subspace method was suggested as an approach for learning ensemble classifiers by Ho (1998) and applied as a method for learning ensembles of nearest-neighbor classifiers by Bay (1999). Randomization was evaluated by Dieterich (2000) and compared with bagging and boosting. Random forests were introduced by Breiman (2001). Rotation forests are a more recent ensemble learning method introduced by Rodriguez, Kuncheva, and Alonso (2006). Subsequent studies by Kuncheva and Rodriguez (2007) show that the main factors responsible for its performance are the use of principal component transformations (as opposed to other feature extraction methods such as random projections) and the application of principal component analysis to random subspaces of the original input attributes.

Freund and Schapire (1996) developed the AdaBoost.M1 boosting algorithm, and derived theoretical bounds for its performance. Later, they provided bounds for generalization error using the concept of margins (Schapire, Freund, Bartlett, & Lee, 1997). Drucker (1997) adapted AdaBoost.M1 for numeric prediction. The LogitBoost algorithm was developed by Friedman, Hastie, and Tibshirani (2000). Friedman (2001) described how to make boosting more resilient in the presence of noisy data.

Domingos (1997) described how to derive a single interpretable model from an ensemble using artificial training examples. Bayesian option trees were introduced by Buntine (1992), and majority voting was incorporated into option trees by Kohavi and Kunz (1997). Freund and Mason (1999) introduced alternating decision trees; experiments with multiclass alternating decision trees were reported by Holmes, Pfahringer, Kirkby, Frank, and Hall (2002). Landwehr, Hall, and Frank (2005) developed logistic model trees using the LogitBoost algorithm.

Stacked generalization originated with Wolpert (1992), who presented the idea in the neural network literature, and was applied to numeric prediction by Breiman (1996a). Ting and Witten (1997a) compared different level-1 models empirically and found that a simple linear model works well; they also demonstrated the advantage of using probabilities as level-1 data. Dzeroski and Zenko (2004) obtained improved performance using model trees instead of linear regression. A combination of stacking and bagging has also been investigated (Ting and Witten 1997b).

12.9 **WEKA IMPLEMENTATIONS**

- Bagging
  Bagging (bag a classifier; works for regression too)
  MetaCost (make a classifier cost-sensitive, in the *metaCost* package)
- Randomization
  RandomCommittee (ensembles using different random number seeds)
  RandomSubSpace (use a different randomly chosen subset of attributes)
  RandomForest (bag ensembles of random trees)
  RotationForest (ensembles using rotated random subspaces, in the
    rotationForest package)
- Boosting: *AdaBoostM1*
- Additive regression:
  AdditiveRegression
  LogitBoost (additive logistic regression)
- Interpretable ensembles:
  ADTree (alternating decision trees, in the *alternatingDecisionTrees*
    package)
  LADTree (learns alternating decision trees using LogitBoost, in the
    alternatingDecisionTrees package)
  LMT (logistic model trees)
- *Stacking* (learns how to combine predictions)

Moving on: applications and beyond

13

CHAPTER OUTLINE

13.1 Applying Machine Learning...504
13.2 Learning From Massive Datasets 506
13.3 Data Stream Learning 509
13.4 Incorporating Domain Knowledge 512
13.5 Text Mining 515
    Document Classification and Clustering...516
    Information Extraction 517
    Natural Language Processing..518
13.6 Web Mining 519
    Wrapper Induction..519
    Page Rank 520
13.7 Images and Speech 522
    Images 523
    Speech 524
13.8 Adversarial Situations 524
13.9 Ubiquitous Data Mining 527
13.10 Further Reading and Bibliographic Notes 529
13.11 WEKA Implementations...532

Machine learning is a burgeoning new technology for mining knowledge from data, a technology that a lot of people are beginning to take seriously. Looking forward, the main challenge ahead is applications. Opportunities abound. Wherever there is data, things can be learned from it. Whenever there is too much data for people to pore over themselves, the mechanics of learning will have to be automatic. But the inspiration will certainly not be automatic! Applications will come not from computer programs, nor from machine learning experts, nor from the data itself, but from the people who work with the data and the problems from which it arises. That is why we have written this book, and that is what the WEKA system described in Appendix B is for—to empower those who are not machine learning experts to apply these techniques to problems that arise in daily working life. The ideas are simple. The algorithms are here. The rest is really up to you!

Of course, development of the technology is certainly not finished. Machine learning is a hot research topic and new ideas and techniques continually emerge. To give a flavor of the scope and variety of research fronts, we close Part II by looking at some topical areas in the world of data mining.

13.1 APPLYING MACHINE LEARNING

In 2006 the International Data Mining Conference took a poll to identify the top 10 data mining algorithms. Although now somewhat dated, it is still instructive to consider the result, shown in Table 13.1. It is good to see that all the algorithms are covered in this book! The conference organizers divided the algorithms into rough categories, which are also shown. Some of the assignments are rather arbitrary—Naïve Bayes, e.g., is certainly a statistical learning method. Nevertheless the emphasis on classification over other forms of learning, which reflects the emphasis in this book, is evident in the table; as is the prominence of C4.5, which we have also noted. One algorithm in Table 13.1 that has not been mentioned so far is the PageRank algorithm for link mining, which we were a little surprised to see in this list. Section 13.6 contains a brief description.

We have repeatedly stressed that productive use of machine learning is not just a matter of finding some data and then blindly applying learning algorithms to it. Of course, the existence of tools such as the WEKA workbench makes that easy to do—and therein lies a danger. We have seen many publications that seem to follow this methodology: the authors run a plethora of learning algorithms on a particular dataset and then write an article claiming that such-and-such a machine learning method is best for such-and-such a problem—with little apparent understanding of what those algorithms do, the nature of the data, or consideration for statistical significance. The usefulness of such studies is questionable.

Table 13.1 The Top 10 Algorithms in Data Mining, According to a 2006 Poll

	Algorithm	Category	Book Section
1	C4.5	Classification	4.3, 6.1
2	K-means	Clustering	4.8
3	SVM	Statistical learning	7.2
4	Apriori	Association analysis	4.5, 6.3
5	EM	Statistical learning	9.3, 9.4
6	PageRank	Link mining	13.6
7	Adaboost	Ensemble learning	12.4
8	kNN	Classification	4.7, 7.1
9	Naïve Bayes	Classification	4.2
10	CART	Classification	6.1

A related but rather different issue concerns the improvements in machine learning methods that have been reported over the years. In a 2006 paper provocatively entitled "Classifier technology and the illusion of progress," David Hand, a prominent statistician and machine learning researcher, points out that a great many algorithms have been devised for supervised classification, and a great many comparative studies have been conducted that apparently establish the superiority of new methods over their predecessors. Yet he contends that the continued steady progress that publication of these studies seems to document is, in fact, to a large extent illusory. This message brings to mind the $1R$ machine learning scheme some 15 years earlier with which we began Chapter 4, Algorithms: the basic methods, which, as pointed out there, was never really intended as a machine learning "method" but was devised to demonstrate that putting high-powered inductive inference methods to work on simple datasets is like using a sledgehammer to crack a nut. That insight underlies the simplicity-first methodology that pervades this book, of which Hand's recent paper is a salutary reminder.

How can progress be largely illusory, given documented improvements in measured classification success? The claim is basically that the differences in performance are very small, and in practical applications are likely to be swamped by other sources of uncertainty. There are many reasons for this. Simple methods may not perform as well as complex ones, but they often perform nearly as well. An extremely simple model—always choose the majority class—sets a baseline upon which any learning method should be able to improve. Consider the improvement over the baseline achieved by a simple method as a proportion of the improvement over the baseline achieved by a sophisticated method. For a variety of randomly-chosen datasets, it turns out that a very simple method achieved more than 90% of the improvement yielded by the most sophisticated scheme. This is not so surprising. In standard classification schemes such as decision trees and rules, a huge proportional gain in predictive accuracy is achieved at the beginning of the process when the first branch or rule is determined, and subsequent gains are small—usually very small indeed.

Small improvements are easily swamped by other factors. A fundamental assumption of machine learning is that the training data is representative of the distribution from which future data will be chosen—the assumption is generally that the data is independent and identically distributed (often abbreviated to IID). But in real life, things drift. Yet training data is always retrospective. And it might be quite old. Consider the loan scenario introduced in Section 1.3. To collect a substantial volume of training data (and thorough training needs a substantial volume), we must wait until many loans have been issued. And then we must wait until the end of the loan period (2 years? 5 years?) for the outcome to be known. By the time we use it for training, the data is quite old. And what has changed in the meantime? There are new ways of doing things. The bank has changed the way it defines measurements on which the features are based. New features have become available. Policies have altered. Is that ancient data really representative of today's problem?

Another fundamental problem is the reliability of the class labels in the training data. There may be small errors—random or even systematic ones—in which case, perhaps, we should stick to simpler models because the higher-order terms of more complex models may be very inaccurate. In determining class labels, someone, somewhere, may be mapping a gray world on to a black-and-white one, which requires judgment and invites inconsistency. And things may change: the notion of a "defaulter" on a loan—say, unpaid bills for 3 months—may be subtly different today than it was before—perhaps, in today's economic climate, hard-pressed customers will be given another couple of month's leeway before calling in the bailiffs. The point is not that learning will necessarily fail. The changes may be fairly subtle, and the learned models may still work well. The point is that the extra few percent gained by a sophisticated model over a simple one may be swamped by other factors.

Another issue, when looking at comparative experiments with machine learning methods, is who is doing the driving. It's not just a matter of firing up the various different methods and recording the results. Many machine learning schemes benefit from tweaking—optimization to fit the problem at hand. Hopefully the data used for tweaking is kept entirely separate from that used for testing (otherwise the results are dishonest). But it is natural that an expert in some particular method—maybe the person who developed it—is able to squeeze more performance out of it than someone else. If they are trying to get their work published, they will certainly want to present the new method in the best possible light. They may not be so experienced at squeezing good performance out of existing, competitive, methods—or so diligent. New methods always look better than old ones; also, more complicated schemes are harder to criticize than simpler ones!

The upshot is that small gains in laboratory performance, even though real, may be swamped by other factors when machine learning is applied to a practical data mining problem. If you want to do something worthwhile on a practical dataset you need to take the entire problem context into account.

Before closing this section, we should note that Hand's paper was written before the breakthrough results obtained using deep learning. These show that extremely complex models can yield substantial benefits in some applications, if sufficient training data is available and sufficient care is taken when learning them.

13.2 LEARNING FROM MASSIVE DATASETS

The enormous proliferation of very large databases in today's companies and scientific institutions makes it necessary for machine learning algorithms to operate on massive datasets. Two separate dimensions become critical when any algorithm is applied to very large datasets: space and time.

Suppose the data is so large that it cannot be held in main memory. This causes no difficulty if the learning scheme works in an incremental fashion, processing one instance at a time when generating the model. An instance can be read from the input file, the model can be updated, the next instance can be read, and so on—without ever holding more than one training instance in main memory. This is "data stream learning," and we discuss it in the next section. Other methods, such as basic instance-based schemes and locally weighted regression, need access to all the training instances at prediction time. In that case, sophisticated caching and indexing mechanisms have to be employed to keep only the most frequently used parts of a dataset in memory and to provide rapid access to relevant instances in the file.

The other critical dimension when applying learning algorithms to massive datasets is time. If the learning time does not scale linearly (or almost linearly) with the number of training instances, it will eventually become infeasible to process very large datasets. In some applications the number of attributes is a critical factor, and only methods that scale linearly in the number of attributes are acceptable. Alternatively, prediction time might be the crucial issue. Fortunately, there are many learning algorithms that scale gracefully during both training and testing. For example, the training time for Naïve Bayes is linear in both the number of instances and the number of attributes. For top-down decision tree inducers, we saw in Section 6.1 that training time is linear in the number of attributes and, if the tree is uniformly bushy, log-linear in the number of instances (if subtree raising is not used).

When a dataset is too large for a particular learning algorithm to be applied, there are three ways to make learning feasible. The first is trivial: instead of applying the scheme to the full dataset, use just a small subset for training. Of course, information is lost when subsampling is employed. However, the loss may be negligible because the predictive performance of a learned model often flattens out long before all the training data is incorporated into it. If this is the case, it can easily be verified by observing the model's performance on a holdout test set for training sets of different size.

This kind of behavior, called the *law of diminishing returns*, may arise because the learning problem is a simple one, so that a small volume of training data is sufficient to learn an accurate model. Alternatively, the learning algorithm might be incapable of grasping the detailed structure of the underlying domain. This is often observed when Naïve Bayes is employed in a complex domain: additional training data may not improve the performance of the model, whereas a decision tree's accuracy may continue to climb. In this case, of course, if predictive performance is the main objective you should switch to the more complex learning algorithm. But beware of overfitting! Take care not to assess performance on the training data.

Parallelization is another way of reducing the time complexity of learning. The idea is to split the problem into smaller parts, solve each using a separate processor, and combine the results together. To do this, a parallelized version of the learning algorithm must be created. Some algorithms lend themselves naturally to parallelization. Nearest-neighbor methods, e.g., can easily be distributed among several processors by splitting the data into parts and letting each processor find the nearest neighbor in its part of the training set. Decision tree learners can be parallelized by letting each processor build a subtree of the complete tree. Bagging and stacking (although not boosting) are naturally parallel algorithms. However, parallelization is only a partial remedy because with a fixed number of processors, the algorithm's asymptotic time complexity cannot be improved—although modern graphics cards contain an enormous number of (very simple) processors!

A simple way to apply any algorithm to a large dataset is to split the data into chunks of limited size and learn models separately for each one, combining the result using voting or averaging. Either a parallel bagging-like scheme or a sequential boosting-like scheme can be employed for this purpose. Boosting has the advantage that new chunks can be weighted based on the classifiers learned from previous chunks, thus transferring knowledge between chunks. In both cases memory consumption increases linearly with dataset size; hence some form of pruning is necessary for very large datasets. This can be done by setting aside some validation data and only adding a model from a new chunk to the committee classifier if it increases the committee's performance on the validation set. The validation set can also be used to identify an appropriate chunk size by running the method with several different chunk sizes in parallel and monitoring performance on the validation set.

The best but most challenging way to enable a learning paradigm to deal with very large datasets would be to develop new algorithms with lower computational complexity. In some cases, it is provably impossible to derive exact algorithms with lower complexity. Decision tree learners that deal with numeric attributes fall into this category. Their asymptotic time complexity is dominated by the sorting process for the numeric attribute values, a procedure that must be performed at least once for any given dataset. However, stochastic algorithms can sometimes be derived that approximate the true solution but require a much smaller amount of time.

Background knowledge can make it possible to vastly reduce the amount of data that needs to be processed by a learning algorithm. Depending on which attribute is the class, most of the attributes in a huge dataset might turn out to be irrelevant when background knowledge is taken into account. As usual, it pays to carefully engineer the data that is passed to the learning scheme and make the greatest possible use of any prior information about the learning problem at hand. If insufficient background knowledge is available, the attribute filtering algorithms described in Section 7.1 can often drastically reduce the amount of data— possibly at the expense of a minor loss in predictive performance. Some of these—e.g., attribute selection using decision trees or the $1R$ learning scheme— are linear in the number of attributes.

To give a feeling for the volume of data that can be handled by straightforward implementations of machine learning algorithms on ordinary microcomputers, we ran WEKA's decision tree learner J48, an implementation of C4.5, on a dataset with 5 M instances, 40 attributes (almost all numeric), and a class with 25 values.[1] We used a reasonably modern machine[2] running a Java virtual machine[3] with 6 Gbytes of heap space (half of this was required just to load the data). The resulting tree, which had 1388 nodes, took 18 minutes to build. In general, Java is a little slower than equivalent C/C++ code—but less than twice as slow.

There are datasets today that truly deserve the adjective *massive*. Scientific datasets from astrophysics, nuclear physics, earth science, and molecular biology are measured in terabytes. So are datasets containing records of financial transactions. Application of standard programs for machine learning to such datasets in their entirety is a very challenging proposition.

13.3 DATA STREAM LEARNING

One way of addressing massive datasets is to develop learning algorithms that treat the input as a continuous data stream. In the new paradigm of data stream mining, which has developed during the last decade, algorithms are developed that cope naturally with datasets that are many times the size of main memory—perhaps even indefinitely large. The core assumption is that each instance can be inspected once only (or at most once) and must then be discarded to make room for subsequent instances. The learning algorithm has no control over the order in which instances are processed, and must update its model incrementally as each one arrives. Most models also satisfy the "anytime" property—they are ready to be applied at any point during the learning process. Such algorithms are ideal for real-time learning from data streams, making predictions in real time whilst adapting the model to changes in the evolving input stream. They are typically applied to online learning from data produced by physical sensors.

For such applications, the algorithm must operate indefinitely yet use a limited amount of memory. Even though we have stipulated that instances are discarded as soon as they have been processed, it is obviously necessary to remember at least something about at least some of the instances, otherwise the model would be static. And as time progresses, the model may continue to grow—inexorably. But it must not be allowed to grow without bound. When processing big data, memory is quickly exhausted unless limits are enforced on every aspect of its use. Moving from space to time, algorithms intended for real-time application must process instances faster than they arrive, dealing with each one within a fixed, constant, preferably small, time bound. This does not allow, e.g., for occasional complex reorganizations of a tree model—unless the cost can be amortized over several instances, which introduces a further level of complexity.

---

[1]We used a version of the 1999 KDD Cup data at http://kdd.ics.uci.edu/databases/kddcup99/kddcup99.html.
[2]Apple OSX with a 4 GHz Intel Core i7 processor.
[3]Oracle's 64-bit Java Virtual Machine (Java 1.8) in server mode.

Naïve Bayes is a rare example of an algorithm that needs no adaptation to deal with data streams—as long as there are no substantial changes in the stream. Training is incremental: it merely involves updating a fixed set of numeric parameters. Memory usage is small because no structure is added to the model. Other classifiers with the same properties include 1R and the basic perceptron. Multilayer neural nets usually have a fixed structure as well, and as we saw in Section 7.2 stochastic backpropagation updates weights incrementally after each training instance has been processed, rather than in a batch operation, and thus is suitable for online learning. Rules with exceptions make modifications incrementally by expressing exceptions to existing rules rather than reengineering the entire set, and thus could be rendered suitable for data stream learning—although care would need to be taken to ensure that memory usage did not increase inexorably as the number of exceptions increased. Instance-based algorithms and related methods such as locally weighted linear regression are also incremental, but need to be adapted to operate within a fixed memory bound.

To convey the flavor of how a standard algorithm might be adapted for stream processing, we will examine the case of decision trees—which have the advantage of evolving structure in a form that is interpretable. Early work on incremental induction of decision trees devised methods for creating a tree and allowing it to be restructured when sufficient evidence had accumulated that an alternative version would be better. However, a large amount of information needs to be retained to support the restructuring operation—in some cases, all of the training data. Furthermore, restructuring tends to be slow—sometimes slower than recreating the entire tree from scratch. Although interesting, these methods do not support indefinite processing of data streams in real time.

Their problem is that they adopt the usual paradigm of squeezing as much information as possible out of the available instances. With data streams, this is not necessarily appropriate—it is perfectly acceptable to discard some information about the instances, because if it is important it will always reappear. A new paradigm of "Hoeffding trees" was introduced in 2000, which builds models that can be proven equivalent to standard decision trees if the data is static and the number of examples is large enough.

Hoeffding trees are based on a simple idea known as the Hoeffding bound. It makes intuitive sense that, given enough independent observations, the true mean of a random variable will not differ from the estimated mean by more than a certain amount. In fact, the Hoeffding bound states that after n observations and with probability $1-\delta$, the true mean of a random variable of range R will not be smaller than the estimated mean minus ε, where

$$\varepsilon = \sqrt{\frac{\ln(1/\delta)}{2n}} \cdot R.$$

This bound holds regardless of the probability distribution that underlies the values. Being general, it is more conservative than distribution-dependent bounds. Although tighter bounds are known for particular distributions, the Hoeffding formulation works well empirically.

The basic issue in decision tree induction is to choose an attribute to branch on at each stage. To apply the Hoeffding bound, first set a small value of δ (say 10^{-7}), the probability that the choice of attribute will be incorrect. The random variable being estimated is the difference in information gain between the best two attributes, and R is the base two logarithm of the number of possible class labels. For example, if the difference in gain between the best two attributes is estimated to be 0.3, and the above formula yields a value for ε of 0.1, the bound guarantees that the actual difference in gain exceeds 0.2 with high probability, which represents positive separation for the best attribute. Thus it is safe to split.

If the difference in information gain between the best two attributes is less than ε, it is not safe to split. However, ε will decrease as n continues to increase, so it is simply a matter of waiting until more examples have been seen—although, of course, this may alter the estimate of which are the two best attributes and how far apart they are.

This simple test is the core principle of Hoeffding trees: to decide, with probability $1-\delta$, that a particular attribute exhibits greater information gain than all the others, i.e., the gap between it and its closest competitor exceeds ε. The bound decays rapidly as more examples are seen: e.g., for a two-class problem ($R = 1$) with $\delta = 10^{-7}$ it falls below 0.1 after the first 1000 examples and below 0.01 after the first 100,000. One might object that as the number of leaves grows indefinitely, the probability of making incorrect decisions will continually increase even though the probability of error at each one falls below δ. This is true—except that, working within finite memory, the number of leaves cannot grow indefinitely. Given a maximum tree size, keeping the overall probability of error within a given bound is just a matter of choosing an appropriate value for δ. The basic principle can be applied to measures other than the information gain, and to learning methods other than decision trees.

There are many other issues. A tie-breaking strategy is advisable to permit further development of the tree in situations where the top two attributes exhibit very similar information gains. Indeed, the presence of two identical attributes could block any development of the tree at all. To prevent this, nodes should be split whenever the Hoeffding bound falls below a small prespecified tie-breaking parameter, no matter how close the next best option. To increase efficiency the Hoeffding test may be performed periodically for each leaf, after k new instances have reached it, and only when a mix of classes have reached the leaf—otherwise there is no need to split. Prepruning is another simple possibility. The algorithm can incorporate this by also evaluating the merit of not splitting at all: i.e., by splitting only if the best attribute's information gain at the node exceeds zero. Unlike prepruning in the batch learning setting, this is not a permanent decision: nodes are only prevented from splitting until it appears that a split will be useful.

Now consider memory usage. What must be stored within a leaf are simply counts of the number of times each class label reaches that leaf, for each attribute value. This causes problems for numeric attributes, which require separate treatment. Unsupervised discretization is easy, but supervised prediscretization is trickier. A Gaussian approximation can be made for numeric attributes on a per-class basis and updated using simple incremental update algorithms for mean and variance. To prevent indefinite growth in memory requirements, a strategy must be devised to limit the total number of nodes in the tree. This can be done by deactivating leaves that look insufficiently promising in terms the accuracy gain that further development might yield. The potential gain is bounded by the expected number of mistakes a leaf might make, so this is an obvious candidate for measuring its promise. Leaves can periodically be ordered from most to least promising and deactivated accordingly. A further possibility for saving space is to abandon attributes that seem to be poor predictors and discard their statistics from the model.

Although this section has focused on decision trees for classification, researchers have studied stream-based versions of all the classical data mining problems: regression, clustering, ensemble methods, association rules, and so on. An open-source system called MOA for Massive Online Analysis, closely related to WEKA, contains a collection of online learning algorithms, as well as tools for evaluation.[4]

13.4 INCORPORATING DOMAIN KNOWLEDGE

Throughout this book we have emphasized the importance of getting to know your data when undertaking practical data mining. Knowledge of the domain is absolutely essential for success. Data about data is often called *metadata*, and one of the frontiers in machine learning is the development of ways to allow learning methods to take metadata into account in a useful way.

You don't have to look far for examples of how metadata might be applied. In Chapter 2, Input: concepts, instances, attributes, we divided attributes into nominal and numeric. But we also noted that many finer distinctions are possible. If an attribute is numeric an ordering is implied, but sometimes there is a zero point and sometimes not (for time intervals there is, but for dates there is not). Even the ordering may be nonstandard: angular degrees have a different ordering to integers because 360° is the same as 0° and 180° is the same as −180° or indeed 900°. Discretization schemes assume ordinary linear ordering, as do learning schemes that accommodate numeric attributes, but it would be a routine matter to extend them to circular orderings. Categorical data may also be ordered. Imagine how much more difficult our lives would be if there were no conventional ordering for letters of the alphabet. (Looking up a

---

[4]http://moa.cs.waikato.ac.nz. The moa, like the WEKA, is a flightless New Zealand bird, but it is very large—and also, unfortunately, extinct.

listing in the Hong Kong telephone directory presents an interesting and nontrivial problem!) And the rhythms of everyday life are reflected in circular orderings: days of the week, months of the year. To further complicate matters there are many other kinds of ordering, such as partial orderings on subsets: subset A may include subset B, or subset B may include subset A, or neither may include the other. Extending ordinary learning schemes to take account of this kind of information in a satisfactory and general way is an active research area.

Metadata often involves relations among attributes. Three kinds of relation can be distinguished: semantic, causal, and functional. A *semantic* relation between two attributes indicates that if the first is included in a rule, the second should be, too. In this case, it is known a priori that the attributes only make sense together. For example, in agricultural data that we have analyzed, an attribute called *milk production* measures how much milk an individual cow produces, and the purpose of our investigation meant that this attribute had a semantic relationship with three other attributes, *cow-identifier*, *herd-identifier*, and *farmer-identifier*. In other words, a milk production value can only be understood in the context of the cow that produced the milk, and the cow is further linked to a specific herd owned by a given farmer. Semantic relations are, of course, problem dependent: they depend not just on the dataset but also on what you are trying to do with it.

Causal relations occur when one attribute causes another. In a system that is trying to predict an attribute caused by another, we know that the other attribute should be included to make the prediction more meaningful. For example, in the agricultural data mentioned previously there is a chain from the farmer, herd, and cow identifiers, through measured attributes such as milk production, down to the attribute that records whether a particular cow was retained or sold by the farmer. Learned rules should recognize this chain of dependence.

Functional dependencies occur in many databases, and the people who create databases strive to identify them for the purpose of normalizing the relations in the database. When learning from the data, the significance of a functional dependency of one attribute on another is that if the latter is used in a rule there is no need to consider the former. Learning schemes often rediscover functional dependencies that are already known. Not only does this generate meaningless, or more accurately tautological, rules, but also other, more interesting patterns may be obscured by the functional relationships. However, there has been much work in automatic database design on the problem of inferring functional dependencies from example queries, and the methods developed should prove useful in weeding out tautological rules generated by learning schemes.

Taking these kinds of metadata, or prior domain knowledge, into account when doing induction using any of the algorithms we have met does not seem to present any deep or difficult technical challenges. The only real problem—and it is a big one—is how to express the metadata in a general and easily understandable way so that it can be generated by a person and used by the algorithm.

It seems attractive to couch the metadata knowledge in just the same representation as the machine learning scheme generates. We focus on rules, which are the norm for much of this work. The rules that specify metadata correspond to prior knowledge of the domain. Given training examples, additional rules can be derived by one of the rule induction schemes we have already met. In this way, the system might be able to combine "experience" (from examples) with "theory" (from domain knowledge). It would be capable of confirming and modifying its programmed-in knowledge based on empirical evidence. Loosely put, the user tells the system what he or she knows, gives it some examples, and it figures the rest out for itself!

To make use of prior knowledge expressed as rules in a sufficiently flexible way, it is necessary for the system to be able to perform logical deduction. Otherwise, the knowledge has to be expressed in precisely the right form for the learning algorithm to take advantage of it, which is likely to be too demanding for practical use. Consider causal metadata: if attribute A causes B and B causes C, we would like the system to deduce that A causes C rather than having to state that fact explicitly. Although in this simple example explicitly stating the new fact presents little problem, in practice, with extensive metadata, it will be unrealistic to 4expect users to express all logical consequences of their prior knowledge.

A combination of deduction from prespecified domain knowledge and induction from training examples seems like a flexible way of accommodating metadata. At one extreme, when examples are scarce (or nonexistent), deduction is the prime (or only) means of generating new rules. At the other, when examples are abundant but metadata is scarce (or nonexistent), the standard machine learning techniques described in this book suffice. Practical situations span the territory between.

This is a compelling vision, and methods of inductive logic programming, mentioned in Section 3.4, offer a general way of specifying domain knowledge explicitly through statements in a formal logic language. However, current logic programming solutions suffer serious shortcomings in real-world environments. They tend to be brittle and to lack robustness, and they may be so computation intensive as to be infeasible on datasets of any practical size. Perhaps this stems from the fact that they use first-order logic, i.e., they allow variables to be introduced into the rules. The machine learning schemes we have seen, whose input and output are represented in terms of attributes and constant values, perform their machinations in propositional logic, without variables—greatly reducing the search space and avoiding all sorts of difficult problems of circularity and termination.

Some aspire to realize the vision without the accompanying brittleness and computational infeasibility of full logic programming solutions by adopting simplified reasoning systems. Others place their faith in the general mechanism of Bayesian networks, discussed in Section 9.2, in which causal constraints can be expressed in the initial network structure and hidden variables can be postulated and evaluated automatically. Probabilistic logic learning offers a way to cope with both the complexity and the uncertainty of the real world by combining logic programming with statistical reasoning. It will be interesting to see whether systems that allow flexible specification of different types of domain knowledge will become widely deployed.

13.5 TEXT MINING

Data mining is about looking for patterns in data. Likewise, text mining is about looking for patterns in text: it is the process of analyzing text to extract information that is useful for particular purposes. Compared with the kind of data we have been talking about in this book, text is unstructured, amorphous, and difficult to deal with. Nevertheless, in modern Western culture, text is the most common vehicle for the formal exchange of information. The motivation for trying to extract information from it is compelling—even if success is only partial.

The superficial similarity between text and data mining conceals real differences. In Chapter 1, What's it all about?, we characterized data mining as the extraction of implicit, previously unknown, and potentially useful information from data. With text mining, however, the information to be extracted is clearly and explicitly stated in the text. It is not hidden at all—most authors go to great pains to make sure that they express themselves clearly and unambiguously. From a human point of view, the only sense in which it is "previously unknown" is that time restrictions make it infeasible for people to read the text themselves. The problem, of course, is that the information is not couched in a manner that is amenable to automatic processing. Text mining strives to bring it out in a form that is suitable for consumption by computers or by people who do not have time to read the full text.

Both data and text mining seek to extract information that is potentially useful. In one sense, this means *actionable*—capable of providing a basis for actions to be taken automatically. In the case of data mining, this notion can be expressed in a relatively domain-independent way: actionable patterns are ones that allow nontrivial predictions to be made on new data from the same source. Performance can be measured by counting successes and failures, statistical techniques can be applied to compare different data mining methods on the same problem, and so on. However, in many text mining situations it is hard to characterize what "actionable" means in a way that is independent of the particular domain at hand. This makes it difficult to find fair and objective measures of success.

As we have emphasized throughout this book, "potentially useful" is often given another interpretation in practical data mining: the key for success is that the information extracted must be *comprehensible* in that it helps to explain the data. This is necessary whenever the result is intended for human consumption rather than (or as well as) a basis for automatic action. This criterion is less applicable to text mining because, unlike data mining, the input itself is comprehensible. Text mining with comprehensible output is tantamount to summarizing salient features from a large body of text, which is a subfield in its own right: *text summarization*.

DOCUMENT CLASSIFICATION AND CLUSTERING

We have already encountered one important text mining problem: *document classification*, in which each instance represents a document and the instance's class is the document's topic. Documents are characterized by the words that appear in them. The presence or absence of each word can be treated as a Boolean attribute, or documents can be treated as bags of words, rather than sets, by taking word frequencies into account. We encountered this distinction in Section 4.2, where we learned how to extend Naïve Bayes to the bag-of-words representation, yielding the multinomial version of the algorithm.

There is, of course, an immense number of different words, and most of them are not very useful for document classification. This presents a classic feature selection problem. Some words—e.g., function words, often called *stopwords*—can usually be eliminated a priori, but although these occur very frequently there are not all that many of them. Other words occur so rarely that they are unlikely to be useful for classification. Paradoxically, infrequent words are common—nearly half the words in a document or corpus of documents occur just once. Nevertheless, such an overwhelming number of words remains after these word classes are removed that further feature selection may be necessary using the methods described in Section 8.1. Another issue is that the bag-of-words (or set-of-words) model neglects word order and contextual effects. There is a strong case for detecting common phrases and treating them as single units.

Document classification is supervised learning: the categories are known beforehand and given in advance for each training document. The unsupervised version of the problem is called *document clustering*. Here there is no predefined class, but groups of cognate documents are sought. Document clustering can assist information retrieval by creating links between similar documents, which in turn allows related documents to be retrieved once one of the documents has been deemed relevant to a query.

There are many applications of document classification. A relatively easy categorization task, *language identification*, provides an important piece of metadata for documents in international collections. A simple representation that works well for language identification is to characterize each document by a profile that consists of the *n-grams*, or sequences of *n* consecutive letters (for some small value such as $n = 3$), that appear in it. The most frequent 300 or so *n*-grams are highly correlated with the language. A more challenging application is *authorship ascription*, where a document's author is uncertain and must be guessed from the text. Here, the stopwords, not the content words, are the giveaway, because their distribution is author dependent but topic independent. A third problem is the *assignment of key phrases* to documents from a controlled vocabulary of possible phrases, given a large number of training documents that are tagged from this vocabulary.

INFORMATION EXTRACTION

Another general class of text mining problems is *metadata extraction*. Metadata was mentioned above as data about data: in the realm of text the term generally refers to salient features of a work, such as its author, title, subject classification, subject headings, and keywords. Metadata is a kind of highly structured (and therefore actionable) document summary. The idea of metadata is often expanded to encompass words or phrases that stand for objects or "entities" in the world, leading to the notion of *entity extraction*. Ordinary documents are full of such terms: phone numbers, fax numbers, street addresses, email addresses, email signatures, abstracts, tables of contents, lists of references, tables, figures, captions, meeting announcements, Web addresses, and more. In addition, there are countless domain-specific entities, such as international standard book numbers (ISBNs), stock symbols, chemical structures, and mathematical equations. These terms act as single vocabulary items, and many document processing tasks can be significantly improved if they are identified as such. They can aid searching, interlinking and cross-referencing between documents.

How can textual entities be identified? Rote learning, i.e., dictionary lookup, is one idea, particularly when coupled with existing resources—lists of personal names and organizations, information about locations from gazetteers, or abbreviation and acronym dictionaries. Another is to use capitalization and punctuation patterns for names and acronyms; titles (*Ms.*), suffixes (*Jr.*), and baronial prefixes (*von*); or unusual language statistics for foreign names. Regular expressions suffice for artificial constructs such as uniform resource locators (URLs); explicit grammars can be written to recognize dates and sums of money. Even the simplest task opens up opportunities for learning to cope with the huge variation that real-life documents present. As just one example, what could be simpler than looking up a name in a table? But the name of the former Libyan leader *Muammar Qaddafi* is represented in 47 different ways in documents that have been received by the Library of Congress!

Many short documents describe a particular kind of object or event, combining entities into a higher-level composite that represent the document's entire content. The task of identifying the composite structure, which can often be represented as a template with slots that are filled by individual pieces of structured information, is called *information extraction*. Once the entities have been found, the text is parsed to determine relationships among them. Typical extraction problems require finding the predicate structure of a small set of predetermined propositions. These are usually simple enough to be captured by shallow parsing techniques such as small finite-state grammars, although matters may be complicated by ambiguous pronoun references and attached prepositional phrases and other modifiers. Machine learning has been applied to information extraction by seeking rules that extract fillers for slots in the template. These rules may be couched in pattern-action form, the patterns expressing constraints on the slot-filler and words in its local context. These constraints may involve the words themselves, their part-of-speech tags, and their semantic classes.

Taking information extraction a step further, the extracted information can be used in a subsequent step to learn rules—not rules about how to extract information but rules that characterize the content of the text itself. These rules might predict the values for certain slot-fillers from the rest of the text. In certain tightly constrained situations, such as Internet job postings for computing-related jobs, information extraction based on a few manually constructed training examples can compete with an entire manually constructed database in terms of the quality of the rules inferred.

There is no real consensus about what text mining covers: broadly interpreted, all natural language processing comes under the ambit of text mining. Since their introduction, conditional random fields have been and remain one of the dominant tools in this area. The problem of extracting meeting information from unstructured emails, mentioned in Chapter 9, Probabilistic methods, is just one example: many other information extraction tasks have similar conditional random field formulations.

NATURAL LANGUAGE PROCESSING

Natural language processing, a rich field of study with a long history, is an active application area for deep learning. We have seen how latent semantic analysis (LSA) and latent Dirichlet allocation (LDA[b]) permit exploratory topic analysis of document collections. More recently, it has been observed that neural language modeling techniques can perform significantly better than LSA for preserving relationships among words; moreover, LDA[b] also has difficulty scaling to truly massive data.

Researchers at Google have created a set of language models called *word2vec*, based on single-hidden-layer networks trained with vast amounts of data—783 million words for initial experiments, and 30 billion for later ones. (Associated software is available online.) One such model produces continuous representations of words by training a neural bag-of-words model to predict words given their context. Because word order in the context window is not captured, this is known as a "continuous bag of words" model. Another model, "skip-gram," gives each word to a log-linear classifier with a linear projection layer—a form of shallow neural network—that predicts nearby words within a certain distance before and after the source word. Here the number of states for the output prediction equals the vocabulary size, and with data at this scale the vocabulary ranges from 10^5 to 10^9 terms, so the output is decomposed into a binary tree known as a "hierarchical softmax," which, for a V-word vocabulary needs to evaluate only $\log_2(V)$ rather than V output nodes.

A particularly noteworthy aspect of this work is that the representations learned yield projections for words that allow inferences about their meaning to be performed with vector operations. For example, upon projecting the words *Paris*, *France*, *Italy* and *Rome* into the learned representation, one finds that simple vector subtraction and addition yield the relationship *Paris−France+Italy* ≈*Rome*! More precisely, *Rome* is found to be the closest word when all words are projected into this representation.

Many research and development groups are mining massive quantities of text data in order to learn as much as possible from scratch, replacing features that have previously been hand-engineered by ones that are learned automatically. Large neural networks are being applied to tasks ranging from sentiment classification and translation to dialog and question answering. The deep encoder-decoder architecture discussed at the end of Chapter 10, Deep learning, represents one such example: Google researchers have used it to learn how to translate languages from scratch, based on voluminous data.

13.6 WEB MINING

The World Wide Web is a massive repository of text. Almost all of it differs from ordinary "plain" text because it contains explicit structural markup. Some markup is internal and indicates document structure or format; other markup is external and defines explicit hypertext links between documents. Both these information sources give additional leverage for mining Web documents. *Web mining* is like text mining but takes advantage of this extra information and often improves results by capitalizing on the existence of topic directories and other information on the Web.

Consider internal markup. Internet resources that contain relational data—telephone directories, product catalogs, and so on—use hypertext markup language (HTML) formatting commands to clearly present the information they contain to Web users. However, it is quite difficult to extract data from such resources in an automatic way. To do so, software systems use simple parsing modules called *wrappers* to analyze the page structure and extract the requisite information. If wrappers are coded by hand, which they often are, this is a trivial kind of web mining because it relies on the pages having a fixed, predetermined structure from which information can be extracted algorithmically. But pages rarely obey the rules. Their structures vary; Web sites evolve. Errors that are insignificant to human readers throw automatic extraction procedures completely awry. When change occurs, adjusting a wrapper manually can be a nightmare that involves getting your head around the existing code and patching it up in a way that does not cause breakage elsewhere.

WRAPPER INDUCTION

Enter *wrapper induction*—learning wrappers automatically from examples. The input is a training set of pages along with tuples representing the information derived from each page. The output is a set of rules that extracts the tuples by parsing the page. For example, the rules might look for certain HTML delimiters—paragraph boundaries (<*p*>), list entries (<*li*>), or boldface (<*b*>)—that the Web page designer has used to set off key items of information, and learn the sequence in which entities are presented. This could be accomplished by iterating over all choices of delimiters, stopping when a consistent wrapper is encountered. Then recognition will depend only on a minimal set of cues, providing some defense against extraneous text and markers in the input. Alternatively, one might follow Epicurus's advice at the end of Section 5.10 and seek a robust wrapper that uses multiple cues to guard against accidental variation. The great advantage of automatic wrapper induction is that when errors are caused by stylistic variants it is a simple matter to add these to the training data and reinduce a new wrapper that takes them into account. Wrapper induction reduces recognition problems when small changes occur and makes it far easier to produce new sets of extraction rules when structures change radically.

PAGE RANK

One of the problems with the Web is that a lot of it is rubbish. In order to separate the wheat from the chaff, a metric called PageRank was introduced by the founders of Google; it is used in various guises by other search engines too, and in many other Web mining applications. It attempts to measure the prestige of a Web page or site, where *prestige* is, according to a dictionary definition, "high standing achieved through success or influence." The hope is that this is a good way to determine authority, defined as "an accepted source of expert information or advice." Recall that the PageRank algorithm was identified in Table 13.1 as one of the top 10 data mining algorithms, the only one that we have not encountered so far. It is perhaps questionable whether it should be classed as a data mining algorithm, but it is worth describing all the same.

The key is external markup in the form of hyperlinks. In a networked community, people reward success with links. If you link to my page, it's probably because you find it useful and informative—it's a successful Web page. If a host of people link to it, that indicates prestige: my page is successful and influential. Look at Fig. 13.1, which shows a tiny fraction of the Web, including links between pages. Which ones do you think are most authoritative? Page **F** has five incoming links, which indicates that five people found it worth linking to, so there's a good chance that this page is more authoritative than the others. **B** is second best, with four links.

Merely counting links is a crude measure. Some Web pages have thousands of outgoing links whereas others have just one or two. Rarer links are more discriminating and should count more than others. A link from your page to mine bestows more prestige if your page has few outlinks. In Fig. 13.1 the many links emanating from page **A** mean that each one carries less weight, simply because **A** is a prolific linker. From **F**'s point of view, the links from **D** and **E** may be more valuable than the one from **A**. There is another factor: a link is more valuable if it comes from a prestigious page. The link from **B** to **F** may be better than the others into **F** because **B** is more prestigious. Admittedly this factor involves a certain circularity, and without further analysis it's not clear that it can be made to work. But indeed it can.

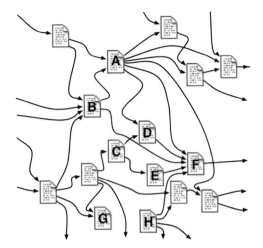

FIGURE 13.1

A tangled web.

Here are the details. We define the PageRank of a page to be a number between 0 and 1 that measures its prestige. Each link into the page contributes to its PageRank. The amount it contributes is the PageRank of the linking page divided by the number of outlinks from it. The PageRank of any page is calculated by summing that quantity over all links into it. The value for **D** in Fig. 13.1 is calculated by adding one-fifth of the value for **A** (because it has five outlinks) to one-half the value for **C**.

A simple iterative method is used to resolve the apparently circular nature of the calculation. Start by randomly assigning an initial value to each page. Then recompute each page's PageRank by summing the appropriate quantities, described earlier, over its inlinks. If the initial values are thought of as an approximation to the true value of PageRank, the new values are a better approximation. Keep going, generating a third approximation, and a fourth, and so on. At each stage, recompute the PageRank for every page in the Web. Stop when, for every page, the next iteration turns out to give almost exactly the same PageRank as the previous one.

Subject to two modifications discussed below, this iteration is guaranteed to converge, and fairly quickly too. Although the precise details are shrouded in secrecy, today's search engines probably seek an accuracy for the final values of between 10^{-9} and 10^{-12}. An early experiment reported 50 iterations for a much smaller version of the Web than today's, before the details became commercial; several times as many iterations are needed now. Google is thought to run programs for several days to perform the PageRank calculation for the entire Web, and the operation is—or at any rate used to be—performed every few weeks.

There are two problems with the calculation we have described. You probably have a mental picture of PageRank flowing through the tangled web of Fig. 13.1, coming into a page through its inlinks and leaving it through its outlinks. What if there are no inlinks (page **H**)? Or no outlinks (page **G**)?

To operationalize this picture, imagine a surfer who clicks links at random. They takes the current page, choose an outlink at random, and go to that link's target page. The probability of taking any particular link is smaller if there are many outlinks, which is exactly the behavior we want from PageRank. It turns out that the PageRank of a given page is proportional to the probability that the random surfer lands on that page.

Now the problem raised by a page with no outlinks becomes apparent: it's a PageRank sink because when surfers comes in they cannot get out. More generally, a set of pages might link to each other but not to anywhere else. This incestuous group is also a PageRank sink: the random surfer gets stuck in a trap. And a page with no inlinks? Random surfers never reach it. In fact, they never reach any group of pages that has no inlinks from the rest of the Web, even though it may have internal links, and outlinks to the Web at large.

These two problems mean that the iterative calculation described above does not converge, as we earlier claimed it would. But the solution is simple: *teleportation*. With a certain small probability, just make the surfer arrive at a randomly chosen page instead of following a link from the one they are on. That solves both problems. If surfers are stuck at **G** they will eventually teleport out of it. And if they can't reach **H** by surfing, they will eventually teleport into it.

The teleport probability has a strong influence on the rate of convergence of the iterative algorithm—and on the accuracy of its results. At the extreme, if it were equal to 1, meaning that the surfer always teleported, the link structure would have no effect on PageRank, and no iteration would be necessary. If it were 0 and the surfer never teleported, the calculation would not converge at all. Early published experiments used a teleportation probability of 0.15; some speculate that search engines increase it a little to hasten convergence.

Instead of teleporting to a randomly chosen page, you could choose a predetermined probability for each page, and—once you had decided to teleport—use that probability to determine where to land. This does not affect the calculation. But it does affect the result. If a page was discriminated against by receiving a smaller probability than the others, it would end up with a smaller PageRank than it deserves. This gives search engine operators an opportunity to influence the results of the calculation—an opportunity that they probably use to discriminate against certain sites (e.g., ones they believe are trying to gain an unfair advantage by exploiting the PageRank system). This is the stuff of which lawsuits are made.

13.7 IMAGES AND SPEECH

Until recently, images and speech signals received less attention from data mining researchers. However, the deep learning renaissance has changed all that. Signal processing in general is an area where massive amounts of data are easily available, and seems to be well suited to the kind of automatic extraction of low-level features that are built up into successively higher levels that deep networks do so well. The world abounds with signal data—but it is generally unlabeled. The production of large collections of *labeled* data is stimulating practitioners to apply deep learning techniques to many signal processing tasks, principally image recognition and face verification and recognition.

IMAGES

Chapter 10, Deep learning, discussed how deep learning techniques have revolutionized aspects of the field of computer vision. This impact has only been possible because academic groups and technology companies made substantial investments in mining and labeling data on a large scale. The availability of carefully curated datasets enables high-capacity supervised or discriminative deep learning techniques to push recognition performance into the realm of usability for many applications. In addition to the examples highlighted below, convolutional neural network architectures have been used on tasks ranging from segmenting brain tumors to computing the depth in a scene from stereo cameras; the *Further reading* section gives pointers to specific examples.

Deep convolutional neural network techniques have transformed the field of object category recognition. On large-scale visual recognition challenges such as ImageNet they can outperform people in terms of agreement with human judgments. ImageNet imagery was mined from the Internet and labeled in a large-scale academic project. Google has prepared a dataset of digits obtained by mining and labeling house numbers in their massive collection of Street View images; again, deep convolutional networks outperform people in terms of agreement with human judgments.

There is an important distinction between recognizing object categories and identifying particular objects: identifying *your car* in a photograph is quite different from recognizing that *a car* is present. Here also deep learning based methods are continually improving recognition performance. An alternative approach, "SIFT descriptors," which are based on the scale-invariant feature transform, are already deployed in systems that recognize specific objects. These descriptors are computed from "interest points" that are found in an image—things like corners, which are easy to find and localize in images of the same object from different viewpoints. Once these points have been found, a descriptor inspired by the human visual system is computed based on a trick that helps select an appropriate scale and orientation. This involves cutting out a patch with a certain orientation and rotation, and then creating a histogram of image gradients using the patch. While SIFT descriptors find their greatest application in 3D reconstruction, panoramic image creation and robotic mapping, they are also widely used for identifying and tracking specific instances of objects.

Face recognition, an important special case of object recognition, has been the subject of intense research for decades—and deep convolutional networks have transformed the field. Better-than-human performance has been achieved on the task of face verification, using databases such as the "Labeled faces in the wild" data collected by the University of Massachusetts. In face verification one is given two photographs of faces and asked whether they belong to the same person or not. Good results are achieved using a special "Siamese network" architecture that takes two images as input and compares them using the internal representation of the convolutional neural network. The images are generally preprocessed to center the faces, crop them, and register them on a common coordinate system. Facial keypoint or landmark detection methods are used to help with the registration and warping process, or to localize key zones to be used as input.

It is worth noting, given the discussion of data mining and ethics in Chapter 1, What's it all about?, that face verification and face recognition raise difficult ethical issues. Federal governments deploy the technology in the fight against international terrorism; airports use it to reduce lineups at immigration. Its potential application in widespread video surveillance has a profound effect on the balance between security and privacy, and other civil liberties. At the individual level, stalkers would welcome end-user web services for face recognition.

SPEECH

Speech recognition is rapidly becoming a widely used technology. Major companies use large datasets to render their systems robust to different speakers and noise sources. The classical architecture uses a signal processing front end to compute features inspired by the human auditory system from a spectral analysis of the audio input, and passes them to a large system of hidden Markov models that have Gaussian mixture models for their observation likelihoods. Sophisticated language models are used to help disambiguate what words are present in the audio. Here again deep learning methods have been having substantial impact, and many large industrial groups are replacing elements of the classic speech recognition pipeline with deep learning techniques such as recurrent neural networks.

13.8 ADVERSARIAL SITUATIONS

A prime application of machine learning is junk email filtering. When we wrote the second edition of this book (late 2004) the scourge of unwanted email was a burning issue; by the writing of the third edition of this book (early 2010), the problem had abated despite the continual growth of spam email (by some estimates it accounts for 95% of all emails). This is largely due to the widespread use of spam filtering, which often uses learning techniques. At first blush junk email filtering appears to present a standard problem of document classification: divide documents into "ham" and "spam" on the basis of the text they contain, guided by training data, of which there are copious amounts. But it differs from ordinary document classification because it involves an adversarial aspect. The documents that are being classified are not chosen at random from an unimaginably huge set of all possible documents; they contain emails that are carefully crafted to evade the filtering process, designed specifically to beat the system.

Early spam filters simply discarded messages containing "spammy" words that connote such things as sex, lucre, and quackery. Of course, much legitimate correspondence concerns gender, money, and medicine: a balance must be struck. So filter designers recruited Bayesian text classification schemes that learned to strike an appropriate balance during the training process. Spammers quickly adjusted with techniques that concealed the spammy words by misspelling them; overwhelmed them with legitimate text, perhaps printed in white on a white background so that only the filter saw it; or simply put the spam text elsewhere, in an image or a URL that most mail readers download automatically.

The problem is complicated by the fact that it is hard to compare spam detection algorithms objectively. Although training data abounds, privacy issues preclude publishing large public corpora of representative email. And there are strong temporal effects. Spam changes character rapidly, invalidating sensitive statistical tests such as cross-validation. Finally, the bad guys can also use machine learning. For example, if they could get hold of examples of what your filter blocks and what it lets through, they could use this as training data to learn how to evade it.

There are, unfortunately, many other examples of adversarial learning situations in our world today. Closely related to junk email is search engine spam: sites that attempt to deceive Internet search engines into placing them prominently in lists of search results. Highly ranked pages yield direct financial benefits to their owners because they present opportunities for advertising, providing strong motivation for profit seekers. Then there are the computer virus wars, in which designers of viruses and virus-protection software react to one another's innovations. Here the motivation tends to be general disruption and denial of service rather than monetary gain.

Computer network security is a continually escalating battle. Protectors harden networks, operating systems, and applications, and attackers find vulnerabilities in all three areas. Intrusion detection systems sniff out unusual patterns of activity that might be caused by a hacker's reconnaissance activity. Attackers realize this and try to obfuscate their trails, perhaps by working indirectly or by spreading their activities over a long time—or, conversely, by striking very quickly. Machine learning is being applied to this problem in an attempt to discover semantic connections among attacker traces in computer network data that intrusion detection systems miss. This is a large-scale problem: audit logs used to monitor computer network security can amount to gigabytes a day even in medium-sized organizations.

Many automated threat detection systems are based on matching current data to known attack types. The U.S. Federal Aviation Administration developed the *Computer Assisted Passenger Pre-Screening System* (CAPPS), which screens airline passengers on the basis of their flight records and flags individuals for additional checked baggage screening. Although the exact details are unpublished, CAPPS is, e.g., thought to assign higher threat scores to cash payments. However, this approach can only spot known or anticipated threats. Researchers are using unsupervised approaches such as anomaly and outlier detection in an attempt to detect suspicious activity. As well as flagging potential threats, anomaly detection systems can be applied to the detection of illegal activities such as financial fraud and money laundering.

Data mining is being used today to sift through huge volumes of data in the name of homeland defense. Heterogeneous information such as financial transactions, health-care records, and network traffic is being mined to create profiles, construct social network models, and detect terrorist communications. This activity raises serious privacy concerns and has resulted in the development of privacy-preserving data mining techniques. These algorithms try to discern patterns in the data without accessing the original data directly, typically by distorting it with random values. To preserve privacy, they must guarantee that the mining process does not receive enough information to reconstruct the original data. This is easier said than done.

On a lighter note, not all adversarial data mining is aimed at combating nefarious activity. Multiagent systems in complex, noisy real-time domains involve autonomous agents that must both collaborate in a team and compete against antagonists. If you are having trouble visualizing this, think soccer. Robo-soccer is a rich and popular domain for exploring how machine learning can be applied to such difficult problems—primarily using reinforcement learning techniques, which are beyond the scope of this book. Players must not only hone low-level skills but must also learn to work together and adapt to the behavior patterns of different opponents.

Finally, machine learning has been used to solve an actual historical literary mystery by unmasking a prolific author who had attempted to conceal his identity. Ben Ish Chai was the leading rabbinic scholar in Baghdad in the late 19th century. Among his vast literary legacy are two separate collections of about 500 Hebrew-Aramaic letters written in response to legal queries. He is known to have written one collection. Although he claims to have found the other in an archive, historians suspect that he wrote it, too, but attempted to disguise his authorship by deliberately altering his style. The problem this case presents to machine learning is that there is no corpus of work to ascribe to the mystery author. There were a few known candidates, but the letters could equally well have been written by anyone else. A new technique appropriately called *unmasking* was developed that creates a model to distinguish the known author's work A from the unknown author's work X, iteratively removes those features that are most useful for distinguishing the two, and examines the speed with which cross-validation accuracy degrades as more features are removed. The hypothesis is that if work X is written by work A's author, who is trying to conceal his identity, whatever differences there are between work X and work A will be reflected in only a relatively small number of features compared with the differences between work X and the works of a completely different author, say the author of work B. In other words, when work X is compared with works A and B, the accuracy curve as features are removed will decline much faster for work A than it does for work B. It was concluded that Ben Ish Chai did indeed write the mystery letters. This technique is a striking example of original and creative use of machine learning in an adversarial situation.

13.9 UBIQUITOUS DATA MINING

We began this book by pointing out that we are overwhelmed with data. Nowhere does this impact the lives of ordinary people more than on the World Wide Web. No-one can keep pace with the information explosion. Whereas data mining originated in the corporate world because that's where the databases are, text and web mining are moving machine learning technology out of the companies and into the home. Whenever we are overwhelmed by data on the Web, mining techniques promise tools to tame it. Applications are legion. Finding friends and contacting them, maintaining financial portfolios, shopping for bargains in an electronic world, using data detectors of any kind—all of these could be accomplished automatically without explicit programming. Already mining techniques are being used to predict what link you're going to click next, to organize documents for you, sort your mail, and prioritize your search results. In a world where information is overwhelming, disorganized and anarchic, text and web mining may be the solution we so desperately need.

Many believe that the Web is but the harbinger of an even greater paradigm shift: *ubiquitous computing*. Small portable devices are everywhere—mobile phones, personal digital assistants, personal stereo and video players, digital cameras, mobile Web access. Already some devices integrate all these functions. They know our location in physical time and space, help us communicate in social space, organize our personal planning space, recall our past, and envelop us in global information space. It is easy to find scores of processors in a middle-class home in the US today, and they often communicate with one another and with the global information infrastructure. Thus the potential for data mining will soar.

Take consumer music. Popular music leads the vanguard of technological advance. Sony's original Walkman paved the way to today's ubiquitous portable electronics. Apple's iPOD pioneered large-scale portable storage. Napster's network technology spurred the development of peer-to-peer protocols. Recommender systems such as Firefly brought computing to social networks.

Content-aware music services are migrating to portable devices. Applications for data mining in networked communities of people are legion: discovering musical trends, tracking preferences and tastes, and analyzing listening behaviors.

Ubiquitous computing weaves digital space closely into real-world activities. To many, extrapolating their own computer experiences of extreme frustration, arcane technology, perceived personal inadequacy, and machine failure, this sounds like a nightmare. But proponents point out that it can't be like that, because, if it is, it won't work. Today's visionaries foresee a world of "calm" computing in which hidden machines silently cooperate behind the scenes to make our lives richer and easier. They'll reach beyond the big problems of corporate finance and school homework to the little annoyances such as where are the car keys, can I get a parking place, and is that shirt I saw last week at Macy's still on the rack? Clocks will find the correct time after a power failure, the microwave will download new recipes from the Internet, kid's toys will refresh themselves with new games and new vocabularies. Clothes labels will track washing, coffee cups will alert cleaning staff to mold, light switches will save energy if no-one is in the room, and pencils will digitize everything we draw. Where will data mining be in this new world? Everywhere!

It's hard to point to examples of a future that does not yet exist. But advances in user interface technology are suggestive. Many repetitive tasks in direct-manipulation computer interfaces cannot be automated with standard application tools, forcing users to perform the same interface actions over and over again. This typifies the frustrations alluded to previously: who's in charge—me or it? Experienced programmers might write a script to carry out such tasks on their behalf, but as operating systems accrue layer upon layer of complexity the power of programmers to command the machine is eroded and vanishes altogether when complex functionality is embedded in appliances rather than in general-purpose computers.

Research in *programming by demonstration* enables ordinary users to automate predictable tasks without requiring any programming knowledge at all. The user need only know how to perform the task in the usual way to be able to communicate it to the computer. One system, called *Familiar*, helps users automate iterative tasks involving existing applications on Macintosh computers. It works across applications and can work with completely new ones never before encountered. It does this by using Apple's scripting language to glean information from each application and exploiting that information to make predictions. The agent tolerates noise. It generates explanations to inform the user about its predictions, and incorporates feedback. It's adaptive: it learns specialized tasks for individual users. Furthermore, it is sensitive to each user's style. If two people were teaching a task and happened to give identical demonstrations, Familiar would not necessarily infer identical programs—it's tuned to their habits because it learns from their interaction history.

Familiar employs standard machine learning techniques to infer the user's intent. Rules are used to evaluate predictions so that the best one can be presented to the user at each point. These rules are conditional so that users can teach classification tasks such as sorting files based on their type and assigning labels based on their size. They are learned incrementally: the agent adapts to individual users by recording their interaction history.

Many difficulties arise. One is scarcity of data. Users are loth to demonstrate several iterations of a task—they think the agent should immediately catch on to what they are doing. Whereas a data miner would consider a 100-instance dataset miniscule, users bridle at the prospect of demonstrating a task even half a dozen times. A second difficulty is the plethora of attributes. The computer desktop environment has hundreds of features that any given action might depend upon. This means that small datasets are overwhelmingly likely to contain attributes that are apparently highly predictive but nevertheless irrelevant, and specialized statistical tests are needed to compare alternative hypotheses. A third is that the iterative, improvement-driven development style that characterizes data mining applications fails. It is impossible *in principle* to create a fixed training and testing corpus for an interactive problem such as programming by demonstration because each improvement in the agent alters the test data by affecting how users react to it. A fourth is that existing application programs provide limited access to application and user data: often the raw material on which successful operation depends is inaccessible, buried deep within the application program.

Machine learning is already widely used at work. Text and Web mining is bringing the techniques in this book into our own lives, as we read our email and surf the Web. As for the future, it will be stranger than we can imagine. The spreading computing infrastructure will offer untold opportunities for learning. Machine learning will be in there, behind the scenes, playing a role that will turn out to be foundational.

13.10 FURTHER READING AND BIBLIOGRAPHIC NOTES

Wu et al. (2008) describe the process of identifying the top 10 algorithms in data mining for presentation at the *International Conference on Data Mining* in 2006 in Hong Kong and have followed this up with a book that describes all the algorithms (Wu and Kumar, 2009). The paper on the "illusion of progress" in classification is by Hand (2006), and it was he who found that a very simple method achieves more than 90% of the classification improvement yielded by the most sophisticated scheme.

There is a substantial volume of literature that treats the topic of massive datasets, and we can only point to a few references here. Fayyad and Smyth (1995) describe the application of data mining to voluminous data from scientific experiments. Shafer, Agrawal, and Metha (1996) describe a parallel version of a top-down decision tree inducer. A sequential decision tree algorithm for massive disk-resident datasets has been developed by Mehta, Agrawal, and Rissanen

(1996). The technique of applying any algorithm to a large dataset by splitting it into smaller chunks and bagging or boosting the result is described by Breiman (1999); Frank, Holmes, Kirkby, and Hall (2002) explain the related pruning and selection scheme.

Early work on incremental work on decision trees is reported by Utgoff (1989) and Utgoff, Berkman, and Clouse (1997). The Hoeffding tree was introduced by Domingos and Hulten (2000). Our description of it, including extensions and improvement, closely follows Kirkby's (2007) PhD thesis. The MOA system is described by Bifet, Holmes, Kirkby, and Pfahringer (2010).

Despite its importance, comparatively little seems to have been written about the general problem of incorporating metadata into practical data mining. A scheme for encoding domain knowledge into propositional rules and its use for both deduction and induction has been investigated by Giraud-Carrier (1998). The related area of inductive logic programming, which deals with knowledge represented by first-order logic rules, is covered by Bergadano and Gunetti (1996). Probabilistic logic learning is covered by de Raedt (2008).

Text mining is a broad area, and there are few comprehensive surveys of the area as a whole: Witten (2004) provides one. A large number of feature selection and machine learning techniques have been applied to text categorization (Sebastiani, 2002). Martin (1995) describes applications of document clustering to information retrieval. Cavnar and Trenkle (1994) show how to use n-gram profiles to ascertain with high accuracy the language in which a document is written. The use of support vector machines for authorship ascription is described by Diederich, Kindermann, Leopold, and Paass (2003); the same technology was used by Dumais, Platt, Heckerman, and Sahami (1998) to assign key phrases from a controlled vocabulary to documents on the basis of a large number of training documents. The use of machine learning to extract key phrases from the document text has been investigated by Turney (1999), Frank, Paynter, Witten, Gutwin, and Nevill-Manning (1999) and Medelyan and Witten (2008).

Appelt (1999) describes many problems of information extraction. Many authors have applied machine learning to seek rules that extract slot-fillers for templates, e.g., Soderland, Fisher, Aseltine, and Lehnert (1995), Huffman (1996), and Freitag (2002). Califf and Mooney (1999) and Nahm and Mooney (2000) investigated the problem of extracting information from job ads posted on Internet newsgroups. An approach to finding information in running text based on compression techniques has been reported by Witten, Bray, Mahoui, and Teahan (1999a). Mann (1993) notes the plethora of variations of *Muammar Qaddafi* on documents received by the Library of Congress.

Chakrabarti (2003) has written an excellent and comprehensive book on techniques of Web mining. Kushmerick, Weld, and Doorenbos (1997) developed techniques of wrapper induction. The founders of Google wrote an early paper that introduced the PageRank algorithm (Brin and Page, 1998). At the same time Kleinberg (1998) described a system called HITS (for hypertext-induced topic selection) that has some superficial similarities but produces strikingly different results.

The first paper on junk email filtering was written by Sahami, Dumais, Heckerman, and Horvitz (1998). Our material on computer network security is culled from Yurcik et al. (2003). The information on the CAPPS system comes from the U.S. House of Representatives Subcommittee on Aviation (2002), and the use of unsupervised learning for threat detection is described by Bay and Schwabacher (2003). Issues with privacy-preserving data mining techniques are discussed by Datta, Kargupta, and Sivakumar (2003). Stone and Veloso (2000) surveyed multiagent systems of the kind that are used for playing robo-soccer from a machine learning perspective. The fascinating story of Ben Ish Chai and the technique used to unmask him is from Koppel and Schler (2004).

A popular early framework for neural probabilistic language models was proposed by Bengio, Ducharme, Vincent, and Janvin (2003): a key element of the approach is to project words into a continuous vector representation. Extending the general idea, Collobert and Weston (2008) present a large unified neural network architecture for performing many natural language processing tasks using the same underlying network and shared word representations, and showed that its performance is competitive across many common tasks. The influential *word2vec* technique was proposed by Mikolov, Chen, Corrado, and Dean, (2013a, 2013b), while Morin and Bengio (2005) explored the hierarchical softmax technique for language modeling.

Russakovsky et al. (2015) reviews the ImageNet challenge and the rise of convolutional neural networks to prominence in object category recognition. The Google Street View house numbers are described by Netzer et al. (2011), who estimate human performance at 98% accuracy—and now many experiments with convolutional neural networks described in the literature exceed this figure. David Lowe invented SIFT descriptors. Lowe (2004) gives details of their implementation and applications: they work well, and have been patented.

Facebook's "DeepFace" Siamese architecture for face verification uses a facial keypoint detector followed by a sophisticated 3D warping procedure to frontalize faces (Taigman, Yang, Ranzato, & Wolf, 2014). Of course, Facebook has access to a huge labeled database—4.4 million labeled faces from 4000 people (about 1000 each, on average). Siamese neural architectures were proposed by Bromley, Guyon, LeCun, Säckinger, and Shah (1994). The first system to produce face verification that rivaled human performance was Sun, Chen, Wang, and Tang (2014)'s convolutional neural network, which used a 200,000-image database of faces of 10,000 celebrities. This system uses fewer facial landmarks, and crops patches out of images centered on the key points; ensembles of many models produced the best performance.

Amongst many other applications, Havaei et al. (2016) used deep convolutional neural networks for brain tumor segmentation; Zbontar and LeCun (2015) present impressive results for stereo vision.

The vision of calm computing, as well as the examples we have mentioned, is from Weiser (1996) and Weiser and Brown (1997). More information on different methods of programming by demonstration can be found in compendia by Cypher

(1993) and Lieberman (2001). Mitchell, Caruana, Freitag, McDermott, and Zabowski (1994) report some experience with learning apprentices. Familiar is described by Paynter (2000). Permutation tests (Good, 1994) are statistical tests that are suitable for small sample problems: Frank (2000) describes their application in machine learning.

13.11 WEKA IMPLEMENTATIONS

- *HoeffdingTree* (creates decision trees and modifies them incrementally).

Appendix A: Theoretical foundations

A.1 MATRIX ALGEBRA

BASIC MANIPULATIONS AND PROPERTIES

A column vector $\mathbf{x}$ with d dimensions can be written

$$\mathbf{x} \equiv \begin{bmatrix} x_1 \\ x_2 \\ \vdots \\ x_d \end{bmatrix} = \begin{bmatrix} x_1 & x_2 & \cdots & x_d \end{bmatrix}^T,$$

where the *transpose* operator, superscript T, allows it be written as a transposed row vector—which is useful when defining vectors in running text. In this book, vectors are assumed to be row vectors.

The transpose $\mathbf{A}^T$ of a matrix $\mathbf{A}$ involves copying all the rows of the original matrix $\mathbf{A}$ into the columns of $\mathbf{A}^T$. Thus a matrix with m rows and n columns becomes a matrix with n rows and m columns:

$$\mathbf{A} \equiv \begin{bmatrix} a_{11} & a_{12} & \cdots & a_{1n} \\ a_{21} & a_{21} & \cdots & a_{2n} \\ \vdots & \vdots & \ddots & \vdots \\ a_{m1} & a_{m2} & \cdots & a_{mn} \end{bmatrix} \Rightarrow \mathbf{A}^T = \begin{bmatrix} a_{11} & a_{21} & \cdots & a_{m1} \\ a_{12} & a_{21} & \cdots & a_{m2} \\ \vdots & \vdots & \ddots & \vdots \\ a_{1n} & a_{2n} & \cdots & a_{nm} \end{bmatrix}.$$

The *dot product* or *inner product* between vector $\mathbf{x}$ and vector $\mathbf{y}$ of the same dimensionality yields a scalar quantity,

$$\mathbf{x} \cdot \mathbf{y} = \langle \mathbf{x}, \mathbf{y} \rangle = \mathbf{x}^T \mathbf{y} = \sum_{i=1}^{D} x_i y_i.$$

For example, the Euclidean norm can be written as the square root of the dot product of a vector $\mathbf{x}$ with itself, $||\mathbf{x}||_2 = \sqrt{\mathbf{x}^T \mathbf{x}}$.

The *tensor product* or *outer product* $\otimes$ between an m-dimensional vector $\mathbf{x}$ and an n-dimensional vector $\mathbf{y}$ yields a matrix,

$$\mathbf{x} \otimes \mathbf{y} \equiv \mathbf{x}\mathbf{y}^T = \begin{bmatrix} x_1 \\ x_2 \\ \vdots \\ x_m \end{bmatrix} \begin{bmatrix} y_1 & y_2 & \cdots & y_n \end{bmatrix} = \begin{bmatrix} x_1 y_1 & x_1 y_2 & \cdots & x_1 y_n \\ x_2 y_1 & x_2 y_2 & \cdots & x_2 y_n \\ \vdots & \vdots & \ddots & \vdots \\ x_m y_1 & x_m y_2 & \cdots & x_m y_n \end{bmatrix}$$

Given an N row and K column matrix $\mathbf{A}$, and a K row and M column matrix $\mathbf{B}$, if we write each row of $\mathbf{A}$ as $\mathbf{a}_n^T$ and each column of $\mathbf{B}$ as $\mathbf{b}_m$, the matrix product $\mathbf{AB}$ (i.e., matrix multiplication) can be written

$$\mathbf{AB} = \begin{bmatrix} \mathbf{a}_1^T \\ \mathbf{a}_2^T \\ \vdots \\ \mathbf{a}_N^T \end{bmatrix} [\, \mathbf{b}_1 \quad \mathbf{b}_2 \quad \cdots \quad \mathbf{b}_M \,] = \begin{bmatrix} \mathbf{a}_1^T\mathbf{b}_1 & \mathbf{a}_1^T\mathbf{b}_2 & \cdots & \mathbf{a}_1^T\mathbf{b}_M \\ \mathbf{a}_2^T\mathbf{b}_1 & \mathbf{a}_2^T\mathbf{b}_2 & \cdots & \mathbf{a}_2^T\mathbf{b}_M \\ \vdots & \vdots & \ddots & \vdots \\ \mathbf{a}_N^T\mathbf{b}_1 & \mathbf{a}_N^T\mathbf{b}_2 & \cdots & \mathbf{a}_N^T\mathbf{b}_M \end{bmatrix}.$$

If we write each column of $\mathbf{A}$ as $\mathbf{a}_k$ and each row of $\mathbf{B}$ as $\mathbf{b}_k^T$, the matrix product $\mathbf{AB}$ can also be written in terms of tensor products

$$\mathbf{AB} = [\, \mathbf{a}_1 \quad \mathbf{a}_2 \quad \cdots \quad \mathbf{a}_K \,] \begin{bmatrix} \mathbf{b}_1^T \\ \mathbf{b}_2^T \\ \vdots \\ \mathbf{b}_K^T \end{bmatrix} = \sum_{k=1}^{K} \mathbf{a}_k\mathbf{b}_k^T.$$

The *elementwise product* or *Hadamard product* of two matrices that are of the same size is

$$\mathbf{A} \circ \mathbf{B} = \begin{bmatrix} a_{11} & a_{12} & \cdots & a_{1n} \\ a_{21} & a_{21} & \cdots & a_{2n} \\ \vdots & \vdots & \ddots & \vdots \\ a_{m1} & a_{m2} & \cdots & a_{mn} \end{bmatrix} \circ \begin{bmatrix} b_{11} & b_{12} & \cdots & b_{1n} \\ b_{21} & b_{21} & \cdots & b_{2n} \\ \vdots & \vdots & \ddots & \vdots \\ b_{m1} & b_{m2} & \cdots & b_{mn} \end{bmatrix}$$

$$= \begin{bmatrix} a_{11}b_{11} & a_{12}b_{12} & \cdots & a_{1n}b_{1n} \\ a_{211}b_{21} & b_{21}b_{21} & \cdots & a_{2n}b_{2n} \\ \vdots & \vdots & \ddots & \vdots \\ a_{m1}b_{m1} & a_{m2}b_{m2} & \cdots & a_{mn}b_{mn} \end{bmatrix}.$$

A square matrix $\mathbf{A}$ with n rows and n columns is *invertible* if there exists a square matrix $\mathbf{B} = \mathbf{A}^{-1}$ such that $\mathbf{AB} = \mathbf{BA} = \mathbf{I}$, where $\mathbf{I}$ is the identity matrix consisting of all zeros except that all diagonal elements are one. Square matrices that are not invertible are called *singular*. A square matrix $\mathbf{A}$ is singular if and only if its determinant, $\det(\mathbf{A})$, is zero. The following equation for the inverse shows why a zero determinant implies that a matrix is not invertible:

$$\mathbf{A}^{-1} = \frac{1}{\det(\mathbf{A})}\mathbf{C}^T,$$

where $\det(\mathbf{A})$ is the determinant of $\mathbf{A}$ and $\mathbf{C}$ is another matrix known as the cofactor matrix. Finally, if a matrix $\mathbf{A}$ is orthogonal, then $\mathbf{A}^{-1} = \mathbf{A}^T$.

DERIVATIVES OF VECTOR AND SCALAR FUNCTIONS

Given a scalar function y of an m-dimensional column vector $\mathbf{x}$,

$$\frac{\partial y}{\partial \mathbf{x}} \equiv \begin{bmatrix} \dfrac{\partial y}{\partial x_1} \\[2ex] \dfrac{\partial y}{\partial x_2} \\[2ex] \vdots \\[2ex] \dfrac{\partial y_1}{\partial x_m} \end{bmatrix} = \mathbf{g}.$$

This quantity is known as the *gradient*, $\mathbf{g}$. We have defined it here as a column vector, but it is sometimes defined as a row vector. Defining the gradient as a column vector implies certain orientations for the other quantities defined below, so keep in mind that the derivatives that follow are sometimes defined as the transposes of those given here. Using the definition and orientation above we can write the types of parameter updates frequently used in algorithms like gradient descent in vector form with expressions such as $\boldsymbol{\theta}^{\text{new}} = \boldsymbol{\theta}^{\text{old}} - \mathbf{g}$, where $\boldsymbol{\theta}$ is a parameter (column) vector.

Given a scalar x and n-dimensional vector function $\mathbf{y}$,

$$\frac{\partial \mathbf{y}}{\partial x} \equiv \begin{bmatrix} \dfrac{\partial y_1}{\partial x} & \dfrac{\partial y_2}{\partial x} & \cdots & \dfrac{\partial y_n}{\partial x} \end{bmatrix}.$$

For an m-dimensional vector $\mathbf{x}$ and an n-dimensional vector $\mathbf{y}$, the *Jacobian matrix* is given by

$$\frac{\partial \mathbf{y}}{\partial \mathbf{x}} \equiv \begin{bmatrix} \dfrac{\partial y_1}{\partial x_1} & \dfrac{\partial y_2}{\partial x_1} & \cdots & \dfrac{\partial y_n}{\partial x_1} \\[2ex] \dfrac{\partial y_1}{\partial x_2} & \dfrac{\partial y_2}{\partial x_2} & \cdots & \dfrac{\partial y_n}{\partial x_2} \\[2ex] \vdots & \vdots & \ddots & \vdots \\[2ex] \dfrac{\partial y_1}{\partial x_m} & \dfrac{\partial y_2}{\partial x_m} & \cdots & \dfrac{\partial y_n}{\partial x_m} \end{bmatrix}.$$

The Jacobian is sometimes defined as the transpose of this quantitiy even given the other definitions above. Watch out for the implications. The derivative of a scalar function $y = f(\mathbf{X})$ with respect to an $m \times n$ dimensional matrix $\mathbf{X}$ is known as a *gradient matrix* and is given by

$$\frac{\partial f}{\partial \mathbf{X}} \equiv \begin{bmatrix} \dfrac{\partial y}{\partial x_{11}} & \dfrac{\partial y}{\partial x_{12}} & \cdots & \dfrac{\partial y}{\partial x_{1n}} \\[2ex] \dfrac{\partial y}{\partial x_{21}} & \dfrac{\partial y}{\partial x_{22}} & \cdots & \dfrac{\partial y}{\partial x_{2n}} \\[2ex] \vdots & \vdots & \ddots & \vdots \\[2ex] \dfrac{\partial y}{\partial x_{m1}} & \dfrac{\partial y}{\partial x_{m2}} & \cdots & \dfrac{\partial y}{\partial x_{mn}} \end{bmatrix} = \mathbf{G}.$$

Table A.1 Quantities That Result From Various Derivatives
(After Minka, 2000)

	Scalar $\dfrac{\partial f}{\cdot}$	Vector $\dfrac{\partial \mathbf{f}}{\cdot}$	Matrix $\dfrac{\partial \mathbf{F}}{\cdot}$
Scalar $\dfrac{\cdot}{\partial x}$	Scalar: $\dfrac{\partial f}{\partial x} = g$	Vector: $\dfrac{\partial \mathbf{f}}{\partial x} \equiv \left[\dfrac{\partial f_i}{\partial x}\right] = \mathbf{g}^T$	Matrix: $\dfrac{\partial \mathbf{F}}{\partial x} \equiv \left[\dfrac{\partial f_{ij}}{\partial x}\right] = \mathbf{G}^T$
Vector $\dfrac{\cdot}{\partial \mathbf{x}}$	Vector: $\dfrac{\partial f}{\partial \mathbf{x}} \equiv \left[\dfrac{\partial f}{\partial x_i}\right] = \mathbf{g}$	Matrix: $\dfrac{\partial \mathbf{f}}{\partial \mathbf{x}} \equiv \left[\dfrac{\partial f_i}{\partial x_j}\right] = \mathbf{G}$	Tensor: $\dfrac{\partial \mathbf{F}}{\partial \mathbf{x}} \equiv \left[\dfrac{\partial F_{ij}}{\partial x_k}\right]$
Matrix $\dfrac{\cdot}{\partial \mathbf{X}}$	Matrix: $\dfrac{\partial f}{\partial \mathbf{X}} \equiv \left[\dfrac{\partial f}{\partial x_{ij}}\right] = \mathbf{G}$	Tensor: $\dfrac{\partial \mathbf{f}}{\partial \mathbf{X}} \equiv \left[\dfrac{\partial f_i}{\partial x_{jk}}\right]$	Tensor: $\dfrac{\partial \mathbf{F}}{\partial \mathbf{X}} \equiv \left[\dfrac{\partial f_{ij}}{\partial x_{kl}}\right]$

Our choice for the orientations of these quantities means that the gradient matrix has the same layout as the original matrix, so updates to a parameter *matrix* $\mathbf{X}$ take the form $\mathbf{X}^{\text{new}} = \mathbf{X}^{\text{old}} - \mathbf{G}$.

While many quantities can be expressed as scalars, vectors, or matrices, there are many that cannot. Inspired by the tabular visualization of Minka (2000), the scalar, vector, matrix, and tensor quantities resulting from taking the derivatives of different combinations of quantities are shown in Table A.1.

THE CHAIN RULE

The chain rule for a function z, which is a function of y, which is a function of x, all of which are scalars, is

$$\frac{\partial z}{\partial x} = \frac{\partial z}{\partial y}\frac{\partial y}{\partial x}$$

where the two terms could be reversed, because multiplication is commutative. Now, given an m-dimensional vector $\mathbf{x}$, an n-dimensional vector $\mathbf{y}$, and an o-dimensional vector $\mathbf{z}$, if $\mathbf{z} = \mathbf{z}(\mathbf{y}(\mathbf{x}))$, then

$$\frac{\partial \mathbf{z}}{\partial \mathbf{x}} \equiv \begin{bmatrix} \dfrac{\partial z_1}{\partial x_1} & \dfrac{\partial z_2}{\partial x_1} & \cdots & \dfrac{\partial z_o}{\partial x_1} \\ \dfrac{\partial z_1}{\partial x_2} & \dfrac{\partial z_2}{\partial x_2} & \cdots & \dfrac{\partial z_o}{\partial x_2} \\ \vdots & \vdots & \ddots & \vdots \\ \dfrac{\partial z_1}{\partial x_m} & \dfrac{\partial z_2}{\partial x_m} & \cdots & \dfrac{\partial z_o}{\partial x_m} \end{bmatrix},$$

where each entry in the $m \times n$ matrix can be computed using

$$\frac{\partial z_i}{\partial x_j} = \sum_{k=1}^{n} \frac{\partial y_k}{\partial x_j}\frac{\partial z_i}{\partial y_k} = \left[\frac{\partial \mathbf{y}}{\partial x_j}\right]\left[\frac{\partial z_i}{\partial \mathbf{y}}\right].$$

The vector form could be viewed as

$$\frac{\partial \mathbf{z}}{\partial \mathbf{x}} = \begin{bmatrix} \dfrac{\partial y_1}{\partial x_1} & \dfrac{\partial y_2}{\partial x_1} & \cdots & \dfrac{\partial y_n}{\partial x_1} \\[2ex] \dfrac{\partial y_1}{\partial x_2} & \dfrac{\partial y_2}{\partial x_2} & \cdots & \dfrac{\partial y_n}{\partial x_2} \\[2ex] \vdots & \vdots & \ddots & \vdots \\[2ex] \dfrac{\partial y_1}{\partial x_m} & \dfrac{\partial y_2}{\partial x_m} & \cdots & \dfrac{\partial y_n}{\partial x_m} \end{bmatrix} \begin{bmatrix} \dfrac{\partial z_1}{\partial y_1} & \dfrac{\partial z_2}{\partial y_1} & \cdots & \dfrac{\partial z_o}{\partial y_1} \\[2ex] \dfrac{\partial z_1}{\partial y_2} & \dfrac{\partial z_2}{\partial y_2} & \cdots & \dfrac{\partial z_o}{\partial y_2} \\[2ex] \vdots & \vdots & \ddots & \vdots \\[2ex] \dfrac{\partial z_1}{\partial y_n} & \dfrac{\partial z_2}{\partial y_n} & \cdots & \dfrac{\partial z_o}{\partial y_n} \end{bmatrix}$$

$$\frac{\partial \mathbf{z}}{\partial \mathbf{x}} = \frac{\partial \mathbf{y}}{\partial \mathbf{x}} \frac{\partial \mathbf{z}}{\partial \mathbf{y}},$$

which yields the chain rule for vectors, where chains extend toward the left as opposed to the right as is often done with the scalar version. For the special case when the final function evaluates to a scalar—which is frequently encountered when optimizing a loss function, we have

$$\frac{\partial z}{\partial x_j} = \sum_{k=1}^{n} \frac{\partial y_k}{\partial x_j} \frac{\partial z}{\partial y_k},$$

$$\frac{\partial z}{\partial \mathbf{x}} = \frac{\partial \mathbf{y}}{\partial \mathbf{x}} \frac{\partial z}{\partial \mathbf{y}}.$$

The rule generalizes, so that if there were yet another vector function $\mathbf{w}$ that is a function of $\mathbf{x}$, through $\mathbf{z}$, then

$$\frac{\partial \mathbf{w}}{\partial \mathbf{x}} = \frac{\partial \mathbf{y}}{\partial \mathbf{x}} \frac{\partial \mathbf{z}}{\partial \mathbf{y}} \frac{\partial \mathbf{w}}{\partial \mathbf{z}}.$$

To find the derivative of a matrix that is the function of another matrix, the chain rule generalizes. For example, for a matrix $\mathbf{X}$ if matrix $\mathbf{Y} = f(\mathbf{X})$, the derivative of a function $g(\mathbf{Y})$ is

$$\frac{\partial g(\mathbf{Y})}{\partial \mathbf{X}} = \frac{\partial g(f(\mathbf{X}))}{\partial \mathbf{X}}$$

$$\frac{\partial g(\mathbf{Y})}{\partial x_{ij}} = \sum_{k=1}^{K} \sum_{l=1}^{L} \frac{\partial g(\mathbf{Y})}{\partial y_{kl}} \frac{\partial y_{kl}}{\partial x_{ij}}$$

COMPUTATION GRAPHS AND BACKPROPAGATION

Computation networks help to show how the gradients required for deep learning with backpropagation can be computed. They also provide the basis for many software packages for deep learning, which partially or fully automate the computations involved.

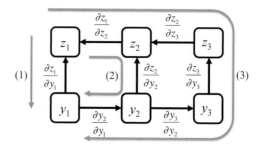

FIGURE A.1

Decomposing partial derivatives using a computation graph.

We begin with an example that computes intermediate quantities that are scalars, and then extend it to networks involving vectors that represent entire layers of variables at each node. Fig. A.1 gives a computation graph that implements the function $z_1(y_1, z_2(y_2(y_1), z_3(y_3(y_2(y_1)))))$, and shows how to compute the gradients. The chain rule for a scalar function a involving intermediate results $b_1, \ldots, b_k$ that are dependent on c is

$$\frac{\partial a(b_1, \ldots, b_k)}{\partial c} = \sum_{k=1}^{n} \frac{\partial a}{\partial b_k} \frac{\partial b_k}{\partial c}.$$

In the example, the partial derivative of z_1 with respect to y_1 therefore consists of three terms

$$\frac{\partial z_1}{\partial y_1} = \underbrace{\frac{\partial z_1}{\partial y_1}}_{(1)} + \underbrace{\frac{\partial z_1}{\partial z_2} \frac{\partial z_2}{\partial y_2} \frac{\partial y_2}{\partial y_1}}_{(2)} + \underbrace{\frac{\partial z_1}{\partial z_2} \frac{\partial z_2}{\partial z_3} \frac{\partial z_3}{\partial y_3} \frac{\partial y_3}{\partial y_2} \frac{\partial y_2}{\partial y_1}}_{(3)}$$

$$= \frac{\partial z_1}{\partial y_1} + \frac{\partial z_1}{\partial z_2} \left[\frac{\partial z_2}{\partial y_2} + \frac{\partial z_2}{\partial z_3} \frac{\partial z_3}{\partial y_3} \frac{\partial y_3}{\partial y_2} \right] \frac{\partial y_2}{\partial y_1}$$

The sums needed to compute this involve following back along the flows of the subcomputations that were performed to evaluate the original function. These can be implemented efficiently by passing them between nodes in the graph, as Fig. A.1 shows.

This high-level notion of following flows in a graph generalizes to deep networks involving entire layers of variables. If Fig. A.1 were drawn using a scalar for z_1 and vectors for each of the other nodes, the partial derivatives could be replaced by their vector versions. It is necessary to reverse the order of the multiplications, because in the case of partial derivatives of vectors with respect to vectors, computations grow to the left, yielding

$$\frac{\partial z_1}{\partial \mathbf{y}_1} = \frac{\partial z_1}{\partial \mathbf{y}_1} + \frac{\partial \mathbf{y}_2}{\partial \mathbf{y}_1} \left[\frac{\partial \mathbf{z}_2}{\partial \mathbf{y}_2} + \frac{\partial \mathbf{y}_3}{\partial \mathbf{y}_2} \frac{\partial \mathbf{z}_3}{\partial \mathbf{y}_3} \frac{\partial \mathbf{z}_2}{\partial \mathbf{z}_3} \right] \frac{\partial z_1}{\partial \mathbf{z}_2}$$

To see this, consider (1) the chain rule for the partial derivative of a scalar function z with a vector $\mathbf{x}$ as argument, but involving the computation of an intermediate vector $\mathbf{y}$:

$$\frac{\partial z(\mathbf{y})}{\partial x_j} = \sum_{k=1}^{n} \frac{\partial y_k}{\partial x_j} \frac{\partial z}{\partial y_k}$$

$$\frac{\partial z}{\partial \mathbf{x}} = \frac{\partial \mathbf{y}}{\partial \mathbf{x}} \frac{\partial z}{\partial \mathbf{y}}$$

$$= \mathbf{D}\mathbf{d},$$

and (2) the chain rule for the same scalar function $z(\mathbf{x})$, but involving the computation of an intermediate matrix $\mathbf{Y}$:

$$\frac{\partial z(\mathbf{Y})}{\partial \mathbf{x}} = \sum_{l=1}^{L} \frac{\partial \mathbf{y}_l}{\partial \mathbf{x}} \frac{\partial z}{\partial \mathbf{y}_l}$$

$$= \sum_{l=1}^{L} \mathbf{D}_l \mathbf{d}_l.$$

DERIVATIVES OF FUNCTIONS OF VECTORS AND MATRICES

Here are some useful derivatives for functions of vectors and matrices. Petersen and Pedersen (2012) gives an even larger list.

$$\frac{\partial}{\partial \mathbf{x}} \mathbf{A}\mathbf{x} = \mathbf{A}^T$$

$$\frac{\partial}{\partial \mathbf{x}} \mathbf{x}^T \mathbf{x} = 2\mathbf{x}$$

$$\frac{\partial}{\partial \mathbf{a}} \mathbf{a}^T \mathbf{x} = \frac{\partial}{\partial \mathbf{a}} \mathbf{x}^T \mathbf{a} = \mathbf{x}$$

$$\frac{\partial}{\partial \mathbf{x}} \mathbf{x}^T \mathbf{A}\mathbf{x} = \mathbf{A}\mathbf{x} + \mathbf{A}^T \mathbf{x}$$

$$\frac{\partial}{\partial \mathbf{A}} \mathbf{y}^T \mathbf{A}\mathbf{x} = \mathbf{y}\mathbf{x}^T$$

$$\frac{\partial}{\partial \mathbf{x}} (\mathbf{a} - \mathbf{x})^T (\mathbf{a} - \mathbf{x}) = -2(\mathbf{a} - \mathbf{x})$$

Notice that the first identity above would be equal to simply $\mathbf{A}$, had we defined the Jacobian to be the transpose of our definition above.

For a symmetric matrix $\mathbf{C}$ (e.g., an inverse covariance matrix),

$$\frac{\partial}{\partial \mathbf{a}}(\mathbf{a}-\mathbf{b})^T \mathbf{C}(\mathbf{a}-\mathbf{b}) = 2\mathbf{C}(\mathbf{a}-\mathbf{b})$$

$$\frac{\partial}{\partial \mathbf{b}}(\mathbf{a}-\mathbf{b})^T \mathbf{C}(\mathbf{a}-\mathbf{b}) = -2\mathbf{C}(\mathbf{a}-\mathbf{b})$$

$$\frac{\partial}{\partial \mathbf{w}}(\mathbf{y}-\mathbf{A}\mathbf{w})^T \mathbf{C}(\mathbf{y}-\mathbf{A}\mathbf{w}) = -2\mathbf{A}^T \mathbf{C}(\mathbf{y}-\mathbf{A}\mathbf{w})$$

VECTOR TAYLOR SERIES EXPANSION, SECOND-ORDER METHODS, AND LEARNING RATES

The method of gradient descent, the interpretation of learning rates, and more sophisticated second-order methods can be viewed through the lens of the Taylor series expansion of a function. The approach presented below is also known as Newton's method.

The Taylor expansion of a function near point x_o can be written

$$f(x) = f(x_o) + \frac{f'(x_o)}{1!}(x - x_o) + \frac{f''(x_o)}{2!}(x-x_o)^2 + \frac{f^{(3)}(x_o)}{3!}(x-x_o)^3 + \cdots$$

Using the approximation up to the second-order (squared) terms in x, taking the derivative, setting the result to zero, and solving for x, gives

$$0 = \frac{d}{dx}\left[f(x_o) + f'(x_o)(x - x_o) + \frac{f''(x_o)}{2}(x-x_o)^2\right]$$

$$= f'(x_o) + f''(x_o)(x - x_o), \text{ thus solving for } \delta x \equiv (x - x_o)$$

$$\Rightarrow \delta x = -\frac{f'(x_o)}{f''(x_o)}, \text{ or } x = x_o - \frac{f'(x_o)}{f''(x_o)}.$$

This generalizes to the vector version of a Taylor series for a scalar function with matrix arguments, where

$$f(\boldsymbol{\theta}) = f(\boldsymbol{\theta}_o) + \mathbf{g}_o^T(\boldsymbol{\theta} - \boldsymbol{\theta}_o) + \frac{1}{2}(\boldsymbol{\theta}-\boldsymbol{\theta}_o)^T \mathbf{H}_o(\boldsymbol{\theta} - \boldsymbol{\theta}_o) + \cdots,$$

$$\mathbf{g}_o = \frac{df}{d\boldsymbol{\theta}_o}, \mathbf{H}_o = \frac{d}{d\boldsymbol{\theta}_o}\frac{df}{d\boldsymbol{\theta}_o} = \frac{d^2 f}{d\boldsymbol{\theta}_o^2}.$$

Using the identities given in the previous section, taking the derivative with respect to the parameter vector $\boldsymbol{\theta}$, setting it to zero and then solving for the point at which the quadratic approximation to the function would be zero, yields

$$\frac{df(\boldsymbol{\theta})}{d\boldsymbol{\theta}} = 0 = \mathbf{g}_o + \mathbf{H}_o(\boldsymbol{\theta} - \boldsymbol{\theta}_o), \Delta\boldsymbol{\theta} \equiv (\boldsymbol{\theta} - \boldsymbol{\theta}_o)$$

$$\Rightarrow \Delta\boldsymbol{\theta} = -\mathbf{H}_o^{-1}\mathbf{g}_o.$$

This means that for the update $\boldsymbol{\theta}^{\text{new}} = \boldsymbol{\theta}_o - \mathbf{H}_o^{-1}\mathbf{g}_o$, the *learning rate* used for gradient descent can be thought of in terms of a simple diagonal matrix approximation to the inverse Hessian matrix in a second-order method. In other words, using a simple learning rate is analogous to making an approximation, so that $\mathbf{H}_o^{-1} = \eta \mathbf{I}$.

Full-blown second-order methods take more effective steps at each iteration. However, they can be expensive because of the need to compute this quantity. For convex problems like logistic regression, a popular second-order method known as L-BFGS builds an approximation to the Hessian. Here, L stands for limited memory and BFGS stands for the inventors of the approach, Broyden–Fletcher–Goldfarb–Shanno. Another family of approaches are known as the conjugate gradient algorithms and involve working with the linear system of equations associated with $\mathbf{H}_o\mathbf{x} = -\mathbf{g}_o$ when solving for $\mathbf{x} = \Delta\boldsymbol{\theta}$ as opposed to computing the inverse of $\mathbf{H}_o$.

One needs to keep in mind that when solving nonconvex problems (e.g., learning for multilayer neural networks) the Hessian is not guaranteed to be *positive definite*, which means that it may not even be invertible. Consequently the use of heuristic adaptive learning rates and momentum terms remain popular and effective for neural network methods.

EIGENVECTORS, EIGENVALUES, AND COVARIANCE MATRICES

There is a strong connection between eigenvectors, eigenvalues and diagonalization of a covariance matrix, and the method of principal component analysis. If λ is a scalar *eigenvalue* of a matrix $\mathbf{A}$, there exists a vector $\mathbf{x}$ called an *eigenvector* of $\mathbf{A}$ such that $\mathbf{A}\mathbf{x} = \lambda\mathbf{x}$. Define a matrix $\boldsymbol{\Phi}$ to consist of eigenvectors in each column, and define $\boldsymbol{\Lambda}$ as a matrix with the corresponding eigenvalues on the diagonal, then the matrix equation $\mathbf{A}\boldsymbol{\Phi} = \boldsymbol{\Phi}\boldsymbol{\Lambda}$ defines the eigenvalues and eigenvectors of $\mathbf{A}$.

Many numerical linear algebra software packages (e.g., Matlab) can determine solutions to this equation. If the eigenvectors in $\boldsymbol{\Phi}$ are orthogonal, which they are for symmetric matrices, the inverse of $\boldsymbol{\Phi}$ equals its transpose, which implies that we could equally well write $\boldsymbol{\Phi}^T\mathbf{A}\boldsymbol{\Phi} = \boldsymbol{\Lambda}$. To find the eigenvectors of a covariance matrix, set $\mathbf{A} = \boldsymbol{\Sigma}$, the covariance matrix. This yields the definition of the eigenvectors of a covariance matrix $\boldsymbol{\Sigma}$ as the set of orthogonal vectors stored in a matrix $\boldsymbol{\Phi}$ and normalized to have unit length, such that $\boldsymbol{\Phi}^T\boldsymbol{\Sigma}\boldsymbol{\Phi} = \boldsymbol{\Lambda}$. Since $\boldsymbol{\Lambda}$ is diagonal matrix of eigenvalues, the operation $\boldsymbol{\Phi}^T\boldsymbol{\Sigma}\boldsymbol{\Phi}$ has been used to *diagonalize* the covariance matrix.

While these results may seem esoteric at first glance, their use is widespread. For example, in computer vision an eigenanalysis-based principal component analysis for face recognition yields what are known as "eigenfaces." The general technique is widely used in numerous other contexts, and classic, well-cited eigenanalysis-based papers appear in many diverse fields.

THE SINGULAR VALUE DECOMPOSITION

The singular value decomposition is a type of matrix factorization that is widely used in data mining and machine learning settings and is implemented as a core routine in many numerical linear algebra packages. It decomposes a matrix $\mathbf{X}$ into the product of three matrices such that $\mathbf{X} = \mathbf{USV}^T$, where $\mathbf{U}$ has orthogonal columns, $\mathbf{S}$ is a diagonal matrix containing the singular values (normally) sorted along the diagonal, and $\mathbf{V}$ also has orthogonal columns. By keeping only the k largest singular values, this factorization allows the data matrix to be reconstructed in a way that is optimal in a least squares sense for each value of k. For any given k, we could therefore write $\mathbf{X} \approx \mathbf{U}_k \mathbf{S}_k \mathbf{V}_k^T$. Fig. 9.10 illustrates how this works visually.

In our discussion earlier on eigendecompositions we developed an expression for diagonalizing a covariance matrix $\mathbf{\Sigma}$ using $\mathbf{\Phi}^T \mathbf{\Sigma} \mathbf{\Phi} = \mathbf{\Lambda}$, where $\mathbf{\Phi}$ holds the eigenvectors and $\mathbf{\Lambda}$ is a diagonal matrix of eigenvalues. This amounts to seeking a decomposition of the covariance matrix that factorizes into $\mathbf{\Sigma} = \mathbf{\Phi}\mathbf{\Lambda}\mathbf{\Phi}^T$. This reveals the relationship between principal component analysis and the singular value decomposition applied to data stored in the columns of matrix $\mathbf{X}$. We will use the fact that the covariance matrix $\mathbf{\Sigma}$ for *mean centered* data stored as vectors in the columns of $\mathbf{X}$ is simply $\mathbf{\Sigma} = \mathbf{XX}^T$. Since orthogonal matrices have the property that $\mathbf{UU}^T = \mathbf{I}$, through the following substitution we can see that the matrix $\mathbf{\Phi}$, known as the right singular vectors of $\mathbf{X}$, corresponds to the eigenvectors of the covariance matrix. In other words, to factorize a covariance matrix into $\mathbf{\Sigma} = \mathbf{\Phi}\mathbf{\Lambda}\mathbf{\Phi}^T$, mean center the data and perform an singular value decomposition on $\mathbf{X}$. Then the covariance matrix is $\mathbf{\Sigma} = \mathbf{XX}^T = \mathbf{USD}^T\mathbf{DS}^T\mathbf{U}^T = \mathbf{US}^2\mathbf{U}^T$, so $\mathbf{U} = \mathbf{\Phi}$ and $\mathbf{S} = \mathbf{\Lambda}^{\frac{1}{2}}$—in other words, the so-called singular values are the square roots of the eigenvalues.

A.2 FUNDAMENTAL ELEMENTS OF PROBABILISTIC METHODS
EXPECTATIONS

The expectation of a discrete random variable X is

$$E[X] = \sum_x xP(X = x),$$

where the sum is over all possible values for X. The conditional expectation for discrete random variable X given random variable $Y = y$ has a similar form

$$E[X|Y = y] = \sum_x xP(X = x|Y = y).$$

Given a probability density function $p(x)$ for a continuous random variable X,

$$E[X] = \int_{-\infty}^{\infty} xp(x)dx.$$

The empirical expectation of a continuous-valued variable X is obtained by placing a Dirac delta function on each empirical observation or example, and normalizing by the number of examples, to define $p(x)$. The expected value of a matrix is defined as a matrix of expected values.

The expectation of a function of a continuous random variable X and a discrete random variable y is

$$E[f(X,Y)] = \int_{-\infty}^{\infty} \sum_{y} f(x,Y)p(x, Y = y)dx.$$

Expectations of sums of random variables are equal to sums of expectations, or

$$E[X + Y] = E[X] + E[Y].$$

If there is a scaling factor s and bias or constant c, that

$$E[sX + c] = sE[X] + c.$$

The variance is defined as

$$\begin{aligned}
\mathrm{Var}[X] &= \sum_{x} (x - E[X])^2 p(X = x) \\
&= E[(X - E[X])(X - E[X])] \\
&= E[X^2 - 2XE[X] + (E[X])^2] \\
&= E[X^2] - 2E[X]E[X] + (E[X])^2 \\
&= E[X^2] - E[X]^2.
\end{aligned}$$

The expectation of the product of continuous random variables X and Y with joint probability $p(x,y)$ is given by

$$E[XY] = \int_{-\infty}^{\infty} \int_{-\infty}^{\infty} xyp(x, y)dxdy.$$

The covariance between X and Y is given by

$$\begin{aligned}
\mathrm{Cov}[X, Y] &= E[(X - E[X])(Y - E[Y])] \\
&= \sum_{x} \sum_{y} (x - E[X])(y - E[Y])p(X = x, Y = y) \\
&= E[XY] - E[X]E[Y].
\end{aligned}$$

Therefore $\mathrm{Cov}[X, Y] = 0 \Rightarrow E[XY] = E[X]E[Y]$, and X and Y are said to be uncorrelated. Clearly $\mathrm{Cov}[X,X] = \mathrm{Var}[X]$. The covariance matrix for a d-dimensional continuous random variable $\mathbf{x}$ is obtained from

$$\mathrm{Cov}[\mathbf{x}] = \begin{bmatrix} \mathrm{Cov}(x_1, x_1) & \cdots & \mathrm{Cov}(x_1, x_d) \\ \vdots & \vdots & \vdots \\ \mathrm{Cov}(x_d, x_1) & \cdots & \mathrm{Cov}(x_d, x_d) \end{bmatrix}.$$

CONJUGATE PRIORS

In more fully Bayesian methods one treats both variables and parameters as random quantities. The use of prior distributions over parameters can provide simple and well justified ways to regularize model parameters and avoid overfitting. Applying the Bayesian modeling philosophy and techniques can lead to simple adjustments to traditional maximum likelihood estimates. In particular, the use of a conjugate prior distribution for a parameter in an appropriately defined probability model means that the posterior distribution over that parameter will remain in the same form as the prior. This makes it easy to adapt traditional maximum likelihood estimates for parameters using simple weighted averages of the maximum likelihood estimate and the relevant parameters of the conjugate prior. We will see how this works for the Bernoulli, categorical, and Gaussian distributions below. Other more sophisticated Bayesian manipulations are also simplified through the use of conjugacy.

BERNOULLI, BINOMIAL, AND BETA DISTRIBUTIONS

The *Bernoulli* probability distribution is defined for binary random variables. Suppose $x \in \{0, 1\}$, the probability of $x = 1$ is given by π and the probability of $x = 0$ is given by $1 - \pi$. The probability distribution can be written in the following way

$$P(x; \pi) = \pi^x (1-\pi)^{1-x}.$$

The *binomial* distribution generalizes the Bernoulli distribution. It defines the probability for a certain number of successes in a sequence of binary experiments, where the outcome of each experiment is governed by a Bernoulli distribution. The probability of exactly k successes in n experiments under the binomial distribution is

$$P(k; n, \pi) = \binom{n}{k} \pi^k (1-\pi)^{n-k},$$

and defined for $k = 0, 1, 2, \ldots, n$ where

$$\binom{n}{k} = \frac{n!}{k!(n-k)!}$$

is the binomial coefficient. Intuitively, the binomial coefficient is needed to account for the fact that the definition of this distribution ignores the order of the results of the experiments—the k results where $x = 1$ could have occurred anywhere in the sequence of the n experiments. The binomial coefficient gives the number of different ways in which one could have obtained the k results where $x = 1$. Intuitively, the term π^k is the probability of exactly k results where $x = 1$, and π^{n-k} is the probability of having exactly $n - k$ results where $x = 0$. These two terms are valid for each of the possible ways in which the sequence of outcomes could have occurred, and we therefore simply multiply by the number of possibilities.

The *Beta* distribution is defined for a random variable π where $0 \le \pi \le 1$. It uses two shape parameters $\alpha, \beta > 0$ such that

$$P(\pi; \alpha, \beta) = \frac{1}{B(\alpha, \beta)} \pi^{\alpha-1}(1-\pi)^{\beta-1}, \qquad (A.1)$$

where $B(\alpha, \beta)$ is the beta function and serves as a normalization constant that ensures that the function integrates to one. The Beta distribution is useful because it can be used as a conjugate prior distribution for the Bernoulli and binomial distributions. Its mean is

$$\pi_B = \left(\frac{\alpha}{\alpha + \beta} \right),$$

and it can be shown that if the maximum likelihood estimate for the Bernoulli distribution is given by π_{ML} then the posterior mean π_* of the Beta distribution is

$$\pi_* = w\pi_B + (1 - w)\pi_{\mathrm{ML}},$$

where

$$w = \frac{\alpha + \beta}{\alpha + \beta + n},$$

and n is the number of examples used to estimate π_{ML}. The use of the posterior mean value π_* as the regularized or smoothed estimate, replacing π_{ML} in a Bernoulli model, is therefore justified under Bayesian principles by the fact that the mean value of the posterior predictive distribution of a Beta-Bernoulli model is equivalent to plugging the posterior mean parameters of the Beta into the Bernoulli, i.e.

$$p(x|D) = \int_0^1 \mathrm{Bern}(x|\pi) \ \mathrm{Beta}(\pi|D)d\pi = \mathrm{Bern}(x; \pi_*).$$

This supports the intuitive notion of thinking of α and β as imaginary observations for $x = 1$ and $x = 0$, respectively, and justifies it in a Bayesian sense.

CATEGORICAL, MULTINOMIAL, AND DIRICHLET DISTRIBUTIONS

The *categorical* distribution is defined for discrete random variables with more than two states; it generalizes the Bernoulli distribution. For K categories one might define $A \in \{a_1, a_2, \cdots, a_K\}$ or $x \in \{1, 2, \cdots, K\}$; however, the order of the integers used to encode the categories is arbitrary. If the probability of x being in state or category k is given by π_k, and if we use a *one hot* encoding for a vector representation $\mathbf{x}$ in which all the elements of $\mathbf{x}$ are zero except for exactly one dimension that is equal to 1, representing the state or category of $\mathbf{x}$, then the categorical distribution is

$$P(\mathbf{x}; \boldsymbol{\pi}) = \prod_{k=1}^{K} \pi_k^{x_k}.$$

The *multinomial* distribution generalizes the categorical distribution. Given multiple independent observations of a discrete random variable with a fixed categorical probability π_k for each class k, the multinomial distribution defines the probability of observing a particular number of instances of each category. If the vector **x** is defined as the number of times each category has been observed, then the multinomial distribution can be expressed as

$$P(\mathbf{x}; n, \boldsymbol{\pi}) = \left(\frac{n!}{x_1! \cdots x_K!} \right) \prod_{k=1}^{K} \pi_k^{x_k}.$$

The *Dirichlet* distribution is defined for a random variable or parameter vector $\boldsymbol{\pi}$ such that $\pi_1, \ldots, \pi_K > 0$, $\pi_1, \ldots, \pi_K < 1$, $\pi_1 + \pi_2 + \ldots, \pi_K = 1$, which is precisely the form of $\boldsymbol{\pi}$ used to define the categorical and multinomial distributions above. The Dirichlet *distribution* with parameters $\alpha_1, \ldots, \alpha_K > 0$, $K \geq 2$ is

$$P(\boldsymbol{\pi}; \boldsymbol{\alpha}) = \frac{1}{B(\boldsymbol{\alpha})} \prod_{i=k}^{K} \pi_k^{\alpha_k - 1}$$

where $B(\boldsymbol{\alpha})$, the *multinomial beta function*, serves as the normalization constant that ensures that the function integrates to one:

$$B(\boldsymbol{\alpha}) = \frac{\prod_{k=1}^{K} \Gamma(\alpha_k)}{\Gamma\left(\sum_{k=1}^{K} \alpha_k\right)}$$

where $\Gamma(\cdot)$ is the gamma function.

The Dirichlet distribution is useful because it can be used as a conjugate prior distribution for the categorical and multinomial distributions. Its mean (vector) is

$$\boldsymbol{\pi}_D = \frac{\boldsymbol{\alpha}}{\sum_{k=1}^{K} \alpha_k}.$$

And it generalizes the case of the Bernoulli distribution with a Beta prior. That is, it can be shown that if the traditional maximum likelihood estimate for the categorical distribution is given by $\boldsymbol{\pi}_{\mathrm{ML}}$, then the posterior mean $\boldsymbol{\pi}_*$ of a model consisting of a categorical likelihood and a Dirichlet prior has the form of a Dirichlet distribution with mean

$$\boldsymbol{\pi}_* = w\boldsymbol{\pi}_D + (1 - w)\boldsymbol{\pi}_{\mathrm{ML}}$$

where

$$w = \frac{\alpha_K}{\alpha_K + n}, \quad \alpha_K = \sum_{k=1}^{K} \alpha_k,$$

and where n is the number of examples used to estimate $\boldsymbol{\pi}_{\mathrm{ML}}$. The use of the posterior mean value $\boldsymbol{\pi}_*$ as the regularized or smoothed estimate to replace $\boldsymbol{\pi}_{\mathrm{ML}}$ in a categorical probability model is therefore justified under Bayesian principles by the fact that the mean value of the posterior predictive distribution of a categorical model with a Dirichlet prior is equivalent to plugging the posterior mean parameters of the Dirichlet posterior into the categorical probability model, i.e.,

$$p(\mathbf{x}|D) = \int_{\pi} \text{Cat}(\mathbf{x}|\pi) \ \text{Dirichlet}(\pi|D)d\pi = \text{Cat}(\mathbf{x}; \pi_*).$$

Again the intuitive notion of thinking of each of the elements α_k of the parameter vector α for the Dirichlet as imaginary observations is justified under a Bayesian analysis.

ESTIMATING THE PARAMETERS OF A DISCRETE DISTRIBUTION

Suppose we wish to estimate the parameters of a discrete probability distribution—of which the binary distribution is a special case. Let the probability of a variable being in category k be π_k, and write the parameters of the distribution as the length$-k$ vector π. Encode each example using a one hot vector $\mathbf{x}_i$, $i = 1, \ldots, N$, which is all zero except for one dimension that corresponds to the observed category, where $x_{i,k} = 1$. The probability of a dataset can be expressed as

$$P(\mathbf{x}_1, \ldots, \mathbf{x}_N; \pi) = \prod_{i=1}^{N} \prod_{k=1}^{K} \pi_k^{x_{i,k}}.$$

If n_k is the number of times that each class k in the data has been observed, the log-likelihood of the data is

$$\log P(n_1, \ldots, n_K; \pi) = \sum_{k=1}^{K} n_k \ \log \pi_k.$$

To ensure that the parameter vector defines a valid probability, the log-likelihood is augmented with a term involving a *Lagrange multiplier* λ that enforces the constraint that the probabilities sum to one:

$$L = \sum_{k=1}^{K} n_k \ \log \pi_k + \lambda \left[1 - \sum_{k=1}^{K} \pi_k \right].$$

Taking the derivative of this function with respect to λ and setting the result to zero tells us that the sum over the probabilities in our model should be 1 (as desired). We then take the derivative of the function with respect to each parameter and set it to zero, which gives

$$\frac{\partial L}{\partial \pi_k} = 0 \quad \Rightarrow \quad n_k = \lambda \pi_k.$$

We can solve for λ by summing both sides over k:

$$\sum_{k=1}^{K} n_k = \lambda \sum_{k=1}^{K} \pi_k \quad \Rightarrow \quad \lambda = \sum_{k=1}^{K} n_k = N.$$

Therefore we can determine that the gradient of the augmented objective function is zero when

$$\pi_k = \frac{n_k}{N}.$$

This simple result should be in line with your intuition about how to estimate probabilities.

We discussed above how specifying a Dirichlet prior for the parameters can regularize the estimation problem and compute a smoothed probability π_k^*. The regularization can equivalently be viewed as imaginary data or counts α_k for each class k, to give an estimate

$$\pi_k^* = \frac{n_k + \alpha_k}{N + \alpha_K}, \qquad \alpha_K = \sum_{k=1}^{K} \alpha_k,$$

which can also be written

$$\pi_k^* = \left[\frac{\alpha_K}{N + \alpha_K} \right] \left(\frac{\alpha_k}{\alpha_K} \right) + \left[\frac{N}{N + \alpha_K} \right] \left(\frac{n_k}{N} \right).$$

This also follows from the analysis above that expressed the smoothed probability vector π_* as a weighted combination of the prior probability vector π_D and the maximum likelihood estimate π_{ML}, $\pi_* = w\pi_D + (1 - w)\pi_{ML}$.

THE GAUSSIAN DISTRIBUTION

The one-dimensional Gaussian probability distribution has the following form:

$$P(x; \mu, \sigma) = \frac{1}{\sigma\sqrt{2\pi}} \exp\left[-\frac{(x - \mu)^2}{2\sigma^2} \right],$$

where the parameters of the model are its mean μ and variance σ^2 (the standard deviation σ is simply the square root of the variance). Given N examples $x_i = 1, \ldots, N$, the maximum likelihood estimates of these parameters are

$$\mu = \frac{1}{N} \sum_{i=1}^{N} x_i, \qquad \sigma^2 = \frac{1}{N} \sum_{i=1}^{N} (x_i - \mu)^2.$$

When estimating the variance, the equation above is sometimes modified to use $N-1$ in place of N in the denominator to obtain an unbiased estimate, giving the standard deviation as

$$\sigma = \sqrt{\frac{1}{N - 1} \sum_{i=1}^{N} (x_i - \mu)^2},$$

especially with sample sizes less than 10. This is known as the (corrected) *sample standard deviation*.

The Gaussian distribution can be generalized from one to two dimensions, or indeed to any number of dimensions. Consider a two-dimensional model consisting of independent Gaussian distributions for each dimension, which is equivalent to a model with a diagonal covariance matrix when written using matrix notation. We can transform from scalar to matrix notation for a two-dimensional Gaussian distribution:

$$P(x_1, x_2) = \frac{1}{\sqrt{2\pi}\sigma_1} \exp\left[-\frac{(x_1 - \mu_1)^2}{2\sigma_1^2}\right] \frac{1}{\sqrt{2\pi}\sigma_2} \exp\left[-\frac{(x_2 - \mu_2)^2}{2\sigma_2^2}\right]$$

$$= (2\pi)^{-1}(\sigma_1^2 \sigma_2^2)^{-1/2} \exp\left\{-\frac{1}{2}(\mathbf{x} - \boldsymbol{\mu})^T \begin{bmatrix} \sigma_1^2 & 0 \\ 0 & \sigma_2^2 \end{bmatrix}^{-1} (\mathbf{x} - \boldsymbol{\mu})\right\}$$

$$= (2\pi)^{-1}|\boldsymbol{\Sigma}|^{-1/2} \exp\left\{-\frac{1}{2}(\mathbf{x} - \boldsymbol{\mu})^T \boldsymbol{\Sigma}^{-1} (\mathbf{x} - \boldsymbol{\mu})\right\},$$

where the covariance matrix of the model is given by $\boldsymbol{\Sigma}$, the vector $\mathbf{x} = [x_1 \ x_2]^T$, and the mean vector $\boldsymbol{\mu} = [\mu_1 \ \mu_2]^T$. This progression of equations is true because the inverse of a diagonal matrix is simply a diagonal matrix consisting of one over each of the original diagonal elements, which explains how the scalar notation converts to the matrix notation for an inverse covariance matrix. The covariance matrix is the matrix with this entry on row i and column j:

$$\Sigma_{ij} = \text{cov}(x_i, x_j) = \text{E}[(x_i - \mu_i)(x_j - \mu_j)]$$

where E[.] refers to the expected value and $\mu_i = \text{E}[x_i]$. The mean can be computed in vector form:

$$\boldsymbol{\mu} = \frac{1}{N} \sum_{i=1}^{N} \mathbf{x}_i.$$

The equation for estimating a covariance matrix is

$$\boldsymbol{\Sigma} = \frac{1}{N} \sum_{i=1}^{N} (\mathbf{x}_i - \boldsymbol{\mu})(\mathbf{x}_i - \boldsymbol{\mu})^T.$$

In general the multivariate Gaussian distribution can be written

$$P(x_1, x_2, \ldots, x_d) = (2\pi)^{-d/2} |\boldsymbol{\Sigma}|^{-1/2} \exp\left\{-\frac{1}{2}(\mathbf{x} - \boldsymbol{\mu})^T \boldsymbol{\Sigma}^{-1} (\mathbf{x} - \boldsymbol{\mu})\right\}.$$

When a variable is to be modeled with a Gaussian distribution with mean $\boldsymbol{\mu}$ and covariance matrix $\boldsymbol{\Sigma}$, it is common to write $P(\mathbf{x}) = N(\mathbf{x}; \boldsymbol{\mu}, \boldsymbol{\Sigma})$. Notice the semicolon: this implies that the mean and covariance will be treated as parameters. In contrast, the "|" (or "given") symbol is used when the parameters are treated as variables and their uncertainty is to be modeled. Treating parameters as random variables is popular in Bayesian techniques such as latent Dirichlet allocation.

USEFUL PROPERTIES OF LINEAR GAUSSIAN MODELS

Consider a Gaussian random variable $\mathbf{x}$ with mean μ and covariance matrix $\mathbf{A}$, $p(\mathbf{x}) = N(\mathbf{x}; \mu, \mathbf{A})$, and a random variable $\mathbf{y}$ whose conditional distribution given $\mathbf{x}$ is Gaussian with mean $\mathbf{Wx} + \mathbf{b}$ and covariance matrix $\mathbf{B}$, $p(\mathbf{y}|\mathbf{x}) = N(\mathbf{y}; \mathbf{Wx} + \mathbf{b}, \mathbf{B})$. The marginal distribution of $\mathbf{y}$ and conditional distribution of $\mathbf{x}$ given $\mathbf{y}$ can be written

$$p(\mathbf{y}) = N(\mathbf{y}; \mathbf{Wx} + \mathbf{b}, \mathbf{B} + \mathbf{WAW}^T),$$
$$p(\mathbf{x}|\mathbf{y}) = N(\mathbf{x}; \mathbf{C}[\mathbf{W}^T\mathbf{B}^{-1}(\mathbf{y} - \mathbf{b}) + \mathbf{A}^{-1}\mu], \mathbf{C}),$$

respectively, where $\mathbf{C} = (\mathbf{A}^{-1} + \mathbf{W}^T\mathbf{B}^{-1}\mathbf{W})^{-1}$.

PROBABILISTIC PCA AND THE EIGENVECTORS OF A COVARIANCE MATRIX

When explaining principal component analysis in Section 9.6 we discussed the idea of diagonalizing a covariance matrix Σ and formulated this in terms of finding a matrix of eigenvectors Φ such that $\Phi^T\Sigma\Phi = \Lambda$, a diagonal matrix. The same objective could be formulated as finding a factorization of the covariance matrix such that $\Sigma = \Phi\Lambda\Phi^T$. Recall that in our presentation of probabilistic PCA in Chapter 9 we saw that the marginal probability for $P(\mathbf{x})$ under principal component analysis involves a covariance matrix given by $\Sigma = (\mathbf{W}^T\mathbf{W} + \sigma^2\mathbf{I})$. Therefore, when $\sigma^2 \to 0$ we can see that if $\mathbf{W} = \Phi\Lambda^{\frac{1}{2}}$ we would have precisely the same $\mathbf{W}$ that one could obtain from matrix factorization methods based on eigen-decomposition. Importantly, for $\sigma^2 > 0$ it can be shown that maximum likelihood learning will produce $\mathbf{W}$s that are not in general orthogonal (Tipping and Bishop, 1999a, 1999b); however, some more recent work has shown how to impose orthogonality constraints during a maximum likelihood−based optimization procedure.

THE EXPONENTIAL FAMILY OF DISTRIBUTIONS

The exponential family of distributions includes Gaussian, Bernoulli, Binomial, Beta, Gamma, Categorical, Multinomial, Dirichlet, Chi-squared, Exponential and Poisson, among many others. In addition to their commonly used forms, these distributions can all be written in the standardized *exponential family form* that makes them easy to work with algebraically:

$$p(\mathbf{x}) = h(\mathbf{x}) \ \exp[\theta^T T(\mathbf{x}) - A(\theta)],$$

where θ is a vector of *natural* parameters, $T(\mathbf{x})$ is a vector of *sufficient statistics*, $A(\theta)$ is known as *cumulant generating function*, and $h(\mathbf{x})$ is an additional function of $\mathbf{x}$. As an example, for the 1D Gaussian distribution these parameters are $\theta = [\mu/\sigma^2 \quad -1/(2\sigma^2)]^T$, $T(\mathbf{x}) = \begin{bmatrix} x & x^2 \end{bmatrix}^T$, $h(\mathbf{x}) = 1/\sqrt{2\pi}$, and $A(\theta) = \mu^2/(2\sigma^2) + \ln|\sigma|$.

VARIATIONAL METHODS AND THE EM ALGORITHM

With a complex probability model for which the posterior distribution cannot be computed exactly, a method called *variational EM* can be used. This involves manipulating approximations to the model's true posterior distribution during an EM optimization procedure. The following variational analysis also helps to show why and how the EM algorithm involving exact posterior distributions works.

Before we begin, when using variational methods with approximate distributions it is helpful to make a distinction between the parameters used to build an approximation to the true posterior distribution and the parameters of the original model. Consider a probability model with a set of hidden variables H and a set of observed variables X. The observed values are given by $\tilde{X}$. Let $p = p(H|\tilde{X}; \theta)$ be the model's exact posterior distribution, and $q = q(H|\tilde{X}; \Phi)$ be a variational approximation, with a set Φ of variational parameters.

To understand how variational methods are used in practice, we first examine the well-known "variational bound." This is created using two tricks. The first is to divide and multiply by the same quantity; the second is to apply an inequality known as Jensen's inequality. These allow the construction of a *variational lower bound* $L(q)$ on the log marginal likelihood:

$$\log p(\tilde{X}; \theta) = \log \sum_H p(\tilde{X}, H; \theta)$$

$$= \log \sum_H \frac{q(H|\tilde{X}; \Phi)}{q(H|\tilde{X}; \Phi)} p(\tilde{X}, H; \theta)$$

$$\geq \sum_H q(H|\tilde{X}; \Phi) \, \log \frac{p(\tilde{X}, H; \theta)}{q(H|\tilde{X}; \Phi)}$$

$$= \mathrm{E}[\log P(\tilde{X}, H; \theta)]_q + \mathrm{H}(q)$$

$$= \mathrm{L}(q).$$

Here, $\mathrm{H}(q)$ is the entropy of q, which is

$$\mathrm{H}(q) = - \sum_H q(H|\tilde{X}; \Phi) \log q(H|\tilde{X}; \Phi).$$

The bound $\mathrm{L}(q)$ becomes an equality when $q = p$. In the case of "exact" EM, this confirms that each M-step will increase the likelihood of the data. However, to make the lower bound tight again in preparation for the next M-step, the new exact posterior must be recomputed *with the updated parameters* as a part of the subsequent E-step.

When q is merely an approximation to p, the relationship between the marginal log-likelihood and the expected log-likelihood under distribution q can be written with an equality as opposed to an inequality:

$$\log P(\tilde{X}; \theta) = \mathrm{E}[\log P(\tilde{X}, H; \theta)]_q + \mathrm{H}(q) + D_{\mathrm{KL}}(q \| p)$$

$$= \mathrm{L}(q) + D_{\mathrm{KL}}(q \| p).$$

$\mathrm{KL}(q \| p)$ is known as the Kullback–Leibler (KL) divergence, a measure of the distance between distributions q and p. It is not a true distance in the mathematical sense, but rather a quantity that always exceeds zero and only becomes zero when $q = p$. Here it is given by

$$D_{\mathrm{KL}}(q||p) = \sum_{H} q(H|\tilde{X}; \Phi) \ \log \frac{q(H|\tilde{X}; \Phi)}{p(H|\tilde{X}; \theta)}.$$

The difference between the log marginal likelihood and the variational bound is given by the KL divergence between the approximate q and the true p. This means that if q is approximate, the bound can be tightened by improving the quality of the approximation q to the true posterior p. So, as we also saw above, when q is not an approximation but equals p exactly, $D_{\mathrm{KL}}(q||p) = 0$ and

$$\log P(\tilde{X}; \theta) = \mathrm{E}[\log \ P(\tilde{X}, H; \theta)]_q + \mathrm{H}(q).$$

Variational inference techniques are often used to improve the quality of an approximate posterior distribution within an EM algorithm, and the term "variational EM" refers to this general method. However, the result of a variational inference procedure is sometimes useful in itself. A key feature of variational methods arises from the existence of the variational bound and the fact that algorithms can be formulated that iteratively bring q closer to p in the sense of the KL divergence.

The *mean-field* approach is one of the simplest variational methods. It minimizes the KL divergence between an approximation, which consists of giving each variable its own separate variational distribution (and parameters), and the true joint distribution. This is known as a "fully factored variational approximation" and could be written

$$q(H|\tilde{X}; \Phi) = \prod_{j} q_j(h_j|\tilde{X}; \phi_j).$$

Given some initial parameters for the separate distributions for each variable $q_j = q_j(h_j)$, one proceeds to update each variable iteratively, given expectations of the model under the current variational approximation for the other variables. These updates take this general form:

$$q_j(h_j|\tilde{X}; \phi_j) = \frac{1}{Z} \mathrm{E}[\log \ P(X, H; \theta)]_{\prod_{i \neq j} q_i(h_i)},$$

where the expectation is performed using the approximate qs for all variables h_i other than h_j, and Z is a normalization constant obtained by summing over the numerator for all values of h_j.

Early work on variational methods for graphical models is well represented in Jordan, Ghahramani, Jaakkola, and Saul (1999). If distributions are placed over parameters as well as hidden variables, variational Bayesian methods and variational Bayesian EM can be used to perform more fully Bayesian learning (Ghahramani and Beal, 2001). Winn and Bishop (2005) gives a good comparison of belief propagation and variational inference methods when viewed as message passing algorithms. Bishop's textbook (Bishop, 2006), as well as Koller and Friedman (2009)'s, provide further detail and more advanced machine learning techniques based on the variational perspective.

Appendix B: The WEKA workbench

The WEKA workbench is a collection of machine learning algorithms and data preprocessing tools that includes virtually all the algorithms described in this book. It is designed so that you can quickly try out existing methods on new datasets in flexible ways. It provides extensive support for the whole process of experimental data mining, including preparing the input data, evaluating learning schemes statistically, and visualizing the input data and the result of learning. As well as a wide variety of learning algorithms, it includes a wide range of preprocessing tools. This diverse and comprehensive toolkit is accessed through a common interface so that its users can compare different methods and identify those that are most appropriate for the problem at hand.

WEKA was developed at the University of Waikato in New Zealand; the name stands for *Waikato Environment for Knowledge Analysis*. Outside the university the WEKA, pronounced to rhyme with *Mecca*, is a flightless bird with an inquisitive nature found only on the islands of New Zealand. The system is written in Java and distributed under the terms of the GNU General Public License. It runs on almost any platform and has been tested under Linux, Windows, and Macintosh operating systems.

B.1 WHAT'S IN WEKA?

WEKA provides implementations of learning algorithms that you can easily apply to your dataset. It also includes a variety of tools for transforming datasets, such as the algorithms for discretization and sampling. You can preprocess a dataset, feed it into a learning scheme, and analyze the resulting classifier and its performance—all without writing any program code at all.

The workbench includes methods for the main data mining problems: regression, classification, clustering, association rule mining, and attribute selection. Getting to know the data is an integral part of the work, and many data visualization facilities and data preprocessing tools are provided. All algorithms take their input in the form of a single relational table that can be read from a file or generated by a database query.

One way of using WEKA is to apply a learning method to a dataset and analyze its output to learn more about the data. Another is to use learned models to generate predictions on new instances. A third is to apply several different learners and compare their performance in order to choose one for prediction. In the interactive WEKA interface you select the learning method you want from a menu. Many methods have tunable parameters, which you access through a property sheet or *object editor*. A common evaluation module is used to measure the performance of all classifiers.

Implementations of actual learning schemes are the most valuable resource that WEKA provides. But tools for preprocessing the data, called *filters*, come a close second. Like classifiers, you select filters from a menu and tailor them to your requirements.

HOW DO YOU USE IT?

The easiest way to use WEKA is through a graphical user interface called the *Explorer*. This gives access to all of its facilities using menu selection and form filling. For example, you can quickly read in a dataset from a file and build a decision tree from it. The Explorer guides you by presenting options as forms to be filled out. Helpful *tool tips* pop up as the mouse passes over items on the screen to explain what they do. Sensible default values ensure that you can get results with a minimum of effort—but you will have to think about what you are doing to understand what the results mean.

There are three other graphical user interfaces to WEKA. The *Knowledge Flow* interface allows you to design configurations for streamed data processing. A fundamental disadvantage of the Explorer is that it holds everything in main memory—when you open a dataset, it immediately loads it all in. That means that it can only be applied to small- to medium-sized problems. However, WEKA contains some incremental algorithms that can be used to process very large datasets. The Knowledge Flow interface lets you drag boxes representing learning algorithms and data sources around the screen and join them together into the configuration you want. It enables you to specify a data stream by connecting components representing data sources, preprocessing tools, learning algorithms, evaluation methods, and visualization modules. If the filters and learning algorithms are capable of incremental learning, data will be loaded and processed incrementally.

WEKA's third interface, the *Experimenter*, is designed to help you answer a basic practical question when applying classification and regression techniques: Which methods and parameter values work best for the given problem? There is usually no way to answer this question a priori, and one reason we developed the workbench was to provide an environment that enables WEKA users to compare a variety of learning techniques. This can be done interactively using the Explorer. However, the Experimenter allows you to automate the process by making it easy to run classifiers and filters with different parameter settings on a corpus of datasets, collect performance statistics, and perform significance tests. Advanced users can employ the Experimenter to distribute the computing load across multiple machines using Java remote method invocation. In this way you can set up large-scale statistical experiments and leave them to run.

The fourth interface, called the *Workbench*, is a unified graphical user interface that combines the other three (and any plugins that the user has installed) into one application. The Workbench is highly configurable, allowing the user to specify which applications and plugins will appear, along with settings relating to them.

Behind these interactive interfaces lies the basic functionality of WEKA. This can be accessed in raw form by entering textual commands, which gives access to all features of the system. When you fire up WEKA you have to choose among five different user interfaces via the WEKA GUI Chooser: the Explorer, Knowledge Flow, Experimenter, Workbench, and command-line interfaces (we do not consider the command-line interface in this Appendix). Most people choose the Explorer, at least initially.

WHAT ELSE CAN YOU DO?

An important resource when working with WEKA is the online documentation, which has been automatically generated from the source code and concisely reflects its structure. The online documentation gives the only complete list of available algorithms because WEKA is continually growing and—being generated automatically from the source code—the online documentation is always up to date. Moreover, it becomes essential if you want to proceed to the next level and access the library from your own Java programs or write and test learning schemes of your own.

In most data mining applications, the machine learning component is just a small part of a far larger software system. If you intend to write a data mining application, you will want to access the programs in WEKA from inside your own code. By doing so, you can solve the machine learning subproblem of your application with a minimum of additional programming.

If you intend to become an expert in machine learning algorithms (or, indeed, if you already are one), you will probably want to implement your own algorithms without having to address such mundane details as reading the data from a file, implementing filtering algorithms, or providing code to evaluate the results. If so, we have good news for you: WEKA already includes all this. To make full use of it, you must become acquainted with the basic data structures.

An extended version of this Appendix, which discusses these opportunities for advanced users and also describes the command-line interface, is available at http://www.cs.waikato.ac.nz/ml/book.html.

B.2 THE PACKAGE MANAGEMENT SYSTEM

The WEKA software has evolved considerably since the third edition of this book was published. Many new algorithms and features have been added to the system, a number of which have been contributed by the community. With so many algorithms on offer we felt that the software could be considered overwhelming to the new user. Therefore a number of algorithms and community contributions were removed and placed into plugin *packages*. A package management system was added that allows the user to browse for, and selectively install, packages of interest.

Another motivation for introducing the package management system was to make the process of contributing to the WEKA software easier, and to ease the maintenance burden on the WEKA development team. A contributor of a plugin package is responsible for maintaining its code and hosting the install-able archive, while WEKA simply tracks the package metadata. The package system also opens the door to the use of third-party libraries, something that we would have discouraged in the past in order to keep a lightweight footprint for WEKA.

The graphical package manager can be accessed from the *Tools* menu of WEKA's *GUI Chooser*. The very first time the package manager is accessed it will download information about the currently available packages. This requires an internet connection, however, once the package metadata has been downloaded it is possible to use the package manager to browse package information while offline. Of course, an Internet connection is still required to be able to actually install a package.

The package manager presents a list of packages near the top of its window and a panel at the bottom that displays information on the currently selected package in the list. The user can choose to display packages that are available but not yet installed, only packages that are installed, or all packages. The list presents the name of each package, the broad category that it belongs to, the version currently installed (if any), the most recent version of the package available that is compatible with the version of WEKA being used, and a field that, for installed packages, indicates whether the package has been loaded success-fully by WEKA or not. Although not obvious at first glance, it is possible to install older versions of a particular package. The *Repository version* field in the list is actually a drop-down box. The list of packages can be sorted, in ascending or descending order, by clicking on either the package or category column header.

The information panel at the bottom of the window has clickable links for each version of a given package. "Latest" always refers to the latest version of the package, and is the same as the highest version number available. Clicking one of these links displays further information, such as the author of the package, its license, where the installable archive is located, and its dependencies. The information about each package is also browsable at the Web location where WEKA's package metadata is hosted. All packages have at least one dependency listed—the minimum version of the core WEKA system that they can work with. Some packages list further dependencies on other packages. For example, the *multi-InstanceLearning* package depends on the *multi-InstanceFilters* package. When installing *multi-InstanceLearning*, and assuming that *multi-InstanceFilters* is not already installed, the system will inform the user the *multi-InstanceFilters* is required and will be installed automatically.

The package manager displays what are known as *official* packages for WEKA. These are packages that have been submitted to the WEKA team for a review and have had their metadata added to the official central metadata repository. For one reason or another, an author of a package might decide to make it available in an unofficial capacity. These packages do not appear in the official list on the Web, or in the list displayed by the graphical package manager. If the user knows the URL to an archive containing an unofficial package, it can be installed by using the button in the upper right-hand corner of the package manager window.

Whenever a new package, or new version of an existing one, becomes available the package manager informs the user by displaying a large yellow warning icon. Hovering over this icon displays a tool-tip popup that lists the new packages and prompts the user to click the *Refresh repository cache* button. Clicking this button downloads a fresh copy of all the package information to the user's computer.

The *Install* and *Uninstall* buttons at the top of the package manager's window do exactly as their names suggest. More than one package can be installed or uninstalled in one go by selecting multiple entries in the list. By default, WEKA attempts to load all installed packages, and if a package cannot be loaded for some reason a message will be displayed in the *Loaded* column of the list. The user can opt to prevent a particular package from being loaded by selecting it and then clicking the *Toggle load* button. This will mark the package as one that should not be loaded the next time that WEKA is started. This can be useful if an unstable package is generating errors, conflicting with another package (perhaps due to third-party libraries), or otherwise preventing WEKA from operating properly.

B.3 THE EXPLORER

WEKA's historically most popular graphical user interface, the Explorer, gives access to all its facilities using menu selection and form filling. To begin, there are six different panels, selected by the tabs at the top, corresponding to the various data mining tasks that WEKA supports. Further panels can become available by installing appropriate packages.

Loading the data into the Explorer

To illustrate what can be done with the Explorer, suppose we want to build a decision tree from the weather data included in the WEKA download. Fire up WEKA to get the *GUI Chooser*. Select *Explorer* from the five choices on the right-hand side. (The others were mentioned earlier: *Simple CLI* is the old-fashioned command-line interface.)

What you see next is the main Explorer screen. The six tabs along the top are the basic operations that the Explorer supports: right now we are on *Preprocess*. Click the *Open file* button to bring up a standard dialog through which you can select a file. Choose the *weather.arff* file. If you have it in CSV format, change from *ARFF data files* to *CSV data files*.

Having loaded the file, the Preprocess screen tells you about the dataset: it has 14 instances and 5 attributes (center left); the attributes are called *outlook*, *temperature*, *humidity*, *windy*, and *play* (lower left). The first attribute, *outlook*, is selected by default (you can choose others by clicking them) and has no missing values, three distinct values, and no unique values; the actual values are *sunny*, *overcast*, and *rainy* and they occur five, four, and five times, respectively (center right). A histogram at the lower right shows how often each of the two values of the class, *play*, occurs for each value of the *outlook* attribute. The attribute *outlook* is used because it appears in the box above the histogram, but you can draw a histogram of any other attribute instead. Here *play* is selected as the class attribute; it is used to color the histogram, and any filters that require a class value use it too.

The *outlook* attribute is nominal. If you select a numeric attribute, you see its minimum and maximum values, mean, and standard deviation. In this case the histogram will show the distribution of the class as a function of this attribute.

You can delete an attribute by clicking its checkbox and using the *Remove* button. *All* selects all the attributes, *None* selects none, *Invert* inverts the current selection, and *Pattern* selects those attributes whose names match a user-supplied regular expression. You can undo a change by clicking the *Undo* button. The *Edit* button brings up an editor that allows you to inspect the data, search for particular values and edit them, and delete instances and attributes. Right-clicking on values and column headers brings up corresponding context menus.

Building a decision tree

To build a decision tree, click the *Classify* tab to get access to WEKA's classification and regression schemes. In the *Classify* panel, select the classifier by clicking the *Choose* button at the top left, opening up the *trees* section of the hierarchical menu that appears, and finding *J48*. The menu structure represents the organization of the WEKA code into modules and the items you need to select are always at the lowest level. Once selected, *J48* appears in the line beside the *Choose* button, along with its default parameter values. If you click that line, the J48 classifier's object editor opens up and you can see what the parameters mean and alter their values if you wish. The Explorer generally chooses sensible defaults.

Having chosen the classifier, invoke it by clicking the *Start* button. WEKA works for a brief period—when it is working, the little bird at the lower right of the Explorer jumps up and dances—and then produces the output for J48.

Examining the output

At the beginning of the output is a summary of the dataset, and the fact that 10-fold cross-validation was used to evaluate it. That is the default, and if you look closely at the *Classify* panel you will see that the *Cross-validation* box at the left is checked. Then comes a pruned decision tree in textual form. The model that is shown here is always the one generated from the full dataset available from the *Preprocess* panel.

The next part of the output gives estimates of the tree's predictive performance. In this case they are obtained using stratified cross-validation with 10 folds. As well as the classification error, the evaluation module also outputs several other performance statistics.

The *Classify* panel has several other test options: *Use training set*, which is generally not recommended; *Supplied test set*, in which you specify a separate file containing the test set; and *Percentage split*, with which you can hold out a certain percentage of the data for testing. You can output the predictions for each instance by clicking the *More options* button and checking the appropriate entry. There are other useful options, such as suppressing some output and including other statistics such as entropy evaluation measures and cost-sensitive evaluation.

Working with models

The small pane at the lower left of the *Classify* panel, which contains one highlighted line, is a history list of the results. The Explorer adds a new line whenever you run a classifier. To return to a previous result set, click the corresponding line and the output for that run will appear in the Classifier Output pane. This makes it easy to explore different classifiers or evaluation schemes and revisit the results to compare them.

When you *right*-click an entry a menu appears that allows you to view the results in a separate window, or save the result buffer. More importantly, you can save the model that WEKA has generated in the form of a Java object file. You can reload a model that was saved previously, which generates a new entry in the result list. If you now supply a test set, you can reevaluate the old model on that new set.

Several items on the right-click menu allow you to visualize the results in various ways. At the top of the Explorer interface is a separate *Visualize* tab, but that is different: it shows the dataset, not the results for a particular model. By right-clicking an entry in the history list you can see the classifier errors. If the model is a tree or a Bayesian network you can see its structure. You can also view the margin curve and various cost and threshold curves, and perform a cost/benefit analysis.

EXPLORING THE EXPLORER

We have briefly investigated two of the six tabs at the top of the Explorer. In summary, here is what all the basic tabs do:

1. *Preprocess*: Choose the dataset and modify it in various ways.
2. *Classify*: Train learning schemes that perform classification or regression and evaluate them.
3. *Cluster*: Learn clusters for the dataset.
4. *Associate*: Learn association rules for the data and evaluate them.
5. *Select attributes*: Select the most relevant aspects in the dataset.
6. *Visualize*: View different two-dimensional plots of the data and interact with them.

Each tab gives access to a whole range of facilities. In our tour so far, we have barely scratched the surface of the *Preprocess* and *Classify* panels.

At the bottom of every panel is a *Status* box and a *Log* button. The status box displays messages that keep you informed about what is going on. For example, if the Explorer is busy loading a file, the status box will say so. Right-clicking anywhere inside this box brings up a little menu with two options: display the amount of memory available to WEKA, and run the Java garbage collector. Note that the garbage collector runs constantly as a background task anyway.

Clicking the *Log* button opens a textual log of the actions that WEKA has performed in this session, with timestamps.

As noted earlier, the little bird at the lower right of the window jumps up and dances when WEKA is active. The number beside the ✕ shows how many concurrent processes are running. If the bird is standing but stops moving, it is sick! Something has gone wrong, and you may have to restart the Explorer.

Loading and filtering files

Along the top of the *Preprocess* panel are buttons for opening files, URLs, and databases. Initially, only files whose names end in *.arff* appear in the file browser; to see others, change the *Format* item in the file selection box.

Data can be saved in various formats using the *Save* button in the *Preprocess* panel. It is also possible to generate artificial data using the *Generate* button. Apart from loading and saving datasets, the *Preprocess* panel also allows you to filter them. Clicking *Choose* (near the top left) in the *Preprocess* panel gives a list of filters. We will describe how to use a simple filter to delete specified attributes from a dataset, in other words, to perform manual attribute selection. The same effect can be achieved more easily by selecting the relevant attributes using the tick boxes and pressing the *Remove* button. Nevertheless we describe the equivalent filtering operation explicitly, as an example.

Remove is an unsupervised attribute filter, and to see it you must first expand the *unsupervised* category and then the *attribute* category. This will reveal quite a formidable list of filters, and you will have to scroll further down to find Remove.

When selected, it appears in the line beside the *Choose* button, along with its parameter values—in this case the line reads simply "Remove." Click that line to bring up a generic object editor with which you can examine and alter the filter's properties.

To learn about it, click *More* button. This explains that the filter removes a range of attributes from the dataset. It has an option, *attributeIndices*, that specifies the range to act on and another called *invertSelection* that determines whether the filter selects attributes or deletes them. There are boxes for both of these in the object editor. After configuring an object it is often worth glancing at the resulting command-line formulation that the Explorer sets up, which is shown next to the *Choose* button.

Algorithms in WEKA may provide information about what data characteristics they can handle, and, if they do, a *Capabilities* button appears underneath *More* in the generic object editor. Clicking it brings up information about what the method can do. In this case it states that *Remove* can handle many attribute characteristics, such as different types (nominal, numeric, relational, etc.) and missing values. It shows the minimum number of instances that are required for *Remove* to operate on.

A list of selected constraints on capabilities can be obtained by clicking the *Filter* button at the bottom of the generic object editor. If the current dataset exhibits some characteristic that is ticked in this list but missing from the capabilities for the *Remove* filter the *Apply* button to the right of *Choose* in the *Preprocess* panel will be grayed out, as will the entry in the list that appears when the *Choose* button is pressed. Although you cannot apply it, you can nevertheless select a grayed-out entry to inspect its options, documentation, and capabilities using the generic object editor. You can release individual constraints by deselecting them in the constraints list, or click the *Remove filter* button to clear all the constraints.

Clustering and association rules

Use the *Cluster* and *Associate* panels to invoke clustering algorithms and methods for finding association rules. When clustering, WEKA shows the number of clusters and how many instances each cluster contains. For some algorithms the number of clusters can be specified by setting a parameter in the object editor. For probabilistic clustering methods, WEKA measures the log-likelihood of the clusters on the training data: the larger this quantity, the better the model fits the data. Increasing the number of clusters normally increases the likelihood, but may overfit.

The controls on the *Cluster* panel are similar to those for *Classify*. You can specify some of the same evaluation methods—use training set, supplied test set, and percentage split (the last two are used with the log-likelihood). A further method, classes to clusters evaluation, compares how well the chosen clusters match a preassigned class in the data. You select an attribute (which must be nominal) that represents the "true" class. Having clustered the data, WEKA determines the majority class in each cluster and prints a confusion matrix showing how many errors there would be if the clusters were used instead of the true class. If your dataset has a class attribute, you can ignore it during clustering by selecting it from a pull-down list of attributes, and see how well the clusters correspond to actual class values. Finally, you can choose whether or not to store the clusters for visualization. The only reason not to do so is to conserve space. As with classifiers, you visualize the results by right-clicking on the result list, which allows you to view two-dimensional scatter plots. If you have chosen classes to clusters evaluation, the class assignment errors are shown. For the *Cobweb* clustering scheme, you can also visualize the tree.

The *Associate* panel is simpler than *Classify* or *Cluster*. WEKA contains several algorithms for determining association rules, but no methods for evaluating such rules.

Attribute selection

The *Select attributes* panel gives access to several methods for attribute selection. These involve an attribute evaluator and a search method. Both are chosen in the usual way and configured with the object editor. You must also decide which attribute to use as the class. Attribute selection can be performed using the full training set or using cross-validation. In the latter case it is done separately for each fold, and the output shows how many times—i.e., in how many of the folds—each attribute was selected. The results are stored in the history list. When you right-click an entry here you can visualize the dataset in terms of the selected attributes (choose *Visualize reduced data*).

Visualization

The *Visualize* panel helps you visualize a dataset—not the result of a classification or clustering model, but the dataset itself. It displays a matrix of two-dimensional scatter plots of every pair of attributes. You can select an attribute—normally the class—for coloring the data points using the controls at the bottom. If it is nominal, the coloring is discrete; if it is numeric, the color spectrum ranges continuously from blue (low values) to orange (high values). Data points with no class value are shown in black. You can change the size of each plot, the size of the points, and the amount of jitter, which is a random displacement applied to X and Y values to separate points that lie on top of one another. Without jitter, a thousand instances at the same data point would look just the same as one instance. You can reduce the size of the matrix of plots by selecting certain attributes, and you can subsample the data for efficiency. Changes in the controls do not take effect until the *Update* button is clicked.

Clicking one of the plots in the matrix enlarges it. You can zoom in on any area of the resulting panel by choosing *Rectangle* from the menu near the top right and dragging out a rectangle on the viewing area like that shown. The *Submit* button near the top left rescales the rectangle into the viewing area.

FILTERING ALGORITHMS

Now we take a closer look at the filtering algorithms implemented within WEKA. There are two kinds of filter: unsupervised and supervised. This seemingly innocuous distinction masks a rather fundamental issue. Filters are often applied to a training dataset and then also applied to the test file. If the filter is supervised—e.g., if it uses class values to derive good intervals for discretization—applying it to the test data will bias the results. It is the discretization intervals derived from the *training* data that must be applied to the test data. When using supervised filters you must be careful to ensure that the results are evaluated fairly, an issue that does not generally arise with unsupervised filters.

Because of popular demand, WEKA allows you to invoke supervised filters as a preprocessing operation, just like unsupervised filters. However, if you intend using them for classification you should adopt a different methodology. A metalearner is provided in the *Classify* panel that invokes a filter in a way that wraps the learning algorithm into the filtering mechanism. This filters the test data using the filter that has been created by the training data. It is also useful for some unsupervised filters. For example, in WEKA's *StringToWordVector* filter the dictionary will be created from the training data alone: words that are novel in the test data will be discarded. To use a supervised filter in this way, invoke the *FilteredClassifier* metalearning scheme from in the *meta* section of the menu displayed by the *Classify* panel's *Choose* button.

Within each type there is a further distinction between *attribute filters*, which work on the attributes in the datasets, and *instance filters*, which work on the instances. To learn more about a particular filter, select it in the WEKA Explorer and look at its associated object editor, which defines what the filter does and the parameters it takes.

LEARNING ALGORITHMS

On the *Classify* panel, when you select a learning algorithm using the *Choose* button the command-line version of the classifier appears in the line beside the button, including the parameters specified with minus signs. To change them, click that line to get an appropriate object editor. The classifiers in WEKA are divided into Bayesian classifiers, trees, rules, functions, lazy classifiers, meta classifiers, and a final miscellaneous category.

Metalearning algorithms take classifiers and turn them into more powerful learners, or retarget them for other applications. They are used to perform boosting, bagging, cost-sensitive classification and learning, automatic parameter optimization, and many other tasks. We already mentioned *FilteredClassifier*: it runs a classifier on data that has been passed through a filter, which is a parameter. The filter's own parameters are based exclusively on the training data, which is the appropriate way to apply a supervised filter to test data.

ATTRIBUTE SELECTION

Attribute selection can be performed in the Explorer's *Select attributes* tab. It is normally done by searching the space of attribute subsets, evaluating each one. A potentially faster but less accurate approach is to evaluate the attributes individually and sort them, discarding attributes that fall below a chosen cut-off point. WEKA supports both methods.

Subset evaluators take a subset of attributes and return a numerical measure that guides the search. They are configured like any other WEKA object. Single-attribute evaluators are used with the *Ranker* search method to generate a ranked list from which *Ranker* discards a given number.

Search methods traverse the attribute space to find a good subset. Quality is measured by the chosen attribute subset evaluator. Each search method can be configured with WEKA's object editor, just like evaluator objects.

B.4 THE KNOWLEDGE FLOW INTERFACE

With the Knowledge Flow interface, users select WEKA components from a tool bar, place them on a layout canvas, and connect them into a directed graph that processes and analyzes data. It provides an alternative to the Explorer for those who like thinking in terms of how data flows through the system. It also allows the design and execution of configurations for streamed data processing, which the Explorer cannot do. You invoke the Knowledge Flow interface by selecting *KnowledgeFlow* from the choices on the *GUIChooser*.

GETTING STARTED

Let us examine a step-by-step example that loads a data file and performs a cross-validation using the J48 decision tree learner. First create a source of data by expanding the *DataSources* folder in the *Design* palette on the left-hand side of the Knowledge Flow and select *ARFFLoader*. The mouse cursor changes to crosshairs to signal that you should next place the component. Do this by clicking anywhere on the canvas, whereupon a copy of the ARFF loader icon appears there. To connect it to an ARFF file, right-click it to bring up a pop-up menu and then click *Configure* to get an editor dialog. From here you can either browse for an ARFF file by clicking the Browse button, or type the path to one in the *Filename* field.

Now we specify which attribute is the class using a *ClassAssigner* object. This is found under the *Evaluation* folder in the *Design* palette, so expand the *Evaluation* folder, select the *ClassAssigner*, and place it on the canvas. To connect the data source to the class assigner, right-click the data source icon and select *dataset* from the menu. A rubber-band line appears. Move the mouse over the class assigner component and left-click. A red line labeled *dataset* appears, joining the two components. Having connected the class assigner, choose the class by right-clicking it, selecting *Configure*, and entering the location of the class attribute.

We will perform cross-validation on the J48 classifier. In the data flow model, we first connect the *CrossValidationFoldMaker* to create the folds on which the classifier will run, and then pass its output to an object representing J48. *CrossValidationFoldMaker* is in the *Evaluation* folder. Select it, place it on the canvas, and connect it to the class assigner by right-clicking the latter and selecting *dataset* from the menu. Next select *J48* from the *trees* folder under the *Classifiers* folder and place a J48 component on the canvas. Connect J48 to the cross-validation fold maker in the usual way, but make the connection *twice* by first choosing *trainingSet* and then *testSet* from the pop-up menu for the cross-validation fold maker. The next step is to select a *ClassifierPerformanceEvaluator* from the *Evaluation* folder and connect J48 to it by selecting the *batchClassifier* entry from the pop-up menu for J48. Finally, from the *Visualization* folder we place a *TextViewer* component on the canvas. Connect the classifier performance evaluator to it by selecting the *text* entry from the pop-up menu for the performance evaluator.

The flow of execution is started by clicking one of the two triangular-shaped "play" buttons at the left side of the main toolbar. The leftmost play button launches all data sources present in the flow in parallel; the other play button launches the data sources sequentially, where a particular order of execution can be specified by including a number at the start of the component's name (a name can be set via the *Set name* entry on popup menu). For a small dataset things happen quickly. Progress information appears in the status area at the bottom of the interface. The entries in the status area show the progress of each step in the flow, along with their parameter settings (for learning schemes) and elapsed time. Any errors that occur in a processing step are shown in the status area by highlighting the corresponding row in red. Choosing *Show results* from the text viewer's pop-up menu brings the results of cross-validation up in a separate window, in the same form as for the Explorer.

To complete the example, we can add a *GraphViewer* and connect it to J48's *graph* output to see a graphical representation of the trees produced for each fold of the cross-validation. Once you have redone the cross-validation with this extra component in place, selecting *Show results* from its pop-up menu produces a list of trees, one for each cross-validation fold. By creating cross-validation folds and passing them to the classifier, the Knowledge Flow model provides a way to hook into the results for each fold.

The flow that we have just considered is actually available (minus the *GraphViewer*) as a built-in template. Example templates can be accessed from the *Template* button, which is the third icon from the right in the toolbar at the top of the Knowledge Flow interface. There are a number of templates that come with WEKA, and certain packages, once installed via the package manager, add further ones to the menu. The majority of template flows can be executed without further modification as they have been configured to load datasets that come with the WEKA distribution.

KNOWLEDGE FLOW COMPONENTS

Most of the Knowledge Flow components will be familiar from the Explorer. The *Classifiers* folder contains all of WEKA's classifiers, the *Filters* folder contains the filters, the *Clusterers* folder holds the clusterers, the *AttSelection* folder contains evaluators and search methods for attribute selection, and the *Associations* panel holds the association rule learners. All components in the Knowledge Flow are run in a separate thread of execution, except in the case where data is being processed incrementally—in this case a single thread of execution is used because, generally, the amount of processing done per data point is small, and launching a separate thread to process each one would incur a significant overhead.

CONFIGURING AND CONNECTING THE COMPONENTS

You establish the knowledge flow by configuring the individual components and connecting them up. The menus that are available by right-clicking various component types have up to three sections: *Edit*, *Connections*, and *Actions*. The *Edit* operations delete components and open up their configuration panel. You can give a component a name by choosing *Set name* from the pop-up menu. Classifiers and filters are configured just as in the Explorer. Data sources are configured by opening a file (as we saw previously) or by setting a database connection, and evaluation components are configured by setting parameters such as the number of folds for cross-validation. The *Connections* operations are used to connect components together by selecting the type of connection from the source component and then clicking on the target object. Not all targets are suitable; applicable ones are highlighted. Items on the connections menu are disabled (grayed out) until the component receives other connections that render them applicable.

There are two kinds of connection from data sources: *dataset* connections and *instance* connections. The former are for batch operations such as classifiers like J48; the latter are for stream operations such as *NaiveBayesUpdateable* (an incremental version of the Naïve Bayes classifier). A data source component cannot provide both types of connection: once one is selected, the other is disabled. When a *dataset* connection is made to a batch classifier, the classifier needs to know whether it is intended to serve as a training set or a test set. To do this, you first make the data source into a test or training set using the *TestSetMaker* or *TrainingSetMaker* components from the *Evaluation* panel. On the other hand, an *instance* connection to an incremental classifier is made directly: there is no distinction between training and testing because the instances that flow update the classifier incrementally. In this case a prediction is made for each incoming instance and incorporated into the test results; then the classifier is trained on that instance. If you make an *instance* connection to a batch classifier it will be used as a test instance because training cannot possibly be incremental whereas testing always can be. Conversely, it is quite possible to test an incremental classifier in batch mode using a *dataset* connection.

Connections from a filter component are enabled when it receives input from a data source, whereupon follow-on *dataset* or *instance* connections can be made. *Instance* connections cannot be made to supervised filters or to unsupervised filters that cannot handle data incrementally (such as *Discretize*). To get a test or training set out of a filter, you need to put the appropriate kind in.

The classifier menu has two types of connection. The first type, namely, *graph* and *text* connections, provides graphical and textual representations of the classifier's learned state and is only activated when it receives a training set input. The other type, namely, *batchClassifier* and *incrementalClassifier* connections, makes data available to a performance evaluator and is only activated when a test set input is present too. Which one is activated depends on the type of the classifier.

Evaluation components are a mixed bag. *TrainingSetMaker* and *TestSetMaker* turn a dataset into a training or test set. *CrossValidationFoldMaker* turns a dataset into *both* a training set and a test set. *ClassifierPerformanceEvaluator* generates textual and graphical output for visualization components. Other evaluation components operate like filters: they enable follow-on *dataset*, *instance*, *training set*, or *test set* connections depending on the input (e.g., *ClassAssigner* assigns a class to a dataset). Visualization components do not have connections, although some have actions such as *Show results* and *Clear results*.

INCREMENTAL LEARNING

In most respects the Knowledge Flow interface is functionally similar to the Explorer: you can do similar things with both. It does provide some additional flexibility—e.g., you can see the tree that J48 makes for each cross-validation fold. But its real strength is the potential for incremental operation.

If all components connected up in the Knowledge Flow interface operate incrementally, so does the resulting learning system. It does not read in the dataset before learning starts, as the Explorer does. Instead, the data source component reads the input instance by instance and passes it through the Knowledge Flow chain.

Selecting the "Learn and evaluate Naive Bayes incrementally" template from the *templates* menu brings up a configuration that works incrementally. An *instance* connection is made from the loader to a class assigner component, which, in turn, is connected to the updatable Naïve Bayes classifier. The classifier's text output is taken to a viewer that gives a textual description of the model. Also, an *incrementalClassifier* connection is made to the corresponding performance evaluator. This produces an output of type *chart*, which is piped to a strip chart visualization component to generate a scrolling data plot.

This particular Knowledge Flow configuration can process input files of any size, even ones that do not fit into the computer's main memory. However, it all depends on how the classifier operates internally. For example, although they are incremental, many instance-based learners store the entire dataset internally.

B.5 THE EXPERIMENTER

The Explorer and Knowledge Flow environments help you determine how well machine learning schemes perform on given datasets. But serious investigative work involves substantial experiments—typically running several learning schemes on different datasets, often with various parameter settings—and these interfaces are not really suitable for this. The Experimenter enables you to set up large-scale experiments, start them running, leave them, and come back when they have finished and analyze the performance statistics that have been collected. They automate the experimental process. The statistics can be stored in a file or database, and can themselves be the subject of further data mining. You invoke this interface by selecting *Experimenter* from the choices at the side of the *GUIChooser*.

Whereas the Knowledge Flow transcends limitations of space by allowing machine learning runs that do not load in the whole dataset at once, the Experimenter transcends limitations of time. It contains facilities for advanced users to distribute the computing load across multiple machines using Java RMI. You can set up big experiments and just leave them to run.

GETTING STARTED

As an example, we will compare the J48 decision tree method with the baseline methods *OneR* and *ZeroR* on the Iris dataset. The Experimenter has three panels: *Setup*, *Run*, and *Analyze*. To configure an experiment, first click *New* (toward the right at the top) to start a new experiment (the other two buttons in that row save an experiment and open a previously saved one). Then, on the line below, select the destination for the results—in this case the file *Experiment1*—and choose *CSV file*. Underneath, select the datasets—we have only one, the Iris data. To the right of the datasets, select the algorithms to be tested—we have three. Click *Add new* to get a standard WEKA object editor from which you can choose and configure a classifier. Repeat this operation to add the three classifiers. Now the experiment is ready.

The other settings are all default values. If you want to reconfigure a classifier that is already in the list, you can use the *Edit selected* button. You can also save the options for a particular classifier in XML format for later reuse. You can right-click on an entry to copy the configuration to the clipboard, and add or enter a configuration from the clipboard.

Running an experiment

To run the experiment, click the *Run* tab, which brings up a panel that contains a *Start* button (and little else); click it. A brief report is displayed when the operation is finished. The file *Experiment1.csv* contains the results, in CSV format, which can be directly read into a spreadsheet. Each row represents 1-fold of a

10-fold cross-validation (see the *Fold* column). The cross-validation is run 10 times (the *Run* column) for each classifier (the *Scheme* column). Thus the file contains 100 rows for each classifier, which makes 300 rows in all (plus the header row). Each row contains plenty of information, including the options supplied to the machine learning scheme; the number of training and test instances; the number (and percentage) of correct, incorrect, and unclassified instances; the mean absolute error, root mean-squared error, and many more.

There is a great deal of information in the spreadsheet, but it is hard to digest. In particular, it is not easy to answer the question posed previously: How does J48 compare with the baseline methods *OneR* and *ZeroR* on this dataset? For that we need the *Analyze* panel.

Analyzing the results

The reason that we generated the output in CSV format was to allow you to explore the raw data produced by the Experimenter in a spreadsheet. The Experimenter normally produces its output in ARFF format. You can also leave the file name blank, in which case the Experimenter stores the results in a temporary file.

To analyze the experiment that has just been performed, select the *Analyze* panel and click the *Experiment* button at the right near the top; otherwise, supply a file that contains the results of another experiment. Then click *Perform test* (near the bottom on the left). The result of a statistical significance test of the performance of the first learning scheme (*J48*) versus the other two (*OneR* and *ZeroR*) will be displayed in the large panel on the right.

We are comparing the percent correct statistic: this is selected by default as the comparison field shown toward the left of the output. The three methods are displayed horizontally, numbered (1), (2), and (3), as the heading of a little table. The labels for the columns are repeated at the bottom—*trees.J48*, *rules.OneR*, and *rules.ZeroR*—in case there is insufficient space for them in the heading. The inscrutable integers beside the scheme names identify which version of the scheme is being used. They are present by default to avoid confusion among results generated using different versions of the algorithms. The value in brackets at the beginning of the *iris* row *(100)* is the number of experimental runs: 10 times 10-fold cross-validation.

The percentage correct is shown for the three schemes: 94.73% for method 1, 92.53% for method 2, and 33.33% for method 3. The symbol placed beside a result indicates that it is statistically better (*v*) or worse (*) than the baseline scheme—in this case J48—at the specified significance level (0.05, or 5%). The corrected resampled *t*-test is used here. Here, method 3 is significantly worse than method 1, because its success rate is followed by an asterisk. At the bottom of columns 2 and 3 are counts (*x/y/z*) of the number of times the scheme was better than (*x*), the same as (*y*), or worse than (*z*) the baseline scheme on the datasets used in the experiment. In this case there is only one dataset; method 2 was equivalent to method 1 (the baseline) once and method 3 was worse than it once.

(The annotation (*v*/ /***) is placed at the bottom of column 1 to help you remember the meanings of the three counts *x*/*y*/*z*.)

The output in the *Analyze* panel can be saved into a file by clicking the "Save output" button. It is also possible to open a WEKA Explorer window to further analyze the experimental results obtained, by clicking on the "Open Explorer" button.

ADVANCED SETUP

The Experimenter has an advanced mode, which is accessed by selecting *Advanced* from the drop down box near the top of the *Setup* panel. This enlarges the options available for controlling the experiment—including, e.g., the ability to generate learning curves. However, the advanced mode is hard to use, and the simple version suffices for most purposes. For example, in advanced mode you can set up an iteration to test an algorithm with a succession of different parameter values, but the same effect can be achieved in simple mode by putting the algorithm into the list several times with different parameter values.

One thing you can do in advanced mode but not in simple mode is run experiments using clustering algorithms. Here, experiments are limited to those clusterers that can compute probability or density estimates, and the main evaluation measure for comparison purposes is the log-likelihood. Another use for the advanced mode for is to set up distributed experiments.

THE *ANALYZE* PANEL

Our walkthrough used the *Analyze* panel to perform a statistical significance test of one learning scheme (*J48*) versus two others (*OneR* and *ZeroR*). The test was on the error rate. Other statistics can be selected from the drop-down menu instead, including various entropy figures. Moreover, you can see the standard deviation of the attribute being evaluated by ticking the *Show std deviations* checkbox.

Use the *Test base* menu to change the baseline scheme from J48 to one of the other learning schemes. For example, selecting *OneR* causes the others to be compared with this scheme. Apart from the learning schemes, there are two other choices in the *Select base* menu: *Summary* and *Ranking*. The former compares each learning scheme with every other scheme and prints a matrix whose cells contain the number of datasets on which one is significantly better than the other. The latter ranks the schemes according to the total number of datasets that represent wins (>) and losses (<) and prints a league table. The first column in the output gives the difference between the number of wins and the number of losses.

The *Row* and *Column* fields determine the dimensions of the comparison matrix. Clicking *Select* brings up a list of all the features that have been measured in the experiment. You can select which to use as the rows and columns of the matrix.

(The selection does not appear in the *Select* box because more than one parameter can be chosen simultaneously.)

There is a button that allows you to select a subset of columns to display (the baseline column is always included), and another that allows you to select the output format: plain text (default), output for the LaTeX typesetting system, CSV format, HTML, data and script suitable for input to the GNUPlot graph plotting software, and just the significance symbols in plain text format. It is also possible to show averages and abbreviate filter class names in the output.

There is an option to choose whether to use the paired corrected *t*-test or the standard *t*-test for computing significance. The way the rows are sorted in the results table can be changed by choosing the *Sorting (asc.) by* option from the drop-down box. The default is to use natural ordering, presenting them in the order that the user entered the dataset names in the *Setup* panel. Alternatively, the rows can be sorted according to any of the measures that are available in the *Comparison field*.

References

Abadi, M., Agarwal, A., Barham, P., Brevdo, E., Chen, Z., Citro, C., et al. (2016). TensorFlow: Large-scale machine learning on heterogeneous distributed systems. *arXiv preprint*, arXiv:1603.04467.

Abe, N., Zadrozny, B., & Langford, J. (2006). Outlier detection by active learning. *Proceedings of the 12th ACM SIGKDD international conference on knowledge discovery and data mining* (pp. 767–772). New York, NY: ACM Press.

Adriaans, P., & Zantige, D. (1996). *Data mining*. Harlow: Addison-Wesley.

Agrawal, R., Imielinski, T., & Swami, A. (1993a). Database mining: A performance perspective. *IEEE Transactions on Knowledge and Data Engineering*, *5*(6), 914–925.

Agrawal, R., Imielinski, T., & Swami, A. (1993b). Mining association rules between sets of items in large databases. In P. Buneman, & S. Jajodia (Eds.), *Proceedings of the ACM SIGMOD international conference on management of data, Washington, DC* (pp. 207–216). New York, NY: ACM Press.

Agrawal, R., & Srikant, R. (1994). Fast algorithms for mining association rules in large databases. In J. Bocca, M. Jarke, & C. Zaniolo (Eds.), *Proceedings of the international conference on very large data bases, Santiago, Chile* (pp. 478–499). San Francisco, CA: Morgan Kaufmann.

Aha, D. (1992). Tolerating noisy, irrelevant, and novel attributes in instance-based learning algorithms. *International Journal of Man-Machine Studies*, *36*(2), 267–287.

Almuallin, H., & Dietterich, T. G. (1991). Learning with many irrelevant features. *Proceedings of the ninth national conference on artificial intelligence, Anaheim, CA* (pp. 547–552). Menlo Park, CA: AAAI Press.

Almuallin, H., & Dietterich, T. G. (1992). Efficient algorithms for identifying relevant features. *Proceedings of the ninth Canadian conference on artificial intelligence, Vancouver, BC* (pp. 38–45). San Francisco, CA: Morgan Kaufmann.

Andrews, S., Tsochantaridis, I., & Hofmann, T. (2003). Support vector machines for multiple-instance learning. *Proceedings of the conference on neural information processing systems, Vancouver, Canada* (pp. 561–568). Cambridge, MA: MIT Press.

Ankerst, M., Breunig, M. M., Kriegel, H.-P., & Sander, J. (1999). OPTICS: Ordering points to identify the clustering structure. *Proceedings of the ACM SIGMOD international conference on management of data* (pp. 49–60). New York, NY: ACM Press.

Arthur, D., & Vassilvitskii, S. (2007). K-means++: The advantages of careful seeding. *Proceedings of the eighteenth annual ACM-SIAM symposium on discrete algorithms. New Orleans, Louisiana* (pp. 1027–1035). Philadelphia, PA: Society for Industrial and Applied Mathematics.

Asmis, E. (1984). *Epicurus' scientific method*. Ithaca, NY: Cornell University Press.

Asuncion, A., & Newman, D. J. (2007). *UCI machine learning repository*. Irvine, CA: University of California, School of Information and Computer Science. <http://www.ics.uci.edu/~mlearn/MLRepository.html>.

Atkeson, C. G., Schaal, S. A., & Moore, A. W. (1997). Locally weighted learning. *AI Review*, *11*, 11–71.

Auer, P., & Ortner, R. (2004). A boosting approach to multiple instance learning. *Proceedings of the European conference on machine learning, Pisa, Italy* (pp. 63–74). Berlin: Springer-Verlag.

Baldi, P., & Hornik, K. (1989). Neural networks and principal component analysis: Learning from examples without local minima. *Neural Networks, 2*(1), 53–58.

Barnett, V., & Lewis, T. (1994). *Outliers in statistical data.* West Sussex: John Wiley and Sons.

Bay, S. D. (1999). Nearest neighbor classification from multiple feature subsets. *Intelligent Data Analysis, 3*(3), 191–209.

Bay, S. D., & Schwabacher, M. (2003). Near linear time detection of distance-based outliers and applications to security. *Proceedings of the workshop on data mining for counter terrorism and security, San Francisco.* Philadelphia, PA: Society for Industrial and Applied Mathematics.

Bayes, T. (1763). An essay towards solving a problem in the doctrine of chances. *Philosophical Transactions of the Royal Society of London, 53,* 370–418.

Beck, J. R., & Schultz, E. K. (1986). The use of ROC curves in test performance evaluation. *Archives of Pathology and Laboratory Medicine, 110,* 13–20.

Belhumeur, P. N., Hespanha, J. P., & Kriegman, D. J. (1997). Eigenfaces vs. fisherfaces: Recognition using class specific linear projection. *IEEE Transactions on Pattern Analysis and Machine Intelligence, 19*(7), 711–720.

Bengio, Y. (2009). Learning deep architectures for AI. *Foundations and Trends® in Machine Learning, 2*(1), 1–127.

Bengio, Y. (2012). *Practical recommendations for gradient-based training of deep architectures. Neural networks: Tricks of the trade* (pp. 437–478). Heidelberg: Springer Berlin Heidelberg.

Bengio, Y., Ducharme, R., Vincent, P., & Janvin, C. (2003). A neural probabilistic language model. *Journal of Machine Learning Research, 3,* 1137–1155.

Bengio, Y., Simard, P., & Frasconi, P. (1994). Learning long-term dependencies with gradient descent is difficult. *IEEE Transactions on Neural Networks, 5*(2), 157–166.

Bergadano, F., & Gunetti, D. (1996). *Inductive logic programming: From machine learning to software engineering.* Cambridge, MA: MIT Press.

Bergstra, J., & Bengio, Y. (2012). Random search for hyper-parameter optimization. *The Journal of Machine Learning Research, 13*(1), 281–305.

Bergstra, J., Breuleux, O., Bastien, F., Lamblin, P., Pascanu, R., Desjardins, G., & Bengio, Y. (2010). Theano: A CPU and GPU math expression compiler. *Proceedings of the python for scientific computing conference (SciPy)* (Vol. 4, p. 3). Austin, TX: BibTeX, June 30–July 3.

Berry, M. J. A., & Linoff, G. (1997). *Data mining techniques for marketing, sales, and customer support.* New York, NY: John Wiley.

Besag, J. E. (1986). On the statistical analysis of dirty pictures. *Journal of the Royal Statistical Society, Series B, 48*(3), 259–302.

Beygelzimer, A., Kakade, S., & Langford, J. (2006). Cover trees for nearest neighbor. *Proceedings of the 23rd international conference on machine learning* (pp. 97–104). New York, NY: ACM Press.

Bifet, A., Holmes, G., Kirkby, R., & Pfahringer, B. (2010). MOA: Massive online analysis. *Journal of Machine Learning Research, 9,* 1601–1604.

Bigus, J. P. (1996). *Data mining with neural networks.* New York, NY: McGraw Hill.

Bishop, C. M. (1995). *Neural networks for pattern recognition.* New York, NY: Oxford University Press.

Bishop, C. M. (2006). *Pattern recognition and machine learning.* New York, NY: Springer Verlag.

Bishop, C.M., Spiegelhalter, D. & Winn, J. (2002). VIBES: A variational inference engine for Bayesian networks. In *Advances in neural information processing systems* (pp. 777–784). Cambridge, MA: MIT Press

Blei, D. M., & Lafferty, J. D. (2006). Dynamic topic models. *Proceedings of the 23rd international conference on machine learning* (pp. 113−120). New York: ACM Press.

Blei, D. M., Ng, A. Y., & Jordan, M. I. (2003). Latent Dirichlet allocation. *The Journal of Machine Learning Research, 3*, 993−1022.

BLI (Bureau of Labour Information) (1988). Collective bargaining review *(November)*. Ottawa, ON: Labour Canada, Bureau of Labour Information.

Blockeel, H., Page, D., & Srinivasan, A. (2005). Multi-instance tree learning. *Proceedings of the 22nd international conference on machine learning, Bonn, Germany* (pp. 57−64). New York, NY: ACM Press.

Blum, A., & Mitchell, T. (1998). Combining labeled and unlabeled data with co-training. *Proceedings of the eleventh annual conference on computational learning theory, Madison, WI* (pp. 92−100). San Francisco, CA: Morgan Kaufmann.

Bottou, L. (2012). Stochastic gradient descent tricksIn (2nd ed.). G. Montavon, G. B. Orr, & K.-R. Muller (Eds.), *Neural networks: Tricks of the trade* (vol. 7700, Heidelberg: Springer, LNCS.

Bouckaert, R. R. (1995). Bayesian belief networks: From construction to inference. *PhD Dissertation*. The Netherlands: Computer Science Department, University of Utrecht.

Bouckaert, R. R. (2004). *Bayesian network classifiers in Weka*. New Zealand: Department of Computer Science, University of Waikato, Working Paper 14/2004.

Bouckaert, R. R. (2010). DensiTree: Making sense of sets of phylogenetic trees. *Bioinformatics, 26*(10), 1372−1373.

Bourlard, H., & Kamp, Y. (1988). Auto-association by multilayer perceptrons and singular value decomposition. *Biological Cybernetics, 59*, 291−294.

Brachman, R. J., & Levesque, H. J. (Eds.), (1985). *Readings in knowledge representation* San Francisco, CA: Morgan Kaufmann.

Brants, T., & Franz, A. (2006). *Web 1T 5-gram Version 1 LDC2006T13. DVD*. Philadelphia, PA: Linguistic Data Consortium.

Brefeld, U., & Scheffer, T. (2004). Co-EM support vector learning. In R. Greiner, & D. Schuurmans (Eds.), *Proceedings of the twenty-first international conference on machine learning, Banff, Alberta, Canada* (pp. 121−128). New York: ACM Press.

Breiman, L. (1996a). Stacked regression. *Machine Learning, 24*(1), 49−64.

Breiman, L. (1996b). Bagging predictors. *Machine Learning, 24*(2), 123−140.

Breiman, L. (1996c). *[Bias, variance, and] Arcing classifiers. Technical Report 460*. Berkeley, CA: Department of Statistics, University of California.

Breiman, L. (1999). Pasting small votes for classification in large databases and online. *Machine Learning, 36*(1−2), 85−103.

Breiman, L. (2001). Random forests. *Machine Learning, 45*(1), 5−32.

Breiman, L., Friedman, J. H., Olshen, R. A., & Stone, C. J. (1984). *Classification and regression trees*. Monterey, CA: Wadsworth.

Bridle, J. S. (1990). *Probabilistic interpretation of feedforward classification network outputs, with relationships to statistical pattern recognition*. *Neurocomputing* (pp. 227−236). Berlin: Springer Berlin Heidelberg.

Brin, S., Motwani, R., Ullman, J. D., & Tsur, S. (1997). Dynamic itemset counting and implication rules for market basket data. *ACM SIGMOD Record, 26*(2), 255−264.

Brin, S., & Page, L. (1998). The anatomy of a large-scale hypertext search engine. *Computer Networks and ISDN Systems, 33*, 107−117.

Brodley, C. E., & Fried, M. A. (1996). Identifying and eliminating mislabeled training instances. *Proceedings of the thirteenth national conference on artificial intelligence, Portland, OR* (pp. 799−805). Menlo Park, CA: AAAI Press.

Bromley, J., Guyon, I., LeCun, Y., Säckinger, E., & Shah, R. (1994). *Signature verification using a "Siamese" time delay neural network. Advances in neural information processing systems* (pp. 737−744). Burlington, MA: Morgan Kaufmann.

Brownstown, L., Farrell, R., Kant, E., & Martin, N. (1985). *Programming expert systems in OPS5*. Reading, MA: Addison-Wesley.

Buntine, W. (1992). Learning classification trees. *Statistics and Computing, 2*(2), 63−73.

Buntine, W. (2002). *Variational extensions to EM and multinomial PCA. Machine Learning: ECML 2002* (pp. 23−34). Berlin: Springer Berlin Heidelberg.

Buntine, W. L. (1994). Operations for learning with graphical models. *Journal of Artificial Intelligence Research, 2*, 159−225.

Burge, C., & Karlin, S. (1997). Prediction of complete gene structures in human genomic DNA. *Journal of Molecular Biology, 268*(1), 78−94.

Burges, C. J. C. (1998). A tutorial on support vector machines for pattern recognition. *Data Mining and Knowledge Discovery, 2*(2), 121−167.

Cabena, P., Hadjinian, P., Stadler, R., Verhees, J., & Zanasi, A. (1998). *Discovering data mining: From concept to implementation*. Upper Saddle River, NJ: Prentice Hall.

Califf, M. E., & Mooney, R. J. (1999). Relational learning of pattern-match rules for information extraction. *Proceedings of the sixteenth national conference on artificial intelligence, Orlando, FL* (pp. 328−334). Menlo Park, CA: AAAI Press.

Cardie, C. (1993). Using decision trees to improve case-based learning. In P. Utgoff (Ed.), *Proceedings of the tenth international conference on machine learning, Amherst, MA* (pp. 25−32). San Francisco, CA: Morgan Kaufmann.

Cavnar, W. B., & Trenkle, J. M. (1994). N-Gram-based text categorization. *Proceedings of the third symposium on document analysis and information retrieval* (pp. 161−175). Las Vegas, NV: UNLV Publications/Reprographics.

Ceglar, A., & Roddick, J. F. (2006). Association mining. *ACM Computing Surveys, 38*(2), ACM, New York, NY.

Cendrowska, J. (1987). PRISM: An algorithm for inducing modular rules. *International Journal of Man-Machine Studies, 27*(4), 349−370.

Chakrabarti, S. (2003). *Mining the web: Discovering knowledge from hypertext data*. San Francisco, CA: Morgan Kaufmann.

Chang, C.-C., & Lin, C.-J. (2001). LIBSVM: A library for support vector machines. Software available at http://www.csie.ntu.edu.tw/∼cjlin/libsvm.

Cheeseman, P., & Stutz, J. (1995). Bayesian classification (AutoClass): Theory and results. In U. M. Fayyad, G. Piatetsky-Shapiro, P. Smyth, & R. Uthurusamy (Eds.), *Advances in knowledge discovery and data mining* (pp. 153−180). Menlo Park, CA: AAAI Press.

Chen, J., & Chaudhari, N. S. (2004). Capturing long-term dependencies for protein secondary structure prediction. *International Symposium on Neural Networks* (pp. 494−500). Berlin: Springer Berlin Heidelberg.

Chen, M. S., Jan, J., & Yu, P. S. (1996). Data mining: An overview from a database perspective. *IEEE Transactions on Knowledge and Data Engineering, 8*(6), 866−883.

Chen, Y., Bi, J., & Wang, J. Z. (2006). MILES: Multiple-instance learning via embedded instance selection. *IEEE Transactions on Pattern Analysis and Machine Intelligence, 28*(12), 1931−1947.

Cherkauer, K. J., & Shavlik, J. W. (1996). Growing simpler decision trees to facilitate knowledge discovery. In E. Simoudis, J. W. Han, & U. Fayyad (Eds.), *Proceedings of* the second international conference on knowledge discovery and data mining, Portland, OR (pp. 315–318). Menlo Park, CA: AAAI Press.

Chevaleyre, Y., & Zucker, J.-D. (2001). Solving multiple-instance and multiple-part learning problems with decision trees and rule sets: Application to the mutagenesis problem. *Proceedings of the biennial conference of the Canadian society for computational studies of intelligence, Ottawa, Canada* (pp. 204–214). Berlin: Springer-Verlag.

Cho, K., & Chen, X. (2014). *Classifying and visualizing motion capture sequences using deep neural networks.*, IEEE international conference on computer vision theory and applications (VISAPP) (Vol. 2, pp. 122–130). Setúbal: SciTePress.

Cho, K., van Merrienboer, B., Gulcehre, C., Bahdanau, D., Bougares, F., Scwenk, H., & Bengio, Y. (2014). Learning Phrase Representations using RNN Encoder–Decoder for Statistical Machine Translation. *Empirical Methods on Natural Language Processing.* arXiv preprint arXiv:1406.1078.

Chollet, F. (2015). Keras: Theano-based deep learning library. Code: https://github.com/fchollet/keras. Documentation: http://keras.io.

Chung, J., Gulcehre, C., Cho, K., & Bengio, Y. (2014). Empirical evaluation of gated recurrent neural networks on sequence modeling. *arXiv preprint*, arXiv:1412.3555.

Ciresan, D. C., Meier, U., Gambardella, L. M., & Schmidhuber, J. (2010). Deep, big, simple neural nets for handwritten digit recognition. *Neural Computation*, 22(12), 3207–3220.

Ciresan, D.C., Meier, U., Masci, J., Maria Gambardella, L., & Schmidhuber, J. (2011). Flexible, high performance convolutional neural networks for image classification. In *Proceedings of the International Joint Conference on Artificial Intelligence (IJCAI).* vol. 22, no. 1, pp. 1237.

Ciresan, D., Meier, U., & Schmidhuber, J. (2012). Multi-column deep neural networks for image classification. In *Proceedings of Computer Vision and Pattern Recognition (CVPR).* pp. 3642–3649.

Cleary, J. G., & Trigg, L. E. (1995). K*: An instance-based learner using an entropic distance measure. In A. Prieditis, & S. Russell (Eds.), *Proceedings of the twelfth international conference on machine learning, Tahoe City, CA* (pp. 108–114). San Francisco, CA: Morgan Kaufmann.

Cohen, J. (1960). A coefficient of agreement for nominal scales. *Educational and Psychological Measurement*, 20, 37–46.

Cohen, W. W. (1995). Fast effective rule induction. In A. Prieditis, & S. Russell (Eds.), *Proceedings of the twelfth international conference on machine learning, Tahoe City, CA* (pp. 115–123). San Francisco, CA: Morgan Kaufmann.

Collobert, R., Kavukcuoglu, K., & Farabet, C. (2011). Torch7: A matlab-like environment for machine learning. In *BigLearn, NIPS Workshop* (No. EPFL-CONF-192376).

Collobert, R., & Weston, J. (2008, July). A unified architecture for natural language processing: Deep neural networks with multitask learning. *Proceedings of the 25th international conference on machine learning* (pp. 160–167). New York, NY: ACM Press.

Cooper, G. F., & Herskovits, E. (1992). A Bayesian method for the induction of probabilistic networks from data. *Machine Learning*, 9(4), 309–347.

Cortes, C., & Vapnik, V. (1995). Support vector networks. *Machine Learning*, 20(3), 273–297.

Cover, T. M., & Hart, P. E. (1967). Nearest neighbor pattern classification. *IEEE Transactions on Information Theory IT*, 13, 21–27.

Cristianini, N., & Shawe-Taylor, J. (2000). *An introduction to support vector machines and other kernel-based learning methods.* Cambridge: Cambridge University Press.

Cybenko, G. (1989). Approximation by superpositions of a sigmoidal function. *Mathematics of Control, Signals and Systems, 2*(4), 303–314.

Cypher, A. (Ed.), (1993). *Watch what I do: Programming by demonstration* Cambridge, MA: MIT Press.

Dasgupta, S. (2002). Performance guarantees for hierarchical clustering. In J. Kivinen, & R. H. Sloan (Eds.), *Proceedings of the fifteenth annual conference on computational learning theory, Sydney, Australia* (pp. 351–363). Berlin: Springer-Verlag.

Dasu, T., Koutsofios, E., & Wright, J. (2006). Zen and the art of data mining. In *Proceedings of the KDD Workshop on Data Mining for Business Applications* (pp. 37–43). Philadelphia, PA.

Datta, S., Kargupta, H., & Sivakumar, K. (2003). Homeland defense, privacy-sensitive data mining, and random value distortion. *Proceedings of the workshop on data mining for counter terrorism and security, San Francisco* (pp. 27–33). Philadelphia, PA: Society for International and Applied Mathematics.

Day, W. H. E., & Edelsbrünner, H. (1984). Efficient algorithms for agglomerative hierarchical clustering methods. *Journal of Classification, 1*(1), 7–24.

de Raedt, L. (2008). *Logical and relational learning.* New York, NY: Springer-Verlag.

Decoste, D., & Schölkopf, B. (2002). Training invariant support vector machines. *Machine Learning, 46*(1–3), 161–190.

Deerwester, S. C., Dumais, S. T., Landauer, T. K., Furnas, G. W., & Harshman, R. A. (1990). Indexing by latent semantic analysis. *JAsIs, 41*(6), 391–407.

Demiroz, G., & Guvenir, A. (1997). Classification by voting feature intervals. In M. van Someren, & G. Widmer (Eds.), *Proceedings of the ninth European conference on machine learning, Prague, Czech Republic* (pp. 85–92). Berlin: Springer-Verlag.

Dempster, A. P., Laird, N. M., & Rubin, D. B. (1977). Maximum likelihood from incomplete data via the EM algorithm. *Journal of the Royal Statistical Society, Series B, 39*(1), 1–38.

Devroye, L., Györfi, L., & Lugosi, G. (1996). *A probabilistic theory of pattern recognition.* New York, NY: Springer-Verlag.

Dhar, V., & Stein, R. (1997). *Seven methods for transforming corporate data into business intelligence.* Upper Saddle River, NJ: Prentice Hall.

Diederich, J., Kindermann, J., Leopold, E., & Paass, G. (2003). Authorship attribution with support vector machines. *Applied Intelligence, 19*(1), 109–123.

Dietterich, T. G. (2000). An experimental comparison of three methods for constructing ensembles of decision trees: Bagging, boosting, and randomization. *Machine Learning, 40*(2), 139–158.

Dietterich, T. G., & Bakiri, G. (1995). Solving multiclass learning problems via error-correcting output codes. *Journal Artificial Intelligence Research, 2,* 263–286.

Dietterich, T. G., & Kong, E. B. (1995). Error-correcting output coding corrects bias and variance. *Proceedings of the twelfth international conference on machine learning, Tahoe City, CA* (pp. 313–321). San Francisco, CA: Morgan Kaufmann.

Dietterich, T. G., Lathrop, R. H., & Lozano-Perez, T. (1997). Solving the multiple-instance problem with axis-parallel rectangles. *Artificial Intelligence Journal, 89* (1–2), 31–71.

Domingos, P. (1997). Knowledge acquisition from examples via multiple models. In D. H. Fisher (Ed.), *Proceedings of the fourteenth international conference on machine learning, Nashville, TN* (pp. 98–106). San Francisco, CA: Morgan Kaufmann.

Domingos, P. (1999). MetaCost: A general method for making classifiers cost-sensitive. In U. M. Fayyad, S. Chaudhuri, & D. Madigan (Eds.), *Proceedings of the fifth international conference on knowledge discovery and data mining. San Diego, CA* (pp. 155–164). New York, NY: ACM Press.

Domingos, P., & Hulten, G. (2000). *Mining high-speed data streams. International conference on knowledge discovery and data mining* (pp. 71–80). New York, NY: ACM Press.

Domingos, P., & Lowd, D. (2009). *Markov logic: An interface layer for AI.* San Rafael, CA: Morgan and Claypool.

Domingos, P., & Pazzani, M. (1997). Beyond independence: Conditions for the optimality of the simple Bayesian classifier. *Machine Learning, 29*, 103–130.

Dong, L., Frank, E., & Kramer, S. (2005). Ensembles of balanced nested dichotomies for multi-class problems. *Proc of the ninth European conference on principles and practice of knowledge discovery in databases, Porto, Portugal* (pp. 84–95). Berlin: Springer-Verlag.

Dony, R. D., & Haykin, D. (1997). Image segmentation using a mixture of principal components representation. *IEE Proceedings—Vision, Image and Signal Processing, 144*(2), 73–80.

Dougherty, J., Kohavi, R., & Sahami, M. (1995). Supervised and unsupervised discretization of continuous features. In A. Prieditis, & S. Russell (Eds.), *Proceedings of the twelfth international conference on machine learning, Tahoe City, CA* (pp. 194–202). San Francisco, CA: Morgan Kaufmann.

Drucker, H. (1997). Improving regressors using boosting techniques. In D. H. Fisher (Ed.), *Proceedings of the fourteenth international conference on machine learning, Nashville, TN* (pp. 107–115). San Francisco, CA: Morgan Kaufmann.

Drummond, C., & Holte, R. C. (2000). Explicitly representing expected cost: An alternative to ROC representation. In R. Ramakrishnan, S. Stolfo, R. Bayardo, & I. Parsa (Eds.), *Proceedings of the sixth international conference on knowledge discovery and data mining. Boston, MA* (pp. 198–207). New York, NY: ACM Press.

Duda, R. O., & Hart, P. E. (1973). *Pattern classification and scene analysis.* New York, NY: John Wiley.

Duda, R. O., Hart, P. E., & Stork, D. G. (2001). *Pattern classification* (2nd ed.). New York, NY: John Wiley.

Dumais, S. T., Platt, J., Heckerman, D., & Sahami, M. (1998). Inductive learning algorithms and representations for text categorization. *Proceedings of the ACM seventh international conference on information and knowledge management, Bethesda, MD* (pp. 148–155). New York, NY: ACM Press.

Dzeroski, S., & Zenko, B. (2004). Is combining classifiers with stacking better than selecting the best one? *Machine Learning, 54*, 255–273.

Edwards, D. (2012). *Introduction to graphical modeling.* New York, NY: Springer Science and Business Media.

Efron, B., & Tibshirani, R. (1993). *An introduction to the bootstrap.* London: Chapman and Hall.

Egan, J. P. (1975). Signal detection *theory and ROC analysis.* New York, NY: Series in Cognition and Perception Academic Press.

Epanechnikov, V. A. (1969). Non-parametric estimation of a multivariate probability density. *Theory of Probability and its Applications, 14*, 153–158.

Ester, M., Kriegel, H.-P., Sander, J., & Xu, X. (1996). A density-based algorithm for discovering clusters in large spatial databases with noise. *Proceedings of the second international conference on knowledge discovery and data mining (KDD-96)* (pp. 226–231). Portland, OR: AAAI Press.

Fan, R.-E., Chang, K.-W., Hsieh, C.-J., Wang, X.-R., & Lin, C.-J. (2008). LIBLINEAR: A library for large linear classification. *J Machine Learning Research, 9,* 1871–1874.

Fayyad, U. M., & Irani, K. B. (1993). Multi-interval discretization of continuous-valued attributes for classification learning. *Proceedings of the thirteenth international joint conference on artificial intelligence, Chambery, France* (pp. 1022–1027). San Francisco, CA: Morgan Kaufmann.

Fayyad, U. M., Piatetsky-Shapiro, G., Smyth, P., & Uthurusamy, R. (Eds.), (1996). *Advances in knowledge discovery and data mining* Menlo Park, CA: AAAI Press/MIT Press.

Fayyad, U. M., & Smyth, P. (1995). From massive datasets to science catalogs: Applications and challenges. *Proceedings of the workshop on massive datasets* (pp. 129–141). Washington, DC: NRC, Committee on Applied and Theoretical Statistics.

Finkel, J. R., Grenager, T., & Manning, C. (2005). Incorporating non-local information into information extraction systems by Gibbs sampling. *Proceedings of the 43rd annual meeting on association for computational linguistics* (pp. 363–370). Stroudsburg: Association for Computational Linguistics.

Fisher, D. (1987). Knowledge acquisition via incremental conceptual clustering. *Machine Learning, 2*(2), 139–172.

Fisher, R.A. (1936). The use of multiple measurements in taxonomic problems. *Annual Eugenics* 7 (part II): 179–188. Reprinted in *Contributions to Mathematical Statistics,* 1950. New York, NY: John Wiley.

Fix, E., & Hodges Jr., J.L. (1951). Discriminatory analysis; non-parametric discrimination: Consistency properties. Technical Report 21-49-004(4), USAF School of Aviation Medicine, Randolph Field, Texas.

Flach, P. A., & Lachiche, N. (1999). Confirmation-guided discovery of first-order rules with Tertius. *Machine Learning, 42,* 61–95.

Fletcher, R. (1987). *Practical methods of optimization* (2nd ed.). New York, NY: John Wiley.

Foulds, J., & Frank, E. (2008). Revisiting multiple-instance learning via embedded instance selection. *Proceedings of the Australasian joint conference on artificial intelligence, Auckland, New Zealand* (pp. 300–310). Berlin: Springer-Verlag.

Foulds, J., & Frank, E. (2010a). A review of multi-instance learning assumptions. *Knowledge Engineering Review, 25*(1), 1–25.

Foulds, J., & Frank, E. (2010b). Speeding up and boosting diverse density learning. *Proc 13th international conference on discovery science* (pp. 102–116). New York, NY: Springer.

Fradkin, D., & Madigan, D. (2003). Experiments with random projections for machine learning. In L. Getoor, T. E. Senator, P. Domingos, & C. Faloutsos (Eds.), *Proceedings of the ninth international conference on knowledge discovery and data mining, Washington, D.C* (pp. 517–522). New York, NY: ACM Press.

Frank, E. (2000). Pruning decision trees and lists. *PhD Dissertation.* New Zealand: Department of Computer Science, University of Waikato.

Frank, E., & Hall, M. (2001). A simple approach to ordinal classification. In L. de Raedt, & P. A. Flach (Eds.), *Proceedings of the twelfth European conference on machine learning. Freiburg, Germany* (pp. 145–156). Berlin: Springer-Verlag.

Frank, E., Hall, M., & Pfahringer, B. (2003). Locally weighted Naïve Bayes. In U. Kjærulff, & C. Meek (Eds.), *Proceedings of the nineteenth conference on uncertainty in artificial intelligence, Acapulco, Mexico* (pp. 249–256). San Francisco, CA: Morgan Kaufmann.

Frank, E., Holmes, G., Kirkby, R., & Hall, M. (2002). Racing committees for large datasets. In S. Lange, K. Satoh, & C. H. Smith (Eds.), *Proceedings of the fifth international conference on discovery science, Lübeck, Germany* (pp. 153–164). Berlin: Springer-Verlag.

Frank, E., & Kramer, S. (2004). Ensembles of nested dichotomies for multi-class problems. *Proceedings of the twenty-first international conference on machine learning, Banff, Alberta, Canada* (pp. 305–312). New York, NY: ACM Press.

Frank, E., Paynter, G. W., Witten, I. H., Gutwin, C., & Nevill-Manning, C. G. (1999). Domain-specific key phrase extraction. *Proceedings of the sixteenth international joint conference on artificial intelligence, Stockholm, Sweden* (pp. 668–673). San Francisco, CA: Morgan Kaufmann.

Frank, E., Wang, Y., Inglis, S., Holmes, G., & Witten, I. H. (1998). Using model trees for classification. *Machine Learning*, *32*(1), 63–76.

Frank, E., & Witten, I. H. (1998). Generating accurate rule sets without global optimization. In J. Shavlik (Ed.), *Proceedings of the fifteenth international conference on machine learning, Madison, WI* (pp. 144–151). San Francisco, CA: Morgan Kaufmann.

Frank, E., & Witten, I. H. (1999). Making better use of global discretization. In I. Bratko, & S. Dzeroski (Eds.), *Proceedings of the sixteenth international conference on machine learning, Bled, Slovenia* (pp. 115–123). San Francisco, CA: Morgan Kaufmann.

Frank, E., & Xu, X. (2003). *Applying propositional learning algorithms to multi-instance data*. Technical Report 06/03. New Zealand: Department of Computer Science, University of Waikato.

Franz, A., & Brants, T. (2006). "All Our N-gram are Belong to You". Google Research Blog. Retrieved 2015-09-14.

Freitag, D. (2002). Machine learning for information extraction in informal domains. *Machine Learning*, *39*(2/3), 169–202.

Freund, Y., & Mason, L. (1999). The alternating decision tree learning algorithm. In I. Bratko, & S. Dzeroski (Eds.), *Proceedings of the sixteenth international conference on machine learning, Bled, Slovenia* (pp. 124–133). San Francisco, CA: Morgan Kaufmann.

Freund, Y., & Schapire, R. E. (1996). Experiments with a new boosting algorithm. In L. Saitta (Ed.), *Proceedings of the thirteenth international conference on machine learning, Bari, Italy* (pp. 148–156). San Francisco, CA: Morgan Kaufmann.

Freund, Y., & Schapire, R. E. (1999). Large margin classification using the perceptron algorithm. *Machine Learning*, *37*(3), 277–296.

Frey, B. J. (1998). *Graphical models for machine learning and digital communication*. MIT Press.

Friedman, J. H. (1996). *Another approach to polychotomous classification. Technical report*. Stanford, CA: Department of Statistics, Stanford University.

Friedman, J. H. (2001). Greedy function approximation: A gradient boosting machine. *Annals of Statistics*, *29*(5), 1189–1232.

Friedman, J. H., Bentley, J. L., & Finkel, R. A. (1977). An algorithm for finding best matches in logarithmic expected time. *ACM Transactions on Mathematical Software, 3*(3), 209–266.

Friedman, J. H., Hastie, T., & Tibshirani, R. (2000). Additive logistic regression: A statistical view of boosting. *Annals of Statistics*, *28*(2), 337–374.

Friedman, N., Geiger, D., & Goldszmidt, M. (1997). Bayesian network classifiers. *Machine Learning*, *29*(2), 131–163.

Fukushima, K. (1980). Neocognitron: A self-organizing neural network model for a mechanism of pattern recognition unaffected by shift in position. *Biological Cybernetics*, *36* (4), 193–202.

Fulton, T., Kasif, S., & Salzberg, S. (1995). Efficient algorithms for finding multiway splits for decision trees. In A. Prieditis, & S. Russell (Eds.), *Proceedings of the twelfth international conference on machine learning, Tahoe City, CA* (pp. 244–251). San Francisco, CA: Morgan Kaufmann.

Fürnkranz, J. (2002). Round robin classification. *Journal of Machine Learning Research*, *2*, 721–747.

Fürnkranz, J. (2003). Round robin ensembles. *Intelligent Data Analysis*, *7*(5), 385–403.

Fürnkranz, J., & Flach, P. A. (2005). ROC 'n' rule learning: Towards a better understanding of covering algorithms. *Machine Learning*, *58*(1), 39–77.

Fürnkranz, J., & Widmer, G. (1994). Incremental reduced-error pruning. In H. Hirsh, & W. Cohen (Eds.), *Proceedings of the eleventh international conference on machine learning, New Brunswick, NJ* (pp. 70–77). San Francisco, CA: Morgan Kaufmann.

Gaines, B. R., & Compton, P. (1995). Induction of ripple-down rules applied to modeling large data bases. *Journal of Intelligent Information Systems*, *5*(3), 211–228.

Gama, J. (2004). Functional trees. *Machine Learning*, *55*(3), 219–250.

Gärtner, T., Flach, P. A., Kowalczyk, A., & Smola, A. J. (2002). Multi-instance kernels. *Proceedings of the international conference on machine learning, Sydney, Australia* (pp. 179–186). San Francisco, CA: Morgan Kaufmann.

Gelman, A., Carlin, J. B., Stern, H. S., & Rubin, D. B. (2014). *Bayesian data analysis* (Vol. 2). London: Chapman and Hall/CRC.

Geman, S., & Geman, D. (1984). Stochastic relaxation, gibbs distributions, and the bayesian restoration of images. *IEEE Transactions on Pattern Analysis and Machine Intelligence*, *6*(6), 721–741.

Genkin, A., Lewis, D. D., & Madigan, D. (2007). Large-scale Bayesian logistic regression for text categorization. *Technometrics*, *49*(3), 291–304.

Gennari, J. H., Langley, P., & Fisher, D. (1990). Models of incremental concept formation. *Artificial Intelligence*, *40*, 11–61.

Gers, F. A., Schmidhuber, J., & Cummins, F. (2000). Learning to forget: Continual prediction with LSTM. *Neural Computation*, *12*(10), 2451–2471.

Ghahramani, Z., & Beal, M. J. (1999). Variational inference for bayesian mixtures of factor analysers. *NIPS*, *12*, 449–455.

Ghahramani, Z., & Beal, M. J. (2001). Propagation algorithms for variational Bayesian learning. *Proceedings of Advances in Neural Information Processing Systems*, *13*, 507–513.

Ghahramani, Z., & Hinton, G. E. (1996). The EM algorithm for mixtures of factor analyzers *(Vol. 60). Technical Report CRG-TR-96-1.* University of Toronto.

Ghani, R. (2002). Combining labeled and unlabeled data for multiclass text categorization. In C. Sammut, & A. Hoffmann (Eds.), *Proceedings of the nineteenth international conference on machine learning, Sydney, Australia* (pp. 187–194). San Francisco, CA: Morgan Kaufmann.

Gilad-Bachrach, R., Navot, A., & Tishby, N. (2004). Margin based feature selection: Theory and algorithms. In R. Greiner, & D. Schuurmans (Eds.), *Proceedings of the twenty-first international conference on machine learning, Banff, Alberta, Canada* (pp. 337−344). New York, NY: ACM Press.

Gilks, W. R. (2005). *Markov chain monte carlo*. New York, NY: John Wiley and Sons, Ltd.

Giraud-Carrier, C. (1996). FLARE: Induction with prior knowledge. In J. Nealon, & J. Hunt (Eds.), *Research and development in expert systems XIII* (pp. 11−24). Cambridge: SGES Publications.

Glorot, X., & Bengio, Y. (2010). Understanding the difficulty of training deep feedforward neural networks. In *AISTATS*. vol. 9, pp. 249−256.

Glorot, X., Bordes, A., & Bengio, Y. (2011). Deep sparse rectifier networks. *AISTATS, 15*, pp. 315−323.

Gluck, M., & Corter, J. (1985). Information, uncertainty and the utility of categories. *Proceedings of the annual conference of the cognitive science society, Irvine, CA* (pp. 283−287). Hillsdale, NJ: Lawrence Erlbaum.

Goldberg, D. E. (1989). *Genetic algorithms in search, optimization and machine learning*. Reading, MA: Addison-Wesley.

Good, I. J. (1953). The population frequencies of species and the estimation of population parameters. *Biometrika, 40*(3−4), 237−264.

Good, P. (1994). *Permutation tests: A practical guide to resampling methods for testing hypotheses*. New York, NY: Springer-Verlag.

Goodfellow, I., Bengio, Y., & Courville, A. (2016). *Deep learning*. Cambridge, MA: MIT Press.

Graves, A. (2012). *Supervised sequence labelling*. Berlin: Springer Berlin Heidelberg.

Graves, A., & Schmidhuber, J. (2005). Framewise phoneme classification with bidirectional LSTM and other neural network architectures. *Neural Networks, 18*(5), 602−610.

Graves, A., Liwicki, M., Fernández, S., Bertolami, R., Bunke, H., & Schmidhuber, J. (2009). A novel connectionist system for unconstrained handwriting recognition. *IEEE Transactions on Pattern Analysis and Machine Intelligence, 31*(5), 855−868.

Graves, A., Mohamed, A.R., & Hinton, G. (2013). Speech recognition with deep recurrent neural networks. In *IEEE international Conference on Acoustics, Speech and Signal Processing (ICASSP)* (pp. 6645−6649).

Green, P., & Yandell, B. (1985). Semi-parametric generalized linear models. In *Proceedings 2nd international GLIM conference*, Lancaster, Lecture notes in Statistics No. 32 44−55. New York, NY: Springer-Verlag.

Greff, K., Srivastava, R. K., Koutník, J., Steunebrink, B. R., & Schmidhuber, J. (2015). LSTM: A search space odyssey. *arXiv preprint*, arXiv:1503.04069.

Griffiths, T. L., & Steyvers, M. (2004). Finding scientific topics. *Proceedings of the National Academy of Sciences, 101*(Suppl. 1), 5228−5235.

Grossman, D., & Domingos, P. (2004). Learning Bayesian network classifiers by maximizing conditional likelihood. In R. Greiner, & D. Schuurmans (Eds.), *Proceedings of the twenty-first international conference on machine learning, Banff, Alberta, Canada* (pp. 361−368). New York, NY: ACM Press.

Groth, R. (1998). *Data mining: A hands-on approach for business professionals*. Upper Saddle River, NJ: Prentice Hall.

Guo, Y., & Greiner, R. (2004). *Discriminative model selection for belief net structures*. Edmonton, AB: Department of Computing Science, TR04-22, University of Alberta.

Gütlein, M., Frank, E., Hall, M., & Karwath, A. (2009). Large-scale attribute selection using wrappers. *Proceedings of the IEEE symposium on computational intelligence and data mining* (pp. 332–339). Washington, DC: IEEE Computer Society.

Guyon, I., Weston, J., Barnhill, S., & Vapnik, V. (2002). Gene selection for cancer classification using support vector machines. *Machine Learning*, *46*(1–3), 389–422.

Hall, M. (2000). Correlation-based feature selection for discrete and numeric class machine learning. In P. Langley (Ed.), *Proceedings of the seventeenth international conference on machine learning, Stanford, CA* (pp. 359–366). San Francisco, CA: Morgan Kaufmann.

Hall, M., & Frank, E. (2008). Combining Naïve Bayes and decision tables. *Proceedings of the 21st Florida artificial intelligence research society conference* (pp. 318–319). Miami, FL: AAAI Press.

Hall, M., Holmes, G., & Frank, E. (1999). Generating rule sets from model trees. In N. Y. Foo (Ed.), *Proceedings of the twelfth Australian joint conference on artificial intelligence, Sydney, Australia* (pp. 1–12). Berlin: Springer-Verlag.

Han, J., Kamber, M., & Pei, J. (2011). *Data mining: Concepts and techniques* (3rd ed.). San Francisco, CA: Morgan Kaufmann.

Han, J., Pei, J., & Yin, Y. (2000). Mining frequent patterns without candidate generation. In *Proceedings of the ACM-SIGMOD International Conference on Management of Data* (pp. 1–12). Dallas, TX.

Han, J., Pei, J., Yin, Y., & Mao, R. (2004). Mining frequent patterns without candidate generation: A frequent-pattern tree approach. *Data Mining and Knowledge Discovery*, *8*(1), 53–87.

Hand, D. J. (2006). Classifier technology and the illusion of progress. *Statistical Science*, *21*(1), 1–14.

Hand, D. J., Manilla, H., & Smyth, P. (2001). *Principles of data mining*. Cambridge, MA: MIT Press.

Hartigan, J. A. (1975). *Clustering algorithms*. New York, NY: John Wiley.

Hastie, T., & Tibshirani, R. (1998). Classification by pairwise coupling. *Annals of Statistics*, *26*(2), 451–471.

Hastie, T., Tibshirani, R., & Friedman, J. (2009). *The elements of statistical learning* (2nd ed.). New York, NY: Springer-Verlag.

Hastings, W. K. (1970). Monte Carlo sampling methods using Markov chains and their applications. *Biometrika*, *57*(1), 97–109.

Havaei, M., Davy, A., Warde-Farley, D., Biard, A., Courville, A., Bengio, Y., ... Larochelle, H. (2016). *Brain tumor segmentation with deep neural networks*. Medical Image Analysis.

Haykin, S. (1994). *Neural networks: A comprehensive foundation*. Upper Saddle River, NJ: Prentice Hall.

He, K., Zhang, X., Ren, S., & Sun, J. (2016). Deep residual learning for image recognition. In *Proceedings of the IEEE Conference on Computer Vision and Pattern Recognition (CVPR)*, pp. 770–778.

Heckerman, D., Geiger, D., & Chickering, D. M. (1995). Learning Bayesian networks: The combination of knowledge and statistical data. *Machine Learning*, *20*(3), 197–243.

Hempstalk, K., & Frank, E. (2008). Discriminating against new classes: One-class versus multi-class classification. *Proceedings of the twenty-first Australasian joint conference on artificial intelligence, Auckland, New Zealand* (pp. 225–236). New York, NY: Springer.

Hempstalk, K., Frank, E., & Witten, I. H. (2008). One-class classification by combining density and class probability estimation. *Proceedings of the European Conference on Machine Learning and Principles and Practice of Knowledge Discovery in Databases, Antwerp, Belgium* (pp. 505–519). Berlin: Springer-Verlag.

Hinton, G. E. (2002). Training products of experts by minimizing contrastive divergence. *Neural Computation, 14*(8), 1771–1800.

Hinton, G. E., & Salakhutdinov, R. (2006). Reducing the dimensionality of data with neural networks. *Science, 313*(5786), 504–507.

Hinton, G.E., & Sejnowski, T.J. (1983, June). Optimal perceptual inference. In *Proceedings of the IEEE conference on computer vision and pattern recognition* (pp. 448–453). Washington, DC.

Ho, T. K. (1998). The random subspace method for constructing decision forests. *IEEE Transactions on Pattern Analysis and Machine Intelligence, 20*(8), 832–844.

Hochbaum, D. S., & Shmoys, D. B. (1985). A best possible heuristic for the k-center problem. *Mathematics of Operations Research, 10*(2), 180–184.

Hochreiter, S. (1991). Untersuchungen zu dynamischen neuronalen Netzen. Diploma thesis, Institut f. Informatik, Technische Univ. Munich. Advisor: J. Schmidhuber.

Hochreiter, S., Bengio, Y., Frasconi, P., & Schmidhuber, J. (2001). Gradient flow in recurrent nets: The difficulty of learning long-term dependencies. In S. C. Kremer, & J. F. Kolen (Eds.), *A field guide to dynamical recurrent neural networks* (pp. 179–206). Piscataway, NJ: IEEE Press.

Hochreiter, S., & Schmidhuber, J. (1997). Long short-term memory. *Neural Computation, 9*(8), 1735–1780.

Hofmann, T. (1999, August). Probabilistic latent semantic indexing. *Proceedings of the 22nd annual international ACM SIGIR conference on Research and development in information retrieval* (pp. 50–57). New York, NY: ACM Press.

Holmes, G., & Nevill-Manning, C. G. (1995). Feature selection via the discovery of simple classification rules. In G. E. Lasker, & X. Liu (Eds.), *Proceedings of the international symposium on intelligent data analysis* (pp. 75–79). Baden-Baden: International Institute for Advanced Studies in Systems Research and Cybernetics.

Holmes, G., Pfahringer, B., Kirkby, R., Frank, E., & Hall, M. (2002). Multiclass alternating decision trees. In T. Elomaa, H. Mannila, & H. Toivonen (Eds.), *Proceedings of the thirteenth European conference on machine learning, Helsinki, Finland* (pp. 161–172). Berlin: Springer-Verlag.

Holte, R. C. (1993). Very simple classification rules perform well on most commonly used datasets. *Machine Learning, 11*, 63–91.

Hornik, K. (1991). Approximation capabilities of multilayer feedforward networks. *Neural Networks, 4*(2), 251–257.

Hosmer, D. W., Jr, & Lemeshow, S. (2004). *Applied logistic regression*. New York, NY: John Wiley and Sons.

Hsu, C. W., Chang, C. C., & Lin, C. J. (2003). *A practical guide to support vector classification*. Department of Computer Science, National Taiwan University.

Huang, C., & Darwiche, A. (1996). Inference in belief networks: A procedural guide. *International Journal of Approximate Reasoning, 15*(3), 225–263.

Huffman, S. B. (1996). Learning information extraction patterns from examples. In S. Wertmer, E. Riloff, & G. Scheler (Eds.), *Connectionist, statistical, and symbolic approaches to learning for natural language processing* (pp. 246–260). Berlin: Springer Verlag.

Hyvärinen, A., & Oja, E. (2000). Independent component analysis: Algorithms and applications. *Neural Networks*, *13*(4), 411−430.

Ihaka, R., & Gentleman, R. (1996). R: A language for data analysis and graphics. *Journal of Computational and Graphical Statistics*, *5*(3), 299−314.

Ilin, A., & Raiko, T. (2010). Practical approaches to principal component analysis in the presence of missing values. *The Journal of Machine Learning Research*, *11*, 1957−2000.

International Human Genome Sequencing Consortium (2001). Initial sequencing and analysis of the human genome. *Nature*, *409*(6822), 860−921.

Ioffe, S., & Szegedy, C. (2015). Batch normalization: Accelerating deep network training by reducing internal covariate shift. *arXiv preprint*, arXiv:1502.03167.

Ivakhnenko, A. G., & Lapa, V. G. (1965). *Cybernetic predicting devices*. New York, NY: CCM Information Corporation.

Jabbour, K., Riveros, J. F. V., Landsbergen, D., & Meyer, W. (1988). ALFA: Automated load forecasting assistant. *IEEE Transactions on Power Systems*, *3*(3), 908−914.

Jia, Y., Shelhamer, E., Donahue, J., Karayev, S., Long, J., Girshick, R., ... Darrell, T. (2014). Caffe: Convolutional architecture for fast feature embedding. *Proceedings of the ACM international conference on multimedia* (pp. 675−678). New York, NY: ACM Press.

Jiang, L., & Zhang, H. (2006). Weightily averaged one-dependence estimators. *Proceedings of the 9th Biennial Pacific Rim international conference on artificial intelligence* (pp. 970−974). Berlin: Springer-Verlag.

John, G. H. (1995). Robust decision trees: Removing outliers from databases. In U. M. Fayyad, & R. Uthurusamy (Eds.), *Proceedings of the first international conference on knowledge discovery and data mining, Montreal, Canada* (pp. 174−179). Menlo Park, CA: AAAI Press.

John, G. H. (1997). Enhancements to the data mining process. *PhD Dissertation*. Stanford, CA: Computer Science Department, Stanford University.

John, G. H., Kohavi, R., & Pfleger, P. (1994). Irrelevant features and the subset selection problem. In H. Hirsh, & W. Cohen (Eds.), *Proceedings of the eleventh international conference on machine learning, New Brunswick, NJ* (pp. 121−129). San Francisco, CA: Morgan Kaufmann.

John, G. H., & Langley, P. (1995). Estimating continuous distributions in Bayesian classifiers. In P. Besnard, & S. Hanks (Eds.), *Proceedings of the eleventh conference on uncertainty in artificial intelligence, Montreal, Canada* (pp. 338−345). San Francisco, CA: Morgan Kaufmann.

Johns, M. V. (1961). An empirical Bayes approach to nonparametric two-way classification. In H. Solomon (Ed.), *Studies in item analysis and prediction* (pp. 221−232). Palo Alto, CA: Stanford University Press.

Jones, M. C., Marron, J. S., & Sheather, S. J. (1996). A brief survey of bandwidth selection for density estimation. *Journal of the American Statistical Association*, *91*(433), 401−407.

Jordan, M. I., Ghahramani, Z., Jaakkola, T. S., & Saul, L. K. (1998). *An introduction to variational methods for graphical models* (pp. 105−161). The Netherlands: Springer.

Jordan, M. I., Ghahramani, Z., Jaakkola, T. S., & Saul, L. K. (1999). An introduction to variational methods for graphical models. *Machine Learning*, *37*(2), 183−233.

Kass, R., & Wasserman, L. (1995). A reference Bayesian test for nested hypotheses and its relationship to the Schwarz criterion. *Journal of the American Statistical Association*, *90*, 928−934.

Keerthi, S. S., Shevade, S. K., Bhattacharyya, C., & Murthy, K. R. K. (2001). Improvements to Platt's SMO algorithm for SVM classifier design. *Neural Computation*, *13*(3), 637−649.

Kerber, R. (1992). Chimerge: Discretization of numeric attributes. In W. Swartout (Ed.), *Proceedings of the tenth national conference on artificial intelligence, San Jose, CA* (pp. 123−128). Menlo Park, CA: AAAI Press.

Kibler, D., & Aha, D. W. (1987). Learning representative exemplars of concepts: An initial case study. In P. Langley (Ed.), *Proceedings of the fourth machine learning workshop, Irvine, CA* (pp. 24−30). San Francisco, CA: Morgan Kaufmann.

Kimball, R., & Ross, M. (2002). *The data warehouse toolkit* (2nd ed.). New York, NY: John Wiley.

Kira, K., & Rendell, L. (1992). A practical approach to feature selection. In D. Sleeman, & P. Edwards (Eds.), *Proceedings of the ninth international workshop on machine learning, Aberdeen, Scotland* (pp. 249−258). San Francisco, CA: Morgan Kaufmann.

Kirkby, R. (2007). *Improving hoeffding trees. PhD Dissertation*. New Zealand: Department of Computer Science, University of Waikato.

Kittler, J. (1978). Feature set search algorithms. In C. H. Chen (Ed.), *Pattern recognition and signal processing*. The Netherlands: Sijthoff an Noordhoff.

Kivinen, J., Smola, A. J., & Williamson, R. C. (2002). Online learning with kernels. *IEEE Transactions on Signal Processing*, *52*, 2165−2176.

Kleinberg, J. (1998) "Authoritative sources in a hyperlinked environment." *Proc ACM-SIAM Symposium on Discrete Algorithms*. Extended version published in *Journal of the ACM*, Vol. 46 (1999), pp. 604−632.

Koestler, A. (1964). *The act of creation*. London: Hutchinson.

Kohavi, R. (1995a). A study of cross-validation and bootstrap for accuracy estimation and model selection. *Proceedings of the fourteenth international joint conference on artificial intelligence, Montreal, Canada* (pp. 1137−1143). San Francisco, CA: Morgan Kaufmann.

Kohavi, R. (1995b). The power of decision tables. In N. Lavrac, & S. Wrobel (Eds.), *Proceedings of the eighth European conference on machine learning, Iráklion, Crete, Greece* (pp. 174−189). Berlin: Springer-Verlag.

Kohavi, R. (1996). Scaling up the accuracy of Naïve Bayes classifiers: A decision-tree hybrid. In E. Simoudis, J. W. Han, & U. Fayyad (Eds.), *Proceedings of the second international conference on knowledge discovery and data mining, Portland, OR* (pp. 202−207). Menlo Park, CA: AAAI Press.

Kohavi, R., & John, G. H. (1997). Wrappers for feature subset selection. *Artificial Intelligence*, *97*(1−2), 273−324.

Kohavi, R., & Kunz, C. (1997). Option decision trees with majority votes. In D. Fisher (Ed.), *Proceedings of the fourteenth international conference on machine learning, Nashville, TN* (pp. 161−191). San Francisco, CA: Morgan Kaufmann.

Kohavi, R., & Provost, F. (Eds.), (1998). Machine learning: Special issue on applications of machine learning and the knowledge discovery process. *Machine Learning*, *30*(2/3), 127−274.

Kohavi, R., & Sahami, M. (1996). Error-based and entropy-based discretization of continuous features. In E. Simoudis, J. W. Han, & U. Fayyad (Eds.), *Proceedings of the second international conference on knowledge discovery and data mining, Portland, OR* (pp. 114–119). Menlo Park, CA: AAAI Press.

Koller, D., & Friedman, N. (2009). *Probabilistic graphical models: Principles and techniques*. Cambridge, MA: MIT Press.

Komarek, P., & Moore, A. (2000). A dynamic adaptation of AD-trees for efficient machine learning on large data sets. In P. Langley (Ed.), *Proceedings of the seventeenth international conference on machine learning, Stanford, CA* (pp. 495–502). San Francisco, CA: Morgan Kaufmann.

Kononenko, I. (1995). On biases in estimating multi-valued attributes. *Proceedings of the fourteenth international joint conference on artificial intelligence, Montreal, Canada* (pp. 1034–1040). San Francisco, CA: Morgan Kaufmann.

Koppel, M., & Schler, J. (2004). Authorship verification as a one-class classification problem. In R. Greiner, & D. Schuurmans (Eds.), *Proceedings of the twenty-first international conference on machine learning, Banff, Alberta, Canada* (pp. 489–495). New York, NY: ACM Press.

Kristjansson, T., Culotta, A., Viola, P., & McCallum, A. (2004, July). Interactive information extraction with constrained conditional random fields. *AAAI, 4*, 412–418.

Krizhevsky, A., Sutskever, I., & Hinton, G.E. (2012). ImageNet classification with deep convolutional neural networks. In *Advances in Neural Information Processing Systems* (NIPS 2012).

Krogel, M.-A., & Wrobel, S. (2002). Feature selection for propositionalization. *Proceedings of the international conference on discovery science, Lübeck, Germany* (pp. 430–434). Berlin: Springer-Verlag.

Kschischang, F. R., Frey, B. J., & Loeliger, H. A. (2001). Factor graphs and the sum-product algorithm. *Information Theory, IEEE Transactions on, 47*(2), 498–519.

Kubat, M., Holte, R. C., & Matwin, S. (1998). Machine learning for the detection of oil spills in satellite radar images. *Machine Learning, 30*, 195–215.

Kulp, D., Haussler, D., Rees, M.G., & Eeckman, F.H. (1996). A generalized hidden Markov model for the recognition of human genes in DNA. In *Proc. Int. Conf. on Intelligent Systems for Molecular Biology* (pp. 134–142). St. Louis.

Kuncheva, L. I., & Rodriguez, J. J. (2007). An experimental study on rotation forest ensembles. *Proceedings of the seventh international workshop on multiple classifier systems, Prague, Czech Republic* (pp. 459–468). Berlin/Heidelberg: Springer.

Kushmerick, N., Weld, D. S., & Doorenbos, R. (1997). Wrapper induction for information extraction. *Proceedings of the fifteenth international joint conference on artificial intelligence, Nagoya, Japan* (pp. 729–735). San Francisco, CA: Morgan Kaufmann.

Lafferty, J., McCallum, A., & Pereira, F. (2001). Conditional random fields: Probabilistic models for segmenting and labeling sequence data. In *The proceedings of the international conference on machine learning (ICML)* (pp. 282–289).

Laguna, M., & Marti, R. (2003). *Scatter search: Methodology and implementations in C*. Boston, MA: Kluwer Academic Press.

Landwehr, N., Hall, M., & Frank, E. (2005). Logistic model trees. *Machine Learning, 59* (1–2), 161–205.

Langley, P. (1996). *Elements of machine learning*. San Francisco, CA: Morgan Kaufmann.

Langley, P., Iba, W., & Thompson, K. (1992). An analysis of Bayesian classifiers. In W. Swartout (Ed.), *Proceedings of the tenth national conference on artificial intelligence, San Jose, CA* (pp. 223–228). Menlo Park, CA: AAAI Press.

Langley, P., & Sage, S. (1994). Induction of selective Bayesian classifiers. In R. L. de Mantaras, & D. Poole (Eds.), *Proceedings of the tenth conference on uncertainty in artificial intelligence, Seattle, WA* (pp. 399–406). San Francisco, CA: Morgan Kaufmann.

Langley, P., & Sage, S. (1997). Scaling to domains with irrelevant features. In R. Greiner (Ed.), *Computational learning theory and natural learning systems* (Vol. 4). Cambridge, MA: MIT Press.

Langley, P., & Simon, H. A. (1995). Applications of machine learning and rule induction. *Communications of the ACM, 38*(11), 55–64.

Larochelle, H., & Bengio, Y. (2008). Classification using discriminative restricted Boltzmann machines. In *Proceedings of the 25th International Conference on Machine learning (ICML)*, pp. 536–543.

Lauritzen, S. L., & Spiegelhalter, D. J. (1988). Local computations with probabilities on graphical structures and their application to expert systems. *Journal of the Royal Statistical Society Series B (Methodological), 50*, 157–224.

Lavrac, N., Motoda, H., Fawcett, T., Holte, R., Langley, P., & Adriaans, P. (Eds.), (2004). Special issue on lessons learned from data mining applications and collaborative problem solving. *Machine Learning, 57*(1/2), 83–113.

Lawrence, N., Seeger, M., & Herbrich, R. (2003). Fast sparse Gaussian process methods: The informative vector machine. In *Proceedings of the 16th Annual Conference on Neural Information Processing Systems* (No. EPFL-CONF-161319, pp. 609–616).

Lawson, C. L., & Hanson, R. J. (1995). *Solving least squares problems*. Philadelphia, PA: SIAM Publications.

le Cessie, S., & van Houwelingen, J. C. (1992). Ridge estimators in logistic regression. *Applied Statistics, 41*(1), 191–201.

Le, Q. V., Jaitly, N., & Hinton, G. E. (2015). A simple way to initialize recurrent networks of rectified linear units. *arXiv preprint*, arXiv:1504.00941.

LeCun, Y., Bengio, Y., & Hinton, G. E. (2015). Deep learning. *Nature, 521*(7553), 436–444.

LeCun, Y., Bottou, L., Bengio, Y., & Haffner, P. (1998). Gradient-based learning applied to document recognition. *Proceedings of the IEEE, 86*(11), 2278–2324.

LeCun, Y., Bottou, L., Orr, G. B., & Müller, K. R. (1998). *Efficient BackProp. Neural Networks: Tricks of the Trade* (pp. 9–50). Berlin: Springer Berlin Heidelberg.

Li, M., & Vitanyi, P. M. B. (1992). Inductive reasoning and Kolmogorov complexity. *Journal Computer and System Sciences, 44*, 343–384.

Lichman, M. (2013). *UCI Machine Learning Repository*. Irvine, CA: University of California, School of Information and Computer Science. <http://archive.ics.uci.edu/ml>.

Lieberman, H. (Ed.), (2001). *Your wish is my command: Programming by example* San Francisco, CA: Morgan Kaufmann.

Littlestone, N. (1988). Learning quickly when irrelevant attributes abound: A new linear-threshold algorithm. *Machine Learning, 2*(4), 285–318.

Littlestone, N. (1989). Mistake bounds and logarithmic linear-threshold learning algorithms. *PhD Dissertation*. Santa Cruz, CA: University of California.

Liu, B. (2009). *Web data mining: Exploring hyperlinks, contents, and usage data*. New York, NY: Springer Verlag.

Liu, B., Hsu, W., & Ma, Y. M. (1998). Integrating classification and association rule mining. *Proceedings of the fourth international conference on knowledge discovery and data mining (KDD-98)* (pp. 80–86). New York, NY: AAAI Press.

Liu, H., & Setiono, R. (1996). A probabilistic approach to feature selection: A filter solution. In L. Saitta (Ed.), *Proceedings of the thirteenth international conference on machine learning, Bari, Italy* (pp. 319–327). San Francisco, CA: Morgan Kaufmann.

Liu, H., & Setiono, R. (1997). Feature selection via discretization. *IEEE Transactions on Knowledge and Data Engineering, 9*(4), 642–645.

Lowe, D. G. (2004). Distinctive image features from scale-invariant keypoints. *International Journal of Computer Vision, 60*(2), 91–110.

Luan, J. (2002). Data mining and its applications in higher education. *New Directions for Institutional Research, 2002*(113), 17–36.

Lunn, D., Spiegelhalter, D., Thomas, A., & Best, N. (2009). The BUGS project: Evolution, critique and future directions (with discussion). *Statistics in Medicine, 28*, 3049–3082.

Lunn, D. J., Thomas, A., Best, N., & Spiegelhalter, D. (2000). WinBUGS—a Bayesian modelling framework: Concepts, structure, and extensibility. *Statistics and Computing, 10*, 325–337.

Mann, T. (1993). *Library research models: A guide to classification, cataloging, and computers*. New York, NY: Oxford University Press.

Marill, T., & Green, D. M. (1963). On the effectiveness of receptors in recognition systems. *IEEE Transactions on Information Theory, 9*(11), 11–17.

Maron, O. (1998). *Learning from ambiguity. Ph.D. thesis*. Massachusetts Institute of Technology.

Maron, O., & Lozano-Peréz, T. (1997). A framework for multiple-instance learning. *Proceedings of the conference on neural information processing systems, Denver, CO* (pp. 570–576). Cambridge, MA: MIT Press.

Martin, B. (1995). *Instance-based learning: Nearest neighbour with generalisation. MSc Thesis*. Department of Computer Science, University of Waikato, New Zealand.

McCallum, A.K. (2002). Mallet: A machine learning for language toolkit. http://mallet.cs.umass.edu.

McCallum, A., & Nigam, K. (1998). A comparison of event models for Naïve Bayes text classification. *Proceedings of the AAAI-98 workshop on learning for text categorization, Madison, WI* (pp. 41–48). Menlo Park, CA: AAAI Press.

McCallum, A., Pal, C., Druck, G., and Wang, X. (2006). Multi-conditional learning: Generative/discriminative training for clustering and classification. In the *proceedings of AAAI* (Vol. 21, No. 1, p. 433). Menlo Park, CA; Cambridge, MA; London; AAAI Press; MIT Press; 1999.

McCullagh, P. (1980). Regression models for ordinal data. *Journal of the Royal Statistical Society. Series B (Methodological), 42*, 109–142.

McCullagh, P., & Nelder, J. A. (1989). *Generalized linear models* (Vol. 37). Boca Raton, FL: CRC Press.

Medelyan, O., & Witten, I. H. (2008). Domain independent automatic keyphrase indexing with small training sets. *Journal American Society for Information Science and Technology, 59*, 1026–1040.

Mehta, M., Agrawal, R., & Rissanen, J. (1996). SLIQ: A fast scalable classifier for data mining. In P. Apers, M. Bouzeghoub, & G. Gardarin (Eds.), Proceedings of the fifth international conference on extending database technology, *Avignon, France*. New York, NY: Springer-Verlag.

Melville, P., & Mooney, R. J. (2005). Creating diversity in ensembles using artificial data. *Information Fusion*, *6*(1), 99–111.

Metropolis, N., Rosenbluth, A. W., Rosenbluth, M. N., Teller, A. H., & Teller, E. (1953). Equations of state calculations by fast computing machines. *Journal of Chemical Physics*, *21*(6), 1087–1092.

Michalski, R. S., & Chilausky, R. L. (1980). Learning by being told and learning from examples: An experimental comparison of the two methods of knowledge acquisition in the context of developing an expert system for soybean disease diagnosis. *International Journal of Policy Analysis and Information Systems*, *4*(2), 125–161.

Michie, D. (1989). Problems of computer-aided concept formationIn J. R. Quinlan (Ed.), *Applications of expert systems* (Vol. 2, pp. 310–333). Wokingham: Addison-Wesley.

Mikolov, T., Chen, K., Corrado, G., & Dean, J. (2013a). Efficient estimation of word representations in vector space. *arXiv preprint*, arXiv:1301.3781.

Mikolov, T., Sutskever, I., Chen, K., Corrado, G. S., & Dean, J. (2013b). Distributed representations of words and phrases and their compositionality. *Advances in Neural Information Processing Systems*, *26*, 3111–3119.

Minka, T. (2000). *Old and new matrix algebra useful for statistics*. MIT Media Lab note.

Minka, T. P. (2001). Expectation propagation for approximate Bayesian inference. *Proceedings of the seventeenth conference on uncertainty in artificial intelligence* (pp. 362–369). San Francisco, CA: Morgan Kaufmann Publishers Inc.

Minsky, M., & Papert, S. (1969). *Perceptrons*. Cambridge, MA: MIT Press.

Mitchell, T. M. (1997). *Machine Learning*. New York, NY: McGraw Hill.

Mitchell, T. M., Caruana, R., Freitag, D., McDermott, J., & Zabowski, D. (1994). Experience with a learning personal assistant. *Communications of the ACM*, *37*(7), 81–91.

Moore, A. W. (1991). Efficient memory-based learning for robot control. *PhD Dissertation*. Computer Laboratory, University of Cambridge, UK.

Moore, A. W. (2000). The anchors hierarchy: Using the triangle inequality to survive high-dimensional data. In C. Boutilier, & M. Goldszmidt (Eds.), *Proceedings of the sixteenth conference on uncertainty in artificial intelligence, Stanford, CA* (pp. 397–405). San Francisco, CA: Morgan Kaufmann.

Moore, A. W., & Lee, M. S. (1994). Efficient algorithms for minimizing cross validation error. In W. W. Cohen, & H. Hirsh (Eds.), *Proceedings of the eleventh international conference on machine learning, New Brunswick, NJ* (pp. 190–198). San Francisco, CA: Morgan Kaufmann.

Moore, A. W., & Pelleg, D. (1998). Cached sufficient statistics for efficient machine learning with large datasets. *Journal Artificial Intelligence Research*, *8*, 67–91.

Moore, A. W., & Pelleg, D. (2000). X-means: Extending *k*-means with efficient estimation of the number of clusters. In P. Langley (Ed.), *Proceedings of the seventeenth international conference on machine learning, Stanford, CA* (pp. 727–734). San Francisco, CA: Morgan Kaufmann.

Morin, F., & Bengio, Y. (2005). Hierarchical probabilistic neural network language model. In *Proceedings of the international workshop on artificial intelligence and statistics* (pp. 246–252).

Murphy, K. P. (2002). Dynamic Bayesian networks: Representation, inference and learning. *Doctoral dissertation*. Berkeley, CA: University of California.

Murphy, K. P. (2012). *Machine learning: A probabilistic perspective*. Cambridge, MA: MIT Press.

Mutter, S., Hall, M., & Frank, E. (2004). Using classification to evaluate the output of confidence-based association rule mining. *Proceedings of the seventeenth Australian joint conference on artificial intelligence, Cairns, Australia* (pp. 538−549). Berlin: Springer.

Nadeau, C., & Bengio, Y. (2003). Inference for the generalization error. *Machine Learning, 52*(3), 239−281.

Nahm, U.Y., & Mooney, R.J. (2000). Using information extraction to aid the discovery of prediction rules from texts. *Proceedings of the Workshop on Text Mining at the Sixth International Conference on Knowledge Discovery and Data Mining* (pp. 51−58). Boston, MA. Workshop proceedings at: http://www.cs.cmu.edu/ ~ dunja/WshKDD2000.html.

Neal, R. M. (1992). Connectionist learning of belief networks. *Artificial Intelligence, 56* (1), 71−113.

Neal, R. M., & Hinton, G. E. (1998). A view of the EM algorithm that justifies incremental, sparse, and other variants. *Learning in graphical models* (pp. 355−368). Netherlands: Springer.

Nelder, J., & Wedderburn, R. (1972). Generalized linear models. *Journal of the Royal Statistical Society. Series A, 135*(3), 370−384.

Netzer, Y., Wang, T., Coates, A., Bissacco, A., Wu, B., & Ng, A.Y. (2011). Reading digits in natural images with unsupervised feature learning. In *NIPS workshop on deep learning and unsupervised feature learning* (Vol. 2011, p. 4). Granada, Spain.

Niculescu-Mizil, A., & Caruana, R. (2005). Predicting good probabilities with supervised learning. *Proceedings of the 22nd international conference on machine learning, Bonn, Germany* (pp. 625−632). New York, NY: ACM Press.

Nie, N. H., Hull, C. H., Jenkins, J. G., Steinbrenner, K., & Bent, D. H. (1970). *Statistical package for the social sciences.* New York, NY: McGraw Hill.

Nigam, K., & Ghani, R. (2000). Analyzing the effectiveness and applicability of co-training. *Proceedings of the ninth international conference on information and knowledge management, McLean, VA* (pp. 86−93). New York, NY: ACM Press.

Nigam, K., McCallum, A. K., Thrun, S., & Mitchell, T. M. (2000). Text classification from labeled and unlabeled documents using EM. *Machine Learning, 39*(2/3), 103−134.

Nilsson, N. J. (1965). *Learning machines.* New York, NY: McGraw Hill.

Nisbet, R., Elder, J., & Miner, G. (2009). *Handbook of statistical analysis and data mining applications.* New York, NY: Academic Press.

Oates, T., & Jensen, D. (1997). The effects of training set size on decision tree complexity. *Proceedings of the fourteenth international conference on machine learning, Nashville, TN* (pp. 254−262). San Francisco, CA: Morgan Kaufmann.

Ohm, P. (2009). Broken promises of privacy: Responding to the surprising failure of anonymization. *University of Colorado Law Legal Studies Research Paper No. 09-12*, August.

Omohundro, S. M. (1987). Efficient algorithms with neural network behavior. *Journal of Complex Systems, 1*(2), 273−347.

Pascanu, R., Mikolov, T., & Bengio, Y. (2013). On the difficulty of training recurrent neural networks. In *Proceedings of the 30th International Conference on Machine Learning (ICML)*, pp. 1310−1318.

Paynter, G. W. (2000). Automating iterative tasks with programming by demonstration. *PhD Diessertation*. Department of Computer Science, University of Waikato, New Zealand.

Pearson, R. (2005). *Mining Imperfect Data.* USA: Society for Industrial and Applied Mechanics.

Pedregosa, F., Varoquaux, G., Gramfort, A., Michel, V., Thirion, B., Grisel, O., ... Cournapeau, D. (2011). Scikit-learn: Machine learning in Python. *Journal of Machine Learning Research*, *12*, 2825–2830.

Pei, J., Han, J., Mortazavi-Asi, B., Wang, J., Pinto, H., Chen, Q., ... Hsu, M. C. (2004). Mining sequential patterns by pattern-growth: The PrefixSpan approach. *IEEE Trans Knowledge and Data Engineering*, *16*(11), 1424–1440.

Petersen, K. B., & Pedersen, M. S. (2012). *The matrix cookbook*. Technical University of Denmark, Version Nov. 2012.

Piatetsky-Shapiro, G., & Frawley, W. J. (Eds.), (1991). *Knowledge discovery in databases* Menlo Park, CA: AAAI Press/MIT Press.

Platt, J. (1998). Fast training of support vector machines using sequential minimal optimization. In B. Schölkopf, C. Burges, & A. Smola (Eds.), *Advances in kernel methods: Support vector learning*. Cambridge, MA: MIT Press.

Platt, J. (1999). Probabilistic outputs for support vector machines and comparisons to regularized likelihood methods. *Advances in Large Margin Classifiers*, *10*(3), 61–74.

Power, D. J. (2002). What is the true story about data mining, beer and diapers? *DSS News*, *3*(23). <http://www.dssresources.com/newsletters/66.php>.

Provost, F., & Fawcett, T. (1997). Analysis and visualization of classifier performance: Comparison under imprecise class and cost distributions. In D. Heckerman, H. Mannila, D. Pregibon, & R. Uthurusamy (Eds.), *Proceedings of the third international conference on knowledge discovery and data mining, Huntington Beach, CA* (pp. 43–48). Menlo Park, CA: AAAI Press.

Pyle, D. (1999). *Data preparation for data mining*. San Francisco, CA: Morgan Kaufmann.

Quinlan, J. R. (1986). Induction of decision trees. *Machine Learning*, *1*(1), 81–106.

Quinlan, J. R. (1992). Learning with continuous classes. In N. Adams, & L. Sterling (Eds.), *Proceedings of the fifth Australian joint conference on artificial intelligence, Hobart, Tasmania* (pp. 343–348). Singapore: World Scientific.

Quinlan, J. R. (1993). *C4.5: Programs for machine learning*. San Francisco, CA: Morgan Kaufmann.

Quinlan, J. R. (1996). Improved use of continuous attributes in C4.5. *Journal of Artificial Intelligence Research*, *4*, 77–90.

Rabiner, L. R. (1989). A tutorial on hidden Markov models and selected applications in speech recognition. *Proceedings of the IEEE*, *77*(2), 257–286.

Rabiner, L. R., & Juang, B. H. (1986). An introduction to hidden Markov models. *ASSP Magazine, IEEE*, *3*(1), 4–16.

Ramon, J., & de Raedt, L. (2000). Multi instance neural networks. *Proceedings of the ICML workshop on attribute-value and relational learning* (pp. 53–60). Stanford, CA.

Ray, S., & Craven, M. (2005). Supervised learning versus multiple instance learning: An empirical comparison. *Proceedings of the International Conference on Machine Learning, Bonn, Germany* (pp. 697–704). New York, NY: ACM Press.

Read, J., Pfahringer, B., Holmes, G., & Frank, E. (2009). Classifier chains for multi-label classification. *Proc 13th European conference on principles and practice of knowledge discovery in databases and 20th European conference on machine learning, Bled, Slovenia* (pp. 254–269). Berlin: Springer Verlag.

Rennie, J. D. M., Shih, L., Teevan, J., & Karger, D. R. (2003). Tackling the poor assumptions of Naïve Bayes text classifiers. In T. Fawcett, & N. Mishra (Eds.), *Proceedings of the twentieth international conference on machine learning, Washington, DC* (pp. 616–623). Menlo Park, CA: AAAI Press.

Ricci, F., & Aha, D. W. (1998). Error-correcting output codes for local learners. In C. Nedellec, & C. Rouveird (Eds.), *Proceedings of the European conference on machine learning, Chemnitz, Germany* (pp. 280−291). Berlin: Springer-Verlag.

Richards, D., & Compton, P. (1998). Taking up the situated cognition challenge with ripple-down rules. *International Journal of Human-Computer Studies, 49*(6), 895−926.

Richardson, M., & Domingos, P. (2006). Markov logic networks. *Machine Learning, 62* (1−2), 107−136.

Rifkin, R., & Klautau, A. (2004). In defense of one-vs-all classification. *Journal of Machine Learning Research, 5*, 101−141.

Ripley, B. D. (1996). *Pattern recognition and neural networks.* Cambridge: Cambridge University Press.

Rissanen, J. (1985). The minimum description length principleIn S. Kotz, & N. L. Johnson (Eds.), *Encylopedia of statistical sciences* (Vol. 5, pp. 523−527). New York, NY: John Wiley.

Robbins, H., & Monro, S. (1951). A stochastic approximation method. *The Annals of Mathematical Statistics, 22*, 400−407.

Rodriguez, J. J., Kuncheva, L. I., & Alonso, C. J. (2006). Rotation forest: A new classifier ensemble method. *IEEE Transactions on Pattern Analysis and Machine Intelligence, 28*(10), 1619−1630.

Rojas, R. (1996). *Neural networks: A systematic introduction.* Berlin: Springer.

Rousseeuw, P. J., & Leroy, A. M. (1987). *Robust regression and outlier detection.* New York, NY: John Wiley.

Roweis, S. (1998). EM algorithms for PCA and SPCA. *Advances in Neural Information Processing Systems, 10*, 626−632.

Rumelhart, D. E., Hinton, G. E., & Williams, R. J. (1986). Learning internal representation by error propagation. *Parallel Distributed Processing, 1*, 318−362.

Russakovsky, O., Deng, J., Su, H., Krause, J., Satheesh, S., Ma, S., . . . Fei-Fei, L. (2015). Imagenet large scale visual recognition challenge. *International Journal of Computer Vision, 115*(3), 211−252.

Russell, S., & Norvig, P. (2009). *Artificial intelligence: A modern approach* (3rd ed.). Upper Saddle River, NJ: Prentice Hall.

Sahami, M., Dumais, S., Heckerman, D., & Horvitz, E. (1998). A Bayesian approach to filtering junk e-mail. *Proceedings of the AAAI-98 Workshop on Learning for Text Categorization, Madison, WI* (pp. 55−62). Menlo Park, CA: AAAI Press.

Saitta, L., & Neri, F. (1998). Learning in the "real world.". *Machine Learning, 30*(2/3), 133−163.

Salakhutdinov, R., & Hinton, G. E. (2009). Deep Boltzmann machines. *International Conference on Artificial Intelligence and Statistics, 9*, 448−455.

Salakhutdinov, R., & Hinton, G. E. (2012). An efficient learning procedure for deep Boltzmann machines. *Neural Computation, 24*(8), 1967−2006.

Salakhutdinov, R., Roweis, S., & Ghahramani, Z. (2003). Optimization with EM and expectation-conjugate-gradient. *ICML, 20*, 672−679.

Salzberg, S. (1991). A nearest hyperrectangle learning method. *Machine Learning, 6*(3), 251−276.

Schapire, R. E., Freund, Y., Bartlett, P., & Lee, W. S. (1997). Boosting the margin: A new explanation for the effectiveness of voting methods. In D. H. Fisher (Ed.), *Proceedings of the fourteenth international conference on machine learning, Nashville, TN* (pp. 322−330). San Francisco, CA: Morgan Kaufmann.

Scheffer, T. (2001). Finding association rules that trade support optimally against confidence. In L. de Raedt, & A. Siebes (Eds.), *Proceedings of the fifth European conference on principles of data mining and knowledge discovery, Freiburg, Germany* (pp. 424–435). Berlin: Springer-Verlag.

Schmidhuber, J. (2015). Deep learning in neural networks: An overview. *Neural Networks*, *61*, 85–117.

Schölkopf, B., Bartlett, P., Smola, A. J., & Williamson, R. (1999). *Shrinking the tube: A new support vector regression algorithm*, Advances in Neural Information Processing Systems (Vol. 11, pp. 330–336). Cambridge, MA: MIT Press.

Schölkopf, B., & Smola, A. J. (2002). *Learning with kernels: Support vector machines, regularization, optimization, and beyond*. Cambridge, MA: MIT Press.

Schölkopf, B., Williamson, R., Smola, A., Shawe-Taylor, J., & Platt, J. (2000). *Support vector method for novelty detection*, Advances in Neural Information Processing Systems (12, pp. 582–588). MIT Press.

Schuster, M., & Paliwal, K. K. (1997). Bidirectional recurrent neural networks. *IEEE Transactions on Signal Processing*, *45*(11), 2673–2681.

Sebastiani, F. (2002). Machine learning in automated text categorization. *ACM Computing Surveys*, *34*(1), 1–47.

Seewald, A. K. (2002). How to make stacking better and faster while also taking care of an unknown weakness. *Proceedings of the Nineteenth International Conference on Machine Learning, Sydney, Australia* (pp. 54–561). San Francisco, CA: Morgan Kaufmann.

Seewald, A. K., & Fürnkranz, J. (2001). An evaluation of grading classifiers. In F. Hoffmann, D. J. Hand, N. M. Adams, D. H. Fisher, & G. Guimarães (Eds.), *Proceedings of the fourth international conference on advances in intelligent data analysis, Cascais, Portugal* (pp. 115–124). Berlin: Springer-Verlag.

Sha, F., & Pereira, F. (2003). Shallow parsing with conditional random fields. In Proceedings of the Conference of the North American Chapter of the Association for Computational Linguistics on Human Language Technology Volume 1 (pp. 134–141). Association for Computational Linguistics.

Shafer, R., Agrawal, R., & Metha, M. (1996). SPRINT: A scalable parallel classifier for data mining. In T. M. Vijayaraman, A. P. Buchmann, C. Mohan, & N. L. Sarda (Eds.), *Proceedings of the second international conference on very large databases, Mumbai (Bombay), India* (pp. 544–555). San Francisco, CA: Morgan Kaufmann.

Shalev-Shwartz, S., Singer, Y., & Srebro, N. (2007). Pegasos: Primal estimated subgradient solver for SVM. *Proceedings of the 24th international conference on Machine Learning* (pp. 807–814). New York, NY: ACM Press.

Shawe-Taylor, J., & Cristianini, N. (2004). *Kernel methods for pattern analysis*. Cambridge: Cambridge University Press.

Shearer, C. (2000). The CRISP-DM model: The new blueprint for data mining. *J Data Warehousing*, *5*, 13–22.

Simard, P.Y., Steinkraus, D., & Platt, J.C. (2003). Best practices for convolutional neural networks applied to visual document analysis. In *Proceedings of 7th International Conference on Document Analysis and Recognition (ICDAR)*, vol. 3, pp. 958–962.

Simonyan, K., & Zisserman, A. (2014). Very deep convolutional networks for large-scale image recognition. In *the proceedings of ICLR* 2015. arXiv preprint arXiv:1409.1556.

Slonim, N., Friedman, N., & Tishby, N. (2002). Unsupervised document classification using sequential information maximization. *Proceedings of the 25th international ACM SIGIR conference on research and development in information retrieval* (pp. 129–136). New York, NY: ACM Press.

Smola, A. J., & Scholköpf, B. (2004). A tutorial on support vector regression. *Statistics and Computing, 14*(3), 199–222.

Smolensky, P. (1986). Information processing in dynamical systems: foundations of harmony theory. In D. E. Rumelhart, & J. L. McClelland, and the PDP Research Group (Eds.), *Parallel distributed processing: explorations in the microstructure of cognition* (Vol. 1, pp. 194–281). Cambridge, MA: MIT Press.

Snoek, J., Larochelle, H., & Adams, R. P. (2012). Practical Bayesian optimization of machine learning algorithms. *Advances in neural Information Processing Systems, 464,* 2951–2959.

Soderland, S., Fisher, D., Aseltine, J., & Lehnert, W. (1995). Crystal: Inducing a conceptual dictionary. *Proceedings of the fourteenth international joint conference on artificial intelligence, Montreal, Canada* (pp. 1314–1319). Menlo Park, CA: AAAI Press.

Spiegelhalter, D., Thomas, A., Best, N., & Lunn, D. (2003). *WinBUGS user manual.*

Srikant, R., & Agrawal, R. (1996). Mining sequential patters: Generalizations and performance improvements. *Proceedings of the Fifth International Conference on Extending Database Technology.* Avignon, France. P. M. Apers, M. Bouzeghoub, and G. Gardarin, Eds. *Lecture Notes In Computer Science*, Vol. 1057. Springer-Verlag, London, 3–17.

Srivastava, N., Hinton, G. E., Krizhevsky, A., Sutskever, I., & Salakhutdinov, R. (2014). Dropout: a simple way to prevent neural networks from overfitting. *Journal of Machine Learning Research, 15*(1), 1929–1958.

Stevens, S. S. (1946). On the theory of scales of measurement. *Science, 103,* 677–680.

Stone, P., & Veloso, M. (2000). Multiagent systems: A survey from a machine learning perspective. *Autonomous Robots, 8*(3), 345–383.

Stout, Q. F. (2008). Unimodal regression via prefix isotonic regression. *Computational Statistics and Data Analysis, 53,* 289–297.

Su, J., Zhang, H., Ling, C. X., & Matwin, S. (2008). Discriminative parameter learning for Bayesian networks. *Proceedings of the 25th International Conference on Machine Learning* (pp. 1016–1023). Helsinki: ACM Press.

Sugiyama, M. (2007). Dimensionality reduction of multimodal labeled data by local fisher discriminant analysis. *The Journal of Machine Learning Research, 8,* 1027–1061.

Sun, Y., Chen, Y., Wang, X., & Tang, X. (2014). Deep learning face representation by joint identification-verification. In *Advances in Neural Information Processing Systems* (pp. 1988–1996).

Sutskever, I., Vinyals, O., & Le, Q.V. (2014). Sequence to sequence learning with neural networks. In *Advances in neural information processing systems* (pp. 3104–3112).

Sutton, C., & McCallum, A. (2004). Collective segmentation and labeling of distant entities in information extraction. University of Massachusetts Amherst, Dept. of Computer Science *Technical Report TR-04-49.*

Sutton, C., & McCallum, A. (2006). An introduction to conditional random fields for relational learning. *Introduction to statistical relational learning, 93–128.*

Swets, J. (1988). Measuring the accuracy of diagnostic systems. *Science, 240,* 1285–1293.

Szegedy, C., Liu, W., Jia, Y., Sermanet, P., Reed, S., Anguelov, D., ... Rabinovich, A., (2015). Going deeper with convolutions. In *Proceedings of the IEEE Conference on Computer Vision and Pattern Recognition (CVPR)*, pp. 1–9.

Taigman, Y., Yang, M., Ranzato, M.A., & Wolf, L. (2014). Deepface: Closing the gap to human-level performance in face verification. In *Proceedings of the IEEE Conference on Computer Vision and Pattern Recognition (CVPR)*, pp. 1701–1708.

Teh, Y.W., Newman, D., & Welling, M. (2006). A collapsed variational Bayesian inference algorithm for latent Dirichlet allocation. In *Advances in neural information processing systems*, pp. 1353–1360.

Theano Development Team, Al-Rfou, R., Alain, G., Almahairi, A., Angermueller, C., Bahdanau, D.,Belopolsky, A. (2016). Theano: A Python framework for fast computation of mathematical expressions. arXiv preprint arXiv:1605.02688.

Tibshirani, R. (1996). Regression shrinkage and selection via the lasso. *Journal of the Royal Statistical Society. Series B (Methodological)*, 267–288.

Ting, K. M. (2002). An instance-weighting method to induce cost-sensitive trees. *IEEE Transactions on Knowledge and Data Engineering, 14*(3), 659–665.

Ting, K. M., & Witten, I. H. (1997a). Stacked generalization: When does it work?. *Proceedings of the fifteenth international joint conference on artificial intelligence, Nagoya, Japan* (pp. 866–871). San Francisco, CA: Morgan Kaufmann.

Ting, K. M., & Witten, I. H. (1997b). Stacking bagged and dagged models. In D. H. Fisher (Ed.), *Proceedings of the fourteenth international conference on machine learning, Nashville, TN* (pp. 367–375). . San Francisco, CA: Morgan Kaufmann.

Tipping, M. E. (2001). Sparse Bayesian learning and the relevance vector machine. *The Journal of Machine Learning Research, 1*, 211–244.

Tipping, M. E., & Bishop, C. M. (1999a). Mixtures of probabilistic principal component analyzers. *Neural Computation, 11*(2), 443–482.

Tipping, M. E., & Bishop, C. M. (1999b). Probabilistic principal component analysis. *Journal of the Royal Statistical Society: Series B (Statistical Methodology), 61*(3), 611–622.

Turk, M., & Pentland, A. (1991). Eigenfaces for recognition. *Journal of Cognitive Neuroscience, 3*(1), 71–86.

Turney, P. D. (1999). *Learning to extract key phrases from text. Technical Report ERB-1057*. Ottawa, Canada: Institute for Information Technology, National Research Council of Canada.

U.S. House of Representatives Subcommittee on Aviation. (2002). Hearing on aviation security with a focus on passenger profiling, February 27, 2002. <http://www.house.gov/transportation/aviation/02-27-02/02-27-02memo.html>.

Utgoff, P. E. (1989). Incremental induction of decision trees. *Machine Learning, 4*(2), 161–186.

Utgoff, P. E., Berkman, N. C., & Clouse, J. A. (1997). Decision tree induction based on efficient tree restructuring. *Machine Learning, 29*(1), 5–44.

Vafaie, H., & DeJong, K. (1992). Genetic algorithms as a tool for feature selection in machine learning. *Proceedings of the international conference on tools with artificial intelligence* (pp. 200–203). Arlington, VA: IEEE Computer Society Press.

van Rijsbergen, C. A. (1979). *Information retrieval.*. London: Butterworths.

Vapnik, V. (1999). *The nature of statistical learning theory* (2nd ed.). New York, NY: Springer-Verlag.

Venables, W. N., & Ripley, B. D. (2000). *S Programming*. Springer.

Venables, W. N., & Ripley, B. D. (2002). *Modern Applied Statistics with S* (4th ed.). New York, NY: Springer.

Venter, J. C., et al. (2001). The sequence of the human genome. *Science, 291*(5507), 1304−1351.

Vincent, P., Larochelle, H., Lajoie, I., Bengio, Y., & Manzagol, P. A. (2010). Stacked denoising autoencoders: Learning useful representations in a deep network with a local denoising criterion. *The Journal of Machine Learning Research, 11,* 3371−3408.

Vitter, J. S. (1985). Random sampling with a reservoir. *ACM Transactions on Mathematical Software, 1*(11), 37−57.

Wang, J., Han, J., & Pei, J. (2003). CLOSET + : Searching for the best strategies for mining frequent closed itemsets. *Proceedings of the International Conference on Knowledge Discovery and Data Mining (KDD'03)*, Washington, DC.

Wang, J., & Zucker, J.-D. (2000). Solving the multiple-instance problem: A lazy learning approach. *Proceedings of the international conference on machine learning, Stanford, CA* (pp. 1119−1125). San Francisco, CA: Morgan Kaufmann.

Wang, Y., & Witten, I. H. (1997). Induction of model trees for predicting continuous classes. In M. van Someren, & G. Widmer (Eds.), *Proceedings of the of the poster papers of the european conference on machine learning* (pp. 128−137). Prague: University of Economics, Faculty of Informatics and Statistics.

Wang, Y., & Witten, I. H. (2002). Modeling for optimal probability prediction. In C. Sammut, & A. Hoffmann (Eds.), *Proceedings of the nineteenth international conference on machine learning, Sydney, Australia* (pp. 650−657). San Francisco, CA: Morgan Kaufmann.

Webb, G. I. (1999). Decision tree grafting from the all-tests-but-one partition. *Proceedings of the sixteenth international joint conference on artificial intelligence* (pp. 702−707). San Francisco, CA: Morgan Kaufmann.

Webb, G. I. (2000). MultiBoosting: A technique for combining boosting and wagging. *Machine Learning, 40*(2), 159−196.

Webb, G. I., Boughton, J., & Wang, Z. (2005). Not so naïve Bayes: Aggregating one-dependence estimators. *Machine Learning, 58*(1), 5−24.

Webb, G. I., Boughton, J. R., Zheng, F., Ting, K. M., & Salem, H. (2012). Learning by extrapolation from marginal to full-multivariate probability distributions: decreasingly naive Bayesian classification. *Machine Learning, 86*(2), 233−272.

Wegener, I. (1987). *The complexity of Boolean functions.* New York, NY: John Wiley and Sons.

Weidmann, N., Frank, E., & Pfahringer, B. (2003). A two-level learning method for generalized multi-instance problems. *Proceedings of the European conference on machine learning, Cavtat, Croatia* (pp. 468−479). Berlin: Springer-Verlag.

Weiser, M. (1996). Open house. *Review,* the web magazine of the Interactive Telecommunications Program of New York University.

Weiser, M., & Brown, J. S. (1997). The coming age of calm technology. In P. J. Denning, & R. M. Metcalfe (Eds.), *Beyond calculation: The next fifty years* (pp. 75−86). New York, NY: Copernicus.

Weiss, S. M., & Indurkhya, N. (1998). *Predictive data mining: A practical guide.* San Francisco, CA: Morgan Kaufmann.

Welling, M., Rosen-Zvi, M., & Hinton, G.E. (2004). Exponential family harmoniums with an application to information retrieval. In *Advances in neural information processing systems* (pp. 1481−1488).

Werbos, P. (1974). *Beyond Regression: New Tools for Prediction and Analysis in the Behavioral Sciences. PhD thesis.* Harvard University.

Wettschereck, D., & Dieterich, T. G. (1995). An experimental comparison of the nearest-neighbor and nearest-hyperrectangle algorithms. *Machine Learning, 19*(1), 5–28.

Wild, C. J., & Seber, G. A. F. (1995). *Introduction to probability and statistics.* New Zealand: Department of Statistics, University of Auckland.

Williams, C. K., & Rasmussen, C. E. (2006). *Gaussian processes for machine learning.* MIT Press, 2(3), 4.

Winn, J. M., & Bishop, C. M. (2005). Variational message passing. *Journal of Machine Learning Research, 6*, 661–694.

Winston, P. H. (1992). *Artificial intelligence.* Reading, MA: Addison-Wesley.

Witten, I. H. (2004). Text mining. In M. P. Singh (Ed.), *Practical handbook of internet computing.* Boca Raton, FL: CRC Press, 14-1–14-22.

Witten, I. H., & Bell, T. C. (1991). The zero-frequency problem: Estimating the probabilities of novel events in adaptive text compression. *IEEE Transactions on Information Theory, 37*(4), 1085–1094.

Witten, I. H., Bray, Z., Mahoui, M., & Teahan, W. (1999a). Text mining: A new frontier for lossless compression. In J. A. Storer, & M. Cohn (Eds.), *Proceedings of the data compression conference, Snowbird, UT* (pp. 198–207). Los Alamitos, CA: IEEE Press.

Witten, I. H., Moffat, A., & Bell, T. C. (1999b). *Managing gigabytes: Compressing and indexing documents and images* (second edition). San Francisco, CA: Morgan Kaufmann.

Wolpert, D. H. (1992). Stacked generalization. *Neural Networks, 5*, 241–259.

Wu, X., & Kumar, V. (Eds.), (2009). *The top ten algorithms in data mining* London: Chapman and Hall.

Wu, X. V., Kumar, J. R., Quinlan, J., Ghosh, Q., Yang, H., Motoda, G. J., . . . Steinberg, D. (2008). Top 10 algorithms in data mining. *Knowledge and Information Systems, 14*(1), 1–37.

Xu, B., Wang, N., Chen, T., & Li, M. (2015). Empirical Evaluation of Rectified Activations in Convolutional Network. *arXiv preprint,* arXiv:1505.00853.

Xu, X., & Frank, E. (2004). Logistic regression and boosting for labeled bags of instances. *Proceedings of the 8th Pacific-Asia conference on knowledge discovery and data mining, Sydney, Australia* (pp. 272–281). Berlin: Springer-Verlag.

Yan, X., & Han, J. (2002). gSpan: Graph-based substructure pattern mining. *Proceedings of the IEEE international conference on data mining (ICDM '02).* Washington, DC: IEEE Computer Society.

Yan, X., & Han, J. (2003). CloseGraph: Mining closed frequent graph patterns. *Proceedings of the Ninth ACM SIGKDD International Conference on Knowledge Discovery and Data Mining.*

Yan, X., Han, J., & Afshar, R. (2003). CloSpan: Mining closed sequential patterns in large datasets. *Proceedings of the SIAM International Conference on Data Mining (SDM'03), San Francisco, CA.*

Yang, Y., Guan, X., & You, J. (2002). CLOPE: A fast and effective clustering algorithm for transactional data. *Proceedings of the Eighth ACM SIGKDD International Conference on Knowledge Discovery and Data Mining,* pp. 682–687.

Yang, Y., & Webb, G. I. (2001). Proportional k-interval discretization for Naïve Bayes classifiers. In L. de Raedt, & P. Flach (Eds.), *Proceedings of the Twelfth European Conference on Machine Learning, Freiburg, Germany* (pp. 564–575). Berlin: Springer-Verlag.

Yu, D., Eversole, A., Seltzer, M., Yao, K., Huang, Z., Guenter, B., Droppo, J. (2014). An introduction to computational networks and the computational network toolkit. *Tech. Rep. MSR-TR-2014-112*, Microsoft Research, Code: http://codebox/cntk.

Yurcik, W., Barlow, J., Zhou, Y., Raje, H., Li, Y., Yin, X., ... Searsmith, D. (2003). Scalable data management alternatives to support data mining heterogeneous logs for computer network security. *Proceedings of the workshop on data mining for counter terrorism and security, San Francisco, CA*. Philadelphia, PA: Society for International and Applied Mathematics.

Zadrozny, B., & Elkan, C. (2002). Transforming classifier scores into accurate multiclass probability estimates. *Proceedings of the eighth ACM international conference on knowledge discovery and data mining, Edmonton, Alberta, Canada* (pp. 694–699). New York, NY: ACM Press.

Zaki, M.J., Parthasarathy, S., Ogihara, M., & Li, W. (1997). New algorithms for fast discovery of association rules. *Proceedings Knowledge Discovery in Databases* (pp. 283–286).

Zbontar, J., & LeCun, Y. (2015). Computing the stereo matching cost with a convolutional neural network. *Proceedings of the IEEE conference on computer vision and pattern recognition* (pp. 1592–1599).

Zeiler, M. D., & Fergus, R. (2014). Visualizing and understanding convolutional networks. *Proceeding of ECCV 2014* (pp. 818–833). New York, NY: Springer International Publishing.

Zhang, H., Jiang, L., & Su, J. (2005). Hidden Naïve Bayes. *Proceedings of the 20th national conference on artificial intelligence* (pp. 919–924). Menlo Park, CA: AAAI Press.

Zhang, T. (2004). Solving large scale linear prediction problems using stochastic gradient descent algorithms. *Proceedings of the 21st international conference on machine learning* (pp. 919–926). Omni Press.

Zhang, T., Ramakrishnan, R., & Livny, M. (1996). BIRCH: An efficient data clustering method for very large databases. *Proceedings of the ACM SIGMOD international conference on management of data, Montreal, Quebec, Canada* (pp. 103–114). New York, NY: ACM Press.

Zheng, F., & Webb, G. (2006). Efficient lazy elimination for averaged one-dependence estimators. *Proceedings of the 23rd international conference on machine learning* (pp. 1113–1120). New York, NY: ACM Press.

Zheng, Z., & Webb, G. (2000). Lazy learning of Bayesian rules. *Machine Learning, 41*(1), 53–84.

Zhou, Z.-H., & Zhang, M.-L. (2007). Solving multi-instance problems with classifier ensemble based on constructive clustering. *Knowledge and Information Systems, 11*(2), 155–170.

Zhu, J., & Hastie, T. (2005). Kernel logistic regression and the import vector machine. *Journal of Computational and Graphical Statistics, 14*(1), 185–205.

Zou, H., & Hastie, T. (2005). Regularization and Variable Selection via the Elastic Net. *Journal of the Royal Statistical Society, Series B, 67*, 301–320.

Index

Note: Page numbers followed by "*f*" and "*t*" refer to figures and tables, respectively.

0-9, and Symbols

0 − 1 loss function, 176
0.632 bootstrap, 170
1R (1-rule), 93
  discretization, 296
  example use, 94*t*
  missing values and numeric data, 94−96
  overfitting for, 95
  pseudocode, 93*f*
11-point average recall, 191

A

Accuracy, of association rules, 79, 120
  minimum, 79, 122, 124
Accuracy, of classification rules, 102, 115
Activation functions, 270, 424−426, 425*t*
Acuity parameter, 152
AD trees. *See* All-dimensions (AD) trees
AdaBoost, 487−489
AdaBoost.M1 algorithm, 487
Additive logistic regression, 492−493
Additive regression, 490−493
ADTree algorithm, 501
Adversarial data mining, 524−527
Agglomerative clustering, 142, 147
Aggregation, 438
Akaike Information Criterion (AIC), 346
AlexNet model, 435
All-dimensions (AD) trees, 350−351
  generation, 351
  illustrated examples, 350*f*
Alternating decision trees, 495
  example, 495*f*, 496
  prediction nodes, 495
  splitter nodes, 495
Analysis of variance (ANOVA), 393
Analyze panel, 568, 570−571
Ancestor-of relation, 51
AND, 262
Anomalies, detecting, 318−319
Antecedent, of rule, 75
AODE. *See* Averaged one-dependence estimator (AODE)
Applications, 503
  automation, 28
  challenge of, 503
  data stream learning, 509−512

  diagnosis, 25−26
  fielded, 21−28
  incorporating domain knowledge, 512−515
  massive datasets, 506−509
  text mining, 515−519
Apriori algorithm, 234−235
Area under the curve (AUC), 191−192
Area under the precision-recall curve (AUPRC), 192
ARFF files, 57
  attribute specifications in, 58
  attribute types in, 58
  defined, 57
  illustrated, 58*f*
Arithmetic underflow, 344−345
Aspect model, 378−379
Assignment of key phrases, 516
Association learning, 44
Association rules, 11−12, 79−80. *See also* Rules
  accuracy (confidence), 79, 120
  characteristics, 79
  computation requirement, 127
  converting item sets to, 122
  coverage (support), 79, 120
  double-consequent, 125−126
  examples, 11−12
  finding, 120
  finding large item sets, 240−241
  frequent-pattern tree, 235−239
  mining, 120−127
  predicting multiple consequences, 79
  relationships between, 80
  single-consequent, 126
  in Weka, 561
Attribute evaluation methods, 562
  attribute subset evaluators, 564
  single-attribute evaluators, 564
Attribute filters, 563
  supervised, 563
  unsupervised, 563
Attribute selection, 287−295. *See also* Data transformations
  backward elimination, 292−293
  beam search, 293
  best-first search, 293
  filter method, 289−290
  forward selection, 292−293
  instance-based learning methods, 291

Attribute selection (*Continued*)
  race search, 294
  recursive feature elimination, 290–291
  schemata search, 294
  scheme-independent, 289–292
  scheme-specific, 293–295
  searching the attribute space and, 292–293
  selective Naïve Bayes, 295
  symmetric uncertainty, 291–292
  in Weka, 562
  Weka evaluation methods for, 562
  wrapper method, 289–290
Attribute subset evaluators, 564
Attribute-efficient learners, 135
Attributes, 43, 53–54, 95
  ARFF format, 58
  Boolean, 55–56
  causal relations, 513
  combination of, 120
  conversions, 94
  date, 58
  difference, 135–136
  discrete, 55–56
  evaluating, 94*t*
  highly branching, 110–113
  identification code, 95
  interval, 55
  irrelevant, 289
  nominal, 54, 357
  normalized, 61
  numeric, 54, 210–212
  ordinal, 55
  ratio, 55
  relations between, 83
  relation-valued, 58
  relevant, 289
  semantic relation between, 513
  string, 58, 313
  string, conversion, 313
  types of, 44, 61–62
  values of, 53–54
  weighting, 246–247
AUC. *See* Area under the curve (AUC)
AUPRC. *See* Area under the precision-recall curve
      (AUPRC)
Authorship ascription, 516
AutoClass, 156, 359
  Bayesian clustering scheme, 359–360
Autoencoders, 445–449
  combining reconstructive and discriminative
      learning, 449
  denoising autoencoders, 448
  layerwise training, 448
  pretraining deep autoencoders with RBMs, 448

Automation applications, 28
Averaged one-dependence estimator (AODE),
      348–349
Average-linkage method, 147–148

B

Background knowledge, 508
Backpropagation, 263, 426–429
  checking implementations, 430–431
  stochastic, 268–269
Backward elimination, 292–293
Backward pruning, 213
Bagging, 480
  algorithm for, 483*f*
  bias-variance decomposition, 482–483
  with costs, 483–484
  idealized procedure versus, 483
  instability neutralization, 482–483
  for numeric prediction, 483
  as parallel, 508
  randomization versus, 485–486
Bagging algorithm, 480–484
Bags, 156–157
  class labels, 157
  instances, joining, 474
  positive, 475–476
  positive probability, 476
Balanced iterative reducing and clustering using
      hierarchies (BIRCH), 160
Balanced Winnow, 134–135
Ball trees, 139
  in finding nearest neighbors, 140
  illustrated, 139*f*
  nodes, 139–140
  splitting method, 140–141
  two cluster centers, 145*f*
Batch learning, 268–269
Batch normalization, 436
Bayes Information Criterion, 159–160
Bayes' rule, 337, 339, 362–363
Bayesian clustering, 358–359
  AutoClass, 359
  DensiTree, 359, 360*f*
  hierarchical, 359
Bayesian estimation and prediction, 367–370
  probabilistic inference methods, 368–370
Bayesian Latent Dirichlet allocation (LDA[b]),
      379–380
Bayesian multinet, 349
Bayesian networks, 158, 339–352, 382–385
  AD tree, 350–351, 350*f*
  algorithms, 347–349
  conditional independence, 343–344

data structures for fast learning, 349–352
EM algorithm to, 366–367
example illustrations, 341*f*, 342*f*
for weather data, 341*f*, 342*f*
K2 algorithm, 411
learning, 344–347
making predictions, 340–344
Markov blanket, 347–348
predictions, 340–344
prior distribution over network structures, 346–347
specific algorithms, 347–349
structure learning by conditional independence tests, 349
TAN, 348
BayesNet algorithm, 416
Beam search, 293
Belief propagation. *See* Probability propagation
Bernoulli process, 165
BestFirst method, 334
Best-first search, 295
Bias, 33–35
language, 33–34
multilayer perceptron, 263
overfitting-avoidance, 35
search, 34–35
Bias-variance decomposition, 482–483
Binary classification problems, 69
Binary events, 337
BIRCH. *See* Balanced iterative reducing and clustering using hierarchies (BIRCH)
Bits, 106–107
Block Gibbs sampling, 454
Boltzmann machines, 449–451
Boolean attributes, 55–56
Boolean classes, 78
Boosting, 486–490
AdaBoost, 487–489
algorithm for, 487, 488*f*
classifiers, 490
in computational learning theory, 489
decision stumps, 490
forward stagewise additive modeling, 491
power of, 489–490
Bootstrap, 169–171
Bootstrap aggregating. *See* Bagging
Box kernel, 361
"Burn-in" process, 369
"Business understanding" phase, 28–29

C
C4.5, 113, 216, 219–220, 288–289
functioning of, 219
MDL-based adjustment, 220

C5.0, 221
Caffe, 465
Calibration, class probability, 330
discretization-based, 331
logistic regression, 330
PAV-based, 331
Capabilities class, 561
CAPPS. *See* Computer-Assisted Passenger Prescreening System (CAPPS)
CART system, 210, 283
cost-complexity pruning, 220–221
Categorical and continuous variables, 452–453
Categorical attributes. *See* Nominal attributes
Category utility, 142, 154–156
calculation, 154
incremental clustering, 150–154
Causal relations, 513
CBA technique, 241
CfsSubsetEval method, 334
Chain rule, 327, 343–344
Chain-structured conditional random fields, 410
Circular ordering, 56
CitationKNN algorithm, 478
Class boundaries
non-axis parallel, 251
rectangular, 248–249, 249*f*
Class labels
bags, 157
reliability, 506
Class noise, 317
Class probability estimation, 321
dataset with two classes, 329, 329*f*
difficulty, 328–329
overoptimistic, 329
ClassAssigner component, 564–565
ClassAssigner filter, 564–565, 567
Classes, 45
Boolean, 78
membership functions for, 129
rectangular, 248–249, 249*f*
Classical machine learning techniques, 418
Classification, 44
clustering for, 468–470
cost-sensitive, 182–183, 484
document, 516
k-nearest-neighbor, 85
Naïve Bayes for, 103–104
nearest-neighbor, 85
one-class, 319
pairwise, 323
Classification learning, 44
Classification rules, 11–12, 75–78. *See also* Rules
accuracy, 224

Classification rules (*Continued*)
  antecedent of, 75
  criteria for choosing tests, 221–222
  disjunctive normal form, 78
  with exceptions, 80–82
  exclusive-or, 76, 77*f*
  global optimization, 226–227
  good rule generation, 224–226
  missing values, 223–224
  multiple, 78
  numeric attributes, 224
  from partial decision trees, 227–231
  producing with covering algorithms, 223
  pruning, 224
  replicated subtree, 76, 77*f*
  RIPPER rule learner, 227, 228*f*, 234
ClassifierPerformanceEvaluator, 565, 567
ClassifierSubsetEval method, 334
Classify panel, 558–559, 563
  classification error visualization, 559
Cleansing
  artificial data generation, 321–322
  detecting anomalies, 318–319
  improving decision trees, 316–317
  one-class learning, 319–320
  outlier detection, 320–321
  robust regression, 317–318
"Cliques", 385
Closed-world assumptions, 47, 78
CLOSET + algorithm, 241
Clustering, 44, 141–156, 352–363, 473
  agglomerative, 142, 147
  algorithms, 87–88
  category utility, 142
  comparing parametric, semiparametric and
      nonparametric density models, 362–363
  with correlated attributes, 359–361
  document, 516
  EM algorithm, 353–356
  evaluation, 200
  expectation maximization algorithm, 353–356
  extending mixture model, 356–358
  for classification, 468–470
  group-average, 148
  hierarchical, 147–148
  in grouping items, 45
  incremental, 150–154
  iterative distance-based, 142–144
  k-means, 144
  MDL principle application to, 200–201
  number of clusters, 146–147
  using prior distributions, 358–359
  and probability density estimation, 352–363
  representation, 88*f*

statistical, 296
two-class mixture model, 354*f*
in Weka, 561
Cobweb algorithm, 142, 160, 561–562
Co-EM, 471
"Collapsed Gibbs sampling", 380–381
Column separation, 325
Comma-separated value (CSV)
  data files, 558
  format, 558
Complete-linkage method, 147
Computation graphs and complex network
      structures, 429–430
Computational learning theory, 489
Computational Network Toolkit (CNTK), 465
Computer-Assisted Passenger Prescreening System
      (CAPPS), 526
Concept descriptions, 43
Concepts, 44–46. *See also* Input
  defined, 43
"Condensed" representation, 473
Conditional independence, 343–344
Conditional probability models, 392–403
  generalized linear models, 400–401
  gradient descent and second-order methods, 400
  using kernels, 402–403
  linear and polynomial regression, 392–393
  multiclass logistic regression, 396–400
  predictions for ordered classes, 402
  using priors on parameters, 393–395
    matrix vector formulations of linear and
        polynomial regression, 394–395
Conditional random fields, 406–410
  chain-structured conditional random fields, 410
  linear chain conditional random fields, 408–409
  from Markov random fields to, 407–408
  for text mining, 410
Confidence
  of association rules, 79, 120
  intervals, 173–174
  upper/lower bounds, 246
Confidence limits
  in error rate estimation, 215–217
  for normal distribution, 166*t*
  for Student's distribution, 174*t*
  on success probability, 246
Confusion matrix, 181
Consequent, of rule, 75
ConsistencySubsetEval method, 334
Constrained quadratic optimization, 254
Contact lens problem, 12–14
  covering algorithm, 115–119
  rules, 13*f*
  structural description, 14, 14*f*

Continuous attributes. *See* Numeric attributes
Contrastive divergence, 452
Convex hulls, 253
Convolution, 440–441
Convolutional neural networks (CNNs), 419,
    437–438
  convolutional layers and gradients, 443–444
  deep convolutional networks, 438–439
  from image filtering to learnable convolutional
    layers, 439–443
  ImageNet evaluation, 438–439
  implementation, 445
  pooling and subsampling layers and gradients, 444
Corrected resampled *t*-test, 175–176
Cost curves, 192–194
  cost in, 193
  cost matrixes, 182, 182*t*, 186
Cost of errors, 179–180
  cost curves, 192–194
  cost-sensitive classification, 182–183
  cost-sensitive learning, 183
  examples, 180
  lift charts, 183–186
  problem misidentification, 180
  recall-precision curves, 190
  ROC curves, 186–190
Cost–benefit analyzer, 186
Cost-complexity pruning, 220–221
Cost-sensitive classification, 182–183, 484
Cost-sensitive learning, 183
  two-class, 183
Co-training, 470
  EM and, 471
Counting the cost, 179–194
Covariance matrix, 356–357
Coverage, of association rules, 79, 120
  minimum, 124
  specifying, 127
Covering algorithms, 113–119
  example, 115
  illustrated, 113*f*
  instance space during operation of, 115*f*
  operation, 115
  in producing rules, 223
  in two-dimensional space, 113–114
CPU performance, 16
  dataset, 16*t*
Cross-correlation, 440–441
Cross-validation, 167–168, 432–433
  estimates, 173
  folds, 168
  leave-one-out, 169
  repeated, 175–176
  for ROC curve generation, 189

stratified threefold, 168
tenfold, 168, 286–287
threefold, 168
CrossValidationFoldMaker, 565, 567
CSV. *See* Comma-separated value (CSV)
CuDNN, 465–466
Customer support/service applications, 28
Cutoff parameter, 154

D

Data, 38
  augmentation, 437
  evaluation phase, 29–30
  linearly separable, 131–132
  noise, 7
  overlay, 57
  scarcity of, 529
  sparse, 60–61
  structures for fast learning, 349–352
Data cleansing, 65, 288, 316–322. *See also* Data
    transformations
  anomaly detection, 318–319
  decision tree improvement, 316–317
  methods, 288
  one-class learning, 319–320
  robust regression, 317–318
Data mining, 5–6, 9, 28–30
  adversarial, 524–527
  applying, 504–506
  as data analysis, 5
  ethics and, 35–38
  learning machine and, 4–9
  life cycle, 29*f*
  scheme comparison, 172–176
  ubiquitous, 527–529
Data preparation. *See also* Input
  ARFF files, 57–60
  attribute types, 61–62
  data gathering in, 56–57
  data knowledge and, 65
  inaccurate values in, 63–64
  missing values in, 62–63
  sparse data, 60–61
Data projections, 287, 304–314
  partial least-squares regression, 307–309
  principal components analysis, 305–307
  random, 307
  text to attribute vectors, 313–314
  time series, 314
Data stream learning, 509–512
  algorithm adaptation for, 510
  Hoeffding bound, 510
  memory usage, 511–512

Data stream learning (*Continued*)
  Naïve Bayes for, 510
  tie-breaking strategy, 511
Data transformations, 285
  attribute selection, 288−295
  data cleansing, 288, 316−322
  data projection, 287, 304−314
  discretization of numeric attributes, 287, 296−303
  input types and, 305
  methods for, 287
  multiple classes to binary ones, 288−289, 315−316
  sampling, 288, 315−316
"Data understanding" phase, 28−29
Data warehousing, 56−57
Data-dependent expectation, 451
DataSet connections, 566−567
Date attributes, 58
Decimation, 438
Decision boundaries, 69
Decision lists, 11
  rules versus, 119
Decision stumps, 490
Decision tree induction, 30, 316
  complexity, 217−218
  top-down, 221
Decision trees, 6, 70−71, 109*f*
  alternating, 495−496, 495*f*
  C4.5 algorithm and, 219−220
  constructing, 105−113
  cost-complexity pruning, 220−221
  for disjunction, 76*f*
  error rate estimation, 215−217
  examples, 14*f*, 18*f*
  highly branching attributes, 110−113
  improving, 316−317
  information calculation, 108−110
  missing values, 71, 212−213
  nodes, 70−71
  numeric attributes, 210−212
  partial, obtaining rules from, 227−231
  pruning, 213−215
  with replicated subtree, 77*f*
  rules, 219
  in Weka, 558−559
DecisionStump algorithm, 490
DecisionTable algorithm, 334
Dedicated multi-instance methods, 475−476
Deep belief networks, 455−456
Deep Boltzmann machines, 453−454
Deep feedforward networks, 420−431
  activation functions, 424−426, 425*t*
  backpropagation, 426−429
    checking implementations, 430−431

computation graphs and complex network structures, 429−430
  deep layered network architecture, 423−424
  feedforward neural network, 424*f*
  losses and regularization, 422−423
  MNIST evaluation, 421−422, 421*t*
Deep layered network architecture, 423−424
Deep learning, 418
  autoencoders, 445−449
  deep feedforward networks, 420−431
  recurrent neural networks, 456−460
  software and network implementations, 464−466
  stochastic deep networks, 449−456
  techniques, 418
  three-layer perceptron, 419
  training and evaluating deep networks, 431−437
    batch normalization, 436
    cross-validation, 432−433
    data augmentation and synthetic transformations, 437
    dropout, 436
    early stopping model, 431−432
    hyperparameter tuning, 432−433
    learning rates and schedules, 434−435
    mini-batch-based stochastic gradient descent, 433−434
    parameter initialization, 436−437
    pseudocode for mini-batch based stochastic gradient descent, 434, 435*f*
    regularization with priors on parameters, 435
    unsupervised pretraining, 437
    validation, 432−433
Deeplearning4j, 465
Delta, 314
Dendrograms, 87−88, 147
Denoising autoencoders, 448
Denormalization, 50
  problems with, 51
DensiTree, 359, 360*f*
  visualization, 359, 360*f*
Diagnosis applications, 25−26
  faults, 25−26
  machine language in, 25
  performance tests, 26
Difference attributes, 135−136
Dimensionality reduction, PCA for, 377−378
Direct marketing, 27
Directed acyclic graphs, 340
Discrete attributes, 55−56
  1R (1-rule), 296
  converting to numeric attributes, 303
  discretization, 287, 296−303. *See also* Data transformations
  decision tree learners, 296

entropy-based, 298–301
error-based, 301
global, 296
partitioning, 94–95
proportional *k*-interval, 297–298
supervised, 297
unsupervised, 297
Discrete events, 337
Discretization-based calibration, 330
Discriminative learning, 449
Disjunctive normal form, 78
Distance functions, 135–136
difference attributes, 135–136
generalized, 250
for generalized exemplars, 248–250
missing values, 136
Diverse-density method, 475–476
Divide-and-conquer, 105–113, 289
Document classification, 516. *See also*
    Classification
in assignment of key phrases, 516
in authorship ascription, 516
in language identification, 516
as supervised learning, 516
Document clustering, 516
Domain knowledge, 19
Double-consequent rules, 126
Dropout, 436
Dynamic Bayesian network, 405

E

Early stopping, 266–268
model, 431–432
Eigenvalues, 306
Eigenvectors, 306
"Elastic net" approach, 394
EM algorithm, 416
EM for PPCA, 375–376
END algorithm, 334
"Empirical Bayesian" methods, 368
Empirical risk, 422–423
Ensemble learning, 479
additive regression, 490–493
bagging, 481–484
boosting, 486–490
interpretable ensembles, 493–497
multiple models, 480–481
randomization, 484–486
stacking, 497–499
Entity extraction, in text mining, 517
Entropy, 110
Entropy-based discretization, 298–301
error-based discretization versus, 301
illustrated, 299f

with MDL stopping criterion,
    301
results, 299f
stopping criteria, 293, 300
Enumerated, 55–56
Enumerating concept space, 32–33
Equal-frequency binning, 297
Equal-interval binning, 297
Error rate, 163
decision tree, 215–217
repeated holdout, 167
success rate and, 215–216
training set, 163
Error-based discretization, 301
Errors
estimation, 172
inaccurate values and, 63–64
mean-absolute, 195
mean-squared, 195
propagation, 266–268
relative-absolute, 195
relative-squared, 195–196
resubstitution, 163
squared, 177
training set, 163
Estimation error, 172
Ethics, 35–38
issues, 35
personal information and, 37–38
reidentification and, 36–37
Euclidean distance, 135
between instances, 149
function, 246–247
Evaluation
clustering, 200–201
as data mining key, 161–162
numeric prediction, 194–197
performance, 162
Examples, 46–53. *See also* Instances;
    specific examples
class of, 45
relations, 47–51
structured, 51
types of, 46–53
Exceptions, rules with, 80–82, 231–233
Exclusive-or problem, 77f
Exclusive-OR (XOR), 262
Exemplars, 245
generalizing, 247–248
noisy, pruning, 245–246
reducing number of, 245
Exhaustive error-correcting codes,
    326
ExhaustiveSearch method, 496

Expectation, 357
Expectation maximization (EM) algorithm,
    353–356, 365–366, 468
  and cotraining, 471
  maximization step, 469
  with Naïve Bayes, 469
  to train Bayesian networks, 366–367
Expected gradients, 364–365
  for PPCA, 375
Expected log-likelihoods, 364–365
  for PPCA, 374
Experimenter, 554, 568–571. *See also* Weka
    workbench
  advanced setup, 570
  Analyze panel, 568–571
  results analysis, 569–570
  Run panel, 568
  running experiments, 568–569
  Setup panel, 568, 571
  simple setup, 570
  starting up, 568–570
Expert models, 480
Explorer, 554, 557–564. *See also* Weka
    workbench
  ARFF format, 560
  Associate panel, 561–562
  association-rule learning, 234–241
  attribute selection, 564
  automatic parameter tuning, 171–172
  Classify panel, 558
  Cluster panel, 561
  clustering algorithms, 141–156
  CSV data files, 558
  decision tree building, 558–559
  filters, 560–561, 563
  introduction to, 557–564
  J48, 558–559
  learning algorithms, 563
  loading datasets, 557–558, 560–561
  metalearning algorithms, 558
  models, 559
  Preprocess panel, 559–560
  search methods, 564
  Select Attributes panel, 562, 564
  Visualize panel, 553, 562
EXtensible Markup Language (XML), 57, 568

F

Factor analysis, 373
Factor graphs, 382–385
  Bayesian networks, 382–385
  logistic regression model, 382–385
  Markov blanket, 383*f*

False negatives (FN), 180–182, 191*t*
False positive rate, 180–181
False positives (FP), 180–182, 191*t*
Familiar system, 528
Feature map, 439–440
Feature selection, 331–333
Feedforward networks, 269–270
  feedforward neural network, 424*f*
Fielded applications, 21–28
  automation, 28
  customer service/support, 28
  decisions involving judgments, 22–23
  diagnosis, 22–23
  image screening, 23–24
  load forecasting, 24–25
  manufacturing processes, 27–28
  marketing and sales, 26–27
  scientific, 28
  web mining, 21–22
File mining, 53
Files
  ARFF, 58–60
  filtering, 560–561
  loading, 560–561
  opening, 560
Filter method, 289–290
FilteredClassifier algorithm, 563
FilteredClassifier metalearning scheme, 563
Filtering approaches, 319
Filters, 554, 563
  applying, 561
  attribute, 562–564
  information on, 561
  instance, 563
  supervised, 563, 567
  unsupervised, 563, 567
  in Weka, 559
Finite mixtures, 353
Fisher's linear discriminant analysis, 311–312
Fixed set, 54, 510
Flat files, 46–47
F-measure, 191, 202–203
Forward pruning, 213
Forward selection, 292–293
Forward stagewise additive modeling, 491
  implementation, 492
  numeric prediction, 491–492
  overfitting and, 491–492
  residuals, 491
Forwards-backwards algorithms, 386
FP-growth algorithm, 235, 241
Frequent-pattern trees, 242
  building, 235–239
  compact structure, 235

data preparation example, 236*t*
header tables, 237
implementation, 241
structure illustration, 239*f*
support threshold, 240
Functional dependencies, 513
Functional trees, 71–72
Fundamental rule of probability. *See* Product rule

G

Gain ratio, 111–112
Gaussian distributions, 373, 394
Gaussian kernel, 361
Gaussian process regression,
    272
Generalization
    exemplar, 247–248, 251–252
    instance-based learning and, 251
    stacked, 497–499
Generalization as search, 31–35
    bias, 33–35
    enumerating the concept space, 32–33
Generalized distance functions, 250
Generalized linear models, 400–401
    link functions, mean functions, and
        distributions, 401*t*
Generalized Sequential Patterns (GSP),
    241
Generalizing exemplars, 247–248
    distance functions for, 248–250
    nested, 248
Generative models, 371
Gibbs sampling, 368–369
Global optimization, classification rules for,
    226–227
Gradient ascent, 476
Gradient clipping, 457–458
Gradient descent, 266–268
    illustrated, 265*f*
    and second-order methods, 400
    stochastic, 270–272
    subgradients, 270–271
Graphical models, 352, 370–391
    computing using sum-product and max-product
        algorithms, 386–391
    factor graphs, 382–385
    LDA, 379–381
    LSA, 376–377
    Markov random fields, 385–386
    PCA for dimensionality reduction, 377–378
    and plate notation, 371
    PPCA, 372–376
    probabilistic LSA, 378–379

Graphics processing units (GPUs), 392
GraphViewer, 565
Greedy method, for rule pruning,
    219
GreedyStepwise method, 334
Group-average clustering, 148
Growing sets, 224
GSP. *See* Generalized Sequential Patterns (GSP)

H

Hamming distance, 325
Hausdorff distance, 475, 477
Hidden attributes, 340
Hidden layer, multilayer perceptrons, 263,
    266–268, 267*f*
Hidden Markov models, 404–405
Hidden variable models, 363–367
    EM algorithm, 365–366
        to train Bayesian networks, 366–367
    expected gradients, 364–365
    expected log-likelihoods, 364–365
Hidden variables, 355–356, 363
Hierarchical clustering, 147–148, 359. *See also*
    Clustering
    agglomerative, 147
    average-linkage method, 147–148
    centroid-linkage method, 147–148
    dendrograms, 147
    displays, 149*f*
    example, 148–150
    example illustration, 153*f*
    group-average, 148
    single-linkage algorithm, 147, 150
HierarchicalClusterer algorithm, 160
Highly branching attributes, 110–113
Hinge loss, 271, 271*f*
Histogram equalization, 297
Hoeffding bound, 510
Hoeffding trees, 510
HTML. *See* HyperText Markup
    Language (HTML)
Hyperparameter
    selection, 171–172
    tuning, 432–433
Hyperplanes, 252–253
    maximum-margin, 253–254
    separating classes, 253*f*
Hyperrectangles, 247–248
    boundaries, 247–248
    exception, 248
    measuring distance to, 250
    in multi-instance learning, 477
    overlapping, 248

Hyperspheres, 139
HyperText Markup Language (HTML)
  delimiters, 519–520
  formatting commands, 519

I

IB1 algorithm, 160
IB3. *See* Instance-Based Learner version 3 (IB3)
IBk algorithm, 284
Id3 algorithm, 160
ID3 decision tree learner, 113
Identification code attributes, 95
  example, 111*t*
Image screening, 23–24
  hazard detection system, 23
  input, 23–24
  problems, 24
ImageNet evaluation, 438–439
ImageNet Large Scale Visual Recognition
        Challenge (ILSVRC), 438–439
Inaccurate values, 63–64
Incremental clustering, 150–154
  acuity parameter, 152–154
  category utility, 150–151
  cutoff parameter, 154
  example illustrations, 151*f*, 153*f*
  merging, 151–152
  splitting, 152
Incremental learning, 567
Incremental reduced-error pruning, 225, 226*f*
IncrementalClassifierEvaluator, 567
Independent and identically distributed (i.i.d.), 338
Independent component analysis, 309–310
Inductive logic programming, 84
Information, 37–38, 106–107
  calculating, 108–110
  extraction, 517–518
  gain calculation, 222
  measure, 108–110
  value, 110
Informational loss function, 178–179
Information-based heuristics, 223
Input, 43
  aggregating, 157
  ARFF format, 57–60
  attribute types, 61–62
  attributes, 53–56
  concepts, 44–46
  data assembly, 56–57
  data transformations and, 304
  examples, 46–53
  flat files, 46–47
  forms, 43

  inaccurate values, 63–64
  instances, 46–53
  missing values, 62–63
  preparing, 56–65
  sparse data, 60–61
  tabular format, 127
Input layer, multilayer perceptrons, 263
Instance connections, 566–567
Instance filters, 563
Instance space
  in covering algorithm operation, 115*f*
  partitioning methods, 130*f*
  rectangular generalizations in, 86–87
Instance-Based Learner version 3 (IB3),
        246
Instance-based learning, 84–85, 135–141
  in attribute selection, 291
  characteristics, 84–85
  distance functions, 135–136
    for generalized exemplars, 248–250
  explicit knowledge representation
        and, 251
  generalization and, 244–252
  generalizing exemplars, 247–248
  nearest-neighbor, 136–141
  performance, 245–246
  pruning noise exemplars, 245–246
  reducing number of exemplars, 245
  visualizing, 87
  weighting attributes, 246–247
Instance-based representation, 84–87
Instances, 43, 46–47
  centroid, 142–143
  misclassified, 132–133
  with missing values, 212–213
  multilabeled, 45
  order, 59–60
  sparse, 61
  subset sort order, 212
  training, 198
Interpretable ensembles, 493–497
  logistic model trees, 496–497
  option trees, 494–496
Interval quantities, 55
Iris example, 14–15
  data as clustering problem, 46*t*
  dataset, 15*t*
  decision boundary, 69, 70*f*
  decision tree, 72, 73*f*
  hierarchical clusterings, 153*f*
  incremental clustering, 150–154
  rules, 15
  rules with exceptions, 80–82, 81*f*, 231–233,
        232*f*

Isotonic regression, 330
Item sets, 120–121
  checking, of two consecutive sizes,
      126
  converting to rules, 122
  in efficient rule generation, 124–127
  example, 121*t*
  large, finding with association rules, 240–241
  minimum coverage, 124
  subsets of, 124–125
Items, 120
Iterated conditional modes procedure, 369–370
Iterative distance-based clustering, 142–144

J

J48 algorithm, 558, 565, 567–568
  cross-validation with, 565
Java virtual machine, 508–509
Joint distribution, 367, 452–453
Judgment decisions, 22–23

K

K2 algorithm, 411
*K*2 learning algorithm, 347
Kappa statistic, 181
KD-trees, 136
  building, 137
  in finding nearest-neighbor, 137–138, 137*f*
  for training instances, 137*f*
  updating, 138–139
Keras, 465–466
Kernel density estimation, 361–362
Kernel logistic regression, 261
Kernel perceptron, 260–261
Kernel regression, 403
Kernel ridge regression, 258–259
  computational expense, 259
  computational simplicity,
      259
  drawback, 259
Kernels, conditional probability models using,
      402–403
Kernel trick, 258
K-means algorithm, 355
K-means clustering, 142–143
  iterations, 144
  k-means + +, 144
  seeds, 144
K-nearest-neighbor method, 85
Knowledge, 37
  background, 508
  metadata, 513
  prior domain, 513

Knowledge Flow interface, 554–555, 564–567.
      See also Weka workbench
  Associations panel, 566
  Classifiers folder, 566
  Clusters folder, 566
  components, 566
  components configuration and connection,
      566–567
  dataSet connections, 566–567
  evaluation components, 566
  Evaluation folder, 564–565
  Filters folder, 566
  incremental learning, 567
  starting up, 564–565
Knowledge representation, 91
  clusters, 87
  instance-based, 84–87
  linear models, 68–70
  rules, 75–84
  tables, 68
  trees, 70–75
KStar algorithm, 284

L

L_2 regularization, 399
Labor negotiations example, 16–18
  dataset, 17*t*
  decision trees, 18*f*
  training dataset, 18
LADTree algorithm, 501
Language bias, 33–34
Language identification, 516
Laplace distribution, 393–394
Laplace estimator, 99, 358–359
Large item sets, finding with association rules,
      240–241
Lasagne, 465–466
LatentSemanticAnalysis method, 376–377
Latent Dirichlet allocation (LDA), 379–381
Latent semantic analysis (LSA), 376–377
Latent variables. *See* Hidden variables
LaTeX typesetting system, 571
Lattice-structured models, 408
Law of diminishing returns, 507
Layerwise training, 448
Lazy classifiers, in Weka, 563
Learning
  association, 44
  batch, 268–269
  classification, 44
  concept, 54
  cost-sensitive, 65–66
  data stream, 509–512

Learning (*Continued*)
  deep. *See* Deep learning
  ensemble, 479
  incremental, 567
  instance-based, 84−85, 135−141, 244−252
  locally weighted, 281−283
  machine, 7−9
  multi-instance, 53, 156−158, 472−476
  one-class, 288, 319−320
  in performance situations, 21
  rote, 84−85
  semisupervised, 468−472
  statistics versus, 30−31
  testing, 8
Learning algorithms, 563
  Bayes, 563
  functions, 563
  lazy, 563
  miscellaneous, 563
  rules, 563
  trees, 563
Learning Bayesian networks, 344−347
Learning paradigms, 508
Learning rate, 267−268
  and schedules, 434−435
Least-squares linear regression, 70, 129
Least Absolute Shrinkage and Selection Operator
  (LASSO), 394
Leave-one-out cross-validation, 169
Level-0 models, 497−498
Level-1 model, 497−498
LibLINEAR algorithm, 284
LibSVM algorithm, 284
Lift charts, 183−186
  data for, 184*t*
  illustrated, 185*f*
  points on, 194
Lift factor, 183−184
Likelihood, 337
Linear chain conditional random fields, 408−409
Linear classification
  logistic regression, 129−131
  using the perceptron, 131−133
  using Winnow, 133−135
Linear discriminant analysis, 310
Linear machines, 159
Linear models, 68−70, 128−135
  in binary classification problems, 69
  boundary decision, 69
  extending, 252−273
  generating, 252
  illustrated, 69*f*, 70*f*
  kernel ridge regression, 258−259
  linear classification, 129−131

  linear regression, 128−129
  local, numeric prediction with, 273−284
  logistic regression, 129−131
  maximum-margin hyperplane, 253−254
  in model tree, 280*t*
  multilayer perceptrons, 261−269
  nonlinear class boundaries, 254−256
  numeric prediction, 128−129
  perceptron, 131−133
  stochastic gradient descent, 270−272
  support vector machine use, 252
  support vector regression, 256−258
  in two dimensions, 68
Linear regression, 128−129, 392−393
  least-squares, 70, 129
  locally weighted, 281−283
  matrix vector formulations, 394−395
  multiple, 491
  multiresponse, 129
Linear threshold unit, 159
LinearForwardSelection method, 334
LinearRegression algorithm, 160
LMT algorithm, 160
Load forecasting, 24−25
Loading files, 560−561
Locally weighted linear regression, 281−283
  distance-based weighting schemes, 282
  in nonlinear function approximation, 282
Logic programs, 84
Logistic model trees, 496−497
Logistic regression, 129−131, 398−399
  additive, 492−493
  calibration, 330
  generalizing, 131
  illustrated, 130*f*
  model, 382−385
  two-class, 131
LogitBoost algorithm, 492−493
Log-likelihood, 338
Log-normal distribution, 357−358
Log-odds distribution, 357−358
Long short-term memory (LSTM), 457−458
Loss functions
  0 − 1, 176
  informational, 178−179
  quadratic, 177−178
LWL algorithm, 284

M

M5P algorithm, 284
M5Rules algorithm, 284
Machine learning, 7−9
  applications, 9

in diagnosis applications, 25
expert models, 480
modern, 467
schemes, 209–210
statistics and, 30–31
Manufacturing process applications, 27–28
Market basket analysis, 26–27, 120
Marketing and sales, 26–27
    churn, 26
    direct marketing, 27
    historical analysis, 27
    market basket analysis, 26–27
Markov blanket, 347–348
Marginal likelihood, 355, 363
Marginal log-likelihood for PPCA, 374
Marginal probabilities, 387
Markov blanket, 347–348, 348f, 369
Markov chain Monte Carlo methods, 368–369
Markov models, 403–404
Markov networks, 352
Markov random fields, 385–386, 407–408
Massive datasets, 506–509
Massive Online Analysis (MOA), 512
Max-product algorithms, 391
Max-sum algorithm. *See* Max-product algorithms
Maximization, 357
Maximum-margin hyperplane, 253–254
    illustrated, 253f
    support vectors, 253–254
Maximum likelihood estimation, 338–339
Maximum posteriori parameter estimation, 339
MDL. *See* Minimum description length (MDL) principle
Mean-absolute errors, 195
Mean-squared errors, 195
Mean function, 401
Memory usage, 511–512
MetaCost algorithm, 484
Metadata, 56, 512
    application examples, 512–513
    knowledge, 513
    relations among attributes, 513
Metalearners, 563
Metalearning algorithms, in Weka, 563
Metric trees, 141
Metropolis–Hastings algorithm, 368–369
MIDD algorithm, 478
MILR algorithm, 478
Mini-batch-based stochastic gradient descent, 433–434
    pseudocode for, 434, 435f
Minimum description length (MDL) principle, 179, 197–200
    applying to clustering, 200–201

metric, 346
probability theory and, 199
training instances, 198
MIOptimalBall algorithm, 478
MISMO algorithm, 478
Missing values, 62–63
    1R, 94–96
    classification rules, 223–224
    decision trees, 70–71, 212–213
    distance function, 136
    instances with, 212
    machine learning schemes and, 63
    mixture models, 358
    Naïve Bayes, 100
    partial decision trees, 230–231
    reasons for, 63
MISVM algorithm, 478
MIWrapper algorithm, 160
Mixed-attribute problems, 11
Mixed National Institute of Standards and Technology (MNIST), 421–422, 421t
Mixture models, 353, 370
    extending, 356–358
    finite mixtures, 353
    missing values, 357
    nominal attributes, 357
    two-class, 354f
Mixture of Gaussians
    expectation maximization algorithm, 353–356
Mixtures, 353
    of factor analyzers, 360–361
    of principal component analyzers, 360–361
MOA. *See* Massive Online Analysis (MOA)
Model's expectation, 451
Model trees, 75, 273–275
    building, 275
    illustrated, 74f
    induction pseudocode, 277–281, 278f
    linear models in, 280t
    logistic, 496–497
    with nominal attributes, 279f
    pruning, 275–276
    rules from, 281
    smoothing calculation, 274
Multiclass prediction, 181
MultiClassClassifier algorithm, 334
Multiclass classification problem, 396
Multiclass logistic regression, 396–400
    matrix vector formulation, 397–398
    priors on parameters, 398–400
Multi-instance learning, 53, 156–158, 472.
    See also Semisupervised learning
    aggregating the input, 157
    aggregating the output, 157–158

Multi-instance learning (*Continued*)
  bags, 156–157, 474
  converting to single-instance learning, 472–474
  dedicated methods, 475–476
  hyperrectangles for, 476
  nearest-neighbor learning adaptation to, 475
  supervised, 156–157
  upgrading learning algorithms, 475
Multi-instance problems, 53
  ARFF file, 60*f*
  converting to single-instance problem, 157
Multilabeled instances, 45
Multilayer perceptrons, 261–269
  backpropagation, 264–269
  bias, 263
  datasets corresponding to, 262*f*
  as feed-forward networks, 269
  hidden layer, 263, 266–267, 267*f*
  input layer, 263
  units, 263
MultilayerPerceptron algorithm, 284
Multinomial logistic regression, 396
Multinominal Naïve Bayes, 103
Multiple classes to binary transformation,
  322–328, 324*t. See also* Data
  transformations
  error-correcting output codes, 324–326
  nested dichotomies, 326–328
  one-vs.-rest method, 323
  pairwise classification, 323
  pairwise coupling, 323
  simple methods, 323–324
Multiple linear regression, 491
Multiresponse linear regression, 129
  drawbacks, 129
  membership function, 129
Multistage decision property, 110

N

Naïve Bayes, 99, 289
  classifier, 347
  for document classification, 103–104
  with EM, 469
  independent attributes assumption, 469
  locally weighted, 283
  missing values, 100–103
  multinominal, 103
  numeric attributes, 100–103
  selective, 295
  semantics, 105
NaiveBayes algorithm, 160
NaiveBayesMultinomial algorithm, 160
NaiveBayesUpdateable algorithm, 566–567

NAND, 263
Nearest-neighbor classification, 85
  speed, 141
Nearest-neighbor learning, 475
  attribute selection, 290
  Hausdorff distance variants
    and, 477
  instance-based, 136
  multi-instance data adaptation, 475
Nested dichotomies, 326–328
  code matrix, 327*t*
  defined, 327
  ensemble of, 328
Neural networks, 445
  approaches, 471–472
Neuron's receptive field, 440
N-fold cross-validation, 169
N-grams, 403–404, 516
Nnge algorithm, 284
Noise, 7
"Noisy-OR" function, 476
Nominal attributes, 54
  mixture model, 356–358
  numeric prediction, 276
  symbols, 54
Nonlinear class boundaries, 254–256
Nonparametric density models for classification,
  362–363
Normal distribution
  assumption, 103, 105
  confidence limits, 166*t*
Normalization, 184, 408
Norm clipping. *See* Gradient clipping
NOT, 262
Novelty detection. *See* Outlier—detection of
Nuclear family, 50
Null hypothesis, 59
Numeric attributes, 54, 296–303
  1R, 94
  classification rules, 224
  converting discrete attributes to, 303
  decision tree, 210–212
  discretization of, 287
  Naïve Bayes, 100
  normal-distribution assumption for, 105
Numeric prediction, 16, 44
  additive regression, 490–493
  bagging for, 483
  evaluating, 194–197
  linear models, 128–135
  outcome as numeric value, 46
  performance measures, 195*t*, 197*t*
  support vector machine algorithms
    for, 256

Numeric prediction (local linear models),
  273−284
  building trees, 275
  locally weighted linear regression, 281−283
  model tree induction, 277−281
  model trees, 274−275
  nominal attributes, 276
  pruning trees, 275−276
  rules from model trees, 281
Numeric thresholds, 211
Numeric-attribute problems, 11

O

Obfuscate filter, 304−305, 525
Object editors, 553−554
Occam's Razor, 197, 200, 489−490
One-class classification. *See* Outlier—detection of
One-class learning, 288, 319−320
  multiclass classifiers, 320−321
  outlier detection, 320−321
One-dependence estimator, 348−349
"One-hot" method, 393
OneR algorithm, 568
One-tailed probability, 166
One-vs.-rest method, 323
Option trees, 494−496
  as alternating decision trees, 495, 495*f*
  decision trees versus, 494
  example, 494*f*
  generation, 494−495
OR, 262
Order-independent rules, 119
Ordered classes, predictions for, 402
"Ordered logit" models, 402
Orderings, 54
  circular, 56
  partial, 56
Ordinal attributes, 55−56
  coding of, 55−56
Orthogonal coordinate systems, 305
Outliers, 320
  detection of, 320−321
Output
  aggregating, 157
  clusters, 87−88
  instance-based representation, 84−87
  knowledge representation, 91
  linear models, 68−70
  rules, 75−84
  tables, 68
  trees, 70−75
Overfitting, 95
  for 1R, 95

  backpropagation and, 268
  forward stagewise additive regression and,
    491−492
  support vectors and, 255
Overfitting-avoidance bias, 35
Overlay data, 57

P

PageRank, 21, 504, 520−522
  recomputation, 521
  sink, 522
  in Web mining, 521
Pair-adjacent violators (PAV) algorithm, 330
Paired *t*-test, 173
Pairwise classification, 323
Pairwise coupling, 323
Parabolas, 249
Parallelization, 507−508
Parameter initialization, 436−437
Parametric density models for classification,
    362−363
Partial decision trees
  best leaf, 230
  building example, 230*f*
  expansion algorithm, 229*f*
  missing values, 230−231
  obtaining rules from, 227−231
Partial least squares regression, 307−309
Partial ordering, 56
Partitioning
  for 1R, 95
  discretization, 94
  instance space, 86*f*
  training set, 213
Partition function, 385
Parzen window density estimation, 361
PAV. *See* Pair-adjacent violators (PAV) algorithm
Perceptron learning rule, 132
  illustrated, 132*f*
  updating of weights, 134
Perceptrons, 133
  instance presentation to, 133
  kernel, 260−261
  linear classification using, 131−133
  multilayer, 261−269
  voted, 261
Performance
  classifier, predicting, 165
  comparison, 162
  error rate and, 163
  evaluation, 162
  instance-based learning, 246
  for numeric prediction, 195*t*, 197*t*

Performance (*Continued*)
  predicting, 165
  text mining, 515
Personal information use, 37–38
PKIDiscretize filter, 334
"Plate notation", 370–371
PLSFilter filter, 334
Poisson distribution, 357–358
Polynomial regression, 392–393
  matrix vector formulations, 394–395
Posterior distribution, 337
Posterior predictive distribution, 367–368
Postpruning, 213
  subtree raising, 214
  subtree replacement, 214
Prediction
  with Bayesian networks, 340–344
  multiclass, 181
  nodes, 495
  outcomes, 180–181, 180*t*
  three-class, 181*t*
  two-class, 180*t*
Prepruning, 213
Pretraining deep autoencoders with RBMs, 448
Principal component analysis (PCA), 305–307, 372
  of dataset, 306*f*
  for dimensionality reduction, 377–378
  principal components, 306
  recursive, 307
Principal components regression, 307
PrincipalComponents filter, 334
Principle of multiple explanations, 200
Prior distribution, 337
  clustering using, 358–359
Prior knowledge, 514
Prior probability, 98–99
PRISM rule-learning algorithm, 39, 110, 118–119
Probabilistic inference methods, 368–370
  probability propagation, 368
  sampling, simulated annealing, and iterated
    conditional modes, 368–370
  variational inference, 370
Probabilistic LSA (pLSA), 376, 378–379
Probabilistic methods, 336
  Bayesian estimation and prediction, 367–370
  Bayesian networks, 339–352
  clustering and probability density estimation,
    352–363
  conditional probability models, 392–403
  factor graphs, 382–385
  foundations, 336–339
  graphical models, 370–391
  hidden variable models, 363–367
  maximum likelihood estimation, 338–339

maximum posteriori parameter estimation, 339
  sequential and temporal models, 403–410
  software packages and implementations, 414–415
Probabilistic principal component analysis
    (PPCA), 360–361, 372–376
  EM for, 375–376
  expected gradient for, 375
  expected log-likelihood for, 374
  inference with, 373–374
  marginal log-likelihood for, 374
Probabilities
  class, calibrating, 328–331
  maximizing, 199
  one-tailed, 166
  predicting, 176–179
  probability density function relationship, 177
  with rules, 13
Probability density estimation, 352–363
  clustering and, 352–363
  comparing parametric, semiparametric and
    nonparametric density models, 362–363
  expectation maximization algorithm, 353–356
  extending mixture model, 356–358
  Kernel density estimation, 361–362
  two-class mixture model, 354*f*
Probability density functions, 102
Probability estimates, 340
Probability propagation, 368
Probability theory, 336–337
Product rule, 337, 343–344
Programming by demonstration, 528
Projection. *See* Data projections
Projections
  Fisher's linear discriminant analysis, 311–312
  independent component analysis, 309–310
  linear discriminant analysis, 310
  quadratic discriminant analysis, 310–311
  random, 307
"Proportional odds" models, 402
Proportional k-interval discretization, 297–298
Pruning
  cost-complexity, 220–221
  decision trees, 213–215
  example illustration, 216*f*
  incremental reduced-error, 225, 226*f*
  model trees, 275–276
  noisy exemplars, 245–246
  postpruning, 213
  prepruning, 213
  reduced-error, 215, 225
  rules, 219
  subtree lifting, 218
  subtree raising, 214
  subtree replacement, 213

Pruning sets, 224
Pseudoinverse, 394

Q

Quadratic discriminant analysis, 310–311
Quadratic loss function, 177–178

R

Race search, 294
RaceSearch method, 334
Radial basis function (RBF), 270
    kernels, 256
    networks, 256
    output layer, 270
Random projections, 307
Random subspaces, 485
RandomCommittee algorithm, 501
RandomForest algorithm, 501
Randomization, 484–486
    bagging versus, 485–486
    rotation forests, 486
RandomSubSpace algorithm, 501
Ranker method, 564
Ratio quantities, 55
RBF. *See* Radial basis function (RBF)
RBFNetwork algorithm, 284
RBMs, pretraining deep autoencoders with, 448
Recall-precision curves, 190
    area under the precision-recall curve, 192
    points on, 194
Reconstructive learning, 449
Rectangular generalizations, 86–87
Rectified linear units (ReLUs), 424–425
Rectify() function, 424–425
Recurrent neural networks, 269, 456–460
    deep encoder-decoder recurrent network, 460*f*
    exploding and vanishing gradients, 457–459
    recurrent network architectures, 459–460
Recursive feature elimination, 290–291
Reduced-error pruning, 225, 269
    incremental, 225, 226*f*
Reference density, 322
Reference distribution, 321
Regression, 68
    additive, 490–493
    isotonic, 330
    kernel ridge, 258–259
    linear, 16, 128–129
    locally weighted, 281–283
    logistic, 129–131
    partial least-squares, 307–309
    principal components, 307

    robust, 317–318
    support vector, 256–258
Regression equations, 75
Linear regression, 16
Linear regression equation, 16
Regression tables, 68
Regression trees, 72, 273–274
    illustrated, 74*f*
Regularization, 273
Reidentification, 36–37
RELAGGS system, 477
Relations, 47–51
    ancestor-of, 51
    sister-of, 48*f*, 49*t*
    superrelations, 50
Relation-valued attributes, 59
    instances, 61
    specification, 59
Relative absolute errors, 196
Relative squared errors, 195–196
RELIEF (Recursive Elimination of Features), 331
Repeated holdout, 167
Replicated subtree problem, 76
    decision tree illustration, 77*f*
Representation learning techniques, 418
Reservoir sampling, 315–316
Residuals, 308
Restricted Boltzmann machines (RBMs), 451–452
Resubstitution errors, 163
RIPPER algorithm, 227, 228*f*, 234
Ripple-down rules, 234
Robo-soccer, 526
Robust regression, 317–318
ROC curves, 186–190
    area under the curve, 191–192
    from different learning schemes, 189
    generating with cross-validation, 189
    jagged, 188–189
    points on, 194
    sample, 188*f*
    for two learning schemes, 189*f*
Rotation forests, 486
RotationForest algorithm, 501
Rote learning, 84–85
Row separation, 325
Rule sets
    model trees for generating, 281
    for noisy data, 222
Rules, 10, 75–84
    antecedent of, 75
    association, 11–12, 79–80, 234–241
    classification, 11–12, 75–78
    computer-generated, 19–21
    consequent of, 75

Rules (*Continued*)
  constructing, 113–119
  decision lists versus, 119
  decision tree, 219
  efficient generation of, 124–127
  with exceptions, 80–82, 231–233
  expert-derived, 19–21
  expressive, 82–84
  inferring, 93–96
  from model trees, 281
  order-independent, 119
  perceptron learning, 132
  popularity, 78
  PRISM method for constructing, 118–119
  probabilities, 13
  pruning, 218–219
  ripple-down, 234
  trees versus, 114

S

Sampling, 288, 315–316. *See also* Data
      transformations
  with replacement, 315
  reservoir, 315–316
  procedure, 366, 368–370
  without replacement, 315–316
"Scaled" kernel function, 361
Schemata search, 294
Scheme-independent attribute selection, 289–292
  filter method, 289–290
  instance-based learning methods,
      291
  recursive feature elimination, 290–291
  symmetric uncertainty, 291–292
  wrapper method, 289–290
Scheme-specific attribute selection, 293–295
  accelerating, 294–295
  paired *t*-test, 294
  race search, 294
  results, 294
  schemata search, 294
  selective Naïve Bayes, 295
Scientific applications, 28
Screening images, 23–24
SDR. *See* Standard deviation reduction (SDR)
Search, generalization as, 31–35
Search bias, 34–35
Search engines, in web mining, 21–22
Search methods (Weka), 413, 564
Second-order analysis, 435
Seeds, 144
Selective Naïve Bayes, 295
Semantic relationship, 513

Semiparametric density models for classification,
      362–363
Semisupervised learning, 467–472. *See also*
      Multi-instance learning
  clustering for classification, 468–470
  co-EM, 471
  cotraining, 470–471
    EM and, 471
  neural network approaches, 471–472
Separate-and-conquer algorithms, 119, 289
Sequential and temporal models, 403–410
  conditional random fields, 406–410
  hidden Markov models, 404–405
  Markov models, 403–404
  N-gram methods, 403–404
Set kernel, 475
Shapes problem, 82
  illustrated, 82*f*
  training data, 83*t*
Sigmoid function, 264*f*
Sigmoid kernel, 256
SimpleCart algorithm, 242
SimpleKMeans algorithm, 160
SimpleLinearRegression algorithm,
      160
SimpleMI algorithm, 160
Simple probabilistic modeling, 96–105
Simulated annealing, 369
Single-attribute evaluators, 564
Single-consequent rules, 126
Single-linkage clustering algorithm, 147, 149
Skewed datasets, 139
Sliding dot product, 440
Smoothing calculation, 274
"Sobel" filters, 441
Soft maximum, 475
Softmax function, 397
Soybean classification example, 19–21
  dataset, 20*t*
  examples rules, 19
Sparse data, 60–61
Splitter nodes, 495
Splitting, 152
  clusters, 146
  criterion, 275
  model tree nodes, 277–278
Squared error, 178
Stacking, 319, 497–499
  defined, 159, 497
  level-0 model, 497–498
  level-1 model, 497–498
  model input, 497–498
  output combination, 497
  as parallel, 507–508

Standard deviation from the mean, 166
Standard deviation reduction (SDR), 275–277
Standardizing statistical variables, 61
Statistical clustering, 296
Statistical modeling, 406
Statistics, machine learning and, 30–31
Step function, 264*f*
Stochastic backpropagation, 268–269
Stochastic deep networks, 449–456. *See also*
      Convolutional neural networks (CNNs)
   Boltzmann machines, 449–451
   categorical and continuous variables, 452–453
   contrastive divergence, 452
   deep belief networks, 455–456
   deep Boltzmann machines, 453–454
   restricted Boltzmann machines, 451–452
Stochastic gradient descent, 270–272
Stopwords, 313, 516
Stratification, 167
   variation reduction, 168
Stratified holdout, 167
Stratified threefold cross-validation, 168
String attributes, 58
   specification, 58
   values, 59
StringToWordVector filter, 290, 563
Structural descriptions, 6–7
   decision trees, 6
   learning techniques, 9
Structure learning, 349
   by conditional independence tests,
      349
"Structured prediction" techniques, 407–408
Student's distribution with k-1 degrees of freedom,
      173–174
Student's *t*-test, 173
Subgradients, 270–271
Subsampling, 444
Subtree lifting, 218
Subtree raising, 214
Subtree replacement, 213
Success rate, error rate and, 215–216
Sum rule, 337
Sum-product algorithms, 386–391
   example, 389–390
   marginal probabilities, 387
   probable explanation example, 390
Super-parent one-dependence estimator, 348–349
Superrelations, 50
Supervised discretization, 297, 332
Supervised filters, 563
   attribute, 563
   instance, 563
   using, 563

Supervised learning, 45
   multi-instance learning, 472–476
Support, of association rules, 79, 120
Support vector machines (SVMs), 252, 403, 471
   co-EM with, 471
   hinge loss, 271
   linear model usage, 252
   term usage, 252
   training, 253–254
   weight update, 272
Support vector regression, 256–258
   flatness maximization, 256–257
   illustrated, 257*f*
   for linear case, 257
   linear regression differences, 256–257
   for nonlinear case, 257
Support vectors, 253–254
   finding, 254
   overfitting and, 255
Survival functions, 402
Symmetric uncertainty, 291–292
Synthetic transformations, 437

T

Tables
   as knowledge representation, 68
   regression, 68
Tabular input format, 127
TAN. *See* Tree-augmented Naïve Bayes (TAN)
Teleportation, 522
Tenfold cross-validation, 169
Tensor flow, 464–465
Tensors, 420, 464–465
Testing, 163–164
   test data, 163
   test sets, 163
TestSetMaker, 566–567
Text mining, 515–519
   conditional random fields for,
      410
   data mining versus, 515
   document classification, 516
   entity extraction, 517
   information extraction, 517–518
   metadata extraction, 517
   performance, 515
   stopwords, 516
Text summarization, 515
Text to attribute vectors, 313–314
Theano, 464
Theory, 197
   exceptions to, 197
   MDL principle and, 198

Threefold cross-validation, 168
3-point average recall, 191
"Time-homogeneous" models, 405
Time series, 314
   Delta, 314
   timestamp attribute, 314
Timestamp attribute, 314
Tokenization, 313
Top-down induction, of decision trees, 221
Torch, 465
Training, 163–164
   data, 164
   instances, 198
   support vector machines, 261
Training sets, 162
   error, 215
   error rate, 163
   partitioning, 213
TrainingSetMaker, 566–567
Tree diagrams. *See* Dendrograms
Tree-augmented Naïve Bayes (TAN), 348
Trees, 70–75. *See also* Decision trees
   AD, 350–351, 350*f*
   ball, 139, 139*f*
   frequent-pattern, 235–239
   functional, 71–72
   Hoeffding, 511
   kD, 136–137, 137*f*
   logistic model, 496–497
   metric, 141
   model, 74*f*, 75, 273
   option, 494–496
   regression, 72, 74*f*, 273
   rules versus, 114
True negatives (TN), 180–181, 190–191
True positive rate, 186–188
True positives (TP), 180–181, 190–191
T-statistic, 174–176
T-test, 173
   corrected resampled, 175–176
   paired, 173
Two-class mixture model, 354*f*
Two-class problem, 82
Typographic errors, 63–64

U

Ubiquitous computing, 527
Ubiquitous data mining, 527–529
Unbalanced data, 64–65
Unmasking, 526–527
Unsupervised attribute filters, 563. *See also* Filters
Unsupervised discretization, 297–298
Unsupervised pretraining, 437
User Classifier (Weka), 72

V

Validation, 432–433
Validation data, 164
Validation sets, 508
   for model selection, 201–202
Variables, standardizing, 61
Variance, 482
Variational bound, 370
Variational inference, 370
Variational parameters, 370
Venn diagrams, in cluster representation, 87–88
Visualization, in Weka, 562
Visualize panel, 562
Viterbi algorithms, 386
Voted perceptron, 261

W

Weather problem example, 10–12
   alternating decision tree, 495*f*
   ARFF file for, 58*f*
   association rules, 11–12, 123*t*
   attribute space, 292*f*
   attributes evaluation, 94*t*
   attributes, 10
   Bayesian networks, 341*f*, 342*f*
   clustering, 151*f*
   counts and probabilities, 97*t*
   data with numeric class, 47*t*
   dataset, 11*t*
   decision tree, 109*f*
   expanded tree stumps, 108*f*
   FP-tree insertion, 236*t*
   identification codes, 111*t*
   item sets, 121*t*
   multi-instance ARFF file, 60*f*
   numeric data with summary statistics, 101*t*
   option tree, 494*f*
   tree stumps, 106*f*
Web mining, 21–22, 519–522
   PageRank algorithm, 520–522
   search engines, 22
   teleportation, 522
   wrapper induction, 519–520
Weight decay, 269, 393, 399, 435
Weighting attributes
   instance-based learning, 246–247
   test, 247
   updating, 246–247
Weights
   determination process, 16
   with rules, 13

Weka workbench, 504, 553–555
  advanced setup, 570
  association rules, 561–562
  attribute selection, 562
  clustering, 561–562
  components configuration and connection,
      566–567
  development of, 553
  evaluation components, 566
  Experimenter, 554, 568–571
  Explorer, 554, 557–564
  filters, 554, 563
  GUI Chooser panel, 556
  how to use, 554–555
  incremental learning, 567
  interfaces, 554
  ISO-8601 date/time format, 59
  J48 algorithm, 558–559
  Knowledge Flow, 554, 564–567
  learning algorithms, 563
  metalearning algorithms, 563
  User Classifier facility, 72
  visualization, 562
  visualization components, 565, 567
Winnow, 133–135
  Balanced, 134–135
  linear classification with, 133–135
  updating of weights, 134
  versions illustration, 134*f*
Wisdom, 38
Wrapper induction, 519–520
Wrapper method, 289–290
Wrappers, 519

X

XML (eXtensible Markup Language), 57, 568
XOR (exclusive-OR), 262–263
XRFF format, 57

Z

Zero-frequency problem, 178–179
ZeroR algorithm, 568–569